ADVANCES IN AI AND SIMULATION

Titles in the *SIMULATION SERIES*

ADVANCES IN AI AND SIMULATION

Proceedings of the SCS Multiconference on
AI and Simulation
28-31 March, 1989
Tampa, Florida

Edited by
Ranjeet Uttamsingh
Synetics
and
A. Martin Wildberger
General Physics Corporation

Simulation Series
Volume 20
Number 4
March 1989

A Society for Computer Simulation International (Simulation Councils, Inc.) publication
San Diego, California

ISBN 0-911801-50-2

PRINTED IN THE UNITED STATES OF AMERICA

CONTENTS

CONTENTS

PREFACE

The combination of Artificial Intelligence (AI) and Simulation technologies provides synergistic benefits for certain applications development in both fields. This is becoming increasingly recognized by both the simulation and AI communities. One manifestation of this recognition is the rapid growth and increase in the overall technical quality of the AI and Simulation components of the recent Society for Computer Simulation International (SCSI) sponsored simulation multiconferences.

Simulation and AI technologies are combined in a wide variety of applications to provide:

- Expert system components embedded into conventional simulations
- AI object oriented programming techniques for the development of discrete event and continuous simulations
- Qualitative simulation
- Neural networks
- Programmed heuristics used in the actual development of mathematical models
- Natural language front-ends for model development and simulation execution.

The primary motivation for combining the two technologies arises from the recognition by the applications developer that certain applications require both the analytical techniques afforded by simulation technology, as well as the flexibility and heuristic modeling capabilities provided by AI. In general, the benefits of combining the technologies for these applications include:

- Faster development of the application through the use of productivity enhancing techniques such as frame based object representation
- Significantly decreased resources required for the maintenance of simulation through the use of the inheritance capability of object oriented programming
- Increased speed of application execution by implementation on advanced parallel hardware architectures
- Improved developer's and user's interfacing through natural language and object oriented windowing interface systems
- Decreased simulation knowledge requirements for the developers through the use of heuristic aids for model development.

These and other benefits are reported in the papers presented in the second Artificial Intelligence and Simulation Conference, part of the Eastern Multiconference (EMC) '89. This year, the AI and Simulation Conference will consist of approximately double the number of paper and panel discussion sessions as last year. The conference will also present four tutorials, including one on neural networks. The papers in the conference cover the threoretical aspects as well as real applications. The theoretical aspects are reported in the following groups of paper sessions:

- Methodology and Concepts by Paul Fishwick, *University of Florida*
- AI and Modeling Process by Wanda Austin, *The Aerospace Corporation*
- AI Techniques for Discrete Event and Continuous Simulation by Sumitra Reddy, *West Virginia University.*

Applications are reported in the following groups of paper sessions:

- AI and Simulation for Control and Training by Andrew Kornecki, *Embry Riddle Aeronautical University*
- Agricultural Applications by Harbans Lal, *University of Florida*
- AI and Simulation in Telecommunications by Ina Ghaznavi Collins, *GTE Government Systems Corporation.*

The tutorials, plenary speeches, papers and panel discussion sessions will provide a wealth of current and relevant information to the curious as well as experienced practitioners in the field. Attendees to the conference will have the unique opportunity to mingle with contributors to the conference, who represent a cross-section of researchers and applications developers; university staff, government staff, government contractors and commercial industry personnel.

Non-contributing attendees of this year's Conference are most welcome to consider active participation in next year's AI and Simulation Conference. This annual event is rapidly gaining recognition as "the place to be for AI and Simulation."

Ranjeet Uttamsingh
Chairman of the AI and Simulation Conference
1989 Eastern Multiconference

ADVANCES IN AI AND SIMULATION

Advances in AI and Simulation
© 1989 By The Society for Computer
Simulation International
ISBN 0-911801-50-2

Knowledge acquisition for the air traffic control training

Andrew J. Kornecki
Computer Science Department, Embry Riddle Aeronautical University
Daytona Beach, Fl. 32014

ABSTRACT

Air Traffic Control System (ATC) represents one of the services of the Federal Aviation Administration to accomplish a safe and expeditious flow of air traffic. It is not an easy task to achieve full harmony and cooperation in such a complex system based on a multitude of individual human decisions, requiring fault-free communication, and using sophisticated computer and electronics gadgets supplied by different vendors.

The presented research is related to the project funded by the Florida High Technology and Industrial Council [Gonzalez et al. 1988]. Since 1987, the University of Central Florida has been working on an Intelligent Simulation Training System (ISTS). The General Electric Company has been involved in the preparation of an ATC Radar Simulator. The Embry Riddle Aeronautical University has been engaged in building the Air Traffic Expert Controller (ATEC) representing the ATC Knowledge Base and Expert System. The ERAU activities have dealt with two aspects:

- to build a system capable of intelligent preprocessing of the ATC Radar Simulator output and create some consistent factual description of a simulated air traffic situation,

- to acquire the ATC expert operational knowledge and build a system capable of imitating the expert controller decision process.

The operational knowledge to be acquired will be represented in a rule-based form. Each controller action is activated by a set of situation facts. There are thus three problems with the operational knowledge acquisition: to identify controller actions, to identify situation facts, and to build rules binding situation facts with either the controller actions or other situation facts. The problems of knowledge acquisition to build an ATC expert system capable of recognizing traffic situation and generating an appropriate action are described in the paper.

INTRODUCTION

The best way to train an AT controller on a terminal radar position is to request the trainee to actually control the traffic in real life conditions. An experienced AT controller would constantly supervise the trainee and intervene whenever a problem situation would develop. In such a case, we need to have access to the real ATC terminal, and need to have one experienced controller (a scarce resource nowadays) for each trainee. Therefore, a much better way is to substitute the real ATC radar system by a simulator, and the expert by an intelligent computer program simulating the human expert behavior [Kornecki 1988].

To design such an expert program there is a need to extract the ATC knowledge. The sources of the operational knowledge are ATC manuals describing the system, regulations, phraseology, etc. There is, however, a vast amount of knowledge that can be extracted from the human experts by a process of careful interviewing [Liebowitz 1988]. Although the rules in manuals are designed to avoid ambiguity, there is still room for interpretation, heuristic, or rules of thumb. Handling a complex traffic situation is a subjective issue, and various controllers can act in different ways, without breaking related regulations.

The computer software we consider represents a well known concept of an expert system. In an excellent review of knowledge acquisition related problems [Hayes-Roth et al. 1980], we read that the power of intelligent systems derives primarily from the knowledge of human experts. Knowledge acquisition refers to the transfer of expertise from a human expert to a machine. Only a formal knowledge representation scheme will allow the expert to express the knowledge in a domain-specific terms.

The currently being implemented computer expert systems [Michaelsen et al. 1985] are capable of:

- applying expertise to the problem solutions,
- explaining and justifying what they do,
- communicating with other and acquiring new knowledge.

Such human expert capabilities as knowledge reorganization, breaking rules, graceful degradation, or determining relevance, for computer expert systems are still in an initial development phase.

The subsequently outlined user specification and requirements phase for the ATC software design includes these concepts in AI literature, facilitating knowledge acquisition in building an expert system.

KNOWLEDGE ACQUISITION FOR THE ATC EXPERT

The premise of any ATC action comprises some known to the controller facts about the current traffic situation. Some of these facts are extracted from incoming simulated verbal communication, some are available as a text on a CRT. Most of the information is given in a visual form from the simulated radar screen. Only the human mind is capable of merging these complex information coming from various sources, and detecting relevant facts on which the controller action is based. To identify how the expert recognizes traffic situation requires a great deal of interviews. The concepts of perceptual filtering, and partitioned dialogue [Brown 1988] may be very helpful. Once such information is extracted, an appropriate intelligent pre-processor can be designed which uses the simulation output to create the facts representing the factual knowledge about the current state of the system and predicted conflicts.

The ATC system represents a classical expert system approach, in which the solution is driven by forward chaining rules. The system evidently conforms to the cause-effect paradigm. The controller's knowledge can be represented as production rules, where the situation facts constitute premises (IF clause), and the action facts constitute conclusions (THEN clause). In some cases, a rule conclusion may be yet another situation fact. An inference engine is responsible for searching the knowledge base and firing the rules. Asserting facts to and/or retracting facts from the knowledge base constitutes a principal knowledge control handling mechanism. The knowledge control issues are crucial for the efficiency and correct performance of an expert system. To facilitate the ATEC development the Automated Reasoning Tool – an available expert system shell – has been used in the initial project phase.

The ISTS project activities proved the feasibility of the system as presented in an initially designed demo program, and subsequently an advanced prototype using LISP Symbolics machine. Since in both cases the stress was on exploring the feasibility of the presented approach, the expert part of the system has been limited to a few in-flight separation and hand-off rules. The addition of further rules, case by case, without a more rigorous formalized approach could lead to creation of the expert system which is not fully competent and effective in executing complex ATC actions.

In order to address this issue, a serious effort has been undertaken to study the ATC literature and manuals related to the terminal control area. After detailed analysis of the relevant sections and discussions with ATC experts, a more rigorous approach has been proposed.

As shown above, it is clear that most of the controller actions result in a verbal communication to a pilot, another controller, or an aviation authority. Examples of some other controller actions are to file some written information, or to record a change in e.g. flight strip. Each of these actions has a unique phraseology. Some of them will require parameters given in either symbolic or numeric form, (e.g. airport, airway name, aircraft identification, altitude, heading, etc.). In interviewing the ATC experts, we have found that each action is originated by some primary situation fact, (e.g. radar contact, pilot request, predicted separation violation, need for hand-off). The goal of the controller's action is to eliminate this triggering fact. The controller action depends, however, on some other secondary situation facts describing the situation at the moment of decision – (e.g. other fraffic, type of aircraft, flight plan, weather, airport situation, knowledge of area, etc.).

Air Traffic Expert Controller is a dynamically driven Expert System with its Knowledge Base consisting of rules and facts. The rules reflect ATC operational procedures and regulations enhanced by the experience of the domain experts – air traffic controllers. The facts represent the ATC situation and/or required course of action. The facts on the current situation are asserted and/or retracted dynamically as the result of external inputs. These inputs come (in the current settings) from the simulation module responsible for imitating the aircraft and pilot behavior, weather, environment (radio, navigational aids, restricted areas, runways, airports), and emergency events. For the aircraft, treated as a simulation object, such data as aircraft heading, exact X-Y position, or speed are known object attributes. Acquiring data from the simulation, the expert program can base its knowledge of situation on all these available details. Complex arithmetic computations, based on geometric relation of aircraft in three dimensional space, produce exact values when the given separation violation may take place. To base an expert decision on such data does not simulate a human expert behavior. Nevertheless, it seems to be permissible when the ATEC is simulation driven.

A slightly different situation might arise assuming we want to use the ATEC as a real life ATC consultant – advisor. The air traffic controller sitting in front of the radar screen does not know the details known only to the simulation program. The ATC action is based on a subjective evaluation of the situation rather than on a specific projection of the aircraft courses and computation of the future possible separation violation. The mentioned subjectivity reflects the fact that the controller compares the current situation with the past one. The controller does so in some frequent, easy to define time intervals, sometimes subconsciously, testing whether there is a possible future separation violation. The flight strips and information about the pilot intentions play an important role in this evaluation. There is no extensive arithmetic computation involving geometric relation between objects in three dimensional space.

As pointed out by ATC experts [McKinnon 1987] it is within the capabilities of modern technology to have an access to the aircraft data from tracking beacons. Thus even in the consultant-advisor mode, in connection with the real time system, the presented expert program would perform similarly as for the system which is simulation based.

ATC EXPERT SYSTEM KNOWLEDGE STRUCTURE

As we try to present the acquisition of domain specific knowledge, we discuss here the activities of terminal area radar controller. However, a similar analysis may be repeated for en-route, tower, and ground controller. The presented considerations are general enough to constitute a base for building an expert system for any controller-dispatcher type of activities.

A detailed analysis of ATC manuals and interviews with the experts allow us to identify several groups of controller action related to various phases of the flight:

* Initial clearance before the take-off.
When the aircraft is ready to take-off, this readiness is reported to the tower. The tower controller contacts the terminal area radar controller (departure position, if separate) to get the departure clearance. The radar controller analyzes the traffic situation in the vicinity of the initial path of the aircraft. The analysis gives a base to issue clearance to release, hold, or release with some restrictions. This clearance is then reported to the pilot by the tower (clearance delivery).

* Departure.
After an aircraft is airborne, a blip is shown on the radar screen. At that time the pilot is supposed to contact the controller. After this happens the controller acknowledges the radar contact and gives initial instructions (if necessary) based on the filed flight plan and current traffic situation. There are several other actions in case there is no radar contact, no voice communication, etc.

* Pilot requests and emergencies.
At any time a pilot can contact the controller requesting some action. In most cases, the action is an authorization of altitude/course change. In some cases it is a request for some information. Depending on the request and the traffic situation, the controller decision is communicated to the pilot (making a note about the change in the flight plan). In this category we may have emergencies (the type of emergency is reported) resulting in a pre-defined sequence of the controller action (for example: call airport authority, FBI, etc.).

* Separation.
Continuously the controller monitors separation standards. In case any two aircraft are on the course and altitude that may result in violating these standards the controller evaluates the traffic in the vicinity and communicates his decision to one of the pilots involved about a requested change of altitude, heading, or speed. Such change has to be made to eliminate the possible violation. There are

some other actions related to filing a "near miss" report, etc.

* Hand-offs.
When the aircraft is close to the next sector the hand-off procedure to the next sector is originated. The sequence of actions include communication with the other sector controller and the pilot to give him the next sector contact. The communication from the other sector controller will originate the hand-off from the neighboring sector. These actions are completed with a communication to the pilot who enters the given sector.

* Weather.
The controller monitoring the weather may detect that the predicted path of an aircraft leads through a heavy turbulence area. Such situation will result in a communication to a pilot suggesting the change in the flight plan. The decision is left to the pilot, and his/her answer is treated as pilot request.

* Arrivals.
The pilot handed-off to the arrival controller will get the necessary sequence of recommended actions based on the controller knowledge about the airport, traffic situation, position, speed, and altidude of the aircraft, etc. The sequence is originated by the pilot communication about his readiness to land. The initial controller action is to give the airport altimeter and weather information (confirm ATIS). In most cases the sequence includes vectors, altitude, and speed requirements to intercept the final approach course. The sequence of actions is completed when the aircraft is on the final approach and handed-off to the tower.

* Traffic advisories.
While monitoring the traffic the controller might issue advisories about the traffic based on the information from the radar screen. The resulting advice is communicated to the pilot.

The short description presented above should facilitate a rigorous approach in building the terminal radar ATC expert. For all groups introduced above specific actions with their respective phraseology have been identified. These actions need to be represented as facts identified by name, appended with possible parameters (symbolic or numeric) including time of issue, time of validity etc. The analysis of ATC manuals and expert interviews allow us to identify the primary situation fact that originates the specific action. Additional secondary situation facts are conditions to launch the specific action. It should be emphasized that the set of the same conditions may sometimes result in two or more different actions. Also, different conditions may result in the same action.

EXAMPLE

The following example representing the operational knowledge acquisition for selected group of the terminal radar controller actions is not complete. For the sake of brevity only limited rules, situation, and action facts corresponding to the initial clearance before take-off have been summarized. The example, however, should give a flavor of the presented approach. The action and situation facts will be identified by the upper and lower case letters respectively.

This group of controller action deals with giving a clearance either to the tower or to the clearance delivery controller, in order either to release unconditionally, release with constraints, or hold the aircraft requesting the take-off clearance. The primary situation fact triggering this action is a request from the tower that the given aircraft is ready to take-off. This fact will be asserted by the pre-processor module based on the data from the simulation module. The time of assertion (curr-tim) as well as other time stamps may constitute parameters for the facts. Both the situation and action facts may have defined time-of-validity (t-of-v) identifying the interval in which controller action is to be taken. Some additional facts having impact on the controller action will be situation facts to be detected by the pre-processing module such as: no-conflicting-traffic, traffic-above, traffic-right, traffic-left, conflicting-traffic, no-flight-plan, heavy-ahead, etc.

The possible controller actions related to the aircraft release for departure are:

A. (release aircraft-id t-of-v)
B. (restricted-release-alt aircraft-id
                    alt-data t-of-v)
C. (restricted-release-dir aircraft-id
                    dir-data t-of-v)
D. (hold aircraft-id delay)
E. (request-flight-plan aircraft-id)

The triggering situation fact is a communication from the tower (clearance delivery) about the aircraft readiness. As long as this fact is not asserted there is no need for the controller to do anything in the matter of releasing the aircraft. After the action is taken the primary situation fact should disappear (to be retracted).

a. (ready-for-departure aircraft-id curr-tim)

The secondary fact to be considered is an existence of filed flight plan for the aircraft in question.

b. (flight-plan-filed aircraft-id)

The facts (a and b) are the necessary conditions for the expert to consider one of the first four actions (A - D). Now, the pre-processing module must be activated to detect the traffic on predicted flight route in the close vicinity of the airport - immediately after the take-off. The result of these computation will be assertion of one of the following facts:

c. (no-conflicting-traffic curr-tim t-of-v)
d. (traffic-above altitude curr-tim t-of-v)
e. (traffic-right dir-data curr-tim t-of-v)
f. (traffic-left dir-data curr-tim t-of-v)

g. (conflicting-traffic curr-tim delay)
h. (heavy-craft-ahead curr-tim delay)

Reviewing the controler actions related to the departure clerances we can see that to generate one of the possible actions (A, B, C, D, or E) we may use one of the following rules:

RULE 1: ; unconditional release
         IF a and b and c and not h THEN A

RULE 2: ; restricted altitude release
         IF a and b and d and not h THEN B

RULE 3: ; restricted direction release (right)
         IF a and b and e and not h THEN C

RULE 4: ; restricted direction release (left)
         IF a and b and f and not h THEN C

RULE 5: ; file the flight plan
         IF a and not b THEN E

RULE 6: ; delay take-off after heavy aircraft
         IF a and b and c and h THEN D

RULE 7: ; hold
         IF a and b and g THEN D

CONCLUSIONS

The presented considerations review the scope of the ATEC project concentrating on the domain knowledge representation and acquisition problems. Using formalized approach for the specified domain knowledge acquisition we have identified facts and rules as the components of the ATC Expert System. Most of the situation facts represent knowledge about the current system state and are acquired from the simulation module. A subsequent modifications, modules interfacing, verification, and validation of the system represent the future tasks in the project realization.

REFERENCES

Brown J.R:"Knowledge Acquisition Methodologies for Visual Experts", Proceedings of the FLAIRS, Florida Artificial Intelligence Research Symposium, Orlando, Fl., May 1988, pp. 228-230,

Gonzalez A., Kornecki A., Ransom A, Bauert P., Phinney R.:"A Simulation Based Expert System for Training Air Traffic Controllers", Proceedings of the FLAIRS, Florida Artificial Intelligence Research Symposium, Orlando, Fl., May 1988, pp. 231-235,

Hayes-Roth F.,Klahr P., Mostow D.J.:"Knowledge Acquisition, Knowledge Programming, and Knowledge Refinement", The Rand Corporation, R-2540-NSF, 1980, in "Expert Systems-Techniques, Tools, and Applications" ed.by P.Klahr and D.Waterman, Addison-Wesley, 1986, pp.310-349,

Kornecki A.:"Simulation and AI as Tools in Aviation Education", Proceedings of the SCS Conference on AI and Simulation, April 1988, Orlando, Florida, pp.121-125,

Liebowitz J.:"Introduction to Expert Systems", Mitchel Publishing, Inc., Santa Cruz, California, 1988,

McKinnon P.:"Living with Artificial Intelligence", Journal of ATC, October-December 1987, pp.23-25,

Michaelsen R.H., Michie D., Boulanger A.:"The Technology of Expert Systems", Byte, April 1985, pp. 303-312,

Advances in AI and Simulation
© 1989 By The Society for Computer
Simulation International
ISBN 0-911801-50-2

PROLOG for an integrated simulation and expert system*

Harbans Lal and R.M. Peart
Department of Agricultural Engineering
University of Florida
Gainesville, FL 32611

ABSTRACT

The paper discusses application of logic programming as means for developing an integrated decision support system. It allows development of Expert Systems and Simulation in one single environment. The main advantage of using logic programming for simulation over conventional languages is that the inferencing capability of the logic programming can be utilized to diagnose causes for poor performance of the model. The system can then help the user in the process of parameter estimation for the model. The paper also presents FARMSYS--an intelligent farming system tool for multicrop production systems developed using this approach. It combines the capability of expert systems and logic-based simulation in a seamless decision-aid tool. It is the first agricultural application of logic-based simulation. The program is written in Turbo Prolog, a PC-based logic programming language.

SIMULATION AND ITS LIMITATIONS

Simulation is one of the most powerful techniques available for analyzing and predicting the behavior of complex systems (Umphress and Udo 1987). Simulation, like other data processing programs, does not provide optimal solutions. The scarcity and the cost of expert advice for output interpretation is a disadvantage of simulation as a management tool.

KNOWLEDGE-BASED SYSTEMS

Knowledge-Based Systems (KBS) are integrated packages which combine the capability of expert systems and simulation, including the necessary data bases (Peart et al. 1988). They use rule-based paradigms of expert systems and are tightly integrated to the conventional analytical tools. They provide the power of mathematical equations which are often worth thousands of rules and also that of production rules which show their strength when the real world does not conform to rigid equations. So KBS are tools which can intelligently apply analytical tools to deal with real world problems.

APPROACHES TO KBS DEVELOPMENT

The approaches to KBS development can be divided into two broad categories; 1) Hybrid approach and 2) Knowledge-based Simulation approach (Beck and Jones 1988).

Hybrid Approach

The hybrid approach is the most popular approach. In this approach the expert systems

---

*This paper approved as Journal Paper No. _____ of the Florida Agricultural Experiment Station.

and conventional analytical or simulation models, developed separately, are combined to act as a single program. The simulation model available for a particular system or specially developed for the purpose is written using one of the procedural languages such as FORTRAN, BASIC or PASCAL to implement an algorithm. The expert systems are written in one of the AI languages or specialized shells. In this combination, the model provides the knowledge about the system for the defined set of circumstances and an expert system interprets its results for the user. Such systems have made significant contributions as decision-aid tools (McKinion and Lemmon 1985 and Batchelor et al. 1987). However, the language incompatibilities and requirements of powerful computers are disadvantages.

Knowledge-Based Simulation

In recent years there have been attempts to develop knowledge-based systems where both the simulation and expert systems are written using one single environment, thus providing a seamless system. In such systems, also referred to as Knowledge-based Simulation, components of many models are organized into a model base (Reddy et al. 1986). The model base acts as a library which can be consulted for developing a specific model which addresses a particular problem. AI techniques are used to organize the model base and to identify those models needed for a specific goal and design. In addition, models can be integrated with databases and other application programs. Two approaches used to develop such systems are listed below.

Object-Oriented Approach. Applications using the object-oriented approach are developed using an object-oriented programming (OOP) environment and language. In such an environment, the objects become the principal focus of attention. The whole world of interest is expressed as a collection of objects with a mechanism by which they can communicate with each other and generate new objects (Stefik and Bobrow 1986; Gabriel 1987; Lal et al. 1987). The representation of knowledge in different classes and subclasses in a hierarchical manner facilitates the development, utilization and maintenance of knowledge based systems. However, PC-based systems are not yet sufficiently powerful to handle operational scale applications using this approach.

Logic-Based Approach. The logic-based approach uses PROgramming in LOGic (PROLOG) environment and language for developing its applications. PROLOG is one of the most widely used languages for writing knowledge-based expert systems in Japan and Europe. It is considered as a development tool. It contains a basic scheme for representing knowledge (a common characteristic of a language) and also has a built-in inference engine which conducts its searches.

A program in this language is a collection of facts and rules and the predicates may be formed to describe different objects of the world of interest. From this collection PROLOG derives solutions to the questions. The recursion, symbol and list processing capabilities of PROLOG facilitate handling qualitative knowledge, in addition to quantitative knowledge, for the given system effectively and efficiently.

In recent years there have been attempts to develop simulation programs and simulation languages using PROLOG as a base language (Korencki 1986 and Yokoi et al. 1986). Attempts have also been made to develop object-oriented programming languages using PROLOG (Futo and Gergerly 1987 and Fan and Sackett 1988). The simulations developed using the logic programming approach also have been referred to as goal-oriented simulation or logic-based simulation.

PROLOG provides a unique environment for developing a seamless knowledge-based system. Both simulation and expert systems can be developed under one single environment. In addition, it provides the following advantages for designing the simulation:

1) It enables the modeler to specify qualitative, in addition to quantitative, knowledge about the system.

2) The system may be defined in a much more descriptive manner than with most procedural languages.

3) It provides a convenient design facility as it permits natural language-like sentences which allows nonprogrammers a better understanding of program logic.

4) The inferencing capability of PROLOG can be utilized to diagnose causes for poor performance of the model. The system can then help the user in the process of parameter estimation for the model.

In this paper we describe an agricultural application which has been developed using the logic programming approach. It is the first of its kind. It combines the capability of expert systems and logic-based simulation.

FARM DECISION-AID TOOLS AND THEIR TYPES

Crop production is one of the principal activities of most farm systems. This activity can be described as a system of n-stage decision problems. These n-stages are differentiated by weather, availability of man and machinery, and state of the crop and/or fields. At each decisive moment farmers consider all these factors consciously or subconsciously to decide their actions. They select some man and machine to perform certain operation(s) on crops and/or fields.

The stochastic nature of the weather and complexity of other factors, both endogenous and exogenous, responsible for crop production really makes the job of the farmers complex and challenging. They are always concerned about selection, efficient utilization, and management of the resources at their disposal in order to have better control over the production process at different problem stages. To help farmers make decisions under such conflicting and complex situations, agricultural scientists have been developing Decision-Aid Tools (DATs) which could be utilized by farmers to increase their farm yields and profits.

The Farm Decision-Aid Tools, both analytical and simulation models, can be broadly classified into: 1) biological plant scale models, 2) field scale models, and 3) farm-scale models.

The biological plant scale models study the behavior of the individual plant and extrapolate it for the whole field or farm. The examples of such models are the crop growth simulation models (Jones et al. 1988) designed to study the physiological development and growth of plants. These models have been commonly used to better understand the development process of the plant. However, in recent years there have been attempts to use them as decision-aid tools (Boggess et al. 1983; Boote and Jones 1986; Hoogenboom et al. 1987).

The field-scale models study the behavior of an individual field in terms of its adaptability to different cropping systems (a combination of crops over time) to suit its environmental and soil characteristics. These models generally do not consider the operational constraints (machinery and labor requirements) to implement the candidate or the selected cropping systems (Tsai et al. 1987).

The farm-scale models capture the behavior of the farm as a whole. These models consider the operational constraints of the farm and can help farmers make strategic planning and/or tactical management decisions. Quantitative techniques such as linear programming and simulation have been used to model the operational behavior of the whole farm.

All three types of models are important in developing decision-aid tools for the farm. They should be considered as complementary rather than competitive or substitutes for one another. The plant-based models should serve as the basic tools for developing field-scale models. The field scale models can then serve as a starting point for farm-scale models.

FARMSYS, discussed in this paper, is a farm-scale model. It can utilize the actual or optimum farm situation to study and analyze its operational behavior. The optimum farm situation could be obtained using field-scale models or other farm-scale models such as linear programming.

FARMSYS KNOWLEDGE BASES

FARMSYS is an object-oriented, knowledge-based decision system for crop production systems. It has been developed using a logic-programming approach and is written in Turbo Prolog.

It combines the capability of expert systems and simulation in a seamless decision-aid tool. The simulation of the field operations uses a one-day time step. The front and tail end expert systems of FARMSYS are designed to interact with the user in a friendly manner.

The tail end expert system also analyzes the simulation reports in the context of the available farm resource base to identify bottlenecks and/or availability of excess machinery and labor and makes appropriate cost-effective recommendations for their remedies. The operations simulator also has many built-in expert systems which are called upon to make heuristic decisions prior to carrying out actual tasks.

The knowledge-bases of FARMSYS, like most other knowledge-based systems, can be broadly lumped into three broad categories; input knowledge, procedural knowledge, and output knowledge.

The knowledge about the farm and the region is supplied as input to FARMSYS. It (FARMSYS) then manipulates the input knowledge with procedural knowledge captured within the Operations Simulator and produces another body of knowledge in the form of simulation reports. These reports are then analyzed by the Expert Advisor to develop appropriate recommendations (Fig. 1).

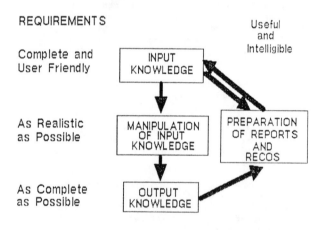

Figure 1. Functional relationships in FARMSYS.

The input and output knowledge of FARMSYS is stored in the form of dynamic databases of the PROLOG. Lal et al. (1988) provide a detailed discussion about the structure and contents of these knowledge-bases, including the procedural knowledge captured in the Operations Simulator.

Farm knowledge is the most critical component of the knowledge-bases supplied by the user for his specific farm setting. Fig. 2 presents a semantic net representation of the farm knowledge.

The farm has crops, fields, labor, tractors and implements. The crops are grown on the fields. Each crop has a list of operations which need to be carried out to grow it. Each operation needs to meet agronomic requirements prior to its execution. The implements are characterized by their types (self-propelled or tractor-powered type). The tractor-powered type implements

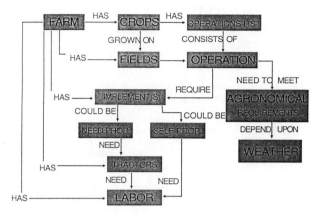

Figure 2. Semantic representation of farm knowledge.

require a power unit for them to be operational. The power unit (tractor or animals) in turn requires an operator. On the other hand, self-propelled implements do not require any power unit. They become operational with an operator.

The actual work hours for the day for an operation are decided by a built-in expert system based upon the scheduled work hours, working hours conditions associated with the operation, and the rainfall of the day. The work for the day, in turn, is calculated using working width and speed of the implement, operational efficiency of the operation, and the actual work hours for the day as follows.

Actual Work Done, area per day = Width*Speed*Op.Eff.*Actual Work Hrs.

COMPONENTS OF FARMSYS

FARMSYS consists of three principal components; Farm Info Manager, Operations Simulator, and Expert Analyzer.

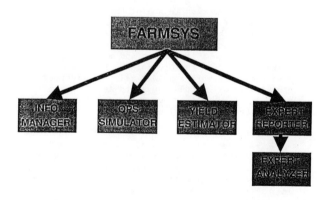

Figure 3. FARMSYS hierarchical components.

Farm Info Manager

It is designed to collect farm information. It works as an intelligent front end for the Operations Simulator. It receives information from the user for the farm setting concerning crops, fields, machinery, labor and other power sources and sequence and details of different operations associated with each crop in a friendly and interactive manner.

The user fills in information on the specially designed forms on the computer screen. Once any information such as tractor make or model is entered, it need not be typed in again, but it will appear on a "pop-up" menu the next time it is a possible selection as input. The information thus collected is then stored in different files.

The Info Manager also permits the user to access any file in a developed set and let him make changes such as addition or deletion of an entity or modification of one or more attributes of the selected item of any entity.

A built-in file manager keeps track of the status of different farm files as affected by any change in the related files. The Info Manager also presents messages to the user about these effects prior to letting him make any changes and also advises him to take appropriate action.

Though Info Manager is presently structured to collect farm information, its basic concepts can be utilized to collect information about many more types of industrial applications.

Operations Simulator

The Farm Field Operations Simulator is the real heart of the system which simulates field operations for all fields of the farm for a complete growing season with one-day time steps and produces both work and no-work reports.

Structure of the Simulator. The Operations Simulator is structured into two distinct components; namely, a) farm specific knowledge and b) procedural simulation knowledge.

The farm specific knowledge consists of the number of ASCII files containing knowledge about the farm setting, actual weather for the location for the selected years, and expert knowledge for the region. This component needs to be developed by the user for his specific regional and farm setting and is stored in the form of dynamic data base files. The correct format and structuring of the database entries is essential for successful running of the program. Therefore, it is highly recommended to use Info Manager to generate and modify any farm information for operating the simulator.

The procedural simulation knowledge is a PROLOG program consisting of predicates and clauses (discussed briefly later in the paper) which carry out the actual simulation. The compiled version of the program cannot be accessed by user for any modification.

Simulation with Logic Programming. The Operations Simulator of FARMSYS is a unique agricultural application developed in logic programming. Therefore, we present a part of the code (Table 1) and discuss briefly how we have used PROLOG for simulating field operations.

Table 1. Part of code for field operation simulation.

```
doSimulation:-
    getFarmKnowledge(labor,field,equipment,crop,
      irrigate,operation,tractor,implement),
    getOtherKnowledge(expertfile,weatherfile,
      workhrsfile),
    findSimulationDuration(SDay,FDay),
    simulateSeason(SDay,SDay),message_work(14),
    writeResultFiles(result1,result2,result3,
      result4).

simulateSeason(SDay,FDay):-
    asserta(currentday(Sday)),repeat,
      currentday(SimDay),
    makeAvailAll,
    simulateADay(Simday,"Irrigation"),
    simulateADay(Simday,"HarvestingOps"),
    simulateADay(Simday,"PlantProtectionOps"),
    simulateADay(Simday,"PlantFertiOps"),
    simulateADay(Simday,"LandPrepOps"),
    Sday1=Simday+1,
    changeDay(Sday1),
    Sday1>Fday.

simulateADay(SDay,OpsType):-
    fieldc(FieldN,CropN),
    chkCondAndWork(FieldN,CropN,Sday,OpsType),fail.

simulateADay(_,_):-!.
```

The simulation has been carried out utilizing the backtracking (repeat-fail combination) property of PROLOG as discussed by Flowers (1988). This develops an effect similar to looping in conventional procedural languages.

The code given consists of three principal predicates, "doSimulation", "simulateSeason" and "simulateADay" which work in an hierarchical order. They can be thought of as subroutines in procedural languages.

The predicate "doSimulation" creates the necessary conditions for the simulation by bringing the farm and other knowledge to the memory using predicates "getFarmKnowledge" and "getOtherKnowledge", calls "simulateSeason", and writes reports on successful completion of the season's simulation.

The "simulateSeason" predicate has the two arguments start day (SDay) and finish day (FDay). The Turbo Prolog predicate "asserta" puts "SDay" into the dynamic database "currentday". Then it collects the same day value by use of the database predicate "currentday(SimDay)". Then it calls "simulateADay" five times with the current day and different operation types. The order of calling the predicates with different operation types determines their priority. Under the current format the irrigation gets the highest priority, followed by harvesting, plant protection, plant and fertilizer application, and land preparation operations.

On the successful completion of the one-day simulation, the current day is updated by one day (Sday1=Sday+1), and the content of the "currentday" database is changed by the use of predicate "changeDay". Finally, a check is made to see if the updated day is greater than the last day for the simulation (Sday1>Fday). This condition is satisfied when the simulation for the whole period is completed, otherwise the condition fails and backtracking begins.

The backtracking proceeds up through different predicates until it encounters "repeat". The "repeat" predicate is a nondeterministic clause which always reverses the backtracking process. On the reversal of the process, Prolog finds the content of the "currentday" database changed and picks it up for further actions of calling the "simulateADay" predicate with the new day. The process is repeated with one day increments until (Sday1>Fday) becomes true and the execution of the predicate "simulateSeason" is successfully completed.

The "simulateADay" predicate is designed to carry out one-day simulation for the current day (Sday) and the given Operation Type (OpsType). The dynamic database "fieldc" consists of entries of all the fields with the crops being grown on them. These entries are made in order of priorities of fields to be served by the simulator. During execution of this predicate, the first field (FieldN) and the crop (CropN) being grown on it are picked up and are passed to predicate "chkCondAndWork" to carry out its task. The predicate ""chkCondAndWork" checks various conditions which need to be satisfied prior to carrying out the actual task and then calculates the amount of work done based upon the available machinery set.

On successful completion of the task of "chkCondAndWork" for the current field, crop and operation type, the predicate "fail" causes the clause to fail and forces it to backtrack.

In this case, the backtracking occurs up to the database predicate "fieldc" which acts like a nondeterministic clause. At this stage Prolog picks the contents (FieldN and CropN) of the next entry in the database and repeats the steps of this clause in a hope to succeed. However, because of the "fail" predicate, it fails again. The process is repeated until all the entries of the "fieldc" database have been tried. Having worked on all the entries of the database "fieldc", the clause fails even prior to calling predicate "chkCondAndWork". Then, Prolog searches for an alternative "simulateADay" clause or rule, and finds "simulateADay(_,_):-!.", which always succeeds for any value of SDay and OpsType, thus successfully completing the task of simulating the instantiated value of the OpsType for the day for all crops and fields.

Expert Analyzer

The Expert Analyzer analyzes the simulation reports of the Operations Simulator in context of a resource base available on the farm. It advises the user to take appropriate action to improve his farming operation. Three reports prepared and presented by the analyzer are 1) Machinery Usage Report, 2) Operations Analysis Report, and 3) Accumulated Work Report.

Machinery Usage Report. This report deals with the monthly and overall utilization of farm implements, tractors and laborers. It identifies the excess of labor or machinery available on the farm. It provides the user with a performance report of the selected entity for the entire cropping season.

It separates the most and the least utilized items for the selected entity type (laborers, tractors or different types of implements). It then analyzes the importance of the least utilized item for the farm, based upon its allocation strategy, to carry out different tasks. The least utilized item is considered important for the farm if it is the unique item and does not have any complementary unit for most of the tasks it is assigned to carry out. Based upon the relative importance of the item, recommendations are made to keep it or to remove it from the system.

Operations Analysis Report. This report analyzes different operations for their timely start and completion. It identifies the bottlenecks for different operations and makes recommendations to overcome them in a cost-effective manner. This report works in a manner contrary to the Machinery Usage Report. While the Machinery Usage Report identifies and recommends reducing the under-utilized labor and machinery resource from the farm, the Operation Analysis Report identifies and recommends to upgrade the needed machinery sets (implement, tractor and operator). It can do that by increasing working hours during critical periods or increasing operational capacity through changing the speed of operation if possible or the working width up to the power limit of the power unit. The criteria for deciding for delays can be either user input or based upon a built-in default heuristic.

Accumulated Work Report. This report is designed to provide the user with an aggregate usage report for any combination of items of different farm entities over a desired interval. It can be used in analyzing the performance of one or more entities in combination with other entities. Utilizing this report the user can get answers to questions such as; how many hours did Tractor_1 work with the soybean crop during the whole year? and how many hours did Laborer_1 work with Tractor_2 during Jan 1 to Jun 30?, etc., for his farm setting based upon the simulation results.

VERIFICATION AND QUALIFICATION

The development of a knowledge-based system, like most computer software, is not complete until it has been tested for its functions. Software testing can be divided into verification and validation. However, in the case of knowledge-based systems like FARMSYS, the latter might more correctly be termed as "qualification".

The verification and qualification of FARMSYS has been carried out at two levels; 1) professional level and 2) operational level.

For the professional level qualification, we hosted a one day mini-conference on Knowledge-based Decision Systems using Logic Programming at the Department of Agricultural Engineering of the University of Florida. It was attended by 12 professionals interested in farm operations management from different parts of the U.S. and from overseas. We presented them FARMSYS and discussed its structure, components and logic in great details. They also witnessed a demonstration of FARMSYS with a real farm example. They were then asked to evaluate FARMSYS and its different components using a questionnaire which contained statements concerning various features of FARMSYS. The participants had 5 options ranging from "strongly disagree" to "strongly agree" to chose for each statement. The analysis of the questionnaire suggested that all participants appreciated the general structure of FARMSYS and the approach taken for its development. However, they had valid concerns about the relevance of the general heuristics utilized in different components of FARMSYS for their specific location.

For the operational level, we have collected the real farm data of some selected farms from north Florida and have utilized FARMSYS for analyzing their machinery and power resources for scheduling their field operations. In this analysis we have been able to identify some of their over-sized and under-sized implements for their farming operation. The farmers really like the expert analyzer part of FARMSYS which presents them the specific report of the selected combination of entities.

The complete details about the qualification procedures and their reports are available in the senior author's doctoral thesis (Lal, 1988).

REFERENCES

Batchelor, W.D.; R.W. McClendon; J.W. Jones; and D.B. Adams. 1987. An Expert Simulation System for Soybean Insect Pest Management. ASAE Paper 87-4501. ASAE, St. Joseph, MI 49085.

Beck, H.W. and J.W. Jones. 1988. Simulation and Artificial Intelligence Concepts. Paper presented at the Expert Systems Workshop, Orlando, FL, Feb. 1988. ASAE, St. Joseph, MI 49085.

Boggess, W.G. and C.B. Amerling. 1983. "A Bioeconomics Simulation Analysis for Irrigation Investments." Southern Journal of Agricultural Engineering, Dec. 1983: 85-91.

Boote, K.J. and J.W. Jones. 1986. Application of and Limitations of Crop Growth Simulation Models to fit Crops and Cropping Systems to Semi-Arid Environment. Depts. of Agronomy and Agricultural Engineering, University of Florida, Gainesville, U.S.A.

Fan, I.S. and P.J. Sackett. 1988. "A PROLOG Simulator for Interactive Flexible Manufacturing Systems Control." Simulation 50, no. 6: 239-247.

Flowers, E.B. 1988. "Failing with Grace." Turbo Technix 1, no. 5: 76-85.

Futo I. and T. Gergerly. 1987. "Logic Programming in Simulation." Trans. of the Society of Computer Simulation 3, no. 3: 195-216.

Gabriel, R.P. 1987. "What Computer Can't Co (And Why)." Moments 1, no. 3.

Hoogenboom, G.; J.W. Jones; and J.W. White. 1987. Use of Models in Studies of Drought Tolerance. Paper presented at the Workshop on Drought in Dry Beans. Centro Internacional de Agricultura Tropical, Cali, Colombia.

Jones, J.W.; K.J. Boote; S.S. Jagtap; G. Hoogenboon; and G.G. Wilkerson. 1988. SOYGRO 5.4: Soybean Crop Growth Simulation Model-User's Guide. Florida Agri. Expt. Sta. Paper no. 8304. IFAS, University of Florida, Gainesville, FL.

Kornecki Andrzej. 1988. "Simulation and Artificial Intelligence as Tools in Aviation Education." In: AI Papers, ed. R.J. Uttamsingh, SCS, San Diego, California. Simulation Series 20, no. 1: 121-126.

Peart, R.M.; Harbans Lal; and J.W. Jones. 1988. Developing Integrated Decision Support Systems using PROLOG. AAAI Workshop on AI in Agr., Aug. 1988, Univ. of Texas, San Antonio, TX, U.S.A.

Lal, Harbans. 1988. Engineering Farm Knowledge for Logic-Based Decision Support System. Ph.D. dissertation. Univ. of Florida, Gainesville, Fl, U.S.A. (in preparation).

Lal, H; R.M. Peart; and J.W. Jones. 1987. Expert Systems for Technology Transfer, ASAE Summer Meeting, Paper no. 87-5028, 12 pgs.

Lal, Harbans; R.M. Peart; J.W. Jones; and B. Jacobson. 1988. An Intelligent Field Operations Simulator, ASAE Summer Meeting, Paper No. 88-5020, 26 pgs.

McKinion, J.M. and H.E. Lemmon. 1985. "Expert Systems for Agriculture." Computers and Electronics in Agriculture 1: 31-40.

Reddy Y.V.; M.S. Fox; N. Hussain; and M. Roberts. 1986. "The Knowledge-Based Simulation Systems." IEEE Software, March 1986, pp. 26-37.

Stefik Mark and D.G. Bobrow. 1986. "Object Oriented Programming: Themes and Variations." AI Magazine 6, no. 4: 40-59.

Tsai, Y.J.; J.W. Jones; and J.W. Mishoe. 1987. "Optimizing Multiple Cropping Systems: A Systems Approach." Trans. of the ASAE 30, no. 6: 1554-1561.

Umphress, D.A. and Udo W. Pooch. 1987. "A Goal Oriented Simulation." In: Methodology and Validation, Simulation Series, Society for Computer Simulation 19, no. 1: 44-49.

Yokoi Shinji. 1986. "A PROLOG Based Object-Oriented Language and its Compiler. In: Lecture Notes in Computer Science. ed. G. Gobs and J. Hartmanis, Logic Programming' 86. Proc. of the 5th Conf. Tokyo, Japan.

Advances in AI and Simulation
© 1989 By The Society for Computer
Simulation International
ISBN 0-911801-50-2

Object-oriented and AI techniques for laboratory training

Jose M. Giron-Sierra and Jose G. Wagner-Lopez

Departamento de Informatica y Automatica
Facultad de Fisicas
Universidad Complutense de Madrid
Paraninfo
28040 Madrid, Spain

ABSTRACT

Corresponding to new theoretical courses on modern Automatic Control Engineering, for Graduate and Doctoral purposes, we constructed a new Digital Control Laboratory. The Experimental Devices reflect aspects of Chemical Industrial processes, and are under computer control: as a result the practices are complicated and risky for the equipment. In view of the difficulties confronted by the students, we developed a training system. This system is based on dynamic simulations of the controlled processes. We used Object-Oriented programming with emphasis on animated graphics for the simulations. The training is conducted by a hierarchical structure of expert systems, following a schedule of training tasks: we identify diverse knowledge domains which confluence in the experiments, and the training system observe an ordered strategy giving control to the suitable expert system. The students are trained also for malfunctions diagnostic and safety reactions. Knowledge is extracted from laboratory teachers. The paper describes the developing and characteristics of the expert training system, with details about software engineering.

A CONTROL SYSTEMS LABORATORY

We are engaged in a coordinated set of actions, to adapt our education activities about Control Systems, to modern circumstances. Non-classical control strategies before considered of only academic interest, are now becoming applicable, in view of the technological advances over the instrumentation and computer fields, together with low prices. This means an opportunity for the industrial plants, in order to attain high levels of quality, safety and competence, making use of better control systems. The consequence in educational terms is that we have to consider advanced theory, with algorithmic formulations ,and prepare the students for industrial practical situations. So we developed new courses, and implemented a new laboratory for digital control.

The purpose of the Laboratory is to introduce to the students the real problems, so we designed experimental devices that capture, at manageable scale and complexity, important aspects of industrial processes, which require automatic control solutions. We selected problems of pedagogical impact, and began the construction of first prototypes (Astrom and Ostberg 1986). These initial experimental devices are a heat exchanger, an AC motor - DC generator system, and a two-tank system. The prototypes serve as a basis for subsequent construction of some replicas with adequate variations. We associate a PC computer to each experimental device by means of an intermediate electronic unit: the PC acts as master, and the unit as slave. Each unit is made by a generic module, with a microprocessor; and a specific module, with interface electronics corresponding to one of the experimental devices. The PC sends to the slave the control algorithm, coded in BASIC; the slave's generic module receives and stores this program, and under the supervision of the master executes the control strategy, interacting through the specific module with the experimental device. The PC receives streams of experimental data from the slave during the practice. Each set of master (PC), slave, and experimental device, constitutes an experimental system (including measurement apparatus too).

Three different groups of students are contemplated by the Laboratory: beginners, initiated, and doctoral. The objectives are also different: the beginners will study standard control algorithms; the initiated will develop control algorithms; and the doctoral students will employ the experimental system for research purposes (for example: identification, adaptive control, intelligent control). The master (PC) units help to develop new programs to be executed by the slave units.

Considering that Chemical Industry has an important place and is showing great interest in automatic control application, and that some of the students will obtain a degree in Chemical Engineering (others will anyway get an industry-related job); the general path to increase the provision of Laboratory experimental systems is to concentrate on Chemical Industry facets.

THE PROBLEM

The problem now is that the experimental systems portray complex scenarios, requiring a team of students to carry out scheduled and coordinated activities. A minimal organization of the team is needed, so each member adopts specific responsibilities during the practice. There are also risks for the experimental systems components, if the correct procedures are not observed; for instance, a bad start of a motor may well provoke overheating and perhaps destructive effects on power electronics. For reasons of time consumption, safety, too much repetitive work for the laboratory assistants, effective help to the team, we decided to build a training system.

CHARACTERISTICS OF THE TRAINING SYSTEM

The purpose of the training system is to prepare teams of students to carry out determined Laboratory experimental practices. We incorporate intelligent tutoring system properties, so the training system recognizes the team learning status, and adapts the training process to the observed deficiencies (Wenger 1987; Park 1988). A code assigned to each team, informs to the training system which level (beginner, initiated, doctoral) and which practice marks the training track to be run.

When a practice is assigned to a team of students, they receive laboratory guides with information and worksheets. These guides consist of two volumes; the first gives a description of the experimental system, along with instructions of use; the second covers all the details about the practice to be effectuated. Once ready to come to the laboratory, they enter the training process, which follows a sequence of three phases. The first concern of the training system refers to the static knowledge the team must extract from the laboratory guides: in consequence the goal of the training phase 1 is to assure the team understands the relevant aspects of the experimental system (components, causal interaction, use of the computer, safety rules), and about the practice (objectives, theory and methods, experimental procedure, work distribution, data processing). The second phase of the training concentrates on dynamic knowledge (behaviour, control, limits, dangers) about each component, then about the experimental device, and finally about the experimental system. The third phase is dedicated to the dynamic and operational aspects of the experimental practice. Basically the phases 1 and 2 attempts to relieve the laboratory assistants from a tedious work, while the phase 3 run simulations, displayed by animated graphics, of what will happen in the real experiment: aiming to prevent difficulties and problems.

The success of a training system depends heavily upon superficial aspects: we have to pay special attention to a motivating, realistic, intuitive human interface (Rasmussen 1983; Alessi 1988). This is facilitated by the use of the PC graphic capabilities. In addition to that, considering the practices demand tasks distribution and coordination, we took advantage of the PC open architecture to connect a panel of

lamps and switches, so the training system reproduces the mechanical controls of the experimental devices.

TRAINING SYSTEM FUNDAMENTALS

While other training systems require a teacher to handle the training process, we aim to embody the educator functions into the system, by using artificial intelligence.

We conceive our training system in a form very natural for us - university teachers -, using the metaphor of an educational organization. Each team of students follows a training track, along several sessions, preparing for a practice. Several teams use the same training system. Inside the training system a "secretary", using identity codes assigned to the teams, keeps a record of their following-up, and sends instructions to the "scheduler" in order to begin a session (detailing students level, which practice, final point of the last session). There are three "teachers", one for each phase of the training. The scheduler directs the work of these teachers, to proceed along the training track as convenient; for instance, when beginning a session in the middle of the track, it is useful to recall some traits of the previous training. There are some educational resources to the disposition of the teachers: the most important are simulations and animated graphics (Kulikowski et Al. 1988). There is also a blackboard where the teachers write information and judgments, for several uses: contribution to a model of the team, coordination with the scheduler. The teacher's responsibility is to transmit a set of knowledge units to the team; which units and how to instruct depend on the practice considered, the team level, and his previous training memorandum. When the training track comes to an end, a "referee" issues final judgments and recommendations about the team, for the laboratory assistants.

The three phases of the training represent an ordered strategy to cover several knowledge domains, that are important for a good preparation before the practices: theory concepts and methods stated in practical form for each practice, measurement apparatus manipulation and using, composition and behaviour of the experimental system, planning and execution of the practices, identification and prevention of possible problems, etc.. One of the factors the "teachers" weigh to select knowledge units, is the team level: for instance, the teachers presume the high level students know how to use standard components and apparatus. Moreover, the team level influence the way the selected knowledge units are handled by the teacher: following the example of high level students, they will need only a quick refresh when surveying some conventional facets of the practice.

Motivation is a very important property we have to focus on. When teaching a knowledge unit, the training system adopts interactive and challenging manners, knowing the probable weak flanks of the students before the practices. For instance, one of the frequent laboratory pathologies is the blind switch on of power with independence of apparatus initial setting and connections. Corresponding to this problem, the training system displays figures on the screen showing any of the apparatus with incorrect initial disposition: the students have to realize it and fix the arrangement. Later on, in the phase 2, the training system will touch dynamic matters, using animated graphics; one of the activities alludes to apparatus behaviour

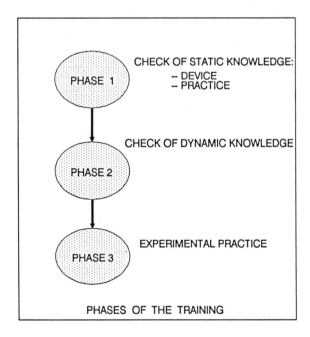

PHASE 1 — CHECK OF STATIC KNOWLEDGE:
– DEVICE
– PRACTICE

PHASE 2 — CHECK OF DYNAMIC KNOWLEDGE

PHASE 3 — EXPERIMENTAL PRACTICE

PHASES OF THE TRAINING

and handling: provided the initial setting is correct, the students can play with the simulated apparatus until they consider they are ready to use the real apparatus, telling so to the system; when this happens, the system places some problems: for example, to measure a current with a multimeter, that requires a non-risky procedure (if the students take a wrong route, the system will detect it and alert to the students).

Many other pedagogical considerations could be mentioned (Merrill 1987; Merrill 1988), but let us stop here. The important result is that each of the knowledge units owns an associated peculiar set of pedagogical strategies, tailored to the subject treated and the students conditions (Ercoli and Lewis 1988). The general pattern of the strategies is to begin with an introductory exposition (there are graphic oriented resources, such block models, circuit equivalents, causal flow diagrams), attempting to make the students get a rational vision of the phenomena that will take place during the practice: so they will acquire common sense for the real experimental action; the strategy continues with a simulation part under the students initiative (testing, piloting); finally, the system takes the initiative, placing problematic situations (for instance, the failure of a component).

OBJECT ORIENTED DEVELOPING

The training system has been implemented using the SMALLTALK/V language and programming environment (Digitalk 1986). We took the decision of using Smalltalk because it offers very good support and facility to create animated graphics and modern man-machine interface, having also many advantages from the software engineering point of view. Like the specialized literature about object-oriented programming insists (Cox 1984), we get a positive working and reasoning discipline helping as well to economize efforts, as the software modules developed are re-usable. Being a new point of departure about programming, it means the drawback of facing a learning curve; but the time saved along a complete development compensates for it.

For simulation purposes object-oriented programming is specially adequate. We created objects such Tank, Valve, Pump, etc.. Smalltalk makes easy the creation of these objects and, once defined, their interconnecting reproducing the experimental device reality: by interchanging messages among the objects, they also reproduce the dynamics of the experiment, being displayed on the screen with good animation facilities.

The definition of an object includes variables and behaviours; for instance a tank has a liquid level (variable), and a dynamics of filling (behaviour). The behaviours of the objects are activated by sending messages to the objects, for instance: fillTank (indicating the quantity of liquid entering the tank). In our training system the object Tank, and others, serves for various uses: to study in particular this experimental device element (phases 1 and 2), to cooperate with other elements for the experimental device simulation, and to provoke a problematic situation with a malfunction.

Let us consider the educational metaphor again. The secretary, scheduler, teachers and referee are also objects, with specific behaviours. For instance, the teachers respond to the messages: teach and recall. The work of teachers is really

simple, because the knowledge units are objects including what to transmit to the students and how (the complete set of pedagogical strategies for this unit), the teachers select the appropriate knowledge units in an ordered fashion (perhaps reiterating).

ARTIFICIAL INTELLIGENCE

The training system detects holes in the conceptual and procedural knowledge of the team: gives advice to the team, elaborates a model of the team, adapts the teaching.

During the simulations of the experiment, the training system detects problems derived from the control algorithm under test and the team actions: alerts the team, indicates possible causes (Astrom et al. 1986; Sripada et al. 1987; Efstathion 1987).

Along the training activities targeted to prepare the team for malfunctions and failures, the system consciously introduces defects and problems, and help the team to diagnose (Milne 1987; Yuan-Liang and Govindaraj 1986).

For these activities the training system employs several mechanisms of intelligence, organized as a hierarchy of expert systems.

The objects corresponding to elements of the experimental system, embody a small expert system, so it is possible to ask to an object whether it has any problem (message: seeifproblem) and the reason of it. For instance a Tank may in-

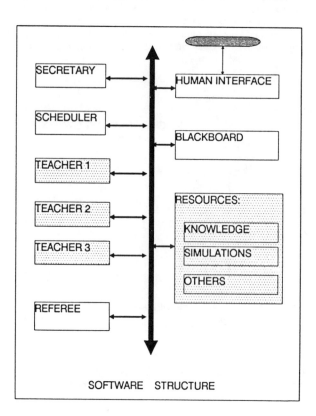

SOFTWARE STRUCTURE

form (predict) that the input/output dynamics can drive the Tank to overflow, or the Pump may prompt that has been working too hard for a long time (that means the objects keep some history vectors, with the possibility of pattern-recognition).

One of the training facets relates to measurement apparatus handling. In the universe of objects we designed, for the training system, these apparatus are included too as objects, which recognize (expert systems) correct procedures of use. The objects keep internal variables that denote a status, allowing in this case to remember the apparatus setting: a decisive factor for examining the correctness of the students procedures.

Some of the practices embrace the development and test of control algorithms. This is made with the assistance of the third "teacher", who uses a resource consisting in a set of programming tools (editor, lexical analyzer) for the restricted dialect of BASIC interpreted by the slave units. Once written, the program is executed interacting with the simulated experimental device. There are objects corresponding to the slave unit modules, which take charge of executing the program, sending the appropriate messages to the simulated experimental device, which in turn is an object. What will happen in real life in applying the control algorithm, can be seen on the screen in normal or accelerated time: the objects (Tank, Pump, etc.) called to interaction by the simulated experimental device, issue status information and deductions: the teacher elaborates with these data a report for the students, adding remarks and advice concerning the control algorithm. For these functions the teacher applies two knowledge units: one for the code developing, and the other to carry out the simulation-based study: this unit uses an expert system for heuristic judgments about the control algorithm, considering the effects. There is a resource associated with the simulated experimental device, consisting of a causal net which describes the cause-effect chaining of the phenomena in the device (Kuipers 1984; Morris and Rouse 1985).

When the team is trained for diagnosis skills, the knowledge unit in charge uses three resources: the causal net, and two simulations of the experimental device. One of the simulations operates as reference, while the other exhibits ill behaviour. The knowledge unit introduces malfunctions in the objects included in this second simulation, thus originating the ill behaviour. The screen shows the bad conduct of the device, until the students notice something is going wrong and stop the simulated experiment: from now on they receive assistance from the training system to locate the failures. The knowledge unit has an expert system for diagnosis, which consults the three resources. Naturally the training system knows where the failures are, but what we want to transmit is the strategy (rules) for locating them, and this is done by the dialogue of the expert system with the students. The simulation of reference is a duplicate of the other simulation with a difference: the objects are simpler, with no provision for malfunctions and intelligence.

We employed conventional shells to develop and test the expert systems. In general the inference mechanism is of hybrid nature: backtracking is predominant for diagnosis functions, while the high level members of the hierarchy exert planning activities, requiring forward chaining. The software development has been divided into several pieces of diverse difficulty, and achieved with the help of students, so we choose VP-Expert (Paperback 1987) and Exsys (EXSYS 1985) be-

cause they are not expensive, easy to learn, and work on PC computers. Once validated, each small expert system has been codified in Smalltalk, and added as methods to the pertinent objects.

A previous step of knowledge engineering is needed in order to build the knowledge base for each expert system (Davis and Lenat 1982; Hayes-Roth et al. 1983; Hu 1987). The training process mirrors in some extent the dialogue between the laboratory assistant and the students: so in fact we decided to record the conversations during the practices, and circulated some tests. The primary source of knowledge is the exercised laboratory assistant; with the complement of the knowledge and expertise of the experimental systems designers and integrators, together with the teachers of theory and the designers of the practices; furthermore, we have to consider the ignorance and common mistakes of the students. The general rule for knowledge capture is to take note of everything when developing the experimental device and the practices: things that are clear in the beginning, become trivial when solved, and tend to be forgotten if you try to capture this knowledge afterwards. Impartial observers are useful too, as they make questions about perhaps overlooked matters.

CONCLUSIONS

From the first time we tested Smalltalk performances it was seen the programs execute slowly: the main delays come from accesses to disk and inheritance mechanisms: for this reason it is convenient to organize hierarchies of not many levels, giving more responsibilities to the objects (enrich their behaviour). Likewise, we keep the expert systems as simple as possible, and use them only in the proper stages of the training process: this is guaranteed by the distribution of intelligence among knowledge units and other objects. The graphical representation is simple and colourful, easy to animate with quick routines.

Our first objective has been the implementation of a basic prototype with all the functions, for the purposes of feasibility study and to get operational references for subsequent research. We are now developing a version in C language, with the help of C_talk (CNS 1987) and other software tools: we want to obtain a compact package (an application created with "make") enjoying good execution speed, so the students could have a copy for personal use (this is a de facto pedagogical method, perhaps not formally admitted, but very real because computer diffusion).

The way we attack the incorporation of intelligence to the training system, enacts a practical example of divide-and-conquer strategy: we distinguish different knowledge domains, and identify attachments of these domains to objects and stages of the training process (Woolf and Cunningham 1987). The object-oriented programming promotes this kind of strategy. Hierarchies arise naturally when using objects representation, and inheritance. Functions of the resultant organizations, are duties assigned to the pertinent objects: including in this case intelligent specialized activities.

Objects could be born with primitive characteristics and begin to interact, showing for instance the basic comportments of a simulated system. Then it is possible to feed the objects with more capabilities, so the simulation seizes more refined performances. That means object-oriented programming induces an interactive and additive way of developing software, around an initial prototype where the important agents are present. The literature about expert systems cites as a general remark of programmers, that expert systems never attain a definitive status: the users asking continually for improvements and performance quantum leaps. This is a welcomed never-ending ambition, motivating more cycles of research and development. Our research is not an exception: we have to introduce improvements (in particular factors cooperating to good educational impact, demanding some psychological art), and to explore new significative intelligence enhancements.

REFERENCES

Alessi, S.M. 1988. "Fidelity in the Design of Instructional Simulations". Journal of Computer-Based Instruction 15, no. 2: 40-47.

Astrom, K.J.; J.J. Anton; and K.E. Arzen. 1986. "Expert Control". Automatica 22, no. 3: 277-286.

Astrom, K.J., And A.B. Ostberg. 1986. "A Teaching Laboratory for Process Control". IEEE Control Systems Magazine, (October): 37-42.

Cox, B.J. 1984. "Message/Object Programming: An Evolutionary Change in Programming Technology". IEEE Software 1, no. 1, (June): 51-61.

CNS Inc. 1987. C_talk.

Davis, R. And D. Lenat. 1982. Knowledge Based Systems in Artificial Intelligence. McGraw-Hill.

Digitalk Inc. 1986. Smalltalk/V.

Efstathion, J. 1987. "Knowledge-Based Systems for Industrial Control". Computer-Aided Engineering Journal, (February): 7-20.

Ercoli, P. And R. Lewis, eds. 1988. Artificial Intelligence Tools in Education. North-Holland.

EXSYS Inc. 1985. Exsys.

Hayes-Roth, F.; D.A. Waterman; and D.B. Lenat. 1983. Building Expert Systems. Addison-Wesley.

Hu, D. 1987. Programmer's Reference Guide to Expert Systems. Howard W. Sams & Co..

Kuipers, B. 1984. "Commonsense Reasoning About Causality: Deriving Behavior from Structure". Artificial Intelligence 24: 169-203.

Kulikowski; Huber; and Ferrate, eds. 1988. Artificial Intelligence, Expert Systems and Languages in Modelling and Simulation. North-Holland.

Merrill, M.D. 1987. "Prescriptions for an Authoring System". Journal of Computer-Based Instruction 14, no. 1: 1-10.

Merrill, M.D. 1988. "The Role of Tutorial and Experimental Models in Intelligent Tutoring Systems". Educational Technology, (July): 7-14.

Milne, R. 1987. "Artificial Intelligence for Online Diagnosis". IEE Proceedings 134, D, no. 4: 238-244.

Morris, N.M. And W.B. Rouse. 1985. "The Effects of Type of Knowledge upon Human Problem Solving in a Process Control Task". IEEE T. Systems, Man and Cybernetics 15, no. 6: 698-707.

Paperback Software International. 1987. VP-Expert.

Park, O. 1988. "Functional Characteristics of Intelligent Computer-Assisted Instruction: Intelligent Features". Educational Technology, (June): 7-13.

Rasmussen, J. 1983. "Skills, Rules, and Knowledge: Signals, Signs, and Symbols, and Other Distinctions in Human Performance Models". IEEE T. Systems, Man and Cybernetics 13, no. 3: 257-266.

Sripada, N.R.; D.G. Fisher; and A.J. Morris. 1987. "AI Application for Process Regulation and Servo Control". IEE Proceedings 134, D, no. 4: 251-259.

Wenger, E. 1987. Artificial Intelligence and Tutoring Systems. Morgan Kaufmann.

Woolf, B. And P.A. Cunningham. 1987. "Multiple Knowledge Sources in Intelligent Teaching Systems". IEEE Expert, (Summer): 41-54.

Yuan-Liang, Su. And T. Govindaraj. 1986. "Diagnosis in Large Dynamic System: Experiments in a Training Simulator". IEEE T. Systems, Man and Cybernetics 16, no. 1: 129-141.

Advances in AI and Simulation
© 1989 By The Society for Computer
Simulation International
ISBN 0-911801-50-2

Simulating decision processes in the rule-based paradigm

Stan Szpakowicz[†], Gregory E. Kersten[††], Zbig Koperczak[†]

Artificial Intelligence Research Group, Department of Computer Science, University of Ottawa
Ottawa, Ontario, Canada   K1N 6N5
[††] Decision Analysis Laboratory, School of Business, Carleton University
Ottawa, Ontario, Canada   K1S 5B6

ABSTRACT

Decision processes with dynamically changing information interact with the environment and adapt the decision problem to reflect the varying requirements. Such processes can be modelled by different approaches, such as games, meta-games, or multiple-criteria decision models. We describe a rule-based approach, with rules used at several levels to represent the problem itself, its potential for change and its actual modifications in response to signals from the environment. This approach stems from our experiments with the expert system shell NEGOPLAN in supporting decisions with strategic interactions. We present the power of NEGOPLAN on a simple example of a robot that explores a planet.

1. INTRODUCTION

Simulation has been traditionally considered as a numerical technique for conducting experiments (Naylor et al. 1966). Rule-based formalism and logic programming contribute to the extension of the scope of simulation to both qualitative and quantitative modelling, experimentation, and analysis of the system's behaviour (Arons 1983; Lavery 1986; Shannon et al. 1985). Shannon (1987: p.16) states that expert systems technology "will follow a different paradigm ... the modeller will declare the knowledge about the system, define the goal and let the computer work to find the solution...". This seems possible in the long run, but here we only consider how this technology can be used to develop models and to organize experiments.

We present a rule-based approach to simulating decision processes that involve identification of the environment, self-analysis and readiness for action, and identification of the local decision rules. This approach is the extension of a method and its implementation in the expert system shell NEGOPLAN (Kersten et al. 1988, Matwin et al. 1987, Szpakowicz et al. 1987). NEGO-PLAN has been applied to the modelling and support of negotiation processes. We have tested it on several examples, including union-management negotiation (Matwin et al. 1989) and negotiation with a hostage taker (Michalowski et al. 1988).

We apply NEGOPLAN to the simulation of discrete decision processes in an environment for which the set of all possible states can be determined but the current state cannot be predicted. The decisions are made by a (human or machine) system according to its current status, the recent history of its decisions, and the state of the environment. For these purposes we have extended the capabilities of NEGOPLAN with random modelling of the environment, simple arithmetic, and the recording of the history of the system's decisions.

The paper has four more sections. In section 2 we show how we simulate the system's responses to challenges posed by the environment in order to achieve goals defined a priori. The system we consider is a robot sent to take pictures and collect samples on a planet with known characteristics but unknown probabilities or their distribution. A rule-based model of the robot and its environment is given in section 3, and experiments with this model are discussed in section 4. We use a very simple example to demonstrate our approach, its flexibility and capability of simulating decision process, but NEGOPLAN at its present stage can be applied to much more complex and more realistic problems. It can also be expanded to accommodate new requirements, some of which are discussed in the concluding section.

2. THE NEGOPLAN APPROACH

We distinguish the static and dynamic aspect of the simulation of the robot decision problem. They correspond to the structure of the problem at various stages of the simulation, and to the "atomic" changes that can be combined to bring the system closer to its goals. Simulation ends when the current principal goal has been achieved and no further goal can be inferred form the present situation.

The static aspect. The problem is seen as a set of loosely coupled subproblems that eventually reduce to elementary facts about the system and its environment. The principal goal is hierarchically decomposed into subgoals, with *facts* at the lowest level. This decomposition is represented in a *goal representation tree* such as those in Figures 2 and 3. The dependence of a goal/subgoal on one or more of lower-level subgoals or facts is captured by a *rule*, for example

local_goals <- reach_target & take_picture & take_sample.

This rule can be read "local goals of a robot consist of reaching the target, taking its photograph and collecting a sample".

At any given moment, the planet and the robot are in a certain state whose characteristics are expressed by facts. Logical values of facts are described by *metafacts*. A metafact of the form "$A : F ::= v$" means that agent A considers fact F as having the value v. For example:

planet : heat(normal) ::= true.

This metafact reads "it is presently true that the heat, as the characteristics of the planet, is normal".

Three values are possible: *any*, *true*, and *false*. *any* means that a fact may be assigned the value *any* or *true* and that both must be taken into consideration when this fact is considered. Metafacts characterizing the environment (e.g. planet : sun(hidden) ::= true) may be randomly generated from a given repertory, and they always assign *true* to the facts they describe. Fact values may also be fixed, and the user may, in particular, use *any* to express the *flexibility* of the robot's reaction (its indifference) to a particular environmental parameter.

Metafacts that describe the initial situation are given *a priori*. Other metafacts are generated in two ways. First, they result from an analysis of the GRT, following a process of finding the necessary truth values that facts must have in order for the overall goal to be true, i.e. achieved. Second, new metafacts are produced by *metarules*.

The dynamic aspect. The dynamic aspect of the decision problem is captured by metarules. They model local decisions in sequences of decisions that lead to modifications of the robot's goals. There are two types of metarules: *response rules* and *goal modification rules*. Response rules model changes in the current status of the robot in response to the current state of the environment which is defined by metafacts. For example, the robot's reaction to the sun being exposed is to decrease the expected amount of energy necessary to take a picture or a sample.

Response rules, although not used here for this purpose, may also model changes in the environment if it reacts to the robot's

actions. Goal modification rules formalize changes in the goal representation tree caused by the environment's metafacts or by the robot's status. (Many examples of metarules will be given in the next section.)

Simulation - chaining. A forward-chaining inference engine takes the environment metafacts and uses metarules to determine the robot's new status. The status is specified by the robot's remaining energy, and the number of pictures and samples yet to be taken. We use a standard, agenda-driven algorithm for the chaining of metarules. Changes in the robot status are modelled by adding special metafacts to metarules, as in XCON (McDermott 1982).

NEGOPLAN knowledge base. The relationships between elements of the NEGOPLAN knowledge base for the planet exploration problem are presented in Figure 1. The history consists of metafacts describing previous status of the robot and it is updated when a new status is generated. The new status is caused by changes in the state of the environment. These changes, described by metafacts, are used by metarules which modify or generate rules representing the robot. The rules and the history are used to generate a new status of the robot.

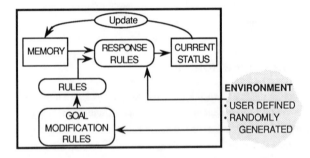

Fig. 1. Relations between elements of the knowledge-base

3. A DETAILED EXAMPLE: PLANET EXPLORATION

We use NEGOPLAN to simulate the decision-making processes and the behaviour of a robot that collects samples and takes photographs on a planet, and responds to the changing environment. The robot's initial goal is described by two rules with an intuitive reading:

```
goals( robot ) <-   global_goals.
global_goals <-     pictures_missing( 5 ) &
                    samples_missing( 5 ) &
                    energy_left( 8 ).
```

These rules are shown in Figure 2 as a Goal Representation Tree.

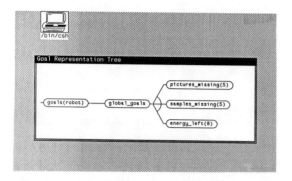

Fig. 2. The Goal Representation Tree
for the initial decision problem

The robot's mission can be broken down into four *phases* characterized by different types of goals. Initially, the robot is in the *starting* phase during which the quantitative aspects of the mission are defined. After the original goal (actually, its GRT) has been transformed into a set of initial metafacts, the robot moves on to the *exploration* phase. In this phase, if the conditions allow it, the robot takes one sample and one picture are taken at each step. The amount of energy used depends on the environment. When energy becomes low, the robot enters the *energy_scarce* phase, in which it minimizes the energy expenditure by quasi-randomly alternating between picture-taking and sample-taking or by asking the user to make a choice. The mission ends when the robot enters the *return* phase, after collecting all the prescribed material or running out of energy.

This simple model can be naturally expressed by NEGOPLAN rules, and it is easy to modify the mission characteristics. For example, the rules presented below could be easily augmented by new rules that would take into account the possibility of replenishing energy resources via solar batteries (operating in the presence of a strong sunlight).

The behaviour of the robot is determined by its status (three counters: the number of pictures and samples still needed, and the level of energy), by metafacts specifying its immediate goals, and by metafacts that represent the state of the environment. (Please refer to Figure 4 for the list of characteristics we have used in our experiment.) Metafacts that represent the counters and those that represent goals are generated by metarules. Metafacts that characterize the environment are supplied by NEGOPLAN from a composite description of the environment's variability.

We begin our presentation with a goal modification rule that redefines the initial goal. The global goals are left unchanged, but "local" goals are added: reach the current target, collect one sample and take one picture. The decision as to the estimated energy use is made by looking at the environment parameters. Here, with the sun hidden, energy consumption is high (2 units). An analogous metarule, with *sun(exposed)* replacing *sun(hidden)* among the preconditions in the lefthand side, has 1 as the estimated energy use.

```
robot : phase( robot, starting ) ::= true &
planet : sun( hidden ) ::= true &
planet : terrain( rough ) ::= true &
planet : heat( normal ) ::= true &
planet : radiation( normal ) ::= true
==>
modify (
    goals( robot ) <-  local_goals & global_goals ,
    local_goals <-     reach_target &
                       take_picture &
                       take_sample ,
    reach_target <-    estimated_energy_use( 2 ) ) .
```

These new goals form a GRT, and facts from this GRT are transformed into metafacts. For example, the fact *take_picture* is put into the knowledge base as the metafact

```
robot : take_picture ::= true
```

The following response rule expresses the phase change that can take place after this metafact has been added:

```
robot : phase( robot, starting ) ::= true &
robot : take_picture ::= true
==>
robot : phase( robot, exploration ) ::= true &
robot : phase( robot, starting ) ::= false .
```

An analogous metarule describes the reaction to the metafact

```
robot : take_sample ::= true
```

As another example of phase change consider this metarule:

```
robot : phase( robot, exploration ) ::= true &
planet : energy_left( 5 ) ::= true
==>
robot : phase( robot, energy_scarce ) ::= true &
robot : phase( robot, exploration ) ::= false .
```

The quantitative changes in the robot's status, such as the number of samples yet to be taken, are modelled by metarules with a special metafact *perform_arithmetic*. The form we show here is very simple, as it only allows elementary integer operations. The response rule shown below adjust the number of pictures still missing; an analogous rule exists for samples.

```
robot  : phase( robot, exploration )  ::=  true &
planet : picture_taken  ::=  true &
robot  : pictures_missing( N )  ::=  true
==>
robot  : perform_arithmetic( subtract, N, 1, N1 )  ::=
                                    true &
robot  : pictures_missing( N )  ::=  false &
planet : pictures_missing( N )  ::=  false &
planet : pictures_missing( N1 )  ::=  true &
planet : picture_taken  ::=  false .
```

When a picture or a sample has been taken, the appropriate response rule records the fact that part of the current step has been successfully completed:

```
robot  : phase( robot, exploration )  ::=  true &
planet : sample_taken  ::=  false &
robot  : take_sample  ::=  true
==>
robot  : take_sample  ::=  false &
planet : sample_taken  ::=  true .
```

Similarly, a change in the energy level after the current step is recorded, as anticipated for the given configuration of the environment:

```
robot  : phase( robot, energy_scarce )  ::=  true &
robot  : estimated_energy_use( N )  ::=  true
==>
robot  : estimated_energy_use( N )  ::=  false &
planet : energy_used( N )  ::=  true .
```

With all the changes properly recorded in the knowledge base, the system is ready to redefine global goals. Local goals remain unchanged (take one picture and one sample).

Global goals specify the quantitative data for the next step. The new characteristics of the environment affect the estimated use of energy. In the response rule analogous to the following one, if the sun were hidden, the use of energy would be 1.

```
robot  : phase( robot, exploration )  ::=  true &
planet : sun( hidden )  ::=  true &
planet : terrain( rough )  ::=  true &
planet : heat( normal )  ::=  true &
planet : radiation( normal )  ::=  true &
```

```
planet : energy_left( K )  ::=  true &
planet : pictures_missing( L )  ::=  true &
planet : samples_missing( M )  ::=  true
==>
modify (
    goals( robot ) <-   local_goals &
                        global_goals ,
    global_goals <-     energy_left( K ) &
                        pictures_missing( L ) &
                        samples_missing( M ),
    reach_target <-     estimated_energy_use( 2 ) ) .
```

This modification rule replaces the GRT of Figure 2 with a new GRT that we show in Figure 3. The new tree represents the robot's decision problem at the beginning of the *exploration* phase.

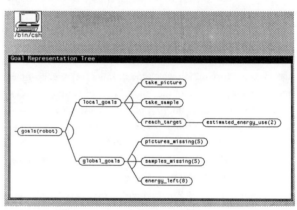

Fig. 3. The Goal Representation Tree
for the new decision problem

Decision making is slightly different if the robot is in the *energy_scarce* phase. To conserve energy, only one picture **or** one sample is taken at a time, with the assumption that with the sun exposed the robot will not need energy (say, its solar batteries will get an additional charge sufficient to perform one action only). If the sun is hidden, the estimated energy use is 1.

```
robot  : phase( robot, energy_scarce )  ::=  true &
planet : sun( exposed )  ::=  true &
planet : terrain( rough )  ::=  true &
planet : heat( normal )  ::=  true &
planet : radiation( normal )  ::=  true &
planet : energy_left( K )  ::=  true &
planet : pictures_missing( L )  ::=  true &
planet : samples_missing( M )  ::=  true
```

```
==>
modify (
    goals( robot ) <-   local_goals & global_goals ,
    global_goals <-     energy_left( K ) &
                        pictures_missing( L ) &
                        samples_missing( M ),
    local_goals <-      reach_target & take_picture
                        #
                        reach_target & take_sample ,
    reach_target <-     estimated_energy_use( 0 ) ) .
```

Both in the *exploration* phase and in the *energy_scarce* phase the
robot is watching for the conditions prompting it to move to the
return phase. This happens if all the material has been collected,
or when the energy level drops below 2 (i.e. the mission is
aborted). Two of the several relevant response rules follow:

```
robot : phase( robot, exploration ) ::= true &
planet : pictures_missing( 0 ) ::= true &
planet : samples_missing( 0 ) ::= true
==>
robot : phase( robot, return ) ::= true &
robot : phase( robot, exploration ) ::= false .

robot : phase( robot, energy_scarce ) ::= true &
planet : energy_left( 0 ) ::= true
==>
robot : phase( robot, return ) ::= true &
robot : phase( robot, energy_scarce ) ::= false .
```

Once in the return phase, the robot changes its goals completely:
it initiates the return operation regardless of the number of
pictures or samples still missing in its collection:

```
robot : phase( robot, return ) ::= true &
planet : pictures_missing( L ) ::= true &
planet : samples_missing( M ) ::= true
==>
modify (
    goals( robot ) <-   global_goals ,
    global_goals <-     return &
                        pictures_missing( L ) &
                        samples_missing( M ) ) .
```

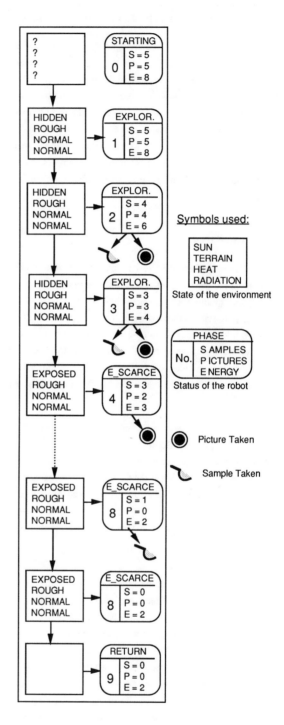

Fig. 4. A trace of a simple experiment with NEGOPLAN

4. NEGOPLAN AT WORK: AN EXPERIMENT WITH ROBOT SIMULATION

The modelling of the robot's behaviour has been discussed in the previous section. We have shown that partial decisions are made on the basis of the current state of the environment and the robot's status. In Figure 4 we present an experiment in which the variability of the environment has been reduced to a minimum - just one of four characteristics can assume more than one randomly chosen value. The drawing should be self-explanatory. The mission begins with 5 pictures and 5 samples to collect, and with 8 units of energy. It is successfully completed after nine steps.

5. CONCLUSION

We have discussed here the rule-base paradigm used to model and simulate the behaviour of a system acting in a dynamically changing environment where it may have to adapt and respond to the changing state of the environment. This approach is flexible and simple. It is possible to model both the quantitative and qualitative aspects of the system. Although we introduced here only very simple calculations, it is possible to integrate much more complicated quantitative models within the rule-based paradigm.

The example we have presented introduces the main concepts of the NEGOPLAN approach. Because NEGOPLAN is basically a tool to support negotiations, it does not have built-in time other than that measured with iterations of the forward chaining machine. It is possible to introduce time as a separate mechanism and to measure the flow of time for particular actions of the system (e.g. time between taking samples) and for changes in the environment.

Another simplification is that the system makes decisions based only on the current state of the environment and its own most recent history. First, the system may base its decisions on the future states - here the use of the value *any* seems to be promising because it gives the flexibility of reactions to the future states. Second, the system may use the whole history in an attempt to determine correlations between states. Still another possibility is to introduce trade-offs in decision making. The system may, for example, choose a different type of terrain because, at a certain moment, taking pictures is more important than taking samples.

The example presented in this paper is simple but it illustrates the use of NEGOPLAN in simulation. We claim that NEGOPLAN makes it possible to model complex systems and to simulate their behaviour in an unknown and changing environment.

REFERENCES

Arons, H. de Swann (1983), "Expert Systems in the Simulation Domain". *Mathematics and Computers in Simulation*, vol. 25.

Kersten, G. E., W. Michalowski, S. Matwin, S. Szpakowicz (1988), "Representing the Negotiation Process with a Rule-Based Formalism". *Theory and Decisions*, vol. 22, pp. 1-33.

Lavery, R. G. (1986), "Artificial Intelligence and Simulation: An Introduction". *Proceedings of the 1986 Winter Simulation Conference*, J. Wilson, *et al.* (eds.), Washington, DC.

Matwin, S., S. Szpakowicz, Z. Koperczak, G. E. Kersten, W. Michalowski (1989), "NEGOPLAN: An Expert System Shell for Negotiation Support". *IEEE Expert*.

Matwin, S., S. Szpakowicz, G. E. Kersten, Z. Koperczak, W. Michalowski (1987), "Logic-Based System for Negotiation Support". *Proceedings of the 1987 Symposium on Logic Programming*, San Francisco: IEEE Computer Society Press, pp. 499-506.

McDermott, J. (1982), "R1: A Rule-based Configurer of Computer Systems". *Artificial Intelligence*, vol. 19, no. 1.

Michalowski, W., G. E. Kersten, Z. Koperczak, S. Matwin, S. Szpakowicz (1988), "Negotiation with a Terrorist: Can an Expert System Help?", *Managerial Decision Support Systems. Proceedings of the 1st IMACS/IFORS Colloquium on Decision Support Systems and Knowledge Based Systems*, Amsterdam: North-Holland, pp. 193-200.

Naylor, T. H., J. L. Balintfy, D. S. Burdic, Kong Chu (1966), *Computer Simulation Techniques*. New York: Wiley.

Shannon, R. E. (1987), "Models and Artificial Intelligence". *Proceedings of the 1987 Winter Simulation Conference*, A. Thesen *et al.* (eds.), Atlanta, GA, December 14-16, pp. 16-23.

Shannon, R. E., R. Mayer, H. Adelsberger (1985), "Expert Systems and Simulation". *Simulation*, vol. 44, no. 6, pp. 275-284.

Szpakowicz, S., S. Matwin, G. E. Kersten, W. Michalowski (1987), "RUNE: An Expert System Shell for Negotiation Support". *Expert Systems and their Applications. Proceedings of the 7th International Workshop*, Avignon, May 13-15, pp. 711-726.

Advances in AI and Simulation
© 1989 By The Society for Computer
Simulation International
ISBN 0-911801-50-2

An intelligent instructor support system
for training simulators

BY

AVELINO J. GONZALEZ, PH.D.   and   HARLEY R. MYLER, PH.D.
UNIVERSITY OF CENTRAL FLORIDA
COMPUTER ENGINEERING DEPARTMENT
ORLANDO, FLORIDA 32816

ABSTRACT

Training Simulators provide an environment in which a student can practice tasks that are either impractical, expensive, or impossible to exercise in a real environment. In general, however they inherently provide little or no feedback on student performance, skill deficiencies or coaching on correct behavior. Such tasks are performed by an instructor from the Instructor/Operator Station (IOS), which is analogous to the control console of a simulator.

In a tactical training task, the instructor can take on several roles in addition to monitoring the trainee. The instructor may have to prepare the training scenario to present to the trainee for his/her solution. This scenario may be partially based on the observation of the performance of the student during exercises. Additionally, some simulators have the ability to modify the scenario dynamically; i.e., introduce additional complications in the middle of the scenario. In such cases, the instructor has to quickly decide what new variables to introduce during the course of the exercise itself. Other roles that can be played by the instructor are that of an adversary or that of a team member.

The instructor's job in such a training environment can be very demanding if the system is large and complex. In addition, instructors are often unfamiliar with the features of a simulator and the latter is thus not used to its full potential.

The advent of Artificial Intelligence as a proven technology in the last decade provides a unique opportunity to provide support to the instructor in his mission. Such assistance will allow him to more efficiently and effectively plan and conduct the training session.

This paper discusses the elements of an Intelligent Instructor Support System (IISS) which can assist the instructor in performing his duties. Such a system is also compared to Intelligent Computer Aided Instruction (ICAI).

1.0 INTRODUCTION

The U. S. Department of Defense spends millions of dollars annually for the training of its personnel. A significant portion of this sum is invested in simulation-based training devices, whose objective is to provide the student with a realistic, yet safe and inexpensive environment in which to acquire skills. The complexity of these simulators can range from the simple ones such as a CRT displaying dial readings, to the sophisticated ones containing motion platforms coupled with highly realistic visual image generation.

The computer hardware required to perform the latter type of simulation in real time has to be fast and powerful.

Simulators tend to provide an environment in which a student can practice tasks that are either impractical, expensive, or impossible to exercise in a real environment. In general, however, they inherently provide little or no feedback on student performance, skill deficiencies or coaching on correct behavior. Human instructors are therefore required to provide these services. The instructors usually perform these tasks from the Instructor/Operator Station (IOS), with little or no performance measuring facilities other than direct output of student actions.

In a tactical training task, the instructor can take on several roles in addition to monitoring the trainee. One of these is to prepare the training scenario to present to the trainee for his/her solution. Design of the scenario may depend on the instructors observation of the performance of the student during previous exercises. Such observations must be either held in the instructors memory or jotted down on paper for later reference. This gives less than optimal consistency to a scenario intended for a particular student, or student group. If instructors change during a training sequence, continuity in training can be lost.

For complex systems or multiple player games, the instructor's job can be very demanding. In addition, instructors are rarely good at simulator operation unless they have had extensive experience with it. As a consequence, advanced features of a simulator may not be used, or the simulator, in general, may not be utilized to its fullest potential. Therefore, a means to allow the instructor to increase his effectiveness while using the simulator to its maximum capability must be found. The use of artificial intelligence makes such a tool possible.

2.0 ARTIFICIAL INTELLIGENCE

Artificial Intelligence (AI) is the branch of computer technology that seeks to provide computers with the ability to solve problems whose solutions are generally considered to require human intelligence.

Computers historically have been used mostly to perform rather simple repetitive tasks. It has normally taken a human with a certain amount of training to be able to arrange these rather simple instructions into a sequence which performed a useful task or solved a problem. Thus, computers traditionally excelled at solving numerical programs and manipulating large quantities of data (data bases), but were rather useless in solving ill-posed problems, or problems with incomplete data.

What these numerical programs have had in common was that they were algorithmic in nature. That is, they are precise and logically-designed set of instructions that yield a single correct answer. The human mind on the other hand can more easily solve some problems using heuristic means. In fact, human expertise is largely a heuristic processing of knowledge rather than an algorithmic processing of data.

AI deals with giving computers this ability to deal with symbols and manipulate them so that they can solve problems not easily solved through algorithms. A branch of AI called Expert Systems has as its goal the solution of problems through a computer system which previously could only be solved by an expert in the domain of interest.

An expert system is composed of three major parts:

- an inference mechanism
- a knowledge base
- support functions

An inference mechanism is the vehicle used for manipulating the knowledge. There are many types, but the most common one is based on rules expressed symbolically and processed using a variation of predicate calculus. Such rules state a conditional production (in the form of if-then) and a fact, such that if the antecedent (IF part) of the production is satisfied, then the consequent action executed by the production (THEN part) would be equivalent to, and therefore replace, the production as well as the original fact.

The inference engine is very closely interrelated to the knowledge that is contained in the knowledge base. Such knowledge can be represented in the form of rules, frames, objects, or a combination of these. Rules are again the most common.

There are two basic types of rule based reasoning mechanisms:

- forward chaining
- backward chaining

A forward chaining (FC) system starts with a set of initial inputs, and proceeds forward through the activation (firing) of rules toward the goals. When the goals have been reached and/or there are no other rules to fire, then the inferencing is complete. Another name for an FC system is "input driven." It normally employs a breadth-first type of search algorithm.

A backward chainer (BC), on the other hand, makes an assumption about the goals, and then works backward attempting to justify the assumption. It determines which rules would affect the goal and then goes to find out whether the conditions for these rules to fire are satisfied. If so, then the rules are fired and the goal is either justified or contradicted. It then proceeds to do the same for another goal (if there are any more) and so on.

If, however, the rules affecting the original goal are not matched, then the mechanism will go backwards one more level and establish which other rules would "create" the data patterns required to match the antecedent of the original (goal level) rules. Once this is done, then it looks for the presence of that data. If present, the rules would fire and chain for-

ward until the goal is either satisfied or contradicted.

If it doesn't find the data patterns required to fire the 2nd level rules, then the mechanism continues to chain backwards until these are found, or until it runs out of rules. In the latter case, it would not be able to justify the goal and either go to the next goal or stop if there are no others. This methodology looks more like a depth-first search algorithm.

Frames are a somewhat more passive knowledge representation paradigm. They offer a structure which defines the relationship between different symbols being represented. They feature attribute-value pairs for a symbol as well as inheritance of attributes for related frames. External procedures are generally required to generate the action.

Objects are similar to frames in that they can represent attributes to the symbols with values attached and they can also show inheritance and other relations between objects. The major difference, however, is that they can cause action to be generated as far as the object itself is concerned.

AI (or expert systems) can be used to assist an instructor in the training environment. The knowledge or expertise of an instructor can be represented in rules and/or frames and used to carry out his instructional functions.

3.0 INTELLIGENT INSTRUCTOR SUPPORT SYSTEM SPECIFICATION

But what exactly are some of the things that an IISS can do for an instructor? This section will describe in more detail tasks in which a system such as this can assist the instructor.

3.1 AUTOMATED PERFORMANCE MONITORING AND ANALYSIS

One of the most important functions which an instructor or a training simulator performs is that of monitoring and analyzing a student's performance. This task, however, can be rather intensive as well as demanding on the instructor. In the words of Charles [Charles 82], "The quantity of data far exceeds the capacity of any Instructor Pilot to access and utilize effectively during training and still be able to monitor and evaluate student performance."

There exist various systems that accomplish some measure of automated performance monitoring. [Seidensticker 82] [Semple et al 82] [Halley 82]. Such systems, however, only appear to check for rather simple measurements such as climb rate, altitude and speed deviation, etc., and merely report instances during flight in which the tolerance of a specific parameter was violated during a simulated exercise. These available functions only seem to exist in standardized tasks where the requirements on the student performance are set previously.

The IIPP should contain automated performance measurement capability which can monitor the student's more subtle actions in complex, non-standard, situations. Such situations normally require the equivalent experience of the pilot, and such experience can best be represented using heuristic programming techniques such as those used in expert systems.

An IIPP can also be used to evaluate the student's performance based on the above measurements and point out to the instructor each student's weaknesses. If the instructor desires, the Intelligent Instructor Support System can update the student model accordingly. Otherwise, the instructor can use the evaluation made by IISS merely as one of a number of inputs and update the student model himself.

The heuristic-based performance monitoring and evaluation is most useful in situations where the tasks are not standard. In such cases, it can be even more important to recognize the situation the student is in than to determine what to do about it. This is particularly true in weapons system trainers where the adversaries are autonomous and intelligent.

A rule-based blackboard architecture is the knowledge representation paradigm of choice for this particular feature. although rules can be slow and difficult to generate and fire, they best simulate the kind of thinking process found in pilots and instructors in a training scenario. The challenge, therefore, is to develop a technique by which the system uses a limited set of rules and procedures to classify the situation and then activates another set of rules which are used to monitor the performance under the proper situation. This process may actually exist in more than two levels, where the lower the rule, the more specific it is. A scheme such as this would be computationally fast because only a limited number of rules are investigated at any one time. Additonally, it could also be a manageable effort to develop these rules, since the low level rules would not have to cover every possible situation.

Performance monitoring is a real-time process for which computational speed is a concern. The evaluation function does not have the same demanding requirements since that process could run off-line, after the simulation exercise is completed.

3.2 SCENARIO GENERATION AND ADAPTIVE TRAINING

Adaptive training is the term used for a flexible and dynamic training method which will train each student individually, based on his abilities as well as weaknesses. The opposite of this concept, of course, is standardized training in which all students receive the same training, regardless of their abilities or performance.

It is clear that, to some degree or another, adaptive training is superior to standardized training. But there is significantly more effort required, since lessons have to be designed individually. This additional effort falls squarely on the shoulders of the instructor, who in the case of military trainers, is severely overloaded as well as in high demand. Thus, adaptive training is not a common feature of military training.

In order to make adaptive training feasible, means of automatically consulting the student progress and generating a customized lesson plan is required. Such a lesson plan would be of a complexity level which would challenge the student, concentrate on weak points, yet not overwhelm him at his stage of progress.

An intelligent instructor support system should be able to access the student model and assemble a lesson plan (or simulation scenario) that would fill these needs, yet be diverse enough so that no two students have experienced the exact same situation.

The student model could be represented by a frame (or object) which would have as slots descriptions of the syllabus items. These, in turn, would represent other frames which would contain the skills making up the particular item. This idea of hierarchically breaking down the student's profile would give the instructor a much improved ability to design custom-made scenarios.

3.3 DYNAMIC SCENARIO MODIFICATION

An extension of the automated scenario generation would be that of dynamically modifying the scenario, if a student shows either a high or low level of proficiency in carrying it out.

This feature would place the additional requirement on the performance monitoring subsystem to evaluate the student's performance prior to the completion of the simulation session. If deviations in the expected performance take place, the evaluation subsytem would take note and replace a yet undisplayed part of the simulation scenario with another one which has a level of difficulty more in line with the student's present level of proficiency.

The challenge in developing this feature is in the performance monitoring and evaluation, which would now have to evaluate in real time just like the monitor. Changing the scenario itself may or may not be difficult from a systems standpoint, dependng on how the simulation scenario is built and represented originally. Some complications added could be bad weather, equipment malfunction or equipment/personnel loss during a battle.

3.4 INTELLIGENT ADVERSARY

Simulators used for training crew members in the tactical use of weapon systems often display the presence of adversaries. The presentation of the adversary is in such a way that will allow th student to make tactical decisions as to the use of the weapon system within the general constraints defined, such as weather, equipment damage, adversary's weapon, teammates, etc. While such features can be highly sophisticated in their fidelity and realism, they generally treat the adversary in a generally pre-determined way, reacting only in a basic manner to the student's action. In actual warfare, however, the opponent is assumed to be equally well trained, and thus capable of reacting to the student's tactics in subtle ways. Reaction could also actually be pro-action, where an opponent anticipates the action of the student and may even attempt to pre-empt it.

The concept of intelligent adversaries is an important one if the student is to be placed in a trainer which simulates actual warfare conditions as closely as possible. As part of the IISS, it would allow the instructor to choose different levels of expertise in order to properly reflect the level of progress of the student. This has to do with the adaptive training feature described above.

4.0 COMPARISON OF IISS TO ICAI

The function of an instructor in a simulation based trainer is to transfer his expertise on the system to the students. Military instructors therefore, are generally experienced people who are pulled from line duty to use their knowledge in training new personnel. Thus, they are a very scarce resource which has to be employed as efficiently and effectively as possible.

There are two approaches to this problem. The first one has traditionally been to make his job easier by automating some tasks and facilitating others. This approach has centered on human factors engineering, whereby the instructor can more easily interact with the simulator and the trainee. Some advances brought about by such approaches are replay/ debrief features [Carter 82], menu-driven commands for the operator, and advanced instructor/operator interfaces (i.e. touch screen, pointers, etc.).

The shortcoming with this approach, conversely, is that while the instructor has more time to devote to his real task, which is to use his experience to instruct, it doesn't go far enough in accomplishing this. There are still various tasks which can be automated. IISS extends this concept through the application of Artificial Intelligence.

The second approach has been to simply replace the instructor altogether. This area of research is Intelligent Computer Aided Instruction (ICAI) applied to simulation based trainers. [Beigel 88a], [Beigel 88b] [Gonzalez 88] [Holmes 88].

The purpose of this section is to compare both approaches and point out the advantages and disadvantage of each.

The advantages of ICAI are obvious. By ideally having no instructor, the efficiency of an instructor is increased infinitely. The scenario generation, performance evaluation and student record upkeep are just some of the functions performed by such a system. However, the level of effort involved in developing such a system is very high indeed, and its re-usability on a different type of training mission in the same simulator without making significant changes is questionable. Additionally, the concept of incremental development, where a partially completed system could be used prior to development of the entire project, does not seem feasible in an ICAI environment. Nevertheless, the end goal of ICAI is a commendable one and research should clearly continue in order to reach these objectives.

The Intelligent Instructor Support System alternative to ICAI described here is considerably more modest in scope. Rather than replace the instructor, it attempts to provide him with tools which liberate him from doing some of the tasks that presently require his intelligence and experience.

The efficiency of an instructor can be measured in how long is the simulator/instructor system used for a single training session. Naturally, the shorter that session is, the more sessions that can be scheduled on a simulator per day. Presently, some off-line work on the simulator by the instructor is necessary in order to prepare for the session as well as to debrief the student. The actual simulation exercise has a finite duration, and that will not change regardless of the instructor. Therefore, the area which can be cut down in order to shorten the duration of a training session is in the preparation and debriefing. These are the areas in which the IISS can be of help.

Another consideration is that not all the features of an IISS need to be developed before the system can be placed in operation. Any help at all for the instructor is an achievement. Lastly, incremental development of an IISS can make the entire project more easily justified since it can be broken down into manageable chunks.

5.0 SAMPLE IMPLEMENTATION OF IISS

In an effort to demonstrate the capability, a mock-up of an IOS exhibiting the features described above was developed at the University of Central Florida. It represents the main IOS monitor used by an instructor in a flight simulator trainer.

It was developed on a Texas Instruments Explorer LISP system connected to a Gould 32/67 through Flavors Technology bus link as shown in Figure 1. The simulation is diven by an F-4 simulator program running in ADA on the Gould. It generates the coordinates of the student craft in real time and passes them to the Explorer through the bus link.

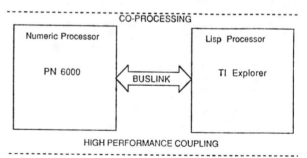

FIGURE 1

The display is a "God's eye" view of the student craft (an F-4) taking off from Andrews Air Force base and engaging oncoming intruders. It has a number of display windows used to depict various vital information about the flight, as well as a menu which allows the instructor to activate the functions discussed in Section 3.0. Figure 2 shows the basic display.

-- The Washington D.C. Region

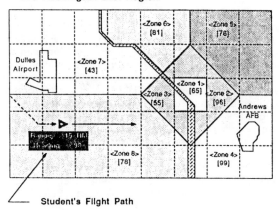

Student's Flight Path

FIGURE 2

Upon activation of one of the system features, additional menu windows may pop up to inquire further from the instructor. Although at present there is no intelligence in such inquiries, the demonstration can show the power and functionality of such a fully-developed system. Additionally, by linking the Explorer to a conventional processor running an ADA simulator, it verifies the feasibility of such a technology in the training environment.

6.0 SUMMARY

There are two basic ways in which to increase the productivity of simulator training: a) replacing the instructor by an intelligent tutor which can perform all the functions of an instructor, or b) developing intelligent tools for use by an instructor.

A case is made in this paper for the advantages of using artificial intelligence techniques to develop the tools in option b above. It is believed that such an approach is technically feasible at present, and has the greatest promise in the near term.

7.0 BIBLIOGRAPHY

[Charles 82] Charles, J. P., "Operational Problems in Instructor Operator Station Design," presented at the NTEC Instructional Features Workshop, October 1982, Orlando, Florida.

[Semple et al. 82] Semple, C. P., and Cross, B. K., "The Real World Instructional Support Features in Flying Training Simulators," presented at the NTEC Instructional Features Workshop, October 1982, Orlando, Florida.

[Halley 82] Halley, R., "They Can Make you or Break You: Considering the Instructor as a User in Automated Training Systems," presented at the NTEC Instructional Features Workshop, October 1982, Orlando, Florida.

[Carter 82] Carter, V. E., "Conceptual Design of an Instructional Support System for Fighter and Trainer Aircraft Flight Simulators," presented at the NTEC Instructional Features Workshop, October 1982, Orlando, Florida.

[Beigel 88a] Beigel, J. E., Interrante, L. D., Sargiant, J. M. et al, "Input and Instruction Paradigms for an Intelligent Simulation Training System." Proceedings of the first Florida Artificial Intelligence Research Symposium, May 1988, Orlando, Florida.

[Beigel 88b] Beigel, J. E., Draman, M., Nadoli, G., Brooks, G., "Control and Inferencing Paradigms for an Intelligent Simulation Training System." Proceedings of the first Florida Artificial Intelligence Research Symposium, May 1988, Orlando, Florida.

[Gonzalez 88] Gonzalez, A. J., Kornecki, A., Ransom, A., et al, "A Simulation-based Expert System for Training Air Traffic Controllers." Proceedings of the first Florida Artificial Intelligence Research Symposium, May 1988, Orlando, Florida.

[Holmes 88] Holmes, Williard, "Why the Marriage Between Simulation and Knowledge-based Systems?" Talk presented at the 1988 Southeastern Simulation Conference, October 1988, Orlando, Florida.

Advances in AI and Simulation
© 1989 By The Society for Computer
Simulation International
ISBN 0-911801-50-2

An intelligent simulation environment for control system design

James T. Robinson
Oak Ridge National Laboratory
Oak Ridge, TN 37831-6364

ABSTRACT

The Oak Ridge National Laboratory is currently assisting in the development of advanced control systems for the next generation of nuclear power plants. This paper presents a prototype interactive and intelligent simulation environment being developed to support this effort. The environment combines tools from the field of Artificial Intelligence; in particular object-oriented programming, a LISP programming environment, and a direct manipulation user interface; with traditional numerical methods for simulating combined continuous/discrete processes. The resulting environment is highly interactive and easy to use. Models may be created and modified quickly through a window oriented direct manipulation interface. Models may be modified at any time, even as the simulation is running, and the results observed immediately via real-time graphics.

INTRODUCTION

The capabilities and limitations of current computer aided control system design and simulation software are well documented in the literature (see for example Rimvall 1988). For the most part, current software emphasizes linear analysis as automated methods for linear systems have been available for some time. For non-linear systems and rule-based systems (such as fuzzy control), general automated design methods are not available and development depends heavily on simulation. However, the potential benefit of simulation as a design tool has not been fully realized in the past due to the high costs of developing and maintaining models. This paper describes a prototype simulation environment which has been designed explicitly for exploratory modeling of power plant processes and control systems. The ease of use, flexibility, and interactive nature of the environment should allow simulation to be incorporated more completely into the design process.

DESCRIPTION

The environment was originally developed on a LMI Lisp Machine using the FLAVORS object-oriented language (Stallman, Weinreb, & Moon 1984) and has recently been installed on a Macintosh-II based Texas Instruments microExplorer. The advantages of the LISP programming environment for developing advanced simulation systems have been noted by other researchers (Stairmon and Kreutzer 1988, Pliske and Halley 1988). LISP environments were developed for exploratory programming and most feature an interpreter (and/or incremental compiler) and many built in tools for advanced user interfaces. The use of an interpreted language such as LISP frees the user from the tedious compile-link-load cycle. This is especially important during the design process, when many alternative plant and control system configurations may be explored.

Object-oriented programming has been successfully applied to discrete-event simulations by a number of researchers (for example Khlar 1986; Ziegler 1987; Stairmong and Kreutzer 1988; Ghaznavi-Collins and Thelen 1988). However, its extension to a predominantly continuous process, such as a power plant, is not straightforward due to the tightly coupled nature of such systems. In particular, simulation by direct message passing between component level objects, as in a round-robin scheme, leads inevitably to numerical instabilities. Our approach to deal with this problem has been to introduce special classes which implement traditional numerical integration algorithms for simulating groups of interconnected objects. This is described below.

Class library

The core of the simulation environment consists of a library of class definitions. These classes may be categorized into the following levels of abstraction:

(1) component-level classes,

(2) physical-system classes, and

(3) numerical-methods classes.

At the lowest level are component-level classes. These are the basic building blocks from which simulation models are constructed. They may represent either actual plant components (such as pumps, pipes, and valves) or abstractions such as heat conductors, flow sources, and time delays. FLOW-CONTROL-VALVE is a good example of a component level class. This class is a member of the VALVE family and inherits the following instance variables from the GENERIC-VALVE class:

inlet-connection
outlet-connection
valve-position
flow-rate
pressure-drop

The variables *inlet-connection* and *outlet-connection* specify the classes' ports and are used to record the names of connected objects. The last three instance variables are dynamic in nature and specify the instantaneous state of the valve. In addition to these inherited instance variables, FLOW-CONTROL-VALVE includes a parameter related to the flow capacity of the valve, *Cvmax*. The methods for FLOW-CONTROL-VALVE include accessor functions for all instance variables as well as *:compute-flow-rate* and *:compute-pressure-drop*.

During an actual simulation, interconnected component-level objects are automatically collected and treated as a group by objects of the higher level *physical-system* classes. This group includes THERMAL-NETWORK, which solves the heat conduction/convection equations for temperature, and HYDRAULIC-LOOP, which solves a loop momentum equation for flow rate. These classes inherit integration methods from *numerical-methods* classes such as LINEAR-SYSTEM and NON-LINEAR-ODE.

THERMAL-NETWORK is an example of a *physical-system* class. Objects of this class solves the energy conservation equations (heat conduction and convection) for groups of thermally connected objects. These equations are represented in the form

$$\frac{d\vec{T}}{dt} = A(t)\,T + \vec{f}(t)$$

where T represents the vector of temperatures, A(t) is a time-varying coefficient matrix, and f(t) is a time varying forcing function. The instance variables of class THERMAL-NETWORK include:

> *components*
> *A-matrix*
> *f-vector,* and
> *T-vector.*

At instantiation an object of class THERMAL-NETWORK automatically creates and initializes the matrix A and vectors f and T of the appropriate dimensions and assigns a row index number to each component. At each time step the THERMAL-NETWORK object sends messages to all components instructing them to update their slot(s) in the coefficient matrix A or forcing vector f, and then advances the resulting equation system one time step according to the integration method inherited from the class LINEAR-SYSTEM.

It should be noted that the user does not have to deal directly with objects of the physical-system or numerical-methods classes. They are automatically constructed prior to a simulation run based on the connections between component-level objects and remain transparent unless the user chooses to modify them.

User Interface

The user-interface is highly interactive and makes use of multiple windows, pull-down menus, icons, etc. A model is constructed by placing icons on the screen and specifying interconnections with the aid of a mouse. Connections are made by specifying a series of horizontal and vertical line segments between ports by dragging and clicking the mouse. Ports and connecting lines are automatically aligned. Connections between ports of unlike type are protected against

Parameters for individual objects are usually entered and/or changed through forms accessed by choosing edit-object from a pull down menu and selecting an objects icon with the mouse. A form for a controller of type SISO-CONTROLLER is illustrated in Figure 1. The forms provide current access to an objects instance variables and may be used to inspect or modify an object during a simulation run. The effects of the change are reflected immediately in the simulation.

```
┌─────────────────────────────────────────┐
│ SISO-CONTROLLER                           │
│ INPUT-TYPE: ··········· :READING          │
│ OUTPUT-TYPE: ·········· :SET-VALVE-POSITION│
│ OUTPUT-OFFSET: ······· 0.0                │
│ CONTROL-TYPE: ········ PI                  │
│ SET-POINT: ·········· 300.0               │
│ PROPORTIONAL-GAIN: -0.02                  │
│ INTEGRAL-GAIN: ······ -0.01               │
│ DIFFERENTIAL-GAIN: 0.0                     │
│ ERROR: ··············· -0.12158203        │
│ INTEGRAL-ERROR: ····· 47.154587           │
│ NAME: ················ PRESSURE-CONTROLLER │
│ ───────────────────────────────────────── │
│ INPUT-CONNECTION:    PRESSURE-SENSOR       │
│ CONTROL-OUTPUT-TO:   A-VALVE               │
│ Do It  ▭                                   │
└─────────────────────────────────────────┘
```

Figure 1. Example form editor for a SISO-CONTROLLER.

Hierarchial zooming. To help manage system complexity the interface implements a hierarchial zooming concept similar to that presented by Elmqvist and Mattson (1986) which allows individual objects to be arranged into a hierarchy of systems and subsystems. A system is simply a collection of objects (which may include other systems). When collapsed it is represented by a rectangular box which may be manipulated as any other object. However, the edit-object operation opens a window into the system rather than a form for editing its attributes. System objects may (and usually do) have ports. These ports are visible on the system icon but in reality belong to one of its components. They are created by connecting a component of the system to a special SYSTEM-PORT object. This causes a port of an appropriate type to be created automatically and made visible upon viewing the system from the next higher level. This port possesses all the characteristics of the original object's port to which it is connected and will accept appropriate connections from other systems or objects. This allows SYSTEM objects to be interconnected freely with component-level objects.

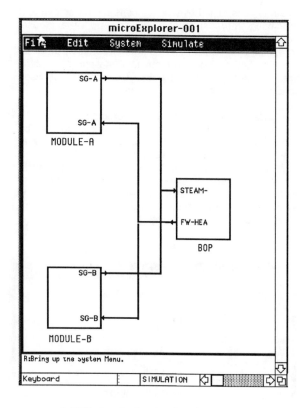

(a) Window for top level system.

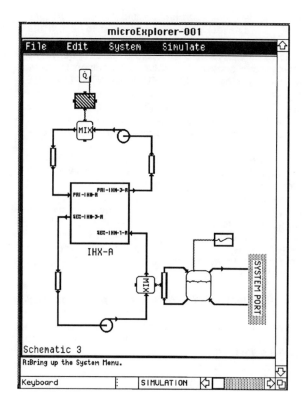

(b) Window for MODULE-A.

Figure 2. Example of hierarchial zooming.

The use of hierarchial zooming is illustrated in Figure 2. Figure 2(a) contains three system boxes, MODULE-A, MODULE-B, and BOP (these correspond to two power blocks of a modular liquid metal reactor and the balance of plant). Editing MODULE-A would open a window into that system as illustrated in Figure 2(b). This system is composed of a number of interconnected component-level objects and yet another system, IHX-A. Note that the icon at the lower right, which represents the steam generator SG-A, is connected via input and output ports to a SYSTEM-PORT object. Thus these ports are visible on the system icon for MODULE-A.

The purpose of the hierarchial organization scheme is to allow the concentration of modeling effort on individual systems. To aid in this, object names are made relative to the system in which they are defined This permits the duplication of names from system to system without conflict.

Scripts.   A simulation scenario is prescribed through the use of scripts, accessed through the SIMULATE pull-down menu. The INIT script contains a series of messages which are sent upon simulation initialization. The RUN script is a series of messages which are repeated each time step. This script may be used to prescribe the default behavior of the plant or an entire simulation scenario. The run script is analogous to the main program of a traditional simulation, with the important difference that it may be changed at any time (even during a simulation run) without recompilation.

Output.   Simulation results are observed through gauges or strip charts. These objects may be connected to the interior of any object and may display any of its parameters. During a simulation, they are expanded and displayed on a special output window. The user interface as it appears during a typical simulation is illustrated in Figure 3. This is a typical layout with the menubar at the top, a process schematic window on the left, and an output window on the right.

File System Interface

The permanent storage of models is achieved through the file system interface. The options available are SAVE-MODEL, SAVE-SYSTEM, LOAD-MODEL, and LOAD-SYSTEM. The SAVE-MODEL command saves all systems of the current model along with the INIT and RUN scripts. The SAVE-SYSTEM command saves the current system (the system whose window is currently active) and all its subsystems. The SAVE-MODEL and SAVE-

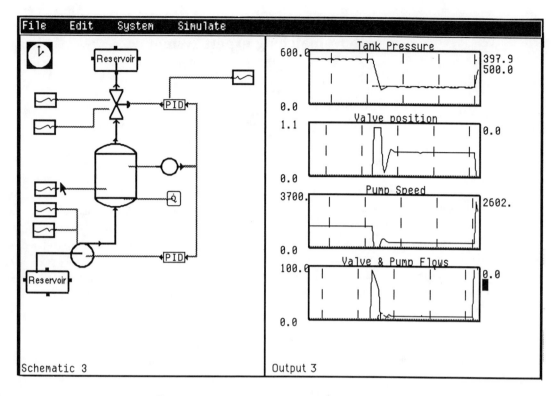

Figure 3. Typical run-time user interface.

SYSTEM options may be executed at any time, and saves each object of the model or system in its current state. This allows simulations to be frozen in their current state and later recreated with the LOAD-MODEL or LOAD-SYSTEM commands.

CONCLUSIONS

This paper describes a prototype interactive and intelligent simulation environment being developed to support the development through exploratory modeling of advanced control systems for power plants. The environment combines tools from the field of Artificial Intelligence; in particular object-oriented programming, LISP programming environments, and direct manipulation user interfaces; with traditional numerical methods for the simulation of continuous systems. This synergistic approach appears to us to be a promising alternative to traditional programming techniques for developing advanced simulation environments.

REFERENCES

Elmqvist, H. and Mattsson, S.E. 1986, "A Simulator for Dynamical Systems Using Graphics and Equations for Modeling," Proceedings of the Third Symposium on Computer-Aided Control System Design, Arlington, VA, September 24-26, 134-140.

Ghaznavi-Collins, I. and Thelen, D. 1988, "An object oriented approach toward system architecture simulation," AI PAPERS,1988 (R.J. Uttamsingh ed.) Simulation Series (20) 4. SCS, San Diego, CA. 103-107.

Khlar, P. 1986. "Expressibility in ROSS, an Object-Oriented Simulation System," Artificial Intelligence in Simulation , (G.C. Vansteenkiste; E.J.H. Kerchoffs; B.P. Zeigler eds.). SCS, San Diego, CA, 147-156.

Pliske, D.B, and Halley, M.R. 1988, "Queing Lab - A Workflow Modeling System for Decision Support," AI PAPERS,1988 (R.J. Uttamsingh ed.) Simulation Series (20) 4. SCS, San Diego, CA, 42-46.

Rimvall, M. 1988, "Computer-Aided Control Systems: Techniques and Tools," in Systems Modeling and Computer Simulation (N.A. Kheir, ed.), Marcel Dekker, Inc., New York, 631-679.

Stairmong, M.C. and Kreutzer, W. 1988, "POSE: a Process-Oriented Simulation Environment embedded in SCHEME," Simulation (50)4, 143-153.

Stallman, R., Weinreb, D. and Moon, D. 1984, Lisp Machine Manual. Lisp Machine Incorporated, Los Angeles, CA.

Zeigler, B.P. 1987, "Hierarchical, modular discrete-event modelling in an object-oriented environment," Simulation (49)5. 219-230.

Advances in AI and Simulation
© 1989 By The Society for Computer
Simulation International
ISBN 0-911801-50-2

Parallel implementation of a pattern matching expert system

Geoffery Guisewite
David L. Hall
Daniel Heinze

HRB Systems, Inc.
Science Park Road
State College, PA 16804

ABSTRACT

This paper describes a pattern matching expert system, which detects patterns in sparse binary images in the presence of noise. The approach combines image processing algorithms and statistical pattern recognition techniques. Initializing the system to correctly remove the image noise (and, hence, recognize patterns in the image) requires a knowledge of the algorithms and of the image characteristics. An expert system was developed which would correctly initialize the system, given a set of characteristics describing the image patterns. Tests with both simulated and actual data demonstrated that this expert system made correct inferences approximately 96% as well as human experts.

The original system was prototyped on a Symbolics 3650 computer and required up to 20 minutes of processing time per image. Subsequently, the algorithms and expert system were reformulated to take advantage of a parallel computer architecture. The architecture utilized a forty-two processor system of microprocessors. Reformulation and rehost of the expert system resulted in an improvement in throughput by a factor approaching 400 to 1.

INTRODUCTION

An occasionally encountered signal processing problem involves noise introduced as multiple false readings which corrupt each "true" data point. For example, at discrete intervals, a measurement device provides multiple values only one of which is the true data point. The remaining false values are noise or false alarms. The data thus represents a multi-valued time sequence in which noise may be distributed various ways, e.g., randomly, uniformly, etc. Such data could result, for example, from an analog-to-digital device or a corrupted data transmission process.

If the underlying ("true") data are aperiodic, then noise removal may be difficult, especially if the data follows a discontinuous pattern. In addition the measurement process may exhibit data dropouts, or false dismissals. Traditional noise reduction methods, such as frequency domain filtering are not applicable for two reasons; first, the data are multi-valued, and second, the true data are aperiodic. Identification of the true data becomes a pattern recognition problem involving recognizing one dimensional patterns (e.g., discontinuous lines) from a sparse binary image. An example of such a data set is shown in figure 1. The true data can be readily identified visually, but are difficult to extract using automatic signal processing techniques. The top of figure 1 illustrates the noisy data, while the bottom portion of the figure is noise free.

We have developed an expert system which utilizes image processing techniques to automatically extract data from noise. The system utilizes a two dimensional convolution filter and a pruning process to remove noise. A rule-based expert system selects control parameters for the convolution filter. The optimal parameters vary depending on the level and type of noise, and the nature of the true data. Tests of the expert system against real data demonstrated that the system could automatically remove noise as well as humans can for 96% of the test cases.

Originally, the expert system was developed to operate on a DEC VAX 11/780 computer and a Symbolic 3650 computer. While proven to be an effective and useful system, the system had a slow response time. A typical data set involves 1024 discrete intervals, with up to forty noise (false) values at each

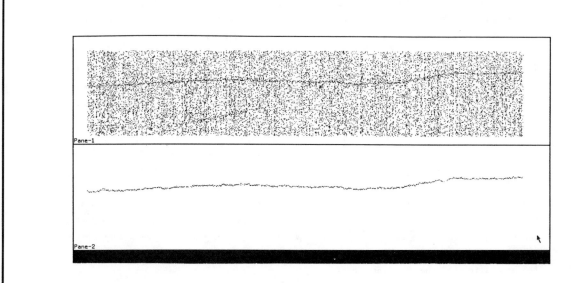

Figure 1 Sample Data Set

measurement interval. For such a data set, the original system required approximately 10 to 20 minutes of processing time. In order to reduce this processing time, we reformulated the algorithms and ported the system to a 42 processor Transputer system. This parallel processing implementation resulted in a significant improvement in throughput, reducing the required processing time to a few seconds.

This paper describes the expert system and noise reduction algorithms, summarizes the parallel implementation, and the test results.

IMAGE PROCESSING ALGORITHMS

In order to remove noise from the noise corrupted multi-valued time series, the data are treated as a two dimensional, sparse binary image. The separation of data from noise is approached as an edge detection, pattern recognition problem (see, for example, Dawson, 1987, Jain, 1986, and Kanal, 1986). Three algorithms are utilized; (1) a two dimensional convolution filter selects likely data (vs. noise) based on a Gaussian weighting scheme; (2) a pruning algorithm distinguishes clusters of data from clusters of noise, and (3) a fill-in process interpolates empty data positions by identifying data within a threshold of the linearly interpolated data values.

The convolution filter, (Huertas, 1986), operates on an image by replacing a picture element's (pixel's) value with the sum of the pixel's value and its neighbors, each weighted by an a priori factor. In essence, a two dimensional weighting matrix is overlaid on the image. The pixel at the center of the weighting matrix is replaced by a weighted sum. The weighting matrix is systematically moved throughout the image until all original pixel values are replaced by new weighted values. Note, a uniform binary image would be unaffected by such a transformation. A Gaussian weighting scheme was used, viz.

$$\text{Weight} = \frac{1}{\sqrt{2\pi}\ \sigma} e^{-x^2/2\sigma^2} \qquad (1)$$

where x is the mean distance between the point being convolved to the point being weighted, and σ is the standard deviation of x.

For our application, in any column (other than that of the point being convolved), the probability of encountering the noise point closest to the point being convolved increases with distance. In order to be distinguishable by human or machine, true data points must have a mean interpoint distance less than that between noise and data, or between noise and noise. Thus, over an extended range of x values, the

33

closest point to the point being convolved will more frequently be data than noise. For this reason, only the point in each column which is closest to the point being convolved contributes to the weight of the point being convolved. This may be expressed as:

$$cw = \sum_{cx-1/2kx}^{cx-1} \max(wx_1, .., wx_j) + \sum_{cx+1}^{cx+1/2kx} \max(wx_1, .., wx_j) \quad (2)$$

where:

- cw is the convolved weight of the point being convolved

- cx is the x value of the point being convolved

- kx is the size-1 in x of the convolution kernel

- wx is the assigned weight of the jth point inside the kernel in x

Where there is no data point in a column, or a noise point is chosen for some other reason, an error will result which will be corrected by the ensuing clustering algorithm.

Subsequent to applying the convolution filter, noise may still remain. In particular, if the original noise forms small, dense clusters, then the convolution algorithm will select noise versus data. In addition, if there are data dropouts (i.e., no true data point), then the convolution algorithm will select noise. In order to distinguish noise from true data, Zahn's (Zahn, 1971, and Duda, 1973) graph theoretic Gastalt technique is applied. The remaining pixels in the image space are treated as nodes of a minimum spanning tree (MST). Random correlations of noise points are small. Thus knowing the density of the original binary image, it is possible to calculate the mean and standard deviation for the size of clusters of noise points.

Being formed from random correlations of random noise points, the noise clusters will be spaced at distances proportional to the distances observed for the single noise points in the original image. This being the case, on the basis of size and distance, the subtrees of the MST may be classified as either noise or data, and the noise clusters may be pruned from the tree.

APPLICATION OF EXPERT SYSTEMS

A difficulty in applying these algorithms is to properly optimize the control parameters for the input data set. The algorithms employed in our application require eight input parameters with about 2**40 possible combinations. Most, however, would be very poor selections. Because the parameters are interdependent and cannot effectively be independently varied, the range of possible inputs can be greatly restricted. Still, to effectively select the parameters an operator would need a detailed understanding of the algorithms, how the parameters are interrelated, and how the parameters relate to the characteristics of the pattern. Even with experience, the accurate selection of parameters over an extended period of time is tedious.

While implementing an expert system (see for example Hall and Sporkin, 1986, and Hall and Heinze, 1988) for parameter selection, extensive records were maintained of the relation between the pattern characteristic, the input parameters, and system performance. Based on these records, rules were developed for parameter selection. The expert system operates at three levels. The first level sets the initial values of the parameters. The second level of rules determines if the system is capable of correctly editing the pattern. If it is determined that there are elements of the signal which cannot be correctly edited, a manual editor is invoked, and the operator is asked to do limited manual pre-editing of the pattern to remove portions which may prove troublesome. The third level is coded into the various algorithms and is used to modify the original parameter values on the basis of characteristics measured during the editing process.

The input to the expert system is made via a mouse sensitive menu which allows the operator to specify a range of values for each of five pattern characteristics - Rate of change; Range of change; Pattern strength; Range of discrete steps in the pattern; Noise level. It is not necessary that the pattern characteristics be uniform over the entire area to be edited. The operator is allowed to specify more than one value for each of the pattern characteristics. For example, part of the pattern may have a high rate of change and part of the pattern may be flat; the noise level may range from high to none; the pattern strength may range from medium to low.... All of the characteristic ranges are taken into account by the expert system, and a worst case parameter selection is made. Figure 2 illustrates the input menu for the expert system.

Using this system, the operator need know nothing of the theory of the algorithms involved in the editing process. Tedious calculations and cross referencing are eliminated while mistakes and retries are minimized. Because the pattern characteristics which must be described are easily observed by a novice, no special skills or expertise are required for editing all but the most difficult patterns. Even where some manual editing is required, it is not the tedious tracing of the pattern with a cursor, but is rather a simple matter of using the mouse to select the corners of rectangular areas in the image to be either erased or saved.

The system was tested on patterns which ranged from low-noise, unperturbed patterns to patterns with up to 20% loss and up to 2% perturbation of each

pixel from its proper position within the possible positioning range. Noise levels ranged from a low of eight noise points per data point to a high of 40 noise points per data point. In all cases, the system performed within 4% of the accuracy of a human editor working completely manually.

A PARALLEL IMPLEMENTATION

While the implemented expert system was effective at performing noise reduction, the response time was relatively slow, requiring approximately 10 to 20 minutes (depending on noise conditions) for each input data set. In order to significantly improve the throughput, we investigated applying multiple general-purpose microprocessors to the process (for a discussion of parallel processing, see Denning, 1988). A system of 20 Transputers (Trademark of INMOS, reference (10)) T414 fixed processors, was used as a parallel processing test bed. This approach was used over a vector solution (e.g., an array processor), because the majority of the processing is integer processing, and not vectorizable due to the sparsity of the data.

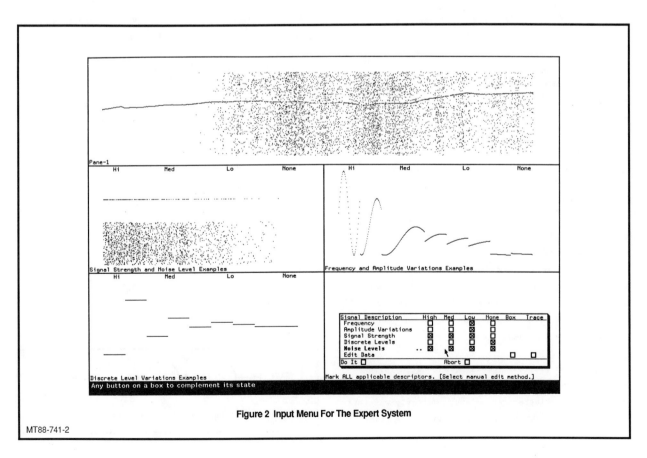

Figure 2 Input Menu For The Expert System

MT88-741-2

Analysis of the processing bottlenecks revealed that both the expert system parameter selection and the interpolation processes required a relatively small amount of processing time. Hence, these processes were each allocated to a single T414 processor. Both the convolution and prime algorithms, however, required significant time and were attacked utilizing one to twenty processors. The main processing issues to resolve were:

(1) Load balancing for the convolution filter

(2) Problem partitioning for pruning

(3) Data distribution for both

Load balancing involves partitioning the problem so that each processor acquires roughly the same workload. This was complicated for this problem by the waves of noise occurring in the data. The processing time for a frame of data depends directly on the number of noise points within the window of each point in the frame. We developed a simple heuristic which partitioned the data based on frames, so that each processor contained roughly the same 'weight' of work. The 'weight' of a frame was

Weight of current frame = (points in current frame)*
                                    (sum of the points in
                                     surrounding window)

This weighting scheme is accurate unless the noise points within a frame are extremely nonuniform. To minimize the effects of nonuniformly distributed points, a damping factor was added. The overall processing speedup is limited by the overhead associated with this data partitioning process.

The pruning process represented a challenge in terms of obtaining a partition which allowed us to exploit multiple processors. This was a result of the asymmetry of the pruning process. The prune-point subset of the processing involved a maximum distance which pruned points must exceed. This allowed us to search backwards in time until an unpruned point occurred. Processing could continue as normal from that point.

The prune cluster processing was not as simple. Again, a threshold distance was used to identify small disjoint clusters of points. Not only was this process asymmetric, but there were no simple criteria

to identify a good starting point for each sub-block of data. The resulting algorithm picked a good candidate for a starting point, performed the processing, and then received the processing results from the left neighbor. If the results indicated the starting point was bad (i.e., it got pruned) then the processing was repeated with a new starting point. The process terminates after a fixed number of iterations.

The data distribution problem can be described as choosing a processor interconnection scheme which allows for efficient distribution of data and interprocessor communication. For the convolution processing, we simply distribute the data to processors as a function of the load balancing results. Processors which contain time-adjacent data can be located contiguously in this case. The prune processing distribution requires that an equal number of frames be distributed to each processor. Again, common data can be located in contiguous processors. Moreover, the shared data can usually be located in two adjacent processors. These requirements led us to a linear array of processors, with data pipelined into the array. Since the number of points input to each processor is roughly the same, this pipelined approach to data distribution is near optimal for a distributed memory machine with a single input source and a limited number of data links per processor.

Our multiprocessor overhead for the data load required less than 0.2 milliseconds, which is small compared to the data movement term which ranges from .1 to .2 seconds depending upon our data rates.

The architecture is depicted in figure 3. The processing approach was to use the additional processors as a coprocessor and implement compute-intensive subsets of the processing on the coprocessor. Each processor executes the identical sequence of functions and synchronizes automatically when communication is required. The parallel language OCCAM was used for the Transputer implementation.

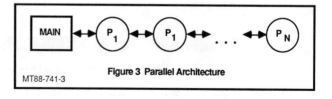

MT88-741-3   Figure 3 Parallel Architecture

TIMING RESULTS

Timing results were measured for various data, architecture and processing parameters. A typical data set involved between 600 and 1,000 measurement intervals with 10 to 40 false noise values per measurement interval. Using a single T414 processor, we obtained a speedup in the range from 3-to-1 up to 12-to-1.

The variance in speedup can be directly related to the parameters of the filtering process. This speedup includes the differences in machine performance and any differences in the efficiency of implementation. We obtained an additional speedup in the range from 11-to-1 up to 17-to-1 by applying 20 processors in the linear array configuration. This resulted in the overall speedup (over the Symbolics solution) ranging from 48-to-1 up to 136-to-1. Speedup results for 1,2,5,10, and 20 T800 processors over the Symbolics are summarized in figure 4. This figure shows the speedup factor versus number of processors for several data sets (i.e., each line in figure 4 corresponds to a separate data set). The overall speedup is significantly less than the convolution speedup. This is a result of our inability to accelerate the prune processing beyond

3-to-1. Fortunately, this has a small impact overall as the prune and fill-in functions account for less than 5% of the original processing.

For the T800 processors, we obtained an overall speedup of 165-to-1 up to 400-to-1 over the Symbolics processor. This results from a roughly 4-to-1 improvement of the T800 over the T414 for this application. This indicates that the floating-point subset of the problem was more significant than originally suspected.

The decrease in processing time has made the T800 multiprocessing more sensitive to the I/O overhead (viz. the processing time decreased while the I/O remained constant), resulting in a decrease in processor utilization.

Obstacles to fully utilizing the twenty processors include communication overhead and load balancing. The performance of the system without load balancing is dramatically decreased. This is expected: if one processor works longer than the others, then the remaining processors sit idle for some period. Our results indicate that we do a reasonably good job of balancing the data, yet we can

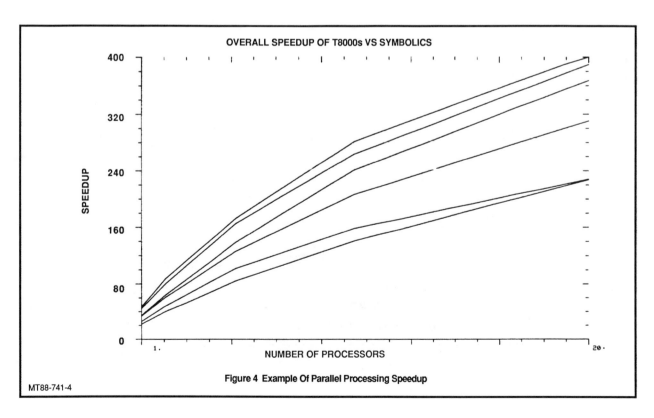

Figure 4 Example Of Parallel Processing Speedup

MT88-741-4

37

attribute half of our utilization limitation to load balancing (including the time to compute the balance partition).

The remainder of our speedup limitation can be attributed to data communications and the inability to successfully accelerate the prune function. The communication overhead is small (maximum of roughly .2 seconds) while the prune and fill-in time account for roughly 0.1 to 1 seconds (on the T414).

The overall intent of the multiprocessor approach was to rapidly process the data. The speedup numbers give an indication of how well we utilized the processors, but does not show the relationship for processing time. The overall processing times as a function of the number of processors used is given in figure 5. Each line in figure 5 corresponds to a separate data set. When compared to the speedup numbers in figure 4, we see we are more successful in speeding up the process when we require more processing originally. This is primarily due to the fixed overhead. We find speedup to be approximately

$$\frac{\text{original time}}{((\text{original time})/N) + \text{Sigma} + \text{Sigma}(N)}$$

where N is the number of processors, Sigma denotes fixed overhead, and Sigma(N) denotes overhead which varies with N.

SUMMARY

The processing results presented here indicate that parallel processing can be exploited for removing noise from sparse binary images. Speedups for both the T414 architecture and the T800 based architecture indicate near-linear speedup for the data files processed. Extended results for the 40 processor case indicate that utilization drops off quickly for the T800 system. Simulated data was used to project results for increased noise densities. Results indicate that as the noise level increases, the processing required increases, and the number of processors which can be effectively utilized increases.

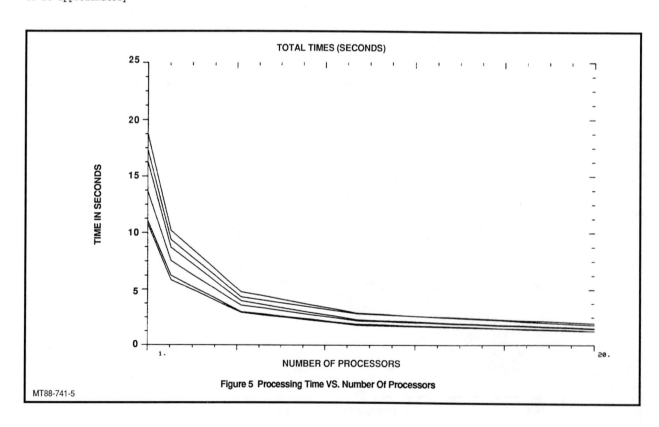

Figure 5 Processing Time VS. Number Of Processors

MT88-741-5

38

REFERENCES

1. Dawson, B. M. "Introduction to Image Processing Algorithms." _Byte_, March 1987, pp. 169-186.

2. Jain, Anlin K. "Cluster Analysis." _Handbook of Pattern Recognition and Image Processing_. Academic Press Inc., 1986, pp. 33-57.

3. Kanal, Laveen N. "Problem Solving Methods for Pattern Recognition." _Handbook of Pattern Recognition and Image Processing_. Academic Press Inc., 1986, pp. 143-165.

4. Huertas, Andreas, Gerard Mendoni. "Detection of Intensity Changes with Subpixel Accuracy Using Laplacian-Gaussian Masks." _IEEE Transactions on Pattern Analysis and Machine Intelligence_, vol. PAMI-8, No. 5, September 1986, pp. 651-664.

5. Zahn, Charles T. "Graph-Theoretical Methods for Detecting and Describing Gestalt Clusters." _IEEE Transactions on Computers_, vol. C-20, No. 1, January 1971.

6. Duda, Richard O., Peter E. Hart. _Pattern Classification and Scene Analysis_. 1973.

7. Hall, D. L. and Sporkin, D. "Expert Systems: Technology's Answer to Information Overload." _Journal of Electronic Defense_, October 1986.

8. Hall, D. L. and Heinze, D. "Introduction to Expert Systems." _AIAA Softalk_, July 1988.

9. Denning, P.J., "Speeding Up Parallel Processing." _American Scientist_, July-August, 1988, pp. 347-349.

10. "This CPU Does Floating Point Faster Than Any Two Chip Sets." _Electronics_, November 1986, pp. 51-55.

Advances in AI and Simulation
© 1989 By The Society for Computer
Simulation International
ISBN 0-911801-50-2

A transputer-based parallel sensor fusion implementation

by Chinh Hoang and David G. Findley

GENERAL DYNAMICS
Fort Worth Division
P.O. Box 748
Fort Worth, Texas 76101

Abstract

The need for target-tracking has led to increasingly complex and expensive hardware/software solutions which involve integrating information from multiple sources (e.g., sensors, remote data link, and a priori). The resulting conflict between the areas of real-time performance, quality and quantity of track information, and expense has often resulted in less than desirable systems. This paper will address some of these areas through a parallel implementation of a report-integration paradigm sensor-fusion/target-tracker (SF/TT) design that uses the INMOS™ Transputer®. A serial multisensor multitarget tracker has been translated from FORTRAN. The tracker was redesigned and reimplemented as two versions of an occam program. The first version is implemented as a single processor sequential tracker running on a T-414 Transputer of an IMS B004 board. The second version as a parallel occam program running on an INMOS™ ITEM-40 System with two IMS B003 boards (8 T-414 Transputers). The ITEM-40 System also contains an IMS B007 board providing the graphics display capability for both versions of the redesigned tracker. The goal for the parallel version of the tracker is to maintain a central track-file at 50 hertz update rate using cost-effective hardware. The parallel approach used maps one track file data-structure to one B003's T-414 Transputer. The track data structure, along with its covariance matrix, is stored local in each B003 Transputer's on-chip 2K bytes 50ns SRAM and local tracking operation algorithms (Rotate, Kalman Filter, Smooth, etc.) are replicated and stored in each B003 Transputer's local 256K byte 120ns DRAM. The resultant parallel tracking testbed represents an almost linear performance improvement over the single-transputer sequential version.

Problem

Sensor-fusion and target-tracking are becoming increasingly important for aircraft to both attack and survive. Previous SF/TT systems have used mainframes for temporally-update-tolerant targets (non-maneuvering commercial aircraft, satellites) or have resorted to special-purpose hardware processors for temporally-update-intolerant targets (maneuvering aircraft, missiles)[1], [3].

Typical threats for military aircraft self-defense systems will be Mach 6+ missiles and projectiles. These threats require the use of fast target-tracking hardware/software. However, the use of such special-purpose processors is economically prohibitive. The design studied here uses the INMOS Transputer, a low-cost parallel processor.

Report Integration Sensor Fusion Paradigm

After studying [7] the advantages and disadvantages of several sensor fusion methods (Track Correlation, Track

Composition and Report Integration), we selected the report-integration paradigm as the foundation for our SF/TT system.

The report-integration paradigm is shown in Figure 1. A central tracking system receives reports from all sensors in the system and then develops a central integrated system track file. Within the central tracking function is a main tracking loop for each sensor. Integrated tracking is done very much like single-sensor tracking, except that each sensor tracking loop operates on the same system track file. Report files, contact files, and association files are still unique to each sensor. Only the system track file is common.

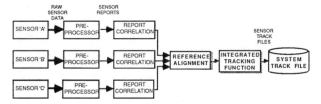

Figure 1 Report Integration Paradigm

In an integrated tracking system, tracks initiated by one sensor may be updated by reports from any other sensor in the system. The integration tracking algorithm is simple. In principle, the code for each sensor is unique. But in practice, much of the code will be common from one sensor to another, and generally will vary only in parameters. Integration is not accomplished by a complex algorithm but simply by having each sensor track loop operate on the same track file. The tracking loop (Figure 2) contains the following seven processes.

1. Track Prediction
2. Track-Report Association
3. Track-Report Resolution
4. Track Update
5. Track Promotion
6. Saved-Report Association
7. Saved-Report Entry

We used a Symbolics 3675® Lisp machine to test the detecting and tracking capabilities of the SF/TT program with many computer simulation runs. The test cases covered different tracking scenarios including the cases of maneuvering and crossing tracks. Results from the runs showed the tracker performed satisfactorily in most cases, especially in the track crossing case where the tracker correctly recognized all the tracks before and after they

Symbolics, Symbolics 3675, Zetalisp® and Flavors are trademarks of Symbolics Inc.
INMOS and occam are trademarks of the INMOS Group of companies

crossed each other. In the runs with tracks making high-g turn maneuvers, we reduced the time step interval of the program in order to maintain the tracking accuracy required (the case of aggressively maneuvering tracks is a fertile area for application of AI techniques, e.g., maneuver anticipation). Track confidence is also included in our study and is currently based upon Baysian techniques (future versions of the SF/TT software will be augmented by target ID-dependent heuristics - e.g. track confidence will vary radically for a missile versus that for a transport aircraft).

Implementing and testing the sequentially executed SF/TT software within other projects revealed that it was the limiting factor in the performance of these systems. Performance requirements led to our re-host and redesign of the sensor fusion software to exploit parallel execution. The host machine chosen was an INMOS ITEM-40 transputer evaluation system, configured with two INMOS B003 boards [4], [5]; occam [6] was chosen as the implementation language since it was designed to facilitate parallel process execution.

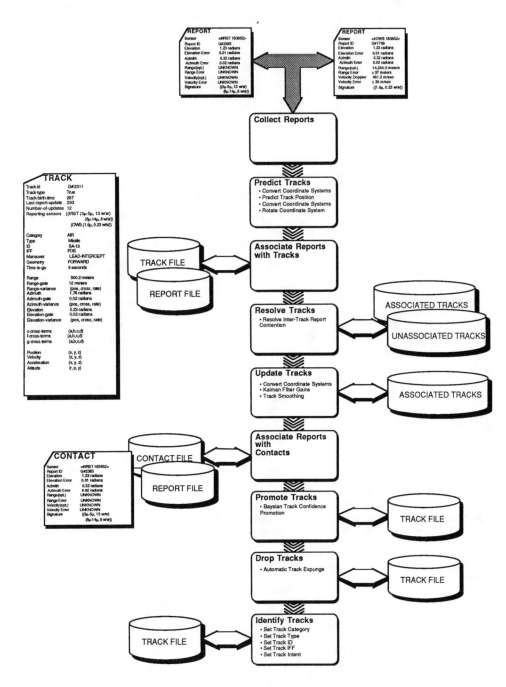

Figure 2 SF/TT Functions

Parallel Target Tracker Design

Our goal for the target tracker implementation on the transputer system was to utilize parallel processing to maintain and update all target track files at 50 hertz.

The target tracker operates upon these files, one of each: contact, saved-contact and association. Besides these files which are common to all the tracks, each track has its own track file containing parameters pertaining to that track (position, speed, heading, etc...). Among the seven processes of the tracker, the Track Update process is the most computation extentive. The process contains a 6-state Kalman filter operating on a 6 x 6 covariance matrix for track smoothing. The Kalman recursive smoothing algorithm contains these five sequenced steps:

1. Predict state variables
2. Predict covariances
3. Compute gains
4. Smooth state variables
5. Smooth covariances

The Track Update process, besides being time consuming, is parallel in nature since it operates upon only the unique track files of each track. These facts make the process become the focus of our tracker parallelization effort (Figure 3).

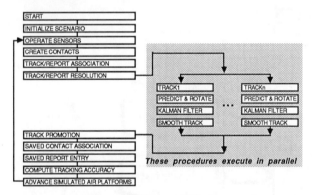

Figure 3 Application of parallel processing to SF/TT algorithm

At the heart of the parallel tracker is the main tracking loop containing three simulated sensors. The sensors, one active and two passive, reside within and are controlled by the main program driver . The driver along with the timing and all the input/output functions reside in the B004 's T-414 (host) transputer (Figure 4). The host transputer also contains all the tracking processes, except the Track Update. The Track Update process , in order to become parallel, is copied and sent to all the B003's T-414 track transputers. Our system contains two B003 boards each having four T-414 transputers. On each B003 board, one transputer handles the data multiplexing task and the other three are for Track Update.

At the begining of a run, the program driver issues commands to all the sensors to perform the scanning and detecting functions. The results are then fed into the target tracker. The tracker now performs the tracking processes (predict, associatrion, etc...) on the host transputer. Once a track is created, its track file is send to one of the B003's Track Update transputer. One transputer is dedicated to each track so the number of tracks in the system is limited

only by the number of transputers available. A single command, broadcast from the host transputer, causes each system track transputer to simultaneously perform the Track Update operations on its track data structure. Upon completion, the track data stuctures are sent back to the host processor for the tracker to continue the tracking process.

Results

Results of our six-track simulation runs represent an almost linear performance improvement of the parallel version over the sequential version of the tracker. On the average, it takes the single transputer version 120 seconds to complete a 300- second, six-track run. The multiple transputer parallel tracker completes the same run in about 24 seconds. A parallel run time of 20 seconds (120/6) is considered as our goal of linear performance improvement. The 4-second difference between the actual and ideal run times of the parallel tracker is primarily due to the I/O overhead between the host, multiplexing, and track processors.

The System Track File as a Temporal Data/Knowledge Base

Within the our Lisp-based Self-Defense expert system [2], the track file has been adopted as a temporal data/knowledge base for the representation of objects in the ownship environment. In the history of target-tracking, the track file data structure has been rather sparse in the amount of information that it contained. This information has been restricted to bearing, azimuth, range, and a track confidence. There are, however, many other types of data or "knowledge" that should be included in the track. In the past, this data/knowledge have been excluded because (1) the information would require additional amounts of "fast" static RAM, an expensive proposition in the 1950-1980 time period and (2) the avionic architectures that would have acted upon this additional temporal object knowledge were limited in terms of functionality. The resulting track data-structure (Figure 5) is now a large (~2K bytes) resulting in a track file of ~335K bytes.

Future Extensions To This Work

Future extensions to this work will involve co-location of our previously developed Lisp-based Self-Defense expert system [2] at each track-transputer node for real-time AI response.

Each SF/TT track file will be extended to contain target posture and processed sensor information concerning an object that is being tracked. The information belonging to the track will include ID, threat level, dynamics, kinematics, time, and accuracy. Temporal histories of many track data items will be maintained for several consecutive track update intervals (e.g., position, velocity, acceleration, and track quality). In this manner, it will be possible to observe how a track has maneuvered with time, how its velocity has changed with time, and how its track quality has changed with time. This knowledge will be used to derive a prediction of target intent. Finally, self-defense expert system recommendations will be associated with each threat-track, which the pilot will assess and approve for employment against the threat (Figure 6).

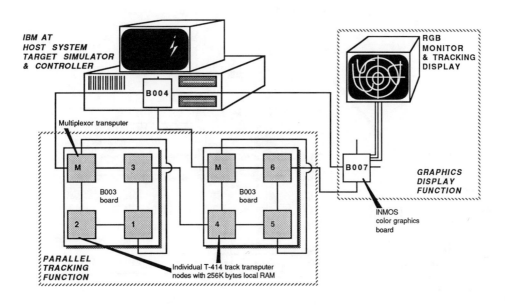

Figure 4   Multiple Transputer Parallel Tracking Hardware Processing Diagram

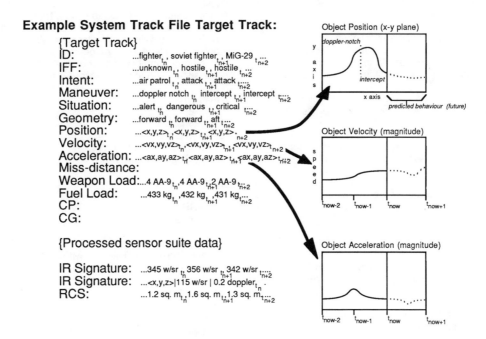

Figure 5 Example System Track File

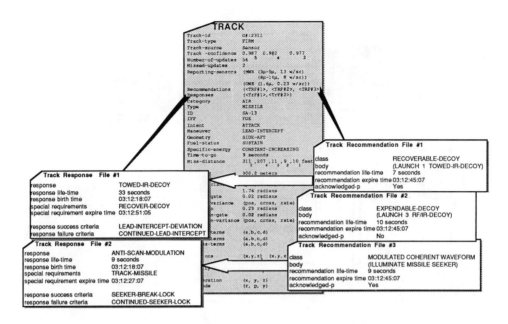

Figure 6 System Track with associated Recommendations and Responses

Observations on the TDS, occam, and rehosting sequential software

(1) The Transputer Development System (TDS™) has an excellent editor that utilizes a folding technique. The folding technique allows a global perspective of the program and greatly facilitates editing and debugging.

(2) The d700c version of the occam compiler we used lacks functions, forcing the use of awkward procedure calls for the same effect.

(3) Due to the large number of separate compilation folds, linking gradually assumed the largest share of the program development time.

(4) Each time the program crashed, we had to resort to rebooting the TDS. This becomes very annoying after few crashes.

Conclusions

The parallel transputer sensor fusion/target-tracker met our expectations of performance. We met several goals in the implementation:

• The redesign and recoding of an existing FORTRAN SF/TT program into parallel occam 2.

• An almost linear performance improvement (for the six target tracking test case, a single transputer required 120 seconds vs. 24 seconds for the parallel eight -transputer example).

Acknowledgments

We received help from many individuals at General Dynamics Fort Worth Division. The foundation of our sensor-fusion/target-tracking algorithms are directly based upon ideas, algorithms, and source code previously developed by William Wilsterman. We would also like to thank Uday Desai, Larry Cockrell, and Jim Stewart for their own unique contributions, and finally INMOS' David Bye, for his assistance in many Transputer related areas.

References

[1] Stimson, G.W.,
Introduction To Airborne Radar
Hughes Aircraft Company,
El Segundo, CA 1983

[2] Darnall, S.P.,
Self-Defense Expert System
ERR-FW-2816, General Dynamics,
January 1988

[3] Blackman, S.S.,
Multiple Target Tracking with Radar
Applications, Artech House, Inc. 1986,
Norwood, MA, 02062

[4] Jones, G.,
Programming In Occam
Prentice-Hall International (UK) Ltd. (1987)
Hemel Hempstead, Hertfordshire, HP2 4RG

[5] Transputer Reference Manual
INMOS Corporation
Colorado Springs, CO 80935

[6] The Transputer Family
INMOS Corporation
Colorado Springs, CO 80935

Advances in AI and Simulation
© 1989 By The Society for Computer
Simulation International
ISBN 0-911801-50-2

Parallel implementation of autonomous target recognition algorithm on a reconfigurable transputer array

B. L. Nicholson
General Dynamics Corporation
Convair Division
San Diego, Ca. 92138

and

G. R. Orr
General Dynamics Corporation
Data Systems Division
San Diego, Ca. 92138

ABSTRACT

An imaging-based autonomous target recognition (ATR) algorithm was implemented on a parallel architecture. This paper describes the techniques employed in adapting a serial algorithm to a parallel computing environment: a reconfigurable array of Transputers. The goal of this effort was to achieve significant performance enhancement and to expand the general knowledge base in exploiting parallel processing.

The approach analyzed the ATR algorithm for computational bottlenecks, data dependencies, and data throughput requirements. Several methods were used to fashion the algorithm for execution of its many parts in parallel and to effectively make use of the specific hardware resources. These methods included data and computation partitioning, static load balancing, static/dynamic memory utilization, and optimal configuration of Transputer connections.

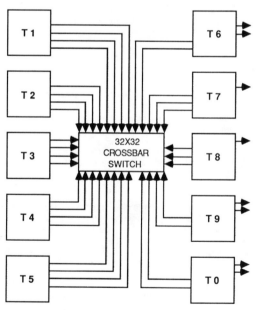

Figure 1

Diagram of the Reconfigurable Transputer Array Board. Ten T800 Transputers, each with 128K bytes external RAM. Transputer's serial links are routed to programmble crossbar switch. Eight serial links, shown on right, can be connected to external devices or to each other. Maximum computational power of the board is 100 MIPS and 15 MFLOPS.

INTRODUCTION

Image processing applications, in general, are well suited for parallel computing. Sections of the picture area can usually be assigned to individual processors for repetitive operations in a pipelined or mesh architecture. The algorithm discussed in this paper locates and identifies naval ships from single frames of Forward Look Infrared (FLIR) imagery. Most of the tasks performed in this ATR algorithm can be logically extended to concurrent processes. The Transputer, with its ability to simultaneously communicate and compute, and to hardware multi-task, provides a low cost, powerful, and flexible parallel processing platform for image computing.

The processor array is based on the T800, the floating point version of the Transputer. It consists of a 32-bit integer processor, 4K bytes of static RAM, 64-bit floating point unit, four high speed serial links, and an external memory interface. The hardware, shown in Figure 1, is a single board with ten Transputers, each with 128K bytes of external static RAM. Thirty two of the forty serial links are connected to a 32x32 programmable crossbar switch, allowing the Transputers to be configured in a variety a ways, even while executing. The remaining eight serial links are used for connections external to the board.

The algorithm was written in the Transputer's native parallel language, OCCAM.

ALGORITHM DESCRIPTION

Figure 2 shows a block diagram of the major algorithm components. A FLIR image, 8-bit gray scale and 256x128 pixels in size, is used as input. The edge map generator operates vertically and horizontally to produce vertical and horizontal edge maps. The target is initially cued from the edge map containing horizontal features. This information is then used to register the target (precisely locate the ends of the ship) to take care of scale, translation, and rotation. Next, a low-resolution profile is extracted from the target. This information, along with height/width ratio, is used to partition the reference database (eliminating consideration of reference profiles that could not correlate with the target). The correlator forms a combined edge map, and the remaining candidates in the reference profile database are partially 2-D correlated with the combined edge map. The output of the algorithm includes detection confidence, ship class, angle, and estimated range to target.

ANALYSIS

The algorithm was initially developed on a VAX 11/750 and was written in FORTRAN. First, the software was directly converted into OCCAM to execute serially on one Transputer. Each section of the algorithm was then timed (Table 1). The time for the algorithm to operate on the VAX 11/750 was 55 seconds. As Table 1 shows, even a single Transputer offers a significant improvement in performance.

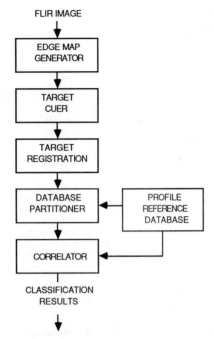

FLIR IMAGE

↓

EDGE MAP
GENERATOR

↓

TARGET
CUER

↓

TARGET
REGISTRATION

↓

DATABASE
PARTITIONER ← PROFILE
                REFERENCE
                DATABASE

↓

CORRELATOR ←

↓

CLASSIFICATION
RESULTS

↓

Figure 2   ATR Algorithm Functions

Edge map generation	3.44	(sec)
Target cuer	0.49	
Target registration	0.08	
Database partitioning	0.90	
Correlation	1.07	
	5.98	Total

Table 1   ATR execution time on one T800 Transputer

The most computationally intensive portion of the algorithm is edge map generation. Since this is a local operator, multiple processors can execute the same code on different sections of the input image. The target cueing algorithm uses the horizontal edge map to detect and cue the target. The first part of this algorithm is an operation on each scan line of one edge map. This consumes about 40 percent of the time cueing the target and is easily done on multiple processors. The remainder of the target cuer must be executed serially. Target registration consists of precisely locating the ends of the target. The search on both ends can be performed in parallel. During database partitioning, an intermediate edge map is formed by combining all other edge maps and a target profile is extracted from this map. If the edge maps are already distributed over several processors, these operations can be done in parallel. Each reference profile not partitioned out of the database can be correlated with the combined edge map independently of the others.

Ideally, using ten Transputers should provide a 10x speed improvement over a single processor. The following section describes how the algorithm was partitioned over ten processors.

IMPLEMENTATION

Figure 3 shows a diagram of the development environment. The Transputer array board, with processors T0, T1, ..., T9, is interfaced to an IBM PC host. Processor T0 is connected to a

Transputer, housed inside the PC, through one of its external serial links. The PC contains a commercially available Transputer plug-in card used for software development, and downloading executable code and image data to the 10-processor board. Digitized FLIR image frames and reference databases are stored on the PC hard disk.

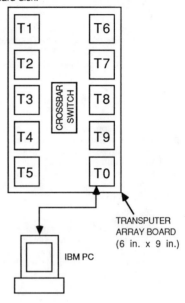

Figure 3

The development environment. The PC contains a Transputer that connects directly to one of the Transputers on the array board.

The profile reference database used in this discussion contains 10 different ship profiles at various angles. The profiles are read from the PC hard disk and dispersed among five Transputers: T2, T3, T4, T6, and T8, each with two profiles.

Figure 4 graphically summarizes the parallel implementation of the ATR algorithm.

The edge map generator is implemented on every Transputer except T1. The input image is broken into nine sections and assigned to separate processors. After the horizontal feature edge map has been formed, each processor passes its results to T1. The nine processors pass their edge maps while performing the first phase of the target cueing algorithm.

Each processor passes cueing data to T1. Processor T1 executes the rest of the target cuer while the other Transputers generate vertical feature edge maps. The edge maps are passed to T1 and T6. By this time T1 has finished with the target cuer and now starts target registration along with processor T6.

Processors T1 and T6 do not execute target registration in parallel. Both processors are used because of memory requirements for the edge maps. While T1 and T6 are performing the registration function, the remaining processors are generating an intermediate edge map needed for database partitioning. The resulting edge map is combined in processor T0 and the target registration points are also passed to T0, where database partitioning statistics are calculated.

After processor T0 has computed partitioning data and tagged candidate profiles in the reference database, T1 calculates the final combined edge map, using data from all other processors. The partitioning statistics and combined edge map are then passed to Transputers T2, T3, T4, T6, and T8. These processors correlate their reference profiles (those not eliminated from consideration) with a limited area in the final combined edge map. The correlation scores are passed to T0, where confidence levels are calculated and target class rankings are made.

HARDWARE/SOFTWARE UTILIZATION

The previous section describes in a high level way how the algorithm was spread over ten Transputers. There were instances where the unique features of the hardware and parallel language were exploited to gain performance increases.

The Transputer's 4K of internal RAM can be accessed in fewer processor cycles than external memory. Part of this fast memory was used as a cache in implementing the edge map generator. Most often used variables in other parts of the algorithm were also identified on each processor and explicitly placed in on-chip RAM when possible.

The algorithm generates several images during its execution stages. The total amount of code and data necessary to execute the algorithm serially exceeds 350K bytes. Because each processor must have duplicate copies of some portions of code and data, the 128K bytes of memory space on each processor must be managed in such a way that identical sections of memory are used for different data items (usually areas of an image) at different times without conflict and without degrading overall algorithm performance. Three features of the Transputer make this possible: the ability to communicate and compute concurrently, very fast hardware multi-tasking, and facilities in the OCCAM language to easily map different items of any data type to the same memory area. At the simplest level, once the original image array has been used on a given processor to generate the edge maps, this memory area can then be utilized for other data. The majority of the processors require much more extensive data remapping.

Figure 5 shows the parallel implementation of processes on each Transputer. The OCCAM statement PRI PAR means that one process is to execute at high priority and one at low priority. The

PRI PAR
  PAR
    ...Process to manage communications through link 0
    ...Process to manage communications through link 1
    ...Process to manage communications through link 2
    ...Process to manage communications through link 3
    ...Process to interface communications with calculations
  SEQ
    ...Calculating process

Figure 5

The top level OCCAM structure on each Transputer. Six processes execute in parallel. Four processes handle I/O through the serial links, one performs calculations, and the sixth handles interface chores. The calculation process executes at low priority. All other processes run at high priority.

following statement, PAR, actually says that there are several processes executing in parallel at high priority. The statement SEQ identifies the low priority process. Four parallel processes executing at high priority pass data in and out of each serial link. The fifth process acts as the controller for all activity on the Transputer. It signals the low priority calculating process that data is available to operate on and receives signals from the computing process when operations are complete. This process also buffers data from the calculating process, signals all the communicating processes when to execute a data transfer in or out of the Transputer, and synchronizes this data movement with the calculating process so there are no conflicts with globally defined, multi-mapped memory areas.

The interface process is carefully written for each Transputer so that the four communicating processes and calculating process are actually executing in parallel as much as possible, not waiting for data or waiting to send data. The processors are also connected to each other (configured via the crossbar switch) in such a way as to minimize the number of Transputers a given data item must pass in order to reach its destination. This not only decreases communication latency, but preserves memory for local uses on each Transputer.

LOAD BALANCING AND PERFORMANCE MEASUREMENT

The major decisions on how to partition the algorithm were based on static load balancing techniques. Sections of the input image were routed to the processors, operations performed on the image, and calculation times computed. This process continued through many iterations, changing parameters such as subimage size, configuration of the serial links, operations to perform concurrently, and the number of Transputers allocated to a task.

Figure 4 illustrates the partitioning of the main algorithmic functions. Notice that processor T1 was idle during vertical edge generation and part of the target cueing task. This was necessary because T1 executes the remainder of the target cuer and target registration tasks, which require memory in excess of that available if the edge map generation is also performed. The idle time on processors T1 and T6, just before target registration, was due to receiving edge maps from the other Transputers. Also, this idle time included initiating data transfers between T1 and T6, needed for executing target registration. Processor T0 combined edge maps that it generated and edge maps contained on processor T6. The remainder of database partitioning and final edge map combination are functions that cannot be parallelized because of data dependencies. The five Transputers that were idle during the correlation phase could have been utilized for this task had the database contained more profiles.

The main approach of this implementation was: once a processor received input data, to perform as many operations as possible on the data. Also, to perform all possible calculations on the results.

An optimal load balance was determined by measuring the execution time for calculations, data transfers, and idleness on each Transputer relative to the other Transputers. This was accomplished by synchronizing the processors using the crossbar switch. Before processor T0 receives the input image from the host system, the switch can be programmed to connect the output of one of T0's links to the inputs of a link on each of the other nine processors. Processor T0 sends a signal simultaneously to the other processors. Each processor reads its clock when the signal is received and the processors are synchronized. The crossbar switch can then be reprogrammed to the configuration for

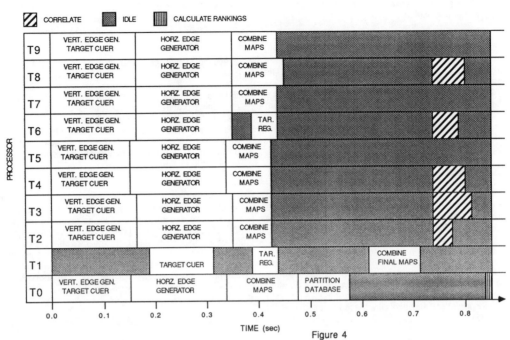

Figure 4
Parallel execution of the ATR algorithm. This implementation requires 0.85 sec to recognize the target.

executing the algorithm. The controlling process on each Transputer obtained all timing information. This method was used to load balance the processors for different implementations by generating a task execution graph as shown in Figure 4.

CONCLUSION

This parallel implementation of the ATR algorithm is only one of many possible. It is not fully optimized in its present form. There is a sizeable amount of processor idle time, but a very significant increase in performance was achieved over a single processor. Alternative approaches are possible and may work as well or better. We have attempted to demonstrate the flexibility and compute power of the Transputer architecture in developing parallel algorithms for imaging applications. Also, the Transputer and OCCAM language are powerful tools in logically describing concurrent processes and then extending processes to physical hardware.

ACKNOWLEDGEMENTS

We would like to acknowledge Mike Patrick and Brad Dunagan, of General Dynamics, Convair Division, for their design and fabrication of the Transputer array board. This work is a small part of a larger effort at General Dynamics in the development of signal/image processing algorithms and hardware design.

REFERENCES

Atkin, P. 1987. "Performance Maximisation." Technical Note 17. INMOS Corporation (Mar)

Hill, G. 1987. "Design and Applications for the IMS C004." Technical Note 19. INMOS Corporation (Jun)

May, D. 1987. "Communications processes and occam." Technical Note 20. INMOS Corporation (Feb)

Advances in AI and Simulation
© 1989 By The Society for Computer
Simulation International
ISBN 0-911801-50-2

Intelligent modeling of telecommunication networks using knowledge based simulation

Ajay Waghray
Rafal Dziedzic
Bell Atlantic Knowledge Systems Inc.
145 Fayette Street
Morgantown, WV 26505

ABSTRACT

LASER/SIM, a powerful knowledge based simulation system, makes it possible to apply traditional simulation methodologies using artificial intelligence techniques. LASER/SIM is used to 1) test the performance of Public Data Packet Switching Networks and 2) test the price competitiveness and performance of private Voice Data networks.

The price evaluation will exploit the ability of LASER/SIM to provide a comparative analysis of the proposed alternatives by managing variants of a model (scenarios) at various points in time (checkpoints).

The performance assessments will take advantage of the modeling and simulation capabilities of LASER/SIM to estimate performance given varying customer requirements.

These simulations can be used to: 1) predict potential response time or delay problems and their effect on long term client system needs; 2) configure the network to meet acceptable criterion; and 3) predict likely consequences when existing networks are modified. The user will have the ability to pose "what-if" questions when assessing the impact of cost-based concerns and prices.

INTRODUCTION

Simulation is one of the most widely used planning techniques for studying the behavior of complex systems. As an analysis tool, simulation can be used to predict the results of changing an existing system. As a design tool, simulation can be used to predict the performance of new systems under varying sets of circumstances. Knowledge Based Simulation (KBS) (Reddy et al. 1986), combines traditional simulation methodologies and artificial intelligence (AI) techniques, making simulation a more flexible, adaptable, and effective tool.

The design, deployment and maintenance of telecommunication networks is made difficult by the variety of equipment that must be interconnected and distributed over widespread areas. A telecommunication network commonly uses electronic gears (switches) and a transmission medium to provide a multiplicity of channels over which customer messages and associated control signals can be transmitted concurrently (Goyal and Worrest 1988). Experiences with using KBS in domains such as manufacturing (Ford and Schroer 1987) and decision support (Moser 1986), have shown that a similar effort in the area of network design/management should result in more efficient, reliable, and cost effective systems.

In this paper we propose the use of KBS to develop a Telecommunication Network Simulation Module (**TNSM**) to be used by System Design Consultants and Marketing Personnel to assess the performance implications of customer proposals and to explore price/performance alternatives.

In the next section we review LASER/SIM (LASERSIM 1986), the modeling environment used in the application development. The Packet Switching and Telecommunication Networks, and the problems of designing and managing them will be discussed next. The Network Modeling Application will then be described in detail, showing how it can be to used address the prior discussed challenges and problems.

THE LASER/SIM MODELING ENVIRONMENT

LASER (Dziedzic 1985) is an efficient, portable programming environment that provides a unified approach to AI programming. LASER includes a frame-based knowledge representation scheme with inheritance, object oriented programming facilities, multiple worlds for reasoning, and both data driven and rule based programming capabilities. A typical object in the LASER environment follows:

```
{
comline
    linespeed : 10
    state :
    contents : "packet1"
}
```

The object comline has three properties linespeed, state, and contents. The value of the property linespeed is 10.

LASER/SIM is a discrete event knowledge based simulation system developed in the LASER environment. The LASER/SIM kernel provides the basic functionality to execute a discrete event simulation model. The LASER/SIM system includes the Blocksworld and the Model Management sub-systems that are built on top of the kernel.

The LASER/SIM Blocksworld (Waghray 1987) subsystem provides a high level modeling framework based on the process interaction and network modeling approach to discrete event simulation. It uses the object-oriented knowledge representation of LASER to provide the modeler with simple and powerful prototypical concepts called **blocks.** These blocks can be instantiated, related, and refined as desired to capture the significant qualities of the system being modeled. Blocks are the basic class entities used to represent and define a model of a system. Blocks in the LASER/SIM environment are represented by LASER objects. Thus we can say that models are represented as a collection of interacting objects. The interactions between the system components are represented by relationships between the objects. The attributes of the model elements are represented by properties of the block objects. The state of the model at any time is given by the values of the properties of these objects.

The library of block objects reduces the model creation activity to one of instantiating the prototypical objects using the LASER inheritance mechanism and then relating them as desired. The instantiated objects can be specialized to meet the model's requirements by changing the values of the object properties. For example, a fibre_optic_line can be a specialization of a comline which in turn might be a specialization of the server block.

The user can expand upon the library of basic blocks provided. Any number of new blocks may be defined by using a predefined sequence of steps. Additional blocks have been defined for developing the Network Modeling Application discussed later.

The LASER/SIM Model Management (Singh, Butcher, and Reddy 1987) subsystem provides the ability to manage multiple variants of a model (scenarios) at various points in time (checkpoints). Hence its is possible to create variants of a model, explore the alternatives, and select the best alternative for the given situation.

Graphic Model Builder

LASER/GMB (Hayhurst 89), the LASER graphic model builder, facilitates the graphical construction and manipulation of object networks. Each generic block object is represented by icons and can be graphically instantiated to represent a desired model component. The model components can be networked together via simple graphic operations. The instantiated model components can be specialized by interactively modifying or adding properties and values.

TELECOMMUNICATIONS NETWORKS

The TNSM module deals with two types of telecommunication networks: Packet Switching Public Data Networks (PDN) and private T1 Voice-Data Networks.

The PDN in question is a public telecommunications network consisting of a number of packet concentrators (PADs) and a single switching node. Each PAD has a number of data terminals attached to it. Data sent into the network is assembled into packets of certain size that contain, in addition to the data itself, information about the destination of the

packet. The topology of the network is fixed, i.e., the number of PADs and the configuration of the network does not change.

Metrics important to a customer wanting to tie into such a network are: data transit times (response time), future expansion capabilities, and cost. The response time depends upon the capacity of communication lines connecting a given PAD with the switch (expressed in kbits/s), the data traffic load in a the PAD, and existing traffic patterns in the communication lines. The costs associated with using the network depend on the amount of transmitted data, the time of day that the transmissions take place, and the protocol used for data transmission.

T1 Voice-Data networks consist of high bandwidth links that can be subdivided in a number of different ways. Each link consists of 24 basic channels. Individual channels can be multiplexed or combined to meet specific customer requirements.

In addition to the items listed for PDN networks, a T1 network customer can be interested in the quality of voice transmission, reliability, and the flexibility to change the characteristics of the network such as the ability to change a voice channel into a data channel.

It is difficult and cumbersome to calculate response time, particularly in public networks where projected customer traffic must be superimposed over existing data transmission traffic patterns (Fernandez and Liddy 1988). Network design is an incremental process, that must be repeated for the designer to observe the effects of changes in network topology and characteristics (Sharma 1988).

Rather than analyzing telecommunication network cost and performance using traditional computational methods, the more efficient and flexible alternative of network simulation can be used.

TELECOMMUNICATION NETWORK SIMULATION MODULE

The TNSM is a part of a larger application called EPIC/MATRIX, which is being developed for a Regional Bell Operating Company. It is a network modeling, configuration, and marketing assistance tool used by sales/marketing personnel. It integrates expert systems, simulation, graphics, and multiple database access using a common interface.

The system is being deployed on an IBM 9370 mainframe under VM/IS and has access to databases containing information about products, existing network topologies, tariffs, and pricing. Certain graphics modules are delivered on CAD workstations. Figure 1 shows the basic architecture of the system.

50

VM/IS		
COMMUNICATION SYSTEM		
LASER/SIM	LASER/RPS	
PROFS	GDDM	A/S
QMF	SQL	BATCH
C	COBOL	REXX
SAA FRONT END PROCESS CONTROLS		

Figure 1: EPIC/MATRIX Architecture.

The user communicates with EPIC/MATRIX through a common front end that uses the SAA protocol and 3270 terminals. Embedded in the system are simulation and expert system modules LASER/SIM and LASER/RPS, a common interface to office automation facilities (PROFS), and graphics modules (GDDM). There are also provisions for SQL database access and programming language extensions (C, COBOL).

The simulation module can simulate communication traffic in an existing Public Data Network (PDN) whose configuration is stored in a database or Voice/Data networks that are configured by the Expert System module.

Public Data Network Simulation

Figure 2 shows a simplified topology of the Philadelphia LATA (Local Access and Transport Area) Public Data Network.

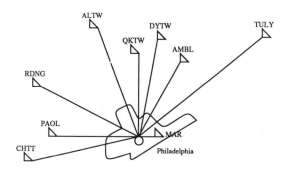

Figure 2: Philadelphia LATA Public Data Network (PDN).

A customer with sites located near access concentrators (PADs marked as triangles in Figure 2) connects to the existing network. Packets of data are transmitted from one PAD to another via a single central switch.

A typical session with TNSM will consist of an interactive part in which customer information such as packet arrival rate, packet size, transmission protocol, and service rate is entered. This is followed by an animated simulation which displays the network and the flow of data, along with statistics on response time at each location. The statistics are broken up to show delays at each component of a packet's path: the data terminal to PAD link, in the PAD itself, the PAD to switch link, and the switch. Fixed values such as pricing information are also displayed for reference. The simulation results reflect the actual state of the PDN because existing network usage is taken into account. Based on the information presented by the PDN simulation module, the customer can decide whether to use the PDN.

T1 Voice/Data Network Simulation

TNSM can also be used as an automated tool for designing networks based on customer specifications. Knowledge Based Systems have been used for network design and simulation (Ferguson and Zlatin 1988; Van Norman 1988). However, in most cases, existing systems provide neither the functionality to design, change and simulate networks in a single package, nor access to real pricing, tariff, and routing data stored in mainframe databases.

The problem of network design lies beyond the scope of this article, instead we will concentrate on simulation of configured networks and graphical interfaces for direct manipulation of network models.

Figure 3 shows a graphical representation of a network configured by TNSM presented through the Graphical Model Builder display.

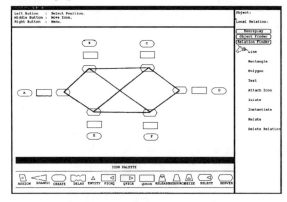

Figure 3 : GMB Display Of a Telecommunications Network.

Each graphical icon on the display is associated with an object in the LASER system and represents a component of a telecommunications network. All aspects of the communication network and the simulation model are represented as LASER objects. The characteristics of network components are acquired either from user input or from relational databases. There is a mapping between fields in database records and values associated with LASER objects.

Figure 4 shows the relationships between objects in the telecommunications network model.

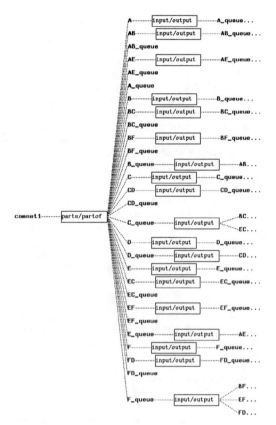

Figure 4: Network Model Relation Display.

Another aspect of the object representation is the ability to store programs (methods) as data. These methods can be used to define the behavior of a network component. For example, the process of transferring a packet through a communications line is encoded in the method P_transmit, stored in the property transmit of object COMLINE shown in Figure 5. This ability of objects to exchange messages that change the model state is utilized by the simulation module to implement the event execution mechanism.

```
{ COMLINE
    instances # : AB AE BC BF CD EC EF FD
    isa # : server
    input * (output) :
    output * (input) :
    contents :
    linespeed :
    transmit : P_transmit
    operation :
    service_time : comservice
    state : 0
}

{ AB
    instanceof # : COMLINE
    GMB$ICON * (GMB$USE) : GMB$LINE1
    input * (output) : AB_queue
    output * (input) : B_queue
    partof * (parts) : comnet1
    linespeed : 20.000000
    GMB$COLOR_INDEX : 2
    GMB$GRAPHICS : 287 197 412 339 0 0 1
}
```

Figure 5: Inheritance Relations.

Displayed are two relations: parts/partof and input/output. The first relation is used to determine which components (objects) constitute the telecommunication network. The second relation determines the flow of data in the network. One can change the configuration of the network model by simply changing relations between objects.

Another type of relation between objects is the inheritance relation. Figure 5 shows objects related through the relation instance/instanceof.

This kind of relation causes inheritance of properties and values between objects. Because object AB is related through the instanceof relation to object COMLINE, all the properties of COMLINE that are not redefined locally are available to object AB.

Because objects can be dynamically modified, the user can modify the network configuration and physical characteristics of the network components by changing values associated with properties of objects. For example, the bandwidth of the communication line between nodes A and B of the network displayed in Figure 3 can be changed by setting the value of the property linespeed of the object AB (see Figure 5).

The end user normally does not modify objects directly, but uses the Graphics Model Builder and a custom menu interface. GMB provides a very high level interface that allows for direct manipulation of the model without the need to know about the underlying data representation. The user can remove or add elements in the network, change the configuration of the network and modify the properties of all elements of the network. A icon palette of building blocks is provided for ease of interaction.

The model can be analyzed by simulating data traffic flow in the network. Each network component has a price associated with it. The system also has access to tariff information. The simulation provides statistical data on response times, delays and other parameters of the network. By comparing results from simulating various network configurations, the user can perform price and performance analyses of the network. This process is facilitated by the Model Management module of LASER/SIM. Model Management tools allow the user to generate scenarios, checkpoint simulation runs and compare results.

To better understand the use of model management, consider the Figure 6. The original network model corresponds to the node marked BASE_NETWORK. The network modeler can now create plausible variations of the original model by making several changes. These variations are represented by creating a scenario for each of them. In Figure 6 the variations correspond to scenarios S1 and S2. After creation of a scenario further modifications can be made to the model. The child scenarios inherit the unchanged information from the parent scenarios. In the current example, the scenarios S1 and S2 would inherit information from the BASE_NETWORK model. Checkpoints may be thought of as a "core dump image" of the simulation at a particular time. At the time corresponding to each scenario at the furthest simulated point, a checkpoint would be created to save the state of the scenario. For example checkpoints CK1, CK2 and CK3.

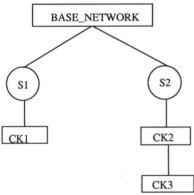

Figure 6: Model Management.

Various model management commands can be used to manage these scenarios and checkpoints. The results in each of the scenarios may be analyzed and compared. The best applicable scenario can then be chosen to give the desired network design.

CONCLUSIONS

In this paper we combined knowledge based simulation techniques and telecommunications knowledge expertise to create a prototype tool for network planning and design. Traditional simulation usually require experts to set up the problem, program the simulation, and interpret the results. Frame based knowledge representation, object oriented programming, and the graphic representation and manipulation of network model simplified the development and deployment of the prototype.

The development of this network management tool is characterized by:

* rapid network model construction, reduced costs, and improved performance

* minimization of user input due to the use of a library of application specific modeling blocks and the object inheritance mechanism.

* the ability to quickly alter design data and evaluate alternatives -- while still maintaining a consistent design -- by using the graphic model builder and the LASER/SIM model management system.

* the ability to directly access network data from mainframe databases.

The object structure of the modeling concepts (blocks) represents the model and its behavior in a way that is familiar to the analyst. The flexibility and adaptability gained by using the object-oriented paradigm extends beyond its representation capabilities. By exploiting data driven programming procedures (demons) and the procedural methods, the dynamic modeling framework makes it possible to execute optional instrument, trace, and display functions associated with an event's occurrence. Additional programming paradigms such as the rule based programming sub-system can easily be incorporated to capture the experienced sales person's heuristics.

This prototype of TNSM has shown the potential for significant time savings, a more consistent and unified approach to network design, and greater customer satisfaction.

When completed and deployed in the field, the TNSM tool should perform as an intelligent assistant to a network marketing person in the design and sales of the PDN and voice-data networks. Varied marketing scenario models will be created and saved, making it possible to bring up particular scenarios. Individual marketing expertise might then be saved and restored later when required by others in a similar situation.

ACKNOWLEDGMENTS

The authors thank Paul Guenther for providing valuable reference resources, and Rick Mace, Brian Cafferty, and John Ballerini for major contributions to the system design.

REFERENCES

Banks, Jerry and John S. Carson. 1984. *Discrete-Event System Simulation*, Prentice Hall, New Jeresy.

Ford, Donnie R and Bernard J. Schroer. 1987. "An expert manufacturing simulation system", *Simulation* 48, no 5 (May): (223 -- 229).

Goyal, Shri K. and Ralph W. Worrest. 1988. "Expert System Applications to Network Management." In *Expert System Applications to Telecommunications*, Jay Liebiwitz editor. John Wiley and sons, New York, 3-44.

Hayhurst, Brett. 1989. LASER/GMB : The Graphic Model Builder, Bell Atlantic Knowledge Systems, Inc. (to be released : spring 89).

Dziedzic, Rafal T. 1985. LASER 1.0 Manual, Artificial Intelligence Laboratory, West Virginia University, Morgantown, WV. (May).

Ferguson, Innes A. and Daniel R. Zlarin. 1988. "Knowledge Structures for Communications Networks Design and Sales" *IEEE Network,* (September): 52-58.

Fernandez, Joseph I. and David E. Liddy. 1988. "Is your packet network a 'model' of response-time efficiency?" *Data Communications*, (May): 139-153.

LASERSIM. 1986. LASER/SIM : A System For Temporal Reasoning, Artificial Intelligence Laboratory, West Virginia University. June 1986.

Moser, Jorge G. 1986. ''Integration of artificial intelligence and simulation in a comprehensive decision-support system'', *Simulation* 47 , no. 6 (Dec): (223 -229).

Reddy, Y. V.; Mark S. Fox; Nizwer Husain; and Malcolm McRoberts. 1986. ''The Knowledge-Based Simulation System.'' *IEEE Software*, (March): 26-37.

Sharma, Ranjana. 1988. "T1 network design and planning made easier." *Data Communications*, (September): 199-207.

Singh, Hawa; Alan Butcher; and Y. V. Reddy. 1987. ''Model Management in Knowledge Based Simulation.'' In *Proceedings of the Eastern Simulation Conference* (Florida, April): (11-14)

Van Norman, Harnell J. 1988. "A user's guide to network design tools" *Data Communications*, (April): 115-133.

Waghray, Ajay. 1987. LASER/SIM BLOCKSWORLD : a network modeling framework for the LASER/SIM knowledge based simulation environment, Master's problem report, West Virginia University.

Advances in AI and Simulation
© 1989 By The Society for Computer
Simulation International
ISBN 0-911801-50-2

SEIMOAR: A function-oriented simulation shell for modeling behavior of high-level system descriptions

Richard M. Adler
The MITRE Corporation
Bedford, MA 01730

ABSTRACT

SEIMOAR is a discrete–event simulation shell for modeling systems at the functional requirements level of description. Most simulators ascribe behaviors to model system components or states. In contrast, SEIMOAR simulates function–oriented models: behaviors represent the simulated effects of executing functions, such as modifying model system or data object attribute values. System descriptions from early phases in the development cycles are more easily modeled from the functional perspective because baseline functionality is established before explicit architectures or state machine models are defined. This paper describes the ingredients of behavioral simulation models and the architecture and operation of the current SEIMOAR prototype.

INTRODUCTION

MITRE assists the U.S. Air Force in procuring complex electronic systems such as communications networks and radars. We are currently developing knowledge–based tools to help automate our activities in the early phases of acquisitions. These activities include defining functional requirements specifications (FRSs) and assessing contractor proposals and high–level system architectural models (HLASs).

Our basic strategy is to represent system specifications in the form of explicit symbolic models that can be manipulated and analyzed via an integrated set of utilities and tools. Specification models are constructed by copying and customizing model system functions, architectural components, and data objects from library knowledge bases (LKBs). These elements can be connected by decomposition, data flow, and control flow relations. The resulting static models are symbolic, knowledge–based analogs to the data–based models that can be assembled using current Computer–Aided Engineering (CAE) tools.

Static control and data flow models, while clearly important, are insufficient to represent dynamic phenomena such as state changes in model systems or data objects. Dynamic models also need to be executable in order to examine connected sequences of state changes over time. Discrete–event simulation tools have been used widely to represent and execute dynamic system models (Kreutzer 1986).

Unfortunately, most discrete–event simulation shells are not readily usable for analyzing very early specifications such as FRSs. Simulators generally assign executable behaviors to model system architectural elements, or to finite state machine model nodes or transition arcs. However, FRSs deliberately omit such ingredients to avoid constraining alternative design approaches. Modifying existing simulators runs the risk of interfering with the original modeling capabilities. A more appealing strategy is to build a simulator with the expressed purpose of modeling early system specifications.

Accordingly, MITRE has developed SEIMOAR, a discrete–event simulation shell that adopts a functional perspective: executable behaviors are ascribed to system functions rather than to system components, states, or data objects. A function behavior specifies a set of events that simulate the effects of executing the function on the model system and data objects. For example, a function can induce (simulated) transformations on sensor data or messages, or a switch of operational modes in a model system.

The functional perspective enables SEIMOAR to simulate system models from very early in the development cycle. Minimal dynamic model ingredients include: a functional decomposition hierarchy; networks of data flow relations among functions at each decomposition level; and test scenarios that represent external inputs to the model. As models are refined to include specific functional behaviors and internal data object and system structures, SEIMOAR supports more detailed simulation.

This paper discusses the current status of the SEIMOAR project. The next section sketches the static system modeling framework underlying the simulator. The following two sections describe behavioral model ingredients and the architecture and operation of the SEIMOAR prototype. The final sections review planned extensions to the simulator and discuss SEIMOAR in relation to other system simulation tools.

STATIC MODELING

MITRE's prototyping testbed is called Automated System Design Library (ASDL). This testbed was developed in Common LISP and KEE, and runs on Symbolics LISP Machines. ASDL models are constructed by copying and editing elements from library knowledge bases (LKBs). Historical LKBs contain specification models for previous acquisitions, while a template LKB depicts generic system functions components, data objects, and connector relations. Example templates include operating system and signal processing functions, processors and interfaces, messages and sensor signals.

Model elements are represented as frames, which define sets of descriptive attributes, or slots, with optional default values, cardinality and legal values restrictions. Copied frames can be customized by adding new attributes or by modifying attribute values. Edited model elements are then connected together with decomposition, data flow, and control flow relations.

ASDL's model editor resembles the menu–driven graphic interfaces provided by current CAE tools: users can browse the LKBs, copy and customize templates or fragments of historical models, and connect these elements to one another. Decompositions are modeled as block diagrams containing boxes and lines. These icons are dynamically linked to specification model KB frames that represent system elements and relations.

INGREDIENTS OF DYNAMIC MODELS

SEIMOAR is built on top of ASDL (see fig. 1). It consists of a set of editors and an object–oriented simulation shell, which are invoked from the main ASDL menu. The editors are used to extend ASDL's static specification models with behavioral ingredients and to create test scenarios that drive model simuations (see fig. 2). The current SEIMOAR prototype simulates the behavior for FRS models. To date, partial FRS models have been simulated for a radar system, a military message processing system, and a hospital patient telemetry station.

ASDL Interface	SEIMOAR Interface
Static Analysis Utilities Library KB/Model Editors	Simulation Shell Behavior Item Editors
Historical Library KB Generic Library KB	Dynamic Specification Model KBs
Common LISP	KEE
Symbolics LISP Machine	

Figure 1. ASDL/SEIMOAR System Architecture

Functional Decomposition	Function Time.Expended
Functional Flow Networks	Function Data.Flow.Actions
Data Object Classes	Scheduler Priorities
Function Behaviors	Test Event Scenarios

Figure 2. Ingredients of Extended FRS Models

The primary ingredient of an ASDL FRS model is a hierarchical decomposition of functions (see fig. 3). The model also defines the classes of data objects that the system will process, such as messages, radar pulse trains or other sensor data, and keyboard inputs. System users and interfaces to the external environment can also be represented. ASDL models can incorporate structural decomposition hierarchies as well. SEIMOAR can manipulate (attributes of) model architectural elements, but does not require them for FRS model simulations.

The critical ingredient for behavioral models is a set of transition networks that represent data flow relations among functions. Individual flow networks connect the top–level functions to one another, the sets of decomposing subfunctions for each top–level function, and so on (see fig. 4). Each flow relation depicts a single transition between a

pair of functions. (The first and last function in a network have no explicit predecessor or successor, respectively.) Flow relations can represent unconditional sequential transitions, conditional branches, and iterative loops. The last two kinds of relations require expressions that describe branching or loop termination conditions (see fig. 5a). FRS flow relation networks are constructed via an extension to the ASDL graphic editor.

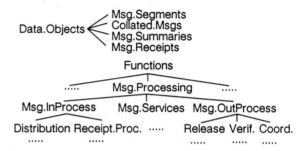

Figure 3. Example FRS Model (partial)

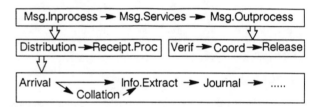

Figure 4. Example Function Flow Networks (partial)

a. **Arrival.Collation.Flow.Relation**
   Predecessor   Arrival
   Successor   Collation
   Flow.Condition (> 1 (get.value *thisevent*
                          nmbr.segs))

b. **Collation.Behavior**
```
(cond
   ((= (get.value *thisevent* nmbr.segs)
       (get.value  *thisevent* msg.seg.nmbr))
    (let* ((msgsegs (find.all.segs *thisevent*))
           (numsg (create.unit collated.msgs
                     (gensym "Col.msg-"))))
     (copy.msg.slots *thisevent* numsg)
     (put.value numsg text
       (loop for seg in msgsets
         collect (get.value seg text) in alltext
         (put.value seg colmsg numsg)
            return alltext)))
   (t nil)))
(print.trace *thisevent*)
```

c. **Collation.Time.Expended**
   (truncate (* 1.4 (get.value *thisevent* nmbr.segs)))

d. **Collation.Data.Flow.Actions**
   (extract *thisevent*)
```
(cond ((= (get.value *thisevent* nmbr.segs)
          (get.value  *thisevent* msg.seg.nmbr))
       (inject (get.value *thisevent* colmsg)))
      (t nil)))
```

Figure 5. Example Flow Relation, Function Attributes

SEIMOAR's other editors extend the FRS model with ingredients that further enrich its behavioral content. The first attribute, Behavior, is an expression that the simulator evaluates to determine the actions to perform when the model function is executed. Possible actions include changing the values of one or more event or system attributes, creating new events, and printing messages to the simulator interface (see fig. 5b). The default Behavior simply prints a notice that the function has executed on a given event at a given time, thus providing an automatic trace of events percolating through the flow networks.

The second attribute, Time.Expended, is an expression that represents the amount of simulated time required for the function to execute. Time.Expended defaults to one simulator clock pulse, the smallest time interval allowed. A template-based editor allows users to specify an integer or a functional expression that evaluates to an integer (see fig. 5c). The global variable (*thisevent*) is bound to the latest event processed for convenient reference in these expressions.

The third attribute, Data.Flow.Actions, specifies special actions for manipulating events after executing a function Behavior, such as inserting or extracting them from the flow networks. For example, lengthy messages are often transmitted across networks in numbered segments. A message collation function Behavior would append the ordered, partitioned segments together into a collated message object upon receipt of the last segment. Data.Flow.Actions would remove message segment objects from the flow network and substitute the collated message object in their place (see fig. 5d). The default action is to pass the event that entered the node through to the next node.

SIMULATION SHELL ARCHITECTURE

The simulation shell consists of three frames: a synchronous Clock; a Simulation Manager; and a Scheduler. In addition to queue lists and other state attributes, these frames contain object-oriented methods invoked by message-passing protocols (Cox 1984) that control the simulation and the display interface.

The shell executes an extended FRS model in conjunction with a test scenario. Each FRS model KB has an associated KB of scenarios, one of which is selected from a menu at initialization and copied into the FRS model. Scenarios consist of sets of events that represent external inputs to the model. Each event consists of an instance of a data object class combined with a "mix-in" set of simulation attributes. Recall that data object classes are defined within the original ASDL FRS model.

Scenario events are edited using a template that displays the attributes of a selected data object class plus two additional mix-in attributes, Injection.Time and Flow.Entry.Point. The former takes an integer value representing the simulated time for injecting the event into the model. The latter specifies the initial function node into which the event is injected. Events also inherit noneditable attributes that hold internal bookkeeping, such as a pointer to the next function node to visit and a record of the event's current state and execution history.

SEIMOAR's primary control cycle: advances the Clock by one increment; injects timely events from the scenario and the future events queue; executes Behaviors for the events' current functions; and dequeues the events (see fig. 6). After each event is executed, its history is updated and its Time.Expended and Data.Flow.Actions expressions are evaluated. The event (or events that result from nondefault Data.Flow.Actions) is updated to reflect the next function to execute and the next Injection.Time, which is the sum of the current time plus the value of Time.Expended. The resulting event is placed on the Future Events queue.

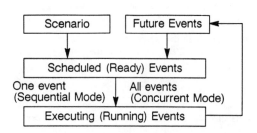

Figure 6. Simulator Control Cycle for FRS Models

An event's next function to execute is determined from its current function's outgoing flow relations. If the successor function is decomposable, the next function is determined to be the (unique) entry node in the subnetwork. If this node is also decomposable, the recursive descent continues. When an event is finished with the last node in a subnetwork, the next function is determined by recursive ascent, returning to the next highest level and determining the successor to the latest decomposing node. Events are removed from the network either through a Data.Flow.Action or upon reaching a terminal node in the top level flow network.

At initialization, the Simulation Manager prompts users to select which functions in the FRS model to decompose. During execution, the simulator ignores decomposition relations for all unselected function nodes, passing events directly through the the given node and network level. This option facilitates selective exploration of large behavioral models, permitting testing and refining of specific decomposition flow subnetworks as desired.

The Scheduler contains a Priorities attribute, which it uses to order events awaiting execution. Priorities consists of a set of declarative conditions that are specified through a specialized menu-driven editor. Minimally, each condition specifies an event attribute, such as the data object's class type or one of its slots, and a sort direction, either increasing or decreasing.

During each clock cycle, the Scheduler sorts the list of queued events with respect to a predicate obtained by transforming the first Priorities condition. Events with identical priorities are sorted with respect to the predicate form of the second condition, if one is defined, and so on recursively. More complex sorting criteria can be specified in terms of rank orderings of attribute values and/or functions of multiple event attribute values. Priorities defaults to First In First Out event ordering, which is represented as ((Injection.Time) Increasing).

At initialization, the Simulation Manager prompts users to select one of the two available simulation modes. In Concurrent mode, ALL queued events are executed by the Scheduler, in prioritized order. In Sequential mode, only the highest priority event is executed. The remaining events remain enqueued on the Scheduler for the next clock cycle. Running the simulation once in each of the modes establishes a performance envelope for the extended FRS model, even though no explicit system architecture has been specified. Intuitively, the Sequential mode represents a "worst case" floor, corresponding to a single server architecture. Similarly, the Concurrent mode represents an idealized infinite resource "best case" performance ceiling, where all ready events are always processed within a clock cycle.

Simulations can be suspended by mouse action at the beginning of each clock cycle, enabling users to examine system state and data object attributes. A graphic trace interface displays the various queue contents and remaining scenario events, while a textual trace logs event executions in another window. Dynamic breakpoints make it easy to study the details of qualitative model behavior. This contrasts with more typical batch simulators that run to completion without interruption and compute aggregate performance statistics.

FUTURE WORK

This section outlines a set of planned extensions that will greatly enhance SEIMOAR's utility. The present prototype tool provides a kernel functional capability to simulate only FRS models. However, SEIMOAR was designed to be extendable to simulate more complex HLAS models as well. The extension involves adding a third operational mode to the simulation shell, plus some additional representational elements (see fig. 7).

Functional Decomposition	Function Time.Expended
Functional Flow Networks	Function Data.Flow.Actions
Data Object Classes	Scheduler Priorities
Function Behaviors	Test Event Scenarios
Structural Decomposition	Server Queue Priorities
Config.Allocation Relations	Server Class Assignments

Figure 7. Ingredients of HLAS Models

HLAS models require explicit structural decompositions, which are optional ingredients in FRS models. To support simulation, all architectural model elements will inherit special mix-in "server" attributes, including a queue, Priorities, and numbers of total and occupied processing channels. Server queues will maintain not only the current events awaiting processing, but also a history of past queue contents for subsequent collection of statistics. Second, HLAS model functions will be allocated explicitly to particular model subsystem or component servers through "Configuration Allocation" relations. Model system architectures and allocation relations will be edited via the ASDL editor, while queue Priorities and other server attributes will be edited through the SEIMOAR interface.

The third simulation mode, called Server mode, will modify the original Scheduler control cycle, which causes events to be executed immediately after the Scheduler queue is prioritized. In Server mode, events will be routed instead

to server or server class queues, based on the Configuration.Allocation pointers for the current function for each event (see fig. 8). Any nonempty Server class queues are processed to route events to instance queues. Class queues are used in situations when dynamic "run-time" allocation among multiple candidate servers is required. Routing of events from class queues to appropriate class member servers will be driven by declarative Assignment conditions analogous to Priorities.

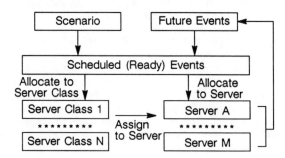

Figure 8. Simulator Control Cycle for HLAS Models

During each control cycle, all nonempty server queues will be processed to completion, in random order. Events in each server queue will be sorted with respect to that queue's Priorities and then executed serially. Future events will be determined and added to the global future events queue, as before, and queue histories updated. To simulate resource allocation, server channels will be locked or inaccessible for the Time.Expended intervals during which they are "processing" events.

Three further enhancements will increase the utility of the current prototype. First, the existing test scenario editor only allows users to create events one at a time, which is obviously tedious. A generator of bulk statistical event populations will be added to simplify creating realistic, extended scenarios.

Execution histories are currently maintained for each event processed by the simulator in a log of lists of the form (function time-started time-stopped). A statistics post-processor utility is planned for computing and displaying performance data, such as mean execution time, standard deviation, and server queue traffic profiles. Such metering instrumentation, commonly available in "batch" simulation tools, is of obvious importance for quantitative analysis.

Currently, expressions for Behavior, Time.Expended, Flow.Condition, and Data.Flow.Actions are specified in terms of LISP and KEE functions. The LISP editor interface is unsuitable for SEIMOAR's intended users, who are system engineers rather than AI programmers. A simpler declarative interface has been designed, based on an intelligent menu-driver coupled to a dedicated language. This editor will automatically compile declarative behavioral expressions into executable code.

Finally, we will investigate integrating design constraints into the modeling and simulation framework. The simulator would check for violations of performance constraints, such as throughput requirements, when executing an FRS or

HLAS model against a test scenario. Violations would be logged to a file for later manual analysis. This capability would allow analysts to study the feasibility of time–sensitive requirements and the plausibility of Time.Expended estimates under varying test scenario traffic loads.

RELATED WORK

SEIMOAR can be used to simulate a wide variety of systems, in contrast to customized tools that are dedicated to modeling communication networks, distributed radar systems (Barry 1987), or resource allocation and queueing systems (Paul 1987). Second, SEIMOAR employs a library–based approach to building new system models, which reflects and supports the typical manual "cut–and–paste" approach to writing new specifications. Knowledge–based technology encourages not only reusability, but also easy adaption of existing templates and system fragments through class specialization and inheritance. CAE tools grounded in database models or non–object–oriented specification languages offer less adaptability and productivity leverage.

SEIMOAR models system dynamics in terms of functional flows and functional behaviors. This approach highlights the behavior of data objects (events) as they flow through the system functional network and are transformed by the actions of model functions. In contrast, finite state machine (Harel 1988), Petri net (Blumofe 1988, Dahler 1987, Razouk 1983) and object–oriented simulators (Stelzner 1987, Adelsberger 1986, Ziegler 1987) generally depict behavior from the perspective of model system architectures and system states.

While system–oriented simulation is problematic for early specification models, function–oriented simulation appears to be inappropriate for system descriptions that are more detailed than HLAS models. Functional modeling provides little insight into low–level hardware and software system architecture and implementation issues. Generally, functional flows change little between HLAS and later models, so traceability is not a significant concern. The most serious problem is the amount of detail and expressiveness required to depict functional behaviors for post–HLAS models. In particular, SEIMOAR's current event–handling mechanisms are inadequate to cope with language–specific models of concurrency, such as Ada tasking (Booch 1983), and re–entrant software modules.

This suggests that function– and system–oriented simulation perspectives can be complementary, together providing a better understanding of the dynamics of system models than could be obtained with either separately. One approach would be to integrate both kinds of simulators into a single framework. For example, SEIMOAR is very compact, and would be easy to reconstruct within a state machine, Petri net, or object–oriented framework. Such tools already contain the basic representational prerequisities: state transition network models; class hierarchies; and message–passing communications.

Simulators that execute system models expressed in a formal specification language (Kato 1987) have an advantage over SEIMOAR with respect to rigor (if not with respect to ease of use). In particular, they often support verification capabilities that SEIMOAR lacks, such as reachability and deadlock checks on real–time system models (Blumofe 1988). The simulation shell enforces the semantics of decomposition and flow relations, but the editor currently does not. Moreover, SEIMOAR executes any Behavior that is a syntactically well–formed LISP/KEE expression.

The current SEIMOAR prototype is also limited to static management of queues: Events can enter the Scheduler queue only at the start of a clock cycle, and events are dequeued only following actual execution. Also, function Behaviors cannot in general change the contents of the Scheduler or Future Events queues. SEIMOAR assumes implicitly that events are mutually independent, an assumption that is unrealistic in many real–time and concurrent processing systems (Misra 1986, Ahuja 1986). However, once the Server mode is implemented, we intend to investigate dynamic queue handling and its impact on event semantics (e.g., race conditions), and predictable termination of queue processing cycles.

CONCLUSIONS

SEIMOAR is a discrete–event simulation shell for modeling and analyzing dynamic aspects of early system specifications from the functional perspective. Ascribing executable behaviors to system functions allows specification models to be simulated before explicit architectures or state machine models have been developed. SEIMOAR exercises such models using scenarios of exogenous test events.

SEIMOAR establishes a uniform methodology or discipline for representing and analyzing the behavioral characteristics of early system specifications. The process of building, executing, and verifying models in SEIMOAR amounts to debugging early system specifications. The process is analogous to writing, compiling, executing, and verifying software programs.

For example, SEIMOAR was used to analyze portions of an FRS for a message processing system. In formulating the behavioral model from specification text and flow charts, a basic inconsistency was uncovered: prioritization of incoming messages required information obtained by executing a function that extracted a subset of message fields. However, messages were being prioritized immediately upon arrival, BEFORE the field extraction function was executed. The corrected model was then executed against test scenarios of incoming messages to analyze message distribution functionality.

A second major theme of the SEIMOAR effort is our attempt support dynamic simulation of behavioral models at multiple stages of system development within a single framework. An integrated simulation shell is a necessary prerequisite for COMPARING behaviors across levels of description.

Our basic strategy will be to simulate extended FRS and HLAS system models against one and the same test scenario, producing a pair of trace logs of event executions. Logs can then be compared to isolate discrepancies, such as HLAS events that have no correlates or are ordered incorrectly with respect to the FRS event log. The major obstacle to automating this process is the fact that the mapping must reflect differences in the level of descriptive resolution or granularity of events across models. This mapping will have to be derived from decomposition and configuration allocation relations and other symbolic system model ingredients. For example, the mapping will require a set of pointers that trace functions in HLAS models to their correlates in FRS models.

Detecting and correcting discrepancies between requirements and subsequent system specifications is critical to the success of a development project. Verifying the consistency of dynamic behavior across a succession of system development models is an important part of this process. SEIMOAR represents an initial step towards automating this important system analysis task.

REFERENCES

Adelsberger, H.; U. Pooch; R.E. Shannon; and G.N. Williams. 1986. "Rule-based object oriented simulation systems." In *Proceedings of the Conference on Intelligent Simulation Environments* (San Diego, CA, Jan 23–25). Society for Computer Simulation, San Diego CA, 107–112.

Ahuja, A.; N.Carriero; and D. Gelernter. 1986, "Linda and Friends." *Computer* 19, no. 8 (Aug.): 26–34.

Barry, B; J.R. Altoft; D.A. Thomas; and M. Wilson. 1987. "Using Objects to Design and Build Radar ESM Systems." *Conference Proceedings for Object-Oriented Programming Systems, Languages, and Applications* (Orlando, FL, Oct. 4–8). ACM, New York, NY, 192–201.

Blumofe, R. and A. Hecht. 1988. "Executing Real-Time Structured Analysis Specifications." *ACM SIGSOFT Software Engineering Notes* 13, no. 3 (July), 32–40.

Booch, G. *Software Engineering in Ada.* Benjamin/Cumming Publishing Co. Menlo Park, CA, 1983.

Cox, B. "Message/Object Programming: An Evolutionary Change in Programming Technology." 1984. *IEEE Software* 1, no.1 (Jan.) 50–61.

Dahler, J; P. Gerber; H.P. Gisiger; and A. Kundig. 1987. "A Graphical Tool for the Design and Prototyping of Distributed Systems." *ACM SIGSOFT Software Engineering Notes* 12, no. 3 (Apr.), 25–36.

Harel, D. 1988. "On Visual Formalisms." *Communications of the ACM* 31, no. 5 (May), 514–529.

Kato, J. and Y. Morisawa. 1987. "Direct Execution of a JSD Specification." *Proceedings of Computer Software and Applications 11th Conference* (Tokyo, Japan, Oct. 7-9). IEEE Computer Society, Washington, D.C. 30–37.

Kreutzer, W. 1986. *System Simulation Programming Styles and Languages.* Addison–Wesley, Reading, MA.

Misra, J. 1986. "Distributed Discrete-Event Simulation." *Computing Surveys* 18, no. 1 (March): 39–65.

Paul, R.J. and G.I. Doukidis. 1987. "Artificial intelligence aids in discrete-event digital simulation modelling" *IEEE Proceedings 134, Pt. D,* no. 4, (July): 278–286.

Razouk, R.; C.V Phelps. 1983. "Performance Analysis Using Timed Petri Nets." Technical Report #206. Department of Computer Science, University of California, Irvine, CA. (Aug).

Stelzner, M.; Y. Dynis; and F Cummins. 1987. "The SimKit System: Knowledge–Based Simulation and Modeling Tools in KEE." Technical Report, Intellicorp, Inc, Mountain View, Ca.

Ziegler, B. 1987. "Hierarchical, modular discrete-event modelling in an object-oriented environment." *Simulation* 49, no. 5 (Nov.), 219–230.

Advances in AI and Simulation
© 1989 By The Society for Computer
Simulation International
ISBN 0-911801-50-2

AIM: An AI-based decision support system

William L. Bewley and David A. Rosenberg
ISX Corporation
Thousand Oaks, California 91360

ABSTRACT

Decision-makers responsible for allocating resources to perform complex missions require easy access to a variety of databases, support in specifying requirements, assumptions, and constraints, an integrated system combining a variety of existing and new software to generate design options and cost-performance predictions, and assistance in evaluating model results and defining and conducting sensitivity analyses and trade studies. AIM is an example of an AI-based system that provides such support. It is an intelligent decision-support system developed for USAF Space Division space transportation system planners. It provides access to databases of requirements, constraints, and resources, and it supports "what-if" analysis of alternative space transportation architectures. It integrates AI modules written in Lisp with Fortran costing algorithms. Functions include specification of requirements, resource selection, allocation, and evaluation. A user-friendly MMI supports use by high-level decision-makers. AIM illustrates many of the functions that should be included in a system supporting system acquisition and management of complex engineering projects, including functions appropriate for AI technology. Extensions of the system will be described which suggest additional high-leverage applications of AI technology to modeling and simulation of complex systems.

INTRODUCTION

- *The government program manager responsible for acquisition of a large weapons system must monitor the design of competing teams of contractors. She needs to compare design features, examine dependencies on key technologies, review mission scenarios, predict the performance of competing designs on alternative mission scenarios, and predict the cost of each design, both development cost and life-cycle cost. She also needs to manipulate designs, constraints, and assumptions in order to conduct sensitivity tests that will help her understand the dynamics and key factors influencing performance and cost.*

- *A division manager of a large manufacturer is responsible for monitoring the performance of his division on the development and marketing of several products. He needs to allocate materials and manpower resources to products such that critical milestones are met as cost-effectively as possible and profit is maximized. He also needs to review available resources and project schedules. He would like to experiment with alternative materials-availability assumptions and manpower loadings to understand the effect of resource allocation options on his division's performance.*

- *The manager of a software development group needs to develop project schedules and assign equipment, manpower, and software assets to tasks. She needs assurance that her assignments will allow her to meet project schedules within cost. If she cannot meet milestones with the current plan, she would like to understand the problem areas in the plan and test her plan repairs.*

These three cases, though describing problems in different domains, in different organizations, and at different levels of an organization, are all examples of high-level decision-making applied to a resource allocation task. In all situations, the decision-maker has one or more well-defined missions, a set of resources to apply to perform the mission, and several assumptions and constraints on how resources may be applied. The task is often, but not always, to find an optimum or satisficing resource allocation. The task may also be to understand the system that applies resources to perform the mission. Resources interact with other resources, assumptions, and mission requirements in complex ways, making it difficult to predict the effect of a changed assumption, relaxed constraint, or different resource mix on mission performance and cost. Expertise in decision-making involves understanding the system sufficiently to allow prediction of the effects of such changes and to identify the factors that drive certain classes of performance and cost.

This paper describes and presents an example of a class of intelligent systems designed to support decision makers working on complex resource-allocation tasks like those described above. These systems are called intelligent systems rather than AI systems because they combine the capabilities of conventional software with those of AI-based modules. ISX believes that the significant DOD applications of today and the future require intelligent systems that integrate conventional software modules and languages with components and techniques based on AI technology to solve problems that would be impossible or impractical with any single technology.

The next section discusses the general characteristics of intelligent decision-support systems for complex resource allocation problems. Following this is a section describing AIM, an example of an intelligent decision-support system for space transportation planning. The paper ends with a discussion of future directions.

INTELLIGENT DECISION-SUPPORT SYSTEMS

An intelligent decision-support system must provide the following capabilities:

Integration with Existing Software

Decision-makers are probably using a variety of existing software applications and databases. The existing software may be effective, and users may trust it. The intelligent decision-support system should use effective existing software and all relevant databases to the greatest possible extent, integrating them with new software, which will mix conventional and AI modules.

Easy Database Access

Perhaps the most important existing facilities to be integrated into the intelligent decision-support system are databases. Decision-makers obviously need access to data; one of the major problems in decision-making is the accessibility of data on which to base a decision. Accessibility of data requires more than mere integration, however. To be truly accessible, access must be fast and it must be through a friendly user interface.

Specification Support

Decision-makers need to specify mission requirements, resource parameters, assumptions, and constraints. This specification must be supported by a friendly user interface. In addition, the decision-maker must be able to define a high-level specification, leaving the detailed specification to the system. For example, the user should be able to specify general requirements of a mission and let the system specify supporting activities, dates, and dependencies on other missions. The system should also detect inconsistencies between missions, e.g., if the user changes the date of a mission the system should detect and report dependent missions invalidated by the date change.

Glass-Box Modeling

Intelligent decision-support must provide predictions of the effect of user specifications and assumptions on outcomes, including performance on the mission and cost. These predictions are based on a model of the system the decision-maker is managing. The model is used to simulate the system in order to generate predictions for the decision-maker. It should be a glass-box model (as opposed to a black-box) so that the decision-maker can view its operation and understand the mechanism that generates the outcomes.

Evaluation

The predictions of the model must be evaluated, at the very least by comparing outcomes to measures of effectiveness or comparing predictions based on different user specifications and assumptions. An intelligent decision-support system should do more than compare MOEs, however. The decision-maker should be assisted in interpreting the results of the evaluation and in selecting appropriate actions based on those interpretations. The intelligent decision-support system should, for example, identify likely causes of MOE shortfalls and suggest changes in specifications, assumptions, or constraints that may improve performance or cost results. This level of evaluation may be based on a qualitative simulation of the modeled process which applies selected resources to specified missions, identifies constraint violations and MOE failures as they occur, and traces the causes of failure for the decision-maker.

Friendly User Interface

Although the term has been so overused that it has become a cliche, user friendliness is still an important characteristic of any computer system, particularly those providing intelligent decision-support. Decision-makers responsible for allocating resources to solve complex problems are usually generalists who deal with problems at a high level. They are also usually expensive. Such people do not have the time or the inclination to deal with a system that is difficult to learn and use. The usual features of a "friendly" user interface -- well-designed graphics, icons, windows, and menus -- are an absolute requirement. In addition, a more individualized user interface based on user models, task models, and error monitors, capabilities of an intelligent user interface (Rouse et al. 1987), should be provided.

AIM: AN EXAMPLE

AIM is an example of an intelligent decision-support system that provides many of the capabilities described above. It was developed for USAF Space Division for use by space transportation planners. The prime contractor was ECON, Inc., and ECON's president, John P. Skratt, was the expert. ISX Corporation staff supported ECON by performing knowledge engineering, architecture and software design, and all software development but a Fortran routine for cost calculation.

Mr. Skratt's guidance was vital to the success of the project. He is one of the few people in the country with the breadth and depth of knowledge required to develop AIM. In a very real sense, AIM is Mr. Skratt in that the model generating the system's predictions represents a portion of Mr. Skratt's expertise. In addition, the user interface design was based on Mr. Skratt's knowledge of the users and domain, as well as his excellent sense for good graphics.

Most of AIM was developed in Symbolics Common Lisp, Release 7.0. The Transportation System database was implemented in KEE, a product of Intellicorp, Inc. The Architecture Cost Module was written in Symbolics Fortran 77. The system runs on a Symbolics 3650.

AIM is composed of three major elements: the user interface, the space transportation model, and evaluation. These are described in the following sections.

User Interface

The AIM user-interface is highly graphic with menu-based and directly manipulable icons for user input. There are six categories of user input: Space Transportation Demand, Transportation Systems, Technology Plans, Objectives and Constraints, Initiation, and Check Points. All but Check Points are invoked by mouse-selecting a button on the main AIM screen shown in Figure 1.

Space Transportation Demand defines the mission to be performed by the space transportation architecture, the schedule of payloads to be delivered to specified orbits. The space transportation community calls this the mission model. AIM aggregates missions into space operational assets (SOAs), major space programs such as space stations, kinetic energy weapons, and interplanetary missions. The SOA concept was invented by

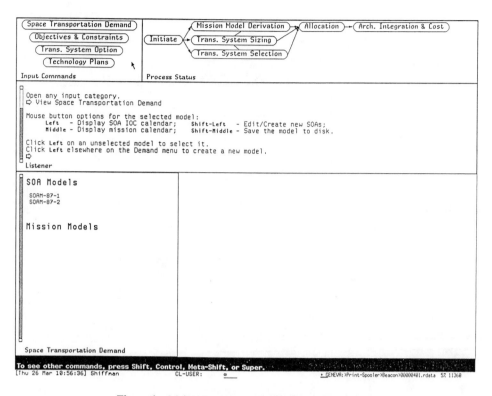

Figure 1: Main AIM Screen, With User Input Buttons.

Mr. Skratt and was first applied in AIM. It is a fundamental part of AIM's approach to space transportation modeling. SOAs are represented as icons, as shown in Figure 2. The user can change initial operational capability (IOC) dates by selecting the icon with the mouse pointing device and moving it on the screen, or by opening a property sheet for the icon, which displays a set of editable parameters defining the SOA, including IOC date.

Transportation Systems defines the launch vehicle resources available to perform the mission defined by Space Transportation Demand. The launch vehicles are represented as icons on a calendar indicating IOC date for each vehicle (Figure 3). As with SOAs, the user can select and move the icons to change IOC dates, or open a property sheet for the icon. The launch vehicle property sheet shown in Figure 4 contains parameters defining payload capacities, available flight rates, development and operational costs as a function of payload capacity and flight rate, and enabling technologies.

Technology Plan defines the cost over time of technologies enabling the launch vehicles over time. The technology plan for a vehicle is a set of cost curves, one for each relevant technology. The user can change data points by selecting and moving points with the mouse or add new points by a mouse selection on the desired location.

Objectives and Constraints are displayed as a menu listing cost objectives and constraints on the application of launch vehicle resources to payload delivery. The user changes constraints by selecting parameter value options.

Initiation is a menu listing additional constraints, including minimum and maximum annual flight rates, launch facility, e.g., Kennedy Space Center. Some constraints are edited by selecting options; others require the user to edit textual values.

Check Points is a menu command that appears during the operation of the model. It permits the user to view the calculation or reasoning behind any interim result produced by the model. After invoking the Check Points command, the user selects the point, e.g., a point on a curve or a bar on a barchart, and the background data or computation is displayed in an overlaid window.

The Model

The AIM Model is based on knowledge derived from the expertise of John P. Skratt. It simulates the construction of a space transportation architecture that will provide the most cost-effective application of launch vehicle resources to the payloads defined by the mission model within the constraints set by the user. The AIM model uses the classic problem-solving strategy of dividing the problem into subproblems. The overall goal of the model is to successfully allocate launch vehicle resources to mission model payloads. To break the problem into more manageable subproblems, the model defines one major subgoal: the selection of transportation systems. The objective is to reduce the set of possible transportation systems to the subset of systems most likely to be used in the final allocation of vehicles to payloads. This final allocation is computationally expensive, and the AIM model reduces the cost by reducing the number of vehicles to be

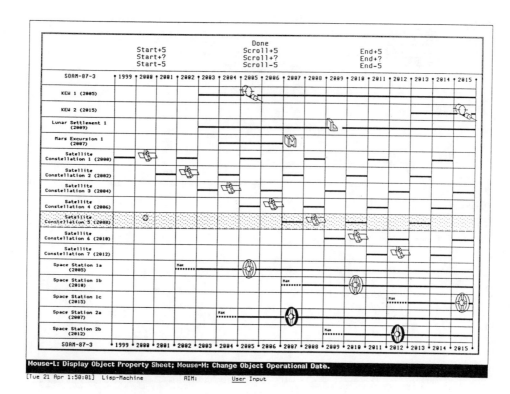

Figure 2: Space Transportation Demand, With SOA Icons.

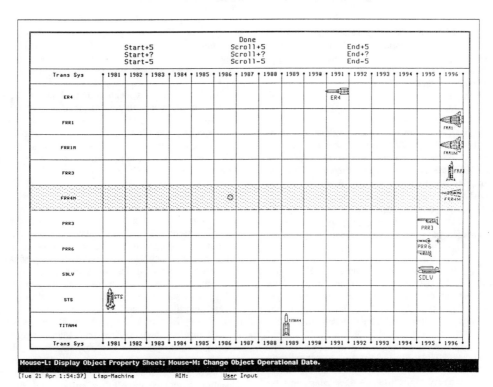

Figure 3: Transportation Systems, With Launch Vehicle Icons.

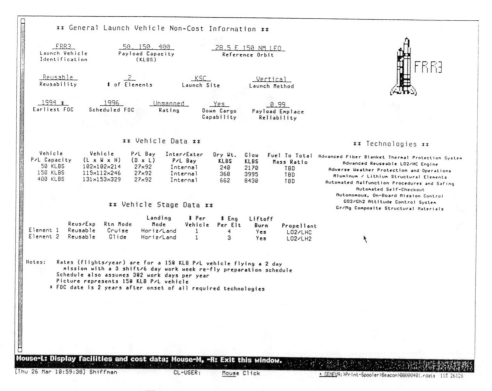

```
    ** General Launch Vehicle Non-Cost Information **

        FRR3            50, 150, 400        28.5 E 150 NM LEO
  Launch Vehicle       Payload Capacity       Reference Orbit
  Identification          (KLBS)

     Reusable              2                KSC           Vertical
   Reusability       # of Elements      Launch Site    Launch Method

    1994 *            1996        Unmanned      Yes         0.99
  Earliest FOC    Scheduled FOC    Rating    Down Cargo   Payload Emplace
                                             Capability     Reliability


            ** Vehicle Data **                          ** Technologies **

  Vehicle      Vehicle      P/L Bay  Inter/Exter  Dry Wt.  Glow  Fuel To Total   Advanced Fiber Blanket Thermal Protection System
 P/L Capacity  (L x W x H)  (D x L)   P/L Bay     KLBS    KLBS   Mass Ratio           Advanced Reusable LO2/HC Engine
   50 KLBS    102x102x214    27x92    Internal     240    2170      TBD            Adverse Weather Protection and Operations
  150 KLBS    115x112x246    27x92    Internal     368    3995      TBD                Aluminum / Lithium Structural Elements
  400 KLBS    131x153x329    27x92    Internal     662    8430      TBD            Automated Malfunction Procedures and Safing
                                                                                        Automated Self-Checkout
            ** Vehicle Stage Data **                                                Autonomous, On-Board Mission Control
                                                                                      CO2/GH2 Attitude Control System
                            Landing   # Per  # Eng  Liftoff                         Gr/Mg Composite Structural Materials
            Reus/Exp  Rtn Mode  Mode   Vehicle Per Elt  Burn    Propellant
 Element 1  Reusable  Cruise  Horiz/Land    1      4     Yes    LO2/LHC
 Element 2  Reusable  Glide   Horiz/Land    1      3     Yes    LO2/LH2


  Notes:   Rates (flights/year) are for a 150 KLB P/L vehicle flying a 2 day
           mission with a 3 shift/6 day work week re-fly preparation schedule
           Schedule also assumes 302 work days per year
           Picture represents 150 KLB P/L vehicle
         * FOC date is 2 years after onset of all required technologies
```

Mouse-L: Display facilities and cost data; Mouse-M, -R: Exit this window.

[Thu 26 Mar 10:59:30] Shiffman   CL-USER: Mouse Click   + GENEVA:>Print-Spooler>Beacon>00000401.rdata 11% 26128

Figure 4: A Launch Vehicle Property Sheet.

considered in the allocation. To achieve the transportation-system selection subgoal, an additional subgoal is defined: the estimation of required cargo bay size. The use of an estimate of required cargo bay size -- *independent* of available vehicles -- to select a set of feasible vehicles is another of Mr. Skratt's concepts first applied in AIM. Mr. Skratt's estimate of cargo bay size, called the Theoretical Cargo Bay (TCB), is combined with the payload frequency and size profile defined by the mission model to predict flight rate, from which a rough estimate of architecture performance and cost can be calculated. This rough estimate is used to select the most feasible vehicles for further analysis. These goals are addressed by the three software modules comprising the AIM model: Transportation System Sizing, Transportation System Selection, and Allocation.

Transportation System Sizing. The AIM model's first step is to determine the Theoretical Cargo Bay (TCB): an estimate of the cargo bay size required to deliver the payloads specified by the mission model while obeying constraints, particularly the constraints on flight rate. Figure 5 shows the display of estimated cargo bay sizes. The top of the figure shows a frequency distribution of payload package sizes derived from the mission model. The curves show cargo bay size as a function of flight rate for two payload modularities: minimum (the largest package sizes derivable from the mission model) and maximum (the smallest derivable package sizes). The left end of each curve is the smallest cargo bay size estimated by the model to be able to deliver the mission model within flight-rate constraints; the right end of each curve is the largest estimated cargo bay size. The display shown in Figure 6 illustrates the relative sizes of the cargo bay extremes and summarizes the diameter, length, and weight of each extreme with predicted flight rate.

Transportation System Selection. Given the cargo bay size ranges, the model calculates the cost of each transportation system for the largest and smallest cargo bay size and then selects the most economical systems predicted to be able to deliver the mission model. This is the subset of vehicles to be considered in allocation of vehicles to payloads.

Allocation. The last step of the model is to allocate launch vehicles to payloads, using only the set selected by the Transportation System Selection module. The Allocation module uses a search procedure which iterates over each successive year of the mission model. For each year, the module determines which missions begin in that year and then generates all possible combinations of mission-to-vehicle assignments, taking constraints including maximum and minimum yearly flight rate, missions restricted to fly on certain vehicles, and the vehicle's IOC date. For each combination, the discounted cost is computed, estimating the cost of future missions by assigning future payloads to vehicles in order of cost per flight. The module then picks the lowest-cost combination to complete the allocation. The current status of allocation is displayed as shown in Figure 7.

Evaluation

AIM's evaluation is conducted by the Architecture Cost module, ECON's Fortran cost calculation program. Based on the number of flights per vehicle per year per launch site, detailed data generated by the Allocation module, Architecture Cost generates annual and total cost for each vehicle used and over all vehicles. Cost categories include vehicle costs (RDT&E, production, facilities, expendable hardware, spares, vehicle overhaul, propellant and infrastructure costs (payload processing, base support, mission control, and flight support).

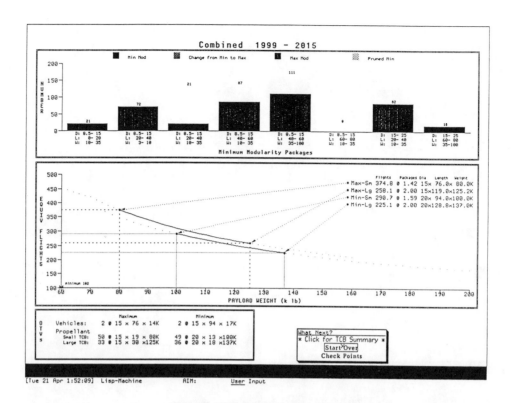

Figure 5: Estimating Cargo Bay Sizes.

Combined TCB Summary						
Max-Sm	Max-Lg	Maximum Modularity				
		TCB	Total Flights	Average Packages	Diameter	Length	Weight
		Smallest	374.8	1.4	15.0	76.0	80.0
		Largest	258.1	2.0	15.0	119.0	125.2
Min-Sm	Min-Lg	Minimum Modularity				
		TCB	Total Flights	Average Packages	Diameter	Length	Weight
		Smallest	290.7	1.6	20.0	94.0	100.0
		Largest	225.1	2.0	20.0	128.8	137.0

What Next?
* Click for Yearly Equivalent Flights *
Start Over

[Tue 21 Apr 1:52:32] Lisp-Machine   AIM: User Input

Figure 6: The Summary of Cargo Bay Sizes.

FUTURE DIRECTIONS

AIM was a proof of concept prototype intended to demonstrate the applicability of AI and advanced user interface concepts to the space transportation architecture domain. Extensions are planned to support application to specific space-transportation domains, including design of the Advanced Launch System and studies of architectures for interplanetary missions. Extensions to the design and functionality of the system are also planned, to support space applications and to generalize the concept and system to non-space domains involving resource application. Design and functionality extensions are discussed below.

Intelligent User Interface

AIM's user interface is highly graphic and features icons, windows, and menus. Users consider it "friendly." It is not yet an intelligent user interface, however. It has the beginnings of features that would provide intelligence, including restrictions on commands based on user types and some error checking based on consistency with model states, but it needs real user and task modeling and a knowledge-based display manager and error monitor.

Simulation

AIM's evaluation, currently based on general performance and cost results, must be extended to support detailed sensitivity analyses, system trades, and suggestions for improvement. This will require the use of object-oriented, qualitative simulation. Because of the detail required, the scale of the simulation(s) will be large, requiring consideration of distributed architectures. In addition, the simulation model represents valuable knowledge that should be reusable, by other decision-makers concerned with different aspects of the same problem or by decision-makers dealing with different but similar problems.

Intelligent Control

Many of the decisions currently required of human decision-makers can be automated. A prime candidate for automation are the control decisions, in which activities of modules are monitored, errors detected, results interpreted, and processing is revised based on errors and results. In AIM, this process monitoring and control is performed by the user. The user should continue to provide overall control and interpretation of results, but many of the lower-level decisions and data interpretation should be performed by the system to support the human decision-maker and free him to focus on the truly difficult decisions.

Knowledge-Based Mission Design

The SOA concept permits the development of knowledge-based mission design modules. These modules would support space transportation users, e.g., the SDI community, in generating mission requirements from SOA designs. The specification of a kinetic energy weapon, for example, could drive more detailed specifications, including payload sizes, sequencing, and required delivery dates. The SOA could then be plugged into the intelligent decision-support system to supply the mission data. More important, SOAs could be plugged into a variety of decision-support systems, providing a reusable knowledge base as well as a support to definition of mission requirements.

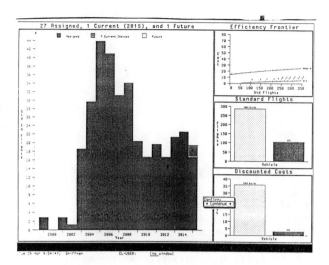

Figure 7: The Allocation Display.

Knowledge-Based Vehicle Design

The concept described above for knowledge-based mission design could also be applied to vehicle design. The vehicles (or other resources) are objects. High-level specification could generate lower level specifications. The objects could be plugged into intelligent decision-support systems.

Infrastructure Model

AIM deals primarily with vehicles. The ground operations infrastructure, including mission planning, the launch processing system, and post-flight refurbishment, must be added to the model.

REFERENCES

Rouse, W. B., N. D. Geddes, and R. E. Curry. 1987. "An Architecture for Intelligent Interfaces: Outline of an Approach to Supporting Operators of Complex Systems." *Human-Computer Interaction*, 3, No. 2: 87 - 122.

Advances in AI and Simulation
© 1989 By The Society for Computer
Simulation International
ISBN 0-911801-50-2

A knowledge-based approach to
planning the design of space systems

April Gillam
Computer Science Laboratory
The Aerospace Corporation
Los Angeles, CA 90009

1   ABSTRACT

We are exploring planning strategies which are particularly relevent to the conceptual design of space systems. The expert system planner must address issues of control, ordering of tasks, how to handle conflicting goals and contradictory results. Another issue is the question of how to evaluate the final design as well as the partial designs. That information should feed back into the design strategy, which means that the plan is actually a dynamic process and not just a static recipe. The difficulty and complexity of design lead to the combination of a creative designer complemented by a machine which searches past cases and supplies analysis tools.

2   INTRODUCTION

The VEHICLES knowledge-based software environment being developed will support the conceptual design of space systems. Conceptual design is a preliminary stage of design during which the requirements and constraints themselves are what has to be developed, as well as exploring multiple design alternatives. The planner must address issues of control, ordering of tasks and how to handle conflicting goals. Another issue is the question of how to evaluate the final design and the partial designs. That information should feed back into the design strategy, which means that the plan is actually a dynamic process and not just a static recipe. The system must decide when a strategy has failed and when another strategy would be more appropriate or effective.

We will start with a discussion of what the design task involves, look at how a couple expert systems have approached planning in the context of design, and then discuss how we are developing planning capabilities for the design of spacecraft at the early conceptual level within a knowledge based framework.

3   PLANNING FOR DESIGN

Chandrasekaran and Brown identify many levels of design, ranging from the very innovative creation of a totally new design to the fairly routine and well specified process of making modifications to an existing design. Most of the work that has been done on automating and assisting design has focussed on the more routine aspects of design.

We depart from this in attempting to develop a knowledge-based system to aid in the conceptual design of space systems. Although some of the tasks may fall into the routine category, many of them require a fair amount of innovation and creativity. The primary feature of conceptual design is that the problem is not well specified. Developing requirements, identifying tradeoffs, and characterizing the family of possible solutions are fundamental processes of conceptual design.

Although knowledge acquisition and the representation of that knowledge is not discussed here, it should be noted how very important these issues are. Their selection may decide how tolerant or flexible the system is to differences between designs, and ultimately to the designers. Realizing that each designer may have a different strategy, our attempt has been to build a system which provides an environment with many capabilities at one's fingertips, rather than rigidly constraining the designer with limitations imposed by the machine.

The main stages of planning a design and attendent difficulties are:

- problem definition
  - some goals are only partially specified
  - some information is only partially known
  - the relative importance of requirements and constraints should be included
- plan creation or selection

- goal decomposition must take into account interactions
- goals or resources may be time dependent
- context dependency should be considered

- controller orchestration of developing design

  - alternative strategies need to be accommodated
  - ordering of tasks should be addressed

- execution of steps in design (tasks)

- evaluation and decision making

  - partial or complete designs need to be evaluated
  - need to distinguish important decisions from details
  - it must be decided if the goal is achievable

- feedback and iteration

Defining the problem is often overlooked. It is assumed to be well known, however there is often a hidden agenda or the main goal might be to develop a well specified problem. Frequently the designer only sees the requirements which were derived from the very top level mission, which means that the motivation and context or scenario is not available to the designer. Design in these cases may translate to an under-constrained problem. The designer must then make reasonable and hopefully educated guesses to make the problem well formed.

The order in which tasks are executed is a part of what the planner must control. There are many different strategies to accomplish this. One method is to prioritize the tasks, so that more important tasks are the first to be acted upon. Another possible method is to keep track of dependencies. The input to a task must be satisfied previous to executing the task. This frequent will give at least a partial ordering of the tasks. A third method is to encapsulate heuristics as rules, which set the order. One heuristic we have frequently come across is that the most stressful aspect of a design is worked early in the design, whereas the routine design tasks may not need to be addressed until much later.

Evaluation is critical in making and refining designs. Designs must be evaluated with respect to the goals and requirements and need some kind of "sanity check". The latter check tests for reasonability. Building a power system to meet specified load levels and peak usage requirements may satisfy the subset of design requirements which have been set. However,

there is a problem if the thermal subsystem has not yet been considered and no thought has been given to that aspect of the design. It may be fairly difficult or impossible to incorporate heat management features at a later stage due to weight and launchability requirements. This is also a place where knowledge of previous spacecraft power and thermal subsystems may be used to flag a deficiency, as well as supplying some reasonable estimates to size the thermal subsystem.

4 PLAN STRATEGIES

Although the design process is extremely complex, experienced human designers perform remarkably well. To deal with the complexity of the design problem they often use the experience of past cases to guide the search for acceptable solutions. This knowledge can be encoded as heuristic rules or may be incorporated as processes for the selective retrieval and modification of previous cases (e.g. [1] and [2]).

Decomposition is another technique that designers use to deal with complexity in design. A complex problem, such as spacecraft design, may be broken down into separate problems or subsystems, for which a solution is developed independently for each one. Then the solutions are integrated. A key problem is whether it is possible to fully specify ahead of time the interactions between the subsystems [3] and whether the problem areas are sufficiently separable for the assumption of their independence to be valid.

One other technique that can be used to deal with the complexity of the design problem is to initially focus on a subset of the problem[4]. Simplifying the problem may not result in a 'simple' problem, but it does reduce the complexity. This is a standard approach at the conceptual stage of spacecraft design where only the subsystems which are most difficult to design are considered. Such techniques are, of course, not guaranteed to produce an optimal solution, but they are useful in finding solutions which satisfy requirements in an acceptable amount of time.

There are critical elements which have great impact on the design and should be considered early on in the design. These elements may drive the design. When using an extremely high data rate, which is the case when transmitting high resolution imagery, it is the communications segment (the downlink) which will be the design driver. It is the most stressful feature of the design. Tong[5] considers this problem as focusing attention on "bottleneck tasks". He takes the relative use of resources as being indicative of a bottleneck.

There may also be cases where the constraints or

the data will drive the design. This might occur when we want to explore the new capabilities that a breakthrough in technology will provide. Here the goal is really to evaluate what the implications are, i.e. what is the performance gain.

There has recently been significant interest in planning and design[6], especially when the design tasks are repetitive and do not stress the creativity of the designer or where the interactions between components are so complex that computer assistance is welcomed. Both of the expert systems briefly presented below have well defined design areas. MOLGEN[7] plans for the design of gene cloning experiments. The goals, constraints, and interactions between components are well known and are enumerable. PRIDE[8] designs paper transports for copy machines.

The two strategies used in MOLGEN are "least commitment" and "heuristic planning". In the case of least commitment, when a decision cannot be made, the planner suspends the task and can move on to another plan step or task. In this way decisions may be deferred "in case other factors are found to bear" [7] on that decision. When more information is available the suspended task may be reactivated.

Heuristics, as used in MOLGEN, are called into play when there is not sufficient information, i.e. the problem is underconstrained, to make a unique decision. The planner uses heuristics to identify the available options and then to rank them so that the task with the highest priority may be activated.

When the problem has become over-constrained MOLGEN performs an undo, or selective backtracking, setting higher priority on steps which were "guessed" or assumed(using the heuristics) as candidates to be undone.

Interactions, represented via constraints, are handled by creating, propagating and trying to satisfy the constraints. However, if the constraints cannot be evaluated, due to missing information, or if the constraints are not propagated, there will be interference between planning decisions which may require devoting the resources to backtracking, and so delaying(possibly forever) the reaching of a solution.

MOLGEN is one of the most highly developed planning schemes, but Stefik points out that there is a major caveat in applying it to a real world situation, which Stefik does point out. The whole scheme is very knowledge intensive. A substantial amount of information must be known to develop heuristics and to manage the constraints. In the case of a well specified design domain it may be possible to give such a complete specification, however significant resources would have to be committed to the development of such a planning scheme.

The expert system PRIDE designs paper transports in copy machines, specifically those that use pinch rolls to move the paper. The domain is well specified, however, as with many real world problems, expertise from many specialists must be consolidated in a single design. Mittal's approach is to consider the problem as constraint-driven. This accesses a large search space with distributed expertise. It is an "underconstrained space of possible designs". Knowledge is used to prune the search space, suggest alternatives at decision points, and modify and make modification decisions about the design when an unsatisfactory design is developed.

In PRIDE the design goals themselves have plans associated with them. Thus the decomposition of the goals has already been characterised as a top-down hierarchy, which works toward achieving the goals. The relevent design methods map out the search space, which, as mentioned above, uses knowledge and constraints to bound the possiblities.

When a design does not meet all the constraints PRIDE uses dependency-directed backtracking, thus retracing the steps, backwards, which it took to reach the faulty conclusion. The steps are retraced back to a decision point at which another decision may be made or some advice may redirect the action at that point.

Another strategy used in PRIDE is case-based reasoning. The cases contain information about how similar systems were planned and what to do when those plans did not succeed, so they provide another mechanism for handling conflicts or failures.

5 VEHICLES APPROACH

In space systems, there are many characteristics of the design process which are similar to the above design tasks, though the degree of their importance may be fairly different. The main difference in our task is that the problem is not well defined and the knowledge used in design and in planning design may only be pertinent in one or a few contexts. For example, the radar equation is different for search and for track. The following list presents some issues which are important for either a human or machine based planner to consider.

- multiple domains are involved

- the components are interdependent

- there is a need for multiple design approaches

- the performance is sensitive to unknown parameters

- the design process is not completely specified

- the design drivers are usually, but not always, known

- goals, constraints, and requirements may be conflicting

- system design is context or scenario dependent

- creativity on the part of the designers is very important and necessary

- there may be a competition for a limited amount of resources

No one approach alone seems to cover all the design situations, so we have developed a very flexible structure which may reason from a high level goal, using goal decomposition, or may start at a low level, with a description of a new technology, and see how that drives the design. A third design approach involves a very quick sizing and characterization of one or two subsystems in isolation. In the first two cases the planner controls the design flow, whereas in the third case the user is the controller and may guide the design step by step or may set the tasks and the order of their execution.

Use of a goal driven planner has some very beneficial side effects. It gives an accountability of how a design was derived and actually helps the designers clarify what is involved and what has not been considered. The explicit nature of having goals and the design path also provides documentation and a mode in which to keep track of what design alternatives have already been explored.

Currently we are using an interactive approach which relies on the user to make hard decisions until we gain sufficient expertise for the system's knowledge base to handle the various considerations. Before decisions can even be made, some evaluation must take place. We have implemented "sanity checks" to test for reasonability of the design results and are adding a case-based perspective to flag the design features which are significantly different from past designs. One scheme compares resource usage(power, weight, etc.) by a subsystem with the resources used in previous spacecraft.

Interdependencies between components are partly handled by how the knowledge is represented. The links, or connections, between subsystems may be inherent in equations or may be overtly tied between subsystems. Thus the impact of work in a given area is posted to other areas which are linked to it. It may be desirable, which analyzing tradeoffs, to limit the scope or propagation distance throughout the design.

One does not want to redesign the entire spacecraft each time a design iteration of the thrusters is made, only when the designer accepts the design solution should its impact be propagated throughout the entire design.

A major part of design is studying tradeoffs. In planning this must be taken into account. When a decision point is reached it may be necessary to do some sort of parametric analysis or sensitivity analysis. Thus, we have taken a semi-automatic semi-interactive tack for our planner. It should be able to proceed with a design on its own, but know when it should ask the user for help or go off on a tangent, such as a trade study, to have more information from which to make the decision.

In designing a space system using the planner we have captured knowledge about goals, subgoals, and the strategies to meet the goals as well as how to evaluate the output. If the goal is to design an infrared sensor for a satellite to map the earth's resources, one must consider the subgoal of area coverage and spatial resolution. The latter parameter will constrain the pointing accuracy which will impact the attitude control system (acs). Thus the planner must consider if the new acs requirement is feasable. This will feed back to the sensor payload, which may need a number of iterations until a reasonable design develops.

In figure 1 the basic planner functionality is presented. The user enters the goals and requirements and also makes decisions when the VEHICLES planner requests help. The planner, in box 1, actually contains the functions given, separately, for increased clarity, in boxes 2 through 5. In box 2, the goals and requirements are analyzed. Heuristics and known goal hierarchies are used to break the goals into more manageable subproblems which have their own goals. The planner then orders the goals and selects the appropriate one to start work on, as seen in box 3. A plan or strategy to accomplish that goal is either selected, as in box 4, from a database or the goal may be further decomposed until either an available plan is appropriate or a plan can be created from available tasks, or the problem is too difficult and must be either presented to the user to decide how to proceed, or another goal may be selected.

Once the goal and plan are set the tasks within that plan are ordered, as seen in box 5. The ordering is not unique because it is dependent on what information is currently known (which may affect which parameters are taken as independent and dependent) and the context or scenario chosen as well as the goal. The goal may direct flow from the detailed level up to a higher level functionality, or may start with functionality and work towards specifying the power and

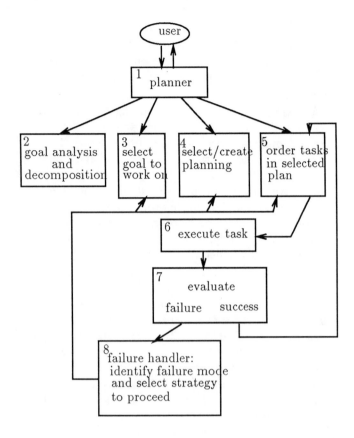

Figure 1: Basic planner functionality.

other characteristics.

Once the ordering is set the planner starts executing the highest priority task, as in box 6. A set of tools are brought into play here. The toolbox includes a flexible equation solver, a trade study tool, a mechanism to apply heuristics and check that assumptions are met, and a few other tools to query the knowledge and data bases as to context, history, or any other relevent information. Evaluation of the partial design, in box 7, uses a set of criteria based on the requirements, constraints and various analysis of performance, cost and risk. If the design evaluation is successful the planner is queried for another task to work on. When all the tasks for a goal have been accomplished the next goal is worked on, until all the goals have been considered and the entire design is evaluated. When the (partial) design does not meet all the evaluation criteria the failure handler decides on a course of action. This my involve backtracking to an earlier decision, selecting a new strategy, reordering the tasks, or even selecting another goal to work on.

6   STATUS

Before beginning to build our system, we spent a year interviewing designers. This period was used to assess how they currently design systems, what a "system" is, what tools they use, and what capabilities would further facilitate the design process. Since then we have spent 18 months writing the conceptual design support system called VEHICLES [9] in Quintus Prolog and C on a SUN 3/160. Presently we are supporting work on the design of three space systems. Two involve designing spacecraft and the third is using VEHICLES to implement a model for resource allocation. the constellation with the provides the necessary coverage.

At this stage we have developed a knowledge base which contains detailed information on communications, a couple kinds of sensors, and some less detailed information on attitude control, orbital mechanics and electrical power. In total, VEHICLES contains over 125 equations, 200 parameters, about 10 satellites and 75 rules. The rule base is in its infancy. Most of the work to this point has been building a platform to support research into design, planning, multi-criteria decision making, trade studies, external tool linking, self documentation, explanation, and evaluation of designs.

The planner in VEHICLES has taken a single design from the initial mission through the few subsystems we currently support. Much of what is mentioned above has been partially implemented at this time. Since we are designing a software system to design space systems we are being fairly self-conscious about the process. Strategies, at the abstract level, for design of spacecraft work well in software design. The satellite designers frequently select the most stressful, or difficult, aspect of the satellite to design first, which is what we had done in designing a parametric equation solver with the freedom to solve for any variable in an equation. This supported our initial decision to emphasize flexibility and was a fairly difficult part which would have hampered design had we not solved the problem of how to implement it.

7   CONCLUSION

Before planning can proceed, one must have an in depth understanding of what is needed, what resources are involved and what impact decisions will have. In analyzing the kinds of information and the diversity of approaches used by experts in the design of spacecraft, we have found that it is essential to interact with a large number of designers. Talking with only one or two experts does not give a broad enough picture of the many-faceted nature of design. Each designer brings his or her own perspective towards how design is done and how important each aspect of the design process is. We software designers certainly do this as well. A key to this has been to recognize that teamwork is vital in the development of both the software and the engineering systems being designed. By having multiple points of view we try to avoid imposing a perspective of how design is done. The aim is to support and enhance the creative process, not pigeon-hole it. As a consequence, the initial reaction to our design aid by actual designers has been quite favorable.

Designers are creative and innovative, whereas computers are good at storing and keeping track of a large amount of detailed information, such as past design successes and failures, and strategies for design and analysis. We hope that the complementary nature of a machine supporting a person will foster the development of designs more rapidly, more numerously, and of a more optimum nature, and also free the designer to concetrate on the more creative aspects of design.

References

[1] K. Hammond, *Case-based Planning: An Integrated Theory of Planning, Learning and Memory*. Ph.D. dissertation, Yale University, 1986.

[2] J. Kolodner, "Extending problem solver capabilities through case-based inference," in *Proceedings of the Fourth International Machine Learning Workshop*, (Irvine, CA), 1987.

[3] L. Steinberg, "Design = top down refinement plus constraint propagation plus what," in *Proceedings of the IEEE Systems Man and Cybernetics Conference*, (Fairfax, Va.), 1987.

[4] D. J. Wilde, *Globally Optimal Design*. John Wiley and Sons, Inc., 1978.

[5] C. Tong, "Goal-directed planning of the design process," in *Proceedings of the Third Conference on AI Applications*, pp. 284–289, Feb.23-27 1987.

[6] W. Swartout, "Darpa workshop on planning," *AI Magazine*, vol. 9, pp. 115–131, Spring 1988.

[7] M. J. Stefik, *Planning with Constraints*. Ph.D. dissertation, Stanford University, 1980.

[8] S. Mittal, C. Dym, and M. Morjaria, "Pride: An expert system for the design of paper handling systems," *IEEE COMPUTER*, vol. 18, pp. 102–114, July 1986.

[9] K. Bellman and A. Gillam, "A knowledge-based approach to the conceptual design of space systems," in *Proceedings of the 1988 Eastern Multi-Conference*, pp. 23–27, Mar. 1988.

Advances in AI and Simulation
© 1989 By The Society for Computer
Simulation International
ISBN 0-911801-50-2

Studying how models evolve: An emphasis on simulation model engineering

Paul A. Fishwick

Department of Computer and Information Sciences

University of Florida

Bldg. CSE, Room 301

Gainesville, FL 32611

INTERNET: fishwick@ufl.edu

Abstract

In this paper, we discuss the problem of the evolution of system simulation models. We formulate a hierarchy of methods that can be used as a template for defining evolving models and we use an example of a transistor circuit to demonstrate the levels of system description that can be associated with this physical model. By better understanding the procedure used when formulating models from the very beginning, we gain insights into how we may augment our existing simulation languages to allow for models at different levels of description.

1 Introduction

The methods for starting with physical system data and proceeding iteratively to create a simulation model have been explored within various segments of the simulation literature; however, much more work needs to be done in focusing directly on effective and cost-saving methods for developing and maintaining models. Just as there is an emphasis in studying the evolution of programs to fit user requirements in the discipline of software engineering, there should also be a similar emphasis in simulation.

The purpose of this paper is to attempt to shed light on the method by which simulation and system models evolve over time. We will focus primarily on the example of the simple transistor circuit shown in Fig. 1. We name our concern for the evolution of models, "simulation (or system) model engineering" (denoted, hereafter, as simply SME). This term is essentially borrowed from the area of software engineering (denoted as SE) in computer science. The goal of our research represented in this paper is to better understand the various processes that occur over a time span as a result of the modeling procedures taken up by the systems analyst. We do not claim that we have solved the problem of finding a unique, precise methodology for model evolution, but rather, we hope to delineate certain general methods which seem to be characteristic of the modeling problem. We have seen related endeavors within SE, for example, and we believe that similar research within systems and simulation might yield useful procedures for model evolution.

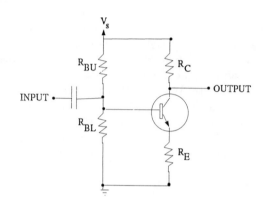

Figure 1: Transistor Circuit

2 The Characteristics of Model Evolution

2.1 General Characteristics

There is no evidence for the existence of a singular method for model evolution. This is due to many factors such as the expertise of the analyst constructing the model and the variety of choices that one has when considering the plethora of modeling techniques available. If there isn't a singular method then the best that we can do is to specify various types of models that are characteristic of a model evolving using a sequence of stages. It is safe to declare that models evolve as we add more *information* to our accumulated system knowledge. When we begin to create a simulation model, our knowledge may be fairly weak; and as we add more information we can tune the model or perhaps graduate to another paradigm for representing system behavior. We define essentially three general types of evolutionary steps: *change in instance, change in structure*, and *change in paradigm*. Changes to simulation models can be seen to fall into one of these three categories. We first outline the categories:

- Category I: Change in Instance
  - Parameter Modification & Estimation
  - Monte Carlo Analysis
  - Fuzzy and Coarse Variables
  - Conditions (Initial and Boundary)
- Category II: Change in Structure
  - New Observational Data
  - Structure Growth or Decay
  - Lumping (abstraction,aggregation), Homomorphism
- Category III: Change in Paradigm
  - Metaphors
  - Analogies
  - Alternate Perspectives

Perhaps the simplest method of changing a model is to change an initial condition or a parameter associated with a system variable. These instantiations of the system components can be real valued, stochastic, fuzzy, interval valued or symbolic in nature. As an analyst better understands a model, he may choose to gradually refine his estimates of some specific variable from a fuzzy value to a real value. The next fundamental level in model evolution relates to the model structure. If our model is a system of equations, we might add a variable or an entire equation to better model system behavior. If our model is a Petri net then we might add extra places and transitions. In category II, we are not simply changing an instance; we are molding the system structure. We might also change the system structure through process abstraction[4,5] or system morphism[16] so that we can maintain an overall preservation of behavior and still have a simpler model. In category III, we dramatically change the model by resorting to knowledge about system analogies and metaphors[8]. Modeling methods such as system dynamics (which uses a fluids metaphor) and compartmental modeling[10] (which uses a metaphor with interconnected, physical compartments) are just two examples of modeling methods that rely on metaphors to create a useful simulation model. Of course, analog simulation methods in general (using discrete electronic components as analogs) are quite popular when digital systems are too slow. The term "alternate perspective" in category III represents the evolution to models by choosing a new model structure not using analogy or metaphor. Instead, the choice can be made from an organized list or in a random fashion. Zwicky's morphological box structure[17] is indicative of this type of evolution (or discovery). To a great extent, we can view model evolution by alternative perspective to represent an intuitive stage that comes before analogical reasoning.

Now that we have briefly discussed basic methods of the evolutionary process, we now discuss the characteristics of models that represent stopping points along the evolutionary timeline. Consider Table 1. We specify a sample set of model types with their associated levels that represent stages during evolution. Most modeling methods can be reduced to a canonical form

Level	Model Type	Graph Type	Characteristics
1	Natural Language	total order	vertex=word, arc=left to right order
2	Semantic Graph	partial order	vertex=semantic concept
3	Symbolic Data Table	simple relational	vertex=symbolic value,
3	Real Data Table	simple relational	vertex=numeric value,
4	Causal Graph	homogeneous graph	vertex type is same throughout graph
5	Petri Net Graph	bipartite graph	two types of nodes: places and transitions
6	First Order Logic	normal form (CNF)	vertices are predicates
6	System of Equations	data flow graphs	vertices are operations and operands
7	Bond Graph	heterogeneous graph	generalized power elements
8	Network Model (SLAM,GPSS)	heterogeneous graph	Turing machine capability

Table 1: A Hierarchy of Sample Modeling Methods

such as a graph. In this way we can compare graph attributes as a rough measure of the level that is indicated by the model type. For instance, note that a semantic graph has hardly any constraints in its definition — it is simply a partially ordered set of nodes each of which represent some semantic concept. Contrast this with a bond graph which intrinsically contains much more detailed and constrained information about the system. A typical bond graph will contain definitions of causality, relationships among generalized effort and flow variables, parameter values (the ohm rating of a resistor, for instance) and conservation principles (the serial and parallel junctions). This is not to say that a bond graph is "better" than a semantic graph, but just that the bond graph contains more structured information about a system and is therefore at a "higher level" in terms of model structure.

2.2 A Transistor Example

A model in natural language format represents, in itself, the simplest and most abstract form of model. According to many natural language researchers, it is natural to equate the notions of natural language and thought. The way that we think and the language concepts that we use to explain and characterize those thoughts are intertwined so that it is often difficult to separate thought from natural language. It is with natural language, then, that we can find our first simulation models for a system[1,2]. For instance, the statement "An incoming electronic signal is amplified and remains relatively stable over small temperature fluctuations" represents a simulation model, in itself, for an electronic device capable of amplification. To utilize the natural language form for simulation, though, we must first construct a mathematical model that crudely represents the semantics of the sentence. Some questions arise immediately:

- What is the quantitative equivalent of "small?"
- How large are the fluctuations in temperature?
- What is the frequency and amplitude of the signal? We need to know both if we are to design the correct filters and include the proper operational amplifier(s) or transistor(s).

- What kinds of controls are present?

- How many stages of amplification are present?

- What are the tolerances (in ambient temperature, etc.) that are associated with the stability of the circuit?

- What are the power requirements?

It is clear that we can continue to ask many questions about the construction of a simulation model for this sentence. It is precisely for this reason that the natural language sentence is appropriate only as a crude simulation characterization — the sentence is ambiguous and has many possible interpretations (or models). A simulation language that incorporates natural language as a viable input must include a great deal of domain knowledge within frames. Also, an interactive question-answer session is often necessary to disambiguate initial conditions or parameter values. For these reasons, one might question the efficacy of using natural language at all; however, we note that there exist a plethora of textbooks discussing system behavior in natural language, and having the capability of translating text into math models with an accompanying interactive session with the analyst would be a very useful capability

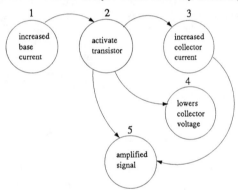

Figure 2: Concept Graph

given the vast numbers of "knowledge bases" waiting to be processed[2]. In addition, natural language is often used by laymen to describe system behavior; in this sense, natural language models are useful from a computer aided instructional perspective.

What kind of model would be more structured than the natural language text? We must add structure to create a slightly more detailed simulation model. We choose a concept (or 'semantic') graph as depicted in Fig. 2. A concept graph is structured enough to provide for arcs and nodes; however, we note the type of each node may be different. For instance: $type(node1) = state$ while $type(node2) = action$. The arcs are left unlabeled. Admittedly, there is little that we can do with this model unless we add more syntactic and semantic detail to the model.

The next step in our evolutionary trail leads us to create a data structure[11] for the real system. The data is often in the form of a table but it can also be represented as a relation. Table 2 depicts a symbolic data table that is created

	R_{CE}				R_B			
	R_C		R_E		R_{BU}		R_{BL}	
	+	-	+	-	+	-	+	-
V_C	-	+	+	-	+	-	-	+
V_B	0	0	0	0	-	+	+	-
V_E	0	0	0	0	-	+	+	-

Table 2: Symbolic Circuit Values

as an experimenter would test the transistor to determine its functionality. The resistors serve as the control variables for the system. When we increase, for instance, R_E (represented in the table by $R_E = +$) then voltage V_C is also increased whereas voltages V_B and V_E remain relatively unchanged (represented by a voltage having a zero value). What values do symbols such as '+','-', and '0' actually represent in real space **R**? This is not clearly specified intentionally so we can view the qualitative aspect of this system description. Such a system description would rarely be used for serious analysis; however, we note that symbolic tables commonly represent human thinking *about* system behavior. Therefore, the symbolic system is useful for aiding humans in the way they reason about the circuit – the table demonstrates its utility specifically in computer aided instruction and training tools.

Now, we need models with which to break the table into even more relations. One simple method is to use a simple causal graph as shown in Figs 3(a-c). Fig. 3(a) represents the most detailed causal model since the graph contains more vertices. Figs 3(b) and 3(c) are created by mapping $V_{BE} \rightarrow \{V_B, V_E\}$ and $V \rightarrow \{V_C, V_{BE}\}$. Graph vertices represent components and voltages while arc labels show general proportionality. For instance, in Fig. 3(a), resistor R_{BU} when increased causes a decrease in voltages V_B and V_E and an increase in V_C (i.e. demonstrating inverse proportionality).

At the next level of evolutionary specification, we can create Petri net model (see Fig. 4) which accentuates the relationship between base control, collector current and gain. The Petri net operates as follows:

1. We insert the number of tokens in place *Base_Control* that represents the quantity of base current through the transistor. Note that the black dot represents a marker and the number to the left of the marker represents the number of markers in a place.

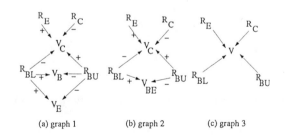

(a) graph 1   (b) graph 2   (c) graph 3

Figure 3: Causal Graphs - Refined and Lumped

2. We insert the number of tokens in place *Gain* that represents the typical current gain for the transistor. β represents the degree of current gain.

3. As place *Base_Control* loses tokens to place *Base_Current_Amount*, we note that our collector current increases linearly. We will assume that we are operating on the linear portion of the characteristic curve for the transistor.

4. Transition *Current_Flow* simply serves to get the Petri net operating at its nominal flow rate. In this sense, the firing of transition *Current_Flow* qualitatively represents the transient response of the transistor to an increase in base current.

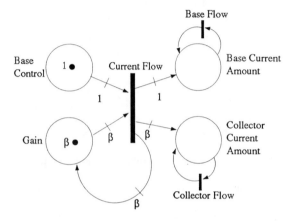

Figure 4: Petri Net Model of Transistor

If we take the symbolic data table discussed earlier, we can induce a set of predicate logic statements that represents the behavior of the circuit. Logical models of the transistor based on human experience are equivalent to "expert systems." The most obvious choice of an expert system that might characterize system behavior is now given. Recall that "unchanged" does not mean zero change, but rather "relatively little change or no change."

IF $resistance(R_C)$ is high THEN $voltage(V_C)$ is low.
IF $resistance(R_C)$ is high THEN $voltage(V_B)$ is unchanged.
IF $resistance(R_C)$ is high THEN $voltage(V_E)$ is unchanged.
IF $resistance(R_C)$ is low THEN $voltage(V_C)$ is high.
IF $resistance(R_C)$ is low THEN $voltage(V_B)$ is unchanged.
IF $resistance(R_C)$ is low THEN $voltage(V_E)$ is unchanged.
IF $resistance(R_E)$ is high THEN $voltage(V_C)$ is high.
IF $resistance(R_E)$ is high THEN $voltage(V_B)$ is unchanged.
IF $resistance(R_E)$ is high THEN $voltage(V_E)$ is unchanged.
IF $resistance(R_E)$ is low THEN $voltage(V_C)$ is low.
IF $resistance(R_E)$ is low THEN $voltage(V_B)$ is unchanged.
IF $resistance(R_E)$ is low THEN $voltage(V_E)$ is unchanged.
IF $resistance(R_{BU})$ is high THEN $voltage(V_C)$ is high.
IF $resistance(R_{BU})$ is high THEN $voltage(V_B)$ is low.
IF $resistance(R_{BU})$ is high THEN $voltage(V_E)$ is low.
IF $resistance(R_{BU})$ is low THEN $voltage(V_C)$ is low.
IF $resistance(R_{BU})$ is low THEN $voltage(V_B)$ is high.

IF $resistance(R_{BU})$ is low THEN $voltage(V_E)$ is high.
IF $resistance(R_{BL})$ is high THEN $voltage(V_C)$ is low.
IF $resistance(R_{BL})$ is high THEN $voltage(V_B)$ is high.
IF $resistance(R_{BL})$ is high THEN $voltage(V_E)$ is high.
IF $resistance(R_{BL})$ is low THEN $voltage(V_C)$ is high.
IF $resistance(R_{BL})$ is low THEN $voltage(V_B)$ is low.
IF $resistance(R_{BL})$ is low THEN $voltage(V_E)$ is low.

Clearly, the above expert system is somewhat primitive since we have failed to group antecedents or consequents in each rule. We can reduce the number of rules by considering simplifying expressions such as the following example which replaces six of the above rules:

IF $resistor\_class = R_{CE}$ THEN $voltage(V_B) = unchanged \wedge voltage(V_E) = unchanged$

Bond graphs represent an even more sophisticated model due primarily to all of the semantics associated with defining the notion of a generalized function or component[15,14]. A bond graph for the circuit is shown in Fig. 5. Note that p refers to the 'p'arallel junction where KCL applies. In some texts, 0 is used instead of p to denote a parallel junction. The transistor is modeled by defining the transistor as a controlled resistance. Note that, in a bond graph, the causality inherent within the system structure is shown in addition to the mathematical relationship among effort and flow variables. Causality is depicted by adding a short line perpendicular to the bond half-arrows.

The most complicated and most general modeling method would be to use a general algorithm with the power of a Turing machine. Essentially, then, the graph or program developed to model the system is unrestricted in its semantics. Programs written in simulation languages such as SLAM II[13], GPSS[3] and SIMSCRIPT[9] are examples of such methods. Even though these programs are not appropriate for the particular domain chosen in this paper (electronic circuits), in general such programs represent methods by which complex and detailed models may be invented. Models based on these programs are at the "end" of an evolutionary method — it is most likely that simpler methods will be used to model the system at the very beginning.

3   Toward More Comprehensive Modeling Tools

We have discussed some of the descriptive levels that can be used during system modeling. We now ask, "How can we change current system modeling and simulation development systems to reflect a more comprehensive approach to modeling (i.e. system evolution from the ground up to the most detailed model)?" We have shown that there are a number of modeling methods that can be used for the same physical system such as a transistor circuit. How can the study of such methods

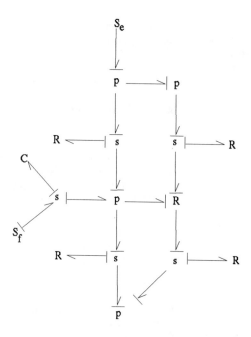

Figure 5: Bond Graph for Circuit

help us to build more comprehensive tools? We list some of the items that a comprehensive tool kit should contain:

- The primary goal of a comprehensive system is that it should help to "lead the user" through each phase of the entire system modeling process given any particular methodology.

- The user should have help in deciding what particular methodology to use. Should the methodology be based on bond graphs, causal graphs, or system dynamics for instance?

- The user should be able to enter information in several quantitative and qualitative[7] forms to the system: symbolic, numeric, probabilistic, and natural language. It is the system's responsibility to map these values into a single framework (such as the real number system). In addition to standard data items, it is important for the user to be allowed to enter geometric constraints associated with the system — the output of a CAD (Computer Aided Design) program is most appropriate for constraining the types of system models that can be subsequently constructed. Many of the manufacturing simulation languages have adopted this approach; however, it should be a widespread phenomenon since the geometry of the system, if easily defined, is often mentally associated with the system behavior.

- In the course of the user entering information as just specified, the user may enter only a <u>partial</u> system description. Some of the constraint based languages such as those reflecting general logic capabilities and specific constraint languages[12] may be appropriate as building blocks. Of-

ten a user's knowledge will be specified in terms of constraints and not as a complete prescription. If, of course, the system does not have enough information for a simulation then the user must be queried for additional input.

- The user should be allowed to enter goals to be met such as "design a small amplifier whose total harmonic distortion is less than X%." The program would then run a variety of simulations using different numeric conditions and slightly different model structures automatically to satisfy the goal. In discrete systems, a user is often interested in minimizing access time to the server in a queue. It therefore seems appropriate that an analyst should be able to run the simulation by specifying a "minimization criterion" instead of manually running and re-running many different simulations with different parameters.

- The user should be permitted to hypothesize a model if he does not require all of the assistance that the comprehensive system allows in creating models from very basic concepts.

- The user should have help in deciding which analysis methods to use to analyze the data. If possible, the system should allow for a presentation of the data using many formats: time series graphs, phase portraits, real and imaginary axis specifications, three dimensional plots. The eventual goal in analyzing simulation data is to be able to ask the program if the physical system is "stable" and have the system use whatever methods necessary to automatically determine an answer and explanation for the user. In other words, the user should not have to manually run regression analyses, followed by frequency analysis, etc. The user is not interested in a particular analysis method per se; he is interested, rather, in determining if the system has some type of qualitative characteristic whose determination is accomplished by the analyses.

4   Conclusions

We have set out to demonstrate three points: 1) That there is a need for research in simulation model engineering (SME) as much as there is one for software engineering (SE), 2) To demonstrate the different levels of complexity that can be used in defining the same system such as a transistor circuit, and finally 3) To describe the components and capabilities that a "next generation" simulation language should contain. We need to further understand the ways in which system model are originally created, modified, utilized, and maintained (just as in software engineering). We believe that a first step to creating a better environment for developing successful system models is to take a general systems perspective toward the modeling problem. We will develop better system model engineering (SME) methods if we look at the variety of modeling methods (from simple causal graphs to bond graphs) found in different disciplines. It is only by viewing systems in a holistic fashion that we see the general characteristics that future simulation and system languages must contain. To cite a specific example, we often see differences between applications using, say expert system representations in AI and equational representations in simulation. If we take a holistic view then we see that expert system rules represent "early" forms of more quantitatively specified systems in an evolutionary system timeline. Research in symbolic methods of "reasoning" and equational methods of "calculation" are often unnecessarily separated when they are actually two methods to be used at different times during system development[6]. Although we have taken some initial steps towards a more productive simulation environment by implementing a system with natural language interfacing, we have not implemented all of the features discussed in this paper. We plan on creating better system modeling tools that conform to sound SME principles, and we hope to see more of these features in future languages for system and simulation modeling.

References

[1] Wanda Austin and Behrokh Khoshnevis. Intelligent simulation environments for system modeling. In *Institute of Industrial Engineering Conference*, May 1988.

[2] Howard Beck and Paul A. Fishwick. Incorporating natural language descriptions into modeling and simulation. (submitted to the Simulation Journal).

[3] IBM Corporation. *General Purpose Simulation System 1360 Introductory User's Manual, Report H20-0304*, 1967.

[4] Paul A. Fishwick. A taxonomy for process abstraction in simulation modeling. In *IEEE International Conference on Systems, Man and Cybernetics*, volume 1, pages 144 – 151, Alexandria, Virginia, October 1987.

[5] Paul A. Fishwick. The role of process abstraction in simulation. *IEEE Transactions on Systems, Man and Cybernetics*, 18(1):18 – 39, January/February 1988.

[6] Paul A. Fishwick. A study of terminology and issues in qualitative simulation. *Simulation*, 50(12), December 1988. (to be published).

[7] Paul A. Fishwick and Paul A. Luker, editors. *Qualitative Simulation Modeling and Analysis*. Springer Verlag, Inc., 1989. (in preparation).

[8] P. Hezemans and L. van Geffen. *Justified use of Analogies in Systems Science*, pages 61 – 67. Elsevier North-Holland, 1985. Volume IV: IMACS Transactions on Scientific Computation-85.

[9] Consolidated Analysis Centers Inc. *SIMSCRIPT II.5 Reference Handbook*, 1972.

[10] John A. Jacquez. *Compartmental Analysis in Biology and Medicine*. University of Michigan Press, 2nd edition, 1985.

[11] George J. Klir. *Architecture of Systems Problem Solving*. Plenum Press, 1985.

[12] William Leler. *Constraint Programming Languages: Their Specification and Generation*. Addison Wesley, 1988.

[13] A. A. B. Pritsker. *Introduction to Simulation and SLAM II*. Halsted Press, 1986.

[14] Ronald C. Rosenberg and Dean C. Karnopp. *Introduction to Physical System Dynamics*. McGraw Hill, 1983.

[15] Jean Thoma. *Bond Graphs: Introduction and Application*. Pergamon, 1975.

[16] Bernard P. Zeigler. *Theory of Modelling and Simulation*. John Wiley and Sons, 1976.

[17] Fritz Zwicky. *Discovery, Invention, Research: Through the Morphological Approach*. MacMillan, 1969.

Advances in AI and Simulation
© 1989 By The Society for Computer
Simulation International
ISBN 0-911801-50-2

Artificial intelligence validation of simulation models

D. Deng*
Dept. of Computer Science
and Systems Science
Xiamen University
Xiamen, China

J.O.Jenkins
The Management School
Imperial College of Science,
Technology and Medicine
London Sw7 2PG, UK

ABSTRACT
    This paper discusses the validation of simulation models using an artificial intelligence(AI) approach. Validation is a vital phase in the simulation life cycle and is a concern of both simulation specialists and managers. Traditionally, validation of a simulation model involves testing for consistency between the behaviour of the model and that of the real world. By the validity of the model we mean an acceptable level of confidence that inferences drawn from the behaviour of the model are correct or acceptable to the real system. Simulation and AI both attempt to model reality; there have been a number of efforts to apply AI techniques to simulation and vice versa, and, to some extent, both have benefited from each other.

    The work reported here focuses on the validation phase of the simulation life cycle. With AI techniques, a knowledge-based system for simulation can be built up by means of which new models can be validated. First, the literature on the validation of simulation models is reviewed. Second, an approach to validation of simulation models is represented. Next, the illustration is given, and finally, suggestions are made for further work.

INTRODUCTION
    The validation of simulation models plays a vital role in a simulation life cycle. However, it is generally agreed that the validation of a simulation model is very difficult. " Validating of a computer simulation is one of the most difficult, and most important, aspects of the simulation process (Lehman 1977)". "The problem of validating computer simulation models is indeed a difficult one because it involves a host of practical, theoretical, statistical, and even philosophical complexities (Naylor, et al. 1968)". The main difficulties in validating simulation models are:
    (1) No model replicates the real world. Hence there can be no absolute validation;
    (2) There is no single set of criteria for validating models;
    (3) There is a conflict between subjective and objective methods;
    (4) There is a difference in experimental and nonexperimental environments;
    (5) There is a disagreement between rationalist and empiricist viewpoints.

    By validity, we mean an acceptable level of confidence that inferences drawn from the behaviour of the model are correct or acceptable to the real system. To validate a model means to develop an acceptable level of confidence that inferences drawn from the performance of the model are correct or

* Mr. Deng is currently working at The Management School, Imperial College of Science, Technology and Medicine

applicable to the real world system (Shannon 1975). Shannon has suggested that the concept of validation should be considered one of degree, and that we must consider the validity of a model as falling on a scale from 0 to 1, where 0 represents absolutely invalid and 1 repersents absolutely valid. There are many viewpoints on the term "validation". For example, "validation is an atempt to demonstrate that the simulatiun behaves like the actual system (Schruben 1980)", "validation is the determination of how adequately the simulation reflects those aspects of the real world it has been designed to model (Lehman 1977)". Obviously, either "likeness" or "adequacy" is the degree to which the model is equivalent to the real world system and hence validity is a relative property. Since there are a great variety of real world systems and information from observations is usually incomplete (due to simplification), and because there are different levels of belief in the validity of a model, it is impossible to set up a single set of criteria for validating models. Shannon(1975) points out that there is an apparent conflict when we are designing and validating simulation models between the need to be objective (ignoring our subjective beliefs or prejudgements and only consider the experimental evidence) and the need to make constructive and intelligent use of our subjective beliefs (intuition, opinions, impressions, etc.). However, there is not always an experimental environment available for validating simulation models, for example, in the field of ecnometrics. Nevertheless, it is unreasonable to regard a non-experimental research as unscientific.

    It is our philosophy that we do not pursue a universal acceptable set of criteria for validation of simulation models, but rather we validate models in terms of their purpose. We pay attention to both subjective judgement and objective tests for validity of models. We consider both experimental and nonexperimental researches as scientific methods. Nevertheless, some general rules must be followed. Lehman (1977) maintains that (1) the theory that underlies or is embodied in, the simulation must meet the general stardards expected of scientific theory; (2) the translation from theory to operating model must be accurate so that the model is a valid representation of theory, and (3) the results of the simulation must agree with data gathered from the real system. These three aspects of validation are called "Comprehensive validation" by Lehman. In practice, an eclectic multistage approach (Naylor 1968) to the validation problem is highly recommended which incorporates the viewpoints of the rationalist (synthetic apriorism in Lehman's terms), the empiricist (ultraempiricism according to Lehman) and the absolute pragmatist. In stage 1, a set of postulates or hypotheses describing the behaviour of the system of interest is formulated; stage 2 calls for an attempt on the part of the analyst to "verify" the postulates on which the model is based, subject to the limitations of existing statistical tests; the third stage consists of testing the model's ability to predict the behaviour of the system under study. These three stages are usually iterative throughout the model development and implementation. Shannon (1975) suggests that even if the model or one of its hypotheses is contradicted by empirical data, it is usually not rejected unless a better model or hypothesis is available. Generally, if the model or hypothesis has any reasonable body of supporting data or theory, finding facts that do not fit it usually leads to refinement and/or redefinition of the hypothesis rather than its complete rejection. There exists a continuing interplay among rationalist, empiticist and pragmatist philosophies throughout the process until the model is validated.

VALIDATION PROCEDURE

Having discussed the validation of simulation models in theory, let us first turn to the procedure for validating simulation models in practice and then to the recent trends in simulation. To achieve the greatest possible validity, the following steps are suggested by Shannon (1975):

(1) Use of common sense and logic;
(2) Taking maximum advantage of the knowledge and insight of those most familiar with the system under study;
(3) Empirically testing, by the use of appropriate statistical techniques and hypotheses;
(4) Paying close attention to details and checking and rechecking each step of the model building progress;
(5) Assuring ourselves that the model performs the way we intend it to by using test data, etc., during the debugging process;
(6) Comparing the input-output transformation of the model and the real world system (whenever possible), using statistical and Turing-type tests;
(7) Running field tests or peripheral research where possible;
(8) Performing sensitivity analysis on input variables and parameters;
(9) Checking carefully the predictions of the model and actual results achieved with the real world system.

These steps can be used as guidelines for validating simulation models. For a specific model, use of these guidelines and domain knowledge enables a specific validation procedure to be obtained.

Given there are some common rules or procedures in the validation process, and there is a criterion for validity -- in the sense of an acceptable of degree to which the behaviour of the model is similar to that of the real world system-- it is possible to develop an expert system for validation of simulation models. Recently, there have been a number of attempts to apply artificial intelligence(AI) techniques to simulation (Chaharbaghi, et al. 1988; Levary and Lin 1988; Lirov, et al. 1988; Murray and Sheppard 1988; Haddock 1987; Moser 1986; Flitman and Hurrion 1987; O'Keefe and Roach 1987).

AI AND SIMULATION

Traditionally, a simulation model is built in a general-purpose language or a specific simulation language such as GPSS (Gordon 1969). Murray and Sheppard(1988) have shown how a model can be built up automatically, using a Knowledge-Based Model Construction(KBMC) system. This consists of a rule base of basic concepts used by simulationist for the construction of SIMAN models of queuing systems. The expert system building tool OPS83 was used to implement the rule base. The underlying KBMC system rule base incorporates knowledge of queuing systems and the target language SIMAN with general simulation modelling language. The KBMC can only automate the model constrction phase of the simulation life cycle. To accomplish a whole simulation process, Levary and Lin (1988) proposed a hybrid expert simulation system (HESS), which is composed of 4 subsystem. These are 1) simulation model; 2) input expert system (IES); 3) output expert system (OES) and 4) Knowledge-Based Management System (KBMS). IES is designed to check the consistency of components of the input vectors; OES is designed to help the user analyze the results of simulation runs and make suggestions regarding the characteristics of additional runs; the KBMS is designed to improve the efficiency of the decision making process for the system under study. Based on a simulation generator, Haddock (1987) proposed an expert system framework, which first initiates the simulation generator to receive information from user, then creates a SIMAN model, and finally, executes the simulation model. The system can make inferences based on 95% confidence level. All of the three systems described above have the ability to accomplish some portions of a simulation life cycle, but very little is mentioned about the validity of a simulatioin model. The objective of this paper is to provide the validation of simulation models with an artificial intelligence approach by means of which a knowlege-based system for validation can be built up. Other authors including Doukidis(1987) hold that there is a close relationship between simulation and AI and that there are models and techniques which are mutually beneficial to each other. Murray and Sheppard(1988) are of the opinion that simulation amd expert systems are complementary technologies that can be combined to provide powerful decision support functions. A typical expert system (ES) is composed of:

. a knowledge base
which contains knowledge such as facts, rules, etc., and is the source from which inferences are drawn;
. an inference engine
which selects rules and uses relevant facts to give solutions or recommendations;
. a control mechanism
which is the manager of the system and is in charge of activities in the system;
. a knowledge acquisition subsystem
which has (shoule have) the ability to learn new knowledge and thus is interfaced with experts;
. a user interface

The validation process can be shown as in Fig.1.

KNOWLEDGE ANALYSIS

It is perfectly possible to develop an expert system for performing the validation process. In this paper, a model of expert system is presented as shown in Fig.2. In this study, we concentrate our attention on the knowledge base and knowledge acquisition subsystem. To begin with, let us discuss what knowledge is needed for model validation.

(1) Knowledge about the behaviour of the real world system
This knowledge should be completely obtained during the specification phase.
(2) Knowledge about the model
This kind of knowledge is obtained during model construction phase. It includes information about variables (dependent,

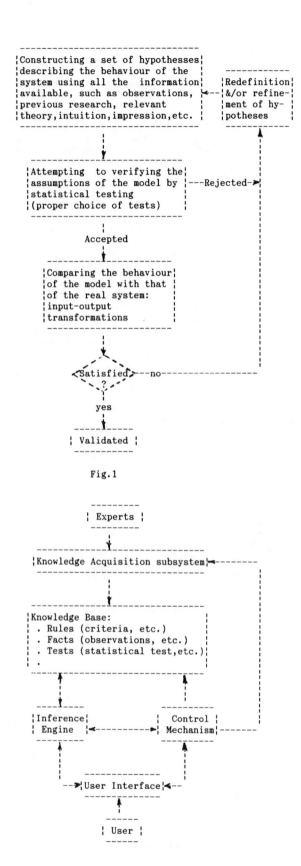

Fig.1

Fig.2

independent, exogenous, endogenous), major assumptions, objectives, applications. For example, if we are validating an inventory system model, it is characterized by the elements:
D----Demand;
K----Reorder cost;
H----Carrying cost;
Q----Quantity to order;
R----Reorder point(time);
EOQ----Economic order quantity(quantity).
The major assumptions are: the need to minimise costs, demand is known with certainty or more likely with some sort of probability distribution, and so on. The model is used to determine the optimal re-order quantity or the timing of ordering so that the total cost of carrying inventory is minimised.

(3) Knowledge about the validation criteria, if any.
   Though there is no single set of criteria, as discussed above, it has been found (Lehman 1977) that the criteria can be divided into two sets:
i). General criteria (rules) applicable to all types of models
   .If the simulation results agree with the real data, if the theory that underlies or is embedded in simulation meets the general standards expected of scientific theory, and if the model is an adequate represen-tation of the theory,
   then
      the simulation can be a valuable contribu-tion to the scientific understanding;
   .If the theory is satisfactory and the results do not agree,
   then
      the theory might be erronous;
   .If the model produces results that are at variance with the data from actual system,
   then
      the simulation model cannot be regarded as valid;
   .If relevant assumptions are accepted at a given confidence level x, and if the results agree,
   then
      the model is valid with confidence level x%

ii). Specific criteria
   A model is validated for a specific purpose. It should have some specific criteria, so its validity or adequacy should be evaluated in terms of its purpose. Take the inventory system as a example, we have
1) In structure, the model, expressed as a function of quantity-to-order Q, ie. Total-cost(Q), must include the two parts: inventory-carrying cost and ordering cost;
2). $0<EOQ<D$;
3). Total-cost'(EOQ)=0;
4). Total-cost''(EOQ)>0.
   Where 3) and 4) are based on mathematical analysis.

(4) Knowledge about statistical validation methods
   This kind of knowledge is relatively easy to obtain, but proper use of it is not easy, for

instance, a proper choice of a specific test from various tests.
(Illustration is given later.)

KNOWLEDGE REPRESENTATION

In this section, a method for knowledge representation is discussed. In a knowledge base, all the knowledge can be classified as rules and facts. Rules can be represented using the Programming-in-logic language Prolog.

Cross-Referencing Method (CRM)

In real world, there are cause-effect relationships . Usually, these are of m-n relationships, rather than m-1 or 1-n relationships between causes and effects. It looks like:

For each effect, it will be represented as

    effect(Effect-id,Cause-list,Effect-description)

where Cause-list is a set of pointers to relevant causes; for every cause, it will be represented as

    cause(Cause-id,Effect-list,Cause-description)

where Effect-list contains a set of pointers to relevant causes. For example, the criteria for inventory model given above can be represented as

    criterion(Cn,According-to,Description)

where According-to contains a set of pointers to some theorems and/or some assumptions, whereas the theorem and assumption can be expressed as

    theorem(Thi,Assump,According-to,Descrip,Used-to)
    assumption(Asj,Desription,Related-to)

where According-to again contains some pointers to other theorems or axioms, Assump contains pointers to some assumptions, and Used-to contains pointers to some applications, the criteria above, for instance, and Related-to tells where the assumption is applied to.

The advantage is that the reduadance caused by IF-THEN rule structure can be reduced and that it provides the inference engine with efficiency.

KNOWLEDGE ACQUISITION

The acquisition process is similar to a human being's learning process. In validating a new model, some new knowledge will be used. After the validation is finished, new knowledge about the model itself and about the methods used to validate it will be stored into the knowledge base. A model is described by the following:

    model(Mno,Component,Assumption,Objective,Application)
    where
      . Component is defined as
          component(Mno,Variable,Relation)
          where Variable is a set of vaiables in the model Mno and Relation is a representation of the relationships between the variables in the model;
      . Assumption is a set of postulates or hypo-

theses under which the model is constructed;
  . Objective is a set of purposes that the model is for;
  . Application indicates what typical applications are suitable.
Obviously, all of the information about the model should be saved, if automatic validation is required. Otherwise, some of the information can be dropped. If a new method is used in validating, a new record for the method should be created.

ILLUSTRATION

Consider the example of testing means. There are two samples from two populations:

    sample(A,-,N1,X1,S1), population(A,-,M1,V1);
    sample(B,-,N2,X2,S2), population(B,-,M2,V2).

where N is the sample size, X is the sample mean, S is the sample variance, M is the population mean, and V is the population variance. Several tests are available. How to choose a appropriate test is depends on the knowns and unknowns about the model and on the hypothesis. For example, under the null hypothesis: HO: m1=m2, one of the following actions might be taken:
    a) v1 and v2 are kown, using test-1;
    b) v1 and v2 are unkown, but equal, using test-2;
    c) v1 and v2 are unkown and unequal, using test-3.
In prolog, we have

    test-of-means(A,B):-
        sample(A,-,N1,X1,S1), population(A,-,-,V1),
        sample(B,-,N2,X2,S2), population(B,-,-,V2),
        test(1,-,V1,N1,X1,S1,-,V2,N2,X2,S2).
    test-of-means(A,B):-
        sample(A,-,N1,X1,S1), population(A,-,-,X),
        sample(B,-,N2,X2,S2), population(B,-,-,Y),
        X=Y,
        test(2,-,-,N1,X1,S1,-,-,N2,X2,S2).
    test-of-means(A,B):-
        sample(A,-,N1,X1,S1), population(A,-,-,-),
        sample(B,-,N2,X2,S2), population(B,-,-,-),
        test(3,-,-,N1,X1,S1,-,-,N2,X2,S2).

where test(*) is defined somewhere else.

DISCUSSION

In this paper, we have discussed validation in theory and presented the architecture of an expert system for validation of simulation models. To validate a model, three kinds of knowledge are needed. First, common sense is used for face validity. Second, objective tests are needed to test the hypotheses on which the model is built. For knowledge representation, this kind of knowledge is relatively easy, but how to choose an appropriate method for a specific model is a key issue. Third, subjective judgements are employed. This kind of knowledge originates from common sense and appears as intuition or impressions.

In discussing the expert system for validation of simulation models, the main concerns are with the knowledge representation and knowledge acquisition. To represent the multiple relationships between causes and effects, a cross-referencing method is described. The main advantage of using this structure is that whenever there is an update operation (usually the knowledge acquisition process requires such a kind of operation), only some changes of pointers is needed and that it is more economical than the IF-THEN structure. Moreover, it is a natural way to represent the real world phenomena. New knowledge is acquired during validation process. There are two sourses from which the knowledge can be obtained: experts and users. From experts, general knowledge is acquired, and from users, specific knowledge is obtained.

The knowledge used for validation can be classified as subjective judgement and/or objective tests. By use of an expert system for validation, the conflict between subjective beliefs and objective tests can be avoided by using subjective knowledge and objective knowledge iteratively (the multistage method). Under an intelligent simulation environment, the validation process of simulation models can be completed automatically, and because the subjective knowledge comes from various experts, this validation tool as a whole is more objective and therefore the validation is more credible.

However, there are some aspects which should be further considered in developing an expert system for validation of simulation models, for instance: 1) The refinement and representation of general criteria (used as guides) and the representation of specific criteria (according to the particular purpose of a model) are needed, and hence, 2) a formal description of validation is desirable.It seems that the later is rather difficult, but we cannot avoid it if we want to build an expert system for a wide range of models.

So far we have only discussed an artificial intelligence approach to the validation phase of a simulation life cycle. By integretation of subjective judgement and objective methods using expert system for validation of simulation models, the validation can be more satisfactory than only by judgement or by subjective testing. Especially, under the nonexperimental environment, the validation of a model can be more reliable because the expert system could view a problem in all directions after it has learnt from various real experts. However, the expert system is only a part (a subsystem) of the intelligent simulation environment and the processes of model construction, validation, and implementation are inseparable(Shannon 1975). Therefore, it is desirable to develop an intelligent simulation environment.

REFERENCES

Chaharbaghi, K.; B.L.Davies; H.Rahnejat and P.J.Dobbs. 1988. "An Expert System Approach to Discrete-Change Simulation." International Journal of Operational and Production Management, Vol.8, No.2: 15-34.

Doukidis, G.I. 1987. "An Anthology on the Homology of simulation with Artificial Intelligence." Journal of Operational Research Society Vol.38, No.8: 701-712.

Flitman,A.M. and R.D.Hurrion.1987."Linking Discrete-Event Simulation Models with expert systems." Journal of Operational Research Society, Vol.38,no.8:723-733.

Gordon, G. 1969. System Simulation. Prentice-Hall, Inc., Englewood Cliffs, N.J., USA

Haddock, J. 1987. "An expert system framework based on a simulation generator",Simulation, Vol.48,No.2 (Feb.):45-53.

Lehman, R.S. 1977. Computer Simulation and Modeling: An Introduction. Lawrence Erlbaum Associates. Publishers, Hillsdale, New Jersey, USA.

Levary, R.R. and C.Y.Lin. 1988. "Hybrid Expert Simulation System (HESS)." Expert Systems, Vol.5, No.2 (May): 120-129.

Lirov,Y; E.T.Rodin; B.G.McElhaney and L.W.Wilbur. 1988 "Artificial intelligence modelling of control systems." Simulation, Vol.50, No.1 (Jan.): 12-24.

Moser, J.G. 1986. "Integration of artificial intelligence and simulation in a comprehensive decision-support system."Simulation, Vol.47, No.6 (Dec.):223-229.

Murray, K.J. and S.V.Sheppard. 1988. "Knowledge based simulation model specification." Simulation, Vol.50, No.3 (March): 112-119.

Naylor, T.H.; J.L.Balintfy; D.S.Burdick and K.chu. 1968. Computer Simulation Techniques. John Wiley & Sons, Inc., New York.

O'Keefe, R.M. and J.W.Roach. 1987. "Artificial Intelligence Approaches to Simulation." Journal of Operational Research Society, Vol.38, No.8: 713-722.

Schruben, L.W. 1980. "Establishing the credibility of simulations." Simulation, Vol.34, No.3(Mar.):101-105.

Shannon, R.E. 1975. Systems Simulation: The Art and Science. Prentice-Hall, Englewood Cliffs, N.J.

Advances in AI and Simulation
© 1989 By The Society for Computer
Simulation International
ISBN 0-911801-50-2

Decision support system for crop production operations scheduling

Surendranath Thangavadivelu   and   Thomas S. Colvin
Dept. of Agric. Engr.   Agricultural Engineer
Iowa State University   USDA-Agrl. Res. Service
Ames, IA 50011   ISU, Ames, IA 50011

ABSTRACT

Crop production is influenced by many complex, dynamic and interdependent factors like weather, soil condition, crop maturity. It often involves making high risk decisions requiring considerable effort and expertise in the management of crop production resources. Providing the expertise of Agricultural Engineers, other experts and simulation models through computing aids could help farm managers make better decisions.

A decision support system, Tillage-Manager, is being developed to plan a sequence of tillage operations, monitor the progress and suggest alternatives when deviations to the original plan occur. This paper reports the progress achieved towards the development of Tillage-Manager. Mathematical models to simulate tillage operations have been developed and integrated with knowledge base modules to schedule a sequence of tillage operations based on recorded weather data. The system with a combination of simulation models for tillage operations and knowledge base modules will be a valuable tool for making tillage management technology easily available to end users.

INTRODUCTION

Decision making in farm situations is a challenging task requiring considerable effort and expertise. To illustrate the complexity of decision making on farms - consider the recent trend among farmers to cut crop production costs and conserve soil by adopting no till or conservation tillage. This necessitates the use of chemical herbicides for effective weed control. On the other hand, environmentalists consider contamination of ground water by chemicals leached below the root zone to be of serious concern. The requirement for chemicals and the concern over contamination need to be balanced against each other to avoid harmful effects. This will require experts to devise an appropriate solution that considers weather, soil condition, crop growth and other influences. Research work has generated an enormous amount of information, which means farm managers have to process a large amount of information every time they have to make a decision.

In agriculture, the problems that occur are ill structured requiring the use of factual, heuristic, incomplete and uncertain information and knowledge for their solution. Farmers and farm managers face many such situations in crop production and often wise decisions have to be made within a short time when the availability of experts is generally questionable. What is needed therefore is a tool to provide the expertise to farmers easily when needed.

REVIEW OF PREVIOUS RESEARCH WORK

Systems Engineering Approach

Several attempts have been made to analyze sequences of agricultural operations using systems engineering approaches. Link et al. (1964) developed an analytical approach to the problem of scheduling a system of farm field machinery taking into consideration the requirements of the farm and constraints imposed on the system. The procedure considers a series of agricultural operations as a sequence and their scheduling is based on the probability of suitable days to carry out the operations in the sequence.

Link (1967) developed a modified form of PERT (Program Evaluation and Review Technique) called a 'Tree Network' which allows for a wide range of random variation in durations and reduces the complexity of network analysis. The analysis of agricultural operations represented in the form of events in a network can be approached easily using this procedure.

Peart et al. (1970) demonstrated the use of project completion and project selection, and network analysis techniques in scheduling crop production operations modelled as a network. Singh et al. (1979) developed an algorithm to design a machinery system based on farm, machinery, equipment and crop data. The simulation algorithm specifies machinery and equipment required and a week-by-week work schedule based on the available and required field working days for each operation. The fraction of calendar time suitable for work during N successive weeks was assumed to be normally distributed in order to arrive at the available field work time.

Simulation Approach

Simulation models have been widely used in managing crop production operations. They have been used for profit maximizing, scheduling, minimizing crop production inputs etc. Whitson et al. (1981) developed a procedure to include the weather risk factor in the selection of profit maximizing crop and machinery selection. The model uses an Evapo-transpiration - Soil moisture balance model to include weather risk in terms of the number of days available for field work within the critical crop production periods.

Chen and McClendon (1985) developed a computer simulation model for soybean and wheat double cropping system. The model determines economic returns for various planting and harvesting rates.

planting dates and proportion of total farm area involved in double cropping. Chen (1986) developed a computer simulation model to budget farm operations and evaluate different farming alternatives. The model can be used for scheduling field operations and to decide which crop to produce based on break even yields and prices computed by the model.

Expert Systems Approach

Meyer et al. (1987) developed a region specific Expert System to classify soil into a particular tillage management group and suggest a tillage system. The system also computes an estimated yield. The system developed in the 'C' language, offers better explanation facilities than what the commonly available expert system shells offer. The fact that expert systems are efficient tools of transferring technology to the end users was also emphasized by Meyer et al. (1987).

Decision Support System

A different and recent approach in the management of agricultural operations is through the development and use of Decision Support System (Lal et al. 1987, Levary & Lin 1988, Lal et al. 1988). The concept behind such systems being the combined use of simulation models with capability to predict and handle time varying inputs and knowledge based systems which are capable of reasoning and are suitable for time independent inputs.

Halterman et al. (1988) developed one such Decision Support System in the domain of double cropping. The system is capable of evaluating soil, crop and other relevant conditions before planting and arrives at a decision on planting soybeans as a double crop following winter wheat.

FINDS (Farm-level Intelligent Decision Support System), (Kline et al. 1987), is a decision support system which combines linear programming and simulation modules for farm machinery management. FINDS uses an LP model to plan machinery management strategies and then formulates a simulation model evaluate the machinery management strategy under variable weather conditions. The advantage of such a system is that is can be a valuable decision support system for users who are not familiar with LP and simulation models and thereby facilitates the evaluation of alternate farm machinery plans.

The fact that expert systems are computer software applications that are capable of carrying out reasoning and analysis has been made use of in the development of a decision support system for crop management, COMAX (CrOp Management EXpert system) (McKinion and Lemmon 1985). COMAX is a production rule system being developed on a LISP machine. The system uses a FORTRAN based cotton growth model GOSSYM for its knowledge base development. The system aims at determining optimum recommendations for management decisions on a daily basis to maximize cotton yields while minimizing user input to the crop system. COMAX provides scenarios for GOSSYM to predict the growth and development of the crop which is used to determine optimum recommendations.

WHY A DECISION SUPPORT SYSTEM?

Mathematical modelling, simulation and such analytical techniques are not always efficient problem solving approaches in agricultural situations. Most of the problems faced by farmers and farm managers do not have well defined procedures for solution and most often heuristic knowledge is combined in arriving at a solution. The use of an expert system is ideal for problem solving under such situations. Diagnosing problems, selecting alternatives, and planning are some of the problem domains in which expert systems can be successfully used. The problem of tillage management is a typical agricultural problem. No analytical procedure devised so far has been a break through in helping farmers manage tillage.

A common approach followed in scheduling agricultural operations is to model them as sequences in a network with the probability of the number of suitable days for carrying out the operations as the basis for scheduling. Agricultural systems are ill-structured (Halterman et al. 1988) and the fact that agricultural operations scheduling must be done under conditions of uncertainty and as a system of interdependent operations does not lend itself easily for solutions by available operations research techniques alone.

The use of simulation techniques for solving agricultural problems is also widely followed. In spite of having capabilities of prediction and handling time varying inputs, as often encountered in agricultural situations, simulation models result in a rigid system as they operate under a set of assumptions specified by the model builder. In many situations, the assumptions and conditions under which the model is applicable are often ignored resulting in unrealistic results.

In practice agricultural problems are often solved using judgmental or subjective logic. Expert systems with heuristic knowledge have been developed to deal with such problems, but without complete success in solving the problems. Expert systems are generally designed to deal with time neutral inputs whereas the problems generally faced in crop production are influenced by time varying and interdependent factors such as weather, soil and crop condition, etc. On the other hand simulation models have predictive ability and handle time varying inputs. Therefore for solving problems such as the one we are faced with i.e. scheduling crop production operations, what is needed is a tool that combines the reasoning ability of expert systems and predictive ability of simulation models. Decision support systems, which are combinations of expert systems and simulation models are ideal in such circumstances. With such a tool it is possible to predict the behavior of the system being modelled for time varying inputs and interpret the simulation results, from which recommendations can be made.

Problem Domain

Dealing with the entire set of crop production operations is not within the scope of this article, hence the problem domain was restricted to the sequence of tillage operations by machinery.

The information required to plan a sequence of tillage operations i.e. farm, equipment, process and environmental data can be generated either from user interaction or through simulation of the system(s) under consideration. However, scheduling tillage operations involve decision making using these data giving due consideration to the constraints involved. This decision making process requires effort and expertise to an extent that the use of a decision support system may be justifiable.

SYSTEM COMPONENTS

The Decision Support System is essentially composed of three sub-systems.

(i)   a knowledge based module (Kbm)
(ii) simulation module
(iii) weather module

Knowledge Based Module

The interactions between the three sub-systems are shown in Fig. 1. The knowledge based module constitutes the heart of the decision support system and performs the function of scheduling tillage operations based on weather and soil condition. The Kbm was developed using PC Plus[*] as the development tool and has both procedural and declarative facts in the knowledge base. Information regarding the different tillage systems, the operations involved in each and their sequence, ideal conditions for the various operations are the kind of information encoded in the knowledge base. The inference engine is essentially that provided in PC Plus using a backward chaining inference mechanism to arrive at solutions. The Kbm generates other relevant information regarding farm, machinery and equipment used, etc. through user interaction. The Kbm also has a possible range of values for input parameters and warns the user when it encounters values outside the range. It also serves as control unit. The execution of the tillage operations simulation sub-module is decided by the Kbm in order to avoid unnecessary runs of the simulation models. On days when tillage operations cannot be performed, the operations simulator is not invoked to update the operation done and area covered. The simulation module consists of two units one for simulating tillage operations and another to keep track of soil moisture on a daily basis. Details regarding simulation module are provided in subsequent sections. The decision support system requires weather data in order to decide whether a day is workable or not. It also requires the forecasted weather in order to determine the possibility of completing current and future operations.

Simulation Module

Moisture Balance Sub-module. Moisture content of soil is a major factor which influences pre-planting operations. It is therefore essential to track soil-moisture variations on a daily basis to determine workability and therefore the scheduling of operations. A computer simulation model based on a simplified moisture balance equation developed earlier (Babeir 1984) was modified for use with this system. The model has been verified (Babeir 1986) and found to predict the moisture content of the soil reasonably well. Figure 2 is a detailed

---

[*]Reference to a company or product name is for specific information only and does not imply approval or recommendation of the product by Iowa State University or USDA to the exculusion of others that may be suitable.

diagram of the system being modeled, which is essentially the interaction between selected aspects of soil and weather. The system considers the top 45 cm layer of soil, divided into three zones each of 15 cm thickness. However the decision support system represents a larger system which is the influence of the interaction between weather and soil layers considered on machine operations schedule. The conceptual boundary encloses the soil medium and machinery required for the operations under the tillage systems. This is a deterministic model, based on the moisture balance equation

$$MC_i = MC_{i-1} + Precipitation$$

$$-(Runoff + Evaporation - Diffusion + Drainage)$$

where MC_i is the soil moisture content on the ith day. The components of the sub-module to calculate the rate variables of the system are empirical in nature.

The movement of water is fully described by the rate functions that determine the quantity of water in each soil layer which is an essential state variable of this sub-module. The rate functions used in this model are given below.

Runoff. $Runoff = 0.344 * Precipitation - 0.334$ (if precipitation is greater than 3 cm)

This function was estimated for Iowa corn fields (Kanwar 1981; Shaw 1963).

Evaporation. During the preplanting stages the evaporation from the field was assumed to be 0.035 cm/day (Kanwar 1981).

Diffusion. The diffusion of small amounts of soil water towards the soil surface as the top layer was depleted by surface drying was modeled as shown below

$$Diffusion_i = [(SM_n / FC_n) - (SM_{n-1} / FC_{n-1})] * FC$$

where $Diffusion_i$ is the soil moisture moving from layer n-1 to n on day i, mm
SM_n is the soil moisture content of soil layer 'n' during day i, mm;
FC_n is the field capacity of layer n, mm;
RDC is the soil moisture redistribution co-efficient

For the condition of corn field in Ames the redistribution coefficient was taken as 0.8 (Kanwar et al. 1983).

Drainage. In order to account for the time taken for draining of gravity water, which is generally considered to take place instantaneously, the following function was used to model the effects of drainage.

$$Drainage_n = (SM_n - FC_n) * DRS$$

Where DRS is the drainage co-efficient taken as 1.25 cm/day as suggested by Kanwar (1984).

Tillage Operations Simulation Sub-module. A modified version of a validated computer simulation program (TERMS) modeling tillage operations

(Colvin et al. 1984) is also a part of the simulation module. TERMS, acquires field, machinery and equipment, and operation data required for the simulation from user interaction. Based on these input data it predicts time, fuel and other costs involved in each operation on a per acre basis. Simulation on a per acre basis allows the model to account for the shape of the field, thereby increasing the precision of predictions. The form of input field data required for TERMS allows it to simulate operations on an approximated regular polygon equivalent to the shape of the field specified.

The program section for simulating tillage operations alone was used in the decision support system for scheduling tillage operations. Provision to store field, machinery and implement data separately was incorporated to limit user input of data each successive time the simulation is performed. The program was modified so that it can be used to predict the time required for a given operation on the specified field or to determine the area that can be covered in a given time and other resources consumed during the operation. The computation logic used in the simulation sub-module is presented in figure 3.

Weather Module. Weather information required for scheduling tillage operations was obtained using a commercial software package, 'Accu-Weather Forecaster'*. Accu-Weather Forecaster provides weather information for places within a 500 mile radius of any weather station chosen by the user. Both current, past and forecasted weather information can be obtained using Accu-Weather Forecaster. The software provides weather data from the National Weather Service through a weather information database, Accu Data.

The types of weather information used by the decision support system are the precipitation and temperature data. Both current and detailed forecast for a period of up to sixty hours can be obtained, which includes six and twelve hour quantity and probability of precipitation and temperature data.

WORKING OF THE SYSTEM

The execution pattern of the decision suppoprt system was designed to emulate discussion with an expert. A typical consultation with an expert would basically involve three phases of information gathering, computation & inference, and formulation of a solution to the problem. A consultation with the decision support system includes gathering of background information at the beginning. Based on the period of interest of the user the system identifies the stage in crop production the user ought to be in. If found to be in the middle of a tillage sequence, it further ascertains if the earlier operations in the sequence have been done.

Data regarding the size of field, machinery and equipment for appropriate operations to be carried out are obtained from the user. The knowledge

---

*Reference to a company or product name is for specific information only and does not imply approval or recommendation of the product by Iowa State University or USDA to the exclusion of others that may be suitable.

based module invokes the simulation module to determine the time and other resources like fuel, lubricant, etc. required to carry out various operations in the tillage sequence. The weather information (temperature and precipitation in particular) is then examined by the knowledge based module on a daily basis and the moisture content of the three soil layers is recalculated by the moisture balance sub-module depending upon precipitation and temperature readings.

Forecasted weather information is used by the decision support system to verify the feasibility of completing the ongoing operation during the forecast period. The current weather information is used to update the operations information. The feasibility of carrying out an operation is checked based on precipitation and soil moisture criteria. When there is the possibility of carrying out a tillage operation, the knowledge based module invokes the operations simulation to update the area covered. A record of planned operations and progress made is maintained for comparison.

Figure 4 shows the window of operation for mold board plowing in fall mold board plowing tillage system. The figure also includes the number of days required to perform the operation on a 100 acre plot if the operation was carried out at a stretch assuming the conditions are favorable. It also shows the number of days it may take based on simulated weather data due to interruptions caused by precipitation or excess soil moisture. The problem is magnified for larger fields. The decision support system performs simulations on a daily basis based on the weather data, arrives at a feasible schedule, and indicates if the completion of an operation is in jeopardy.

CONCULSIONS

The decision support system, Tillage-Manager can be used to evaluate different tillage systems on the basis of time and other resources like fuel, labor, lubricants, etc. required for the operations involved. Using real time weather data and accepted forecasting makes it a valuable tool for scheduling tillage operations. The combined use of simulation models and knowledge base facilitates two way communication between the user and Tillage-Manager. In its fully developed form, Tillage-Manager will have capabilities of dynamic scheduling, analyzing and suggesting alternatives when a planned sequence of tillage operations is interrupted.

REFERENCES

Accu-Weather, Inc. 1987. Accu-Weather's Accu-Data - Complete Computerized Data Base (User's Manual). Accu-Weather, Inc. State College, PA 16801.

Babeir, A.S. 1984. Simulation Model for Predicting Trafficability Condition for Crop Production. Unpublished Ph D. Dissertation. Iowa State University, Ames, IA.

Babeir, A.S., T.S. Colvin, and S.J. Marley. 1986. "Predicting Field Tractability with a Simulattion Model." TRANSACTIONS OF THE ASAE, Vol 29(6):

Chen, L.H., and R.W. McClendon. 1985. "Soybean and Wheat Double Cropping Simulation Model."

TRANSACTIONS OF THE ASAE, Vol. 28(1):65-69.

Chen, L.H. 1986. "Microcomputer Model for Budgeting and Scheduling Crop Production Operations." TRANSACTIONS OF THE ASAE, Vol. 29(4):908-911.

Colvin, T.S., K.L. McConnell, and B.J. Catus. 1984. "A Computer Model for Field Simulation." ASAE Paper 84-1523. American Society of Agricultural Engineers, St. Joseph, MI 49805-9659.

Halterman, S.T., J.R. Barrett, and M.L. Swearingin. 1988. "Double Cropping Expert System." TRANSACTIONS OF THE ASAE, Vol. 31(1):234-239.

Kanwar, R.S. 1981. Hydrologic Simulation of Nitrate Losses with Tile Drainage Water. Unpublished Ph D. Dissertation. Iowa State University, Ames, IA.

Kanwar, R.S., H.P. Johnson, and J.L. Baker. 1983. "Comparison of Simulated and Measured Nitrate Losses in Tile Effluent." TRANSACTIONS OF THE ASAE, Vol. 26:1451-1457.

Kline, D.W., and B.A. McCarl. 1987. "Farm-Level Machinery Management Using Decision Support System." ASAE Paper No. 87-1046. American Society of Agricultural Engineers, St. Joseph, MI 49805-9659.

Lal, H., R.M. Peart, and J.W. Jones. 1987. "Expert Systems for Technology Transfer." ASAE Paper No. 878-5028, American Society of Agricultural Engineers, St. Joseph, MI 49805-9659.

Lal, H., R.M. Peart, and J.W. Jones. 1988. "An Intelligent Field Operations Simulator." ASAE Paper No. 88-5020. American Society of Agricultural Engineers, St. Joseph, MI 49805-9659.

Levary, R.R. and C.Y. Lin. 1988. "Hybrid Expert Simulation System (HESS)." Expert Systems, Vol. 5(2):120-129.

Link, D.A. 1964. "Mathematical Approach to Farm Machinery Scheduling." TRANSACTIONS OF THE ASAE, Vol. 7:13-16, 18.

Link, D.A. 1967. "Activity Network Techniques Applied to a Farm Machinery Selection Problem." TRANSACTIONS OF THE ASAE, Vol. 10(3):310-317.

McKinion, J.M. and H.E. Lemmon. 1985. "Expert Systems for Agriculture." Computers and Electronics in Agriculture, No. 1:31-40.

Metacomet Software, Inc. 1988. Accu-Weather Forecaster (User's Manual). Metacomet Software, Inc. Hartford, Connecticut 06103.

Meyer, R.C., D.R. Griffith, J.V. Mannering and S.D. Parsons. 1987. "Tillage System Selection Software for Maximum Corn/Soybean Yield." ASAE Paper No. 87-5538. American Society of Agricultural Engineers, St. Joseph, MI 49805-9659.

Peart, R.M., K. Von Bargen and D.L. Deason. 1970. "Network Analysis in Agricultural Systems Engineering." TRANSACTIONS OF THE ASAE,

Vol. 13(6):849-853.

Shaw, R.H. 1963. Estimation of Soil Moisture Under Corn. Iowa Agriculture and Home Economics Experiment Station Research Bulletin #520.

Singh, D. and J.B. Holtman. 1979. "An Heuristic Agricultural Field Machinery Selection Algorithm for Multicrop Farm." TRANSACTIONS OF THE ASAE, Vol. 22(4):763-770.

Texas Instruments, Inc. 1987. Personal Consultant Plus (User's Manual). Texas Instruments, Inc. Austin, TX. TI Part No. 2232456-0001.

Whitson, R.E., R.D. Kay, W.A. LePori, and E.M. Rister. 1981. "Machinery and CXrop Selection with Weather Risk." TRANSACTIONS OF THE ASAE, Vol. 24(2):288-291.

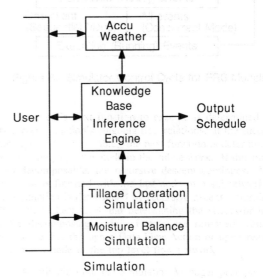

Fig. 1. Components of decision support system

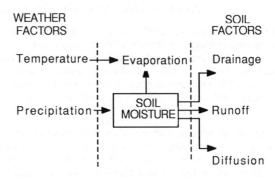

Fig. 2. Components of Moisture Balance Model

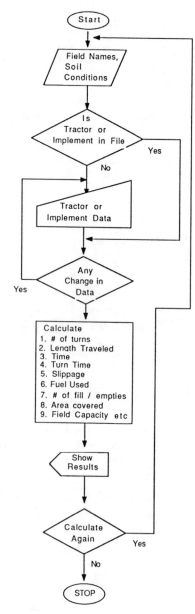

Fig. 3. Flow Chart of TERMS Model

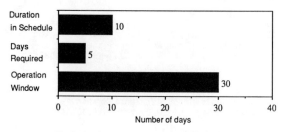

Fig. 4. Number of days taken up in Operation Window

Advances in AI and Simulation
© 1989 By The Society for Computer
Simulation International
ISBN 0-911801-50-2

A modelers encounter with AI
— AIM, a case history

John P. Skratt
ECON, Incorporated
4020 Moorpark Avenue, Suite 216
San Jose, California 95117

Those of us involved with building and implementing tools to support decision making concerned with problems of significant scope or depth and/or requiring large doses of judgment must continually strive to improve the "understandability" of our models. These models must communicate to their users by providing results in an understandable client perspective and they must provide the simplifying assumptions that limit the fidelity of their answers.

The building of tools for such purposes has a long history filled with successes and failures. At various points in time, it has not been evident whether the successes have outweighed the failures, or vice-versa. For the purpose of this presentation, I'll refer to this occupation of tool building and implementation as modeling for decision support systems. In this context, modeling can range from the literal "back-of-the-envelope", to applications requiring truly elegant programming solutions and magnificently large computer hardware. Providing pertinent and accurate information that can aid in a defined decision process requires innovation, modeling and programming expertise, a thorough understanding of potentially applicable tools and solution processes, as well as a significant measure of management skills oriented to the client's perspective.

From this viewpoint the world of AI offers a set of new tools and a saleable label. Years ago, embedding "if-then" judgment rules in FORTRAN or designing a clever user interface, had no other label than good modeling and programming. Today the applications of the mysteries surrounding AI must strive to avoid the results of the over-promised operations research solutions which occurred in the 1960's.

Seeking to separate the "wheat from the chaff" for some pieces of the AI world, our company recently conducted a study for the Air Force Space Division in Los Angeles. Our job was to recognize the chaff and apply the productive items given the AI label to the problem of assessing alternative Space Transportation Architectures (STAs). More specifically, the study objective was to develop a prototype of an eventual full scale model of STA assessment. The requirement for this prototype was to demonstrate the value of applying AI technologies to this particular decision support problem. I participated directly in this effort providing project management as well as a portion of the technical support, to the challenge of "boxing-up" the broad spectrum of STA evaluation in an AI environment. We at ECON recognized this study as an opportunity to consolidate and innovatively apply our many years of experience in the evaluation of space transportation systems.

However, I do not, as a result of this particular study, suggest that we have the insight necessary to determine whether our experience in developing this prototype model to demonstrate the applicability of AI techniques is particularly unique or significant. Nonetheless, we did accomplish our objectives. We were supervised by very bright, knowledgeable people who provided a great deal of support and guidance. As a result of our background, and our team's performance on this study, it was suggested by some of those who provided project oversight that presenting our experiences and observations would be useful to others undertaking similar challenges.

ECON is a small, teenage (15 years old) consulting company specializing in the economics of technology. Our staff has a respected reputation for knowledge, analytical skills and support to government and private sector management for questions dealing with the economics of new and alternative designs for future spacecraft and space transportation systems. The background as to how we at ECON came to work this study is as follows. In early 1984, a group of young Air Force officers, a multi-talented colonel and some far-sighted senior Aerospace Corporation personnel saw the need to develop a model of STA for "in-house" use. ECON's proposal for this effort was unique amongst respondents due to the suggested application of expert systems to help solve some of the difficult "boot-strapping" challenges when the problem of defining the "best" STA is considered in its broadest context. The focus of this new idea was a process for making reasonable assumptions about inter-dependent relationships in the architecture problem so that a manageable, logical evaluation process could be defined and executed. Due to the inability to find an appropriate and cooperative existing contractor to develop this concept, ECON failed to receive one of the original studies awarded by the Air Force. However, the expert system concept was deemed worth pursuing by both Space Division and ECON, Inc. Nine months later, an industry briefing for full and open competition on the prototype development of an STA tool incorporating state-of-the-art AI techniques drew 30 companies, including many large aerospace firms. Recognizing that what was once a focused, innovative idea that we had marketed to a prospective government client, had been turned into a free for all which attracted many AI advocates, we decided it was imperative that we find a recognized AI subcontractor.

As a result of a significant search, the individuals at Teknowledge Federal Systems (now with ISX) proved to have the unique combination of AI technical and government contracting experience necessary to support this effort. Released as a PRDA, Space Division's request for proposal on the prototype development, test and documentation for the Artificially Intelligent Model (AIM) drew 7 responses in January 1986. In simple terms the technical question to be answered was, "what is the best time-phased series of transportation systems including launch vehicles, ground and space-based support elements, manufacturing facilities/processes and technology development programs for a given set of design drivers?" These design drivers included: the designation of a number of existing and currently planned launch systems; a variety of size and configurations for new technology-limited space transportation systems; a demand for transportation that could be defined in an infinite variety of specifications; and a variable set of overall objectives and constraints.

The prototype version of the AIM Software and supporting documentation was delivered and the program successfully demonstrated in May of 1987. The program was written in COMMON LISP and FORTRAN 77, incorporated KEE, and was delivered on a Symbolics 3650 AI workstation. The program made extensive use of Man-Machine Interface (MMI) techniques, a limited number of rules, many objects, consistency checking, audit trail plus run documentation and an overall analytical technique we referred to as "refined solutions." As we had preliminarily designed during the prototype development, the full

scale version of AIM would have fully implemented a blackboard architecture and the emerging capabilities of ABE as it was being developed for DARPA by TFS. For those who may be interested, there exists a video which demonstrates how the prototype works by showing the screen inputs and outputs of a representative run.

What was learned from this exercise? From my perspective, it appears advantageous to capitalize on several aspects of the AIM prototype development process in taking on similar applications. Initially, it should be noted that, as is true in any endeavor, the characteristics of the people involved in the project - their capabilities, professionalism and, most of all, their clarity of thought are essential ingredients to success. Beyond these, several aspects of this endeavor were, in my judgment, critical elements in a productive approach.

The first of these elements was the mixture of skills brought together in this effort. The broad understanding of the domain (Space Transportation System Evaluation); the ability to conceive of new processes for modeling this domain within a decision support framework; the insight into, and implementation of, appropriate AI techniques; and the experience of knowledge engineering for actual applications comprised the necessary mixture of required skills. ECON provided the first two elements while TFS provided the latter two. This particular configuration of skills resulted in a substantial amount of give and take where the knowledge engineering aspects forced clarity of the why and how of the procedures while the domain/modeling expertise invented fresh ways to solve old problems using new, productive avenues offered by the AI experts. This approach helped insure that AI was being implemented only when there was a real benefit in the design and development of a decision support tool. Where this skill mix can be replicated for future applications, a significant benefit may be realized in terms of "boot-strapping" past the blank canvas state and incorporating the flexibility of the tools to handle questions raised by answering the original questions. The ability to anticipate and allow for growth in the scope and/or depth of the problems solved by good-decision support tools is directly related to the next productive element - rapid prototyping.

While it is difficult to draw distinct lines separating these elements and their benefits, the ability to realistically implement rapid prototyping is, from my perspective, the principal beneficial characteristic of AI software in support of this type of application. While rapid prototyping eases the boot-strapping process, its principal contribution is in allowing for trial, error, redesign, retrial, etc., in a framework which does not insist on knowing the ultimate dimensions of the software solution before modeling is initiated. To be able to add in an efficient, repetitive manner new relationships and rules to the process of solving a complex problem is a significantly valuable asset to those seeking to develop a client-oriented decision support tool sooner, rather than later.

In addition to the value associated with the general concept of rapid prototyping, a subsidiary productive concept emerged during the development of the AIM prototype. Figure 1 illustrates this concept by indicating the relationship between "general area" and "local area" expert knowledge.

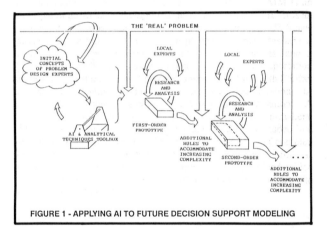

FIGURE 1 - APPLYING AI TO FUTURE DECISION SUPPORT MODELING

Solutions to complex problems necessitating the use of decision support tools have an inherent characteristic - the need to directly touch a level of detail which can be verified by individual experts in all of the component disciplines which make up the general problem. Traditionally, there exist several challenges in solving complex problems of great scope related to the participation of local area experts. Either they are asked to unbiasedly cooperate with other local area experts in democratically developing solutions to the general problem or they are presented the global model for their seal of approval after it has been cast in rigid code. Neither of these situations is particularly productive. Project recognition of the value associated with: 1) separate general area experts (boot-strapping) and local area experts (verification through valid representation of details) working in conjunction with; 2) a planned, sequential growth in the model as the local area experts flesh out the prototype skeleton represents a feasible management approach to the historical prob-

lem of delivering a workable decision support tool on time. In the AIM case the general area experts had to also possess the modeling expertise in order to quickly develop an appropriate, lasting structure that would support local area expert refinement.

Consistent with this organizational and management approach was the implementation of the "refined solutions" technique employed in the AIM prototype development. As has been previously alluded to, complex problems requiring the use of decision support tools are characterized as having many inter-related variables and many, often conflicting objectives. The challenge of putting these problems in a box, any box, is two-fold: first where and how to make the simplifying assumptions such that the problem solution can be started and, second, once a solution is derived, verifying that it is indeed a valid solution (i.e., represents a global optimum or an appropriately "satisficing" answer). Figure 2 shows the underlying design philosophy of the prototype and full scale version of AIM.

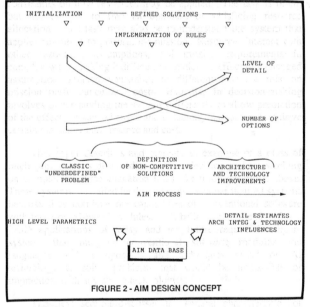

FIGURE 2 - AIM DESIGN CONCEPT

The prototype development activity demonstrated that a workable application of this process could be applied to the STA evaluation problem. Through the implementation of several rules and the consequential simplifying organization of various design drivers, an initial solution set of architectural elements was defined from the very large set of all potential answers. This smaller group of candidate solutions was then subjected to a more rigorous analytical technique employing a sophisticated search algorithm. Extrapolating this process to the planned full scale AIM system, we suggested that as an increasing number of potential solutions were discarded, an increasing level of detail could be added to the remaining set. In this manner refinements added by local area experts could be used to progressively identify the best architecture in terms of stated objectives and constraints. The confidence we placed in this approach stemmed from the structured application of general and local area experts and the basic qualities of rapid prototyping. If, during the sequence of refined solutions in which increasing levels of detail were to be evaluated, it became apparent that good solutions were discarded early in the process, then the general software structure and capabilities applied in the prototype development of AIM would allow for new rules and relationships to correct this problem to be added in a timely and effective manner. Management recognition and planning for this sequence supports the most important aspect in the development of decision support tools - the search for, and understanding of, counter-intuitive relationships and consequences.

One other element not discussed in detail but worthy of mention is the application of state-of-the-art MMI techniques. In general, it is my observation that in the implementation of decision support tools, MMI capabilities far exceed the decision maker's needs or desires. While high content, iconic, dynamic representation of information, non-model operations, etc., can be highly productive, they can also distract the client with "gimmickry" or capabilities which were previously unused and are perceived as, by and large, non-essential. A development process which plans for the graceful growth of MMI capabilities may also be an appropriate design principle for AI applications to decision support tools.

While there are many interesting technical space transportation aspects to the AIM system, I have, for this presentation, chosen to focus on the development, design, organization and management characteristics with the intent that they will provide a useful framework for future similar endeavors. In summary, the list of key, productive ingredients derived from the success of the AIM prototype development were: organization of the team of prototype developers recognizing the existence and role of general versus local area experts; reliance on rapid prototyping capabilities; employing general area experts who possess proven modeling skills to boot-strap the initial version of the model; and implementing a program development schedule that accounts for a refined solution technique which searches for counter-intuitive implications.

Advances in AI and Simulation
© 1989 By The Society for Computer
Simulation International
ISBN 0-911801-50-2

Using expert systems for waste treatment

H. Willard Downs
Department of Agricultural Engineering
Oklahoma State University
Stillwater, Oklahoma 74078

Abstract

An integrated data management system and diagnostic and predictive ES is being developed to assist in operation of wastewater treatment plants. Personal Consultant Plus and dBase III software packages are providing the framework for the development. The data manager stores and analyzes plant operational data, and generates any reports required for documentation. In addition, bio-kinetic process control equations and analysis have been included in the package, and provide daily operational strategies based on a moving analysis of plant performance. Statistical analysis of trends for important parameters and simulation add additional analytical power to the package. The ES operates mainly as a monitor, and takes no action unless a problem is detected or process kinetics need to be updated. Plant personnel are then alerted, and possible corrective strategies identified. The system should be able to anticipate many treatment problems before they become critical, allowing simple and economical corrective measures to be taken. In addition, plant performance can be optimized using the simulation and data analysis capabilities of the package. Finally, the playback and explanation features of the ES allow the user to examine the logic used in arriving at a particular recommendation or decision. This can be useful in helping the user better understand treatment plant operation and problem diagnosis.

Introduction

Biological waste treatment is the primary method of preparing municipal and industrial waste water flows for return to the environment. Increasing wastewater loads on existing plants and more stringent government discharge requirements have put considerable pressure on the waste treatment industry to refine and better understand the design and management of biological waste treatment processes. Though activated sludge and other biological treatment processes are still frequently operated by general guidelines and rules of thumb, facility design and operation must be guided by consideration of both the physical and biological aspects of waste treatment.

During the past several decades many researchers (Eckenfelder and Ford, 1970; Lawrence and McCarty, 1970; McKinney et al. 1968.) have studied the biological dynamics of wastewater treatment. A number of design and predictive relationships have been developed (Gaudy et al. 1967; Gaudy and Gaudy, 1980; Kincannon and Gaudy, 1980; Stover, 1984) which characterize the stabilization and treatment of organically polluted wastewaters through growth of micro-organisms. This bio-kinetic approach can be used to provide a determination of growth rate constants and other treatability parameters for a particular waste flow. Once the biological treatment characteristics of the waste flow have been adequately defined, the physical design of the treatment plant can be accomplished with confidence that it will provide both the capacity and flexibility necessary to meet influent and effluent requirements. Existing waste treatment facilities can also make use of this approach since the kinetic relationships can be used as a predictive or diagnostic tool in identifying and solving problems which occur during plant operation. Existing processes and new waste flows can be analyzed to improve overall treatment efficiency or effluent quality.

The design of new facilities using a bio-kinetic approach is relatively straight forward. However, it is more difficult to apply to existing operations because many of the parameters and qualitative measurements necessary to adequately define the bio-kinetic relationships may not be available, or may be masked by other problems in the treatment facility. In such cases the services of a waste treatment expert who can identify plant problems even where uncertain or missing information is involved is critical. Multiple problems and symptoms must be sorted out using extensive experience and intuition. Unfortunately, the waste treatment expert is not usually called in until the problem has become serious enough to cause a major plant upset and failure to meet treatment standards and effluent guidelines.

One approach to providing the expert knowledge needed to diagnose or predict operational problems may be in the application of Artificial Intelligence, specifically Expert Systems to design and operation of biological waste treatment systems. Diagnosing and trouble-shooting are well suited to the application of an Expert System. Selecting the proper course of action is frequently dependent on a consideration of both well defined physical and chemical relationships, and "expert" knowledge based on experience in biological treatment systems. Ideally such an Expert System (hereafter called an ES) could provide the diagnostic and management capabilities of an expert in a PC based program run in the operations office of any waste treatment plant. With appropriate interfaces, the system could monitor plant operation and assist plant operators in anticipating problems and making the appropriate day-to-day management decisions.

Data Management Requirements for Waste Treatment Plant Operation.

Most waste treatment plants use data management programs to store and manipulate operational data. These programs are used to prepare daily, weekly, monthly or other special reports necessary to document plant operation and efficiency. Maintenance of such a database is also critical to diagnosing operational problems and identifying important trends in the amount and quality of various flows and processes within the waste treatment plant. Thus, planning for the development of an Expert System must necessarily include development of a system for storing, handling and processing plant operational data which will be used by both the Expert System and plant personnel in preparing reports and making decisions.

This paper provides an outline and progress report of efforts to develop an integrated data manager and Expert System to assist in operating a waste treatment plant.

Data Management System

The relationship of the data management system and the interfaces which must be considered are shown in Figure 1. The data manager is the foundation for the system, and must be capable of standing on its own as well as interfacing with other components. It may collect and store data from on-line monitoring systems, key-board input or values calculated by the Expert System. It may also provide data monitoring and processing necessary for input to automatic control systems. The data base manager should also have the capability for statistical analysis to provide trend information for use in process control. All necessary report preparation options which may apply to the plant operation must be included.

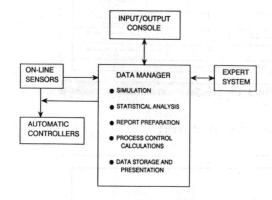

Figure 1. Data manager and advisory Expert System for waste treatment plant operation.

Figure 2 shows a flow chart for a typical biological waste treatment plant along with the various processes parameters which must be monitored and stored in the database. These parameters are all determined by physical or chemical analysis, or by application of the appropriate biological process control equations. The data management system differs from most currently being marketed in that it provides for determining each days operating conditions based on the bio-kinetic characteristics of the plant and wastewater. On a daily basis, these process control calculations provide the plant manager with an operational strategy which will maintain stable, effective treatment even as the quality and quantity of waste flows vary. The bio-kinetic treatment constants can be frequently updated and monitored to determine if there are significant changes occurring in treatability of the wastewater. In addition, these process control equations permit simulations to be run when desired. The impact of changing waste flows and strengths can be estimated before changes actually occur. Similarly, the effect of corrective methods can be approximated before actual implementation.

Some of the bio-kinetic process control calculations use statistical values such as moving and weighted averages. Analysis of historical trends for process parameters such as oxygen uptake can be valuable, in much the same way as statistical process

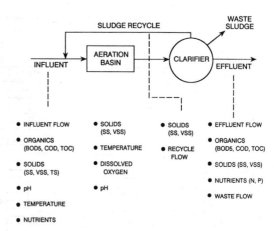

Figure 2. Parameters and locations which must be monitored in a typical waste treatment plant.

control. The trend or performance of a particular variable is analyzed with respect to its deviation from a moving average calculated by several methods. The historical performance of the average is also monitored. No corrective action is taken as long as the fluctuation of the variable stays within an acceptable band. Output from such analysis commonly takes the form of graphical output charting the performance of a variable relative to an acceptable band range. Thus, statistical process monitoring provides an analysis both of the trend of a design average or set point and also the variability of individual observations about that average. Analysis of this type can be very useful in trouble-shooting and optimizing plant performance. Results can be used directly with automatic controllers if appropriate, and will also provide critical information for the ES

Objectives and functions for the data management system are summarized below:

Data Manager Functions

1. Provide for on-line or manual data entry for all pertinent plant operational data.

2. Determine and update bio-kinetic treatment constants and process control calculations.

3. Produce daily operational guidelines and strategies.

4. Perform any statistical calculations or trend analysis needed for operational parameters shown in Figure 2.

5. Run simulations as needed.

6. Generate all reports and documentation required by the plant.

7. Provide data and processing on demand to the ES and plant personnel.

The data management system is 85% complete and has been developed using dBase III.

Expert System

The second area of system development is a diagnostic and predictive ES for plant operation. Under normal conditions, the ES simply monitors plant operational data, kinetic and statistical information and takes no action unless some aspect of plant operation is out of acceptable limits. The goal for the ES is that it be able to provide nearly the same level of analytical, predictive and diagnostic capabilities as would an expert having access to the database. However, there is no need for interaction either by an actual expert, or the ES as long as plant operation is stable. Thus, it is desirable for the ES to be almost totally transparent to the user. The ES can obtain data through the interface with the data management system, or may interact directly with the plant operator through keyboard input. Intermediate results or determinations not requiring immediate action may be returned to the data manager as updates. Examples include monitoring of data trends and bio-kinetic constants.

If some problem or impending upset is identified, the ES may then shift into a more dynamic role, performing some or all of the following tasks:

1. When enough information is available to immediately provide operative suggestions, the system can interact with either the automatic controller or plant personnel.

2. If additional information is required the ES may alert the operator to an impending problem and request the additional information.

3. Provide an alert to plant personnel if necessary.

Where changes will be made in plant operating conditions, or changes in trends are observed which may affect plant operation, the ES may request that the data manager provide simulation to predict performance of the plant for various test conditions. Results of these tests can then be used to formulate management strategies.

Expert System Structure

Texas Instrument's Personal Consultant Plus development shell is being used to develop the prototype ES. PC Plus can interact with dBase III. The knowledgebase is being developed in three frames.

Kinetics. The kinetics frame contains rules which monitor data and trends relating to determination of kinetic process control constants and calculations. Constants and calculations are updated as required by changes in plant performance and wastewater characteristics. If additional information and tests are required to clarify a situation, they are requested. Simulation may be requested. Finally, if changes are observed which suggest a serious disruption of plant operation or capacity, plant personnel are alerted.

Aeration Basin. The aeration reactor is where most of the actual waste treatment takes place. Process parameters such as pH, temperature, oxygen uptake, solids concentration etc. are critical and must be closely monitored. The aeration frame monitors these parameters and their trends, and may make modifications to the daily process control calculations and strategies which result in the most stable operation of the aeration basin. As above, additional information and simulations may be requested, and plant personnel may be alerted if a serious problem seems to be developing.

Clarifier. After the wastewater has been partially cleansed through growth of micro-organisms, the biomass must be settled and removed before the effluent can be discharged. Some of the settled biomass is returned to the aeration basin to maintain the desired ratio of biomass to waste, and the remainder wasted. Obviously smooth and efficient clarification is essential to plant operation. Many plant upsets and problems first manifest themselves in changes in the settling characteristics of the sludge biomass. The clarifier frame closely monitors data from the clarifier such as sludge settling velocity, solids concentration, pH, color etc. If significant changes are observed, additional information is requested from the operator. Frequently the type of micro-organism which is predominant in the sludge provides valuable clues to system operation. Shifts in the predominance and types of micro-organisms can give warning of significant changes in wastewater characteristics and plant operation.

Summary

An integrated data management system and diagnostic and predictive ES is being developed to assist in operation of wastewater treatment plants. Personal Consultant Plus and dBase III software packages are providing the framework for the development. The data manager stores and analyzes plant operational data, and generates any reports required for documentation. In addition, bio-kinetic process control equations and analysis have been included in the package, and provide daily operational strategies based on a moving analysis of plant performance. Statistical analysis of trends for important parameters and simulation add additional analytical power to the package. The ES operates mainly as a monitor, and takes no action unless a problem is detected or process kinetics need to be updated. Plant personnel are then alerted, and possible corrective strategies identified. The system should be able to anticipate many treatment problems before they become critical, allowing simple and economical corrective measures to be taken. In addition, plant performance can be optimized using the simulation and data analysis capabilities of the package. Finally, the playback and explanation features of the ES allow the user to examine the logic used in arriving at a particular recommendation or decision. This can be useful in helping the user better understand treatment plant operation and problem diagnosis.

REFERENCES

Eckenfelder, W.W.Jr., and D.L., Ford 1970. "Water Pollution Control." Pemberton Press, Austin, Texas.

Gaudy, R.F. and E.T. Gaudy. 1980."Microbiology for Environmental Scientists and Engineers." McGraw-Hill Book Company, New York, New York.

Gaudy, A. F. Jr.; M. Ramanathan; and B.S. Rao. 1967. "Kinetic Behavior of Heterogeneous Populations in Completely Mixed Reactors." Biotech, and Bioeng., IX 387.

Lawrence, A.W., and McCarty, P.L. 1970 "Unified Basis for Biological Treatment Design and Operation." J.San. Engineering Division, ASCE, 96, SA3, 757 (1970).

McKinney, Ross E. and O'Brien, Walter J., "Activated Sludge - Basic Design Concepts." J. Walter Pollution Control Federation, 40, 11, 1931 (November 1968).

Stover, E. L., 1984. "Process Control Strategies For Troubleshooting Activated Sludge Plants". Presented at the Virginia Water Pollution Control Association's Seminar on Controlling Activated Sludge: Approaches and Case Histories, Richmond, Virginia (October 25, 1984).

Advances in AI and Simulation
© 1989 By The Society for Computer
Simulation International
ISBN 0-911801-50-2

Some lessons for artificial intelligence and agricultural systems simulation

La Raw Maran
Knowledge-Based Systems Research Laboratory
Department of Agronomy, University of Illinois
1102 South Goodwin, Urbana, IL 61820

Howard W. Beck
Department of Entomology and Nematology
3103 McCarty Hall
University of Florida, Gainesville, FL 32611

ABSTRACT

The computerized simulation of crop plant functions offers important potential for developing practical management tools in agriculture. However, before this potential can be tapped, some formidable problems must be solved. This paper gives a survey of some of these problems within the historical context of simulation techniques. Several suggestions are given toward the development of AI knowledge-based solutions.

SIMULATION AND MODELING

The Issues and Background

In the context of computer applications *simulation* and *modeling* imply the existence either of specific applications, or of technically implementable specifications; however, in the context of *biological systems simulation and modeling*, such an implication does not necessarily follow. In this field the computer-implemented simulation systems will represent only a subset of the available models of plant behavior. The deployment of models for the purposes of research and application far predated the time when the computer first became available as a tool for simulation. (See Rose 1981; Charles-Edwards 1986; Hunt 1978). We will use the terms *modeling* and *simulation* interchangeably since the necessary distinction is not between these two, but whether or not a model or simulation is computerized.

An active cross-fertilization of ideas between model builders in the agronomic plant science domain and a specific segment of specialists in computer application engineering has begun although the onset itself was quite indirect. There exists now an area of mutual concern and new ideas stemming from this interaction have started to appear. Huck and Maran (forthcoming) discuss the circumstances and some of the consequences of this encounter and the following will recapitulate in summary some of their points.

A.   Traditionally, the primary goal of plant science is conceived to be the analysis, description and explanation of plant functions using the general principles of physics and chemistry.

Characteristically, these accounts contain: (1) a description of plant function as processes together with full details regarding the mechanisms of process or plant material components and the dynamic process itself represented as a sequence of event occurrences, such as water intake, photosynthesis, etc. and (2) the recognition of the two fundamental attributes of plant functions - growth and development.

Growth entails continuous metabolic activities and the activities that plant metabolism requires as support, such as fetching water, inorganic solutes, etc. Plant growth also means conducting specific goal-directed activities such that the necessary organic resources can accumulate and engender development. Development means the emergence of new features such as plant organs, whose occurrence follows a preprogram or phenologic model; the appearance of the cotyledon in epigeal germination, of true leaves, of flowers, etc., represent the unfolding of the characteristics called development. Plant growth simulation became the primary target of mathematical modeling in plant biology early on. As Hesketh and Jones (1980) observe, one begins with some conceptual model of some aspect plant function as the base; however, as data collected from this particular function is interpreted for its structure and organization, mathematical tools become indispensible. Mathematics serves the purposes of describing the function, of analysing the component parts, and of synthesizing the separately analysed component systems. These are, even when using powerful mathematical tools, extremely complex tasks, and when the computer became available certain segments among the modelers were eager to enlist its service. The role of the computer in the capacity of scientific data processing began some two decades or more ago.

These developments in biological systems modeling, including the computerized systems, made possible the prediction of the outcome of growth as crop yield, for instance, by using as input a specific physical state description of the crop or its growing environment. This capability became the primary rationale for agronomic simulation efforts.

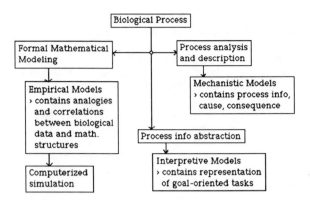

Figure 1. Simulation or Modeling:
The levels of meaning

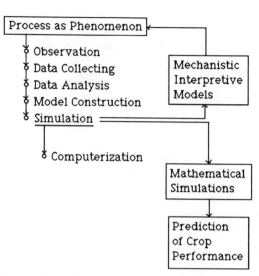

Figure 2. The Development Cycle of Model or Simulation Types

In essence, there are at least three distinct levels of organization of information in the overall scheme of plant science. (1) The traditional concern with the explanation and understanding of plant function as physical process, and the concern with linking growth to development. The model that directly represents the behavior of processes in the descriptive sense is the *mechanistic model* ; this model is characteristically bound to the context of the physical phenomena that it models or simulates. Mechanistic models characteristically describe process-events as being driven by physical causes, and that a specific consequence or goal is realized at the end. A variation of this mechanisitc view is the *interpretive model* which frames in its representation of plant functions the goal-oriented, or task-oriented nature of plant functions. (2) The level of mathematical modeling where, as in the case of growth rate calculation, specific numerical expressions are adopted in an effort to achieve normalization of the raw data about the physical system. At this level a critical line is crossed because we are now representing a process without necessarily explaining that process biologically; it is inconceivable that a polynomial expression, used to calculate the relative growth rate of plants, can preserve in its representation system-like information about enzymes, enzyme actions, cells, cell actions, etc., on up to the plant level functions. (3) The computerized extension of the mathematical model. This last development is catalytic in initiating the discourse between simulationists in the plant sciences and software engineers interested in knowledge-based simulations.

B. Recent activities that have occurred outside the agronomic field but dealing with dynamic modeling have been about the knowledge based approach to simulation (KBS). These events reveal two basic characteristics; first, the approach to simulation that appears to have initiated discourse toward KBS is the approach associated, among others, with the pioneering work of Simon (Simon 1976; Winograd 1986) on decision theory and decision making procedures. This is a highly mathematical (stochastic) approach and to overcome the limitations associated with it the proponents of the KBS approach recommend a series of departures from the strictly numerical to the conceptual representation approach. Secondly, these new developments have occurred in the straightforwardly engineering domains of factory and distribution systems analysis. The problems specifically cited as regards the numerical approach include the complexity of the modeling language, the obscure relationship between modeling concepts and the real systems that are the target of modeling, unmodifiable procedures and procedural organization, remoteness from practical application and the lack of explicitness about the system. In Fox, et al (1988), and Klahr and Fought (1980), a modeling system based on knowledge of the domain of application coupled to a simulation-expertise module is proposed.

This situation is strikingly similar to the kind of developments experienced in agricultural modeling; the bottle-neck in each case is the use of mathematical procedures that represent real-world phenomena without preserving the meaning of the physical or psychological processes themselves. In essence, the situation here appears to be saying that in order for conventional simulation methods to acquire the utility for practical application its procedural systems must be given a transplant of knowledge representation.

SIMULATION AND THE AGRONOMIC GOAL

The goal that underlies all agronomic research, including simulation, is the expectation of relevance to crop production; ultimately, all research must produce something of a practical nature for the crop grower. This goal chains together in the form of a network, abstract and specialized knowledge and the practical needs of crop management in the field. Is agronomic simulation a management tool in this precise sense? The answer, to no one's surprise, is strikingly clear: "No, it is not; at least not yet."

What should be done, or what must occur for simulation to become a practicable management tool? At the outset, it appears that two steps need to be taken; first, recognition must be made of the problems associated with mathematical simulation methods. In the same sense that polynomials cannot preserve the functional meaning of enzymes in relation to cells, and cells in relation to tissues and membranes, etc., they will also be unable to express the meaning of the relationship between seed varieties in relation to soil types, soil types in relation to fertilizers and pesticides, etc. Any effort to attack the problem must begin with the recognition of the fact that the role of mathematics is a critical problem for simulations.

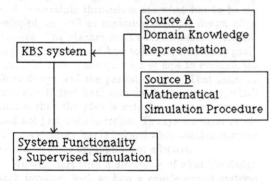

Figure 3. The Hybridized KBS Approach

Secondly, hybridized systems might be pursued so that an expert system type of application can preside over the simulation component. Beck and Jones (n.d.) explored this possibility extensively although they do not deal with the problems of knowledge representation and setting up a domain-specific knowledge base with authority and the

means necessary to supervise the simulation module. Beck and Fishwick (1986) propose the idea of developing procedures that translate the meaning recovered from natural language (NL) expressions into corresponding mathematical expressions, with the simulation task being preformed via the second representation.

These are interesting and admirable ideas; however some fundamental questions must be tackled before we can commit KBS development research to a specific course or direction. The truth of the matter is that we might not get anything better than supervised simulation out of the hybridized systems; there is no assurance that hosting a strictly numerical system inside an expert system would be problem-free.

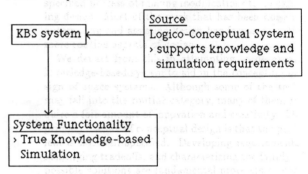

Figure 4. A Purebred KBS System

THE PRIMARY PROBLEMS

There are two fundamentally important problems that confront the development of KBS for agriculture. They are:

I. Although, obviously, an agricultural KBS system must contain the relevant knowledge about plant response to managed growing environments, as well as the know-how to manage the environment for optimal crop yield, the *present* simulation techniques cannot contain such information. In other words, the very information needed to create agricultural KBS systems is excluded, de facto, by the prevailing format of representation. The foremost problem in developing a general utility KBS for agriculture is to find a format of representation that can contain knowledge as well as conduct some form of simulation. Is there such a language?

II. The history behind the development of mathematical simulation methods in both biological and engineering research reveals a serious problem stemming from the inability of mathematical expressions to contain a high degree of information content. What precisely are the reasons underlying this problem? How can this be overcome? Given the readiness of the proponents of the hybridized KBS method to accept a specific simulation component running on mathematical procedures, the question regarding the ability of knowledge-based methods to perform simulation emerges. Is there such a problem in fact?

Perhaps the very concept of simulation should be re-examined; moreover, the well-known AI methods of mechanism modeling, causal representations, model-based reasoning, etc. should be considered for whatever potential they might have for KBS development.

These questions push to the front the issues concerning the unique features and weaknesses of both the numerical method and the conceptual approach. Obviously, there are no ready answers for the reason that no systematic investigations of these questions have been done to our knowledge. Until we acquire some insight into the questions raised it would be quite premature to push the hybridized approach or the "purebred" approach. There are no reasons available to determine the relative appropriateness of one over the other.

OUTLOOK AND SPECULATIONS

In the absence of any clear idea as to whether or not the current methods for plant function simulation should be supplanted or incorporated as an imported subsystem, the best that one can do would be to list the known or preferable properties into the specification of requirements that an agricultural KBS system must have.

(1) The pivotal role of natural language (NL) for communication with the user -qua- crop grower. There is simply no better means of communication than NL for reducing the artefactive barriers that are typical in man-machine interaction.

(2) The recognition of the fact that concept-based representation of domain information will have far more success in supporting NL communication and other services that require intensive NL use, such as data-query and data-management languages.

(3) The fact that hybridized systems with imported components may be more likely to compromise the functional integrity of the system, make modification difficult, conceal system functionality, etc. Grafted relations also invite the possibility of

add-ons that are engineered and lacking in psycholinguistic and epistemological motivations.

(4) Systems with imported subsystems may have a higher tendency to be task-specific, and may lack at a higher level, the capability for interaction with related simulation systems serving related management areas. This spells isolation.

(5) Surely, wherever preserving the mechanistic meaning of the biological process is not a desired criterion, purely mathematical simulation will need to be available (see Fitter 1981). By the same token, wherever containing appropriate knowledge is the accentuated property, a means of representation for this must be found or devised. In all likelihood, hybridization is not the only way to achieve KBS. Cognitively, or in the human model, processes dealing with quantity are not categorially distinct and operationally separate from processes that deal with qualitative information. We should not insist on hybridization to the extent of implying such a separation for the machine-based simulation.

REFERENCES

Beck, H.W. and J.W. Jones (n.d.) *Simulation and Artificial Intelligence Concepts* University of Florida, Gainesville.

Beck H.W. and P.A. Fishwick 1986 *Incorporating Natural Language Descriptions into Modeling and Simulation* UF-CIS Technical Report TR-88-6 Dept. of Computer and Info Science, Univ. of Florida, Gainesville.

Charles-Edwards, D.A., D. Doley, and G.M. Rimmington. 1986 *Modelling Plant Growth and Development* Academic Press, Sydney.

Fitter, A.H. and R.K.M. Hay 1981 *Environmental Physiology of Plants* London, Academic Press

Fox, M.S., N. Husain, M. McRoberts, and Y.V. Reddy 1988 *Knowledge Based Simulation: an Artificial Intelligence approach to System Modeling and Automating the Simulation Cycle* Carnegie-Mellon University, Intelligent Systems Lab. CMU-RI-TR-88-5

Hesketh, J.D. and J.W. Jones, editors 1980 *Predicting Photosynthesis for Ecosystem Models* CRC Press, Inc. Boca Raton, FL.

Huck, M.G. and L.R. Maran (n.d.) Root Decision-Making (to appear) in *Roots: the Hidden Half* Marcel Dekker, Inc. NY.

Hunt, R. 1978 Plant Growth Analysis *The Institute of Biology's Studies in Biology* No. 96; London E. Arnold.

Klahr, P. and W.S. Fought 1980 "Knowledge-based Simulation" *Proceedings* of the First Annual Conference of the American Assoc. for AI, Stanford, CA.

Rose, D.A. and D.A. Charles-Edwards, editors, 1981 *Mathematics and Plant Physiology* Academic Press, London.

Simon, H.A. 1976 *Administrative Behavior* 3rd Edition, NY The Free Press.

Winograd, T. and F. Flores 1986 *Understanding Computers and Cognition* Ablex Publishing, NJ Norwood.

Advances in AI and Simulation
© 1989 By The Society for Computer
Simulation International
ISBN 0-911801-50-2

Architectures for knowledge based simulation and their suitability for natural language processing

Howard W. Beck [1]   La Raw Maran [2]   Paul Fishwick [1]   Ling Li [3]

1 Computer and Information Sciences
University of Florida
Gainesville, Florida 32611
hwb@beach.cis.ufl.edu
fishwick@ufl.edu

2 Department of Agronomy
University of Illinois
Champaign, Illinois 61820

3 Agricultural Engineering Department
University of Florida
Gainesville, Florida 32611

ABSTRACT

We examine several examples in which representational structures used for natural language processing are merged with architectures for knowledge based simulation. The main premise is that in order to adequately support natural language processing, data structures used to represent language meaning must be compatible with the representation used for simulation. We provide examples that include the analysis of text describing temporally related events, analysis of text describing quantitative relationships, and a model base describing model components which can be accessed by a natural language query.

INTRODUCTION

To adequately support language processing, architectures for knowledge based simulation (KBS) must be compatible with data structures used to represent language meaning. To the extent that this compatibility is not achieved, knowledge is hidden within the model and is inaccessible to higher-level reasoning and analysis. The effect of forcing an integrated natural language processing ability onto the KBS architecture is to make explicit all knowledge contained within a model. As a side effect, a versatile user interface is also produced.

In this paper we will examine some examples of merging simulation and representational structures for natural language. There are currently only a few systems which attempt to merge natural language and simulation. PROTEUS uses a recursive transition network (RTN) to represent model components (Ksiezyk and Grishman, 1987). The RTN is also used analyze complex noun phrases. Koshnevis and Austin (1987) provide a natural language front-end to DYNAMO. Models can be constructed from natural language descriptions, but the KBS architecture is separate from the language analyzer. SHOPTALK (Cohen et al., 1988) provides a natural language query facility within a graphical simulation environment. Early work on natural language and simulation was conducted by Heidorn (1974) for queuing models. In the work described in this paper we are stressing a close coupling between natural language representation and KBS architectures, and the utilization of many knowledge sources at various levels of abstraction.

Traditional simulation and modeling techniques are inadequate for supporting natural language processing. For example, it is clear that there is an incompatibility between language meaning representation and mathematical equations. This problem is summarized by the realization, "Equations don't talk." Although equations contain a wealth of domain knowledge, this knowledge is implicit. The meaning of an equation is usually given in external supporting documentation,

variables, parameters, experimental data, and relationships captured by the equation. The equations themselves do not provide this information. This means that the equations cannot have any explanation ability, and have difficulty merging with other knowledge sources.

We do not want to detract anything from the power and usefulness of mathematical models, or imply that they are not valid as knowledge representation languages (Fishwick, 1988b). It is not likely that a new and better representation for physical processes will evolve by using a different representation. Rather, we are interested in finding ways in which the knowledge embedded within models can be shared and combined with other knowledge sources and can be manipulated by higher level reasoning processes.

On the other hand, there are many domains for which detailed, quantitative models have not yet been developed. There will be a continuum of qualitative models which become more sophisticated as more domain knowledge is added. The initial end of this spectrum may be a natural language description of the domain, as illustrated by the first two examples below. In general, knowledge based simulation must utilize existing knowledge for decision making, and not be dependent on missing, lower levels of detail. A knowledge based approach will give the best possible advise on the basis of what is known. Thus we will have models at various levels of abstraction and stages of development.

By natural language representational structures, we mean a logical predicate, graph, or object based representation in which symbols represent concepts, and related concepts are represented by interconnections among the symbols (Sowa, 1984). A computer program is said to "understand" a natural language expression when that expression has been mapped into such a representational structure. At the same time, universal concepts and common sense knowledge can also be represented by such structures and are used in the mapping process. These structures can be manipulated using inferencing techniques such as graph matching. Below we present three examples in which these structures can be merged with representations for temporal relationships, merged directly with quantitative relationships, and used for describing the modules within a model base.

MODELS CAPTURING TEMPORAL RELATIONS

This example attempts to represent temporal events without using mathematical relationships, just by using qualitative relationships expressed in a natural language text. There is a good amount of work on temporal reasoning which can be used for this purpose (Allan, 1983). In this example, we extract knowledge of properties and time directly from a natural language text description of time-varying events in order to build a simple model of the temporal relationships among the events. Properties associated with the entities participating in these events are also extracted and represented explicitly along with the temporal information.

The analysis is performed on the following paragraph which describes the life history of a parasite (T. julis) which attacks an insect pest (Cereal leaf beetle) that feeds on grain crops (Gage and Haines, 1975):

"Adults parasitize cereal leaf beetle larvae feeding on the leaves of small grains. Late instar larvae of T. julis over-winter in the soil within cereal leaf beetle pupal cells formed in late June. An average of 5 parasite larvae can be found within each pupal cell. In late May T. julis larvae complete their development and the adults chew through the pupal cell and make their way to the soil surface where they mate and disperse to grain fields. At this time, T. julis can be seen searching the upper surface of spring grains for cereal leaf beetle larvae."

It is possible for a natural language processor to analyze this text and construct representations for both factual and temporal information directly from the words and grammatical structure of each sentence. For example, the first sentence:

"Adults parasitize cereal leaf beetle larvae feeding on the leaves of small grains."

can be analyzed at a syntactic level, resulting in the following parse tree:

```
SENTENCE
  NOUN PHRASE
    NOUN - Adults
  VERB PHRASE
    VERB - Parasitize
    NOUN PHRASE
      NOUN PHRASE
        PROPER NOUN - Cereal leaf beetle
        NOUN - Larvae
      GERUND PHRASE
        GERUND - Feeding
      PREPOSITIONAL PHRASE
        PREPOSITION - On
        NOUN PHRASE
          NOUN PHRASE
            DETERMINER - The
            NOUN - Leaves
          PREPOSITIONAL PHRASE
            PREPOSITION - Of
            NOUN PHRASE
              ADJECTIVE - Small
              NOUN - Grains
```

The surface semantics of this sentence is represented by a predicate which is constructed by the language processor:

```
Parasitize(Adult T. julis,
    Larvae [Cereal leaf beetle,
        Feeding[Leaves[Grain[Small]]]])
```

which takes the main verb "Parasitize" as the main predicate, and the subject "Adults" and object "Larvae" as arguments. The modifiers (in brackets) "Cereal leaf beetle", and "feeding on the leaves of small grains" are structurally attached to the object. The reference that "Adults" refers to the adults of "T. julis" must be inferred from the context of the paragraph.

The predicate is used to instantiate the generic concept "Parasitize". Prior knowledge of this concept is needed to interpret the sentence. The generic concept is represented by the object:

```
Parasitize
  SUPERCLASS: Action
  ATTRIBUTES
    Parasite: SOME Organism
    Host: SOME Organism
```

which means that Parasitize is an Action involving a Parasite and a Host, both of which are Organisms. Given this object, the action of parasitism expressed in the first sentenced can be used to form the following instance:

```
Parasitize
  SUPERCLASS: Action
  ATTRIBUTES
    Parasite: Adult T. julis
    Host: Cereal leaf beetle
      ATTRIBUTES
        Growth Stage: Larva
        Habitat: Small Grains
        Feeding_Site: Leaves
```

Information about Cereal leaf beetle larvae is also embedded within this object, and is obtained by instantiating the generic concept for Larva.

Temporal relationships concerning the life stages of the insects are implicit in this sentence. Specifically, it is the adult developmental stage of T. julis, rather than some other stage such as eggs or pupae, which does the parasitizing of the larvae. It is the larval stage of Cereal leaf beetle, rather than some other stage, which is attacked. Background knowledge about the life history of insects is needed to understand these relationships. Specifically, all insects begin as eggs, eggs hatch into larvae which progress through several stages or instars, then enter a pupal stage, after which adults emerge and eventually lay eggs.

In a similar fashion, other factual and temporal information described in the paragraph can be represented in predicate form:

```
Overwinter(Larvae, In Soil)
    (In Cereal leaf beetle Pupae)

Be_in(5 Larvae, One Cereal leaf beetle Pupa)

Begin(Life, Cereal leaf beetle Pupa)
    (Time(Late June))

Become(T. julis Larvae, T. julis Adults)
    (Time(Late May))
```

Emerge(Adult T. julis, From Pupa, From Soil)
    (Time(Late May))

Disperse(Adult T. julis, To Grain Fields)
    (Time(Late May))

Search_for(Adult T. julis, Cereal leaf beetle)
    (Location(Spring Grains))

Notice that factual information such as "5 parasite larvae per pupae" is directly associated with other information. Properties associated with each concept are connected structurally, and these properties can include both factual and temporal relationships. For example, all the information associated with the adult T. julis can be expressed by the object:

    T. julis
        SUPERCLASS: Insect, Parasite
        ATTRIBUTES
            Growth Stage: Adult
            Host: Cereal leaf beetle
            Behavior: Emergence, Mating, Dispersion,
                        Searching, Parasitize, Oviposition

where Insect, Parasite, Adult, Cereal leaf beetle, Emergence, etc., are also complex objects. Since the objects associated with Behavior are actions and events, and therefore occur in time, the temporal events can be highlighted as shown in Fig. 1 which emphasizes the dynamic processes which are occurring.

Notice that time is being represented as multiple states by using different objects. Thus, several objects are used to represent the life stages of each insect. There are three different objects for representing T. julis adults. One object represents the newly emergent adult which is in the mating stage, another represents an adult which is exhibiting dispersion activity, and another represents a later stage for ovipositing adults. This notion of time involves objects "predicting" their next state by pointing to another object. Although it is based only on the information expressed in the natural language description, this way of expressing temporal relationships is consistent with later stages of modeling in which each life stage becomes a state variable, and difference equations represent the time progression of the insect population through life stages.

Even with the crude model of Fig. 1 which contains only structural relationships and no quantitative information, questions such as "When will T. julis emerge", or "When will Cereal leaf beetle Pupate?", or "How many parasites are there per pupae?" can be answered. More specific answers can be given as more detailed knowledge is added, but this is a natural result of refining the model.

MODELS CAPTURING QUANTITATIVE RELATIONSHIPS

Another example comes from a one-paragraph description of a nano plankton respiration model taken from a textbook on biological control systems (Milsum, 1966):

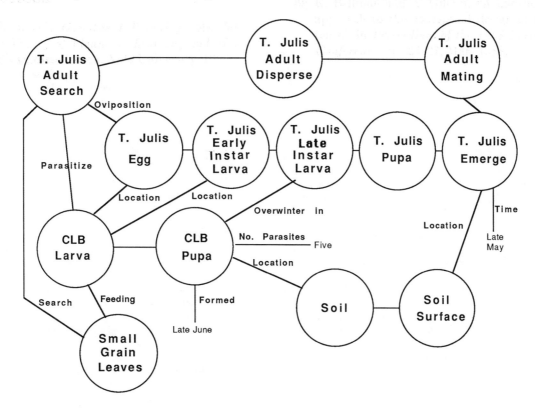

Figure 1. Semantic Network for Temporal Events in the Life History of T. julis.

105

"The sunlight is the input to the system and is represented by a battery of voltage eb. The production rate f of material by photosynthesis is proportional to the difference between eb and a "backup" potential, e, of material in the system, with the constant of proportionality being looked upon as the battery conductance 1/Rb. The community respiration rate fr is assumed proportional to the potential e, and the storage rate fc proportional to the rate of change of potential in the community cellular storage capacity C. Finally, the total production rate f must equal the sum of respiration and storage rates."

We have constructed a system called NATSIM which can generate mathematical equations based on the descriptions given in this paragraph. For example, the sentence:

"The community respiration rate fr is assumed proportional to the potential e."

has the predicate form:

Proportional[Assume, To(e [Potential])]
          (fr [Rate[Respiration[Community]]])

The predicate is used to instantiate the concept "Proportional":

    Proportional
        SUPERCLASS: Equal
        ATTRIBUTES
         Var1: Variable
            Symbol: Fr
            Represents: Rate
                    Type: Respiration
                        Of: Community
         Var2: Multiply
            Var1: Constant
                Symbol: C1
            Var2: Variable
                Symbol: e
                Represents: Potential

Here the generic notion of Proportional implies that a variable is equal to the product of a constant (The constant of proportionality) by another variable. Multiply is a binary relationship between two variables. Notice that as in the previous example additional information is associated with the mathematical terms, namely that fr represents the rate of community respiration, and that e is a potential.

The background knowledge needed to understand this paragraph is contained in a concept generalization hierarchy. Certain classes in the hierarchy represent mathematical operations. For example, proportional is a special case of equal. In addition, there are classes describing electrical components and power sources. These are used to understand the analogy between a battery and sunlight. Also, concepts dealing with biological processes such as photosynthesis and respiration are needed to understand the references in the paragraph.

The generation of mathematical equations is treated as a language translation problem. Just as objects are created through parsing English sentences and instantiating generic

concepts, sentences in any language can be generated by a reverse process. We used a simple context free grammar for generating mathematical equations from objects of class Equal:

    Equal -> exp = exp.
    exp -> exp + exp.
    exp -> exp - exp.
    exp -> exp exp.
    exp -> exp / exp.
    exp -> d exp /d var.
    exp -> (exp).
    exp -> var.
    exp -> cons.
    exp -> numb.

For example, the object for Proportional given earlier can be used to derive an equation:

    Proportional ->
    exp = exp ->
    var = exp
    fr = exp ->
    fr = exp x exp ->
    fr = cons x exp ->
    fr = C1 x exp ->
    fr = C1 x var ->
    fr = C1 x e.

which is the equation form for the sentence about community respiration rate.

Once the equations have been produced, behavioral analysis can be conducted with the help of a natural language query to answer questions such as "Is this a stable system?" or "What is the time constant for the transient behavior?". These can be answered by sending the system equations to a simulator. The simulator could be coupled with a control systems analysis expert system (Cline et al., 1988).

This example illustrates that mathematical expressions can merge directly with natural language expressions. Once again, background knowledge needed to fully understand the system under study must be explicitly represented. However, in this example the mechanics of solving the equations still had to be handled by an external process.

MODEL BASE

Hybrid representations combine two or more different representational approaches. In this example we explore a hybrid representation in which a traditional simulation language is coupled to structural descriptions of simulation components. The simulation, written in FORTRAN, is maintained in its original form. Structural descriptions provide a high-level interface to the simulation.

A model base contains a collection of models and their component modules, creating a library of reusable parts. Modules are represented at varying levels of resolution and abstraction. Such an approach is exemplified by System Entity Structures (Zeigler, 1984) and KBS (Reddy et al., 1986). A module is described by its function, input/output conditions, and coupling requirements. Modules with similar functions are classifed together in a taxonomy.

One service provided by a model base is to help the user determine which modules to apply in a particular situation. In goal directed simulation, modules are assembled which satisfy some goal or provide answers for solving a problem. In model synthesis, the user is a modeler trying to identify modules which can be applied to a new model. As in the previous examples, the module descriptions can be represented using a notation which is compatible with natural language processing. Thus, a natural language query facility can assist users in module selection.

We illustrate this process by building a high level description of a soybean crop model known as SICM (Wilkerson et al., 1983). SICM, Soybean Integrated Crop Model, contains several major components including a plant growth model, evapotranspiration, water balance and irrigation, phenology, and management practices. We created a taxonomy of modules from the original FORTRAN version of SICM (Fig. 2). One advantage of this approach is that SICM is kept in its original FORTRAN form. The high level module descriptions are built externally, avoiding the need to rewrite SICM in a different language.

For example, one of the objects describes an irrigation module which is part of the Water Stress subsystem:

```
Irrigation
   SUPERCLASS: Water Stress
   ATTRIBUTES
      Function: Water Application
                Method: Manual
      Inputs:
         Time:
         Amount:
      Outputs: Soil Moisture Content
      Coupling: Rainfall,Evapotranspiration,Soil-Moisture
```

The instances of a class describe a particular simulation run:

```
Irrigation
   SUPERCLASS: Water Stress
   ATTRIBUTES
      Inputs:
         Time: July 1
      Amount: 1 inch
         Outputs:
            Soil Moisture Content: 12%
```

A natural language query such as:

"If I irrigate today, how much water should be applied?"

is used to instantiate a query object:

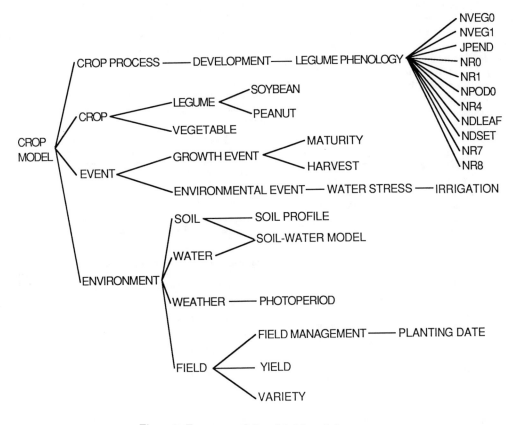

Figure 2. Taxonomy of Crop Models and Components

107

Irrigation
    SUPERCLASS: Water Stress
    ATTRIBUTES
        Inputs:
            Time: Current
            Amount: ?

In a query process technique based on classification (Patel-Schneider et al., 1984; Beck et al., 1989), a search of the taxonomy is made for objects which match the query object. Classification is similar to pruning (Rozenblitz, 1986) in which an experimental frame is used to state the conditions for which a model is needed. The taxonomy of the System Entity Structure (Similar to Fig. 2) is then searched for modules which can address these requirements. In our example, the Irrigation module would be located, and a particular simulation run made to answer the user's question.

In this example, descriptions of the model modules can merge with natural language queries in order to identify relevant model components. However, this representation is less than ideal from a natural language standpoint since the high-level module descriptions tend to be missing much of the detail which is represented implicitly within the FORTRAN code.

CONCLUSIONS

The examples in this paper illustrate some ways of merging knowledge representation techniques used in simulation and natural language processing. This approach intentionally avoids the notion of "natural language interface." Rather, structures representing language meaning are integrated directly with the model. This forces explicit representation of both the information represented by model equations, and background knowledge needed to fully understand the domain being modelled. This will hopefully lead to an intelligent simulation environment; a system that is knowledgeable about all aspects of the model and domain, and can interact with users in natural language to explore problems. This is the service provided by a modeling expert.

Much research lies ahead. We have not adequately represented the "inferencing" process involved in solving equations or simulating their solutions over time. The representations given in the example are declarative in nature, and we have some difficulty with procedural knowledge. Presumably the equations are turned over to a symbolic equation solver or simulator, but then the knowledge base component is left wondering, "What is going on in these external components?"

The process of model reduction can be viewed as a machine learning problem in which additional information is added to take the model to the next stage of refinement. This additional information could be acquired by the system using natural language input. Finally, hybrid approaches must be explored in cases where a uniform representation may not be possible. For example, we would also like databases containing statistical information, documents and pictures to be integrated within this simulation environment. At this point we can only indicate directions to pursue. We have shown that the use of natural language processing will lead to a more effective use of modeling and simulation knowledge.

ACKNOWLEDGEMENTS

This work is supported in part by a grant from the Florida High Technology and Industry Council, #87101421.

REFERENCES

Allan, James F. Maintaining Knowledge about Temporal Intervals. 1983. Communiations of the ACM 26(11):832-843.

Beck, Howard W, Sunit Gala, and Shamkant Navathe. 1989. Classification as a Query Processing Technique in the CANDIDE Semantic Data Model. In Proc. IEEE Conference on Data Engineering. Los Angeles.

Cline, Terry, Hal Abelson, and Warren Harris. 1988. Symbolic Computation and the Analysis, Design, and Simulation of Control Systems. Third AI and Simulation Workshop. AAAI. St. Paul, Minnesota.

Cohen, Philip R., Douglas B. Moran, and Fernando Pereira. 1988. SHOPTALK: An Integrated Interface for Factory Information and Operation. SRI International. Artificial Intelligence Center.

Fishwick, Paul A. 1988a. Automating the Transition from Lumped Models to Base Models. In Proc. of the AI and Simulation Conference, The Society for Computer Simulation. Orlando, Florida.

Fishwick, Paul A. 1988b. A Study of Terminology and Issues in Qualitative Simulation. Simulation. December (To be published).

Gage, S. H. and D. L. Haynes. 1975. Emergence Under Natural and Manipulated Conditions of Tetrastichus julis, an Introduced Larval Parasite of the Cereal Leaf Beetle, with Reference to Regional Population Management. Environmental Entomology 4(3):425-434.

Heidorn, George E. 1974. English as a Very High Level Language for Simulation Programming. In Proc. Symposium on Very High Level Languages. SIGPLAN Notices (April). Pages 91-100.

Khoshnevis, Behrokh, and Wanda Austin. 1987. A Natural Language Interface for Simulation of Multistage Production Distribution Systems. In Second Workshop on AI an Simulation. AAAI. Seattle, Washington.

Ksiezyk, Tomasz, and Ralph Grishman. 1987. Equipment Simulation for Language Understanding. PROTEUS Project Memorandum #11. Department of Computer Science. Courant Institute of Mathematical Sciences. New York University.

Milsum, John H. 1966. Biological Control Systems Analysis. McGraw-Hill.

Patel-Schneider, Peter F., Ronald J. Brachman, and Hector J. Levesque. 1984. ARGON: Knowledge Representation meets Information Retrieval. Fairchild Technical Report No. 654. Fairchild Laboratory for Artificial Intelligence Research.

Reddy, Ramana Y.V., Mark S. Fox, Nizwer Husain, and Malcolm McRoberts. 1986. The Knowledge-Base Simulation System. IEEE Software, 3(2):26-37.

Rozenblit, Jerzy W., Suleyman Sevinc, and Bernard P. Zeigler. 1986. Knowledge-Based Design of LANs Using System Entity Structure Concepts. Proc. 1986 Winter Simulation Conference. J. Wilson, J. Henriksen, S. Roberts (eds.).

Sowa, John F. 1984. Conceptual Structures: Information Processing in Mind and Machine. Addison Wesley.

Wilkerson, G.G, J. W. Mishoe, J. W. Jones, J. L. Stimac, W. G. Boggess, and D. Swaney. 1983. SICM: Soybean Integrated Crop Management Model: Model Description and User's Guide, Version 4.2, Agricultural Engineering Department Research Report AGE-1. University of Florida, Gainesville, FL. 32611.

Zeigler, Bernard P. 1984. Multi-Fascetted Modelling and Discrete Event Simulation. Academic Press.

Advances in AI and Simulation
© 1989 By The Society for Computer
Simulation International
ISBN 0-911801-50-2

Application of an AI simulation tool in the design of a manufacturing process

Nancy S. Skooglund
Westinghouse
Productivity and Quality Center
P. O. Box 160
Pittsburgh, PA 15230-0160

and

Adam C. Peck
Westinghouse
Manufacturing Systems and Technology Center
Mail Stop 6170
9200 Berger Road
Columbia, MD 21046-1602

ABSTRACT

A model is a description of a system that includes both the system's structure and its behavior. The structural aspect represents the system's components and the relationships between them while the behavioral aspect represents how the system's state changes. Simulation provides an understanding of how a system's behavior emerges from the behavior of its interrelated components.

The knowledge-based approach to modeling and simulation includes a number of methodologies directed at representing knowledge: object-oriented programming, frame-based representation, and rule-based reasoning. This artificial intelligence-based approach to simulation provides an environment in which models are rapidly developed and easily extended and understood.

This paper focuses on the use and modification of a knowledge-based simulation system known as SimKit to effect an optimal design of a manufacturing process. After a description of the modeling and simulation software used, an analysis is presented on how the simulation software was modified to model a specific material handling concept in a robotic workstation assembly manufacturing system. The paper provides conclusions of performing this type of analysis and gives advantages and disadvantages of this modeling approach.

1.0 INTRODUCTION

Designing a manufacturing process for optimum low cost and high quality is a challenging task in the continuing goal of being a leader at the competitive edge in manufacturing. Gaining a competitive edge in manufacturing is a strong driver in the current Westinghouse business climate.

Many software/hardware tools are available to help the designer. One of these tools is simulation modeling. Computer simulation modeling provides a cost-effective method for analysis of several approaches or scenarios for manufacturing a lower cost, higher quality product.

1.1 Problem Description

Some of the parts used in products at the Westinghouse Electronic Systems Group are high volume and high cost components. An analysis for the design and producibility of one of these parts was completed and the recommended system included a scenario using robotic workstations and a specialized material handling system. Simulation modeling was used to analyze the parameters of the proposed material handling system and recommend an optimal system.

Specifically, the question was asked, "How many parts should be moved from one workstation to another in a tray for optimal behavior?" The material handling scheme was called a 'tray shuttle' and the

quantity of product per tray was treated as an unknown parameter. The modeling of the system and the subsequent analysis using simulation is the topic of this paper.

1.2 Outline

This paper focuses on the use and modification of an artificial intelligence-based simulation system known as SimKit to effect an optimal design of a manufacturing process. The second section describes the modeling and simulation software that is used and how it was customized for the present model.

The third section presents the results of the simulation. The last section provides conclusions of performing this type of analysis and gives the advantages and disadvantages of this modeling approach.

2.0 MODELING AND SIMULATION SOFTWARE

The simulations were performed using the SimKit software package from IntelliCorp. SimKit is a discrete event simulation tool that includes artificial intelligence (AI) capabilities. It is built on KEE (Knowledge Engineering Environment), which is a general purpose expert systems development system, also from IntelliCorp. SimKit runs on various computers, including Symbolics, Texas Instruments Explorer, and SUN.

Some of the key features of SimKit are:

- Frame-based knowledge representation. All objects in the model are represented as separate entities, or frames. A frame can have any number of attributes, or slots, and each slot can have any number of values. Names of frames and slots are user-specifiable, with no practical restriction on length, and a slot value can be a number, a list, a function, another frame, and so on. Frames are organized into hierarchies, and a child frame inherits default slots and values from its parents. This flexible representation scheme supports development of an easily understandable model, since objects are defined in terms that the user understands. In addition, the flexibility supports development of sophisticated models where new types of objects and their behavior need to be added to the system.

- Rules. Heuristic knowledge, or "rules of thumb," can be encoded in the system using if/then rules. Among the areas where rules can be applied are the control of model behavior during simulation and intelligent post-simulation analysis.

- Object-oriented programming. Because slots can take on values that are functions or include procedural information, slots can represent object behavior in addition to simple declarative information. Objects in the system can interact by "sending messages" to other objects, causing the methods (functions) associated with an object to be executed. This feature results in significant flexibility and extensibility of models.

Graphical model creation. The process of creating a simulation model makes use of a mouse and menu interface, with icons representing the various machines and resources. To create a model the user clicks the mouse on a machine icon to select it, and then moves the mouse to the desired position in the model and clicks again. This places a new machine of that type in the new model. Machine connections are also made by using the mouse. This interface allows the user to quickly and easily create the simulation model.

- Model verification. A model may be verified using several system features:

Valueclass	- specifying types of values which slots may have
Rules	- user-specified rules which, for example, can check inter-object dependencies.
Methods	- user-specified functions for checking model validity.

2.1 QLIB

SimKit is a general purpose simulation tool for queueing applications. The QLIB simulation library contains the basic system functionality. Model objects are defined in terms of the following frames:

Servers	- machines or work stations.
Queues	- groups of items waiting to use servers. Can be FIFO (first-in, first-out) or LIFO (last-in, first-out).
Items	- parts or orders to be processed.
Tasks	- operations to be performed on parts. Includes times--setup, processing, teardown, and transfer times. Can be fixed length duration or variable length.
Sources	- objects that control where items enter the system and the rate of their entry.
Sinks	- data collection points where items exit the system.

Model data, such as processing times, can be represented using random number generators for statistical purposes. The types of distributions which are available include: uniform, exponential, Poisson, normal, lognormal, and step generators. Users can also specify their own generators using functions.

Simulation progresses through the scheduling of events onto a calendar, and the execution of those events. Each event includes the time at which it is to be executed, an object which is the focus of the event, the event type, and any additional arguments as needed. Generic event types include:

Generation	of a new item at a source
Arrival	of an item at a queue, server, or sink
Start	of an item's activity
Completion	of an item's activity
Departure	of an item from a source, queue, server, or sink

These events are represented as methods, or slots

which have functions as their values, on each of the various simulation model objects. Through the use of object-oriented programming, the same message can be sent to two different objects, and each object will respond with the behavior that is appropriate to itself.

2.2 MFGLIB

SimKit's queueing simulation capabilities provide a good base of features from which to build simulation applications. But since SimKit is a general purpose system, MFGLIB, a manufacturing-oriented library, was developed in SimKit by the project team. MFGLIB was created by using menu commands to generate a sublibrary of QLIB. Objects in MFGLIB are related to default objects in QLIB, but their behavior is specialized for the manufacturing environment through the use of LISP functions. Following are the different features in MFGLIB:

Batch Servers	- work stations which process an entire group of orders or parts at the same time, for example ovens.
Shared Resources	- additional resources which must be available to process an order at a work station - tools, fixtures, etc.
Assembly Tasks	- several different parts are assembled together at a station, with only one part resulting as output.
Rework	- test or inspection stations may determine that a part needs rework and must have its routing altered for additional processing.
Machine Failure	- represents random station breakdowns and repair.
Station Yield	- input by user, controls what percentage of items processed at a station are acceptable.
Statistics	- more detailed model simulation results than standard SimKit. Includes the following measures:

Stations:
utilization
down time percentage
average processing time per item
number of items processed
number of items scrapped
umber of station breakdowns
average queue length (over time)
average queue wait time per item (over time)
maximum queue length
maximum queue wait time
Top level:
number of items completed
number of items scrapped
average processing time per item
average throughput time per item
average rework time per item
number of machine breakdowns

2.3 Customization of System for Trays

The detail required in simulating the tray shuttle material handling system necessitates additional modeling capability beyond the generic MFGLIB. Another simulation library was created as a sublibrary of MFGLIB, in order to include this feature. This section describes the new library.

2.3.1 Background

The standard SimKit approach to items moving through a system does not consider the availability of a resource to perform the move. It assumes that any resources required for the move are available when the item finishes processing at a station and is ready to move.

Another feature of SimKit which differs from the tray shuttle model is the use of queues to hold items before stations can process them. In the tray system the trays themselves represent both the material transport mechanism and the queues at stations.

2.3.2 Approach

The tray library is built as a sublibrary of MFGLIB by creating new objects which are subclasses of MFGLIB objects. The default behavior of these new objects is modified as needed by defining new attributes and methods (functions) for the objects. The standard SimKit event types are used (item generation, arrival, start, complete, departure), but an item or station may change what it does when a given event is executed.

As might be expected, the major new object in the tray library is called TRAYS. It represents the generic attributes for a tray, such as:

Contents	- the items currently on the tray
Location	- station where the tray is currently residing
Maximum Quantity	- largest number of items that tray can hold
Possible Locations	- all stations which may use the tray
Function	- indicates whether the tray is currently functioning as an INPUT tray (containing items to be processed at a station), or an OUTPUT tray (holding items after they have completed processing at a station, and then moving them to the next station)

Other objects in the library have new or changed slots and values.

2.3.3 Simulation Events

Changes to system flow will be described in terms of changes to events, since the execution of events controls what happens during simulation.

1. <u>Generation of Items at a Source.</u> Instead of generating items one at a time, the system generates enough items to fill all the output trays at the source. When a tray is filled it is moved to the next station (via the scheduling of departure and arrival events), and the source will start generating items to fill the next tray, if one is available. If no trays are available at the source it will wait until an empty tray returns. Thus the timing of generating new items at a source differs from the standard (non-tray) approach where items arrive one at a time based on the inter-arrival rate specified by the user.

2. <u>Departure of a Tray from a Source, Station, or Sink.</u> The tray is removed from the source, station, or sink's contents. If the source, station, or sink has other trays which it can now process, it will do so. When a tray departs from

a sink, data is collected from all the items in the tray for simulation results calculations, and then the items themselves are deleted. This event remains essentially the same as the standard SimKit departure event.

3. <u>Arrival of a Tray at a Source.</u> This event occurs when a station has processed all the items on an input tray that came from a source, and then sends the tray back to the source where it originated. When the tray arrives at the source, the source will start filling the tray again, if it is not already working on another tray.

4. <u>Arrival of a Tray at a Station.</u> If the station is available (i.e. not busy, and has at least one non-empty input tray and one non-full output tray), a start activity event is scheduled for the first item in the input tray. If the task to be performed is an assembly task, the start activity event will not be scheduled unless there are input trays which contain all of the appropriate parts for assembly.

5. <u>Arrival of a Tray at a Sink.</u> Departure events are scheduled for all the items in the tray, and departure and arrival events are scheduled for the tray to return to the previous station.

6. <u>Start of an Item's Activity at a Station.</u> A completion event is scheduled for the item. If the task to be done is an assembly task, the necessary items are consolidated at this point. This event is similar to the standard SimKit start activity event.

7. <u>Completion of an Item's activity at a Station.</u> The item may be good or bad, depending on station yield (input to model). If the item is bad it is scrapped and leaves the system. If it is good, it is moved from the station's input tray to the output tray. If this causes either the input tray to become empty, or the output tray to become full, or both, the tray(s) will be scheduled to depart the station and arrive at the appropriate upstream or downstream station. Otherwise, a start activity event will be scheduled for the next item in the input tray, based on the same criteria used when a tray arrives at the station.

3.0 SIMULATION RUNS AND RESULTS

In order to run the simulation, a model of the desired manufacturing scenario must be created from the simulation library. This model contains details of the work stations, parts, routings, times, yields, failure rates, etc. For the tray shuttle system, one of the critical input factors is tray capacity. Key output measures to be examined include:

number of parts completed
average time in system per part
work in process (WIP)
station utilization

Four simulation runs were made, each for the same process duration (five 8-hour days) but with varying tray sizes: 1, 5, 15, and 30. Elapsed time for runs varied from 1.5 hours to 4 hours, depending on tray size. The runs were then compared based on the various output measures. Figure 1 shows a graph of number completed over time for one 8-hour day for each scenario. The options with tray sizes of 15 and 30 both produced the greatest number of parts. Average time in system is given in the table below.

Time in system consists of processing time, transport time, and wait time. Processing time per part was 5.8 minutes, and total transport time per tray was 0.5 minute. Wait time was due to either station failure or bottlenecks in the system. As expected, greater tray sizes produced longer waiting times for parts to be completed. Figure 2 illustrates work in process over time for one day of simulation time. Again, work in process levels were consistently higher for larger tray sizes. Finally, figure 3 indicates work station utilization for each scenario. Utilizations were at their highest for the scenarios with tray sizes of 15 and 30. The following table show a summary of the simulation results for the different runs.

	Tray Size (number of parts per tray)			
	1	5	15	30
Number of parts completed daily	408	440	450	450
Average time in system (mins.)	6.8	32.9	96.6	191.4
Average WIP	6.3	30.5	96.6	172.2

Measures for number of parts completed and station utilization indicate that the options with tray sizes of 15 or 30 are preferred over the other two, and the optimum scenario is that with tray size of 15, since it has a lower level of work in process and a shorter length of time in system per part.

4.0 CONCLUSIONS

This paper presents the process of adapting a simulation tool for representing a manufacturing system using tray shuttles for material holding and transport. The project team found the tool effective in developing the model representation to the detail required for the design team's needs, and in providing the output information for analysis in a usable form.

It should be noted that the simulation runs which provided data for this paper were initial runs of intentionally short duration. When the output of the simulation will be used to make decisions it is important to make many runs with varying input distributions, and to be sure that each run continues for an extended length of simulation time. These considerations will help to ensure statistically valid model output.

The remainder of this section discusses the advantages and disadvantages of the simulation tool compared to non-AI simulation packages.

4.1 Advantages

The ability to use if/then rules allows expert knowledge to be simply encoded in the simulation model. Rule-based reasoning can be used during the simulation for intelligent model behavior, and both

Figure 1: Number Completed over Time

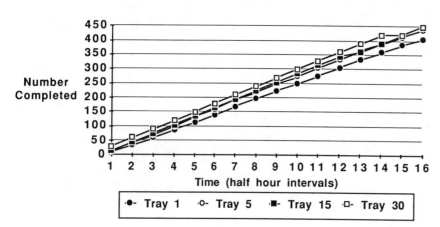

Figure 2: Work in Process over Time

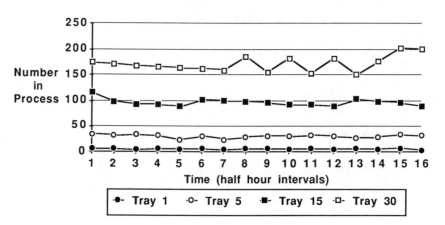

Figure 3: Workstation Utilization vs. Tray Size

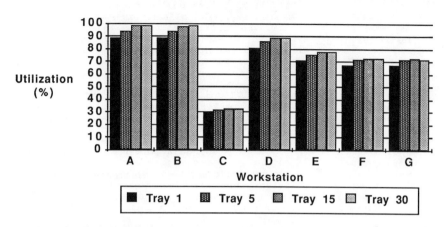

before and after simulation runs. Although this feature has not been used by the project team yet, plans are underway to develop an expert analysis module to analyze the simulation output results and provide suggestions to the user on modifying the model configuration to achieve the optimum.

The flexibility of the tool's knowledge representation capabilities supports the development of sophisticated simulation models. Although other simulation tools have similar flexibility in some aspects, the combination of frame-based representation, object-oriented programming, and rule-based reasoning supports development of structured, modular, consistent models that can be easily modified and extended.

4.2 Disadvantages

Because the underlying software language for the simulation tool is LISP, modifications must also be written in LISP, although C code is also supported via an optional software integration package. This requires specialized training for the simulation library developer. In addition, the tool runs on a limited set of hardware, including LISP computers, which are not part of the mainstream hardware already installed in many locations. The cost of the supporting hardware and software for the system can be prohibitive when compared with non-AI simulation tools which are cheaper and run on more standard hardware.

4.3 Simulation Tool Selection

If faced with the decision today to select a simulation tool for the same application, the project team might not select SimKit. But because the investment had already been made in the past, the system was available, and people who had been trained in the use of the system were available, the team decided to use the tool. The tool does have the advantage of being able to easily incorporate rule-based reasoning in the simulation. An example of this would be the integration of the simulation system with a knowledge-based scheduling system. Simulation could be used to test the validity of the scheduling system output, which would then automatically feed back information to the scheduler to guide the next scheduling runs. This type of application would be greatly benefitted by using a simulation tool with rule-based capabilities.

REFERENCES
Stelzner, M.; J. Dynis; and F. Cummins. 1987. "The SimKit System: Knowledge-Based Simulation and Modeling Tools in KEE." An IntelliCorp Technical Article. IntelliCorp, Mountain View, CA.

Advances in AI and Simulation
© 1989 By The Society for Computer
Simulation International
ISBN 0-911801-50-2

A temporal database for realtime training systems

S. D. Lang

Department of Computer Science
University of Central Florida, Orlando, Florida 32816

Richard E. Reynolds

Human Factors Division
Naval Training Systems Center, Orlando, Florida 32826

ABSTRACT

Realtime simulation systems have been used extensively in the military to provide low-cost simulated environments for training purposes. Students practice on the training devices to get a preview before using the real equipments. Also, students practice to retain proficiency and minimize skill degradation. One important component of a simulation system is a database which maintains the states of the system during training sessions. The database keeps records of the status of various components of the system and the commands issued by the student. In order to provide feedback to the student for error correction, it is essential to have access to the database and detect students' action, or lack of action. This paper describes the design of a temporal database in a naval tactical warfare training testbed system. The database stores the complete history of the training session, and supports a query language interface for a user (instructor or student) to reason about temporal relationship among occurring events.

INTRODUCTION

Realtime simulation systems have been used extensively in the military to provide low-cost simulated environments for training purposes. Students practice on the training devices to get a preview before using the real equipments. Also, students practice to retain proficiency and minimize skill degradation. There is a growing demand for training performance assessment in order to tailor the training scenarios to increase student proficiency in areas where the student appears deficient. Also, as modern weapon and sensor systems become ever more complex, there is a trend towards reducing demands placed upon the instructors and automating part of instructor functions in training scenarios (Narotam and Behnke 1985).

Artificial intelligence and expert system techniques have been proposed and evaluated for incorporation into training systems, particularly in the area of human decision-making such as training in warfare operations and tactics (Daniel 1985). Techniques have been implemented to automate instructor functions (Narotam and Behnke 1985, Williams and Lang 1988), these include (1) performance monitoring and intelligent computer aided instructions which intelligently select appropriate student exercises, (2) automated expository feedback which utilizes a rule base to assess students' error by exposing specific preconditions that were not attended to, and (3) intelligent platforms which utilize expert systems for modeling intelligent behavior of hostile (or friendly) forces.

Central to a simulated training system is a database which maintains the system states during training sessions. The database keeps records of the status of various components of the system, events and exception conditions, and the commands issued by the student. In order to monitor the behavior of the intelligent platforms, and monitor the student performance to provide expository feedback, it is essential to make this database explicitly available, for interfacing with other training system modules or for direct student and instructor queries. An interface to the database should provide access to the complete history of the training session, and should provide logic to reason about the temporal relationship among occurring events. A temporal database is designed for this purpose. The following sections describe a temporal database in a naval tactical warfare training testbed system. In particular, a user query interface is specified that allows the student and instructor to query the system status, and occurring events and processes in the simulated environment.

TEMPORAL DATABASE

As alluded to in the previous section, realtime simulation systems are used extensively in military training. What makes a system realtime? A common definition of realtime means "fast," in the sense that the computer has the ability to guarantee a response after a fixed time has elapsed (Laffey *et al.* 1988). That is, a realtime system can recognize and respond to external events in a timely fashion. In addition, a realtime system models the real world in a realistic fashion. For example, if a submarine is ordered to dive for 100 ft., the simulation system would calculate the kinematics of the submarine and model its change of depth accordingly. Therefore, a realtime system presents to the students an environment in which facts and data need to be interpreted in the context of time, and causal relationships among events and entities are embedded in the temporal information.

Traditionally, the snapshots of a simulation system are recorded in a database, indexed by the time at which the snapshots are taken. This "snapshot database" is used in calculating the performance indicators and tactical variables, such as counter-detection versus range and solution accuracy versus time, in order to provide feedback to the students (Hammell 1983, McDonald *et al.* 1983). Also, the database allows the recorded training sessions be replayed for postgame analysis and alternative tactics illustration.

In order to analyze the dynamic aspects of the evolving simulated environment, we propose to incorporate a temporal logic into the snapshot database, resulting in a temporal database (Allen 1984, McDermott 1982). The temporal database provides an interface to query the facts and properties of the environment at specified time instants, and provides a logic to reason about the occurrences of events and processes. In the database, events describe an activity that involves an outcome and usually occurs instantaneously, such as a helicopter activating a Radar. Processes refer to some activity not involving a culmination or anticipated result and usually occurring over a period of time, such as a helicopter performing evasive maneuvers. The temporal database, providing a complete history of system snapshots and an interface to reason about occurring events and processes, has great potential to enhance current design of training systems. In the next section, we will describe a prototype temporal query language used in a naval tactical warfare training testbed system.

A PROTOTYPE INTERFACE

A training testbed system is used at the Human Factors Laboratory of the Naval Training Systems Center, Orlando, Florida, to develop and evaluate instructional technologies for training Navy officers making tactical decisions in a multi-threat environment. The display system consists of a geographical plot for displaying the platforms, a number of alphanumeric terminals for displaying various status information, and a touch-sensitive plasma panel for inputing commands from the student or instructor. A training scenario may contain a surface ownship, a friendly helicopter performing Over-The-Horizon targeting, a hostile surface ship, and a hostile submarine. Certain platforms (e.g. helicopter and submarine) can be intelligent, in the sense that they are driven by software that exhibits meaningful tactics.

We designed and implemented a prototype interface system that supports a temporal query language. The system runs in an off-line mode and accepts training session data previously recorded on the testbed system for analysis. The interface system is implemented in Turbo Prolog running on an IBM PC. The declarative nature of Prolog allows the programmer to describe problems in terms of facts and rules (Clocksin and Mellish 1981). In our training scenarios, the snapshots form the facts, and Prolog rules are used to parse the user queries and deduce appropriate answers.

The query language supports three types of queries: (1) status queries that ask the status of the system at a given time, (2) time queries that ask when certain event or process occurs, and (3) yes/no queries that ask if certain facts are true at a given time (or in a time interval). The syntax of the query language is described below, using the notation of the Backus-Naur form (Aho *et al.* 1986), each followed by a short annotation.

     (1) F --> speed(p) | location(p) | course(p) | action(p)
          | sensor(p) | distance(p1, p2) | detecting_
          sensor(p1, p2) | detected_sensor(p1, p2)
        (F specifies the speed, location, course, or action
        of platform p, or sensor status of p, distance
        between two platforms p1 and p2, sensors of p1
        detecting p2, or sensors of p2 being detected by p1)

     (2) E --> F=value | detect(p1, p2)
        (E specifies an event when function F has certain
        value, or when platform p1 detects platform p2)

     (3) P --> change_speed(p) | change_course(p)
        (P specifies a process when platform p is changing
        its speed or course)

     (4) U --> E | P
        (U stands for either event E or process P)

     (5) W --> when U | before U | after U
        (W specifies a time when, before, or after U happens)

     (6) S --> ?F | ?FW
        (S specifies a status query that asks the value of
        function F at current time, or at given time W)

     (7) T --> ?U
        (T specifies a time query that asks the time of U)

     (8) Y --> !U | !UW
        (Y specifies a yes/no query that asks whether U
        happens at current time, or at given time W)

     (9) Q --> S | T | Y
        (Q specifies that there are three types of queries,
        status S, time T, and yes/no Y)

Some query examples and their English interpretation are as follows:

    State value queries:
        ?sensor(surface ship) when detect(surface ship,
          missile)
        (What was the surface ship's sensor status when
        the surface ship detected the missile?)

        ?action(surface ship) when action(helicopter)=
        visual
        (What was the surface ship's action when the
        helicopter was performing a visual?)

    Time value queries:
        ?action(helicopter)=visual
        (When did the helicopter perform a visual?)

    Yes/no queries:
        !detect(helicopter, surface ship) when detect
        (surface ship, missile)
        (Did the helicopter detect the surface ship when
        the surface ship detected the missile?)

CONCLUSION

In this report, we considered realtime simulation systems used in military training. We argued that in order to enhance training effectiveness and alleviate demands placed on the instructor, it is essential to provide an interface to allow access to the training system status and performance histories. The interface could be used for post-game analysis and playback, and it could be used as an on-line decision support system. Because of the unique characteristics of realtime simulation systems, this interface must be capable of reasoning temporal relationships among occurring events and processes. We implemented a prototype interface system using Prolog which demonstrated that a simple structured query language could be designed for this purpose. Currently, the prototype system runs in an off-line mode. Further work is planned to enhance the query language to provide more detailed temporal reasoning. Also, work is planned to implement an efficient, on-line temporal database interface.

ACKNOWLEDGEMENTS

The research of the first author was supported by a grant from the Institute for Simulation and Training of the University of Central Florida, IST-20-21-050, 1988.

REFERENCES

Aho, A. V.; Sethi, R.; and Ullman, J. D. 1986. *Compilers -- Principles, Techniques, and Tools*. Addison-Wesley, Reading, Massachusetts.

Allen, J. F. 1984. "Towards a General Theory of Action and Time." *Artificial Intelligence* 23: 123-154.

Clocksin, W. and Mellish, C. 1981. *Programming in Prolog*. Springer-Verlag, New York.

Daniel, D. 1985. "AI Applications for Training -- Seeking the Pragmatic Middle Ground." In *Proceedings of the 7th Interservice/Industry Training Equipment Conference* (Orlando, FL, Nov. 19-21). 51-57.

Hammell, T. J. 1983. "Training Assistance Technology." In *Proceedings of the 5th Interservice/Industry Training Equipment Conference* (Washington, D. C., Nov. 14-16). 181-193.

Laffey, T. J.; Cox, P. A.; Schmidt, J. L.; Kao, S. M.; and Read, J. Y. 1988. "Real-Time Knowledge-Based Systems." *AI Magazine* (Spring). 27-45.

McDermott, D. 1982. "A Temporal Logic for Reasoning about Processes and Plans." *Cognitive Science* 6. 101-155.

McDonald, L. B.; Waldrop, G. P.; and Lambert, E. Y. 1983. "Human Engineering Analysis for the Battle Group Tactical Trainer." In *Proceedings of the 5th Interservice/Industry Training Equipment Conference* (Washington, D. C., Nov. 14-16). 171-180.

Narotam, M. and Behnke, D. 1985. "Performance Monitoring and Intelligent Training." In *Proceedings of the 7th Interservice/Industry Training Equipment Conference* (Orlando, FL, Nov. 19-21). 43-50.

Williams, K. E. and Lang, S. 1988. "Artificial Intelligence for Embedded Training Environments." In *Proceedings of the Conference on AI and Simulation* (Orlando, FL, Apr. 18-21). SCS, San Diego, CA., 126-131.

Advances in AI and Simulation
© 1989 By The Society for Computer
Simulation International
ISBN 0-911801-50-2

Intelligent agents in the simulation of manufacturing systems

Gajanana Nadoli* and John Biegel**
Intelligent Simulation Laboratory
Department of Industrial Engineering and Management Systems
University of Central Florida
Orlando, FL 32816
(407) 275-2111

ABSTRACT

The Control Level functions in a manufacturing system provide the short term and real-time decision making necessary for a smooth operation. We propose a means of incorporating these functions within a simulation in the form of intelligent agents. These agents are represented as objects. They have a set of goals, a knowledge base, an abstraction mechanism, and structural and taxonomical relations with other components of the manufacturing system. The abstraction mechanism of an intelligent agent provides simplified descriptions of the events within the simulation. These simplified descriptions trigger the control actions of an agent. We discuss the necessary characteristics of intelligent agents based on this framework.

INTRODUCTION

The operation of modern manufacturing systems involves a complex interaction of different subsystems. On a broad basis, two distinct levels can be identified within a manufacturing system: a Control Level, and a Performance Level. The decisions provided by the Control Level, either through computers or humans, drive the operation of the Performance Level. The Performance Level consists of production facilities where the actual production activity takes place.

We propose a means of incorporating the Control Level functions in the simulation of manufacturing systems. This involves explicit representation of the Control Level in the form of intelligent agents. The material flow at the Performance Level can be viewed as a system of queues and modelled accordingly. The traditional simulation

----

* Graduate Research Assistant
** Professor and Director, Intelligent
   Simulation Training System (ISTS) Project.

models incorporate the variations caused by Control Level intervention in an aggregate fashion by way of probabilistic branching and/or queueing disciplines. By explicit representation of the Control Level, the decision making processes are simulated in greater detail.

The intelligent agents in a manufacturing simulation provide the short term and real-time decision making processes involved. These agents act based on an abstracted view of the Performance Level. The abstraction process provides simplified descriptions of the events at the Performance Level. These simplified descriptions are the triggering conditions for the actions of intelligent agents. Some of the situations that are caused by or require intervention from intelligent agents are: shortages of parts, machine breakdowns, changes in priorities, and changes in process plans.

We base our representation of the simulation model on an object-oriented approach. An overview of previous research related to representing intelligent agents is presented. The overall framework in which the intelligent agents operate in the simulation of a manufacturing system is described. We concentrate on the required characteristics of the intelligent agents, their structure, and their operation. The role of abstraction in the reasoning process of intelligent agents is briefly outlined.

HIERARCHICAL STRUCTURE OF MANUFACTURING SYSTEMS

The manufacturing systems are organized based on a hierarchical structure. An example system with such a structure is given in figure 1.

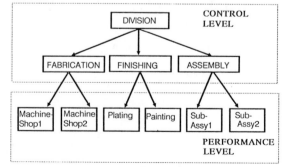

Figure 1. Hierarchical Structure of Manufacturing Systems

In the above example, a manufacturing Division has three major sections: Fabrication, Finishing, and Assembly. Each of these sections has subsections. In this example, machine-shop-1, machine-shop-2, plating, painting, subassembly-1, and subassembly-2 constitute the Performance Level. The Division and the Fabrication, Finishing, and Assembly sections constitute the Control Level. In a simulation model, the Performance Level entities include machines, material handling equipment, and the parts that flow through the system. The Control Level entities in a simulation model include functions such as shop-management (at subsection level), product engineering, scheduling, and progress monitoring (at division level). These functions act independently and they communicate with each other. They can be modelled as a collection of intelligent agents which work together to control the operation of the Performance Level.

Representing the hierarchical structure of a manufacturing system with intelligent agents provides following advantages:
- a) incorporating the hierarchy which is inherent in the system,
- b) analyzing the effect of Control Level functions of the system on the Performance Level,
- c) representing the system at varying levels of abstraction, and
- d) providing answers to qualitative questions such as "Why ?", and "How ?", in addition to "What if?" questions.

There are some issues that have to be addressed in representing the Control Level functions in the form of intelligent agents:
- a) What is the "grain size" of the intelligent agents ?
  For example, the production planning is done by a group of people. Do we consider each member of this team as an agent or the whole group as one agent ?
- b) How are these entities represented ?
- c) What is the interaction of these agents with the lower levels ?

In our view, representing the individuals involved in a function as independent agents would result in a model which is too fine-grained in structure. Representing each of the Control Level functions as a chunk rather than a conglomerate of entities eliminates the problem of dealing with the human element explicitly. Only the collective effect of the function involved is taken into account in the simulation model. This aggregation provides a simplification in representation. The representation and interaction aspects of these agents are discussed in later sections.

LANGUAGES FOR REPRESENTING HIERARCHICAL STRUCTURE

The traditional simulation languages do not provide the expressiveness, modular representation, and control structure necessary to build models with multiple levels. Object oriented languages are well suited for this purpose. In an object oriented approach all the attributes related to an object are encapsulated in a single structure, and the inheritance mechanisms provide the means of describing generic classes of objects. Since object orientation is very close to the way people perceive systems, the development of complex multilevel models and their subsequent mapping to computer code becomes easier. Simulation languages such as ROSS (McArthur et al. 1986) and KBS (Reddy et al. 1986) are based on this approach.

General theories of simulation modelling, and theories of hierarchical representations in simulation modelling have been described in (Zeigler, 1984). Chaudhury and Rao (1988) describe an object-oriented manufacturing simulation of a FMS cell where the resource allocation is handled dynamically. Bond and Soetarman (1988) report an implementation of multilevel abstractions based on predicate logic.

The concept of independently acting agents with varying degrees of intelligence has been reported in Distributed Artificial Intelligence (DAI) literature. DAI is a subfield of AI which deals with the problems of representing multiple intelligent systems that interact with each other (Gasser et al. 1987). The Control Level of manufacturing systems consists of independently acting functions communicating with each other. Hence, the experience with DAI representation techniques is very useful in the simulation modelling of the Control Level functions. The participants of the Sixth Workshop on DAI came to a common definition of different dimensions (see Table 1. for a partial list) of representation of these agents (Huns, 1987).

Dimension	Spectrum of Values	
Agent Dynamism	Fixed Dynamic Autodidactic	Teachable
Agent Autonomy	Controlled Independent	Interdependent
Agent Resources	Restricted	Ample

Table 1. Agent Dimensions

Some relevant aspects of three DAI systems are enumerated next. All these systems have their conceptual roots in object oriented languages. These systems are:
- a) Multi-Agent Computing System (MACE: Gasser et al. 1987),
- b) Activation Framework (AF: Green, 1987), and
- c) EFIGIE (Pattison et al. 1987).

119

a) Multi-Agent Computing System (MACE)

MACE provides knowledge representation and reasoning capabilities for computational units (known as agents) which run in parallel and communicate via messages. MACE agents are self contained, active objects. These agents exist in an environment. They contain knowledge, they sense their environment, and they take actions. Some of the important attributes of MACE agents are: Roles (self, creator, organization-member, my-organization, co-worker), Skills, Goals, Plans, Acquaintances, Local Knowledge (local rules), Memory (local working-memory), Behaviors (procedures), and Model of the world (of itself and other agents). These agents monitor the events using demons and event monitors. The basic structure is similar to objects in other languages.

The MACE agents can be simple or complex. A simple MACE agent may be a production rule, and a complex MACE agent may be a collection of rules. The granularity of agents can thus be controlled. Agents may be organized into structured objects which can respond to particular problems.

b) Activation Framework (AF)

Activation Framework is based on a paradigm of expert objects that communicate by transmitting messages in a manner similar to a community of experts. Some of the AF's ideas were originally from the blackboard architecture of HEARSAY II project (Pattison et al. 1987). Each AF object (AFO) can be considered as a miniature HEARSAY II system with its local blackboard and limited knowledge source procedures. The AFO's are distributed over different processors for achieving parallel processing. The activation of AFO's is done using activation levels which are similar in concept to the certainty factors used in expert systems. An AFO's attributes include name, hypothesis, procedures, local data, input queue, output queue, activation level, threshold level, and time last run. AFOs are attached to higher level structures known as Frameworks. Frameworks are responsible for scheduling the activation of AFOs and providing message transfer mechanisms.

c) EFIGIE

EFIGIE is a language developed for the purpose of instantiating and maintaining large distributed processing networks. The major capability of this language is to specify very complex relations. The organization of network structures is described in terms of their purpose, components, responsibilities of the components, resources of the components, knowledge of components (algorithms, databases, and expertise), and relations between components. The relations between components include communication, authority, location, proximity etc.

In the next section a framework for representing intelligent agents in manufacturing systems is presented. The concepts described in this section are relevant to that framework. Especially, the attributes such as acquaintances, roles, skills, goals, local knowledge, and complex relations are useful in the manufacturing domain.

A FRAMEWORK FOR THE REPRESENTATION OF INTELLIGENT AGENTS

A general framework for modelling of manufacturing systems is shown in Figure 2.

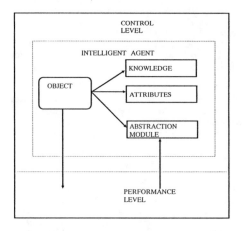

Figure 2. A Representation Framework for Intelligent Agents

In this framework the intelligent agents at higher levels of the system operate on the basis of two functional modes: a) sensing the changes in the lower levels through the process of abstraction, and b) controlling the operation of lower levels through state altering actions. Thus the process of abstraction by these agents is a trigger for the control actions. As mentioned earlier, the typical intelligent agents in the Control Level include shop-level control, scheduling, and progress monitoring. The previous research on abstraction (Bond and Soetarman 1988; Fishwick 1988; McRoberts et. al 1985) deals with the situations where the model of the performance level has to be interpreted/understood by analysts with different points of view. Our approach is to use the concept of abstraction in modelling the control action of intelligent agents. Thus, abstraction is a function used by the agents embedded in the simulation. This function is represented in the form of a separate module attached to the agents. There is an advantage to this approach. Since the abstraction processes are modularized, these modules can also be used as windows to the simulation process. Each of these window should provide the same point of view as that of the agent to whom the abstraction module belongs. For example, consider an abstraction module connected to the intelligent entity representing the shop-level control. This module should also be useful as a window to the simulation for the analyst who wants to study the simulation

120

with a shop-level control viewpoint. The simulation event calendar can also be implemented based on an object-oriented paradigm.

The structural and functional requirements of intelligent agents is discussed next. The issues addressed are communication, abstraction, control, and knowledge.

Communication

The intelligent agents in a simulation are a part of the higher levels of a multilevel structure. The action of these agents is primarily determined by the events on the shopfloor. Some of the examples of such events are: machine breakdowns, part shortages, rush orders, changing priorities, split batches, and part routing. These events are detected by the abstraction modules connected to agents. Such events activate the intelligent agents to take actions that remedy the problems involved. These actions are a part of the reactive mode of operation of these agents. On the other hand, the basic operation of the shopfloor is based on the proactive actions of the intelligent agents. For example, the proactive action of the production engineering department would be to change the process plan of a particular part. This typically is a result of the improved technologies available, and not due to the events on the shopfloor. The proactive action of agents is transmitted to the lower levels where the actual actions are carried out. Thus, the interaction between the multiple levels in a manufacturing system is based on communication of information. The communication from intelligent agents to the lower levels are directives and the communication from lower levels to higher levels are reports. The reports however are interpreted by the abstraction modules.

Abstraction

Abstraction is a fundamental concept in modelling. The real world is represented in an abstract form through a model. The traditional approach has been to develop models at the desired level of detail for a problem at hand. For any new analysis, this approach requires a modelling effort starting from scratch. The previous research on abstraction has concentrated on remedying this situation by providing the capability to view the same model at different levels of abstraction. An abstraction module connected to an agent must be able to incorporate such capabilities.

Process Abstraction: The process abstraction allows the process to be viewed at different levels of detail. This abstraction is closely guided by the structural description of the manufactured products. Each process incorporates the following attributes:
  i) the process-name,
  ii) the time-duration of the process
     (either a constant or a distribution)

and
  iii) the subprocesses (list of subprocesses and corresponding time durations).

In a simulation model, the time required for a process is incorporated as a delay on the simulation clock. If there is a need to consider the details of a process, it is represented as a series of subprocesses, each with a specific time delay distribution. Otherwise, the process is represented as a single time delay with a specific distribution.

Structural Abstraction: Abstraction over structure can be used to view the system being simulated at different levels of detail. Structure, as mentioned earlier, also guides the process abstraction in the case of manufactured products. The main use of structural abstraction is in system representation. Each system entity (including intelligent agents), incorporates following attributes:
  i) part-of, and
  ii) has-parts

The entity shopfloor-1, (See Figure 1) for example is a part of the entity Fabrication. The entity shopfloor-1 has the names of machines, facilities, and material handling equipment in its has-parts slot. Also, the entity shopfloor-1 has an attribute named trancient-entities. This slot holds the information about the parts that are currently being processed or waiting to be processed on the shopfloor.

Relation Abstraction: The simplest relation abstractions would be for reasoning over classes of objects. The inheritance relations such as is-a and a-kind-of provide such capability. Some of relations between agents are given below:
  i) roles,
  ii) proximity,
  iii) in-communication-with,
  iv) in-control-of, and
  v) is-controlled-by.

Property Abstraction: The property abstraction allows the intelligent agents to consider the same object with multiple viewpoints. An individual part on the shopfloor may be a component of a subassembly. This part also represents certain amount of money locked up as work in progress. The amount is calculated based on the monetary value slot in the object representing that part. Other properties over which the abstraction can be carried out include:
  i) weight,
  ii) criticality,
  iii) failure-rate,
  iv) performance-factor, and
  v) roles.

Control

As mentioned earlier, the intelligent agents are acting independently and are in communication with each other. The actions of and the priorities between the agents is a very important issue in achieving synchronization. The organizational concept that can be applied to represent this prioritization is "span of control." The span of control of the intelligent agents is represented in the form of relations (such as (in-control-of and is-controlled-by) between them. This structure implicitly imposes a prioritization scheme between the agents. Also, the priorities are decided based on the problem being handled.

Knowledge

The embedded knowledge is a major distinction between the intelligent agents and the ordinary entities. Since the major responsibility of the intelligent agents is to respond to situations at the Performance Level, the rule based paradigm appears to be a very natural choice to represent the knowledge. A proposed mechanism for connecting rules to agents is shown in Figure 3.

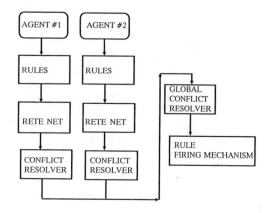

Figure 3. A Mechanism for Connecting Rules to Agents

The rules corresponding to an agent are compiled into a rule network based on the Rete Algorithm. The Rete Algorithm provides one of the most efficient methods for internalizing and interpreting production rules. Each object has its own root node for a rete net. Thus an object's rules are in a form that can be interpreted fast. We propose to use ISTS-IE, an object-oriented implementation of Rete algorithm for this purpose (Nadoli and Biegel 1988). Zalevsky (1988) and Castillo et al (1988) describe mechanisms for embedding rules in a manner consistent with an object-oriented paradigm.

A conflict resolver is responsible for choosing the rule to be fired. This function is implemented as an object in the ISTS-IE. When connecting individual agents with their own rule network, there are two options for implementing the functionality of a Conflict Resolver:
a) a single conflict resolver object which selects the rule to be fired from a global conflict set, or
b) a conflict reslover for each of the intelligent agents (with a local conflict

set) and a global conflict resolver to coordinate these.

In the second case, each of the individual conflict resolvers selects a rule to be fired from its local conflict set. This produces a set of rules. The global conflict resolver chooses the rule to be fired from this set of rules. The actions of the agents can be invoked by means of rule firing, message passing, or demon activations. Rule firing represents the reactive mode of agents whereas message passing and demon activations represent the proactive mode.

CONCLUSIONS

A framework for representing the decision making functions in the simulation of manufacturing systems was presented. Within this framework, a manufacturing system can be described as a hierarchically organized structure with intelligent agents at different levels. The characteristics of the intelligent agents were identified and an object-oriented representation was proposed. The advantages of this approach are twofold:
a) representing decision making functions explicitly provides a vehicle for testing different strategies to be adopted during the operation of the system, and
b) since many systems (other than manufacturing) operate on the basis of a hierarchical structure, the representation paradigms developed in the area of manufacturing are helpful in those areas also.

Currently our focus is on the development of software architecture that can support the concepts presented here.

ACKNOWLEDGEMENTS

This research was carried out using the facilities in the Intelligent Simulation Laboratory at UCF, established for the Intelligent Simulation Training System Project (ISTS). The financial support for the ISTS project comes from the State of Florida through the UCF budget.

REFERENCES

Bond, A.H. and B. Soetarman. 1988. "Multiple Abstraction in Knowledge-Based Simulation." In Proceedings SCS of MultiConference on Artificial Intelligence and Simulation: The Diversity of Applications (San Diego, CA, Feb 3-5):61-66.

Castillo, D.; M. McRoberts; and B. Seik. 1988 "Embedded Expert Systems Improve Model Intelligence In Simulation Experiments." In Proceedings of Summer Simulation Conference (Seattle, July 24-26):591-597.

Chaudhury, A., and H.R. Rao. 1988. "Conceptual Modelling in Computer Integrated Manufacturing Systems." In <u>Proceedings of the Second International Conference on Expert Systems and Leading Edge in Production Planning and Control</u> (Charleston, SC May 3-5):265-276.

Fishwick, P. A. 1988 "The Role of Process Abstraction in Simulation." <u>IEEE Transactions of Systems, Man, and Cybernetics,</u> Vol. 18, No. 1, 18-39.

Gasser, L.; C. Braganza; and N. Herman. 1987. "MACE: A Flexible Testbed for Distributed AI Research." In <u>Distributed Artificial Intelligence</u> (Michael N. Huns, ed.). Morgan Kaufmann, Los Angeles, CA, 119-152.

Green, P. E. 1987 "AF: A Framework for Real-Time Distributed Problem Solving." In <u>Distributed Artificial Intelligence</u> (Michael N. Huns, ed.). Morgan Kaufmann, Los Angeles, CA, 153-175.

Huns, M. N.(ed). 1987. <u>Distributed Artificial Intelligence</u>. Morgan Kaufman, Los Angeles, CA.

McArthur, D.J.; P. Klahr; and S. Narain. 1986. "ROSS: An Object-Oriented Language for Constructing Simulations." In <u>Expert Systems: Techniques, Tools, and Applications."</u> (P. Klahr and D.A. Waterman, eds). Addison-Wesley, Reading, MA, 70-91.

McRoberts, M.; M.S. Fox; and N. Hussain. 1985. "Generating Model Abstraction Scenarios in KBS." In Proceedings of AI, Graphics, and Simulation (San Diego, CA, Feb):29-33.

Nadoli, G., and J. E. Biegel. 1988 "Inferencing In an Intelligent Simulation-Based Training System (ISTS)." In Proceedings of the Southeastern Simulation Conference (Orlando, Oct 17-18):155-159.

Pattison, E.H.; D.D. Corkill; and V. R. Lesser. 1987. "Instantiating Descriptions of Organization Structures." In <u>Distributed Artificial Intelligence</u> (Michael N. Huns, ed.). Morgan Kaufmann, Los Angeles, CA, 59-96.

Reddy, Y.V.R; M.S. Fox; N. Hussain; and M. McRoberts. 1986. "The Knowledge-Based Simulation System." <u>IEEE Software</u> (Mar):26-37.

Zeigler, B.P. 1984. "Multifaceted Modelling Methodology: Grappling With the Irreducible Complexity of Systems." <u>Behavioral Science.</u> Vol. 29, 169-178.

Zalevsky, P. A. 1988. "Knowledge Based Simulation of Manufacturing Facilities." In Proceedings of SCS MultiConference on Artificial Intelligence and Simulation: The Diversity of Applications (San Diego, CA, Feb 3-5): 67-71.

Advances in AI and Simulation
© 1989 By The Society for Computer
Simulation International
ISBN 0-911801-50-2

Hybrid expert system for
beef-forage grazing management

Thomas L. Thompson and Yang Tao
Department of Agricultural Engineering
University of Nebraska
Lincoln, Nebraska 68583-0726

ABSTRACT

A hybrid combination of expert system, database management, and simulation modelling was used to develop a model to assist livestock producers in making pasture grazing management decisions.

Pasture yield was predicted based on pasture species, location, soil type, fertilization level, precipitation, and grazing management. Bi-weekly production of a pasture was determined by distributing the annual pasture yield over the seasonal growth of the species. A rule-based expert system was set up to define the pastures.

Forage demand by a beef animal was estimated based on the animal's age, sex, weight, and milking ability. A set of database management programs was set up to generate the bi-weekly animal inventory and forage demand from generalized producer inputs.

A simulation model was developed to match the pasture supplies and animal forage demand in a time series and project the pasture performance for a specified grazing schedule. Management recommendations on pasture size, pasture stocking rate, animal nutrition, and the earliest starting date for pasture grazing were provided.

INTRODUCTION

One of the most important management aspects to the farmer/rancher is efficient resource management. An efficient production system requires good management of available resources. Many factors related to resource utilization must be properly managed. Balancing forage plant and livestock needs is essential for a beef cattle producer to develop a successful, profitable grazing program (Waller et al, 1986).

The major grazing management decisions include stocking rate, pasture size, grazing schedule and animal nutrition. While making these decisions, many interrelationships about the effect of various management decisions must be understood and balanced. An understanding of how factors such as environment, forage species, and livestock type affect overall performance is necessary to ensure profitable decisions.

Expert systems used in conjunction with database systems and simulation modelling can be an effective technique to represent human expertise and approach livestock-forage balance. The specific knowledge of the experts in the field and their logical decision making power can be organized in an efficient system or knowledge base through computer programs. Users can communicate with the expert system, which will provide proper decisions and recommendations just as the human expert.

The objective of this study was to develop a hybrid expert system with a simulation model to help livestock producers make grazing management decisions. Merging techniques of expert systems, simulation, and databases as a hybrid approach can have more integrated capabilities for building powerful decision support systems (Jones and Beck, 1988). The system has the potential to predict the performance of a year-long forage program and provide recommendations to livestock producers.

AN OVERVIEW

The primary source of knowledge for this development was a Nebraska Extension Circular entitled "A Guide for Planning and Analyzing a Year-Round Forage Program" by Waller et al (1986). This Extension Circular will be referred to as the "Guide" in the following discussion. During development of this model, information in this "Guide" was supplemented with subject matter expertise from specialists from agronomy, animal science, and agricultural engineering. Weekly meetings with this team of domain specialists were used to work on the developmental details.

Throughout the body of this paper, the knowledge is presented as used in the expert system implementation. The representation was based on the background literature in the Guide and the collective expertise of the domain specialists. As needed, the reference literature has been modified and updated for implementation. Each modification was validated in the model to ensure that overall model output was realistic and represented the collective expertise of the research team.

The system was designed to respond like an extension expert in a consultation of how to plan a pasture grazing program with a livestock producer. Expert system techniques in conjunction with a database management system, and simulation modelling were used in the implementation of this Beef-Forage system.

The model consists of three subsystems: Forage, Animal, and Balance. The Forage subsystem uses a rule-based expert system approach to predict pasture production based on the pasture conditions. The Animal subsystem uses a database management system to develop the livestock inventory and estimate animal demand. The Balance subsystem uses the results from the other two subsystems, simulates pasture grazing and balances the pasture production and animal demand. The following sections describe each subsystem. Model implementation details were presented by Tao (1988).

FORAGE SUBSYSTEM

The first step toward development of a model to predict the performance of a beef-forage system was to define the pasture and estimate its productivity. The development efforts were based on the "Guide" (Waller et al, 1986) and recommendations from subject matter experts from this domain.

Pasture Stocking Rate Estimation

The grazing capacity of a pasture is the amount of forage available for grazing; the biological yield potential of the forage resource (Waller et al, 1986). A table of recommended stocking rates for seeded pastures, and seeded annuals provide an estimate of annual forage production. This table was adapted from similar tables developed by the Soil Conservation Service (USDA, 1983) and provide a range of estimates assuming a high level of pasture management. A portion of this table is presented in Table 1.

Pasture season-long production was determined by obtaining suggested pasture stocking rates from the table. These table values were then adjusted for site and environmental conditions and grazing management. Bi-weekly yields were estimated by distributing the annual yield over the growing season according to the growth pattern of the pasture species.

Pasture Yield Potential

Pasture productivity is represented in numbers of Animal Unit Months (AUMs). One AUM is defined as the amount of forage required to sustain a 454 Kg (1000-pound) cow of above average milking ability with a 3 to 4 month old calf for one month. This is equivalent to 309 Kg (680 pounds) of forage dry matter or 341-354 Kg (750-780 pounds) of air-dry forage. From Table 1, pasture productivity is a function of the vegetative zone and soil type. Nebraska is divided into four vegetative zones.

Table 1. Suggested initial recommended stocking rates for two seeded pastures (AUM/acre) (Waller et al, 1986).

Species	Soil Type	I	II	III	IV
		\multicolumn{4}{c}{Vegetative Zone*}			
Smooth brome	Silty lowland	--	2-3	4-5	5-8
	Silty	--	1-3	1-4	2-6
	Limy upland	--	--	2-3	3-5
	Clayey	--	--	2-3	3-4
	Sandy	--	2-3	3-4	4-5
	Sands	--	--	2-3	2-4
Big bluestem	Silty lowland	--	2-3	3-4	4-8
	Silty	--	1-2	1-3	2-6
	Limy upland	--	1	2-3	3-5
	Clayey	--	1	2-3	3-4
	Sandy	--	1-2	3	3-4
	Sands	--	--	2	2-3

* Zones: I = Panhandle, II = West Central, III = Central, and IV = Eastern Nebraska.
Values adapted from the SCS Nebraska Technical Guide (Section II-K). (USDA, 1983).
1 hectare = 2.47 acres

As an example, the productivity for a non-irrigated smooth brome pasture with a silty soil in eastern Nebraska (Zone IV) is 5-15 AUM/hectare (2-6 AUM/acre) per year. The range represents a variation of pasture conditions. Levels of fertilization, precipitation, soil erosion, weed competition, and grazing management are used to define production within this range. The higher value was assumed to represent excellent growing conditions.

Multipliers were used to represent the effect of each factor on a pasture yield potential. Pasture yield was estimated by multiplying the tabular upper AUM value by these multipliers.

Grazing Management. The yield of a pasture depends on the stocking rate and grazing schedule, i.e. grazing management. When cattle continuously graze a pasture for an entire season, the production (AUM/hectare) of the pasture is lower than when the cattle are rotated between pastures. Typically grazing management can be categorized as continuous grazing, simple rotation, or complex rotation.

Seasonal Distribution of Pasture Production

Bi-weekly pasture productivity was used to simulate the pasture response to livestock grazing. The annual pasture forage yield was distributed based on the growth characteristics of the pasture species. Various forage species have different rates and patterns of growth. Figures 1 and 2 illustrate the growth curves of a cool-season and a warm-season species, respectively, as presented in the "Guide" (Waller et al, 1986). The curve pattern of a forage plant's growth and its corresponding quality does not change greatly; it's physiological and morphological characteristics are genetically controlled. Environment and grazing management may have a limited effect on plant response.

These seasonal growth patterns were represented as a vector for each species defining the percentage of the annual growth for each bi-weekly period. The bi-weekly forage production per unit area was calculated by multiplying the pattern vector by the annual pasture yield potential.

During each period, the forage available for grazing consisted of the new growth as presented above plus the carryover of forage that was not grazed during previous periods. The amount of carryover forage is reduced due to wildlife, trampling, weathering, and insects.

Several methods of representing these losses were investigated and discussed by the research group during several meetings. As a compromise, a loss rate of 5% for each 2-week period was selected to be a realistic assumption.

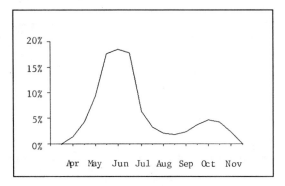

Figure 1. Seasonal growth of a cool season species (smooth brome).

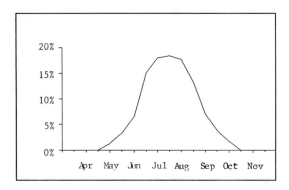

Figure 2. Seasonal growth of a warm season species (big bluestem).

Expert System Implementation

A knowledge base was developed to consult with the user and help the user define the available pastures. VP-Expert (VPX) by Paperback Software Co. was used to develop this expert system. VPX is a rule-based expert system shell with a backward chaining inference technique. All databases were stored using a dBase III format. The knowledge base was stored in the form of IF-THEN rules.

The initial step toward the definition of a user's available pastures was to query the user for the vegetative zone and the expected precipitation. A map of Nebraska was displayed and the user was asked to identify the proper zone. An image illustrating the normal precipitation range throughout Nebraska, was displayed and the user was asked to specify expected precipitation level.

The expert system was setup for user ease and simplicity. The major portion of the forage subsystem was to define, or add, a pasture. The details of each pasture were stored in a database file. Several subsystem utilities were available to initialize (clear) the pasture definitions, delete a pasture and list the pastures that had been previously defined.

Pasture stocking rates for various species as shown in Table 1 were stored in a reference database. The recommended stocking rates were retrieved by searching parameters of species, vegetative zone, and soil type. VPX has a menu command that can dynamically generate menus from the available labels in a specific field of a database file. This feature was used to generate a menu of the available species within the specified vegetative zone. After the user selected the species another menu was generated of the available soil types for that species in that zone. The species available for use with this forage subsystem can be modified by adding (or deleting) the appropriate records to (from) the database.

Multipliers for soil erosion and weeds were determined by symbolic processing of the rules through the levels of selection. The multipliers for fertilizer and precipitation were obtained by linear interpolations which were also performed by the actions of the rules.

After defining a pasture, as described above, the expected yields for the three grazing management schemes were reported to the user. The pasture schedule, which is specified under varying conditions in the balance subsystem, affects the expected yield, thus representation of the grazing management system was deferred to the balance subsystem.

A database was established to store the seasonal growth curves in percentage of annual growth for each species. Bi-weekly pasture yield was generated by distributing annual pasture yield over the seasonal growth pattern. Parameters describing each selected pasture were stored as a record in a database. These records were then used by the balance subsystem.

ANIMAL SUBSYSTEM

A year-round bi-weekly animal demand pattern was needed to match the forage availability. A database management system was programmed to generate the bi-weekly animal inventories and demand from generalized producer inputs.

Livestock Forage Demand Estimation

The forage requirement of animals varies due to differences such as type, age, frame size, and production level. The Animal Unit (AU) was defined as forage intake on the basis of a "standard animal" which is cow-calf pair. The Animal Unit was defined as a 454 Kg (1000-pound) cow of above average milking ability with a calf less than 3 to 4 months postpartum (Waller et al, 1986). Animals consuming more or less forage than the standard animal were assigned AU values based on their intake relative to the standard animal.

Beef cattle were used as the livestock class for this study. A typical 100-cow herd following a replacement policy consists of the following:

Number	Classification	Age, months
85	Mature cows	>36
15	Young cows	24-35
90	Calves	0-11
15	Replacement heifers	12-23
75	Stockers	12-23
2	Young bulls	24-35
3	Mature bulls	>36

The herd consists of animals with a range of ages. 100 cows (85 mature cows and 15 young cows) annually produce 90 calves. At one year of age 15 of the calves are used as replacement heifers, the remaining 75 as stockers. At two years of age the replacement heifers calve and are classified as young cows. With spring calving, all livestock have a birth date of about March 1.

The older and unbred cows are culled during the fall to maintain the desired herd size. As needed, animals can be bought and sold throughout the year to adjust the herd size. Typically, the herd inventory will be maintained at approximately the same levels throughout the year, the only variation being the number of mature cows before and after culling. Adjustments in the above scenario can be made to fit most herd operations with replacement.

Year-round Bi-weekly Animal Demands

Total animal forage demand is estimated from the animal inventory. Animal demand for forage is a function of body weight, milking ability, age, sex, calving date, and animal management activities. The requirements for a standard non-lactating cow increase from 0 at birth to 0.9 AU at 24 months of age. While that for a bull

increases to 1.5 at 36 months. Adjustments are made on these standard requirements for period in the lactation cycle, milking ability and body weight. Forage demand increases for the milk production period.

A multiplier of 1.2 was used as the adjustment for the forage requirement of a cow with superior milking ability. This means that the forage demand is 20% over that of animals with average milking ability (NRC, 1984). The adjustment on animal body weight was made using a weight multiplier which was calculated by dividing the weight kg(lb) of the mature cow by 454 kg (1000 lb) (NRC, 1984).

Model Implementation

Generalized producer input forms (screens) were used to define each herd of beef animals. A database management software package from Paperback Software Inc., VP Info, was used for this subsystem. Database management routines were written to convert the generalized user inputs into an initial year-round inventory of animals. Additional routines allowed the user to modify the generalized inventory. After the inventory for various animal groups was generated, a demand vector was generated for use by the balance subsystem.

The user was presented a screen of default general information. The user was required to enter the herd size (number of cows). As desired the other items could be modified to represent a particular herd. This screen of general information was used to determine the animal inventory for that breed. The user was then asked to separate the herd into several animal groups as different classes of animals would be separated into different pastures. This allowed the simulation of various grazing management practices by allowing the user to select herd groups for a pasture schedule. Another screen was developed to allow the user to specify when animals are bought or sold. The animal inventory of the breed is adjusted to represent this buy or sell activity.

After the animal inventory was defined, the animal demands were generated and stored in a database through a set of database management procedures. This database was available for use by the balance subsystem.

BALANCE SUBSYSTEM

A simulation of pasture production interacting with animal grazing was developed to match the pasture supplies and livestock forage requirements under specified grazing management schedules. Forage quality and animal nutritional needs were projected to compare the animal diet with its nutritional requirements.

Pasture Supply and Animal Forage Demand

The method used to analyze pasture performance under animal grazing was by using accumulative pasture production and accumulative animal demand for forage over the growing season. The forage carryover is subject to loss due to weathering, wildlife, trampling, and insects.

Figure 3 illustrates the results with simple rotation management with a balanced 81 hectares (200 acres) of cool season pasture (Smooth Brome, 8.9 AUM/hectare [3.6 AUM/acre]) and 40 hectares (100 acres) warm season pasture (Big bluestem, 9.26 AUM/hectare [3.75 AUM/acre]) with the typical herd described above. The herd grazes the cool season pasture from May 1 through June 30 (line AB), then moves to the warm season pasture until August 31 (line CD), and back to the cool season pasture until November 1 (line EF). Obviously, the only way this grazing schedule can be carried on these two forage resources is to under utilize the cool-season pasture in the spring and allow carryover to the fall.

Management Recommendations

Management information and recommendations were provided by this balance subsystem. These include: grazing pressure for a pasture, comparison of forage quality in animal diet and animal nutrition requirement, animal average daily gain, and pasture earliest starting grazing date.

Determination of Pasture Size and Herd Size. Total production is directly proportional to the size of the pasture. The number of

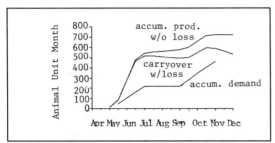

Figure 3. Rotational grazing on a cool-season pasture.

hectares (acres) needed depends on the demand of the herd and the grazing schedule. The pasture supply is considered to be balanced with animal demand if the minimum value of the forage excess (with loss) is zero within the scheduled grazing time.

A balance of pasture production with animal forage demand is a function of (1) the pasture size, (2) the herd size, and (3) the grazing schedule. Based on this criteria of balance, the size of the pasture needed and the herd size can be determined when two of the three parameters are specified. Under a specified animal grazing pressure (herd size) and grazing schedule, the required pasture size can be determined by adjusting the accumulative production (i.e. increasing or decreasing number of hectares) so that it equals the accumulative demand at the end or the middle of the grazing schedule without any deficit within the schedule. Likewise, herd size can be determined by adjusting animal demand which results in a change of the slope of the demand line, when pasture size and grazing schedule are specified. The pasture performance or the relationship of production and demand during the season can be predicted when all three parameters are specified.

The search for the desired pasture size needed to balance the demand from a specific herd was iterative. The search procedure for determining the root of a monotonically decreasing function was used (Thompson, 1968).

Table 2 illustrates the system output for 100 cows with the pasture size balanced to the animal demand. The availability in the second column is the forage available to date; it equals the production during this period plus the carryover with loss from the previous period. From the output, 89 hectares (220 acres) of the pasture are needed to balance the demand by Herd 1 with the grazing schedule from May 1 to October 31. At the end of the specified grazing schedule pasture supply and animal demand are balanced.

Forage Quality and Animal Nutrition. Forage quality provided by the pasture and the nutritional requirement of the herd during the season were matched to identify periods of nutritional deficiency. Pasture quality is presented in Table 2 as TDN (total digestible nutrients) and CP (crude protein). The Diet TDN and CP columns represent the pasture quality for the specified time period. The animal requirements are based on nutritional requirements for the lactating cow and the calf. Table 3 illustrates the model output with 75 stockers on the same cool season pasture. Animal growth rate is directly related to quality of the forage. The projected average daily gain (ADG) is used to relate pasture quality. The projected growth is represented as growth for this period and accumulated for the growing period to date.

Earliest Pasture Grazing Starting Date. The earliest pasture grazing date was suggested by this model as a management recommendation. A minimum level of pasture vegetation should accumulate before animals can be put on the pasture. The earliest grazing starting date was determined based on the condition that pasture vegetation was established and could support the group of animals during the initial period (2 weeks) of grazing.

SUMMARY AND CONCLUSION

An expert system and simulation model was developed to assist livestock producers in pasture grazing management. Pasture yield was estimated according to the "Guide For Planning and Analyzing a

Table 2. Model output for 100 cows on a cool season pasture.

Smooth brome: 8.9 AUM/hectare (3.61 AUM/acre). Herd 1: 85 mature cows, 15 young cows, and 90 calves; average 113.2 AU/mo. With continuous grazing management schedule from 5/1 to 10/31.

| Period starting | -----Pasture AUM------ | | | ---TDN--- | | ---CP-- | |
	Avail- ability	Demand	Deficit	Diet %	Req. %	Diet %	Req. %
Apr 16	15.8	76		20			
May 1	94.5	54.6		70	61.1	18	9.9
May 16	252.4	55.6		67	62.2	15	10.2
Jun 1	401.5	56.5		65	62.9	13	10.4
Jun 16	399.2	57.5		63*	63.1	11	10.4
Jul 1	340.5	58.4		55*	62.7	11	10.3
Jul 16	275.9	60.3		54*	61.8	10*	10.1
Aug 1	213.7	61.2		53*	60.5	10	9.8
Aug 16	153.6	62.1		52*	58.8	11	9.4
Sep 1	111.6	62.1		54*	56.9	11	8.9
Sep 16	110.6	63.1		61	54.9	12	8.4
Oct 1	108.7	56.5		65	52.9	13	7.9
Oct 16	57.5	57.5	0.0	65	51.1	14	7.5

Recommendations:

- 89 hectares (220 acres) would be needed,
- Grazing should NOT be started prior to 4/25,
* The requirement for young cows or high producing cows slightly exceeds the available diet. Performance may be less than maximum during this period.

Table 3. Model output for 75 stockers on a cool-season pasture.

For Smooth brome: 8.9 AUM/hectare (3.61 AUM/acre), with 75 stockers, under schedule of 5/1 -- 10/31.

| Period starting | ----Pasture AUM------ | | | TDN Diet % | CP Diet % | -Steer ADG+- | |
	Avail- ability	Demand	Deficit			this period	to date
Apr 16	7.3			76	20		
May 1	43.3	22.0		70	18	2.9	2.9
May 16	118.6	22.8		67	15	2.5	2.7
Jun 1	189.3	23.6		65	13	2.2	2.5
Jun 16	190.2	24.4		63	11	1.9	2.4
Jul 1	164.8	25.2		55	11	0.9	2.1
Jul 16	136.2	26.0		54	10	0.7	1.8
Aug 1	108.3	26.9		53	10	0.6	1.7
Aug 16	81.0	27.7		52	11	0.5	1.5
Sep 1	61.5	28.5		54	11	0.7	1.4
Sep 16	60.5	29.3		61	12	1.7	1.4
Oct 1	58.3	30.1		65	13	2.2	1.5
Oct 16	30.9	30.9	0.0	65	14	2.2	1.6

Recommendations:

- 40.8 hectares (100.8 acres) would be needed.
- Grazing should NOT be started prior to 4/25.
+ Heifers gain at 20% lower rate.

Year-round Forage Program" (Waller et al, 1986) and adjusted by factors, such as fertilizer, precipitation, and grazing management, which affected the pasture yield. Bi-weekly pasture production for a growing season was estimated based on the seasonal growth of the species. This allowed the pasture grazing to be analyzed in a time series.

Animals were classified into seven classes based on their age and sex. Animal forage demand was estimated based on the body weight, breed, milking ability, class, and number of animals. A year-round animal inventory was predicted based on animal calving date and rate, culling date and rate, buying or selling, and the factors that would reflect the change of the inventory during the year. Animals were grouped into herd groups for grazing management simulation and analyses.

Pasture supplies and animal forage demand were matched by simulating the pasture grazing management. Grazing management was simulated by scheduling groups of animals on each pasture. By simulation and balancing, the size of the pasture needed for the specified animal groups (grazing pressure on the pasture) under a specified grazing schedule was determined.

Forage quality and animal nutritional requirements were compared by the model. Recommendation is provided when nutrition supplied by forage is less than that required by the animal.

A hybrid combination of expert system, database management, and simulation modelling was used in the implementation of the system. A rule-based knowledge base in conjunction with databases was developed to define a pasture and predict the yield. Database management system routines were programmed to generate the animal inventory from generalized producer's inputs. A set of active input screens was developed for the information inputs. A simulation model was developed to simulate pasture grazing in a time series and balance the pasture supplies and animal demand. Hierarchical structures with sets of function keys were developed for a user-friendly environment of the model.

Through the testing and verification by specialists, this expert system model was considered to be very useful for the planning of a year-round pasture grazing management program. The following conclusions were made based on the performance of this expert system model:

1. The expert system can be developed to act as a human expert in the beef-cattle grazing management area.

2. It has great potential to be used as a tool in teaching students and ranchers in planning and analyzing grazing programs.

3. It can provide necessary management information and recommendations, and assist in the evaluation of beef-forage management decisions.

REFERENCES

Jones, J. W. and H. W. Beck. 1988. Simulation and artificial intelligence concepts. In *Proceedings of the Workshop on Expert Systems in Agriculture*. Lake Buena Vista, Florida. February, 1988.

NRC. 1984. *Nutrient Requirement of Beef Cattle (6th Ed.)*. National Academy Press. Washington, DC.

Rehm, G. W. and B. Anderson. 1983. Fertilizing grass pastures in Nebraska. *NebGuide G78-406*, University of Nebraska, Lincoln, NE.

Tao, Y. 1988. *Hybrid expert system of beef-forage grazing systems*. M.S. thesis. University of Nebraska-Lincoln.

Thompson, T. L. and R. M. Peart. 1968. Useful search techniques to save research time. *Transactions of the ASAE*. 11(4) 461:467.

USDA, Soil Conservation Service. 1983. *Nebraska Range Site Descriptions and Guide for Determining Range Condition and Suggestive Initial Stocking Rates.*

Waller, S. S., L. E. Moser and B. Anderson. 1986. A guide for planning and analyzing a year-round forage program. *Nebraska County Extension Service EC86-113*, University of Nebraska - Lincoln.

Advances in AI and Simulation
© 1989 By The Society for Computer
Simulation International
ISBN 0-911801-50-2

A kernel system for modelling and simulation Using system entity structure concepts for systems theory knowledge representation

Herbert Praehofer
Deptartment of Systems Theory
Johannes Kepler University of Linz
A-4040 Linz / Austria

ABSTRACT

This paper presents a design of a kernel system to serve as a basis for simulation environments which are based on system theoretical concepts. It derives its ideas from three main sources: the system theoretical approach to modelling and simulation of Zeigler, the project Computer Aided Systems Theory project at the University of Linz, and the object oriented programming paradigm. System theoretical concepts for simulation modelling and their implementation in object oriented languages are discussed. A scheme for the representation of Systems Theory knowledge relevant for simulation modelling is discussed.

1. INTRODUCTION AND MOTIVATION

Systems Theory provides general problem solving concepts for real world situations where the behavior of the system over time is of interest. It provides modelling formalisms to build dynamic models and operations to solve particular problems. A model is built by specifying the system's boundary, namely the input and output interface, the time base and the dynamic behavior of the system in various levels of abstraction and precision.

The task of simulation is to compute the dynamic behavior of real systems using a model-based approach. Although simulation modelling relies on system concepts to furnish its terminology and justify its approaches, a system theoretical approach is taken only in very few cases. This is especially true for discrete event simulation where a system theoretical formalism exists but is not used by the simulation community. Using a system theoretical approach would have several advantages (Pichler 1984, Oren 1984):

1) Models formulated using a system theoretical concepts can be easily translated into a simulation program.

2) A system specification is a good documentation of the simulation program and hence can be used for person to person communication.

3) Validation, the process of showing that the model properly reflects the system behavior, is supported by a model-based approach.

4) Verification, the process of proving that the program correctly implements the model, is made possible.

5) Models formulated using Systems Theory are easier to modify.

6) A simulator constructed by Systems Theory methods is supported by accompanying theories; therefore its behavior and properties are under scientific control.

7) Systems Theory facilitates the algorithmic manipulation of simulation models.

The kernel system for systems theory instrumented modelling and simulation which is proposed here is intended to serve as a basis to set up modelling and simulation environments for different fields of application. It derives its ideas from three different sources: from Zeigler's system theoretic approach to modelling and simulation (Zeigler 1976, Zeigler 1984), from the project Computer Aided Systems Theory (CAST) (Pichler and Schwaetzel 1988, Pichler 1988), and from the object oriented programming paradigm (Meyer 1988, Keene 1988).

Zeigler (1984) developed a systems theoretical formalism for discrete event simulation, the so-called Discrete Event System (DEVS). He showed how these systems can be simulated using the abstract simulator concept. He also developed a knowledge representation scheme, the so-called system entity structure, which is related to the object oriented programming paradigm and the frame concept. It represents a system with its multiplicities of decompositions and variants. The project CAST initiated by Pichler seeks to implement interactive method banks to support system theoretical problem solving. The STIPS (Systems Theory Instrumented Problem Solving) framework is used as the underlying theoretical framework to develop such method banks. One aim of the object oriented programming paradigm is to facilitate the implementation of reusable software. A class system is intended to provide reusable building blocks which can be used as they are or can be extended to meet special needs.

I propose that a kernel system for system theory instrumented modelling and simulation has to provide the following concepts:

1) concepts for model formulation and model construction

2) simulation concepts to run simulation experiments using these models

3) a framework which facilitates the representation of Systems Theory knowledge, i.e, representation of system types and the applicability of operations on a system of a specific type.

It must be emphasized that the formulation of experimental frames are not explicitly included into the kernel system because in this approach experimental frames should be formulated as special kinds of models.

2. SYSTEMS THEORETIC FOUNDATIONS FOR SIMULATION MODELLING

In this section some fundamental system theoretic concepts and formalisms are presented. First the concept of dynamic systems is defined. Then three modelling formalisms relevant for simulation modelling are presented; the Discrete Time System, Differential Equations Specified System and Discrete Event System formalisms. We will see that each formalism implies restrictions on the elements of their system descriptions. Most important is that these formalisms are closed under coupling. That means one can couple systems together so that the resultant specifies, in turn, a system. Thus the construction of hierarchical models is possible. I will illustrate how these hierarchical systems can be simulated using the abstract simulator concepts. Finally it is shown that these modelling and simulation concepts are readily implementable using the object oriented programming paradigm.

Dynamic Systems:

A Dynamic System is a structure

$$S = <T, X, O, Q, Y, \delta, \lambda>$$

where

    T is the time base
    X is the set of inputs
    Ω are the admissable input segments
    Y is the set of outputs
    δ is the state transition function
    λ is the output function

For a dynamic System two restriction must hold. The input process Ω has to be closed with respect to concatenation (= compositions of words). δ has to have the semigroup-property: for all w1, w2 $\in$ Ω and q $\in$ Q the equation $\delta(q, w1w2) = \delta(\delta(q, w1), w2)$ is valid.

To specify a model by an dynamic system is not practical. Models are instead described in a specific modelling formalism. The formalism implies specific constraints on the system and selects a subclass of systems from the set of all systems. Once such a class is chosen, one only has to give information necessary to distinguish the model from the others in the class. Modelling formalisms such as Differential Equation Specified Systems, Discrete Time System and Discrete Event System build such subclasses of systems. Figure 1 shows these constraints on the elements of its dynamic system (Zeigler 1984a). For a more detailed description of these modelling formalisms and how they define dynamic systems the reader is refered to (Zeigler 1976, Zeigler 1984, and Rozenblit 1988).

	Differential equations	Discrete event	Discrete time
time base T	continuous reals	continuous reals	discrete integers
basic sets X, Q, Y	real vector space	arbitrary	arbitrary
input segments	piecewise continous segments	discrete event segments	sequences
state and output trajectories	continuous segments	piecewise constant segments	sequences

Figure 1: Constraints imposed through modelling formalims

Most important is that each of these formalisms is closed under coupling. That means one can couple systems together so that the resultant again specifies a system. With every network we can associate a dynamic system. Thus one can couple systems together, the resultant in turn can be a component in a bigger network. So the construction of modular hierarchical models is possible.

Simulation of Modular Hierarchical Models:

Zeigler (1984) introduced simulation concepts for modular, hierarchical Discrete Event Systems. The abstract simulator for DEVS has a hierarchical structure reflecting the structure of the hierarchical DEVS. It handles all the simulation needs. Thus a DEVS model can be directly transformed into an executable simulation program using the abstract simulator. The abstract simulator consist of two types of objects - simulators and coordinators. With every atomic model we associate a simulator, with every network we associate a coordinator. The simulation proceeds by messages passed among the simulators and coordinators.

One aim of our work is to develop similar simulation concepts for Discrete Time Systems and Differential Equation Specified Systems. We pursue a approach very similar to the DEVS abstract simulator. The abstract simulator for DESS and DTS will also reflect the hierarchical structure of the model. The same methodology and terminology is used. This is mainly done to be compatible to the DEVS simulator and to support the simulation of non-homogeneous specified models whose components are of different system type.

Object Oriented Implementation:

That object oriented programming is well suited for the implementation of system theoretical concepts has been proved by several projects (Zeigler 1985, Mittelmann 1988, Pichler and Praehofer 1988, Praehofer and Spalt 1988). System types can be readily implemented by class definitions, system of a particular type correspond to the instances of these classes. The slot definitions in a class define the parts that the systems of this type consist of. Methods defined for a class of systems represent the operations which can be applied to the systems

With the progress in developing efficient and powerful object oriented languages like CLOS (Keene 1988), Eiffel (Meyer 1988) or C++ (Stroustrup 1986), this programming paradigm has become even more useful for the implementation of Systems Theory instrumented modelling and simulation environments. One benefit is that by using powerful object oriented languages it is possible to implement not only the systems themselves as objects but also the parts of a system and the inputs processed by it. A system always consists of mathematical objects, i.e., of sets and functions. Pursuing a pure object oriented implementation these mathematical objects would be defined by classes and hence by abstract data types. Doing so, the system object itself is relieved from knowing anything of the internal structure of its parts. It only has to have knowledge about the external interface of the object, i.e., which methods are usable for that object. A very high flexibility of the system representation and definition is the result. It does not matter any longer if the state transition function is defined and stored using a table, an algebraic expression or a Lisp program. In the same way it is possible to implement sets by enumerating their elements or by defining a predicate. All types of functions or sets can be treated uniformly just by obeying the interface conventions. It is also easy to integrate new functions and sets into the environment.

As system types are implementable by an object oriented approach, so are the abstract simulators. Each of the abstract simulators consist of a set of objects of different types. How the simulation schedule proceeds is already defined by a message passing scheme readily implementable in an object oriented language. For the simulation part, it is even more important that a powerful object oriented language is available where messages passing and method evaluation is most efficient. This will very much determine the speed of simulation.

3. SYSTEM THEORY KNOWLEDGE REPRESENTATION

What is Systems Theory Knowledge:

The task of Systems Theory is to provide general problem solving concepts by a model based approach. It has to provide techniques for model construction and operations to solve a given problem employing models. By basing model representation on system theoretical formalisms, all the knowledge of Systems Theory is applicable. To accomplish the requirements of different models for different applications and different problem solving tasks, Systems Theory provides a lot of different systems types which are further specializations of the three basic types discussed in section 2. A elaborate framework of systems types has been established. System transformations are intended to transform a system of one type into a system of another type. These system transformations are the basic means for problem solving. They are used either to obtain "better" solutions for a given system description (synthesis operation) or they are used to compute specific properties of a system (analysis operation). A typical synthesis operation is given by the state minimization algorithm for sequential machines. A typical analysis operation is the computation of the stability property of a system of linear differential equations. Among these problem solving concepts, although the most important and most widely used, simulation is only one out of many analysis operations. Using simulation the dynamic behavior of the system is computed and so one tries to infer properties of the model which then get interpreted in the real world situation.

Each system type implicitly encompasses some knowledge about its structure, it imposes constraints on its parts and regulates the principal applicability of the system transformations. The applicability and implementation of an operation depend on the type of system. There are operations which can be applied to most types of systems and there are operations which are only applicable to a systems of a very specific type. The implementation of an operation also may vary considerably with the system type. A method to compute the dynamic behavior should be available for most types of systems but the implementation may be quite different for the different system types. A method for the state space minimization is currently known only for sequential machines. The implementation of it also varies with the type of sequential machine. Different algorithms are known for partial, deterministic and linear sequential machines. For efficiency, always the most appropriate technique should be used.

Constraints imposed on the parts of a system of a specific type are most important for model construction purposes. Having knowledge of the system type and therefore of the constraints, the modelling task can be made most convenient. Parts which are defined implicitly by the system type, need not be specified. For the other parts the most appropriate scheme for definition can be chosen. For instance with the knowledge that a system is linear and it is a Moore type machine (the output only depends on the state), it is possible to choose a program where the matrices A, B and C can be defined. As we have a Moore type system, matrix D need not be defined and is implicitly set to zero.

A kernel system supporting the development of such advanced Systems Theory based environments therefore has to provide the above system theoretical concepts for model construction, the different system types and the basic system transformations for system theoretical problem solving. Computer representation of Systems Theory knowledge in a comprehensive and consistent way is a challenge for known knowledge representation techniques. In (Mittelmann and Praehofer 1988) an approach to this was presented using the object oriented programming paradigm with multiple inheritance and dynamic classes. A similar but even better representation can be accomplished by the system entity structure (Zeigler 1984). This approach will be outlined next.

Systems Theory Knowledge Representation Using System Entity Structure Concepts:

The system entity structure developed by Zeigler (1984) is a means to represent a system to be modelled within a certain choice of system boundary. It is a tree-like graph that encompasses the boundaries, decompositions and taxonomic relationships that have been perceived for the system being modelled. In the graph we distinguish three kinds of nodes: entity, aspect and specialization. An entity signifies a conceptual part of reality. An aspect names a possible decomposition of an entity. A specialization node facilitates the representation of variants of an entity and has the same semantic as specialization in the object oriented programming paradigm. Each of these nodes can have attached variables. A system entity structure obeys the following axioms:

1) uniformity: Any two nodes which have the same labels have the same attached variables and isomorphic subtrees.

2) strict hierarchy: No label appear more than once down any path of the tree.

3) alternating mode: Each node has a mode which is either entity, aspect or specialization. After an entity follows an aspect or a specialization and after an aspect or specialization follows an entity.

4) valid brothers: No two brothers have same labels.

5) attached variables: No two variables attached to the same item have the same name.

To represent System Theory knowledge the system entity structure is used but for convenience some of the axioms are relaxed. Figure 2 represents our structuring of this kind of knowledge graphically. The different kind of arcs symbolize the different relations. A one-line arc symbolizes an aspect while a two-line arrow symbolizes a specialization. A three line arc points to a multiple decomposition, a decomposition of an entity into an unknown number of entities of the same type.

In this application, the children of an aspect represent the parts of an entity. For instance, the aspect I/O-Aspect of System indicates that every system owns an input and output set and a time base. Specialization of an entity represent the different species of this entity. To choose a specific system type from all possibilities represented by the system entity structure, one node from each of the specializations has to be selected. It must be emphasized that all the aspects of an entity are inherited to the specialized entity. Thus in our example, Network is a specialization of system and it has an aspect netwAsp which specifies the parts Comps and Coupl. But Network also inherits the I/O aspect from System. In distinction to the usual interpretation of the system entity structure, for a valid system definition all the aspects have to be unified.

Most important for our application are the concept of specializations. While aspects define the parts of an entity, the specialization define the different system types. The applicable methods are attached the specialized entities. Additionally constraints imposed on the parts of the system are attached to these specialized nodes. Three different types of these constraints can be distinguished. The following must be specified:

1) the type of a part of a system (e.g. state transition function is a linear function)

2) the type of a part of a part of a system (e.g. the domain of the state transition function is a real vector space)

3) identity of a part of a system with other parts (e.g. the domain of the output function is equal to States   Inputs).

To be able to specify the type of a part a similar specialization hierarchy for the mathematical objects in a system definition must be constructed.

To have more convenience in specifying similar specializations of different entities, the uniformity axiom is relaxed. Specialization nodes as well as their children may appear more than once with the same name in the entity structure and their subtrees need not be isomorphic and their attached variables, constraints and methods not equal. These identically named specializations symbolize the same specializations but either of different entities or at different level of description. In Figure 2 we can observe a specialization linSpec under Out-Func, St-Trans and SeqMach. Of course, each of them have the meaning that something can be linear or not, but different methods, constraints and subtrees are attached to the children. The rule for the selection of entities under such an equal named specialization node is as follows: if there already was a selection from a specialization with the same name, then choose the same entity as before. A node labeled by a set of entities (see {DESS, SeqMach} under MemModel) means a selection of one of these entities.

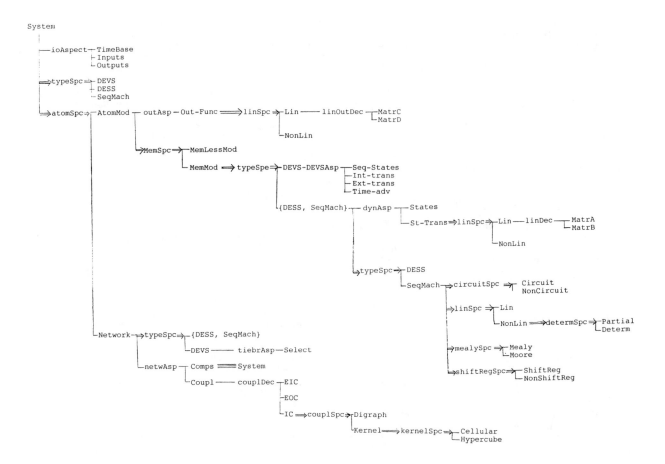

Figure 2: System Entity Structure representing system types

4. CURRENT STATE OF IMPLEMENTATIONS

The first attempt to base simulation program specification upon system theoretical formalisms was Oren's General Systems Theory Implementor GEST (Oren 1971). This 1971 developed simulation environment and its advanced versions GEST81 and MAGEST, facilitate the modelling and simulation of modular and hierarchical discrete and continuous time models.

Most of the ideas presented in this paper are derived from the development of the DEVS formalism, of the abstract simulator for DEVS, and of their implementations. Four different implementations are known to the author: two by Melman and Livny (1984), then DEVS-Scheme by Zeigler (1985) and another by Praehofer and Spalt (1988). Melman and Livny's first implementation was done in Simscript II.5. Recently they implemented DEVS in Modula-2 and applied it to simulation of large scale distributed systems.

Zeigler created his DEVS system in PC-Scheme, a LISP dialect for IBM-PC compatible microcomputers, and its object oriented superset SCOOPS. In this implementation, models as well as abstract simulators are

coded as objects. Simulation proceeds by messages passed among these objects. DEVS-Scheme also incorporates more advanced System Entity Structure concepts which serve as an organizer of a family of models. This part, called ESP-Scheme, helps the modeller to conceptualize and record the decompositions and specializations underlying a model and so assists him in top down design. Recently, new features for testing model morphisms and model simplifications have been incorporated. The next extensions will be to develop a convenient user interface and incorporate the modelling and simulation concepts for Discrete Time Systems and Differential Equation Specified Systems outlined in section 2.

The implementation of Praehofer and Spalt called Systems Theory Instrumented Discrete Event Simulation (STIDEVS) was done in Interlisp-D and its object oriented superset LOOPS. Interlisp-D is a powerful LISP dialect facilitating a display oriented and interactive programming style and therefore provides techniques to implement modern man/machine interfaces. Much emphasis has been laid on the development of a convenient graphical and interactive user interface to support interactive modelling

133

and simulation. In this environment, model bases for different tasks of application can be set up by defining a class system of generic models. To built a model for a specific problem should require only selecting atomic models from these model bases and coupling them together. In distinction to DEVS-Scheme, the abstract simulator is not implemented in an object oriented way but by an recursive program. This was done for efficiency.

The CAST method bank CAST.FSM was one of the first CAST implementations. It supports Finite State Machine methods. It is coded in Interlisp-D/LOOPS and uses a class system for system type representation. Although the project can be regarded as successful, there are some shortcomings in the implementation. The reason is that it evolved out of a small program system and it was never intended to build such a huge program, now 1 MByte of compiled code. The main problem was how to represent the diversity of the system types in a class system. This initiated the studying of how to represent of Systems Theory knowledge and the ideas are outlined in section 3.

ACKNOWLEDGMENT

This paper was written during my stay at the University of Arizona as a Visiting Scholar. I would like to thank Professor Franz Pichler, Professor Jerzy W. Rozenblit and Professor Bernard P. Zeigler for making this visit possible. Special thanks are given to Professor Bernard P. Zeigler, Professor Jerzy W. Rozenblit and Rudolf Mittelmann for their contributions in creating this paper.

This work was partitially supported by SIEMENS Munich, Dept. ZTI.

REFERENCES

Keene, S. (1988)
Object Oriented Programming in CommonLISP
Addison-Wesley 1988.

Melman, M. and M. Livny (1984)
The DISS Methodology for DIstributed System Simulation, Simulation Journal, April

Meyer, B. (1988)
Object Oriented Programming for Software Engineering, Addison Wesley

Mittelmann, R. (1988)
Object Oriented Implementation of Petri Nets Concepts, in: Cybernetics and Systems '88 (ed. R. Trappl) Kluver Academic Publisher

Mittelmann, R. and Praehofer, H. (1988)
Design of an Object Oriented Kernel System for CAST and STIMS, Proc. of the CAST Workshop 1988, University of Linz / Austria (to appear)

Oren, T. (1971)
General Systems Theory Implementor
Doctoral Dissertation, University of Arizona, Tucson.

Oren, T. (1984)
Model-Based Activities: A Paradigm Shift
in: Simulation and Model-Based Methodologies: An Integrative View (eds. Oren et al.)
Springer Verlag Berlin Heidelberg 1984.

Pichler, F. (1984)
Symbolic Manipulation of System Models
in: Simulation and Model-Based Methodologies: An Integrative View (eds. Oren et al.)
Springer Verlag Berlin Heidelberg 1984.

Pichler, F. (1986)
Model Components for Symbolic Processing by Knowledge-Based Systems: The STIPS Framework, in: Modelling and Simulation Methodology in the Artificial Intelligence Era (eds. Elzas, M. et. al.), North-Holland, Amsterdam

Pichler, F. and H. Praehofer (1988)
Computer Aided Systems Theory : Finite State Machines
in: Cybernetics and Systems '88, (ed. Trappl, R.) Kluwer Academic Publishers

Pichler, F. and H. Schwaertzel (1988)
CAST: Computerunterstuetzte Systemtheorie - Konstruktion interaktiver Methodenbanken
Springer Verlag Berlin (to appear)

Pichler, F. (1988)
CAST--Computer Aided Sytems Theory: A Framework for Interactive Method Banks, in: Cybernetics and Systems '88, (ed. Trappl, R.) Kluwer Academic Publishers,

Praehofer H. and A. Spalt (1988)
An Interactive Simulation Environment Using Systems Theory Concepts and Object Oriented Programming, Proc. of the 1988 ESM, Nice, France

Rozenblit, J. W. (1988)
Systems Theory Instrumented Simulation Modelling, Proc. 1988 Winter Simulation Conference San Diego, California

Stroustrup, B. (1986)
The C++ Programming Language
Addison Wesley 1986

Zeigler, B. P. (1976)
Theory of Modelling and Simulation
John Wiley and Sons, New York.

Zeigler, B. P. (1984)
Multifaceted Modelling and Discrete Event Simulation, Academic Press, London.

Zeigler, B. P. (1984a)
System--Theoretic Representation of Simulation Models. IIE Transactions, March, pp. 19-34

Zeigler, B. P. (1984 b)
System Theoretic Foundations of Modellinga and Simulation, in: Simulation and Model-Based Methodologies: An Integrative View (eds. Oren et al.)
Springer Verlag Berlin Heidelberg 1984.

Zeigler, B. P. (1987)
Hierarchical, Modular Discrete Event Modelling in an Object Oriented Environment. Simulation Journal, vol 49:5

Advances in AI and Simulation
© 1989 By The Society for Computer
Simulation International
ISBN 0-911801-50-2

ESP-scheme: A realization of system entity structure in a LISP environment

Tag Gon Kim, ERLab and B.P. Zeigler, ECE Dept.

University of Arizona
Tucson, AZ 85721

ABSTRACT

System entity structure (SES) developed by Zeigler is a structural knowledge representation scheme that contains knowledge of decomposition, taxonomy, and coupling of a system. Formally, SES is a labeled tree with attached variable type that satisfies certain axioms. This paper describes a realization of SES in Scheme (a LISP dialect) called ESP-Scheme. The paper first presents representation of SES and main operations on SES, and then describes facilities in ESP-Scheme. ESP-Scheme acts as a model base management system in DEVS-Scheme, a knowledge-based simulation environment developed by the authors. It supports specification of the structure of a family of models, pruning the structure to a reduced model, and transforming it to a simulation model by synthesizing components models in the model base.

1. Introduction

DEVS-Scheme realizes Zeigler's *DEVS* (Discrete Event System Specification) formalism in Scheme (a LISP dialect) (Kim and Zeigler, 1987; Kim, 1988; Zeigler, 1987). The environment supports building models in a hierarchical, modular manner, a systems oriented approach not possible in conventional languages (Concepcion and Zeigler, 1988). To organize such complex hierarchical structures of models developed using DEVS-Scheme, a model base management system is highly desirable. The *system entity structuring* formalism developed by (Zeigler, 1984) is one such tool for the model base management. ESP-Scheme is a realization of the system entity structuring formalism in the Scheme environment. The ESP-Scheme supports hierarchical specification of the structure of a family of models, pruning the structure to a reduced model, and transforming the structure to a simulation model by synthesizing components models in the model base developed using DEVS-Scheme. This paper first reviews the system entity structuring formalism and then describes overall features of the ESP-Scheme including representation and operations of the system entity structure. It also presents an outline of a knowledge base framework for modelling and simulation based on the entity structure and model base.

2. System Entity Structuring Formalism: A Review

A *system entity structure* (*SES*) is a knowledge representation scheme which contains the decomposition, coupling, and taxonomy information necessary to direct model synthesis (Zeigler 1984; Rozenblit, 1985). Formally, the *SES* is a labeled

tree with attached variable types that satisfies five axioms—alternating mode, uniformity, strict hierarchy, valid brothers, and attached variables. Detail description of the axioms is available in (Zeigler, 1984).

2.1 Three Relationships in SES

There are three types of nodes in the *SES*—*entity, aspect*, and *specialization*—which represent three types of knowledge about the structure of systems. The *entity* node, having several *aspects* and/or *specializations*, corresponds to a model component that represents a real world object. The *aspect* node (a single vertical line in the labeled tree of Fig. 1) represents one *decomposition*, out of many possible, of an entity. Thus the children of an aspect node are entities, distinct components of the decomposition. The *specialization* node (a double vertical arrows in the labeled tree of Fig. 1) represents a way in which a *general* entity can be categorized into *special* entities. As shown in Fig. 1, attached to an *aspect* node is a coupling scheme, which specifies external input, external output, and internal couplings of a system and its components.

A *multiple entity* is a special entity that consists of a collection of homogeneous components. We call such components a *multiple decomposition* of the multiple entity. The aspect of such a multiple entity is called *multiple aspect* (triple vertical lines in the labeled tree of Fig. 1). The representation of such a multiple entity is as follows. A multiple entity A and its components Bs are represented by A, three vertical lines, and B from the top down. Note that instead of presenting all Bs for A's components, only one B is placed in the labeled tree. The number of Bs is specified by a variable, which is attached to the multiple aspect node.

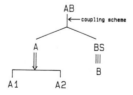

Fig. 1. A System Entity Structure.

2.2 Operations on SES

A *SES* represented by a labeled tree consists of branches and nodes (nodes are also called *items*). An *item* in the *SES* is in one of three types—entities, aspects, or specializations—an ordered pair of which is represented by a branch of the *SES*.

Some operations on the *SES* are: adding an item to the *SES*, deleting an item from the *SES*, attaching variables to items in the *SES*, deleting variables from items in the *SES*, pruning the *SES*, transforming the pruned *SES* into a model.

As the construction of a *SES* is a sequence of adding new items — entities, aspects or specializations — to the *SES*, the most common operation is adding an item. The deletion operation, which deletes entities and associated branches from the *SES*, can be applied only to those entities with no aspects. Variables can be attached to and removed from the items in the *SES*.

The pruning operation extracts a substructure of the *SES* by selecting one aspect and/or one specialization for each entity in the *SES*. The pruning operation ultimately reduces the *SES* to a composition tree that contains all the information about the structure of a model. The transform operation synthesizes a model in a hierarchical fashion from components in the model base developed by using the DEVS-Scheme.

3. Implementation of ESP-Scheme

3.1 Representation of SES in ESP-scheme

The *SES* is implemented by a module called *entity-structure* — a package of hidden variables and associated operations — as shown in Fig. 2. Lists of items and branches are main variables representing a tree structure for the *SES*. The variable *current-item* points to the *current item* in the *SES*, under which new items can be added. Each item in the *items-list* is represented by a structure type called *item*, the fields of which include *type, name, coupling, mult-coup-type,* and *attributes-lst*. Each branch in the *branches-list* is represented by another structure type called *branch* that maintains an *ordered pair* of two items, left- and right-items, in the SES.

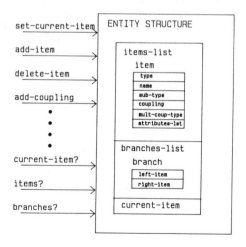

Fig. 2. Representation of System Entity Structure Module.

The field *type* in item structure represents the type of an entity in an entity structure whose range is in {entity, aspect, specialization}. The field *name* is used to identify an entity by its name. The field *coupling* is used to specify coupling scheme of a model specified by a system entity structure. The coupling scheme is a collection of three coupling specifications: external input, external output, and internal coupling. Each of three coupling specifications is represented by a set of ordered pairs of ports. The representation of coupling scheme is compatible with that of DEVS-Scheme. The field *sub-type* with range {multiple-entity, multiple-aspect, multiple-children} represents information on multiple entities and multiple decomposition. The field *mult-coup-type* with range {broadcast, hypercube, cellular} is used to specify the coupling scheme for a kernel model in DEVS-Scheme. Items in *SES* may have attributes that characterize their features. The field *attributes-lst* maintains a list of such attributes, each of which is a pair of variable and its value.

The main operations on the *SES* are *set-current-item, add-item, add-mult, delete-item, add-coupling, prune,* and *transform*. To explain such operations, let us build the *SES* of a system BUF-PROC, a processing element containing a buffer cascaded with a processor. The type of buffer, assumed to be either FIFO (First In First Out) or LIFO (Last In First Out), will be selected by the user in the pruning process. Once the *SES* of the BUF-PROC with an aspect and a specialization is built, we prune the BUF-PROC entity structure and transform the pruned BUF-PROC in a model.

Building the *SES* for the BUF-PROC starts with creating an entity structure, the root of which is an entity BUF-PROC (line (1) of Fig. 3 (a)). Once the *SES* with the root entity BUF-PROC has been created, items are added to the *SES*. However, a sequence of adding items should be such that the resulting *SES* satisfies the axiom of *alternating mode*. *SES* axioms are automatically checked by the *Entity Structure Module* as operations are processed. Since the next items to be added are either aspects or specializations, we add an aspect called *comp-dec* under the root entity BUF-PROC (line (2) of Fig. 3 (a)). To add other items under the aspect *comp-dec* requires setting the current item to the aspect *comp-dec* (line (3) of Fig. 3 (a)). After the current item is set, two components, a buffer and a processor, are added one by one (lines (4) and (5) of Fig. 3 (a)). Note that the current item of the *SES* is still at the aspect *comp-dec*. When an item with type specialization is added under the entity BUFFER, the current item must be set to the BUFFER (line (6) of Fig. 3 (a)). Then line (7) adds a specialization *buf-type* under the entity BUFFER. Similarly, lines (8), (9), and (10) add two items FIFO-BUF and LIFO-BUF under the specialization *buf-type*.

The coupling scheme of the BUF-PROC system, which is attached to the aspect *comp-dec*, can be specified by the operation *add-coupling*. This operation needs to specify the names of two entities and the names of ports in the two entities. The operation *add-coupling* specifies both internal and external coupling of the BUF-PROC system. Lines (12) and (13) of Fig. 3 (a) specify the external coupling scheme, while lines (14) and (15) of Fig. 3 (a) specify the internal coupling scheme of the BUF-PROC.

Fig. 3 (b) shows the resulting *SES* for the BUF-PROC system, which has one aspect under the BUF-PROC entity and one specialization under the BUFFER entity.

Having specified the *SES*, we are ready to prune it to select a particular *pruned entity structure*. The pruning operation queries the user to select one entity under a specialization, if there is one, while traversing all items in the *SES*. One such pruned entity structure is shown in Fig. 3 (c), where the FIFO-BUF has been selected as a specialized buffer.

To automatically construct a simulation model in DEVS-Scheme we apply the *transform* operation to a pruned entity structdure. The operation *transform* retrieves the models from the model base, which correspond to the entities in the pruned entity structure, and then synthesizes them into a simulation model for the BUF-PROC (Fig. 3 (d)). For such models to be available in the model base, we need to specify *atomic DEVS* models for the FIFO-BUF, LIFO-BUF, and PROCESSOR and save them in the model base before applying the transform. Details of the transform operation will be described in section 5.3

3.2 Multiple Entity

The specification of multiple entity and multiple decomposition is powerful for specifying a massively parallel computer architecture with appropriate connection topologies—such as broadcast, hypercube, or cellular—which has been recently introduced as a special-purpose architecture. To demonstrate the power of such specification of the parallel architecture, let us assume that the parallel processor has a collection of processing elements with one of three connections above, each element of which is the BUF-PROC that has already been specified. Let us call the parallel processor BUF-PROCS, meaning that BUF-PROCS consists of a collection of BUF-PROCs.

We can build the *SES* for the BUF-PROCS by adding extra specifications to the one shown in Fig. 3 (a) to create a new root entity BUF-PROCS of type multiple entity. A multiple aspect is added under the BUF-PROCS, and BUF-PROC is added under the multiple aspect by the operation *add-mult*. Once the three items are added, lines (2) through (15) of Fig. 3 (a) can be reused without change for the BUF-PROCS specification. The operation *add-mult-couple* specifies the internal coupling scheme for the kernel models in DEVS-Scheme in contrast to *add-coupling* for digraph models. It sets the slot *mult-coup-type* of the item of type *multiple aspect* to one of subclasses of kernel models (Kim, 1988) in DEVS-Scheme. The resulting *SES*, which has a multiple entity, is shown in Fig. 4. If the broadcast coupling is specified for the multiple decomposition in pruning process, the operation *transform* will create a broadcast model for the BUF-PROCS consisting of one atomic BUF-PROC model. The number of components, BUF-PROCs, can be specified in the initialization process before simulation is begun.

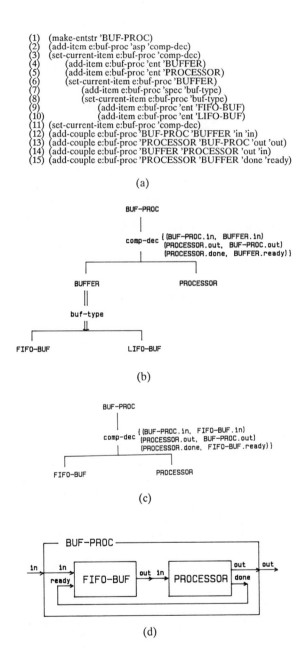

(a)

(b)

(c)

(d)

Fig. 3. (a) ESP-Scheme Code   (b) System Entity Structure
(c) Pruned Entity Structure   (d) Transformed Model

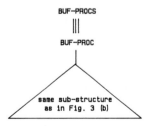

Fig. 4. System Entity Structure with Multiple Entity.

3.3 Hierarchical Model Structuring Operations

To show the power of *SES* hierarchical models structuring formalism we will discuss some advanced operations. Others can be found in (Kim, 1988).

The operation *add-item* is extended to the operation *add-sub-entstr*. This operation adds one entity structure under the current item of type aspect in the original entity structure. Similarly, the operation *delete-sub-entstr* is an extension of the operation *delete-item*. The operation *delete-sub-entstr* needs to specify an item so that a subentity structure consisting of all items under the specified item will be deleted.

The operation *add-mult* is extended such that the level of hierarchy for the multiple entities to be added is arbitrary. The operation *add-mult-mult* allows us to specify a hierarchical construction of different kernel models. Fig. 5 shows the operation that results in three levels of hierarchy of the multiple entities AS, BS, and CS. To specify a different coupling type for different kernel models, we use the operation *set-mult-coup-type*. An application of the operation *add-mult-mult* to modelling a multi-level hypercube architecture can be found in (Kim and Zeigler, 1988). The operation *attach-num-mult-children* attaches the number of components under a multiple entity to the multiple entity.

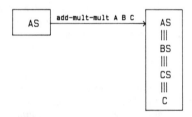

Fig. 5. Construction of Multi-level Multiple Entities.

3.4 Reuse of Pruned Entity Structures

The *Entity Structure Module* provides several operations for reuse of pruned entity structures. The operation *add-spec&ents-at-leaf* searches the entity structure base to find pruned entity structures whose root names are the same as that of a leaf entity in an entity structure. If any are found, the operation adds a specialization under the leaf entity and adds the pruned entities under the specialization (Fig. 6). The operation *mult-asp→asp* changes a multiple aspect in an entity structure to an aspect by specifying the number of children attached under the aspect.

The operation *cut-entstr* makes a non-leaf entity into a leaf entity by cutting all entities under the non-leaf entity, constructing a new entity structure with the entities cut, and saving it in the entity structure base (we shall describe entity strcuture base in section 5.1). The root of the new entity structure is the leaf entity under which all cut entities are connected with the same structure that they used to be. After creating the new en-

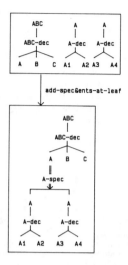

Fig. 6. Addition of Pruned Entity Structure.

tity structure, the operation asks the user to prune the created entity structure as many times as desired. The pruned entity structures are saved in the entity structure base for later use by the operation *add-spec&ents-at-leaf*. Fig. 7 shows the operation *cut-entstr*.

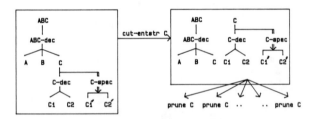

Fig. 7. Cutting Sub Entity Structure.

An entity structure can be constructed in a hierarchically distributed manner so that its leaf entities have their respective entity structures in the entity structure base. The entity structure so built may be merged into one entity structure. The operation *merge-entstr* searches entity structures in the entity structure base with the same root names as leaf entities of an entity structure. If such entity structures are present in the entity structure base, they replace the respective leaf entities.

4. Facilities in ESP-Scheme

SES construction, copying, and other facilities are provided by ESP-Scheme. The facility *make-entstr* creates an entity structure, whose name is the same as its root name except for a prefix "e:". For example, (*make-entstr* system) creates an entity structure e:system with root name system. Since the entity structure so created has only the root entity system, items should be added as required to construct the desired entity structure. The facility *delete-entstr* deletes an existing entity structure.

The facility *copy-entstr* copies one entity structure to another entity structure. For example, the facility create an entity structure that has the same structure as the original one. The facility copies a list of items and a list of branches from the original entity structure and constructs a new entity structure.

Since a list of all entity structures is maintained by the entity structure manager (described in section 5.2), any facility that creates or deletes entity structures should report to the manager about the creation and/or deletion of entity structures so that the manager can update the list of entity structures within it. For example, the facility *rename-entstr* asks the manager to delete the original entity structure from, and add the renamed entity structure to, the list within the manager.

5. Entity Structure Base/Model Base Management

The system entity structures represent the structure knowledge about systems. Such system entity structures are to be saved in the *entity structure base* (*ENBASE*) for later use. To do so, we save an entity structure created in the current Scheme environment into an external storage such as a disk for later use.

5.1 Entity Structure Base

We have implemented ESP-Scheme such that it can save entity structures in, and retrieve them from, the *ENBASE* by using two new facilities, *save-entstr* and *load-entstr*. The facility *save-entstr* saves an entity structure or a pruned entity structure into the *ENBASE* by storing a pair consisting of a list of items and a list of branches for the entity structure in the form of a disk file. A file name in the *ENBASE*, corresponding to an entity structure, is the same as its root entity name except for the extension of the file name, which can be either ".e" for the entity structure or ".p" for the pruned entity structure. The facility *load-entstr* searches for a file corresponding to an entity structure in the *ENBASE*, retrieves the items list and branches list for the corresponding entity structure, and constructs the entity structure.

5.2 Entity Structure Manager

A module *entity structure manager* (*ESM*) is designed to manage all system entity structures in the current environment and/or in the *ENBASE*. The module *ESM* has three local variables. The first variable is a list of entity structures either in the *ENBASE* or in the current environment. The second variable is a list of pruned entity structures either in the *ENBASE* or in the current environment. The third variable is a list of both entity structures and pruned entity structures in the current environment. The operations on the *ESM* include: show entity structures, add entity structure, and delete entity structure.

The operation *show-all:ens* shows all entity structures in the current environment and/or in the *ENBASE*. The operation shows the entity structures and pruned entity structures in the three sperate lists, as described above. The operation add entity structure adds an entity structure to the list in the *ESM* whenever the *ESM* receives a report on the creation of the entity structure from the facilities as described in section 4. The delete entity structure operation deletes an entity structure from the list in the *ESM* as required by the facilities *delete-entstr* or *rename-entstr*.

The initialization routine of the ESP-Scheme initializes the *ESM* when the ESP-Scheme is loaded. The initialization includes searching the *ENBASE* and setting up all lists of entity structures in the *ESM* so that the user can get available entity structures and retrieve some as required. The current *ENBASE* can be moved from one place to the other as requested by the user using *change-dir*. Any change in the *ENBASE* results in the reinitialization of the *ESM*.

5.3 Transform into DEVS Models

A *pruned entity structure* can be synthesized into a simulation model by the operation *transform*. As it visits each entity in the pruned entity structure, *transform* calls upon a *retrieval process* that searches a model corresponding to the *current entity*. If one is found, it is used and transformation of the entity subtree is aborted. The retrieval process proceeds by evaluating the *retrieval rules*, which consist of retrieval rules—pairs of *condition* and retrieval *action*—and *conflict resolution rules* by which a rule is selected if there is more than one with conditions satisfied.

One rule for searching a model that corresponds to the current entity first looks for the model in the working memory, then in the MBASE, and finally, if the current entity is a leaf, in the *ENBASE*. Before searching the model, another rule checks the name of the current entity. If the current entity has a base name and a *non-trivial* extension (the extension starts with numbers or "&"), the base name is used as an entity name for the retrieval process. If more than one rule is satisfied when evaluated, a conflict resolution rule fires only one rule. We employ context specificity—the rule with a more specific condition than other rules is fired—to resolve such a conflict. Details of retrieval rules and conflict resolution rules are available in (Kim, 1988).

If a pruned entity structure is found in the *ENBASE* in the searching process, a *transform* is invoked and executed in a separate Scheme environment so as not to interfere with the current environment. Each recursive invocation can occur in a leaf entity only.

6. Summary and Discussion

We have described an implementation of system entity structure in Scheme, ESP-Scheme, which serves as a model base management system for DEVS models. Our experience with the model management system has shown that it is easier to specify coupled models by defining the appropriate entity structure and applying transform for model synthesis. The transform requires existence of atomic models in the model base defined using DEVS-Scheme.

The utility of ESP-Schem has been demonstrated in construction of several complex hierarchical models for computer networks (Sevinc and Zeigler, 1988) and advanced computer architectures (Kim, 1988).

The above knowledge base framework, implemented in (Kim, 1988), intended to be generative in nature. It is a compact representation scheme which can be unfolded to generate the family of all possible models synthesizable from components in the model base. This knowledge base framework serves as our vehicle for research in knowledge-based system design using variant families of design models (Rozenblit and Zeigler, 1985; Rozenblit, 1986; Sevinc and Zeigler, 1988).

REFERENCES

Concepcion, A.I. and B.P. Zeigler "DEVS Formalism: A Framework for Hierarchical Model Development," *IEEE Trans. Software Engr.*, vol. SE-14, no. 2, pp. 228-241, Feb. 1988.

Kim, Tag Gon "A Knowledge-Based Environment for Hierarchical Modelling and Simulation," Ph.D. Dissertation. Dept. of Electrical and Computer Engr., University of Arizona, Tucson, AZ, 1988.

Kim, Tag Gon and B.P. Zeigler "The DEVS Formalism: Hierarchical, Modular System Specification in an Object-Oriented Framework," In *Proc. of 1987 Winter Simulation Conf.*, Atlanta, GA, 1987, pp. 559-566.

Kim, Tag Gon and B.P. Zeigler "The Class Kernel-Models in DEVS-Scheme: A Hypercube Architecture Example," *ACM SIMULETTER*, vol. 19, no. 2, June, 1988.

Rozenblit, J.W. "A Conceptual Basis for Model-Based System Design," Ph.D. Dissertation. Dept. of Computer Science, Wayne State University, Detroit, MI, 1985.

Rozenblit, J.W. and Zeigler, B.P. "Concepts of Knowledge Based System Design Environments," In *Proc. 1985 Winter Simulation Conf.*, San Francisco, CA, 1985, pp. 223-231.

Rozenblit, J.W., "A Conceptual Basis for Integrated, Model-Based System Design," Technical Report, Dept. of Electrical and Computer Engineering, University of Arizona, Tucson, AZ, Jan. 1986.

Sevinc S. and B.P. Zeigler "Entity Structure Based Design Methodology: A LAN Protocol Example," *IEEE Trans. Software Engr.*, vol. SE-14, no. 3, pp. 375-383, Mar. 1988.

Zeigler, B.P. *Multifacetted Modelling and Discrete Event Simulation*. London, UK and Orlando, FL: Academic Press, 1984.

Zeigler, B.P. "Hierarchical, Modular Discrete-Event Modelling in an Object-Oriented Environment," *Simulation*, vol, 50, no. 5, pp. 219-230, 1987.

Tag Gon Kim is a research engineer at the Environmental Research Lab of the University of Arizona. From 1980 to 1983, he has been a faculty in the Department of Electronics and Communication Engineering at the National Fisheries University of Pusan, Korea. His research interests are in the areas of AI, modelling and simulation, computer architectures, and expert system based real-time control system design. He received his Ph. D. in Electrical and Computer Engineering Department from the University of Arizona. He is a member of IEEE, ACM, and SCS.

Tag Gon Kim
ERLab, The University of Arizona
2601 E., Airport Dr.
Tucson, AZ 85706
(602) 741-1990

Bernard P. Zeigler is a professor of Computer Engineer at the University of Arizona. He is the author of *Multifacetted Modelling and Discrete Event Simulation*, Academic Press, 1984, and *Theory of Modelling and Simulation*, John Wiley, 1976. His research interests include artificial intelligence, distributed simulation, and expert system for simulation methodology.

Bernard P. Zeigler
Dept. of Electr. and Computer Engr.
The University of Arizona
Tucson, AZ 85721
(602) 621-2108

Advances in AI and Simulation
© 1989 By The Society for Computer
Simulation International
ISBN 0-911801-50-2

*FRASES — A knowledge representation scheme for engineering design

Jhyfang Hu, Yuehmin Huang, and Jerzy W. Rozenblit

AI Simulation Group
Dept. of Electrical and Computer Engineering
University of Arizona
Tucson, AZ 85721

ABSTRACT

Along with the rising complexity of design knowledge, knowledge management which includes knowledge acquisition, representation, control, and processing becomes a very difficult task. A good knowledge management scheme is needed to increase the reliability and efficiency of knowledge-based systems. In this paper an efficient knowledge representation scheme for engineering design applications called Frames and Rules Associated System Entity Structure (FRASES) is introduced. With FRASES, complex engineering design knowledge is organized into a hierarchical, entity-oriented tree structure to facilitate control and processing of knowledge. Exploiting well-defined axioms and operations of FRASES, the knowledge acquisition task, accomplished conventionally with time-consuming manual interviewing, can be efficiently automated.

INTRODUCTION

In the last decade the technology of knowledge-based systems has been widely used in solving various engineering problems such as system diagnosis, production scheduling, capacity planning, operation monitoring, design and synthesis, and performance evaluation. In general, the performance of a knowledge-based system is determined by its knowledge management scheme which includes techniques for knowledge representation, acquisition, and inferencing. Up to now, there is no accepted standard, common method for knowledge management in knowledge- based systems. The strategy for knowledge management is usually highly application-dependent. To assure high reliability and efficiency of knowledge-based systems, system designers are responsible to identify the characteristics of a design application and select the most appropriate knowledge management scheme.

Our efforts have focused on entity structure-based system design (Rozenblit and Zeigler 1988, Rozenblit and Huang, 1987). The system entity structure is a knowledge representation scheme that combines the concepts of decomposition, taxonomic, and coupling relationships (Zeigler 1984).

In the following sections we shall present a knowledge representation scheme called Frames and Rules Associated System Entity Structure (FRASES) for engineering design applications. The main objective of FRASES is to facilitate the knowledge management task in knowledge-based engineering design systems. The discussion of this paper will focus on issues of representation, acquisition, refinement, and inferencing.

KNOWLEDGE REPRESENTATION WITH FRASES

Knowledge-based systems are becoming increasing useful in solving complex engineering design problems. Each knowledge-based system may contain one or more knowledge bases for a specific application. For each knowledge base, a certain representation scheme is employed to organize the knowledge acquired from human experts. A good knowledge representation scheme not only efficiently represents all essential knowledge but it also facilitates the knowledge acquisition and inferencing processes. A good knowledge representation scheme for engineering design should be able to represent the following aspects of the design knowledge:

- structural/behavioral characteristic of objects
- taxonomy/decomposition of objects
- constraint checking and design synthesis rules
- generation of design alternatives procedures
- design verification and evaluation procedures

It should also facilitate knowledge management within the system. For example, it should assist in efficient knowledge acquisition, knowledge inferencing, and decision making. Finally, knowledge reflected by the representation scheme must be transparent to domain experts, knowledge engineers, and system users.

The requirement on high quality knowledge-based systems have made the knowledge representation become a major topic in AI research. Different schemes such as production rules (Newell and Simon 1972), frames (Minsky 1977), structure models (Dhar 1987), semantic networks (Quillian 1968), AND/OR trees (Nilsson 1971), and system entity structure (Zeigler 1984, Rozenblit and Huang 1987) have been defined for representing knowledge. These conventional representation schemes may not satisfy all requirements when applied to engineering design domain individually. Based on this observation, we augment the system entity structure into Frame and Rule-Associated System Entity Structure (FRASES). Combined with production rules and frames, FRASES sucessfully represents the knowledge required for engineering design into a hierarchical, entity-oriented knowledge base. FRASES is a superclass of the system entity structure that emcompasses the boundries, decompositions, and taxonomic relationships of the system being designed. All axioms (i.e., Uniformity, Strict hierarchy, Alternating mode, Valid brothers, Attached variables) and operations (i.e. Naming scheme, Distribution and Aggregation, Transformation, Pruning, Inheritance) defined for the system entity structure (Zeigler 1984) are also valid for FRASES-based representations.

In FRASES, an entity signifies a conceptual part of the system which has been identified as a component in one or more decompositions. Each such decomposition is called an aspect. In addition to decompositions, there are relations that facilitate the representation of variants for an entity. Called specialized entities, such variants inherit properties of an entity to which they are related by the specialization relation. A typical example of FRASES representation for a robot design is shown in Figure

* Supported by NASA-Ames Cooperative Agreement No. NOC 2-525.

1. As shown in Figure 1, each FRASES entity is associated with an Entity Information Frame (EIF). Each Entity Information Frame is a frame object containing variable slots of:

$$< N, DATTs, DSF, CRS, CH >$$

where
N: is the name of associated entity or model
DATTs: are design attributes of N
DSF: is the design specification form
CRS: are constraint rules for pruning/synthesis
CH : children entities of N

DSF is a frame used to accept user's design objectives, constraints, and criteria weighting scheme specification. CRS contains pruning and synthesis rules for generating a system configuration. CH indicates the children nodes of the entity. To accomplish a design application, the knowledge given by an Entity Information Frame (EIF) will be extracted and processed by an appropriate inference engine during the design process.

The knowledge representation in FRASES is distinguished from other knowledge representation schemes by the following features:

- Generation of Knowledge: FRASES is a generative representation scheme. Via transformations, new knowledge can be generated.

- Modularity: Axioms of strict hierarchy and alternation assure FRASES to be a hierarchical, modular knowledge representation scheme. This is essential for representing complex knowledge required in engineering design. Knowledge processing (e.g., modifications, updating, deleting) can be localized by focusing on an entity for which the processing is required.

- Efficiency: The characteristic of inheritance and uniformity highly reduces the size of a knowledge base required for the same design application. In FRASES all the attached attributes and substructures are inherited through the specialization of an entity. Every occurrence of an entity has the same Entity Information Frame and isomorphic substructures. The identical nodes located in different paths are updated automatically according to the axiom of uniformity.

- Flexibility: By using the top-down design methodology, the FRASES enables the users to specify design knowledge at the most appropriate design level and to refine the knowledge (or equivalent FRASES structure) as the technology evolves and changes.

KNOWLEDGE ACQUISITION WITH FRASES

Although a number of methodologies such as interviewing, protocol analysis, observing, induction, clustering, prototyping (Waterman 1971, Ritchie 1984, Kahn 1985, Hart 1985, Kessel 1986, Gaines 1987, Olson 1987, etc.) etc., have been proposed for knowledge acquisition, it is difficult to demonstrate their efficiency in engineering design applications. Different design applications require different strategies for knowledge acquisition and representation to avoid misunderstanding and/or loss of important knowledge from human expert. It is very difficult to acquire all aspects of design knowledge simply via the question/answer elicitation process. For example, the knowledge engineer may be unable to question all knowledge required for a design application; or the knowledge to be acquired may be too complicated to be asked in questions, or the human expert may misunderstand the knowledge engineer's questions. All the above situations may result in unnecessary, duplicate, conflicting, or confused knowledge. Acquiring complex knowledge with conventional acquisition methods is costly due to preparation, verification, organization, and traslation of information acquired from human experts. To avoid misunderstanding and/or missing of important facts, knowledge acquisition should be directed or supervised under a certain scheme. The scheme should help in: acquiring knowledge, detecting conflicts, identifying missing facts, and eliminating duplicate or unnecessary knowledge.

FRASES is a complete knowledge representation scheme for engineering design application, which conveys not only the static knowledge (structure and attributes) but also the dynamic knowledge (constraint rules for design, synthesis, verification and evaluation) required for design applications. By using FRASES, the complex knowledge acquisition task can be automated. At each design level, question patterns about decomposition and taxonomy knowledge of design objects can be generated automatically. If an Entity Information Frame (EIF) is missing, this fact will be detected and signaled to design experts. Appropriate verification procedures will be integrated for axiom examination and elimination of conflicting and/or duplicate knowledge. Acquired knowledge will be automatically translated into internal representation without human intervention. Knowledge acquisition assisted or activated by following the FRASES approach is called Knowledge Acquisition based on Representation (KAR). A simplified knowledge acquisition on robot design with KAR approach is shown in Figure 2. At each iterative acquisition, related query rules are referred and interpreted based on the structural nature of FRASES to generate question patterns. Several advantages are expected from the KAR approach:

- Efficiency: Questions patterns required to acquire design knowledge for decomposition, taxonomy, pruning, and synthesis of systems are first predefined into query rules. Based on the structure of FRASES, appropriate questions can be automatically generated to querry knowledge. KAR approach directly translates the acquired knowledge into FRASES representation. By exploiting the defined axioms and operations, the time-consuming acquisition task can be accomplished efficiently.

- Flexibility: FRASES is a flexible knowledge representation scheme. Simple modification of FRASES will fit other AI research applications such as object identification or consultantion systems. As shown in Figure 3, to identify an appropriate robot type for design application, alternative robot designs can be organized into a pure specialization FRASES with selction constraints associated with appropriate specialization entities.

- Controllability and Observability: FRASES will be implemented using extensive graphic facilities. The entity-oriented, hierarchical structure of FRASES allows the represented knowledge to be updated easily.

- Cost-Effectiveness: Unlike the conventional schemes which

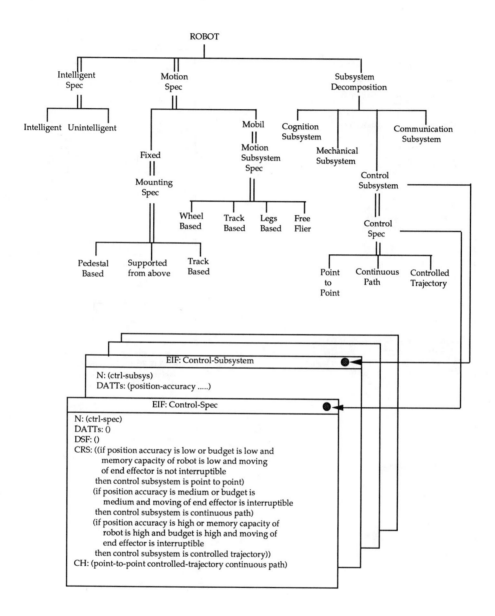

Figure 1 Robot design in FRASES

143

Expert/KAR Interaction	System Internal Conversion

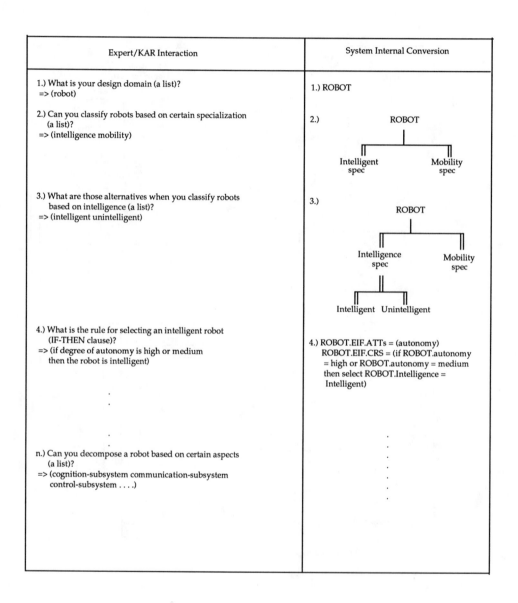

1.) What is your design domain (a list)?
=> (robot)

1.) ROBOT

2.) Can you classify robots based on certain specialization (a list)?
=> (intelligence mobility)

2.) ROBOT — Intelligent spec / Mobility spec

3.) What are those alternatives when you classify robots based on intelligence (a list)?
=> (intelligent unintelligent)

3.) ROBOT — Intelligence spec / Mobility spec; Intelligence spec — Intelligent Unintelligent

4.) What is the rule for selecting an intelligent robot (IF-THEN clause)?
=> (if degree of autonomy is high or medium then the robot is intelligent)

4.) ROBOT.EIF.ATTs = (autonomy)
ROBOT.EIF.CRS = (if ROBOT.autonomy = high or ROBOT.autonomy = medium then select ROBOT.Intelligence = Intelligent)

n.) Can you decompose a robot based on certain aspects (a list)?
=> (cognition-subsystem communication-subsystem control-subsystem . . . .)

Figure 2 KAR with FRASES for robot design

144

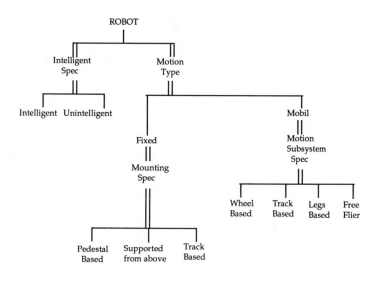

Intelligent-Spec.EIF.CRS:
    ((if desired autonomy is high or medium then select Intelligent Robot)
    (if desired autonomy is low then select Unintelligent ROBOT))

Motion-Type-EIF.CRS:
    ((if budget is low and working area is less than 25 square feet or
        arm carrying capacity is larger than 1000 lbs
     then select Fixed ROBOT)
    (if budget is high and working area is larger than 25 square feet or
        arm carrying capacity is less than 1000 lbs
     then select Mobil ROBOT))

Mounting-Spec.EIF.CRS:
    ((if Motion-type is fixed and power consumption is low and
       working area has a solid ground then select Pedestal-Based mounting)
    (if Motion-type is fixed and power consumption is medium and
      degree of freedom is low and working area has a soft ground
     then select Support-from-above mounting)
      ....
)

Figure 3 Object identification with FRASES

always require human intervention in knowledge acquisition, verification, translation, and organization, the knowledge acquisition task is automated with KAR. The fast turnaround of knowledge acquisition highly reduces the development cost of knowledge-based systems.

DESIGN PROCESS AND VERIFICATION WITH FRASES

After the design knowledge is built into FRASES representation, the system is ready to aid in the design process. A set of design objectives and constraints are accepted through the Design Specification Form (DSF) interface. These user- specified requirements and constraints are employed to derive design configurations. From the view point of problem-solving, aspect and specialization nodes of the system entity structure are the states of the solution space. The process of design generation can be interpreted as a search directed by constraints associated with these states. The mechanism which drives this search is called pruning (Rozenblit and Huang 1987). The resultant design is accomplished by forming a path made of these states through a process of analysis, synthesis, and evaluation. A number of production rules are attached to each state to direct the search. The type of rules can be either selection or synthesis. This depends on the type of a node. The synthesis rules are associated with the aspect node. The selection rules are associated with the specialization node (Rozenblit and Huang 1987). Generally speaking, design constraints are classified into two categories, static and dynamic (Rozenblit and Hu 1988). Without the aid of verification tools such as analytic methods or simulation, the dynamic constraints can not be used for configuration pruning. To save time, all possible design configurations should be generated all at once instead of reapplying searching techniques time after time. As mentioned before, simulation is employed for our design verification. If there exists more than one design configuration, the trade-off design evaluation using techniques of multi-criteria decision making will be activated to suggest the most appropriate design based on the criteria weighting specified in the Design Specification Form (Rozenblit and Hu 1988).

CONCLUSION

Because knowledge-based systems explicitly represent and reason with knowledge supplied by human experts, they offer considerable promise in modern engineering design. This paper has presented a knowledge management scheme used in our system called Knowledge-Based Design Support Environment (KBDSE). A flexible and efficient knowledge representation scheme called FRASES was introduced for representing complicated modern engineering design knowledge. The hierarchical, entity-oriented FRASES representation not only facilitates the knowledge acquisition but also eases control and processing of design knowledge. Knowledge management with FRASES, the time and cost spent in acquisition, verification, translation, organization and application are highly reduced.

REFERENCES

Dhar, V. and H. E. Pople. 1987. "Rule-Based versus Structure-Based Models for Explaining and Generating Expert Behavior," *Communication of the ACM*, vol.30, no.6, p.542-555.

Gaines, B. R. 1987. "An Overview of Knowledge Acquisition and Transfer," *Int. J. Man-Machine Studies*, No.26, p.453-472.

Hart, A. (1985). Knowledge Elicitation: Issues and Methods, Computer-Aided Design, Vol.17, No.9, p.455-462.

Kahn, G. 1985. "Strategies for Knowledge Acquisition," *IEEE Transactions on Pattern Analysis and Machine Intelligence*, No.7, p.511-522.

Kessel, K. L. 1986. "Methodological Tools for Knowledge Acquisition," *Proceedings of the 1986 IEEE International Conference on System, Man, and Cybernetics*, Atlanta, GA.

Newll, A. and H. A. Simon. 1972. *Human Problem Solving*, Englewood Cliffs, NJ: Prentice-Hall.

Nilsson, N. J. 1971. *Problem-Solving Methods in Artificial Intelligence*, New York: McGraw-Hill.

Olson, J. R. and Henry H. Rueter 1987. "Extracting Expertise from Experts: Methods for Knowledge Acquisition," *Expert Systems*, August 1987, Vol.4, No.3, p.152-168.

Quillian, M. R. 1968. "Semantic Memory," In SIP, pp.216-270.

Ritchie, I. C. 1984. "Knowledge Acquisition by Computer Induction," *Proceedings of UNICOM Seminar*, London, England.

Rozenblit, J. W. and Jhyfang Hu. 1988. "Experimental Frame Generation in a Knowledge-based System Design and Simulation Environment", In: *Modelling and Simulation Methodology: Knowledge System Paradigms*, (M. Elzas et. al., eds), North Holland, Amsterdam.

Rozenblit, J. W. and Y. M. Huang. 1987. "Constraint-Driven Generation of Model Structures," *Proceedings of the 1987 Winter Simulation Conference*, Atlanta, Geogia.

Rozenblit, J. W. and B. P. Zeigler. 1988. "Design and Modeling Concepts," *International Encyclopedia of Robotics Application and Automation*, John Wiley and Sons, Inc., New York, p.308.

Waterman, D. A. and A. Newell. 1971. "Protocol Analysis as a Task for Artificial Intelligence," *Artificial Intelligence*, 2, p.285.

Winston, P. H. 1984. Artificial Intelligence, 2nd Ed., Addison Wesley Publishing Company, Massachusetts.

Zeigler, B. P. 1984. Multifacetted Modelling and Discrete Event Simulation, Academic Press, London.

Advances in AI and Simulation
© 1989 By The Society for Computer
Simulation International
ISBN 0-911801-50-2

Using artificial intelligence based system simulation in management information systems research: Three case studies

Bruce C. Herniter
Kung-Chao Liu
Mark O. Pendergast
Department of Management Information Systems
The University of Arizona
Tucson, Arizona 85721

Bitnet: HERNITER or LIUKC or PENDERGAST @ARIZMIS
Internet: HERNITER or LIUKC or PENDERGAST @MIS.ARIZONA.EDU

ABSTRACT

Three facets of Artificial Intelligence Based System Simulation (AISS) are brought together to acquire and test knowledge about information systems: System Entity Structures, which depict the boundaries and decompositions of a system; Discrete Event System Simulation, which is a formalism for hierarchical, modular, discrete event simulation; and Expert Systems.

This paper describes the use of AISS tools in three experimental applications within the PLEXSYS research environment of the Department of Management Information Systems, The University of Arizona. The three cases demonstrate the power and effectiveness of Artificial Intelligence Based System Simulation techniques when applied to the broad range of Management Information Systems research problems.

INTRODUCTION

Management Information Systems (MIS) research has evolved for some forty years, yet its research methodologies are still changing (Cooper 1988). With this evolving nature of MIS research in mind, it is a good idea to fertilize the field by introducing some well-established techniques from other areas.

We have selected a class of Artificial Intelligence Based System Simulation (AISS) techniques originally developed by Zeigler and Rozenblit (Rozenblit 1986) of the Department of Electrical and Computer Engineering of The University of Arizona to test this assertion. The goal is to demonstrate that it is possible for MIS to adopt techniques founded elsewhere, thereby synthesizing its own, new methodologies. Through this paper, we will show how the AISS technique can be infused into MIS research to achieve innovation.

MIS System Development Methodology

Since MIS spans a spectrum of research from behavioral science to engineering, it employs many research methodologies including mathematical simulation, system development, case study, survey, field study, and laboratory experimentation. It is general practice among MIS researchers to employ two or more methodologies to support their work. For example, simulation is often combined with system development to verify a design; field studies are often done in conjunction with laboratory experimentation to provide external generalizability. Vogel and Nunamaker (1987) have documented how the six methodologies have been used to support research work of the PLEXSYS project performed at the MIS Department of The University of Arizona.

In this paper, we show how system development is a research methodology that can benefit from AISS. The process entails five steps (Chen 1988): (1) Construct a conceptual framework, (2) develop a system architecture, (3) analyze and design the system, (4) build the system, and (5) observe and evaluate the system. This methodology is particularly useful in areas that have few or no theoretical guidelines.

Artificial Intelligence Based System Simulation (AISS) Technique

The Artificial Intelligence Based System Simulation (AISS) approach consists of three major conceptual elements: System Entity Structure (SES) technique, Discrete Event System Simulation (DEVS) formalism, and Expert System technology.

Rozenblit (1986) describes SES as a structure which embodies knowledge using three basic relationships: decomposition, taxonomy, and coupling. Decomposition refers to the process of breaking an object into its basic component parts. A taxonomy is a means by which all possible variants of an object can be represented. Coupling refers to how independent model components interact. SES uses a "tree-like" graph to represent the model decompositions and taxonomies. The principles of uniformity and inheritance are employed to create a consistent and concise structure.

Zeigler (1984) details the DEVS formalism. Systems are synthesized from atomic models characterized by state variables. Each model is represented as a vector of external states, internal states, output variables, internal and external transition functions, time advance function, and an output function. DEVS has been implemented on Scheme, a LISP implementation available from Texas Instruments (Zeigler 1987). In addition, Zeigler (1984) defines a separate model type, called the Experimental Frame (EF), that manages the creation of events and collections data on the response of the model. The EF is centralized, there being only one for the entire system or there may be an EF with each atomic model. An EF is made of three conceptual parts: Generator, Transducer, and Acceptor. The Generator creates events for the system to process. The Acceptor monitors the run control segment, while the Transducer gathers summary statistics.

Framework of This Paper

In the ensuing of this paper, we will describe the general approach of using AISS technique in Section 2 and show the application of AISS in three case studies in Section 3. The three cases are: using AISS to conduct research on the planning of Group Decision Support System sessions, then build expert systems for aid in the planning work; using AISS to study the feasibility of implementing Group Decision Support Systems of various network configurations; and using AISS to establish an environment in which an information system development personnel can construct and experiment on information system prototypes. We will then summarize our achievements in Section 4.

THE USE OF AISS TECHNIQUE IN SYSTEM DEVELOPMENT

The AISS process is performed in several stages: SES definition, system instance definition, simulation model definition, and finally the actual running of the system simulation.

SES definition consists of defining a system by first decomposing it into component parts at the level which the simulation is to be performed. This decomposed system is arranged in a tree structure, using the principles of inheritance and uniformity to eliminate redundant aspects. For each component part a taxonomy (enumeration of variations) is created. Finally, system configuration and performance variables are identified and attached to their respective model components. The resulting structure represents all possible configurations of the modeled system.

The second step consists of "pruning" the SES to obtain just those configurations which exhibit desirable characteristics. This pruning can be done manually or with the aid of an Expert System. The pruning operation consists of deciding on which variants for an entity to assume. Once pruning has been completed, the resulting SES represents one possible variation of the original structure which meets specific requirements for a given system. Additional instance models can be built by repeating the pruning step and selecting different options.

The third step consists of taking the pruned SES composition trees and building models which will serve as the basis for running discrete event simulations. Experimental frames are developed for each model to perform simulation run control, event generation, and the measurement and recording of model variable data.

Finally, simulations can be run for each candidate configuration using DEVS-Scheme or any other suitable simulation tool, e.g., NETWORK II.5 (CACI 1987). The simulation results can then be used as a basis for selecting the best candidate configuration.

In summary, the AISS technique can be used at every step in the system development research methodology. SES can be used to develop the taxonomic knowledge required for the conceptual framework. Pruning can be used to guide the development of a system architecture. Simulation results can be used to analyze and design the system and are an aid to analyze observations and evaluate the system.

THE CASE STUDIES

Planning in a Group Decision Support System Environment

The methodology employed uses the concept of AISS as a way of exploring processes, tools, and procedures of a Group Decision Support System (GDSS) implementation. The goal of this case study is a prototype agenda-setting expert system for the use of software tools during a group planning session. An SES was created to classify the different system types of GDSS and pruned to model the PLEXSYS system. Then a prototype expert system to advise the system was constructed. Finally, a simulation was performed.

GDSS research is a response to a common problem: decision makers need to attend meetings to discuss issues and trade information, but those meetings take time away from other important tasks.

GDSS aims to make meetings more efficient (Kraemer and King 1988). Experts in the fields of MIS and Decision Sciences define GDSS as "a set of software, hardware, language components, and procedures that support a group of people in a decision related meeting" (Huber 1984) and "an integrated computer based system which facilitate solution of semi or unstructured problems by a group who has joint responsibility for making the decision" (DeSanctis and Gallupe 1987). Both of these definitions are based on the use of computer systems and fixed procedures to coerce people into using a rational decision process and to ignore intuition, corporate politics, or personal biases.

PLEXSYS is The University of Arizona's GDSS environment, encompassing two computer laboratories (called Plexcenters) and the group software (Dennis et al. 1988; Vogel et al. 1988). Corporate planning is a major use of the Plexcenters.

There are many arrangements that need to be made for a successful meeting to take place at the Plexcenters; a session has many aspects and can take on many specializations. The SES for a Session using the Plexcenters is in Figure 1. For this case study, four specializations were postulated: Group (internal or external to The University of Arizona), Room (choosing between the two Plexcenter rooms, or a networked linking of the two), Range (strategic or tactical issues), and Cooperative (a congenial or an adversarial atmosphere). Each group that wishes to use the facilities will fit into only one option of each of the above categories. Three aspects were chosen. Each meeting may have any number of the options under: Phase (type of activity), Initiation (the software necessary to start a meeting using the software tools provided by the MIS department), and Tool (the optional software tools, any of which may be used during a session).

The selection of these specializations and aspects are driven by the needs of the Session Expert System. The Session Expert System was implemented using the MODSYN rule base and inference engine software (Huang 1987). The rules (through the backward chaining of MODSYN) guide the Plexcenters Session Administrator through four separate aspects of a session: Room selection (based on group size), Cost (based on group size and group specialization–University or non- University), Tool selection (based upon the Phase aspect) and Duration (again, based on the Phase aspect).

The duration of the Analysis Phase was the object of the simulation. The Analysis Phase Tools (Issue Analysis, Vote, and Business Planner) were the only tools for which duration figures were available. Tool use in each PLEXSYS Phase most closely resembles a pipeline process: one tool follows another (Figure 2). There are three processors, each represents one software tool and is characterized by a separate expected time $< T >$. The expected time $< T >$ is used to generate an actual time T, given by the Poisson. The simulation was done on DEVS-Scheme.

In the DEVS-Scheme implementation, hold time T is generated in the subprocessor itself. The Turnaround Time is the sum of all three subprocessor hold times. The Transducer collects statistics on average Turnaround Time (the time to required for one event to work its way through the system) and Thruput (the frequency with which events are processed). Trial results for 10 simulation runs for this simple pipeline model are close to expected values.

This case demonstrates how AISS methodology can be used to first organize knowledge and then create useful expert system and simulations in Group Decision Support Systems. This is quite useful as information on how to plan meetings for the Plexcenters is still being gathered and in many cases the administrators are "flying blind." Further simulation studies will provide more information that can be encoded in the expert system. Even more importantly, the software tools themselves are constantly under revision and are an important area of MIS research. With the SES as a road map,

requirements for new tools will be more easily identified and their purpose more clear.

Construction of Internetworked Group Decision Support System Simulation Models

The following illustrates how the AISS approach is applied to an MIS system design problem. The case concerns the expansion of a local area network (LAN) based GDSS system to include remote work stations and other remote GDSS systems.

As mentioned in the first case study, the MIS department at The University of Arizona is performing on going research into the feasibility and applicability of GDSS. Current systems let participants run GDSS software on PCs in the same room connected with a LAN (IBM PC NET or Token Ring). Communications consists of shared files, file transfer, and program to program datagram exchanges. We would like to extend our GDSS capability to allow remote users to dial-in to a GDSS and the interconnection of different GDSSs, either remote or local. The design and implementation of internet GDSS systems necessitates the research of this question: "Can currently available LAN software meet the throughput and response time requirements of an interactive GDSS? If not, what can be done to change application communication characteristics or LAN gateway performance to make such a system possible?"

The ultimate GDSS system would have the capability to dynamically create a GDSS configuration based on the current capabilities of an organization and the participation requirements for a given GDSS session. This would allow a corporate officer to call a meeting whose members are in remote (or local) sites and have access to the GDSS server via a combination of gateways, bridges, and LANs. Requirements for such a system include: (1) Linking LAN systems via gateways and bridges, (2) performing GDSS applications with users in remote rooms, (3) maintaining or improving current response times (1 or 2 seconds), (4) dynamically configuring systems based on needs of a particular session, and (5) supporting a variety of off the shelf hardware and software.

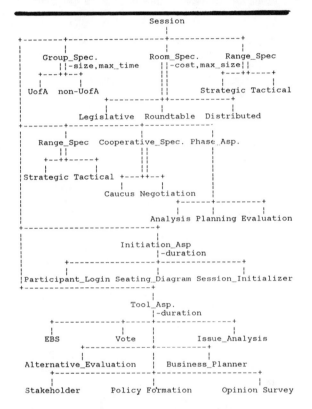

Figure 1: System Entity Structure for GDSS Environment

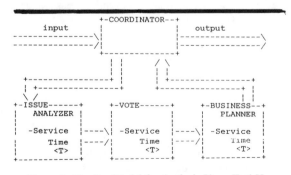

Figure 2: Pipeline Model for Analysis Phase Tool Use

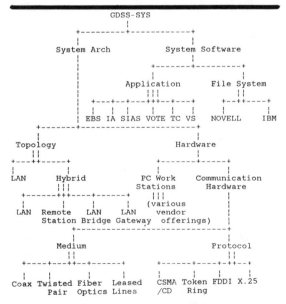

Figure 3: Internet GDSS System Entity Structure

The SES in Figure 3 represents a portion of the proposed internet GDSS system design. Non-pertinent items such as printers and large screen displays have been omitted.

A subset of the rules used to prune the SES to generate GDSS Internet models is presented in Figure 4. The rules presented are grouped according to the decomposition and specialization pruning they perform.

Network Software Selection:

```
1) If throughput_requirements are (medium,low) and
       stand_alone_file_server is not desirable
   then Network_Software is IBM PCNET.

2) If throughput_requirements are high or
       stand_alone_file_server is desirable
   then Network_Software is NOVELL.
```

Network Topology:

```
1) If number_of_existing_lans is greater_than_one and
       distance_between_closest_nodes is small
   then LAN_BRIDGE_LAN is indicated.

2) If number_of_existing_lans is greater_than_one and
       distance_between_closest_nodes is large
   then LAN_GATEWAY_REMOTE_LAN is indicated.
```

Figure 4: Pruning Rules for Internet GDSS SES

NETWORK II.5 simulation package will be used to perform the system simulations. Network II.5 provides an easy means to define a system by specify parameters and linkages for its generic model components, storage devices, processor entities, transfer devices, and modules. Network II.5 automatically collects pertinent data on all model components and separate distribution functions can be defined for each component. Therefore, a Network II.5 model can be viewed as having a separate EF for each component. Network II.5 simulation functions can be mapped into the DEVS EF formalism in the following manner:

X = set of external events = (semaphore setting, message reception, prerequisite module completion, start time, iteration interval)

S = set of internal states = (transfer in progress, awaiting message, awaiting module completion, busy, queue status, processing, delaying, idle)

Y = set of output variables, the following is a partial list: (storage requests granted, file requests, completed accesses, avg/max/std dev usage time, percent time busy, ...)

L = Output function, can be any of the following: (summary report, snapshot report, periodic report, event traces)

dx,di = internal state transitions–internal to Network II.5

ta = time advance function–internal to Network II.5

The SES, rule base, and model structure defined above were used to build three GDSS hardware configurations: two GDSS LANs bridged together, two GDSS LANs connected via a remote gateway, and a remote work station attached to a GDSS LAN. Simulations were performed for each configuration running a variety of tools. The simulation results showed that the current GDSS file structure and interprogram communications methods employed would not be adequate for an internetworked systems. These re-

sults were then used to construct new models which assumed a distributed file structure (as opposed to centralized) and exception updating of files (only transferring new or changed records).

The AISS approach proved to be a useful and effective tool for synthesizing and modeling GDSS Internetworked systems. The model structure and definition technique are easily adapted to networking simulation packages such as Network II.5.

Prototyping of Information Systems

The objective of prototyping is to clarify the characteristics and operation of an information system by constructing a working model that can be exercised. This case study is concerned with how to use an environment that is based on the AISS technique to construct information system prototypes formulated on the data flow model.

The graphical representation of the data flow model, called data flow diagram (DFD) (Page-Jones 1980), has four kinds of elements: external entity, which is the source or sink of data; data flow, which is the data in action; data store, which is the data at rest; and process, which receives data, transforms it, and releases transformed data. It is implied that a process executes only when all its inputs are available, but it does not necessarily produce all its outputs simultaneously.

The requirements for an environment for information system prototyping in data flow model should include:

1. A user can define the structure of the system to be built. The environment should provide means for describing the elements of DFDs, the interconnections between the elements, and the leveling between DFDs.

2. A user can choose a suitable configuration for the system according to certain criteria. The environment should have facilities that help the user to determine on the configuration.

3. A user can derive an executable prototype with respect to the chosen configuration. The environment should supply building blocks for composing the prototype.

4. A user can experiment on the prototype to observe its behavior and gather some statistics for decision making. The information to be captured is, for example, the performance of the whole or some components of the prototype. The environment should have mechanism for collecting statistics and should permit the user to run a prototype in different settings.

5. A user can do prototyping for a partial system. The environment should let the user select the scope of a partial system and build a prototype for it. The environment should also make sure that the prototype for a partial system is valid within the context of the whole system.

An environment that fulfills these requirements can be achieved by imposing a process of fabricating information systems prototypes on top of the AISS technique. The process consists of three phases: decomposition, composition, and evaluation, as shown in Figure 5. A user first enters the decomposition phase and goes through the composition and evaluation phases. He may then decide to return to the decomposition phase or escape from the iteration of prototyping process. The iteration may repeat as many times.

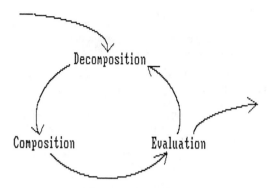

Figure 5: Phases of the Prototyping Process

The goal of the decomposition phase is to derive an SES that represents a specific configuration of an information system that fulfills user's requirements. Given the generic SES that represents the data flow model (Figure 6), a user first expands the generic SES into a specific one that characterizes data stores and elementary processes in more detail. Figure 7 exemplifies typical decompositions of data stores. The user then instantiates the SES to represent the DFDs of the information system being studied. The next work is to specify rules for selecting the types of external entities, data stores, and processes and use the rules to prune the instantiated SES to derive a specific configuration. Figure 8 shows two sample rules for selecting data stores.

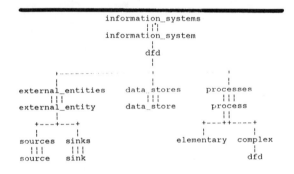

Figure 6: Generic System Entity Structure for Data Flow Modeling

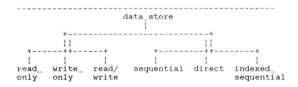

Figure 7: Typical Decomposition of Data Stores

```
If    access_mode=on-line and (volume=high,medium)
Then organization = indexed_sequential

If    access_mode = on-line and volume = low
Then organization = sequential
```

Figure 8: Sample Rules for Selecting a Data Store

The goal of the composition phase is to synthesize an executable prototype in DEVS-Scheme from a set of DEVS-Scheme templates in accordance with the pruned SES from the decomposition phase, and enhance the EFs of the synthesized prototype so that they can catch at appropriate statistics in the evaluation phase. As proposed by Rozenblit (1986), each template should possess a local EF. An EF local to an information system type template is, in fact, the global EF for the whole prototype.

During the evaluation phase a user exercises the information system prototype obtained in the composition phase to determine the quality of the prototype, validate the specifications of the information system being modeled, and so on. To do so, the user executes the prototype in different circumstances and analyzes the information collected by the EFs of the prototype. Based on the result of analysis he decides to go back to the decomposition phase or exit from the prototyping process.

To measure the effectiveness of the proposed information system prototyping environment, it is evaluated against the requirements for an ideal environment. The comparison is tabulated in Table 1.

Ideal Environment	Proposed Environment
Provide means for describing elements of DFDs, interconnections between the elements, and leveling between DFDs.	System entity structure can represent elements of DFD and leveling of DFDs, but not interconnections between the elements of DFDs. The user must refer back to original DFDs.
Provide facilities to help choosing a configuration.	A rule-based expert system (Huang 1987) helps a user to select appropriate configuration.
Supply building blocks for composing prototype.	Each DEVS-Scheme model serves as a building block due to the hierarchical, modular implementation of DEVS-Scheme.
Provide means for experimenting on prototype and have mechanisms for collecting statistics.	DEVS-Scheme environment allows a user to run a prototype in DEVS-Scheme. EFs collect statistics.
Support partial system prototyping.	With the help of local EF any entity on the SES can be executed separately.

Table 1: Comparison of Ideal and Proposed Prototyping Environments

This example has shown the usefulness of AISS technique in administering a prototyping environment for information system development. The AISS technique is flexible and extensible so it can be adapted for prototyping work, which employs both the system modeling and simulation capabilities of AISS.

CONCLUSIONS

Management Information Systems represents the boundary between

151

systems and human beings; between technology and design. The field concerns itself with applying system development methodology to aid and structure of decision processes, the development of network software that implements those tools and finally the design, development and implementation of systems.

Although what we have done is quite preliminary, the three cases do cover a broad spectrum of MIS research: the management of meetings, the design of networks for microcomputers, and creating a user-friendly system design methodology. The application of AISS techniques to the three projects presented here was a success. The AISS techniques permitted the system designers to 1) classify knowledge in a convenient way, 2) put that knowledge into expert systems, and 3) apply that knowledge through the development of simulations.

ACKNOWLEDGMENTS

We would like to thank Drs. J. W. Rozenblit and B. P. Zeigler for their continued guidance for our research. This manuscript could not have been completed without the expert assistance of Irene Hop and the cooperation of the Department of Management Information Systems at The University of Arizona.

REFERENCES

CACI. 1987. Network II.5 User's Manual, Version 3 (June).

Chen, M. 1988. The Integration of Organization and Information System Modeling: A Metasystem Approach to the Generation of Group Decision Support Systems and Computer-Aided Software Engineering. Unpublished Ph.D. dissertation, Department of Management Information Systems, The University of Arizona, Tucson.

Cooper, R.B. 1988. "Review of Management Information Systems Research: A Management Support Emphasis." Information Processing & Management 24, no. 1: 73-102.

Dennis, A.R.; J.F. George; L.M. Jessup; J.F. Nunamaker, Jr.; and D.R. Vogel. 1988. "Information Technology to Support Electronic Meetings." MIS Quarterly 12, no. 4 (Dec.): forthcoming.

DeSanctis, G. and R.B. Gallupe. 1987. "A Foundation for the Study of Group Decision Support Systems." Management Science 33, no. 5 (May): 589-609.

Huang, Y.M. 1987. Building an Expert System Shell for Design Model Synthesis in Logic Programming. Unpublished master's thesis, Department of Electrical and Computer Engineering, The University of Arizona, Tucson.

Huber, G.P. 1984. "Issues in the Design of Group Decision Support Systems." MIS Quarterly 8, no. 3 (Sep.): 195-204.

Kraemer, K.L. and J.L. King. 1988. "Computer-Based Systems for Cooperative Work and Group Decision Making." ACM Computing Surveys 20, no. 2 (June): 115-146.

Page-Jones, M. 1980. The Practical Guide to Structured Systems Design. Yourdon, New York.

Rozenblit, J.W. 1986. "A Conceptual Basis for Integrated, Model-based System Design." Technical Report. Department of Electrical and Computer Engineering, The University of Arizona, Tucson.

Vogel, D.R. and J.F. Nunamaker, Jr. 1987. "Group Decision Support Systems Impact: A Multi-methodological Exploration." Working Paper. Department of Management Information Systems, The University of Arizona, Tucson.

Vogel, D.R.; J.F. Nunamaker, Jr.; J.F. George; A.R. Dennis. 1988. "Group Decision Support Systems: Evolution and Status at The University of Arizona." Center for Management of Information Working Paper CMI- WPS-88-02. Department of Management Information Systems, The University of Arizona, Tucson.

Zeigler, B.P. 1984. Multifaceted Modelling and Discrete Event Simulation. Academic, New York.

Zeigler, B.P. 1987. "Hierarchical Modular Discrete Event Modelling in an Object Oriented Environment." Simulation Journal 49, no. 5: 219-230.

Advances in AI and Simulation
© 1989 By The Society for Computer
Simulation International
ISBN 0-911801-50-2

An AI simulation and modeling tool

Marilyn Golden
Ford Aerospace Corporation
1260 Crossman Avenue
Sunnyvale, CA 94089

ABSTRACT

Software simulation is playing an increasing role in the entire product development life cycle. Traditional software simulation tools have been complex and tedious to use and are not part of an integrated environment. Knowledge representation, knowledge acquisition and reasoning capabilities, resulting from AI research, can alleviate the problems involved with traditional simulation tools and can extend and enhance the capability of software simulation.

Ford Aerospace has developed a software tool that interacts with the user to model the problem domain. The tool, named Paragon, automatically provides a continuous, time-sliced simulation of the modeled domain's behavior. Model-building with Paragon is object oriented and requires no programming. Using the system, a series of integrated graphic screens controlled by mouse selection, requires only a few hours of training.

Once developed, the domain model can serve as the knowledge base for an intelligent, model-based system. A future enhancement is that the model will serve as the "data base" for an integrated environment with an automated interface to a diverse assortment of software tools.

INTRODUCTION

Paragon, the tool described in this paper, was developed as the result of the need for automated satellite control systems that could detect and resolve *unanticipated* satellite anomalies. Traditional approaches such as fault trees and production rule systems were judged inappropriate because all potential faults could not be enumerated for such a complex system that was only "visible" through a fixed set of telemetered data.

The applications research team began investigating the branch of artificial intelligence (AI) known as model based reasoning as a potential method for resolving the problem. The theory was that the human satellite specialist, who currently resolves satellite anomalies, relies on comparing the symptoms observed in the telemetry with his mental model of the satellite. Reasoning about a model of the satellite as it is designed to operate, he hypothesizes the cause of the observed telemetry and justifies his hypothesis. Once the cause is known, a similar reasoning effort can select a command or series of commands to correct or at least mitigate the effects of the fault. It was determined that our system needed to emulate the capability of the human to reason about a correct model of the satellite to achieve our objective of handling unanticipated faults.

The design goal was a system in which the satellite model could be constructed directly by a satellite expert without having to write computer code. In addition, because satellites tend to be one of a kind, but similar, the amount of generic and reusable code was to be optimized.

No software tools or development environments are commercially available to develop such a system; therefore, as our application developed we also developed Paragon, a highly generic tool for creating models and reasoning capabilities.

The remainder of this paper describes the model-building and simulation capabilities of Paragon plus planned enhancements.

MODEL DEVELOPMENT

The goal of allowing a domain expert to develop the domain model interactively with the computer, without the aid of a programmer, mandates a tool that is flexible, yet consistent, and an interface that communicates using domain terms and symbology. The primary features of the model are, for each component in the domain, its attributes, its relationships with other components, and its behavioral description.

First, an underlying representation was developed for Paragon that could adequately represent all the model's features. That representation is a semantic network of nodes and links arranged in a manner that supports domain description and reasoning at various levels of abstraction. To provide a basic structure, classification and composition links and nodes and links that structure behavioral description are predefined within Paragon. To provide flexibility, user-defined relationships are supported. The user names the concepts that comprise the domain, links them using relationships, pre-defined by Paragon or user-defined, and supplies the concepts' behavioral descriptions. The result is a highly structured, consistent model.

Next, a highly-interactive user interface was developed to support both the input and display of model information. A key design goal was that the model builder should only have to use the keyboard to name the various features of the model. After a name is entered, it automatically pops up in menus when needed for additional model description. This Paragon feature avoids confusion caused by misspelling and typing errors and enforces consistency. For example, if the model builder wants to use an attribute from component A as part of the behavioral description for Component B, and the attribute does not pop up in the menu of available attributes, he knows he forgot to link the two components with a functional relationship. Within Paragon, both upward and downward inheritance of attributes facilitate model building, and inheritance of behavior from class level to instance is also supported.

The top level interface, shown in Figure 1, has two main regions. The Concept Graph Interface region, the large window on the left, presents user-selectable views of the classification and composition hierarchies of the model. This window display is scrollable and provides sophisticated techniques for browsing the knowledge base

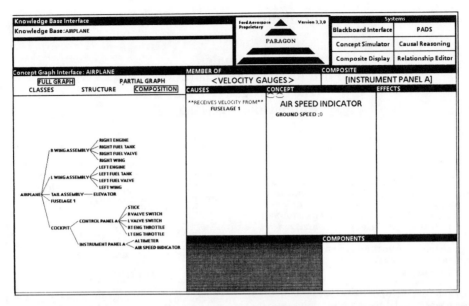

Figure 1. The Top Level Paragon Interface Present User-Selectable Views Of The Knowledge-Base Model.

model; it also provides a pop-up menu for creating new model components, referred to as "concepts" within Paragon. The other major region, to the right of the Concept Graph Interface window, consists of seven windows that display all attributes and relationships of a particular model concept. Mouse buttoning on any concept name in either window causes that concept to be featured in this Concept Display region. A series of menus, accessible via several active regions in the top level interface, aids the model-builder in naming attributes and describing functional relationships between domain concepts. Accessing and inputting behavioral information is accomplished by menu selection of several lower level interfaces.

A unique feature of Paragon is the manner in which the behavioral description of the domain concepts is acquired and represented. The behavioral description captures the dynamics of a concept; that is, when, how and why its attribute values change. In other development environments behavioral descriptions are usually represented using production rules and/or computer code, but within Paragon they are represented within declarative statements. The statements may contain numeric or symbolic parameters.

The structure of the behavioral description is a state transition diagram, as depicted in Figure 2. The model builder first names the states in which the concept may exist and graphically links the states to show possible state transitions. The events or changes in attribute values that occur in each state are then defined along with the conditions under which transition from one state to another will occur. The model builder only needs to type the state names once; afterwards the names appear in a graphic representation and may be linked via mouse selection.

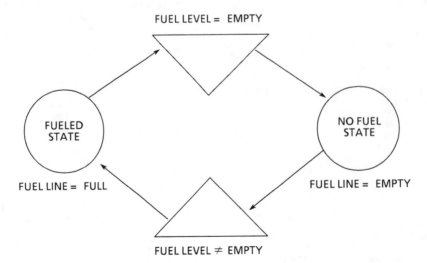

Figure 2. The Behavior Of Domain Concepts Is Described Within A State Transition Diagram.

Describing event statements and transition conditions is performed via mouse selection from menus containing legal attribute names and operators. Legal attributes are those internal to the concept itself or acquired via a functional relationship to another concept. Operators may be arithmetic, logical or one of a series of special operators defined within Paragon.

If a time-stepped simulation is desired by the model builder, behavioral descriptions may assume a time increment that is user selected. Each event description is based on the selected time increment or some multiple of it, selectable by the resolution feature of Paragon. It is not necessary to use the time-based features of Paragon in domain descriptions. If, for example, the problem-solving of the domain can be accomplished with a stimulated reaction network, no time reference is required or desired by the model builder.

SIMULATION

Whenever behavior has been described for a concept, the simulation feature of Paragon can be invoked for verification or to provide simulated output. Simulation can be achieved in either step mode or run mode. In step mode, used primarily for debugging, verification and demonstration, the user controls stepping through each time slice of the simulation. In run mode, Paragon provides a continuous, dynamic simulation that can be paused and continued by the user. Simulation is selectable from the development interface for rapid verification of the behavior of a single concept. Since all the inputs and their current values are displayed, the user can interactively vary inputs to verify the described behavior.

During model development, as each concept's behavior is verified via simulation, it can be combined with other concepts for simulation and the interaction between concepts can be verified. This process can continue, much like hardware build-and-test methodology, until the entire knowledge base is being simulated simultaneously. For simultaneous simulation of more than one concept, the simulator interface is employed.

In its simplest form, the simulator interface provides a window that lists each concept being simulated and the name of its current behavioral state (See figure 3). As the simulation executes, in either step or run mode, the state names are updated in the window. The window also contains a control panel for starting, stopping or stepping the simulation.

If, during simulation, it is desired to observe the change of value of one or more attributes of the system, the user may open additional windows and display the desired attributes, as shown in Figure 4.

To further facilitate data monitoring, a menu of various active images allows the user to attach a number of dials, gauges and indicators to any attribute. The menu provides only those images appropriate for the data type selected. An example of such a display is shown in Figure 5.

In addition, icons can be attached to concepts in the knowledge base to facilitate spatial or positional monitoring. In Figure 6, an icon of an aircraft moves across the screen to indicate its current position, and a circle appears in the display when the radar is "locked on" to a target.

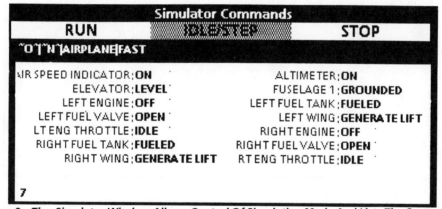

Figure 3. The Simulator Window Allows Control Of Simulation Mode And Lists The Current State Of Each Concept Being Simulated.

LEFT WING:		FUSELAGE 1:		AIR SPEED INDICATOR:	
PLAN AREA:	494	REL VERT FORCE:	0	GROUND SPEED: 435.0	
LIFT COEFF.	0.06	PITCH ANGLE:	0		
LIFT:	0	WEIGHT:	199,764.0		
		DRAG:	0		
		DRAG COEFF:	0.5		
		CS AREA:	7.5	LEFT ENGINE:	
LEFT FUEL TANK:		MASS:	620		
FUEL LEVEL:	3/4	HORIZONTAL VEL:	0	THRUST:	0
FUEL LINE:	FULL	ELEVATION:	0	MAX THRUST:	19000
		VERTICAL VEL:	0.5		

Figure 4. User-selectable Windows Allow Monitoring Of Individual Attributes Of Concepts During Simulation.

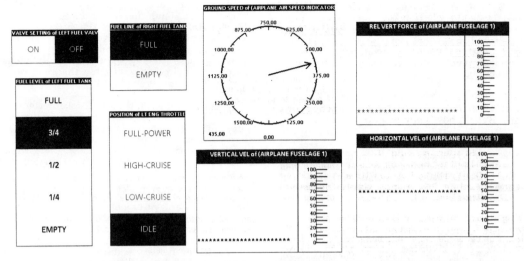

Figure 5. Various User-selectable Active Images May Be Employed To Facilitate Data Monitoring During Simulation.

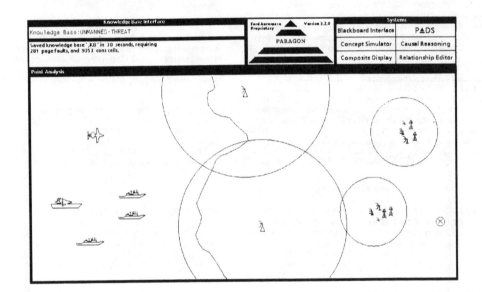

Figure 6. Icons May Be Employed To Facilitate Data Monitoring During Simulation.

INTELLIGENT SYSTEM

To use a Paragon model as a knowledge base for an intelligent system, problem solving or reasoning modules are activated to perform their specific function in the problem solving process. This reasoning capability may be accomplished within the knowledge base by developing decision-making concepts or by executing reasoning modules developed external to the knowledge base. Examples of external reasoning modules that have been developed for Paragon are: (1) Data Monitoring - testing incoming situational data for areas of interest, such as out-of-limits, or wrong discrete state (2) Situation Assessment - focusing on domain concepts of current interest in the problem solving process (3) Causal Diagnostics - determination of cause of current situation, including current actual state (4) Goal Determination - establishing the desired state or attribute values of the domain (5) Planning - determining how to achieve the desired state.

External modules may be domain specific, that is, contain strategies or information pertinent to a specific domain, or they may be generic and useful to many domains.

APPLICATIONS

Paragon has been used to model a variety of domains, including physical systems such as satellites and ground station equipment; processes such as those found in an assembly line or in software programs; qualitative systems, such as the attitudes of the people involved in the operation of a restaurant, and decision systems, such as a controller for intelligent minefields or an unmanned threat emitter.

In addition, Paragon models have been used to provide simulated data for testing an intelligent system. A copy of the model that underlies the intelligent system is executed as a simulation that provides test stimuli to the intelligent system. The simulation model can be altered to provide various desired test outputs and will provide a closed loop response to commands from the intelligent system. While this type of simulation will not suffice in some cases for system validation, it provides an easy and inexpensive test tool during intelligent system development.

FUTURE ENHANCEMENTS

One of the benefits of the model-based approach to building intelligent systems is the diversity of applications that can be supported from the same model (See figure 7). A future enhancement of Paragon, relative to simulation, is to create automated interfaces to a variety of off-the-shelf simulation programs. The Paragon model would be the "data base" of domain information, as described in this paper. When an engineer or designer needs to compute some parameter or statistic, he could set up the scenario via a Paragon interface. Paragon would send the expected inputs to the simulation program, retrieve the output and retain it in the data base.

Planned enhancements also include the development of a wide variety of reasoning functions that can be applied to models to perform more sophisticated problem solving. Examples of such reasoning capabilities already a part of Paragon are the ability to determine the actual state of a system by comparing its output data to the model, a casual analysis function that can explain what caused an attribute to be a certain value, and a spatial reasoning function that can determine the configuration of a group of entities, based on their positions.

CONCLUSION

Paragon is an AI-based tool that already contains robust knowledge representation and acquisition features and automated simulation and documentation capabilities plus an initial set of reusable reasoning capabilities. For distributed processing, Paragon knowledge bases can be linked to each other and have the capability to interface with external programs. Future enhancements will integrate Paragon with other software tools.

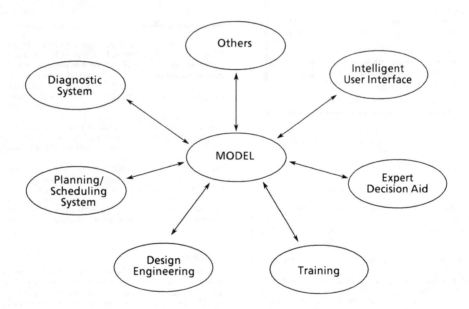

Figure 7. Model-based Reasoning Systems Support Many Diverse Applications.

Advances in AI and Simulation
© 1989 By The Society for Computer
Simulation International
ISBN 0-911801-50-2

Intelligent interfaces for combat simulation

Juliana S. Lancaster and Larry H. Reeker
The BDM Corporation
Advanced Technology Group
7915 Jones Branch Drive, McLean, VA 22102

Abstract

Combat simulations are primarily used to study specific military problems, but their potential usefulness in training has long been recognized. High computational requirements for running realistic scenarios and extensive time requirements for preparing input scenario data and analyzing output data have restricted their practicability in training. Since it now seems likely that parallel processing can bring down simulation run times dramatically, the complexity and extensive time requirements associated with input data preparation and output data analysis become the major remaining stumbling block. Essential to overcoming this obstacle is an intelligent interface that can appropriately display and manipulate scenario data, saving time in scenario preparation and analysis. This paper sketches a cognitively-motivated approach to the development of such an interface.

INTRODUCTION

Combat simulations exist in a variety of levels of specificity, on a variety of machines, and for a variety of purposes. They are primarily used by the Army analytical community to study specific problems relating to doctrine, force structure, weapons effectiveness, mission area requirements, and tactics. Recent work by the Army Research Institute (ARI) suggests that simulations could also be very effective in a training role for military planning (Halpin, 1987). Combat simulations in particular have significant potential for use in one-on-one training of staff officers in the technical aspects of Army tactical planning. Such use would be a substantial improvement over the current time-consuming and tedious method of teaching via programmed text material and would allow students to gain a broader base of experience during their training.

Several factors restrict the actual usability of combat simulations for such purposes: high computational requirements for running realistic scenarios, extensive time requirements for preparing input scenario data, and extensive time requirements for analyzing the output data. Emerging technologies are providing possible relief from these restricting factors. For instance, recent explorations into parallel processing have shown that simulation run times can be improved by several orders of magnitude in parallel implementations. This leaves the complexity and extensive time requirements associated with the preparation of input data and the analysis of output data, each of which can take several man-weeks of effort, as the major remaining stumbling blocks to using combat simulations for training.

Recent advances in artificial intelligence and user interface design suggest that the time involved in preparation and analysis can also be significantly reduced. What is needed is an intelligent interface that can appropriately display and manipulate scenario data, much of which is visual in form (i.e., maps and overlays). This will save time in scenario preparation in two ways. First, it will allow preparation of input scenarios in a familiar procedure. Second, the interface can then assume the burden of converting the visual components into the form required by the simulation. The result will be that the time required for generation of scenario inputs would be reduced to a level of hours rather than weeks. This paper will cover some possible approaches to the development of such interface tools.

This paper describes an approach to applying principles of human cognitive representation to the problems of interface and internal representation of for battle simulations. For this purpose, the interface will need both internal and display representations. It is intended that the display representations facilitate *direct pictorial communication* between user and machine by being *compatible in form and content with the cognitive representations of the users*, and that the internal representations augment this capability by *supporting direct manipulation of imagistic knowledge*.

In illustrating a very simple application of our approach, we will use a single example of the application of a "Hasty Attack" scenario (Figure 1a) to a particular geographic setting (Figure 1b). Though this example is very simple, it will illustrate some of the underlying representations and research issues in developing an intelligent interface. First, however, we will discuss the nature of the knowledge representations required.

VISUAL AND VERBAL KNOWLEDGE

Preparation of a battle scenario or of a course of action for responding to a battlefield situation is a highly visual process. Consequently, the development of systems for rapid generation of battle simulation inputs requires an examination of *visual knowledge*--that part of human knowledge that is difficult to express in spoken or written language, but more easily communicated and/or manipulated through pictorial means such as photographs, diagrams, charts, and graphs. This includes, but is not limited to, information about the details of appearance of objects in a scene, the spatial relationships among objects in a scene, and textural characteristics of objects. Visual knowledge can be considered in contrast to *verbal knowledge*--that part of human knowledge that is easily communicated in spoken or written language. Verbal knowledge includes information about the names and number of objects in a scene, actions, and relationships among actions. While there is no question that visual experience forms a major part of our total fund of knowledge (Chipman, 1987; Larkin & Simon, 1987; Paivio, 1986), our understanding of visual knowledge has remained seriously limited even as psychology, neurology, and

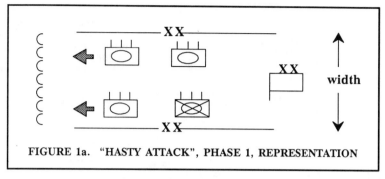

FIGURE 1a. "HASTY ATTACK", PHASE 1, REPRESENTATION

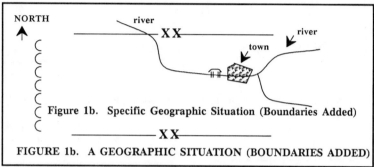

Figure 1b. Specific Geographic Situation (Boundaries Added)

FIGURE 1b. A GEOGRAPHIC SITUATION (BOUNDARIES ADDED)

artificial intelligence have developed a substantial understanding of the nature, content, organization, and representation of verbal knowledge.

This paper addresses several key technical issues that, separately and together, arise due to the absence of a well specified theory of visual knowledge and reasoning. In short, these technical issues are:

• selection of display mode (graphic *vs.* textual) in user interfaces;

• representing non–verbal knowledge in a computer implementation; and

• modeling or replicating reasoning with and about non–verbal information.

The scientific value of a project addressing these technical issues is substantial. The lack of theory–based work on visual knowledge restricts our effectiveness in using visual techniques in training and in communicating ideas that are most easily expressed visually, both among humans and between humans and machines. For example, pictorial materials used in education are often designed or selected on the basis of appeal rather than because of a criterion of compatibility with the learner's existing knowledge.

The lack of understanding of visual knowledge also severely constrains our ability to deal with pictorial information within computers in that, where systems and techniques have been developed for visual understanding tasks, they utilize techniques that do not extend readily to other applications or they are required to translate visual materials into verbal descriptions. Our use of such *ad hoc* techniques underlines the need for a better understanding of visual knowledge at both the theoretical and pragmatic levels, as this understanding provides the major key that we have to effective internal computer implementations.

We will address these issues using an integrated theory of human knowledge that specifies the functions, forms, and manipulations of both visual and verbal

knowledge, specifically a general theory of human knowledge developed over the past 40 years by Professor Lev M. Vekker in the Soviet Union (Vekker, 1974; 1976; 1981). We have begun a study of Vekker's theory[*] and found that it goes beyond any developed in this country in delineating modes and content of human knowledge and interactions among these modes, providing constraints on knowledge representation[†], and also providing specific techniques for eliciting knowledge from experts in order to determine effective representations for particular domains. We believe that, within this theoretical framework, it is possible and feasible to elicit, model, and specify for computer representation the visual knowledge used in the development of force arrays and to encode appropriate and accurate heuristics that will allow the interface to display and accept information during interactions with the user in the same mode(s) the user finds natural, i.e. to be *cognitively compatible* with the user.

Each of the issues created by the absence of a solid theory of visual knowledge can be seen to reside in one component of a man–machine decision system. These are the human, the internal machine knowledge, and the interface itself. Their impact is particularly clear in the design of interfaces for knowledge–based systems where communication and understanding between system and user can be critical. In this application the issues break down into:

---

[*]We have been working with Dr. Vekker, who now resides in the United States, and with Dr. Edward Manukian, of the University of Maryland, who was once a student of Vekker and who contributes many of his own insights on the significance and content of these theories and their relation to North American Psychology.

[†]Vekker's theories postulate at least three modes of cognitive representation, including a tactile/kinesthetic or haptic mode (see Fig. 2). We will not discuss the haptic mode in this paper, though it may also be important in designing certain types of interfaces.

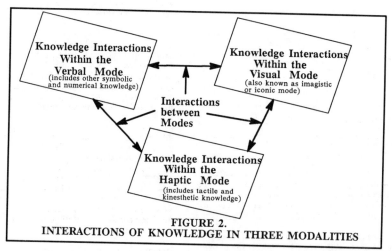

FIGURE 2.
INTERACTIONS OF KNOWLEDGE IN THREE MODALITIES

- knowing when and how humans use visual and/or verbal knowledge
- representing visual knowledge and reasoning within the system; and
- encoding heuristics to allow the system to select appropriate modes for displays.

Figure 3 summarizes each of the units in the human–machine interaction, the types of representations available to humans, machines, and human–machine interfaces, and the technical areas affected by each. We know that humans can deal directly with verbal, visual, and tactile knowledge; but in machines, all knowledge must be represented symbolically. Symbolic representation for computers, because of its discrete nature, is most naturally mapped into (and from) verbal representations. Some of the most interesting work in artificial intelligence has concerned the representation of the underlying semantics of language and there is a need to do the same sort of thing for visual knowledge.

Visual Knowledge and Interface Display Design

Of the knowledge units shown in Figure 3, visual knowledge is in its most tangible form in the human–machine interaction. Relatively recent developments in computer input and output devices emphasize the visual display of information. With the advent of pixel–oriented devices, it became possible -- even natural -- to think in terms of two–dimensional images. But even today, use of this imagistic capability is quite limited. Most programs still utilize visual displays primarily to display verbal information. It may be arranged in two–dimensional displays. It may even be in color. But it is essentially verbal information. Even manipulation of fixed icons, as in certain popular personal computers, is a very limited use of visual information. For the problems considered here, we will need to develop techniques for displaying and manipulating information that is inherently *pictorial* or *imagistic*.

Consider first the input side of the human–computer interface where fixed icons are most often used. A more "natural" approach allows users to enter into the machine images that they have in their minds (for example, a hand–drawn map of some area with which the human is familiar). This can be done by allowing the use of hand–drawn or predrawn and selected iconic inputs, such as a wavy line for a river, that may be combined with words, or replaced by words. This process allows the user to communicate his ideas to the machine in their naturally

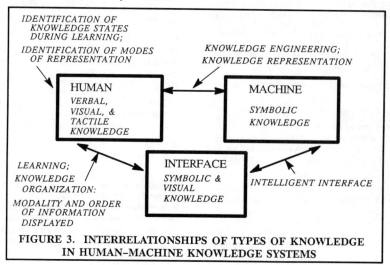

FIGURE 3. INTERRELATIONSHIPS OF TYPES OF KNOWLEDGE IN HUMAN–MACHINE KNOWLEDGE SYSTEMS

```
V4,
{g9,2,0
{g9,2,8
{p6,2,8,16
{g9,2,8
    .{v4,2,32,1.500405,3.297169,1.707699,2.738909,0,0,0}
    .{v4,3,0,1.707699,2.738909,1.79074,2.51515,17,1,0  )
    .{v4,4,0,1.79074,2.51515,2.355828,3.913778,17,1,0}
    .{v4,5,0,2.355828,3.913778,1.416383,3.523558,17,1,0}
    .{v4,6,0,1.416383,3.523558,1.500405,3.297169,17,1,0}}}
.{p6,8,0,16
.{g9,8,8
    {v4,8,32,1.50046,3.297231,1.707699,2.738909,0,0,0}
    {v4,9,0,1.707699,2.738909,1.627013,2.639111,17,1,0}
    {v4,10,0,1.627013,2.639111,1.549216,2.535053,17,1,0}
    ...{etc.}...
```

FIGURE 4. COMPUTER–ENCODED GRAPHIC DATA

pictorial form. Nevertheless, while these inputs can be entered, edited, and stored using existing drawing programs, doing so does not constitute the input of a map that the computer can use in the way the human can use the map. When inputs are converted to a symbolic representation, it tends to be one that is appropriate only for creating the image on a graphic medium such as the example in Figure 4; the objects in the image cannot be recognized, identified, reasoned about, or manipulated. In other words, the display has, and may need, no *knowledge* about the image.

Similar considerations apply to the output side of the interface. · Many of the considerations involved in the effective output of visual information are similar to those germane to traditional graphic representation, such as that found in maps. A very fine study of the nature of graphic representation was done by Bertin (1983). A major point of his treatment is the fact that the characteristics of the visual media and the information need to be matched, in terms of human expectation. In other words, what the user sees as an image should match what the user is comfortable processing visually Here again, it is clear that a valid cognitive model

of human knowledge, built using a good theory–based elicitation methodology will be of major benefit in design.

Visual Knowledge in Computer Systems

The need to manipulate graphic information also governs the design of internal knowledge representations. This fact is equally true for verbal knowledge, visual knowledge, and combinations of modes of knowledge. The ability to manipulate information depends upon both computational capabilities and software engineering considerations. By "computational capabilities", we are not referring to absolute computability considerations, which only peripherally influence choice of internal representations, but to time and memory constraints. These vary with the equipment and the tolerance within an application (some systems needing near–real time response, for instance). Software engineering considerations include the need for *representations* that are convenient to program and comprehensible throughout the life cycle of the software and the availability of *algorithms or heuristics* for reasoning about the represented knowledge.

We often think of visual information as being represented by a set of coordinates in a Euclidean plane. But there are many visual representations where coordinates are unimportant or irrelevant. The *display* representation, as discussed in the last section, may need such information as spatial coordinates; but the *internal representation of the knowledge–based system* needs only the relationships among various instances of schemata that are relevant for the task at hand. Often, a good deal of verbal or temporal or other types of knowledge is needed along with the visual knowledge. Figure 5 shows a *blended* representation, with both verbal knowledge and visual knowledge though expressed in a symbolic form, designed for a task similar to that used in the example presented in the next section.

Typically, visual information is represented internally using *visual primitives*. These differ from system to system in their level of "primitivity"; but for simulation applications, they can be taken to be fairly high level. The

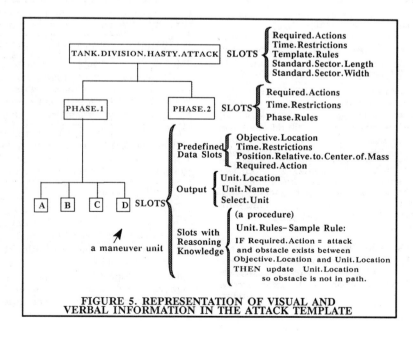

FIGURE 5. REPRESENTATION OF VISUAL AND VERBAL INFORMATION IN THE ATTACK TEMPLATE

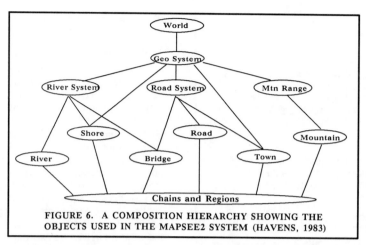

FIGURE 6. A COMPOSITION HIERARCHY SHOWING THE OBJECTS USED IN THE MAPSEE2 SYSTEM (HAVENS, 1983)

components are schemata (not fixed icons, but ones that are variable within bounds set by conventions specified as part of the schema) that can be formed into a tree called a "composition hierarchy", such as that shown in Figure 6. The "chains and regions" shown in the figure are the real primitives -- the basic items that make up the schemata at higher levels, but are themselves meaningless. The next level of the hierarchy contains things like rivers and towns. Above that are systems containing multiple schemata of specified types from the lower level. Thus a river system schema consists of river schemata, shore schemata, and bridge schemata. The degree of complexity of such a hierarchy can be expanded almost arbitrarily. The extent to which it needs to be expanded in a particular task is a matter to be determined by eliciting knowledge from experts. Any particular map (in the example of Figure 6) is represented as an *instance* of the "world" schema (an instance being a fixed representation that falls within the bounds of the schema). A brief but informative explanation of this approach can be found in [Havens, 1983].

Finally, a knowledge–based system must be able to reason about the visual knowledge it holds. While the visual knowledge, like verbal knowledge, will have to be represented appropriately within the computer, the modes of reasoning that the computer uses on it are unlikely to be identical to those used by the human. What is important for designing programs that are adequate from a cognitive perspective is that the internal representations correspond to human representations and that the results of the reasoning be in agreement. This is also an important software engineering consideration, since without it, the program is not likely to be comprehensible. Overall, *the fidelity of the content of the internal representation to the human's cognitive representation and the analogy that this facilitates between the computational operations and the human cognitive operations is one of the few "handles" that we can grasp in trying to bring reasonable software engineering clarity to knowledge–based systems.*

Cognitive Representation as a Unifying Factor

In discussing representations of visual knowledge for interfaces and for internal representation in knowledge–based systems, we have see the *human's cognitive modes of representations* emerge as an central factor. In the interface, the modes of representation must be consistent with the human's expectations and abilities. The internal

computational representations must encode the information contained in human representations accurately and directly, providing a natural mapping into the operations that are important to the human. Figure 7 is a redrawing of Figure 3 indicating the important factors in each representation and the direction of knowledge flow in representation design. This point returns us to our earlier statement that the capabilities for presenting and reasoning with visual knowledge needed by many knowledge–based systems will only develop when they can be based on a well–founded theory of human knowledge representation and reasoning. Vekker's work constitutes an important contribution to the development of such a theory. In the next section, we will present a brief example of one approach to scenario preparation in which we have developed our suggestions for representations based on this work.

EXAMPLE FOR SIMULATION INPUT

Human experts prepare a battle plan using a collection of generic doctrinal templates and apply their knowledge to adapt those procedures and templates to specific situations. One such doctrinal template is a guide to making predictions about how a Soviet tank division will conduct a "hasty attack" and is depicted in Figure 1a. A divisional "hasty attack" refers to an attack made by Soviet forces against a fixed defensive position. This template describes how the subordinate units of the division (tank and motorized infantry regiments) would be deployed in ideal conditions. It also describes doctrinally desirable spacing between them and relative to the enemy position. In addition, the width of unit sectors is specified.

Figures 8 and 9 present an approach to one aspect of applying the "hasty attack" doctrinal template of Figure 1a to the geographic situation of Figure 1b. In Figure 8, the presence of the river and absence of bridges on the west bank means that the northernmost tank regiment of the second echelon will be delayed in assisting the exploitation of possible breakthroughs made during the initial attack. A human expert, interpreting how a Soviet commander would adjust his formation in the face of these terrain conditions, would instead use a maneuver unit configuration similar to that shown in Figure 9. Here the northernmost tank regiment is positioned just to the south of the river, making it easier to exploit any breakthrough made in the initial attack of phase 1. The final troop locations are constrained

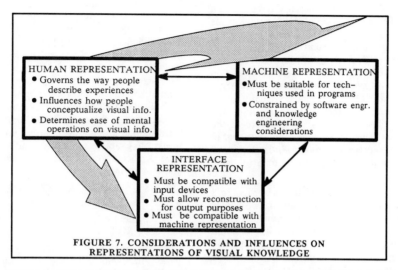

FIGURE 7. CONSIDERATIONS AND INFLUENCES ON REPRESENTATIONS OF VISUAL KNOWLEDGE

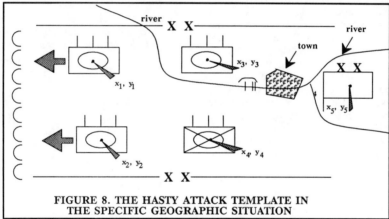

FIGURE 8. THE HASTY ATTACK TEMPLATE IN THE SPECIFIC GEOGRAPHIC SITUATION

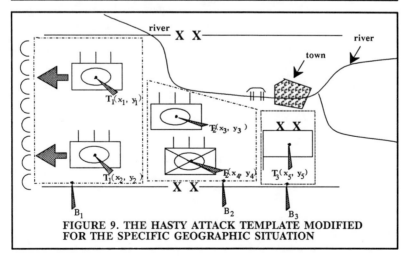

FIGURE 9. THE HASTY ATTACK TEMPLATE MODIFIED FOR THE SPECIFIC GEOGRAPHIC SITUATION

by doctrinal considerations specified in the doctrinal template, but still based on the geographic situation.

There are undoubtedly a number of reasoning processes, based both on verbal and visual information, required to adapt the "Hasty Attack" doctrinal template to a specific situation. The specific geographic situation as depicted in Figure 1b contains a fixed defensive position, division sector boundaries, known unit deployments, and various terrain features (e.g., river, town). Such information would typically be derived from the Intelligence Preparation of the Battlefield (IPB) process done as part of Army tactical planning and would be presented visually using maps and overlays. Similarly, the template specifies the type and number of troops involved and the nature of the attack to be carried out. This information is more verbal in nature. The sample representation shown in Figure 5 contains both forms of information needed to plan using (or against) this template.

The coordinates and transforms shown in Figures 8 and 9 reflect our suggested approach to applying the "hasty attack" doctrinal template to the given geographic situation. In essence, the approach simulates the reasoning that could be executed by a human by first recognizing that terrain obstacles exist to prevent successful execution of the standard template, drawing quadrilaterals B_1, B_2, B_3 in the appropriate positions (ones that one could imagine a human expert drawing similar shapes in his/her "mind's eye"), and then computing the transformations T_1, T_2, and T_3. form the shape and size of the quadrilaterals. In this way, the terrain features are considered in adopting the doctrinal template to the specific situation. This example is oversimplified, since pure shape considerations are not the only ones to be addressed; but it serves to indicates one aspect of using visual information from the geographic schema to develop a situational template and the need to use knowledge engineering techniques for visual knowledge to determine this information and how it is used.

CONCLUSION

As this discussion indicates, the design of good user interfaces is not a simple matter. As the tasks for which computer applications are developed become more complex and more "intelligent", the demands placed on the interface become correspondingly higher. For applications such as combat simulation, much of the information to be processed by the interface and by the simulation, is inherently visual for the human. This includes not only spatial coordinates of units at any given time, but also their relationship to the surrounding terrain and other geographic features. While we do not claim to have solved the problem of building truly "friendly" interfaces for such applications, we believe we have a sound initial approach, founded in a theory of human knowledge and reasoning that drives the selection of both display and internal representations to match the mode and content of the comparable human knowledge. Clearly, a substantial amount of research, both basic and applied, is needed to examine the utility of this, and other theories, for such application and to develop the technologies that will allow us to meet our goals.

REFERENCES

Bertin, J. (1983). *Semiology of Graphs* (trans. by W. J. Berg from the 1967 French edition), University of Wisconsin Press, Madison, WI.

Chipman, S. F. (1987). Visual knowledge, paper presented at American Educational Research Assn., April 20, 1987; available from author at Office of Naval Research.

Havens, W. S. (1983). Recognition mechanisms for schema–based knowledge representations, *Computers and Mathematics with Applications*, 9, 1, 185–199.

Larkin, J. H., and H. A. Simon (1987). Why a diagram is (sometimes) worth ten thousand words, *Cognitive Science*, 11, 65–100.

Paivio, Allan (1986); *Mental Representations: A dual coding approach*; Oxford University Press, New York NY.

Vekker, Lev M. (1974); *Mental Processes*, Vol 1.; Leningrad University Press. (In Russian)

Vekker, Lev M. (1976); *Mental Processes*, Vol 2, Thinking and the intellect; Leningrad University Press. (In Russian)

Vekker, Lev M. (1981); *Mental Processes*, Vol 3, The agent, the experience, action and consciousness; Leningrad University Press. (In Russian)

Advances in AI and Simulation
© 1989 By The Society for Computer
Simulation International
ISBN 0-911801-50-2

CODER: A design tool for aerospace applications

Gordon R. Nelson, Michael A. Johnston, and John L. Blue
The BDM Corporation, Kettering, Ohio 45420

ABSTRACT.

The design of complex systems, such as weapons systems is in itself a complex task. These complex tasks are motivated by the need to design and manage information and new ideas in a systematic and scientific way. Rapid proliferation of new technology is also a driving factor which further complicates the design of these complex systems. The design approach is piecemeal and often not used extensively until full scale engineering development, which causes major problems and expensive engineering changes late in the development program. A solution would be a computer-aided design support tool that would support the early stages of design including mission analysis, functional decomposition, functional allocation, and preliminary design/evaluation of information processing architectures. BDM has developed such a tool. Its name is CODER (COnceptual DEsign Representation) and its purpose is to support early, high-level modeling and analysis of complex weapon systems from a mission effectiveness perspective. CODER is characterized by its object-oriented system description methods and event-stepped simulation techniques and is hosted on a TI Explorer, an Artificial Intelligence (AI) workstation, under the IntelliCorp Knowledge Engineering Environment (KEE) and the Common Lisp programming language.

1 CODER DESCRIPTION.

1.1 CODER Capabilities.

In the early conceptual design stages, many alternative system concepts varying in fundamental ways can be conceived. However, it is impossible to fully develop, test, and evaluate several alternative concepts to determine which is "best" — most cost and operationally effective. Consequently, early conceptual investigations must "prune" all but one or two "good" alternatives on which subsequent development effort can focus. Unfortunately, it is difficult to identify these "good" alternatives in the early conceptual stages of the design. BDM proposed CODER as a means to do just that — to formulate and evaluate alternative system concepts from an operational perspective in the early conceptual stages.

The basic idea of CODER is to work directly with "executable design representations" which are able to simulate their own operations in postulated operational scenarios. Working with executable representations helps designers to develop a thorough understanding of their problem, to systematically evaluate a range of system concepts, to demonstrate and communicate those concepts among workers of varied backgrounds, and to center attention on critical system elements.

Key capabilities of the CODER system are the following: (1) provides a very broad span of modeling and analysis control; (2) promotes exploratory, interactive use; and, (3) enables efficient application of modeling and analysis resources.

1.2 CODER Foundations.

CODER achieves its capabilities by combining object-oriented system description with event-stepped simulation in a powerful symbolic computing environment. These foundations provide visibility into the simulated system structure, traceability of simulated system actions and interactions, and understandability of simulation results.

1.2.1 Object-Oriented System Description.

The basic idea of object-oriented system description is to treat everything as an "active entity" which has its own particular attributes and state values, and which can interact with other such active entities only by sending messages to them. This very simple idea comes from "object-oriented programming", and has important implications for designing, developing, and implementing complex systems which can be understood and used effectively.

Object-oriented programming is currently receiving much attention as an approach to programming which facilitates evolutionary software development and engineering [Bobrow and Stefik 1986a, Bobrow and Stefik 1986b]. The basic ideas of object-oriented programming originated some time ago in the context of computer simulation [Birtwistle, Dahl, Myhrhaug and Nygaard 1973]. Both of these aspects of object-oriented programming are important, and contribute to the utility of CODER as a simulation and analysis support system. However, the most important role of object-oriented programming in CODER is as a framework for the description of complex, interacting systems.

1.2.1.1 Object-Oriented Description is a Natural Way to Specify Complex Systems.

As noted earlier, object-oriented system description methods view everything as an individual active entity which has its own local state values and attributes, and which can interact with other active entities only by sending them messages. Thus, to describe an active entity, one must specify:

- the state variables and parameters which constitute the entity's local state and attributes; and,

- the types of messages it can receive and the actions it should take in responding to them (specified in terms of changing the entity's local state and/or sending messages to itself or other active entities).

For example, an object-oriented specification for an aircraft might include local state variables for its current position (latitude, longitude, and altitude), movement (speed, bearing, and pitch), and velocity (latitude, longitude, and altitude deltas per second); it might also include a method for responding to a "change movement" message by updating the local movement state value, and then recomputing the local velocity state value.

1.2.1.2 Object-Oriented Development Promotes Refinement and Extension.

In practice, it is common to use object-oriented system description methods to define whole classes of active entities rather than specific individual entities. Under this approach, individual active entities can then be created as instances or members of these classes. Thus, a collection of object-oriented class descriptions constitutes a kind of library or catalog of specifications from which individual entities can be constructed as needed. This makes it easy to revise basic features of an active entity by simply modifying its specifications in the class catalog.

In practice, it is also natural to structure these object-oriented class descriptions into hierarchies of classes, subclasses, sub-subclasses, and so on. By letting subclasses "inherit" specifications from their superclasses, new classes of active entities can be described as specializations or refinements of existing classes of entities. Thus, classes of active entities can be incrementally specified and extended, building on previously defined classes. Moreover, in this process, common local state variables, attributes, and method response behavior only have to be specified and maintained in one place — multiple versions of common specifications do not have to be created or maintained.

These practical features of object-oriented system description methods greatly facilitate a rapid process of system development, based on exploratory refinement and extension. They also contribute to the clarity and understandability of the resulting representations.

1.2.1.3 Object-Oriented Implementation Provides Modularity and Uniformity.

Collectively, the overall state of an object-oriented system "resides" in the state variables and parameters of the individual active entities comprising the system. Thus, the system's state is partitioned into smaller, more coherent and manageable "chunks" by the object-oriented specifications. Moreover, these chunks of system state are directly aligned with the design and architecture of the system, since an entity can only change its local state in responding to messages (which, it will be recalled, is the only form of action and interaction permitted in an object-oriented system). As a consequence of these features, systems specified in object-oriented terms can be implemented in a highly modular and uniform manner.

1.2.2 Event-Driven Simulation.

The basic ideas of event-driven simulation are that the state of a simulated situation can change when (but only when) an event occurs, and that the occurrence of an event may cause other future events. Events can be designed into a simulation to mark significant or interesting changes in the state of the simulated situation. Of course, these state changes will reflect the effects of ongoing actions and interactions within the situation.

Event-driven simulation provides many advantages as a CODER foundation. First, and perhaps most importantly, event-driven simulation integrates very nicely with CODER's object-oriented approach to system description. Since object-oriented system specifications organize the actions and interactions of entities in terms of message passing, it is natural to identify events with message receipts by entities. This provides a clear and convenient way to link the occurrence of events (message receipts) to the activities of entities (message response behavior, which may include scheduling other future message receipts as events for other active entities). It also maintains the "local" viewpoint and modular implementation of the object-oriented approach.

Second, event-driven simulation provides good visibility into the dynamics of weapon systems, their subsystems, their functions, and their interactions. Chains of events causing other events causing still other events can be traced, examined, and analyzed. To facilitate such investigations, certain events can be designated as "key events" of particular interest; these key events can be specially noted and recorded for subsequent analysis.

Finally, event-driven simulation supports user refinement and extension, especially in connection with object-oriented system specification. Since events are just message receipts, it is straightforward to expand a single high-level event (e.g., "fire missile") into a more complex sequence of detailed events (e.g., "establish target track", "arm missile", "launch missile"). All that is needed to make such expansions is to add new response methods for each of these message types, insuring that the appropriate message receipt events are scheduled as a part of each response. Thus, users can design their own organization of events to achieve visibility into particular aspects of their problem.

2 CODER STRUCTURE.

In line with its object-oriented foundation and implementation, CODER is itself structured as a system of interacting active entities.

2.1 CODER Simulations.

The top-level working elements in CODER are "simulations" (See Figure 1). CODER simulations are just a special class of CODER active entities which organize the process of building, operating, and modifying simulations in CODER. Users can create simulations, set them up, install them, run them in interactive or batch mode, modify them, copy them, save them, load them, and so on.

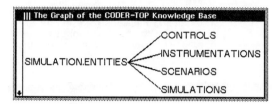

Figure 1: CODER Top-Level Entities.

As discussed in the subsections below, a CODER simulation has three basic components:

1. A scenario, which defines the weapon systems involved in the situation being simulated, the environment in which they are operating, their missions, and so on;

2. An instrumentation, which defines what data should be collected during simulation runs, as well as how it should be collected, handled, and so on; and,

3. A control, which defines simulation options such as repeatability, full event tracing, and so on.

Of course, each of these simulation components is itself just another special kind of CODER active entity with its own local state and message response capabilities. As such, they can be specified, created, and manipulated in the same manner as all other CODER active entities. In particular, users can "swap" whole components in and out of a simulation to change its operation. For example, to make it easy to collect different sets of data during a simulation, a user might simply maintain multiple versions of the instrumentation component for that simulation.

2.1.1 CODER Scenarios.

In many ways, a scenario is the central component of a CODER simulation, for it defines the operational situation of interest. A CODER scenario is an active entity consisting of the weapon systems involved in the situation together with an operational environment in which those weapon systems can interact as they operate. CODER scenarios also include timing information, and make provision to specify particular actions to be performed when the scenario is set up, installed, or initialized (for example, to establish initial values for certain subsystem variables, or to give missions to certain weapon systems).

2.1.2 CODER Instrumentations.

The instrumentation of a CODER simulation defines what data are to be collected during a simulation run, and what is to be done with them. Each CODER instrumentation is an active entity which contains a set of data collection specifications and options. Based on these specifications, the instrumentation entity itself actively manages the creation, installation, attachment, operation and detachment of individual data collector entities which actually collect the data.

2.1.3 CODER Controls.

The control component of a CODER simulation provides a single reference point for managing simulation execution options. For example, users can insure that a particular simulation execution is repeatable by setting a specific random number generator "seed" in the control.

2.2 CODER Event Execution Machinery.

During execution, a CODER simulation is essentially an event-driven simulation. The simulation dynamics involve the scheduling and execution of events.

2.2.1 Event Structure.

Events are implemented as Common Lisp structures having four elements:

1. time — the time at which the event is to occur.

2. actor — the principal entity involved in the event (an individual CODER active entity).

3. action — the action of the event (a message type which can be received by the event actor).

4. information — a list (possibly NIL) of additional information pertinent to the event action (the argument list for the event action as a message).

Using the Common Lisp DEFSTRUCT function to define the EVENT structure yields the basic event handling operations: event predication, event construction, and event field selection. In addition, an event comparator operation is defined to determine whether one event has a strictly earlier (smaller) time of occurrence than another.

An INSERT-EVENT operation is also defined to return the result of inserting an event into a list of events in order of occurrence. The event is inserted after any other events on the list which have the same or earlier time of occurrence. Thus, if two events are scheduled to occur at the same time, the first event scheduled will lie ahead of the other on the list.

The event handling machinery is completed by two functions which deal with the particular list of events maintained in a special event list global variable. The INSERT-NEW-EVENT function constructs a new event with specified time, actor, action, and information, and then resets the event list to the result of inserting that event in the event list using the general INSERT-EVENT function. The EXTRACT-NEXT-EVENT function returns the next event on the event list which should occur, resetting the event list to all the remaining events.

2.2.2 Event Scheduling and Execution.

Events are scheduled directly by individual CODER active entities and are executed as message sends to other (possibly oneself) CODER active entities. The scheduling of an event is accomplished through the use of either a relative or absolute time scheduling macro. These macros cause the specified event to be placed on the current event list after all events with equal or earlier occurrence times.

In essence, event execution simply involves: (1) setting the "current simulation time" to the event's time of occurrence; and then, (2) sending the actor of the event the event's action as a message, with the additional event information as the message arguments. The latter step is accomplished using the basic KEE message send function. However, there are some additional considerations.

- First, since "expired" actors are "out of the game", there must be a check for the expiration of the actor prior to executing the event.

- Second, the event actor may not be the proper performer of the event action. In particular, if the event actor has been allocated an ACM (Active Component Module; see Section 2.3) then the event action should be handed to this ACM to be placed on its processing queue.

- Finally, to account for time used in performing actions, each event is executed in a context including a special "elapsed time" global variable which is initialized at 0 at the beginning of event execution and is incremented by message response methods resulting from the execution of the event. Under ACM allocation, this "elapsed time" represents system response time to the event.

2.3 CODER Systems, Functions, And Components.

Various types of active entities may be involved in a simulation: systems (including weapon systems as well as their subsystems), mission functions, and component modules. The only entities explicitly included in a simulation's scenario are weapon systems. However, weapon systems may have subsystems (which may, in turn, have lower-level subsystems, and so on). Weapon systems (though not subsystems) may also have an organization of mission execution functions which actually operate the weapon system in the simulation. Each of these mission execution functions may be allocated to an active component module which represents "resources" (e.g., information processing capacity) which can perform mission functions.

CODER organizes these different types of active entities into three broad types:

1. Active Scenario Elements (ASEs) represent the weapon systems and subsystems involved in a scenario (See Figure 2); they characterize the physical operations and interactions of systems in scenarios. (ASE interactions are also handled by "operational environments", as described in the next subsection.)

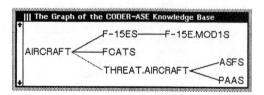

Figure 2: CODER ASE Examples.

2. Active Functional Modules (AFMs) represent the functions performed by weapon systems in executing missions (See Figure 3); they characterize the functional organization and operation of weapon systems in scenarios.

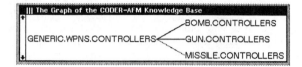

Figure 3: CODER AFM Examples.

3. Active Component Modules (ACMs) represent the "effort" and "capacity" available to perform the mission execution functions represented by AFMs (See Figure 4).

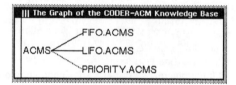

Figure 4: CODER ACM Examples.

Users will work with these three types of active entities in representing new weapon systems, new subsystems, and new concepts of operation.

2.4 CODER Operational Environments.

In accordance with CODER's object-oriented foundations, weapon systems, subsystems, functions, and components operate in a very "localized" way, generally interacting with only a few other specific active entities. There are, however, cases where many entities, possibly unknown to one another, must interact. A good example of this is active sensing as by a radar; here, the radar must propagate a signal out into the environment and then detect reflections back from other entities.

CODER operational environments handle these and other cases where many independent active entities must interact. For example, the radar process is handled in four basic steps:

1. The radar subsystem sends a "propagate" message to the operational environment.

2. The operational environment then sends a "return signal" message to any entities which meet a variety of propagation criteria (e.g., line of sight, field of view, etc.).

3. Entities receiving the "return signal" message respond by telling the operational environment how much radar power they reflect (and, perhaps, by other internal actions such as passing the signal on to an EW receiver for possible detection).

4. The operational environment tells the radar subsystem of any entities whose signal return meets the radar's detection criteria.

CODER operational environments also provide a single reference point for "environmental" information and processes such as terrain and weather parameters.

2.5 CODER Data Collectors.

Active Data Collectors (ADCs) are created and managed by the instrumentation of a CODER simulation. Active Data Collectors can collect any type of information (e.g., numbers, symbols, lists, arrays, structures). Collected information items are time-stamped and maintained in a time-ordered list. Data collectors come in three main varieties (See Figure 5):

1. Data receivers collect any data they are told to collect, thus providing a kind of "note-taking" capability;

2. Data samplers collect the value of a specific local state variable in a specific active entity periodically after a particular sampling interval has passed; and,

3. Data monitors collect the value of a specific local state variable in a specific active entity whenever that variable value changes.

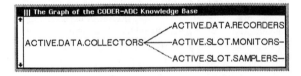

Figure 5: CODER ADC Examples.

Each of these types of active data collectors has its own strengths and weaknesses. Collectively, however, they provide the basis for a broad range of instruments with which to observe and record the execution of CODER simulations. Moreover, in CODER's object-oriented structure, users can easily refine or extend these three types of data collectors to build specialized data collection, processing, and analysis capabilities.

3 CONCLUSION.

CODER has proven to be a very general purpose systems modeling and simulation tool. It has been applied to weapon system design, to the evaluation of candidate weapon system technologies, to the early verification and validation (V&V) of weapon system flight critical software, and, in a very different problem area; to the exploration of design issues surrounding the distribution of data and computation in a large logistics information system. Much of its effectiveness and practicality as a tool for the early operational evaluation of system concepts derives from its merging of object-oriented programming methods with event-stepped simulation techniques in an "AI workstation" environment.

ACKNOWLEDGEMENTS.

The authors wish to acknowledge Dr. J.R. Aldrich as one of the principal designers of CODER.

REFERENCES.

• The BDM Corporation, Cockpit Automation Technology (CAT) Development Phase I, Final Technical Report, (2 Volumes), Dayton, Ohio, March 3, 1986.

• The BDM Corporation, Evaluation of Technology Investment, Volume One — Final Report, Dayton, Ohio, March 25, 1988.

• The BDM Corporation, Evaluation of Technology Investment, Volume Two — Conceptual Design Representation (CODER) Operational Concepts Document — Part One — Management Summary, Dayton, Ohio, March 25, 1988.

• The BDM Corporation, Evaluation of Technology Investment, Volume Three — Conceptual Design Representation (CODER) Operational Concepts Document — Part Two — Analyst's Manual, Dayton, Ohio, March 25, 1988.

• The BDM Corporation, Evaluation of Technology Investment, Volume Four — Conceptual Design Representation (CODER) Software User's Manual, Dayton, Ohio, March 25, 1988.

• The BDM Corporation, Evaluation of Technology Investment, Volume Five — Conceptual Design Representation (CODER) Software Programmer's Manual, Dayton, Ohio, March 25, 1988.

• Birtwistle, B., O. J. Dahl, K. Myhrhaug, and K. Nygaard, Simula Begin, Auerbach, 1973.

• Bobrow, D. G., and M. J. Stefik, "Perspectives on Artificial Intelligence Programming," Science, February 28, 1986, pp. 951-957.

• Bobrow, D. G., and M. J. Stefik, "Object-Oriented Programming: Themes and Variations," The AI Magazine, Vol. 6, No. 4, Winter 1986, pp. 40-62.

Advances in AI and Simulation
ISBN 0-911801-50-2

A computational investigation of expertise in problem solving

Kevin Dunay, Ph.D.
National Exploitation Laboratory
National Photographic Interpretation Center
Washington, D.C. 20024–00967

ABSTRACT

The purpose of this investigation was to develop two computational models of problem solving in the domain of experimental psychology with the intent of investigating the robustness of previous theories of expertise in problem solving. Two simulations of problem solving performance were initially created, precisely emulating the problem solving strategies utilized by an expert and a novice while generating problem solutions for various quasi–experimental problem scenarios. The expert–novice differences uncovered when comparing the problem solutions were, as predicted, consistent with previous investigations of expertise in problem solving. Specifically, even though the number of hierarchical chunks (components of a problem solving schema) was practically equivalent for both subjects, the expert chunks were larger, containing more solution steps for problem solving. These additional solution steps seemed, on the surface, to enhance the problem solving process of the expert. Additionally, implicit solution steps invoked by the subjects during problem solving (those not explicitly stated) were uncovered. A direct test of the predictive capabilities of the computational models, as well as differential expert–novice outcomes was then undertaken. The models were found to have predictive validity, with expert performance being somewhat more enhanced than novice performance. These results are discussed in terms of their consistency with both previous theories of expertise in problems solving, as well as a current theory of human cognition.

INTRODUCTION

Just a few decades ago, our understanding of human intelligent functioning derived from the maligned analysis of measurements on various psychometric intelligence tests (Sternberg, 1986). These techniques, although not trivial, prevented scientists from obtaining a complete and coherent understanding of the complex mechanisms that underlie intelligent functioning. Since the early 1970's, our understanding of these mechanisms has increased significantly due in part to powerful techniques of cognitive science. Cognitive science is the study of the human mind as reflected by the convergence of the disciplines of psychology, computer science, philosophy, linguistics, and artificial intelligence. The global objective of cognitive science is to detail the overall mental operations of the human mind. In order to achieve this, cognitive scientists strive to codify and predict precisely how mental symbols, rules, images, and representations are contrasted, joined, and/or transformed, creating what Fodor (1975) calls a natural "Language of Thought."

At the heart of this endeavor lies the underlying assumption popularized by Newell and Simon (1976) called the physical symbol system hypothesis. This hypothesis states that a physical symbol system, consisting of a set of physical patterns (symbols) that occur as components of an expression (symbolic structure), has the necessary and sufficient means for general intelligent action. The computer provides the perfect medium for testing this hypothesis since computers can serve as arbitrary symbol manipulators, enabling one to simulate most any physical symbol system one desires to create.

Consistent with the idea that computers can collect an array of symbols that allow for intelligent functioning to occur, cognitive science holds to the belief that computers are essential to understaing the underlying mental operations of the human mind. This basic principle of cognitive science suggests that only after a specific theoretical application of human intelligent functioning has been transformed into the natural "Language of Thought" codes, thus creating a working computer model (simulation) of this theory, can the fruitfulness of the theory be validated (Anderson, 1983). Therefore, in order to completely and coherently understand the logical mechanisms that underlie intelligent functioning, one must not solely rely on the cognitive theories developed through the utilization of classic techniques, but must also simulate this cognitive architecture in such a way that emulates the theoretically proposed internal structure of the human mind. It is this approach of cognitive science that enables researchers to unlock at least some of the mysteries of the human mind, paving the way for a more complete and coherent understanding of the cognitive mechanisms that underlie intelligent functioning. As for the specific mental operations of interest, learning, perception, and reasoning are of utmost concern; however, cogntive scientists are particulary interested in problem solving since problem solving captures, in some sense, the epitome of human intelligent functioning.

The present investigation employed expert system techniques to examine the skills used in solving problems of the type usually encountered in basic experimental psychology (research methods) university courses. This problem area meets the criteria outlined in previous computer simulation research (Larkin & Reif, 1979; Gentner, 1980; Prerau, 1985). First, experimental psychology is sufficiently simple to facilitate progress in understanding underlying thought processes. Second, experimental psychology is sufficiently complex to the point of being intellectually challenging, practically significant, and potentially generalizable to more sophisticated problem domains. Third, this problem type primarily requires symbolic reasoning and can be enhanced by the use of heuristics. Lastly, the domain of experimental psychology can be broken down into various content areas (i.e., quasi-experimental designs, observational studies, validity...), thus enabling one to concentrate on a limited piece of the domain. This will serve to constrain the scope of the computational model.

Previous expert-novice research has suggested expert-novice problem solving differences pertaining to both the storage and organization of information in their problem schema knowledge bases as well as the schema-driven cognitive strategies employed (Glaser, in press). The purpose of the dissertation here was to test the robustness of this theory of expertise in problem solving by developing problem solving simulations in the domain of experimental psychology. It was expected that expert-novice differences would also be found for experimental psychology problem solvers.

Consistent with previous literature (Chase & Simon, 1973; Larkin, 1979; Chase & Chi, 1981; Chi, Glaser, & Rees, 1982; Sweller, 1983; Lewis & Anderson, 1985; Glaser, in press), these differences would be in the form of the knowledge base and cognitive strategies used by both individuals. Specifically, the expert and the novice problem solvers both would tend to separate their respective knowledge bases into hierarchical "chunks" containing the necessary domain knowledge (Glaser, in press). For example, they might separate the areas of quasi-experimental techniques into various designs (time-series designs, non-equivalent control groups, regression-discontinuity designs, etc.), with each design controlling for certain threats to validity. However, differential characteristics of the individual problem schemas were predicted. First, the number of chunks would be practically equivalent for both the novice and the expert (Chase & Simon, 1973). Second, the expert chunks would be larger, containing significantly more domain knowledge than that of the novice (Chase & Chi, 1981; Chi, Glaser, & Rees, 1982). Third, the additional information contained in these expert chunks would serve to explicate the general principles already outlined at higher levels of the chunks or problem schemas (Glaser, in press). With respect to the

schema-driven strategies, two predictions were viable. First, the number of possible solutions (rules) for an expert would be greater than that of a novice (Sweller, 1983; Lewis & Anderson, 1985). Second, given that the expert chunks would contain significantly more domain information and rules, the sophistication and accuracy of the schema-driven solutions would be extremely superior for experts (Sweller, 1983; Lewis & Anderson, 1985). These predictions were tested by comparing the problem solutions of the expert with those of the novice. The solutions contained both the generated answer as well as a comprehensive trace of the activities (steps, knowledge, rules, strategies) engaged while solving the problem. Thus, the solutions allowed for a direct comparison of both the knowledge base and cognitive strategies employed by the individuals.

There were two testing phases undertaken in this investigation. The first, called *model development*, concentrated on gathering the necessary information from both the expert and the novice, with the explicit intent of developing a computational model of their problem solving strategies. The objective of the second testing phase, called *model validation*, was to investigate the predictive capability of the computational models constructed during *model development*.

METHOD: MODEL DEVELOPMENT

Subjects
Two subjects (an expert and a novice) participated in this experiment. The expert was a methodology and statistics Professor from the Department of Psychology, University of Notre Dame. The novice was an excellent undergraduate psychology major who completed the required experimental design course offered for psychology majors at Notre Dame.

Material
Four quasi-experimental design problems were used during the *model development* testing phase. Each problem, extracted from previous research, conformed to a different quasi-experimental design technique. For instance, Cook and Campbell (1979) and Howard (1985) have stated that quasi-experimental techniques can be broken down into more specific research designs including interrupted time-series designs, multiple time-series designs, non-equivalent control group designs, and regression-discontinuity designs. The problems used were: **The Big East Conference** (interrupted time-series design), **The Maryland Crackdown** (multiple time-series design), **Teaching Experience For Counselors** (non-equivalent control groups design), and **The Impact of Academic Fellowships** (regression-discontinuity design).

An IBM Personal Computer was used with M.1 software to build the problem solving simulations. M.1 is a knowledge engineering software shell that is used to design, build, and run stand-alone expert systems. These systems are created by building (1) a knowledge base containing the specific facts and rules about some particular problem domain, and (2) an inference engine containing the cognitive strategies used to generate the problem solutions. M.1 contains advanced features that allow for rapid prototyping of problem solving models. Features that facilitate the building of the computer model include an interactive knowledge base (allows for continuous rule and fact modification), an automatic question generator (can ask system to explain why it needs the requested information), and an allowance for certainty factors (ability to represent and use uncertain knowledge). Additionally, M.1 has the capability to trace the flow of inferences and knowledge used during the problem solving activity.

Procedure

Collection of Verbal Protocols. The expert and novice subjects were tested individually by an unbiased interviewer. They were asked to solve the four quasi-experimental design problems while thinking aloud as much as possible. The record of each problem solution (both the answer as well as the detailed set of verbal comments made while generating the answer) for each subject was included in a tape-recorded manuscript of verbal comments made by the subjects. Both sessions lasted approximately one hour each.

Protocol Analysis. The protocols acquired during the *model development* testing phase were analyzed in accordance to the following procedure (which directly corresponds to that outlined by Ericsson and Simon, 1984). First, the protocols were reduced to a more simpler form by extracting the facts and solution steps utilized by the subjects. Thus, encoded protocols were developed from both the novice and the expert protocols. Second, the encoded protocols were aggregated by solution steps, whereby the problem solving steps the subjects used to generate the solutions were outlined. Lastly, these solution steps were aggregated, with the assistance of the subjects, generating a problem schema (model) for each subject. Specifically, the expert and novice subjects were presented with the aggregated solution steps and required to elaborate and precisely specify the strategies they used to solve each problem. The outcome of this was a problem schema (including both facts and rules) that modeled the knowledge base and solution steps utilized by each subject.

Model Development. Two computer models (expert and novice) were developed from these problem schemas in the form of expert system programs. The programs simulated the problem solving steps performed by each subject while generating the problem solutions. The facts and rules of these problem schemas were translated into M.1 software. Specifically, facts precisely define the domain knowledge needed to generate the solution, rules utilize the domain information while adhering to the problem solving

strategies dictated by the subjects and represented in the form of condition–action (IF–THEN) statements. For instance, a fact in a quasi–experimental design simulation could be: Best design = regression–discontinuity. A rule could be: IF no control group, THEN design = interrupted time–series. The outcome of this was an implementable computer model of problem solving in experimental psychology for both the novice and the expert.

Implementation Reliability. In order to enhance the objectivity of the implementation of the problem schemas to M.1 software, a naive observer randomly compared the functionality of the computer models with the given problem schemas. Specifically, the observer was placed at the IBM PC where the novice computational model was already booted. She was given the respective problem schema results and was told to verify and validate the consistency of the computational model with the problem schema. She then compared the problem solutions (solution steps and generated solutions) of the computational model with the problem schema. The observer repeated this comparison with the expert problem schema and respective compuational model. This was consistent with Ericsson and Simon's (1984) test of the reliability of protocol analysis.

Model Testing. After the *model development* testing phase was completed, the problem schemas, as well as the solutions provided by the computer models, were directly compared to test for expert–novice differences in problem solving activity in the domain of experimental psychology. This comparison, performed both within and between problem solutions tested for expert–novice differences with respect to both the knowledge base and schema–driven strategies employed. Again, these comparisons not only investigated the generated solution, but also the detailed set of facts and rules invoked during the problem solving activity.

RESULTS: MODEL DEVELOPMENT

The outcome of this model development phase basically was that two simulations of problem solving performance were created, precisely emulating the problem solving strategies utilized by an expert and a novice while generating problem solutions for various quasi–experimental problem scenarios. The expert–novice differences (pertaining to the knowledge base and control strategies) uncovered when comparing the problem solutions were, as predicted, consistent with previous investigations of expertise in problem solving (Chase & Simon, 1973; Larkin, 1979; Chase & Chi, 1981; Chi, Glaser, & Rees, 1982; Sweller, 1983; Lewis & Anderson, 1985; Glaser, in press). The conclusions to be drawn are: (1) Both problem solvers did separate their respective knowledge bases into hierarchical chunks containing the necessary solution steps (Glaser, in press); (2) The number of hierarchical chunks for both the expert and the novice were practically equivalent (Chase & Simon, 1973); (3) The expert chunks were larger, containing more solution steps (Chase & Chi, 1981; Chi, Glaser, & Rees, 1982); (4) The additional information in the expert problem schema served to enhance the general principles previously outlined at higher levels (Glaser, in press); (5) The expert simulation contained an increased number of possible solutions or rules (Larkin, 1979; Sweller, 1983; Lewis & Anderson, 1985); and (6) Consistent with the idea that a computational approach assesses both the sufficiency and adequacy of the solution steps aggregated from the encoded protocols, as well as requires increased precision in problem schema specification (Larkin, 1979), solution steps implicitly invoked during problem solving were uncovered.

An earlier prediction was made stating that the accuracy of the problem solutions would be superior for the expert. However, we found that there basically was no difference between the expert and novice with respect to the generated solutions for the particular problems used. Both subjects arrived at the same correct conclusions for each problem. However, the present computational approach allowed us to both simulate the problem solving performance of an expert and a novice (as was done in model development), as well as predict the problem solutions these subjects would generate for additional problems (problems not used during model development). Thus, the objective of model validation was to investigate the predictive capabilities of the computational models, while trying to uncover expert enhanced performance. The problems used during model validation were constructed on the basis of what were thought to be two conceptual flaws in the problem schema of the novice. First, if one constructed a problem where pre-experimental data was available however, no pre-intervention trend could be determined from this data, then the computational models would predict two very different solutions, with the expert's being the correct one.

A second conceptual flaw on the part of the novice involves his rule base showing that if one has pre-experimental data, then that rules out a non-equivalent control groups design. Remember, the non-equivalent control groups problem used during model development (problem three) did not have any pre-experimental data. The only possible conclusions for the novice are either a regression-discontinuity design or a multiple time-series design, depending on whether the groups were determined by a discrete cutoff point. However, when this is compared to the expert, the expert's problem schema suggests that if one pre-intervention data point exists, a non-equivalent control groups design is the best solution. Thus, if one constructed a problem where only one pre-experimental data point existed, and the groups were not determined by a discrete cutoff

point, then the best design, according to the expert model, would be a non-equivalent control groups design. However, the novice would have to assume (not explicitly pose the question) that the groups were determined by some discrete cutoff point, since a non-equivalent control groups design can't be used with just one pre-intervention measure; and, according to the novice computational model, no other design is possible.

METHOD: MODEL VALIDATION

Subjects

The same two subjects (the expert and novice) that participated in model development participated in this experiment. Again, the expert was a methodology and statistics Professor from the Department of Psychology, University of Notre Dame. The novice was an excellent undergraduate psychology major who completed the required experimental design course offered for psychology majors at Notre Dame.

Material

For this *model validation* testing phase, two quasi-experimental design problems were used: **The Caribbean Economic Community** (interrupted time-series design) and **Modeling School** (non-equivalent control groups). The two problems constructed highlighted the two conceptual flaws on the part of the novice computational model. Thus, a problem was constructed corresponding to each of the two conceptual flaws discussed above. The first problem, the **Caribbean Economic Community**, was developed so that, on the surface, an interrupted time-series design was the best design. However, if the question was posed to the experimenter concerning a pre-experimental trend, the experimenter was to respond by stating that no pre-experimental trend could be determined from the data. This problem was expected to uncover the first conceptual flaw of the novice -- no accountability for lack of pre-experimental trend. The second problem, **Modeling School**, was developed to address the second conceptual flaw on the part of the novice -- a non-equivalent control groups design can be used with one-pre-experimental data point. If the experimenter was asked whether a discrete cutoff point was used to determine the groups, the answer would be no.

Procedure

Collection of Verbal Protocols. The expert and novice subjects were tested individually by the experimenter. They were asked to solve the two quasi-experimental design problems while thinking aloud as much as possible. These problems were administered in the same order presented in. The record of each problem solution (both the answer as well as the detailed set of verbal comments made while generating the answer) for each subject was included in a tape-recorded manuscript of verbal comments made by the subjects. Both sessions lasted approximately one-half hour each. The procedure during this testing was consistent with that during model development.

Protocol Analysis. The protocols acquired during the model validation testing phase were analyzed exactly like those analyzed in model development; however, no problem schema was generated. First, the protocols were reduced to a more simpler form by extracting the facts and solution steps utilized by the subjects. Thus, encoded protocols were developed from both the novice and the expert protocols. Second, the encoded protocols were aggregated by solution steps, whereby the problem solving steps the subjects used to generate the solutions were outlined.

Model Validation. After the *model validation* testing phase was completed, the problem solutions of the subjects were compared to the problem solutions predicted by the computational models. This comparison, performed both within and between problem solutions tested for expert–novice differences with respect to both the knowledge base and schema–driven strategies employed. Again, these comparisons not only investigated the generated solution, but also the detailed set of facts and rules invoked during the problem solving activity.

RESULTS: MODEL VALIDATION

The objective of this model validation testing phase was to investigate the predictive capabilities of the computational models while trying to uncover enhanced performance on the part of the expert. We can conclude that the models do predict subsequent problem solutions of the respective subjects. This finding enhances our ability to make qualified assessments concerning the differential performance levels between the novice and the expert. Specifically, the conceptual flaws outlined during model development for the novice were illuminated during this model validation testing phase. The novice performed as predicted, but performed incorrectly. Additionally, he seemed somewhat confused duting this problem solving activity. Statements such as "hold on, let me think if I have got this right", "alright, hold on", and "alright, I think I have got it" suggest that he knew something was incorrect, but did not know what to do about it. In other words, he did not have the appropriate strategy (rule) for which to deal with this condition. This showed a degredation in the performance level for the novice. Thus, from this system validation testing phase, we can conclude that the computational models do have predictive validity and the expert performance level is somewhat more sophisticated than the novice.

GENERAL DISCUSSION

The expert–novice differences uncovered in this dissertation were, as predicted, consistent with previous investigations of expertise in problem solving (Chase & Simon, 1973; Larkin, 1979; Chase & Chi, 1981; Chi,

Glaser, & Rees, 1982; Sweller, 1983; Glaser, in press). First, both problem solvers organized their respective knowledge bases into problem schemas. A problem schema is a hierarchically organized knowledge base utilized during problem solving that dictates a schema-driven problem solving strategy in which the individual traverses a "generic to specific" set of solution steps chunks contained additional solution steps that tended to be represented at rather lower levels of the hierarchy, explicating the principles located at higher levels of the problem schema. For example, the expert posed the question concerning the existence of a pre–intervention trend, with the obvious intent of qualifying the presence of usable pre–intervention data. This difference was subsequently highlighted during model validation, resulting in enhanced expert performance. Given that this basic finding is consistent with previous expert–novice research (Larkin, 1979; Glaser, in press), one can conclude that theories of expertise in problem solving are quite generalizable across a variety of domains, including experimental psychology.

that solves the problem in terms of rules for given generated solutions. Within these problem schemas, both subjects separated their knowledge into hierarchical chunks containing the solution steps necessary to solve the problems. This is consistent with Glaser (in press) who states that the major component of knowledge lies in the possession and accessibility of these problem schemas. Second, the number of hierarchical chunks was practically equivalent for both subjects (Chase & Simon, 1973). Third, the expert chunks were larger, containing more solution steps for problem solving (Chase & Chi, 1981; Chi, Glaser, & Rees, 1982). Fourth, the additional information contained in the solution steps seemed, on the surface, to more narrowly define and enhance the problem solving process of the expert (Glaser, in press). Fifth, the expert simulation contained an increased number of possible solutions or rules (Larkin, 1979; Sweller, 1983; Lewis & Anderson, 1985). Lastly, consistent with the computational approach that tests both the sufficiency and adequacy of the generated solution steps invoked by the subjects during problem solving (Larkin, 1979), additional solution steps, not explicitly stated during problem solving, were uncovered. From a direct test of the predictive capabilities of the computational models, as well as the comparative expert–novice outcomes, the models were found to have predictive validity, with the expert performance level being somewhat more enhanced than the novice.

The basic finding of this study was, therefore, that the rules that constitute the problem schema of an expert were found to contain solution steps that seemed to more narrowly define the broader principles outlined at higher levels of the problem schema, leading to enhanced expert performance. Specifically, two simulations of problem solving performance were initially created, precisely simulating the problem solving strategies utilized by an expert and a novice while generating problem solutions for various quasi-experimental problem scenarios.

Earlier in this discussion it was pointed out that the basic finding of this dissertation was that the rules that constitute the problem schema of an expert either contained additional solution steps, or solution steps that seemed to more narrowly define the broader principles of the expert problem schema. The suggestion was made that the novice problem solver should attempt to acquire the detailed rules of the expert problem schema by the utilization of analogical reasoning. This approach dictates that a novice problem schema should be debugged with respect to conceptual flaws, culminating in a revised problem schema with revised rules. A major question now is, is this iterative rule development theoretically justified. Specifically, can this be explained in terms of a theory of human cognition? For the purpose of this discussion, we will concentrate on the work of John Anderson.

John Anderson (1983) developed the ACT* (Adaptive Control of Thought) system which attempts to computationally model the flow of information within the cognitive system. The central notion of the ACT* theory is that an individual acquires a set of productions that correspond to the rules of a given domain. A production is a condition-action rule, just like the rules used in M.1, which performs its action when its conditions are met. Anderson's major theoretical emphasis involves specifying the nature of these rules that reside in memory, as well as the processes (storage, retrieval, encoding, executive) and various factors that build and activate the rules. ACT* is a highly dynamic system in which the rules are discriminantly learned. Specifically, rules are initially learned incorporating the

general information of a given domain, with no emphasis on how to apply them. Lewis and Anderson (1985) suggest that this is consistent with the observation that teachers and textbooks teach general rules. However, rule discrimination applies when ACT* gets feedback that a rule is too general. When a rule fails to solve a problem correctly because of this generality, an attempt is made to add conditions (solution steps) to the rule which will enhance the future success of the rule application. Lewis and Anderson (1985) state that as more solution steps are added to the rule, or additional features of solution steps are specified, the precision of rule application increases. However, this more specific rule might later misapply, and the rule discrimination process would reoccur. Anderson's (1983) notion of rule discrimination seems, on the surface, to be consistent with the iterative rule development cycle undertaken in this dissertation. Thus, the iterative rule development cycle can be theoretically justified in terms of rule discrimination in ACT*.

REFERENCES

Anderson, J. R. (1983). **The architecture of cognition.** Cambridge, Mass: Harvard University Press.

Chase, W. G., & Chi, M. T. H. (1981). Cognitive skill: Implications for spatial skill in large-scale environments. In J. Harvey (Ed.), **Cognition, social behavior, and the environment.** Hillsdale, N. J.: Lawrence Erlbaum Associates.

Chase, W. G., & Simon, H. A. (1973). Perception in chess. **Cognitive Psychology, 4,** 55–81.

Chi, M., Glaser, R., & Rees, E. (1982). Expertise in problem solving. In R. Sternberg (Ed.), **Advances in the psychology of human intelligence.** Hillsdale, N. J.: Erlbaum.

Cook, T. D., & Campbell, D. T. (1979). **Quasi-experimentation: Design and analysis issues for field settings.** Boston, MA.: Houghton Mifflin Company.

Ericsson, K. A., & Simon, H. A. (1984). **Protocol analysis.** Cambridge, Mass.: The MIT Press.

Fodor, J. A. (1975). **The language of thought.** New York: Thomas Y Crowell.

Gentner, D. R. (1979). Toward an intelligent computer tutor. In H.F. O'Neil (Ed.), **Procedures for instructional systems development.** New York: Academic Press.

Glaser, R. (in press). On the nature of expertise. In M. Chi, R. Glaser, and M. Farr (Eds.), **The nature of expertise.** Hillsdale, N. J.: Lawrence Erlbaum Associates.

Howard, G. S. (!985). **Basic research methods in the social sciences.** Glenview, IL.: Scott, Foresman, & Company.

Larkin, J. H. (1979). **Models of strategy for solving physics problems.** Paper presented at the annual meeting of the American Educational Research Association, San Francisco, CA.

Larkin, J. H., & Reif, F. (1979). Understanding and teaching problem solving in physics. **European Journal of Scientific Education, 1,** 191–203.

Lewis, M. W., & Anderson, J. R. (1985). Discrimination of operator schemata in problem solving: Learning from examples. **Cognitive Psychology, 17,** 26–65.

Newell, A., & Simon, H. A. (1976). Computer science as empirical inquiry: Symbols and search. **Communications of the ACM, 19.**

Prerau, D. S. (1985). Selection of an appropriate domain for an expert system. **The AI Magazine, Summer,** 26–30.

Sternberg, R. J. (1986). Inside intelligence. **American Scientist, 74,** 137–186.

Sweller, J. (1983). Control mechanisms in problem solving. **Memory and Cognition, 11,** 32–40.

Advances in AI and Simulation
© 1989 By The Society for Computer
Simulation International
ISBN 0-911801-50-2

Incorporating a crop growth simulation
model in an expert system

R.W. McClendon
W.D. Batchelor
Dept. of Agric. Engr.
University of Georgia
Athens, GA 30602

D.B. Adams
Dept. of Ext. Entomology
Rural Development Center
University of Georgia
Tifton, GA 31793

J.W. Jones
Dept. of Agric. Engr.
University of Florida
Gainesville, FL 32611

J.E. Hook
Dept. of Agronomy
Coastal Plain Exper. Station
University of Georgia
Tifton, GA 31793

ABSTRACT

Detailed crop growth simulation models have been developed for most of the major row crops in the world. These models have proven useful in research as a means of understanding the processes involved and selecting research priorities. However, these models have generally been used only by the model developers or other researchers familiar with modeling. Recent efforts to incorporate crop models in an expert system environment have aided others in using these simulation models. The expert system environment also allows the inclusion of heuristic information from domain experts in crop production. Results from research studies that might not be suitable for crop model development can also be incorporated in the expert system. The expert system environment provides a means to interpret results from the simulation model and select additional runs before offering a recommendation to the user. A case study is included regarding a soybean insect pest management expert system which incorporates a soybean crop growth model in an expert system shell.

INTRODUCTION

Considerable research effort over the past 20 years has been devoted to developing models of agricultural production (Glen 1987). Frequently these models have incorporated computer simulation methodology. When applied to crop production, these models often have taken the form of process-oriented detailed crop growth models. The thrust of these models has largely been to understand the physiology of the crop and to plan future research directions. Unfortunately, these detailed crop growth simulation models have seen only limited use by individuals other than the model developers. Several difficulties frequently encountered in this regard are related to: (1) input requirements (2) limiting assumptions (3) calibration for other locations and (4) simulation output interpretation. The developers of a crop growth model are usually the only ones who completely understand all of its capabilities and limitations. Some large-scale crop modeling efforts, through extensive documentation and standardization, have been able to promote the use of crop models in international research programs (IBSNAT 1986). However, crop growth simulation models have seen relatively little use as direct decision aids or teaching tools.

In order to facilitate the use of crop simulation models to aid growers, several approaches have recently been pursued. In one approach, crop simulation models have been structured in game form to allow the user to make crop management decisions and then interactively see the simulated results (Akbay et al. 1988; Pieters et al. 1981). Another approach has been to incorporate the crop growth model in an expert system. The expert system then assumes the executive role in handling input, running the crop model, and interpreting the output. This expert system can also incorporate traditional expert system rules and facts to aid in decision making (Jones et al. 1987; Shannon et al. 1985; Smith et al. 1985)

COMAX was the first expert system which included a process oriented crop growth simulation model (Baker et al. 1983; Lemmon 1986; McKinion and Lemmon 1985). The COMAX system provides the user with recommendations concerning cotton crop fertilizer, irrigation, and defoliant applications. The expert system allows the user to transmit input information to the GOSSYM crop model, runs the model, and delivers the recommendation based on several runs of the crop model. Another expert simulation system, SMARTSOY (Soybean Management Alternatives using Real-Time Simulation Of Yield), was developed to assist in soybean insect pest management (Batchelor et al. 1988). The creation and evaluation of this system will be discussed herein as a case study of the development of a crop management expert simulation system.

SMARTSOY DEVELOPMENT

The objective of SMARTSOY was to develop a decision support tool which would deliver an expert recommendation regarding insecticide applications in soybean production. Insect pest management thresholds are usually expressed in terms of observed crop damage and/or insect population levels. These thresholds are based on research data and intuition from field experience. The expert for these recommendations in Georgia soybean production is the state Cooperative Extension Service Entomologist. This entomologist prepares extension bulletins and trains county extension agents regarding insect pest management. The rationale for his recommendations regarding when to treat is largely heuristic and his decision process is not easily quantified. It is thus difficult for a county agent who may have a limited entomological background to duplicate the recommendation of the entomologist. However, once the decision is made to treat, the entomologist's recommendation for insecticide selection and rate of application is well defined. SMARTSOY contains two contrasting approaches to knowledge base development. In determining the decision of when to treat, the thought processes of the expert were not followed. However, in determining the insecticide and application rate, the expert's thought process was mimicked.

Treatment Decision

The goal of the SOYGRO crop growth simulation model was to aid in management strategy development for soybean production (Wilkerson et al. 1983a and b). It has been used for several soil types and growing conditions of the Coastal Plain of Georgia (Hood et al. 1987; Fortson et al. 1988; Szmedra et al. 1988). Our approach was to use actual field crop and insect population data and then apply corresponding simulated insect pest damage to the SOYGRO model over a period of time. The SOYGRO model would then be run by the expert system to the end of the season with and without the insect damage. These two runs would represent the cases of treating the insect population with the insecticide or not. The current damage to the crop in terms of immediate leaf or pod damage by an observed insect population is reasonably well understood. Projecting the effects of that damage on yield at harvest is difficult. Therein, the crop growth simulation model is helpful by integrating the insect pest damage effects on final yield.

The entomologist obtained damage rate information for the four primary soybean insect pests in Georgia: soybean looper (Pseudoplusia includens), velvetbean caterpillar (Anticarsia gammatalis), corn earworm (Heliothis zea), and the southern green stink bug (Nazara viridula). Soybean looper (SL) and velvetbean caterpillar (VBC) cause damage by consuming foliage while southern green stink bug (SGSB) causes damage by puncturing seed. Corn earworm (CEW) prefers feeding on seed if present, otherwise it consumes foliage. These damage rates were given in ranges. For example, a VBC population of 26 per row meter will cause a 20-25 percent defoliation over a 14 day period. We therefore created damage application routines for the SOYGRO crop model which would apply the corresponding low (20 percent), high (25 percent) or medium (22.5 percent) damage.

The expert system calculates the difference between the simulated yield with damage (for each level) and the no subsequent damage yield. The value of the yield loss using the current price of soybean is then compared to the cost of an insecticide application to treat the population. From discussions with the entomologist, the treatment recommendation was structured with three alternatives: treat (T), wait three days and check (W3), or wait seven days and check (W7). In the expert system the recommendation took the following form:

if $V \geq C$ then T,

if $C/2 \leq V < C$ then W3,

if $V < C/2$ then W7,

where

V = value of simulated yield loss due to insect populations, and

C = cost to treat the insect populations.

The SOYGRO model was run from the planting date until the decision date with the current season's weather data consisting of daily solar radiation, max/min temperature, and precipitation. From the decision date to the end of the season, the user can select from weather data files for wet,

dry, or average rainfall conditions. Results were presented to the user for each of the three levels of damage. Thus a simulation run was made for each of the three levels assuming each insect population present damaged the crop at that level. The yields from the three damage runs were compared to the run with no-subsequent damage to obtain the associated value of yield loss.

Insecticide Selection

In attempting to duplicate the entomologist's insecticide and application rate selection, the entomologist was interviewed intensively to understand his decision rules. His thought process centered on identifying which insect species of those present would be most harmful. Once that insect species was determined, an insecticide which could control it was selected. The effect of that insecticide on other insect pests present was also considered. The rate at which the insecticide was to be applied was included in the final recommendation. Flow charts of his decision process were used in the interview sessions to help quantify the decision rules.

Expert System Configuration

SMARTSOY was developed using an IBM PS/2 Model 50 microcomputer system with the expert system shell Insight 2+ version 1.2 (Level Five Research Inc., 1986). SMARTSOY consists of five knowledge bases and 12 external programs. The user time required to input a scenario and obtain a recommendation was approximately 11 minutes. Of this time, the execution of SOYGRO and the knowledge bases required approximately 5 minutes.

As an example of the output generated by SMARTSOY a typical insect and crop scenario is included. On August 30 an insect population was assumed consisting of 4 SL, 4 VBC, 1.5 CEW, and 0.5 SGSB per row meter. The agronomic conditions are as follows: Kirby soybean variety, Norfolk loamy sand, May 17 planting date, 43 plants per m^2, 0.73 m row spacing, well irrigated and an average yield of 3.4 t/ha. The leaf mass and seed mass per ha are shown in Fig's. 1 and 2 for the three damage levels and the no subsequent damage case.

SMARTSOY Evaluation

The entomologist selected 30 crop and insect population scenarios which comprised typical decisions faced by growers in South Georgia. The agronomic conditions were also chosen for a typical farm production system. These scenarios were presented to SMARTSOY and the resulting recommendations were compared to those of the entomologist and are given in Table 1. When using the high damage rate, SMARTSOY agreed with the expert in 80 percent of the cases. At the medium and low rate the agreement was 73 and 50 percent, respectively. The insecticide selected and rate of application from SMARTSOY agreed with the entomologist's recommendation in each scenario in which SMARTSOY recommended a treatment. This result was expected due to the quantifiable decision process the entomologist used.

SUMMARY

The objective in this research was to develop a decision support tool for soybean insect pest management in Georgia. SOYGRO, a detailed crop

TABLE 1. Comparison of recommendations of SMARTSOY with the expert for typical insect and crop scenarios using three damage rate levels, soybean value of $220.30/t.

Scenario	SMARTSOY			Expert
	low	med.	high	
1	T	T	T	T
2	W3	W3	W3	W3
3	T	T	T	T
4	W7	W7	W7	W7
5	T	T	T	T
6	T	T	T	T
7	T	T	T	T
8	W3	T	T	T
9	W3	W3	W3	W3
10	W3	W3	T	W3
11	W7	W3	W3	W7
12	W7	W7	W3	W7
13	W3	W3	W3	W3
14	T	T	T	T
15	W7	W3	W3	W3
16	W3	T	T	T
17	T	T	T	T
18	W3	W3	W3	T
19	W3	W3	W3	T
20	W3	T	T	T
21	W3	T	T	T
22	T	T	T	T
23	W3	T	T	T
24	W3	W3	T	T
25	W3	T	T	T
26	W3	W3	W3	T
27	W7	W3	W3	W3
28	W3	W3	T	T
29	W3	W3	T	T
30	W3	W3	T	T
AGREEMENT	50%	73%	80%	

*W7, wait seven days and check; W3, wait three days and check; T treat.

growth simulation model, was incorporated in an expert system shell. Routines were written to apply damage to SOYGRO based on insect damage rate data supplied by the entomologist. In the scheme of the decision support system, information from field scouting reports could then be input to SMARTSOY and the SOYGRO crop model was run with and without the damage. The value of the simulated yield loss was compared to the cost to treat in order to develop a recommendation on the profitability of an insecticide application. The insecticide selection and rate recommendation was based on the entomologist's well defined rules. For evaluation, typical crop and insect pest scenarios were presented to SMARTSOY. SMARTSOY performed well in agreeing with the entomologist when using the medium and high damage rates. The insecticide selection and rate recommendation agreed in all cases.

Future research with SMARTSOY will include testing under actual conditions in soybean fields in South Georgia. The soil types will be determined for the fields and actual planting dates, soybean variety, and irrigation applications will be recorded. Daily weather data will be transmitted from each field to maintain files to run SOYGRO to the current decision date. Field scouts will monitor the crops and all insect pest management decisions will be posed to the entomologist and SMARTSOY. As recommendations are given, any lack of agreement will be analyzed to determine the cause and modifications to SMARTSOY will be made. Additional insect pests will also be included in the damage routines and other soil types will be incorporated for wider applicability.

REFERENCES

Akbay, K.S., R.W. McClendon, and L.G. Brown. 1988. "COTGAME: Cotton Insect Pest Management Simulation Game." *Applied Engineering in Agriculture* 4, no. 3: 201-206, 210.

Baker, D.N., J.R. Lambert and J.M. McKinion. 1983. "GOSSYM: A Simulator of Cotton Crop Growth and Yield." South Carolina Agric. Experiment Sta. Tech. Bull. 1089, Clemson, SC.

Batchelor, W.D., R.W. McClendon, J.W. Jones, and D.B. Adams. 1988. "An Expert Simulation System for Soybean Insect Pest Management." *Transactions of the ASAE* (in press).

Fortson, R.E., R.W. McClendon, and J.E. Hook. 1988. "Managing Irrigation with the SOYGRO Crop Growth Model in the Coastal Plain of Georgia." *Applied Engineering in Agriculture* (in press).

Glen, J.J. 1987. "Mathematical Models in Farm Planning: A Survey." *Operations Research* 35:641-666.

Hood, C.P., R.W. McClendon, and J.E. Hook. 1987. "Computer Analysis of Soybean Irrigation Management Strategies." *Transactions of the ASAE* 30, no. 2: 417-423.

International Benchmark Sites for Agrotechnology Transfer (IBSNAT). 1986. "Decision Support System for Agrotechnology Transfer, Technical Report 5." University of Hawaii at Manoa, Honolulu, Hawaii.

Jones, J.W., P. Jones, and P.A. Everett. 1987. "Combining Expert Systems and Agricultural Models: A Case Study." *Transactions of the ASAE* 30, no. 5:1308-1313.

Lemmon, H.E. 1986. "COMAX: An Expert System for Cotton Crop Management." Science 233, no. 7:29-33.

Level Five Research, Inc. 1986. *Insight 2+*. 503 Fifth Avenue, Indialantic, FL.

McKinion, J.M. and H.E. Lemmon. 1985. "Symbolic Computers and AI Tools for a Cotton Expert System." ASAE Paper No. 85-5520, ASAE, St. Joseph, MI 49085.

Pieters, E.P., K.S. Akbay, L.G. Brown, and R.W. McClendon. 1981. "Use of Computer Game COTGAME in Teaching Entomology." *Environmental Entomology* 10:256-261.

Shannon, R.E., R. Meyer, and H.H. Adelsberger. 1985. "Expert Systems and Simulation." *Simulation* 44, no. 6:275-284.

Smith, R.D., J.R. Barrett, and R.M. Peart. 1985. "Crop production management with expert systems." American Society of Agricultural Engineers Paper No. 85-5521, ASAE, St. Joseph, MI 49085.

Szmedra, P.I., R.W. McClendon, and M.E. Wetzstein. 1988. "Risk Efficiency of Pest Management Strategies: A Simulation Case Study." *Transactions of the ASAE* (in press).

Wilkerson, G.G., J.W. Mishoe, W.G. Boggess, and D.P. Swaney. 1983a. "Modeling soybean growth for crop management." *Transactions of the ASAE* 26, no. 1:63-73.

Wilkerson, G.G., J.W. Mishoe, J.W. Jones, J.L. Stimac, D.P. Swaney, and W.G. Boggess. 1983b. "SICM: Florida Soybean Integrated Crop Management Model. Model Description and User's Guide. Version 4.2." Report AGE 83-1, Department of Agricultural Engineering, Institute of Food Sciences, University of Florida, Gainesville, FL.

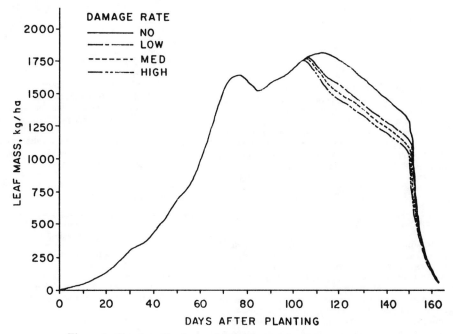

Figure 1. Simulated leaf mass for the damaged and no damage runs.

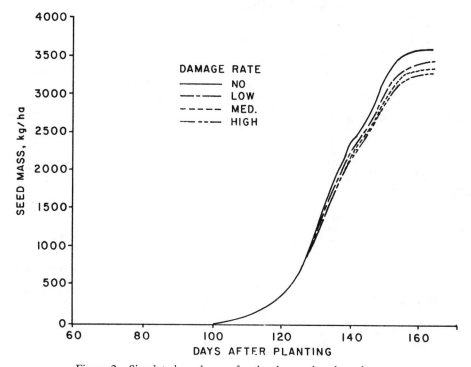

Figure 2. Simulated seed mass for the damaged and no damage runs.

Advances in AI and Simulation
© 1989 By The Society for Computer
Simulation International
ISBN 0-911801-50-2

Conceptual design of chemical processes

David. A. Nelson, Robert L. Kirkwood and James M. Douglas

Department of Chemical Engineering
University of Massachusetts
Amherst, Massachusetts 01003

ABSTRACT

The problem of conceptual design of chemical processes is a very large and open-ended problem. Since experience indicates that less than one percent of the ideas for a new design ever become commercialized, there is a great incentive to undertake conceptual designs to estimate the profitability of a process early in its development. The coupling of artificial intelligence techniques and short-cut design procedures in a software package (PIP, Process Invention Procedure) makes it possible to complete a design in about one hour, as compared to the two day to one-week period required for an experienced designer. This paper describes how PIP uses artificial intelligence techniques in process design.

INTRODUCTION

The rapidly growing success of expert systems in the field of artificial intelligence has generated a strong interest in applying this technology to design problems in a variety of engineering disciplines, see Stephanopoulos (1986), Rychener (1983), and Sriram and Joobbani (1985). The development appears to be moving along two different paths. The first involves the more "classical", qualitative knowledge-based system that use many of the current search, planning and control strategy concepts. The second is to integrate a knowledge-based system on top of computer-aided-design packages. With this configuration the expert system acts as more of an advisor and a guide, assisting the user with the application of very complicated "number crunching" algorithms.

PIP (Process Invention Procedure), a program to perform conceptual design for a limited class of chemical plants, which is discussed in this paper, lies somewhere in between. It relies very heavily on "number crunching" algorithms to analyze the flowsheets generated using rules, but the code is structured and guided in a manner that capitalizes on many of the ideas developed for classical expert systems. Its chief feature is that it can construct a hierarchy of partial solutions to a complex design problem with limited information, and then make decisions on which direction to take in a search based on these partial solutions.

This paper does not provide a complete description of PIP or the methods it uses for conceptual process design. More detailed discussions can be found in Douglas (1985,1988), Kirkwood et al. (1988), and Kirkwood (1987)

In this paper we will first describe conceptual process design, and then examine what expert systems techniques can be used. We will end up discussing some of the advantages and disadvantages of this approach to conceptual design of chemical plants.

CONCEPTUAL PROCESS DESIGN

Conceptual process design of a chemical plant is the act of translating a chemists initial information about a particular reaction pathway into a process flowsheet. The information the chemist will typically know includes:

1. The chemical species being created (primary product)
2. Chemical Reactions
   a. To make the primary product
   b. To make any unwanted secondary products
3. Temperature, pressure and phase of the reactions
4. Some information on the product distribution as a function of reactor operating conditions
5. Available feedstocks

Table 1 shows this information for a plant to produce benzene by the hydrodealkalation of toluene.

Table 1. Initial chemists information for a toluene hydrodealkalation process
Primary Product: Benzene $9.04 per pound mole

Reactions:
    Hydrogen + Toluene = Benzene + Methane
    2 Benzene == Diphenyl + Hydrogen

Reactor Conditions: 1150 F   500 PSIA
Product Distribution: $$S = 1 - \frac{0.0036}{(1-X)^{1.544}}$$ Where S (selectivity) is the amount of benzene produced at the reactor outlet divided by the toluene converted in the reactor and X is the fractional conversion of toluene.
Feed Streams: 1. 96 % (volume) Hydrogen, 4% Methane, 500 PSIA, $1.32 per pound mole 2. 100% Toluene $6.40 per pound mole

A process flowsheet consists of:

1. The particular pieces of equipment required
2. The sizes and costs of the equipment
3. The connections between the equipment

Figure 1 shows a process flowsheet for a plant to produce benzene by the hydrodealkylation of toluene, excluding the energy integration network. This is not the only possible flowsheet structure. For a typical process there are over a million possible process flowsheets (Douglas, 1985), and the goal of conceptual process design is to find the particular flowsheet that maximizes profit.

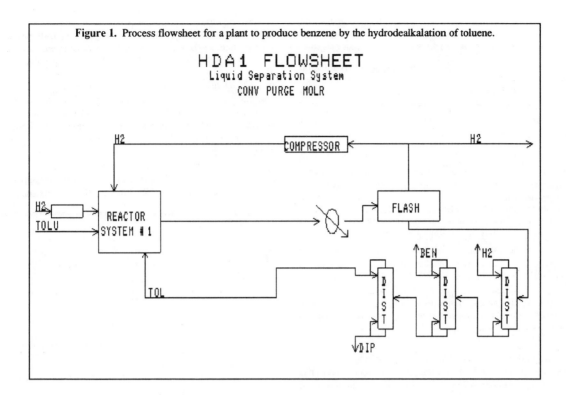

Figure 1. Process flowsheet for a plant to produce benzene by the hydrodealkalation of toluene.

It can be considered as a large optimization problem over both discrete structures and continuous operating variables. Determining how profitable a flowsheet is requires that the material and energy balances be solved, the equipment sizes and costs estimated and the utility costs estimated. These tasks make the problem very computationally intensive. To treat conceptual process design as a pure optimization problem would require this difficult evaluation task be done over all possible structures.

Most possible flowsheet structures are economically unattractive. Less than one percent of the ideas for new designs ever become commercialized (Kirkwood et al., 1988). Even if we ignore structures that are impossible due to physical restrictions (its hard to separate solids in a gas absorber), most structures are not of interest due to economic considerations (gases are very expensive to separate). These feature can be capitalized on during conceptual design to avoid the work involved in creating a complete design for each potential flowsheet. The new work in expert systems has provided some ideas and methodologies that can be used to capitalize on these feature to quickly perform conceptual process designs.

EXPERT SYSTEMS APPLIED TO PROCESS DESIGN

Expert systems provide several techniques for solving conceptual process design problems. In this section we will discuss how tools like generate and test, hierarchical planning and heuristic search are used in the program PIP (Kirkwood et al., 1988) for conceptual design of a restricted class of chemical plants.

To be useful these tools must provide a efficient map of the underlying optimization space. This is the sole rational for using these techniques.

Generate and Test

Conceptual process design is generally considered to consist of two steps, a synthesis step to propose a structure and an analysis step to evaluate the structure. This is very similar to the generate and test paradigm used in the GA1 program to determine DNA structures (Stefik, 1978), and the DENDREL program to determine molecular structures (Buchanan and Feigenbaum, 1978) where candidate solutions are generated, a set of rules are used to prune the solution space, and a physical model is used to evaluate (test) the remaining solutions.

In PIP the procedure is slightly modified. A structure is proposed by answering a series of questions, and then this structure is evaluated by solving the material and energy balance equations, along with the equipment design and cost equations for the proposed structure. A key feature that must be utilized with the generation and test paradigm is early pruning of the search space to eliminate entire regions of the search space. Without this feature, generation and test for PIP would simply be exhaustive enumeration. PIP does not have efficient pruning rules like GA1 and DENDREL, so it depends on a fixed hierarchical plan to efficiently prune the search space.

Hierarchical Planning

PIP utilizes the hierarchical procedure of Douglas (1985) to factor the search space into five distinct levels. By starting at the most abstract (and least complicated) level to generate structures, whole branches of the search space can be eliminated early in the generate and test paradigm. Any structures that survive (the process is profitable) the first level are passed to the second level where they are further refined and then tested at this new more detailed level. The procedure is repeated until either all possible structures are eliminated or the most profitable flowsheet alternatives are identified.

The levels of Douglas's procedure are shown in Table 2. For generate and test to function, the early abstract levels of the procedure must coincide with significant branching in the search space and must provide opportunities for eliminating structures based on little information. Douglas's procedure accomplishes this by adding detail (equipment and streams) at each new level that can only cost more money in an actual plant, along with a structuring of the levels so decisions are made in a descending order of economic importance.

Table 2. Douglas's hierarchical procedure
Level 1: Batch vs. Continuous Operation
Level 2: Input Output Structure of the Flowsheet
Level 3: Recycle Structure of the flowsheet and Reactor Considerations
Level 4: Separation System
Level 4a: Vapor Recovery System
Level 4b: Liquid Separation System
Level 5: Heat Exchanger Network

At the first level we must decide if the plant will run continuously or batch. This decision dictates the design of all further equipment, and hence is required before any equipment design. It is also a decision that is primarily determined by plant capacity. Over a certain level (10 million pounds per year) continues operation is generally cheaper. At Level two, the decisions are made that dictate the input-output structure of the flowsheet. Figure 2 shows an example of a the detail found in a Level two flowsheet. That is, what material streams enter the process and what streams leave. The costs of raw material streams range from 35 to 85% of the total processing costs (Grumer, 1967), and are next in order of economic importance. In Level 3 the decisions regarding the recycle structure of the flowsheet are made. The significant costs found here are for the reactor system and gas recycle compressor (if required). In Figure 3 we see the level of detail in a Level three flowsheet.

The Level 4 decisions include the types of separations required, and the order they are performed. Level 4 is shown in Figure 1. Level 5 determines the heat exchanger network capital and operating costs to utilize energy most efficiently. At the end of Level 5, a complete process flowsheet is created.

Each of these levels is significant in that a higher level cannot be constructed until all of the lower ones have been completed. Except for Level 5, all of the levels only add incremental costs. In the earlier levels, it is always assumed that the tasks performed in the latter levels had no cost. If a flowsheet is not profitable at a early level, no additional work at higher levels is justified. The flowsheet alternative can be rejected with minimum effort.

The key feature of Douglas's hierarchical procedure is that it provides opportunities to make a few decisions about the flowsheet structure, and then to stop and evaluate the results. This ability to construct partial solutions with limited information is the key factor in being able to prune the search space effectively. This is most easily seen in Figure 4, a tree graph of the search space. Whole classes of the search space can be eliminated by constructing a partial solution of a potential flowsheet. Conceptual design of chemical plants is readily amenable to this negative reasoning, since only about one percent of flowsheet ideas ever become commercialized and the physics of the problem allows easy construction of partial solutions.

<u>Heuristic Search</u>

Within each level of Douglas's hierarchical procedure several decisions are made that determine the structure of the flowsheet. We utilize heuristic rules to recommend initial choices for each decision, but the user retains control over the final choice. These heuristics have been traditionally generated by experienced process designers. They can also found by generalizing the results of a large number of computer design case studies, or in most cases it is possible to derive the heuristics (Douglas,1988). This use of heuristics essentially provides a map of the solution space that can be used to provide guidance in finding the optimal structure.

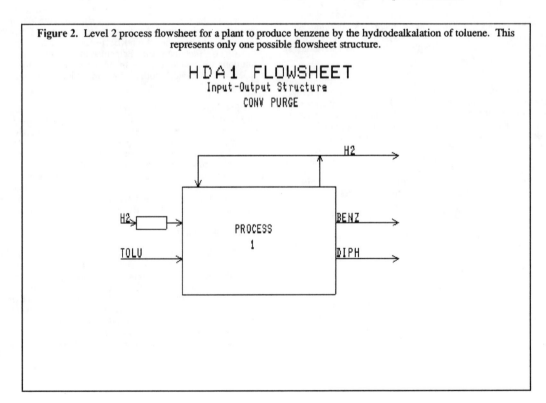

Figure 2. Level 2 process flowsheet for a plant to produce benzene by the hydrodealkalation of toluene. This represents only one possible flowsheet structure.

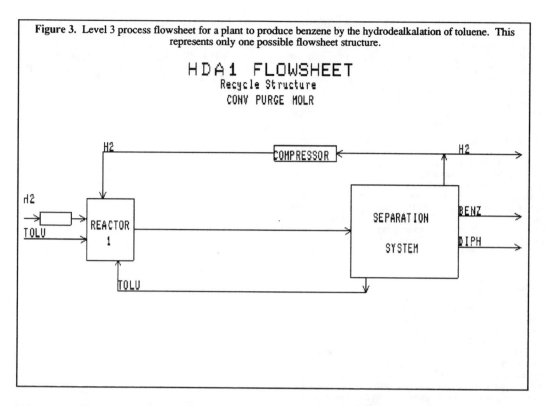

Figure 3. Level 3 process flowsheet for a plant to produce benzene by the hydrodealkalation of toluene. This represents only one possible flowsheet structure.

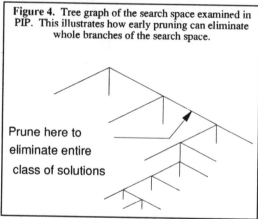

Figure 4. Tree graph of the search space examined in PIP. This illustrates how early pruning can eliminate whole branches of the search space.

One feature of conceptual process design that significantly simplifies the use of heuristics is that the decisions normally involve distinct and isolated choices. The decisions are isolated since they all apply to specific parts of the structure problem. For example the decisions required to select a Level 2 structure are shown in Table 3.

Table 3. Level-2 decisions
1. Should we purify the feed streams before they enter the process?
2. Should we remove or recycle a by-product formed by a reversible side reaction?
3. Should we use a gas recycle and purge stream?
4. Should we recover and recycle each reactant?

The decision about feed stream purification only determines if there will be a unit to remove feedstream impurities. It has no effect on the other decisions. None of the decisions affect each other in the generation of a flowsheet structure within a level. However, it should be pointed out that the decisions will affect each other in the economic evaluation (test phase) as well as some decisions at later levels. For example, the amount of gas recycled in a recycle and purge stream is effected by whether inert gasses are removed by a feed stream purification system.

Since the heuristics are simple and very few in number where they are used to make a decision, we have implemented them in a ad-hoc manner. In most cases, only one heuristic applies to one decision, and there is never any conflict between heuristics. If there are more heuristics (or exceptions to a more general heuristic) that apply to a single decision, the specific ordering of the heuristics fixes the conflict resolution. The user, however, is all ways left with the final decision.

Heuristics assist the user in making initial structural decisions. However, Douglas's hierarchical procedure isolates decisions into manageable numbers (around 5 per level), so that it is not odious to evaluate all of the structures per level. At Level 2 this would result in 24 evaluations. This is a worst case because many of the decisions will be clearly unattractive from a single evaluation and none of the combinations will need to be evaluated.

By keeping track of the decisions made at each level in the hierarchy, which are initially fixed by a heuristic or a user over-ride, the opposite decision represents an alternative structure. It would be possible to evaluate all of the alternatives at each level (breadth-first) as the code proceeds through the hierarchy, but we prefer to use a depth-first search in order to try an discover some reason that would make all of the alternatives unprofitable. However, to find the most profitable alternative, it is necessary to evaluate the alternative decisions. The code automatically identifies these back-tracking points.

THE EVALUATION TASK IN CONCEPTUAL DESIGN

In PIP a significant, and perhaps dominating emphasis is on the evaluation of flowsheet alternatives. The ideas from expert systems provide efficient methods for generating structures, and methods to eliminate complete classes of structures. But the final criteria of a successful design is cost. This significantly affects the structure of the code. The complete design of a chemical plant is not a trivial task. In PIP much more than half the code is involved in structural evaluation. This imposes several restrictions on PIP.

In most expert systems one goal is to interact with a user to input new rules to expand a knowledge base. In PIP, adding new rules is only practical in a limited way. It is relatively simple to add new rules to make the decisions that select a certain structure, but it is very difficult to add rules that create new structures. This requires that the evaluation program also be modified, either by adding complete new equipment models and their connections to the rest of the flowsheet or by connecting existing equipment in non-anticipated orders. This, in effect, limits PIP to searching a known structural search space. For the class of chemical processes that PIP is designed to deal with, this search space is relatively easily defined and complete.

ADVANTAGES OF PIP

Despite the limitations of PIP, the code makes it possible to complete the conceptual design of a limited class of petrochemical processes in about one hour, in contrast to the two-day time period that it takes an experienced designer with simple evaluation techniques. The evaluations require the majority of the time and this leads experienced designers to fix the flowsheet with a very incomplete search. Douglas (1985), after extensive discussions with experienced designers, identifies this early fixing of the flowsheet structure as the major problem in existing designs. The ability to screen many structures with minimum detail (hierarchical plan) makes it possible for PIP to find an optimal flowsheet.

CONCLUSIONS

In this paper we have examined how to solve conceptual process design of chemical process problems using some expert system techniques. Generate and test, hierarchical planning, and heuristic search are used to provide a efficient map of the underlying optimization space. The use of a fixed hierarchical plan and creating partial solutions to a complex problem with limited information are the most significant techniques used in our work.

REFERENCES

Buchanan, B.G., and E.A. Feigenbaum, "Dendrel and Meta-Dendral: Their Applications Dimension", *Artificial Intelligence*, **11** (1978), 5-24

Douglas, J.M., "A Hierarchical Decision Procedure for Process Synthesis," *AIChE J.*, **31**, 353 (1985).

Douglas, J.M., *Conceptual Design of Chemical Processes*. McGraw-Hill (1988).

Grummer, E.L., "Selling Price vs. Raw Material Cost", *Chem. Eng.*, **79**, (1) 190 (1967)

Kirkwood, R.K., Locke, M.H. and Douglas, J.M., "A Prototype Expert System for Synthesizing Chemical Process Flowsheets," *Comp. & Chem. Eng.*, **12**, 329 (1988).

Kirkwood R.K., "PIP -Process Invention Procedure, A Prototype Expert System for Synthesizing Chemical Process Flowsheets," Ph.D Thesis, Department of Chemical Engineering, University of Massachusetts (1987)

Rychener, M.D., " Expert Systems for Engineering Design: Experiments with Basic Techniques", Proceeding, Trends, and Applications, National Bureau of Standards, Gaithersburg, MD (1983)

Sriram, D. and R. Joobbani (Eds.), "AI in Engineering", *SIGART Newsletter*, April, (92) (1985)

Stefik, M., "Inferring DNA Structures from Segmentation Data", *Artificial Intelligence*, **11** (1978), 85-114

Stephanopoulos, G, "Expert Systems and Computing Environments for Process Systems Engineering", *CAST Newsletter*, **9** (1) 8 (1986)

IPSE: A knowledge-based environment
for process simulation

Sumitra M. Reddy*, Richard Turton**, Kevin E. Williams***,
Devendra B. Godbole*, Shailesh M. Potnis*
*Statistics and Computer Science **Chemical Engineering
West Virginia University, Morgantown, WV 26506
***U.S. Department of Energy Morgantown Energy Technology Center
P.O. Box 880 Morgantown, WV 26507-0880

ABSTRACT

In this paper we describe IPSE,[1] (Intelligent Process Simulation Environment) a system that can assist a chemical engineer in all phases of process simulation. The system consists of a number of subsystems: A User Interface, Knowledge base and an Analysis Engine. The user interface serves as a front end for model alteration, perusal and specification of goals. ASPEN was selected as the target process simulation engine.

The IPSE knowledge base consists of knowledge of various types: model-independent generic ASPEN knowledge, current model and goals, rules for model analysis and economic data. The generic IPSE knowledge base which is based on ASPEN's System Definition File (SDF) consists of generic *objects* from which the user-defined models are created by *instantiating* relevant generic objects.

The IPSE analysis engine is goal-driven. At the end of each simulation run, the analyzer checks if all of the model goals are satisfied. If not, it proposes parametric changes to achieve the specified goals.

A prototype of IPSE which integrates ASPEN with the subsystems of IPSE was developed. An example simulation model involving a fluidization process was selected for the prototype. A simple economic analysis package was developed to provide a screening mechanism to evaluate various model alternatives and thus help the engineer to identify a design that is economically viable and technically feasible.

INTRODUCTION

Chemical engineers depend on process simulation models to determine "optimal" plant configurations which are technically feasible and economically viable. Current process simulation technology requires the engineer/designer to follow a lengthy multistep process involving:
1. Development of a flowsheet.

Translation of the flowsheet into a simulation flow diagram for the target process simulation system.

Iterative execution of the model developed in step 2 by altering values of control variables until specified goals (desired values of output variables) are achieved.

Iterative execution of the model determined in step 3 by making structural/topological changes to the flow diagram suggested by exergy and economic analyses until a satisfactory design is identified.

The objective of this project is to assist the engineer in steps 3 and 4 of the process outlined above.

In this paper we describe IPSE, a knowledge based simulation environment that can enhance the productivity of chemical engineers/modelers by serving as an *intelligent* assistant during all phases of process simulation. The goals of this research are:

- Application of knowledge-based techniques to the process modeling domain for enhancement of productivity.

- Archival and distribution of **best experts' knowledge** of process modeling.

- Cross-model inference assistance to modelers not familiar with the process.

- Development of IPSE to serve as an intelligent tutoring system for process simulation.

This system will serve as a research test bed for exploring knowledge based approach to process modeling.

IPSE ARCHITECTURE

The IPSE system consists of three major components: A user interface (front end), an analyzer (back-end) and a knowledge base containing modeling knowledge and rules for analysis. A simplified view of the architecture of IPSE integrated with a process simulation engine is shown in Figure 1.

The IPSE implementation strategy combines a number of knowledge-based programming paradigms: object-oriented knowledge representation, rule-based and data-driven programming.

Object-oriented knowledge representation is used to represent the concepts and modeling entities so that they may be acted upon by the inference engine. It also adds perspicuity to the model. LASER[2], an integrated AI environment is the implementation tool for IPSE. LASER (written in the C language) provides a number of programming paradigms and inference engines to facilitate development of a wide variety of knowledge based systems.

The following subsystems of LASER are currently used to implement IPSE:

1. LASER/KR - for object-oriented knowledge representation.

2. LASER/RPS - the forward chaining inference engine for implementing the IPSE analysis engine.

Each component of IPSE will be described in the following sections.

---

[1]Supported by U.S. Department of Energy, Morgantown Energy Technology Center, Morgantown, WV 26505 under WVU-METC Cooperative agreement, Contract No. DE-FC21-87MC24207.

[2]Trademark of Bell Atlantic Knowledge Systems

IPSE KNOWLEDGE BASE

Knowledge in IPSE has been been classified into following categories:

1. ASPEN knowledge - Generic knowledge about ASPEN blocks and streams (similar to the information contained in the ASPEN System Definition File (SDF).

2. Domain knowledge - Knowledge about generic submodels constructed by grouping ASPEN blocks.

3. Problem knowledge : current model goals and information contained in the ASPEN Problem Definition File (PDF).

4. Analysis knowledge - Rules for the analysis of simulation results and constraint checking.

5. Economic knowledge - knowledge to determine the economic viability of the design.

Regardless of the type of the knowledge, it is represented in the form of LASER objects which form taxonomies (using "isa" hierarchy). Each object may have several properties with multiple values. For example, a *mixer* may be represented as an object that belongs to a class called *block*:

```
{ mixer
    instance-of: block
    inputs : "rmix1" "s3"
    outputs : "rmix2"
}
```

The mixer has two properties: *inputs* with two values "rmix1" and "s3", and *outputs* with one value "rmix2". The generic IPSE knowledge base which is based on the ASPEN System Definition File (SDF) consists of such objects. The user-defined models are represented as the *instances* of these generic objects.

Domain Knowledge

In the IPSE knowledge base, a set of generic submodels (subsection of a flowsheet that represents a process) are stored which serves as templates for submodels employed in a process flowsheet. Each submodel represents an actual piece of equipment for which input/output streams exist and cost information can be obtained. A submodel may consist of several ASPEN units. For example, a submodel called an *inert gas generator* may be simulated using a *mixer* and a *reactor* in ASPEN whereas a *mixer* may be a stand alone submodel. IPSE rules operate at the submodel level instead of ASPEN units because the parametric changes suggested by the IPSE analyzer deals with actual manipulatable input streams.

LASER objects are created based on the ASPEN SDF keywords: Primary keywords, Secondary keywords and the Tertiary keywords. At present, the generic knowledge (i.e. the domain knowledge) about ASPEN *streams* and a limited number of ASPEN *blocks* exists in the IPSE knowledge base. As the system evolves, generic knowledge about <u>all</u> ASPEN blocks will be included in the knowledge base.

Model Goals

IPSE knowledge base contains generic goal objects with a set of properties. Model goals are extracted from the user interactively and transformed into *goal objects* by instantiating the generic goals.

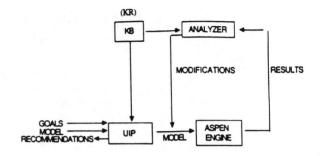

IPSE ARCHITECTURE

Figure 1

FRONT END

The user interface allows the user to perform a variety of tasks: submodel creation by grouping ASPEN units, model alteration, model perusal, examination of model variables and specification of model goals. In the initial phase of the project, the model creation task is not undertaken. Emphasis is given to the goal-driven analysis task. Hence, we begin with a a base case ASPEN flowsheet that is not yet optimized and demonstrate how the IPSE system improves the initial model by using its analysis engine.

Submodel Identification

Normally, an engineer starts from a process flowsheet and from this, he develops a simulation flowsheet. Figure 2 and Figure 3 show examples of this approach. The decomposition of Figure 2, a pictorial representation of the process flowsheet into the ASPEN units in Figure 3 is not unique. Since IPSE starts with a base case ASPEN flowsheet, it is important for the IPSE analyzer to have a knowledge of Figure 2: the initial diagram from which the ASPEN flowsheet was generated. The purpose of extracting this information in terms of the process flowsheet is two-fold: to apply the IPSE rules for analysis which are written in terms of predefined generic submodels, and to provide cost information in terms of the actual physical equipment involved in the flowsheet.

Both graphical and textual routines were developed to interact with the user for submodel identification in an interactive session. An editor using the "pick and place" model allows the user to group ASPEN units that collectively form a predefined submodel.

The flowsheet in Figure 3 consisting of 16 ASPEN units would coalesce into 6 predefined submodels shown in Figure 2. Two mixers (GG-MX1 and GG-MX2) and a reactor (GG-REAC) are grouped to form a gas generator. The process of grouping is continued until all of the ASPEN units are categorized under some predefined submodel. Error checking is performed so that each ASPEN unit belongs to only one submodel to ensure that no ASPEN unit is shared among submodels.

IPSE also ensures that no ASPEN unit in the flowsheet is excluded from membership in a submodel. In this case IPSE would notify the user the names of ASPEN units which had not been assigned to any submodel.

MODEL ANALYSIS

A rule-based programming paradigm is used to express heuristics and logical implications. This forms the heart of the model analysis.

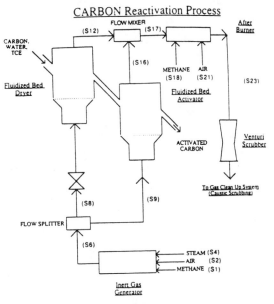

CARBON Reactivation Process

Figure 2

IPSE Rule Base

Rules are formulated in terms of generic submodels so that their application will be general and not specifically tied to a flowsheet. These rules describe the relationship between the inputs and outputs of the submodels.

The rules are written as objects in a standard "(IF <condition> THEN <action>" format so that they can be interpreted by the inference engine of LASER/RPS. Each rule object has two properties : *lhs* (left hand side) to describe conditions and *rhs* (right hand side) to describe actions to be taken when the conditions in the left hand side are satisfied.

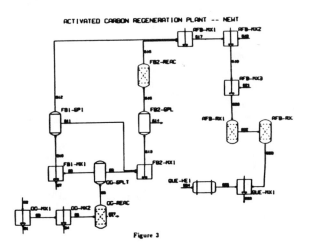

ACTIVATED CARBON REGENERATION PLANT -- NEHT

Figure 3

Analysis Engine

The IPSE analyzer evaluates each goal to determine if it is satisfied. If the goal is not satisfied, it traces through the submodels using rule chaining and identifies the key parameters that can be modified using qualitative reasonings (also the direction of modification such as decrease or increase the parameter) to achieve the goal. The process of analysis is continued for each goal that is not satisfied. The analyzer tabulates all the recommendations from each goal and at the end of the analysis phase, it reports to the user the non-conflicting recommendations.

An example of a recommendation table is given below.

Goal	Can be achieved by	
Goal-1	flow decrease of stream 1	flow decrease of stream 4
Goal-2	flow decrease of stream 1	flow decrease of stream 4
Goal-3	flow increase of stream 2	flow increase of stream 21

Economic Analysis

The IPSE knowledge base incorporates cost information associated with a model. Costs are broken down into two parts: fixed costs and operating costs. Both parts of the cost depend on the model parameters which may vary from simulation run to run. However, every time a process parameter is modified, the analyzer does not compute costs unless the user explicitly asks for the cost information.

This option was implemented using the *data-driven programming* paradigm using *demons*. Demons are procedures that are invoked as a side effect of some actions. In the latter case (that is, when asked by the user) a demon gets activated and it performs the cost calculation only if the parameters contributing to the cost had been updated. If no parameters were updated, it reports the previously calculated cost without repeating the calculation. The IPSE analyzer fetches the parameters contributing to the cost from the IPSE knowledge base containing the current model knowledge.

The cost information is presented to the user in a tabular form: capital costs, utility for each equipment, total utility for each type such as gas, water, and the net present worth of the process using a project life and discount rate supplied by the user.

CONCLUSIONS

The most crucial activity in the project is *Knowledge Engineering* that is, the task of acquisition, representation and archival of the chemical engineering knowledge of the best experts so that it can be applied to broad classes of problems. This is a very difficult and time consuming task because the methods used by human problem solvers are not necessarily implementable on a computer. Knowledge engineers have to deduce the heuristics underlying changes proposed by chemical engineeing experts while analyzing individual models. These heuristics and other process knowledge should be represented and taxonomized so that it could be exploited by the IPSE analyzer in solving a variety of problems.

In this phase we focussed on the parametric and economic analyses. The exergy and economic analysis task involves the development of an analysis engine which examines the flowsheet (which already meets the technical goals specified) from these viewpoints.

However, for this system to be truly useful to a chemical engineer, it should include the capabilities to make topological modifications to further optimize the design. This will be the focus of our research in the later phases.

Successful development of a comprehensive knowledge base and an Exergy and Economic Analysis Engine integrated with the IPSE architecture should result in a truly useful decision support tool for the chemical plant designer. This is the long-term goal of this research.

Advances in AI and Simulation
© 1989 By The Society for Computer
Simulation International
ISBN 0-911801-50-2

An expert systems approach to the analysis of discrete event simulations

Vasile Montan and Y.V. Reddy
West Virginia University
Morgantown, West Virginia

Abstract

Recent advances in the knowledge based approach to simulation have yielded techniques to assist decision makers in dealing with complex systems. There are four main tasks which a simulation expert performs which can can be emulated by an automated simulation system. The first task is designing an appropriate simulation model which would reveal the most about the portion of the system which is of interest. After the model is constructed it needs to be instrumented in such a way that any information which will be needed to properly evaluate the model is recorded while the model is running. Once the model is executed, the results are evaluated by comparing them with the goals for the system. Finally, there must be some way to detect relationships between parameters of the model and the outputs of the model. This paper outlines an approach which interprets a goal for an existing base model, instruments the model based on the goal, designs one or more scenarios of the model, executes each scenario using an existing discrete event simulation engine, and evaluates the results. Once a scenario is found which satisfies the user's goals, the changes from the base model are reported to the user.

1   Introduction

Simulation models afford an increased understanding of the real world system being studied. As a consequence, we are able to predict its behavior under hypothetical conditions. This knowledge may be used to determine how to configure a system so that it produces desirable outputs when given a set of inputs. This is generally the ultimate goal of an expert performing the simulation.

Simulation experts analyze the results of the simulation and determine the effect that changes in an input have on the outputs of the model. Determining the effect that changes in inputs have on the outputs is known as understanding behavior.[4] Using knowledge based programming techniques, it is possible to automate the functions of the simulation expert.

In traditional modeling environments a person who is interested in modeling a system would retain a simulation expert to create the model for him. The modeler would describe the system to the simulation expert as well as the behaviors he wishes to have analyzed. The simulation expert would then construct one or more models which would

have the desired behavior and execute them. The output of the simulation is a string of numbers or a set of graphs which the simulation expert must analyze before reporting back to the modeler [6]. Once the modeler understands the behavior of his system, he may propose a modification which may improve it. The simulation expert will change the model according to the proposed modification and verify that the modification does improve the model.

In the modeling environment described in this paper, the user must describe the system he wishes to model, as well as the results he desires, to the simulation expert program. The program will create one or more scenarios which show the necessary behavior of the system being modeled. Some behaviors may already be partially known to the user or could have been determined from the previous execution of scenarios of the system. Once the behavior is known, the program will attempt to change the model parameters in such a way as to make the results of the model execution fit the desired results. The model will then be executed and the actual results will be compared with the desired results to see if they do fit. If the actual results are not satisfactory, then a new scenario will be tried.

The process of changing the model and testing it is repeated until the desired results are met, or some resource limit has been exceeded. The changes are then translated back into the changes needed in the real world system being modeled. These changes expressed in the terminology of the real world system are known as a prescription, and constitute the final output of the simulation expert program. [7]

2   Overview of System

The simulation analyzer described in this paper is part of a larger system which:

- allows the user to specify his system as well as the results he desires in his own terminology[3];

- creates a simulation model from the description of the system;

- executes the model using an object–oriented, discrete event simulation engine;

- provides a visual representation of the model in action;

- evaluates the results of the simulation and analyzes the behavior of the system, in order to determine what to change in the model if the results are unsatisfactory.

The simulation analyzer is responsible for the last task.

The program is written in the LASER [1] programming environment. Each module communicates with the others through objects (frames) in the knowledge base.

The simulation analyzer has the following responsibilities:

1. **Goal–Directed Modeling** - The analyzer must create scenarios to be executed which show the user what he requests to see in the goal, and aids him in understanding the model [4][3].

2. **Instrumentation** - Once a scenario is created, the analyzer must request that those outputs, which are needed in analyzing the scenario, be measured while the scenario is being executed[4].

3. **Evaluation** - The analyzer must be able to evaluate the results of each scenario's execution and give each scenario a rating which indicates how well it has satisfied the user's goal[4].

4. **Understanding Behavior** - The analyzer must be able to learn what effect changing an input or parameter of a model has on the outputs of the model. It will use this knowledge as a guide in constructing other scenarios [4][5].

3   Goal

A user of the system will have one or more of the following reasons for performing a simulation:

- to see a graphical representation of the system in action;

- to learn the behavior of a system;

- to determine an appropriate setting for the parameters of the system.

All of this is expressed to the analyzer as the goal for the system.

The goal states what the user desires to learn about the system being model, the results he desires, the inputs to test the model with, and any restrictions he may place on modifying the system. All of the restrictions whether they specify the desired results, the inputs to use in testing the model, or limitations in modifying the system are known as constraints. There are three types of constraints: input constraints, parameter constraints and output constraints.

The restrictions which specify the desired results of the model execution are output constraints. These correspond to the desired outputs of the real world system. The less restrictive the output constraints are, the easier it is to find a solution.

The set of inputs for which the model must produce the desired outputs are called the input constraints. Since a system may have any number of inputs and each input can take on many different values, it is impractical to allow anything more than exact values for the inputs. Therefore the input constraints should be quite specific.

The restriction on the parameters of the model are called the parameter constraints. These limit how the model may be constructed.

For instance, a barbershop owner may want to minimize the time customers spend waiting for a barber. This is an output constraint and can be satisfied easily by recommending that the owner add one or more new barbers. The owner, however, may have wanted a different type of solution, and therefore limited the number of barbers to the number currently employed. The number of barbers is a parameter of the model, so this restriction is a parameter constraint.

3.1   Representation

In order for the simulation analyzer to understand and manipulate goals they must be stored in a clear and consistent manner. They must indicate how they relate to the model and to the real world system so that the simulation analyzer can interpret its results back into the user's terminology.

The user will express his constraints in terms that he is familiar with. The program must convert them into the goal object which will be used internally. A goal has the following representation in LASER:

```
{ goal
    display :
    gauge :
    behavior :
    constraints :
}
```

The "display" property indicates whether or not the model should be displayed as it is running. If the user is interested in seeing the graphical representation of his system in action, then he will place the name of the device on which he wants the model to be displayed here. The user will list all of the variables, that he would like displayed, in the property "gauge." A gauge for each of the variables in the list will be displayed on the screen and continuously updated while the simulation is running to show the current value of the variable.

Any variables that the user is interested in learning about will be placed in the "behavior" property. The analyzer will make models which specifically show the behavior of these variables and report its findings back to the user. For each input and parameter variable listed in this property, the analyzer will report how much that variable affects each of the outputs. For each of the output variables listed in this property, the analyzer will report how much that variable is affected by each of the parameters and inputs

The "constraint" property is used to restrict the analyzer in the types of scenarios it may try. The user will specify what range of outputs are acceptable, what range of inputs to experiment with, and what range of parameters are allowable.

A constraint may be any logical combination of conditions or it may be a single condition. A conditions is a relational expression between something which is measured during the simulation and a constant value or something else which is measured during the simulation. Constraints and conditions have the following representation in LASER:

```
{ constraint
    operator :
    operands :
}
{ condition
    LHS :
    rel_op :
    RHS :
}
```

4 Goal-Directed Modeling

The simulation analyzer must determine from the goal what it is the user desires to learn from the simulation. If the user has placed constraints on the inputs and parameters of the model but not on the outputs, the analyzer will construct a scenario which fits those constraints. If the user does place constraints on the outputs of the model, then the analyzer must first learn about the behavior of the model and then construct a scenario which has results that fit those constraints. In either case, the analyzer must report behaviors requested by the user or display the model or gauges while it is running.

Several scenarios of the same model must be constructed in an attempt to find one that satisfies the goal of the user. The user may want to know a good setting for the parameters of the model in order to achieve a desired output. He may want to know the effect that changing a particular parameter will have on all of the outputs. Or, he may just want to know the statistical relationship between a particular parameter and the outputs.

Since the entire model may not be needed, the simulation analyzer must isolate the portion of the model which

would tell the most about the part of the system which is of interest[2].

5 Instrumentation

After the model is constructed it needs to be instrumented in such a way that any information which will be needed to properly evaluate the model is recorded while the model is running. The analyzer must instrument:

- those variables which the user wants to observe during execution,

- those variables which are needed for evaluation,

- and those variables which are needed for analysis of behavior.

The user may observe a variable during the execution of a scenario by requesting a gauge be displayed on a particular device.

6 Scenario Evaluation

Once a scenario has been run, the analyzer must determine how well it has satisfied the goal specified by the user. It does this by rating the scenario according to how well each of the constraints in the goal was met. If a constraint was not met, then the reasons why it was not met are identified so that the analyzer may determine what changes should be made to the model to satisfy that constraint.

For each condition, the scenario evaluator rates how well the final results fit the condition. The condition may be either satisfied or not satisfied. If it is not satisfied, then the rating shows how close it is to being satisfied, and if it is satisfied, then the rating shows how well it is satisfied. Once a rating for each condition is calculated, the weighting of each of the conditions is applied to the evaluation of the corresponding condition to determine a rating for the entire constraint. The rating also depends on how the conditions are combined in the logical expression.

Since each condition is made up of variables, it is necessary for the evaluator to be able to handle values of different types. The different types of values are:

- constants - a value which is precisely expressed by the user.

- property value - a value which may be found in the property of an existing object.

- conditional - a value which may take on a different value depending on some other value.

- functional - an evaluation of a simple expression on other values.

The user may express conditions in terms of equations involving one or more of the variables in the system. Therefore the evaluator must be able to evaluate simple arithmetic operations, such as +, -, *, and / as well as more complex statistical functions, such as minimum, maximum, average, and standard deviation.

The user will specify a condition such as some value to be less than some other value, for example. Once the simulation has been run, the output variable will contain some value. The scenario analyzer must compare that value with the desired value for that variable and rate it according to the specified relation. The evaluator must be able to rate conditions which are made up of any of the relational operators: =, <, <=, <>, >=, >.

The user may wish to combine several conditions with logical operators such as AND, OR, and NOT. The scenario analyzer must be able to combine the rating from each of the individual conditions into a combined rating for the entire constraint. Individual condition evaluations must therefore be consistent so that they may be combined with the logical operators and produce consistent results.

7   Understanding Behavior

When the evaluator finds a condition which has not been met, it indicates how much each of the outputs in the condition need to be modified to cause that condition to be met. When all of the outputs which need to be changed are marked, the analyzer examines its knowledge base to determine what parameters should be changed to attain those changes in the outputs.

The manner in which a parameter affects each of the outputs is known as the behavior of that parameter. There are two ways in which the analyzer can learn the behavior of each of the parameters. Firstly, the user will supply the behavior he knows in advance, and secondly, the analyzer will learn new behaviors by running different scenarios and evaluating the results. Each time a scenario is run the analyzer should acquire more knowledge about the model[4].

The analyzer must store the behavior knowledge in such a way that it is:

- easy to access and use by the analyzer,

- easy for the analyzer to explain to the user in his terminology,

- easy for the user to add and update new information in his terminology,

- and easy for the analyzer to add and update new information.

When the user and the analyzer want to add to or update the behavior knowledge, they will want to do so from the perspective of the parameters. The user will be using his terminology and the analyzer will be using the terminology which it uses internally. The updates will be in the nature of statements such as, "increasing this parameter has this particular effect on that output provided these other conditions are true."

The conditions are necessary since increasing a parameter may increase the value of an output only up to a certain point. After that, futher increase will have a different effect on the output. The conditions may also specify values of other variables. For instance, increasing a parameter may have an effect on an output only if some other parameter has a low value.

When the analyzer uses the behavior knowledge, it will be from the perspective of the outputs. It will want to know to what degree each of the parameters affect a certain output. It will have a particular output which needs to be increased, and will search its knowledge base to find which parameter changes will increase the output. Once it knows all of the parameters which have the desired effect, it will use some selection criteria to pick the best one.

The explanation to the user may be from either perspective. He may want to know the effects of changing a parameter, or he may want to know what parameters affect a particular output. The explanation needs to be more than a display of the behavior objects which involve the specified outputs and parameters. The analyzer must first convert the behavior into the user's terminology.

The effect that a single input or parameter has on a particular output can be represented by a single function provided all other inputs and parameters remain constant. This function can be made more general by specifying under what conditions the function holds. These conditions are expressed in terms of the values of the other inputs and parameters which have an effect on whether or not this function is valid.

Since arbitrary functions are too difficult to determine and store, some simplification is necessary. The effect of a single parameter on a particular output is represented by a series of linear ranges. More conditions are added to specify the values of the parameter for which the range applies. Behavior is represented with the following LASER object:

```
{ behavior
    condition :
    affecting_variable
       (affecting_behavior) *
    affected_variable
       (affected_behavior) *
    amount_effect :
}
```

The relations "affecting_variable" and "affected_variable" allow the behavior object to be accessed from either the perspective of the parameter or of the output.

8 Prescription

If the user specifies constraints on the outputs of the model, then he is looking for a setting of the parameters which makes the model outputs fit those constraints. Once the analyzer has determined enough of the behavior of the model to determine what the appropriate settings for the parameters are, it will create a scenario with those parameters. This scenario will then be executed to prove that it does meet the constraints specified by the user.

The settings for the parameters are then reported back to the user as a prescription. The parameter settings must be described in the user's terminology, so he will know what to change in the real world system. If the model accurately depicts the real world system and that system is changed according to the prescription, then it will indeed produce the desired results.

References

[1] *LASER/KR Knowledge Representation.* Bell Atlantic Knawledge Systems Inc., 145 Fayette St., Morgantown, WV 26505, 1.08 edition, 1988.

[2] Malcolm McRoberts, Mark Fox, and Nizwer Husain. Generating model abstraction scenarios in KBS. In Graham Birtwistle, editor, *Artificial Intelligence, Graphics, and Simulation*, pages 29–33, The Society for Computer Simulation, 1985.

[3] Karen J. Murray and Sallie V. Sheppard. Automatic model synthesis: using automatic programming and expert systems techniques toward simulation modeling. In A. Thesen, H. Grant, and W. David Kelton, editors, *Proceedings of the 1987 Winter Simulation Conference*, pages 534–543, The Society for Computer Simulation, 1987.

[4] Y. V. Reddy, Mark S. Fox, and Nizwer Husain. Automating the analysis of simulations in KBS. In Graham Birtwistle, editor, *Artificial Intelligence, Graphics, and Simulation*, pages 34–40, The Society for Computer Simulation, 1985.

[5] Neena Sathi, Mark Fox, V. Baskaran, and Jack Bouer. *An Artificial Intelligence Approach to the Simulation Life Cycle.* Technical Report, Carnegie Group, Inc., 1986.

[6] Lee Schruben. Using simulation to solve problems: a tutorial on the analysis of simulation output. *Proceedings of the 1987 Winter Simulation Conference*, 40–41, 1987.

[7] Robert E. Shannon, Richard Mayer, and Heimo H. Adelsberger. Expert systems and simulation. *SIMULATION*, 44(6):275–284, June 1985.

Advances in AI and Simulation
© 1989 By The Society for Computer
Simulation International
ISBN 0-911801-50-2

Automated air traffic control sequencing
using expert systems*

Arthur Gerstenfeld, Ph.D.
Department of Management
Worcester Polytechnic Institute
Worcester, MA 01609

ABSTRACT

Because of the massive, often unintelligible publicity, expert systems is almost completely misunderstood (Shank 1987). In some cases it is difficult to determine where software engineering leaves off and where AI or expert systems begins. The primary goal of AI is to build an intelligent machine. An air traffic controller can learn the rules of air traffic in six months (Armstrong 1987). However, for the next four and a half years he is learning technique. Setting up and operating a radar console or using a microphone are easy functions. Deciding which of ten fast moving aircraft should be first for an instrument landing system (ILS) approach can be extremely difficult. Let me list the features I consider to be critical for the air traffic control (ATC) training and airspace design. This paper lists the features that combine artificial intelligence and simulation in order to improve air traffic control training and airspace design.

INTRODUCTION

The features which I consider to be critical for linking an expert system and simulation for air traffic control training are as follows:

1. Communication

An intelligent entity can be communicated with. We cannot talk to rocks or tall trees. We can talk to an intelligent simulator either through a keyboard or by voice. An intelligent simulator can respond by voice (both pilot and instructor voice). Communication is possible (Gerstenfeld, 1988). Figure 1 shows a system alerting a student that a particular aircraft has a noise abatement violation. Communication must be between user and machine and machine to machine. Using the UNIX operating system the communication between machines is extremely fast and reliable.

2. Internal Knowledge

We expect intelligent entities to have some knowledge about themselves. We can embed system knowledge, for example, about noise abatement rules at a particular location and knowledge about surface wind direction and velocity and runway conditions. This is internal knowledge. This can be added to each day as conditions and information changes.

*Much of this work has been supported by the FAA. Particular recognition goes to George Booth, ADS 100 - Advanced Concepts Division, AI Applications to Air Traffic Control.

3. World Knowledge

Intelligence involves being aware of the outside world and being able to find and initialize that information. A knowledge base must be capable of always being added to. For example, altitude restrictions on older 737's should be included. Climb and descent rates varying with temperature and pressure must be included. A procedure cannot be initiated such as an altitude restriction that an aircraft cannot conform to based on performance characteristics at a particular pressure temperature gradient. For example, an aircraft cannot be expected to cross an intersection at or above 10,000 feet if the aircraft cannot reach that altitude in a given distance on a hot summer day. The same aircraft, on the other hand, would not have difficulty reaching 10,000 within the same given distance on a colder day. In this way, the world knowledge has the aircraft respond exactly as it would during active flight. We can embed characteristics of each aircraft so that turn rates, climb rates, descent rates, etc. are always able to be found and utilized. In current simulators without a knowledge base a student could tell a 747 to reduce speed to 100 knots and the system would not have the intelligence to tell the student that cannot be done. An intelligent simulator would explain that a 747 would stall at that slow speed and the pilot's voice would explain that he cannot comply with that clearance.

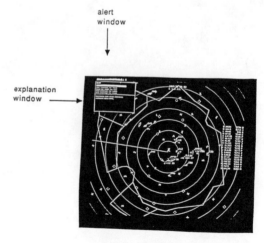

alert window

explanation window

ATCoach alerts student that NYA55 must cross shoreline westbound at altitude of 6000 feet or above noise abatement for Boston.

Figure 1

4. Intentionality

Goal-driven behavior means knowing when one wants something and having a plan to get what one wants. A tree has no plan or goal. An intelligent system has plans, goals, and subgoals. For example, it is not good enough to simply maintain separation, but rather one goal is to utilize good technique. Excessive separation can be costly in terms of fuel and delaying in terms of traffic. A goal in an intelligent system is to go beyond rules and to include the "art" of air traffic control. For example, one goal is not only separation but of tight control so that maximum landings can be achieved. Similarly, a goal of minimum speed changes would mean that altitude or vector changes could be used to increase flight safety and comfort.

5. Explanation Capability

An intelligent system can explain its reasoning. For example, if there is a wake turbulence violation where a small aircraft is directly behind a heavy aircraft at the same altitude and the separation is less than five miles, this rule is explained to the trainee. In this example, the trainee is within rule on separation violation but not within rule on wake turbulence violation and this is explained.

6. Feedback

An intelligent system provides feedback (Brown 1986). The feedback should be organized so that patterns are determined. For example, a trainees error occurring infrequently may be seen as careless errors. However, a repeated error may be seen as basic conceptual misunderstanding. The system should then recommend remedial scenarios. This material should be organized and feedback provided to the student or instructor.

7. Learning

This is perhaps one of the most controversial subjects in AI. One measure of intelligence is the ability to learn. Between the day this paper is written and the day this paper is presented, a learning system will become that much smarter. People are adding knowledge to our system at Logan in Boston, at Montreal, and at Toronto at the very moment that this is being written. If a Standard Instrument Departure (SID) or a Standard Arrival Route (STAR) were to change, this is easily entered into the system. New SIDS and STARS are currently being tested on our system at Logan Airport in Boston.

8. Knowledge Representation

An intelligent system has ways to organize and represent knowledge. Our architecture uses two knowledge bases as shown in Figure 2.

General Knowledge Base	Site Specific
• Air Traffic Control Handbook Rules • Aircraft Performance Characteristics • General Sequencing Techniques	• Letters of Agreement (LOA's) • Standard Operating Procedures (SOP's) • Navigational Aids (NAVAIDS) • Minimum Safe Altitude Warnings (MSAW) Digital Terrain Map • Current Notices to Airmen (NOTAMS)

Site Specific and General Knowledge Bases

Figure 2

DISCUSSION

It is all well and good to know a great deal, but the more you know, the harder it may be to find what you know. Along these same lines, the most knowledgeable person on earth should also be the slowest to say anything. Obviously, people must have a way of organizing their knowledge so they can find what they need when they need it. For any massive system indexing is a central and possibly the central problem. For example, in order to maintain the speed of accessing the system might first search for altitude separation. If aircraft are separated by 1000 feet or more vertically, then it is not necessary to search whether or not the aircraft are separated horizontally. This can be done on a system of Apollos capable of 4 million instructions per second (4MIPS). We expect in the early 1990's to be porting to workstations with 20-25 MIPS.

I shall give two examples of an internal knowledge system. The first example concerns glide slope intercept. As shown in Figure 3 the first C function is to find out if the intercept altitude will be more than 300 feet above the glide slope and if so reject the intercept. The first four lines of code use the tangent C function to determine the glide slope altitude at the point of intercept. We are using the trigonometric function: tan = opp/adj to find the opposite side, which is the altitude in nautical miles converted to feet. Line 5 determines the aircraft altitude in feet at the point of intercept. Line 7 checks if the intercept altitude is greater than the glideslope altitude plus 300 feet. If this is true the message "(Aircarft ID) intercept rejected" will appear in the Alert window and the message "intercept altitude will be (number of feet), that is (number of feet), above glideslope" will appear in the explanation window. The next to

last line of the C function causes the system to
print the messages and sets error number 304 and the
aircraft target ID to be saved for later processing
by the student model.

```
/* Is altitude <= glideslope + 300 feet at the intercept point */

glideslope_altitude =
(decimal)tan(runways[rway].glideslope_angle*M_PI
                        /(decimal)180*stdist2d(runways[rway].x_pos,
                        runways[rway].y_pos,
                        x_intercept,y_intercept))*(decimal)FEET_PER_NM;
intercept_altitude = STtacalt(ac,intercept_time);
if (intercept_altitude >(glideslope_altitude+(decimal)300))
  {
    sprintf(hintstr,"%s intercept rejected.",ac_state[ac].ac_id);
    sprintf(whystr,"intercept altitude will be %04d, that is %04d feet
                    above glideslope.",(int)intercept_altitude,
                    (int)intercept_altitude-glideslope_altitude));
    EX_makehint(hintstr,whystr,304,ac,0);
  return REJECT;
  }


/*  Check for possible wake turbulance application if one is heavy. */
if ((STbehind(other_ac, heavy_ac, behind_tolerance)==YES) &&
        (radar_separation < (decimal)5))
  {
    sprintf(hintstr, "%s and %s wake turbulance violation",
            ac_state[ac],ac_id, ac_state[ac2].ac_id);

    sprintf(whystr, "A small or large operating directly behind heavy
    strcat(whystr," requires 5 miles separation because of wake turb
    EX_makehint(hintstr, whystr, 105, ac1, ac2);
    return YES;

  }
```

Heuristics for Glide Slope and Wake Turbulanc

Figure 3

The second C function checks for a wake
turbulence violation if one aircraft is a heavy and a
small aircraft is behind the heavy at the same
altitude. The "if" statement calls on the C function
"STbehind" passing as arguments the other aircraft,
the heavy aircraft, and the tolerance angle (5
degrees) behind the other aircraft. If the other
aircraft (small or large) is within the tolerance
angle and the radar separation is less than 5 miles,
the Alert window displays the message "(heavy
aircraft ID) and (other aircraft ID) wake turbulence
violation." The explanation window message is
evident. Then the system is called upon to print the
messages and error number 105 is saved together with
the heavy and other aircraft target ID's for use in
the student model.

For an ATC simulator to be really helpful for
both training and plans and procedures it has to be
able to be all of the above. An yet it must do more.
Digitized voice now provides the ability to
accurately reproduce human voices, i.e. the pilot.

Of even more importance is the ability to overlay
several voices simultaneously which is the case of
many air traffic control situations (Singer, 1988).

As we approach the year 2000 and go beyond we
can expect that air traffic will be six times as
dense. Estimates now speak of doubling traffic in
the next ten years. We must utilize ultra high speed
workstation hardware, software which contains highly
accurate simulation and embedded expert systems and
the accumulated knowledge to build intelligent
simulators in order to have safer skies for all.
Workstations are now capable of multiple processing
at speeds unattainable a few years ago. We are
utilizing these capabilities to start to approach the
intelligence needed in order to merge AI and advanced
simulation.

CONCLUSIONS

AI is going through an interesting and important
shift. At the recent AAAI 1988 conference this
became quite clear (AI EXPERT, 1988).. There is a
nascent but important trend toward domain specific
systems. The system described in this paper is a
good example.

I would like to point out that although this
paper has focussed mainly on AI and Simulation for
ATC training, an equally important application is for
airspace management and the system's use for planning
aircraft approaches, departures and airspace
segments.

I see our system as an Expert Support
Environment (ESE) rather than a traditional expert
system. Our system is to develop and amplify the
skills of human experts instead of trying to replace
them. What is my vision for the future? I envision
an ESE that can operate on any of three levels,
depending on the expertise of the user.

1. If the user is a neophyte, the ESE operates as a
   mentor. It focusses mainly on teaching.

2. With more experienced users, the ESE operates
   as a coach. Here the initiative passes to the
   user, with the ESE available to offer whatever
   level of assistance the user requests. The coach
   has the ability to intervene if the user
   unwittingly gets in over his or her head.

3. On the highest level, the ESE can operate an an
   assistant. When this level requires decision
   making, the assistant will operate as a typical
   expert system (AI Expert, 1988).

Our system's ability to explain its conclusions
are notably better than a typical expert system.
Expert systems give the explanation an expert would
use to clarify a decision for another expert. This
explanation generally makes limited sense to a
nonexpert. The system described in this paper is
able to produce explanations appropriate to users
with different experience levels.

The use of AI and simulation provides an
excellent tool for training air traffic controllers
now. In the future I believe this approach will
become the standard. My sincere thanks go to Tom
Moody, friend and colleague, and the controllers at
Logan who have contributed so much to this project.

It is the combination of four items that I

believe has been contributing to the success of this
project:

1. Enhanced graphics
2. Networking capabilities
3. Expert System
4. Air Traffic Control Knowledge

The expert system is an important component but it is
simply a part of the overall system.

REFERENCES

AI Expert, see "Editorial Intelligence AAAI 1988,"
November 1988

AI Expert, November 1988 issue, pages 79-80.

Armstrong, Herbert B., "ATC Training: Teaching of
Screening?" Journal of ATC, July-September, 1987.

Brown, John Seely and RR Burton in Advanced in
Man-Machine Systems Research, JAI Press, Greenwich,
CT 1986.

Gerstenfeld, A., "Speech Recognition Integrated with
ATC Simulation", ICAO, June 1988.

Shank, Roger, Yale University, Head Artificial
Intelligence Project, "What is AI, Anyway?", AI
Magazine, Winter 1987.

Singer, Dr. S. Fred, "R&D Symposium Stresses Need for
Human Factors Research," Journal of ATC,
July-September 1988. (As chief scientist to the
Department of Transportation he said he was apalled
at the state of ATC communications).

Advances in AI and Simulation
© 1989 By The Society for Computer
Simulation International
ISBN 0-911801-50-2

ESMS: An application of distributed cooperating expert systems

Kiet D. Hoang
Research Associate

UFA, Inc.
335 Boylston Street
Newton, MA. 02159

Abstract

This paper describes a software framework for real-time distributed artificial intelligence programming. This framework, called ESMS for Expert System Management System*, supports the implementation of AI systems on multiple interconnected processors that may be geographically distributed. This research project combines both real-time simulation and distributed expert systems. The simulation is based on a suite of avionic systems, and the expert systems are implemented using the ESMS to integrate sensory information from the electronic avionics to make real-time decisions to aid pilots.

Introduction

ESMS stands for Expert System Management System. This work was initiated as an attempt to incorporate expert system technology in an advanced fighter cockpit to reduce pilot workloads and increase mission effectiveness. The increasing complexity of modern avionics systems and mission requirements have imposed tremendous demands on the human pilot, to make decisions quickly and appropriately. One of the problems is the inability of the pilot to assimilate all the information available to him for effective and efficient decision making.

Our application of ESMS is a set of distributed cooperating expert systems connected to an aircraft simulation, involving real-time threat avoidance, route planning and information flow management. These systems consist of three domain-specific expert systems and a manager. Inferences or conclusions reached within a system can be sent to any of the other

---

* This paper describes a ten month research project which focuses on distributed processing and AI applied in the cockpit of an aircraft. This project is funded by the Avionics Lab at Wright-Patterson Air Force Base, Dayton, Ohio. The clearance number is ASD-88-1803.

three over a network. The responsibilities of the three domain-specific expert systems are to make decisions in its own area of expertise, with or without the help from other experts, while the Manager assimilates information and partial solutions from these systems and makes globally sensible decisions, and interfaces with the pilot. The whole system can be visualized in Figure 1.

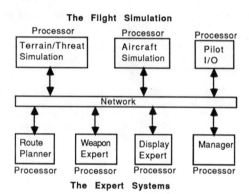

The Distributed Environment of ESMS
Figure 1

Some of the issues that we must address in developing such a distributed cooperating expert system include:

Processor Independence -
In a distributed environment, the execution of an expert system should be independent of the processor it resides on. In fact, for our prototype expert systems, they were first developed on a single Lisp machine, then later ported over to four seperate machines without any modification of the codes. In ESMS, one or more expert systems can be executed in one or more

processors, and the identity of the processor that the expert resides on is unknown until run time.

Control of Cooperating Expert Systems -
Since each expert system is running concurrently on its own processor, the system must be able to handle asynchronous events. In ESMS, the communication between different expert systems is through messages. Since messages can be sent and received asynchronously, an expert will never wait for a reply of a request that it had sent.

Focus of Problem Solving -
Since events in the real world occur asynchronously, a running expert system must be able to focus on the most critical task/event. In our system, the execution of an expert is interruptable based on the states of the world or the criticality of an occuring event. The level/depth of interrupts depends on a machine's available memory.

Fault Tolerance -
Any of the distributed expert systems may fail in a number of ways, such as processor malfunction or network disconnection. Therefore, it is very important that the system possesses the abilities to dynamically reconfigure and to transfer the necessary information among various sub-systems. Since the execution of an expert system in ESMS is independent of the processor it resides on, the level of fault tolerance is very high.

Problem Solving in Real Time -
Due to the nature of our application, it is critical that an expert can communicate with its neighbors in real-time. From our preliminary test program, it had shown that this objective is obtainable. As for the problem-solving process of an expert system, the knowledge base is organized hierarchically, so that a solution can always be found within the time constraint but with different levels of granularity.

Problem Solving in Limited Resource -
The expert systems must be able to make decisions within its own available resources, such as computer time, memory and communication network load. In other words, each system must be able to intelligently allocate tasks in respect to resources. Much work are still needed to be done in this area.

The ESMS Research

Each expert in ESMS is self contained. Its knowledge base consists of domain-specific knowledge to handle both internal and external events. Since each expert is responsible for its own area of expertise, there is no master or slave relationship between any of the four systems, including the Manager. Morever, the whole system is very loosely coupled, so that the addition and deletion of any expert and/or processor will not effect the integrity of the rest of the system.

Instead of production rules of most conventional expert systems, the knowledge base of an expert in ESMS consists of Event-Handlers and Daemons. As the name implies, an event-handler is event-driven, it is a chunk of procedural knowledge that gets invoked whenever an internal or external event occurs. Each handler must be unique and specific for a particular event. It will be triggered whenever the expert is notified of an event by the mean of message. The structure of a handler includes the name of the handler which is global within the expert, the event that it can response to, an area that corresponds to the content of the incoming message, a local data area that is internal to this handler, and a block of procedural knowledge.

Similar to an event-handler, a daemon is also a chunk of procedural knowledge. However, instead of waiting to be triggered by an event, the daemons are data-driven and they are executed continuously one after another. Its primary objective is to monitor the behavior of the system. For example, it can be used to monitor an expert's problem-solving process and the states of the problem space, it can also be used to monitor the health of the processor that the expert resides on, or to monitor some external behaviors/events (such as the states of the aircraft subsystems, etc.) Each daemon has a specific pattern that it matches. Once matched, the body of the daemon will be executed. Typically, it sends out messages to alert or notify others of an impending problems or states.

Each expert in ESMS can communicate with one another via messages. An expert may volunteer to inform others of a newly found information/evidence, if it feels that this information may be valuable to others. Alternatively, an expert can also request other to perform some inferences or to evaluate some pieces of data. In the first case, the expert may not expect a reply from the recipient, while in the later case, it may.

However, An expert would never wait a reply because in a distributed environment, a reply may never come.

As shown in Figure 2, each expert system in ESMS resides on its own processor and communicates with one another over the network. In each system, there is a Control Structure that takes care of executing the knowledge base of the expert (i.e. event-handlers and daemons), a Communication Manager which accepts, maintains and sends messages. In addition, there is a global memory that is shared by all the event-handlers and daemons within the system. This global memory can be used to exchange information and to maintain a global view of the responsible domain space.

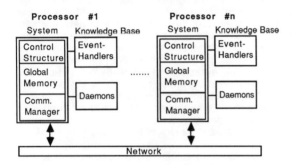

A Framework of Our Distributed ESMS
Figure 2

Messages are sent to an expert by name, so that the sending expert does not need to know the location (i.e. network address) of the recipient in a distributed system. In our system, one or more experts may co-exist on the same processor. This feature of having more than one expert system running on the same processor is particularly important for the fault-tolerance aspect of our application, for example, when a processor is malfunctioned due to battle damage, the Control Structure will reconfigure and allocate the expert on that processor onto another less "busy" processor.

There is a priority and certainty factor associated with each message (an event), so when an expert is handling an event of a particular priority, only the event of higher priority may interrupt it. If the expert is interrupted due to a higher-priority event, it will perform the necessary tasks to handle the interrupting event than resume the previously processed task. The side-effects or results of the interrupting event may preempt or alter the behavior of the resumed event/task.

A message can be sent either from other experts or from within the expert itself. In the latter case, it is seen as setting a subgoal. The content of the messages can be defined arbitrarily depending on the application, as long as there is an understanding between the sender and receiver. Typically, a message must have the name of the sender, the name of the recipient, the message type, a time stamp, a "response-to" id number, a priority value, a certainty factor and application-specific information. Whenever a message is received, its priority is immediately compared with the current priority of the system, if it is higher, the currently running system will be interrupted to handle the newly arrived event. However, if the priority is lower, it will be put on a message queue according to its priority level. Within each prioritized queue, the newer message will be appended to the end of the queue, so that older message will be processed first. There are procedures that the user can provide to manipulate the queues, if the default "First-In First-Out" strategy is inadequate.

The concurrency of ESMS is accomplished by having each expert running on its own processor. Morever, event-handlers and daemons within each system are executed on two seperate processes, so that it can solve problems and monitor its progress simultaneously. In a sense, we have achieved both inter-processor and intra-processor concurrency. Since the whole system is runing asynchronously, each section of code in the system must be self-contained. For example, when a Request-Reply type action is sent, the request is written inside of a daemon or event-handler, and the accept-reply is written in another. In this way there is no need for a piece of code to wait for a reply message, which may never come in a distributed system. The flow of control and interactions between handlers and daemons from one or more expert systems is shown in Figure 3.

Discussion

The ESMS paradigm had been shown to run successfully on four, but not limited to four, independently running Lisp machines. In addition to the communication between the four processors, an expert on any of these systems may also request "raw" data from the flight simulator (as shown in Figure 1). Based on our preliminary analysis, the system seems to handle the real-time communication at least adequately.

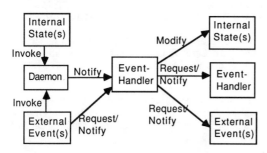

Flow of Control in ESMS
Figure 3

The ESMS system is written in Symbolics CommonLisp. It is still undergoing some evolution. In order to develop a distributed system using this paradigm, one must define each expert using the following system-provided definitions. Some of definitions are:

(Defexpert
  expert name)

(Definit
  procedural code to be executed to initialize the
  system when the expert system is invoked for
  the first time)

(Defevent-handler
  event-handler name.
  event name.
  binding to the content of the message.
  local data area.
  procedural knowledge to handle the event
  indicated by the message)

(Defdaemon
  patterns to be matched.
  procedural knowledge to be executed when the
  above patterns match)

(Defstrategy
  strategy name.
  code to be executed to influence the behavior of
  the underlying inference or search mechanism)

As shown in Figure 1, the flight simulator consists of a terrain/threat simulation, an aircraft simulation, and a graphics and text pilot input/output. Currently, we are in the process of building up the knowledge bases of the four experts of our avionics pilot aiding system. So far, we feel that the ESMS paradigm is very appropriate for this domain. However, as the system evolves and grows in sophistication, we will be certain to provide more features for the system, as well as for the ease of developing and debugging expert systems.

Some of the enhancements that we need in the immediate future will include:

(1) Develop heuristics to allow the system to perform problem-solving intelligently under limited resources. For example, if the system has only five seconds to respond, but heuristics dictates that this particular problem requires six seconds, it must decide whether to pursue this problem and risk failure, or to pursue it with higher level of abstraction, or to solve an entirely different problem instead.

(2) Enrich the knowledge representation of the system.

(3) Develop context-sensitive daemons. Currently, all daemons are considered by the system at any one time. However, depending on the situation or context, the consideration of some daemons may not be relevant.

(4) Provide a global shared memory across all machines, so that the expert systems can easily exchange certain type of information.

(5) Provide more tracing and recording facility for the ease of system debugging.

Conclusion

In summary, the ESMS approach seems to meet the essential criteria that are important for the class of problem that we are addressing, i.e. distributed problem-solving and intelligent avionics pilot aid. Much work remains to be done in refining this paradigm from the lessons we have learned here. Also, the application of this approach to other distributed domains must also be addressed.

Bibliography

[1] L. Erman, F. Hayes-Roth, V.R. Lesser, and R. D. Reddy, "The HEARSAY-II speech understanding system: Integrating knowledge to resolve uncertainty," ACM Computing Surveys, Vol. 12, pp. 213-253, 1980.

[2] P. E. Green, "AF: A Framework for Real-Time Distributed Cooperative Problem-Solving," *Distributed Artificial Intelligence*, pp. 153-175, Morgan Kaufmann, California, 1987.

[3] L. Gasser, C. Braganza and N. Herman, "MACE: A Flexible Testbed for Distributed AI Research," *Distributed Artificial Intelligence*, pp. 119-152, Morgan Kaufmann, California, 1987.

[4] V. R. Lesser, D. D. Corkill, "The Distributed Vehicle Monitoring Testbed: A tool for investigating distributed problem solving networks," AI Magazine, vol 4, no. 3, pp. 15-33, Fall 1983.

[5] E. Durfee and V. R. Lesser, "Incremental Planning to Control a Blackboard-Based Problem-Solver," Proceedings of the Fifth National Conference on Artificial Intelligence, pp. 58-64, August 1986.

[6] E. Durfee, V. R. Lesser, and D. D. Corkill, "Cooperation Through Communication in a Distributed Problem Solving Network," *Distributed Artificial Intelligence*, pp. 29-58, Morgan Kaufmann, California, 1987.

[7] P.E. Green, "Resource Control in a Real Time Target Tracking Process," Proceedings of Fifteenth Asilomar Conference on Circuits, Systems, and Computers, pp. 424-428. Pacific Grove, CA, November 1981.

[8] D. Weinreb and D. Moon, "Flavors: Message Passing in the Lisp Machine," A.I. Memo No. 602, MIT AI Laboratory, Cambridge, MA, November 1980.

[9] B. G. Buchanan and E. H. Shortliffe, *Rule-Based Expert Systems*, Addison Wesley, Reading, MA, 1984.

[10] J. A. Schira, Jr., "Fighter Pilots Aid by Expert Systems," Conference on Intelligent Systems and Machine, pp. 364-369, 1984.

[11] C. C. Hsu, S. M. Wu and J. J. Wu, "A Distributed Approach for Inferring Production System," Proceedings of the Tenth International Joint Conference on Artificial Intelligence, pp. 62- 67, 1987.

[12] S. Berning, D. P. Glasson and J. A. Guffey, "Adaptive Tactical Navigation Concepts," IEEE National Aerospace Electronics, Vol 4, pp. 1235-1242, 1986.

[13] L. D. Pohlmann, and J. R. Payne, "Pilot's Associate Demonstration One: A Look Back and Ahead," IEEE National Aerospace Electronics, Vol 4, pp. 1176-1183, 1986.

[14] J. B. Shelnutt, R. O. Stenerson, P. C. Nelson, and P. S. Marks, "Pilot's Associate Demonstration One: A Look Inside," IEEE National Aerospace Electronics, Vol 4, pp. 1184-1189, 1986.

[15] R. Davis, "Report on the Workshop on Distributed AI," SIGART Newsletter, no. 73, pp. 42-52, October 1980.

[16] R. Davis and R. D. Smith, "Negotiation as a Metaphor for Distributed Problem Solving," Artificial Intelligence, vol 20, no. 1, pp. 63-109, January 1983.

[17] D. McArthur, R. Steeb, and S. Cammarata, "A Framework for Distributed Problem-Solving," Proceedings of the National Conference on Artificial Intelligence, pp. 181-184, Pittsburg, PA, 1982.

[18] T.L. Skillman, Jr., "Distributed Cooperating Processes in a Mobile Robot Control System," Workshop on Blackboard Systems for Robot Perception and Control, June 1986.

[19] R. R. Tenney and N. R. Sandell, "Strategies for Distributed Decisionmaking," IEEE Transactions on Systems, Man, and Cybernetics, vol. SMC-11, no. 8, pp. 527-538, August 1981.

[20] R. G. Smith, "Report on the 1984 Distributed Artificial Intelligence Workshop," The AI Magazine, pp. 234-243, Fall 1985.

Advances in AI and Simulation
© 1989 By The Society for Computer
Simulation International
ISBN 0-911801-50-2

An expert system advisor to aid goal definition for manufacturing system simulation

Thomas K. Joseph
Consultant,

3540 Green Brier Blvd. 448B,
Ann Arbor, MI 48105

ABSTRACT

This paper describes a rule based expert system advisor, which aims to reduce the up-front time spent prior to conducting a simulation study. This upfront study also called pre-simulation study, if planned and conducted properly can greatly reduce delays. Time spend during this phase of the study, is typically devoted to gaining a good understanding of the issues (such as, objectives, constraints, interactions, etc.) considering various factors involved in a manufacturing system. Also, in most cases, the individual responsible for the actual simulation model development has to extract information from members in the team familiar with various design aspects of the system. The expert system proposed with knowledge base from various domains, demonstrates the use of such a tool to help in the simulation study. The structure of the knowledge base to follow in such a system is presented. A prototype implemented in the TI PC-PLUS expert system programming environment with suggestions for future work is described.

INTRODUCTION

Simulation technique is a widely accepted tool for the analysis of manufacturing systems. With the availability of very sophisticated software and supporting hardware, its application has begun to gain acceptance in areas other than the traditional area of design and planning. A simulation study can therefore require knowledge and background in a wide range of fields which goes beyond an individual's expertise, specially for advanced manufacturing systems. This results in unavoidable and seemingly unnecessary delays, as interactions among various people with different backgrounds becomes mandatory for conducting a successful study.

Another major delay associated with conducting a successful study is the upfront time spent in defining the objectives of the study. Contributing to this is the fact that, in many cases the objectives or the goals of the study are never clearly defined. Many times the very exercise of conducting the study and the process of building the model itself can help in this direction. However, this again can be a time consuming process as several iterations may be required prior to defining the final model. Greater benefits can be gained from a simulation study if some effort is devoted to conducting an up front pre-simulation study. Such a study should be directed at narrowing the scope and defining the specific objectives of the study as best as possible, based on the information available at that time.

This paper describes an effort to reduce time in simulation development by using an expert system advisor to help in defining the goals and objectives of the study. A prototype system was developed to demonstrate the concept for using such a system as part of the pre-simulation study. The expert system was developed to accommodate the capability of expanding the knowledge base easily in an evolutionary manner. The possibilities of future studies and development are also discussed.

BACKGROUND

Conducting a Simulation Study

While the benefits to be gained from a simulation are well accepted, one major drawback in its use is that it can be a time consuming process, especially if it is not planned properly. The very flexible nature of simulation technique itself contributes to the overall time requirements. With the availability of sophisticated simulation software, it is possible to incorporate almost any level of detail that might seem necessary. In fact, this is an important advantage of the simulation technique. As the study progresses, problems or issues which may not have been obvious at the time of initiation of the study, can be identified. A deviation from the original objectives mid-way through the study thus may result and could be expected. It is not uncommon for a simulation initiated as a supportive study for evaluation of a design to be broadened in scope to include other issues or incorporate finer detail. These benefits may be characterised as one of the potential gains derived from the exercise of using simulation (Goodhead and Mahoney, 1986).

However, some caution must be exercised in this approach of allowing the study to run its course in this manner. Unnecessary delay can result if the level of detail in the model required to answer certain issues or problems, is increased as they are identified. These delays can be minimized, if not avoided, by some upfront study prior to commencing the actual simulation model development. Based on whatever information is available, the pre-simulation study should be directed at specifying and identifying all possible issues that could potentially arise while analyzing the manufacturing system. There are many factors that can influence the simulation study and it would be to one's advantage to address them prior to commencing the actual simulation study. Some of these factors are listed below.

- The type of manufacturing system environment, (Job-shop, Transfer line or flexible machining system, Assembly system, etc.).

- The life cycle of the manufacturing system under consideration, (Concept, strategic, design, implementation, operational, etc.).

- The material handling system used (conveyor, automated guided vehicles, stacker cranes, etc.).

- General operating philosophies and requirements, (JIT, Low Work-in-process, zero-scrap rate etc.)

- Software design and requirements for implementation of the integrated system (scheduler, control system, MRP etc.)

- The features and capabilities specific to simulation language software planned to be used. (representation of material handling system, statistical analysis, etc.)

- The availability of aggregate (rough cut) system requirements. The minimum machine, manpower and other resource demands required of the system, or equivalent to the *back of the envelope* calculations.

- Experience and background of the people involved in the team responsible for conducting the analysis, including that of the simulation model developer, and the accessiblity of each of them to interact and work as a team.

The above list may not be completely exhaustive but represents most of the factors to be considered. All these must be considered while planning the study, and where applicable, must be addressed. The formal structure for capturing and representing the information in a knowledge base for the expert system and details of the implementation of this structure in a prototype system are presented later.

AI in Manufacturing System Simulation

Considerable interest has been generated in the past few years in the use of artificial intelligence and simulation (Shanon et al, 1985), particularly to manufacturing systems. Most of the applications of AI techniques in simulation are in the use of expert systems in the actual model formulation and development (Doukidis and Paul, 1985, Joseph et al, 1986) or providing the environment for the model representation (Ben-Arieh 1986, Fox et. al, 1986). (Wichmann, 1986), describes an intelligent simulation environment to aid the design and operation of FMSes with the possibility to extend it for objective definition phase as well, within the same environment. The expert system described in this paper is an advisory system to assist in the definition of the objectives of the simulation *study* outside the simulation environment and not restricted to FMS type systems only.

Knowledge Base Structure

The overall structure and the guideline used for representing the knowledge base to follow for the expert system is described. The knowledge base was structured so that the information required for the expert system is extracted from the user in a question-answer session. Decisions or conclusion made during the consultation being conveyed to the user as they occur.

The knowledge base was divided into three main steps or stages, These were:

1. Manufacturing System Identification: This step is intended to classify the manufacturing system under consideration which best fit the users application. The rationale for this is that the type of manufacturing system to a large extent provided various characteristics and problems unique to that specific environment required for the next step. For example, in a Transfer Line system, line balancing and breakdown rates of the machines are important and need to be emphasized.

2. Problem Identification: This step captures some of the specific characteristics associated with the system under consideration. The distinguishing characteristics with various production techniques such as those given in (Gould, 1988), give some guidelines of areas to emphasize in the simulation. Some potential problems that may be associated with the system are pinpointed at this time and the user is queried for more information. Alternatively, the user may be alerted to potential issues or problem areas to incorporate in the simulation studies. All the factors listed earlier that could potentially influence the simulation study, would have to be examined during this stage.

3. Simulation Goals and Methodology: This is the *prescription* part of the advisory system, it outlines a methodology that a user may follow, based on the findings from the preceding stage. The goals of a study for the given system are also provided at this time. The information may be general or specific depending on the knowledge base available in the system. Suggestions to conduct the studies with some tips and pitfalls to be avoided are provided at this time.

The advisor in order to be truly effective should consider all the earlier identified factors associated with manufacturing systems, incorporating multi-disciplinary domains of expertise in the process. Also, any suggestions provided in the prescription part of the advisor should be supported with an explanation by the expert system. This is very essential as it enables to confirm the decisions being made and override them if necessary. This is specially important during the development and verification stage.

The next section describes the prototype expert system advisor developed following the above structure. The prototype as implemented, is meant for demonstration of the concept and does not account for all of the factors listed above. The described expert system would have to evolve over time as the knowledge base is expanded by adding more rules and with more specific guidelines provided in the prescription part of the advisor.

PROTOTYPE DEVELOPMENT

Development Environment

The prototype advisor was developed on the TI PC PLUS (1987) expert system environment on the personal computer (PC AT). One major motivation for selecting this environment was that it provided a very user friendly environment for rapid prototype development. The rules in the knowledge base are easily represented. Knowledge of LISP (PC-SCHEME) is not mandatory for implementing the system. In addition, the environment has the capability to be expand easily. The system allows portability in that the developed system can be delivered on floppy disks for easy access and use later.

Implementation

Backward chaining representation scheme was used for the control structure. The three stages of the scheme were represented in three separate *frames*, with each frame initiated sequentially in the order listed earlier. The first frame was aimed at determining the type of manufacturing system under consideration. Thereafter the second frame was initiated to determine some specifics of the system. Based on the information extracted during the first two stages, the final frame was initiated providing the conclusions: the simulation methodology and the specifications for the objectives of the study to be conducted. For the implemented version, these conclusions and some of the advises and decisions provided during the consultation were printed on the screen. However, for the later version these could be written to an external file for later examination.

Also, using the **Help** property provided in the PC-PLUS shell, an explanation was provided if the user hit the designated help button on the keyboard at any time during a prompt in the session.

The details of each of the stages as implemented in the prototype are described in more detail.

1. Manufacturing System Identification

Three main types of manufacturing system were considered as possible options depending on the characteristics of the system. These were,

- Transfer Line

- Job-Shop

- Flexible Manufacturing System

The criteria used for classifying each were very simplistic and based on numerical values supplied by the user, namely:

- Volume of Production (i.e. number of parts)

- The number of different part types to be produced in the manufacturing system considered. (i.e those with different part sequence)

- Changeover time (or Tool set up) expected for switching from one part type to another if multiple part types were to be produced.

After the manufacturing system type was identified the user was informed of the same and the next step was intiated.

2. Problem Identification

The life cycle of the system was the only factor considered. Two alternatives were provided,

- Greenfield: a brand new facility with new equipments and new building.

- Existing Facility: a facility which is operational with two further options provided,

  o Expansion Plans, such as adding more machines, producing more parts or part type, etc.

  o Study undertaken to determine the cause of a problem, such as, low utilization, high scrap-rate, etc.

3. Simulation Goals and Methodology

This stage is initiated after all the possible questions have been answered and information required for describing the system have been provided. The approach and the goals of the simulation study, for the system described by the user is then provided. This information in the prototype version is provided only for a limited set of all the possibilities and may be general in certain cases. If the knowledge base did not carry any information pertaining to the system described by the the user it would inform user appropriately.

Sample Session

As the session is very screen oriented and interactive, only some of the text in the session is described here.

```
( Step 1 Manufacturing System Identification)
────────────────────────────────────────────

How many different types of parts have to be
produced at the facility?

[2]    (user entered value)

What is the volume of production planned to
be produced at this facility?
HIGH MEDIUM LOW     (user required to select one)

(user selects HIGH)

As per your input, your facility may be
classified as a TRANSFER LINE
────────────────────────────────────────────

(Step 2 Problem Identification )

Which of the following would best describe
 the manufacturing environment of your facility?
GREENFIELD EXISTING_SYSTEM

(user selects  GREENFIELD)

Have you completed the capacity analysis, that
is, the minimum requirements of machines,
manpower, production hours, etc. ?

YES  NO

(user selects NO)
────────────────────────────────────────────

( Step 3 Simulation Goals and Methodology )

Since you haven't completed the capacity analysis
it is reccommended that you conduct some static
analysis to determine one or more of the following:
(1) Equipment (Machines and Material Handling)
    Requirements
(2) Manpower requirements  (3) Line Balance
(4) Minimum time required (hrs.) per day to meet
    required production.
Simulation would be more appropriate and
appropriate after these issues have been
addressed with static (spreadsheet) calculations.
────────────────────────────────────────────
```

CONCLUSION

The expert system described in this paper demonstrated the use of an expert advisor to aid the simulation study. Work still needs to be done in order that the advisor may have the capability to effectively address all the issues to be considered in a manufacturing system simulation. Such a system once developed, can significantly speed up the upfront time needed prior to the simulation model development. The expert system could provide the capability to utilize the knowledge and experience of many experts rather than depend wholly on one individual's. Besides organizing the approach for the simulationist, it could also help the actual user to understand the limitations and the focus on the objectives of the study. For an advanced system this could imply that the user requiring the simulation may acertain this with several iterations on his/her own, prior to even initiating or handing over the responsibility to a specialist.

ACKNOWLEDGEMENT

The initial design and devlopment of prototype expert system was done in 1987 at the Industrial Technology Institute (ITI), Ann Arbor, MI. The author would like to thank many of his friends and colleagues at ITI who helped in this project and the paper.

REFERENCES

Ben-Arieh, David, 1986 "A knowledge based system for simulation and control of a CIM," In Proceedings *European Conference in Artificial Intelligence and Simulation*. July 1986.

Doukidis G.I. and Paul R.J., 1985. "Research into Expert Systems to Aid Simulation Model Formulation", *J. Op. Res. Soc.*, vol 36, no.4, pp 319-325

Fox, Mark, Neena Sathi, V. Bhaskaran, Jack Bouer, 1986, "SIMULATION CRAFT (TM) An Expert System for Discrete Event Simulation". In Proceedings *Eastern Simulation Conference*. Norfolk, VA.

Goodhead, T.C. and T.M. Mahoney, 1986. "Experience in The Use of Computer Simulation for FMS Planning." In *Simulation*. R.D. Hurrion, ed. IFS Publication Ltd, UK

Gould, L., 1988. "Production Management Techniques: Strategic Choices." *Managing Automation*, July 1988, pp 44-48.

Joseph, T.K., M. Patel, H. Gallarda and B. Irish, 1986. "Development of an Expert System Simulator for an Advanced Manufacturing Facility". In Proceedings, *Conference on Intelligent Systems and Machines*, Rochester, MI. pp 300-304.

Shanon R.E., R. Mayer and H.H.Adelsbeger, 1985."Expert Systems and Simulation", *Simulation*, 44:6, pp 275-284

TI PC-PLUS 1987. *Users Manual and Reference*. Texas Instruments Inc., Data Systems Group, Austin, TX. August 87.

Wichmann, K.E., 1986, "An intelligent simulation environment for the design and operation of FMS" In Proceedings, *European Conference on Artificial Intelligence and Simulation*, July 1986, pp 1-11

Advances in AI and Simulation
© 1989 By The Society for Computer
Simulation International
ISBN 0-911801-50-2

DMOD: A logic-based calculus of events
for discrete-event simulation

Sanjai Narain
Rand Corporation
1700 Main Street
Santa Monica, CA 90406
narain@rand.org

ABSTRACT

Discrete-event simulation is an important technique for modeling dynamic systems. We show how dynamic systems can be modeled by Horn clauses in such a way that their interpretation, in a very simple manner, yields a discrete-event simulation computation. Thus, powerful tools of classical logic can be brought to bear upon the synthesis and analysis of models based upon this technique.

An important difference between our implementation and conventional ones is that ours regards simulation as computation of histories, not as a sequence of updates to the current state. This has several advantages. First, information about the past and future can be represented and manipulated in a very simple manner. Second, states are updated in a demand-driven manner, so simulations can terminate more quickly. Third, many useful types of analysis become feasible, which are difficult to perform with conventional implementations.

1.0 INTRODUCTION

By a model of a real world system is meant a representation, or description of that system. By a simulation is meant computation of how the system, particularly its state, evolves with time. Thus, a model is a static entity, while a simulation is a process. The state of a system at time T is the record of values, at time T, of all state parameters of interest. The current simulation time is the value of the variable in the model which represents time. The current state of the system is the data structure in the model which stores the state of the system at the current simulation time.

A well known technique for simulation is the *time-stepped* technique. Simulation time is advanced in fixed increments, and the current state is updated at each resulting instant. This technique is simple to implement. However, it can also be computationally prohibitive, particularly when significant changes in the current state do not occur very frequently. Moreover, all changes between two successive instants are assumed to occur simultaneously at the later instant. This can lead to logical errors, as discussed, for example, in [Evans et al. 1967].

An alternative technique for simulation is the *discrete-event* technique, e.g. [Evans et al. 1967, Zeigler 1984]. It is based on the assumption that to compute the state of the system at any time before time T, it is sufficient to compute only the *events* which occur in the system till T. An event is said to occur when a significant change in the state of the system occurs. Simulation time can now be advanced to the time at which the next event occurs, and only then need the current state be updated. The time between two events can be substantially larger than the fixed time increment in the time-stepped approach. Thus, the number of state updates can be much smaller, and simulation can proceed much more rapidly. Also, state changes are not assumed to be simultaneous, unless actually so, so the logical errors associated with the time-stepped approach do not arise.

A discrete-event model then consists of two main algorithms. The first computes, given a current state, when the next event occurs. The second computes,

given that an event has occurred, what the new, or updated, current state is. In developing these algorithms, two important questions arise.

First, how does one model reference to information about the past? For example, one may wish to model the rule that if at any time T, a commander receives fresh munitions, he orders his troops to advance, only if there has not been any enemy fire between time T1 and time T, T1<T. This rule involves T1 which is in the past of T.

The usual approach to resolving this question is by copying information about the past into the current state. For example, information about enemy fire over a suitable period of time in the past could be copied into the current state. However, this approach can quickly lead to large and complex current states difficult to visualize, reason about, and even efficiently process. In particular, copying can introduce undesirable forms of redundancy.

Second, how does one model reference to information about the future? Many interactions are conveniently stated in terms involving times in the future of the current time. For example, interactions between aircrafts and radars can be represented via the rule: if an aircraft takes off from an airbase at time T, and flies towards a radar, then it will come in that radar's range at time T1, T1>T, unless it is destroyed between T and T1. This rule involves T1 which is in the future of T.

The usual approach to resolving this question is via the device of unscheduling of events. A central event queue is maintained. If at the current time T, there is a possibility that event F will occur at a future time T1, F is scheduled, or inserted into the event queue. If however, between T and T1, an event occurs which invalidates the occurrence of F, F is unscheduled, or deleted from the event queue. For example, if an aircraft takes off from an airbase at time T, and flies towards a radar, then an event of its detection by the radar is scheduled at some future time T1. If however, between T and T1, an event of the aircraft's destruction occurs, then the event of detection is unscheduled.

However, unscheduling of events is a highly procedural device, based upon destructive assignment to a global data structure, namely, the event queue. It is a very unnatural means of expressing the declarative rules involving references to the future. Its use in models, as a substitute for these rules, can make models extremely obscure, particularly as they grow large.

2.0 DMOD: DISCRETE-EVENT SIMULATION IN LOGIC

We now describe a logic-based calculus of events called DMOD (Declarative MODeling). It is an attempt to understand, in purely logical terms, the discrete-event simulation technique, and the ideas surrounding it, such as event, causality, time-varying phenomena. Programs in DMOD are Horn clauses, which can be interpreted in a very simple manner to yield a discrete-event simulation computation. DMOD also proposes answers to the above two questions.

We noted in the previous section that discrete-event simulation was based upon the assumption that to compute the state of a system at any time before time T, it is sufficient only to compute the history, or the sequence of all the events which occur before T. Thus, the history upto T can be regarded as a representation of the state of the system till T. Since simulation is computation of how state evolves, it can also be regarded as computation of histories.

A discrete-event model can now be thought of as consisting of two main sets of rules. The first is a set of *causality* rules. Each causality rule specifies, given the history upto and including event E, what other events will occur. The second is a set of *state-computation* rules. Each state-computation rule specifies, given the history upto and including event E, the state of the system immediately after E.

In writing causality rules it is helpful to take a static point of view. We imagine that the history of a system is already known. Our task is to write some general rules for predicting, given that we know a finite initial segment of the history, the rest of the history. Thus, each of the causality rules is a true statement about the history. Once the causality rules are in place, we can drop the assumption that the history is known. Assuming that the rules form a "complete" description of event occurrences, we can use these to compute the history itself. Exactly how this is done is explained in Section 2.2.

We also propose a new definition of event, different from the one that considers an event as a significant state change. An event is said to occur when one of a set of interesting or unusual conditions is satisfied in the system. These conditions are called event-defining. Each event-defining condition F takes m+1 arguments, m>=0, where the last argument ranges over real-valued time instants. If F is defined for entities a1,..,am,t then F(a1,..,am,t) is said to be an event, and t its time stamp. If F *holds* for entities a1,..,am,t, the event f(a1,..,am,t) is said to occur.

Clearly, the set of event-defining conditions must be chosen in such a way that the assumption of discrete-event simulation is satisfied: given the set of events which have occurred before some time T, the state of the system can be computed at any point of time before T.

Now certain occurrences, difficult to regard as events in the old sense, can be easily regarded as events in the new sense. For example, the occurrence of a tank q occupying the same position as a mine m at time t is difficult to regard as a state change. However, we can think of it as satisfaction of the condition eq_position for q,m,t. Of course, state changes are easy to think of as satisfaction of conditions. For example, change in the velocity of a penetrator p at time t can be regarded as satisfaction of the condition changes_velocity for p and t.

2.1 Definition of DMOD

A DMOD program consists of a set of causality rules, and a set of state-computation rules. Each rule is a Horn clause. A causality rule has the form:

occurs(E,Hist_E,F,Hist_F) if Compute_F,provided(E,Hist_E,F,Hist_F).

where E,Hist_E, and F, are arbitrary terms, Hist_F is a variable, and Compute_F is a set of conditions not involving Hist_F. Compute_F is such that if it succeeds, F becomes ground. Assuming the entire history is known, this rule is to be read as following:

If:

      (a) E is an event which occurs, and
      (b) Hist_E is the history upto but not including E, and
      (c) F is an event which occurs after E, and
      (d) Hist_F is the history upto but not including F, and
      (e) Compute_F computes event F, and
      (f) provided(E,Hist_E,F,Hist_F) holds

Then: event E causes event F.

Hist_E and Hist_F are sorted in decreasing order of time stamps on events. Note that Hist_F includes E and Hist_E. However, references to all three are made available both for convenience and efficiency. As Compute_F does not contain any reference to Hist_F, F is computed purely from information about E and Hist_E.

The condition provided(E,Hist_E,F,Hist_F) is intended to be defined upon the time period starting at the time stamp on E, and ending at the time stamp on F. Procedure provided is defined by clauses of the form:

provided(E,Hist_E,F,Hist_F) if Body.

where Body is an arbitrary set of conditions but *not* involving a call to either occurs, or provided.

A state-computation rule has the form:

value(P,Obj,Val,Hist) if Body.

where Val is the value of parameter P of object Obj immediately after the latest event in history Hist has occurred. Again, Hist is sorted in decreasing order of time stamps on events. Body is a set of conditions for computing Val, but *not* involving a call to either occurs, or provided.

Note that for each parameter P, and event E, if the value of P after E is unchanged from what it was immediately after the predecessor of E, the following rule must be written:

value(P,Obj,Val,Hist) if Hist=[E|OldHist],value(P,Obj,Val,OldHist).

The frame problem [McCarthy & Hayes 1969] now arises, in that the number of such rules can be quite large. However, in practice, these need not actually be written by the model builder. These can be generated either by a compiler, or, as described in the next section, simulated by a single rule. For the purpose of reasoning about models, however, their presence is assumed. Here [A|B] is simply the sequence obtained by attaching A to the front of the sequence B.

An example of a causality rule is the following:

occurs(E,Hist_E,F,Hist_F) if
    E=flies(pen(X),[Px,Py],CT),
    F=in_range(pen(X),radar(R),FT),
    some_radar(radar(R)),
    enters_range(pen(X),[Px,Py],radar(R),FT,[E|Hist_E]),
    provided(E,Hist_E,F,Hist_F).

This rule says that where E is an event of penetrator X commencing flight towards position [Px,Py] at time CT, and Hist_E is history upto but not including E, E will cause, at some future time FT, an event F of a radar R detecting penetrator X, given that provided(E,Hist_E,F,Hist_F) holds. Procedure enters_range computes FT given the information available till E. The definition of provided is:

provided(E,Hist_E,F,Hist_F) if
    E=flies(pen(X),[Px,Py],CT),
    F=in_range(pen(X),radar(R),FT),
    not(occurs_after(E,flies(pen(X),_,_),Hist_F)),
    not(occurs_after(E,destroys(_,pen(X),_),Hist_F)).

This clause states that F occurs if between CT and FT, the penetrator is not diverted from its path (recommences flight), and not destroyed. Procedure occurs_after(A,G,Hist) determines whether there is an occurrence of an event in Hist after A, which matches template G.

An example of a rule for computing the velocity of a penetrator is:

```
value(velocity,pen(X),[Vx,Vy],Hist) if
    Hist=[flies(pen(X),[Px,Py],CT)|_],
    value(position,pen(X),[Mx,My],Hist),
    value(speed,pen(X),Speed,Hist),
    distance(Px,Py,Mx,My,Hyp),
    Vx is Speed*(Px-Mx)/Hyp,
    Vy is Speed*(Py-My)/Hyp.
```

This rule computes velocity of penetrator X immediately after it commences flight to point [Px,Py]. The second and third conditions in the body compute, respectively, the position and speed of penetrator X after it commences flight to point [Px,Py]. Procedure distance(A1,A2,B1,B2,D) computes the distance D between points [A1,A2] and [B1,B2]. The rest of the rule does elementary vector algebra.

Where time(Hist,K) reads off the time stamp K on the latest event in history Hist, the position of a penetrator X at a particular time T can be computed by:

```
value(position,pen(X),[Px,Py],H) if
    H=[clock(CT)|OldH],
    value(position,pen(X),[Ax,Ay],OldH),
    value(velocity,pen(X),[Vx,Vy],OldH),
    time(OldH,T),
    Px is (CT-T)*Vx+Ax,
    Py is (CT-T)*Vy+Ay.
```

If the velocity of a penetrator is the same after an event of its detection by a radar, as it was after its predecessor, one can write:

```
value(velocity,pen(X),V,Hist) if
    Hist=[in_range(pen(X),radar(R),T)|OldHist],
    value(velocity,pen(X),V,OldHist).
```

2.2 Simulation in DMOD

We said in Section 2.0 that when writing occurs clauses, a static point of view may be adopted in that the history of a system may be presumed known, and the occurs clauses regarded as predicting, given an initial segment of the history, the rest of the history. We now show, how once these clauses are in place, they can be used to compute the history itself, or perform simulation.

The history is computed in a bottom-up manner. Let the initial event occur. From the occurs clauses compute which events it causes, then compute the events that these cause, and so on. However, note that an occurs clause is of the form:

```
occurs(A,Hist_A,B,Hist_B) if Compute_B,provided(A,Hist_A,B,Hist_B).
```

Thus, where E is the last computed event, and Hist_E is the history upto, but not including E, we *cannot* obtain the event F which E causes simply by executing the query occurs(E,Hist_E,F,Hist_F), F and Hist_F variables. In Section 2.1 we restricted Compute_B to not contain any reference to Hist_F, so F can be known from Compute_B. However, since Hist_F is not yet known, provided(E,Hist_E,F,Hist_F) cannot be evaluated, so we cannot be sure that F occurs.

To be sure that F occurs we need to delay the evaluation of the condition provided(E,Hist_E,F,Hist_F) till the history till the time stamp on F is computed. We can then bind Hist_F to this history and evaluate the condition.

A delay mechanism is easy to implement. We first transform each occurs clause of the above form into:

```
occurs(A,Hist_A,B,Hist_B,provided(A,Hist_A,B,Hist_B)) if Compute_B.
```

Now, purely from knowledge of E, and Hist_E, the query occurs(E,Hist_E,F,Hist_F,Cond), F, Hist_F, and Cond variables, can succeed. If it does, it returns by binding F to an event, and Cond to provided(E,Hist_E,F,Hist_F), where E,Hist_E, and F are now all ground, but Hist_F is still a variable.

We now insert the pair c(F,provided(E,Hist_E,F,Hist_F)) into an an event queue, each item in which is of the form c(Q,R) sorted in *increasing* order of time stamps of the items. The time stamp of c(Q,R) is that of Q. Along with the event queue we also maintain a history. It contains all the events which have occurred till before the time stamp on the first item in the queue. If the first item in the queue is c(F,provided(E,Hist_E,F,Hist_F)), we can bind Hist_F to this history, and evaluate provided(E,Hist_E,F,Hist_F). If it holds, F occurs, otherwise not.

The simulation algorithm can now be expressed by the following Horn clauses augmented with negation-as-failure, and a facility for computing sets of objects satisfying a given condition:

```
simulate(H,[],H) if true.

simulate(Hist_F,[c(F,C)|R],NewH) if
    is_true(C,Hist_F),
    bag(c(G,Cond),Hist_G^occurs(F,Hist_F,G,Hist_G,Cond),S),
    sort_events(S,Future_Events),
    merge(Future_Events,R,R1),
    simulate([F|Hist_F],R1,NewH).

simulate(Hist_F,[c(F,C)|R],NewH) if
    not(is_true(C,Hist_F)),
    simulate(Hist_F,R,NewH).

is_true(provided(E,Hist_E,F,Hist_F),Hist_F)
    if provided(E,Hist_E,F,Hist_F).
```

In simulate(H,Q,NewH), H is the history associated with the event queue Q, and NewH is the total history. The first clause states that if Q is empty, H is the total history.

The second clause states that if the first item of Q is c(F,C), then determine whether C is true in the light of Hist_F. If so, add F to Hist_F to produce a new history. Determine the set of all pairs c(G,Cond) such that F causes G, conditioned upon Cond, sort them in increasing order of time stamps, merge them into the rest of Q to produce a new event queue, and simulate with the new history, and the new event queue. These tasks are accomplished in order by is_true, bag, sort_events, merge and simulate.

The third clause states that if C is not true, then discard F, and simulate with the present history and the rest of Q. The first argument of is_true is the condition provided(E,Hist_E,F,Hist_F), in which the first three arguments are ground, while the last is a variable. The second argument of is_true is the present history, and is, of course, ground. When is_true is called, Hist_F is bound to this history, and provided(E,Hist_E,F,Hist_F) can be safely evaluated.

The transformed occurs clauses, and value, provided, and simulate clauses can be directly executed as a Prolog program. Thus, a working implementation of DMOD is obtained. The full power of Prolog can be used to define subsidiary procedures, as well as to perform rich types of analysis.

2.3 Two optimizations

Two optimizations are now outlined. The first allows DMOD programs to be more concise. The second improves their efficiency. It is important to stress that these optimizations, and the transformation of occurs clauses described above, are performed automatically by a DMOD to Prolog compiler. The DMOD programmer need not be aware of these.

As we mentioned in Section 2.1, if an event does not affect a parameter, the corresponding value clause need not be written by the model builder. Instead, its presence is simulated. This is done by inserting a cut at the end of the body of each value clause, and placing, at the very end of procedure value, the clause:

$$value(A,B,C,[E|OldH]) \text{ if } value(A,B,C,OldH).$$

Now, given parameter P, object X, and history [E|Hist_E], if Prolog fails to prove the query value(P,X,Val,[E|Hist_E]) by the proper value clauses, it tries this last clause and infers that the value of P for X after [E|Hist_E] is the same as that after Hist_E. If Prolog does succeed, then due to the cut at the end of proper value clauses, it does not try this clause. A more declarative approach based upon Kowalski's resolution of the frame problem [Kowalski 1986] can be employed.

Given that parameter P has been computed after history H, its value is stored, and not recomputed when required again. We have explored some methods of accomplishing this, including use of asserts, binary trees, and difference structures. A much more efficient method seems possible, and is under investigation.

3.0 SOME FEATURES OF DMOD

3.1 Referring to the past

The history upto time T can be used to compute information about both the state, as well as the events till any point of time before T. As histories are "first-class citizens" in DMOD, a procedure can be made to access information about the past of T simply by passing to it the history upto T. For example, we can express the rule that if a commander receives fresh munitions, he orders his troops to advance provided there has been no enemy fire over a period of time in the past, as follows:

```
occurs(E,Hist_E,F,Hist_F,true):-
    E=receive_ammunition(CT),
    F=order_to_advance(CT),
    non_member(enemy_fire(_),[E|Hist_E],Period).
```

Procedure non_member is passed the entire history Hist_E, all events in which are in the past of E. It checks whether an event of the form enemy_fire(_) appears in Hist_E in Period seconds in the past of E.

3.2 Referring to the future

Note that in an occurs clause:

$$occurs(E,Hist\_E,F,Hist\_F) \text{ if } Compute\_F, provided(E,Hist\_E,F,Hist\_F).$$

Hist_F refers to the entire sequence of events which occur before F. Since F is in the future of E, Hist_F can be used to make statements about the future of E, in particular, via the condition provided(E,Hist_E,F,Hist_F). See also the discussion of the provided clause in Section 2.1.

As discussed in Section 2.2, DMOD also has the notions of scheduling and unscheduling of events. When events are inserted into the event queue, they are scheduled. When conditions associated with these do not hold, they are unscheduled. However, these notions appear only within the DMOD interpreter, i.e. procedure simulate, not within DMOD programs. Thus, the model builder need not even be aware of these. He only need specify the declarative causality rules, not how to implement them.

3.3 Demand-driven updating of state

During simulation in DMOD, only those state parameters are computed which are necessary for computing the next event. For example, given that the event E=flies(pen(1),[100,100],1) has occurred, and the history till E is Hist_E, the occurs clause of Section 2.1 is invoked. In it, procedure enters_range computes intersections between the flight path of pen(1) and radars. For this it only computes the position, and velocity of pen(1) after [E|Hist_E]. It does not compute other parameters of pen(1) after [E|Hist_E] such as its commanding aircraft, or its current destination. Thus computation of events is substantially speeded up.

4.0 ANALYSIS WITH DMOD

We now outline the types of analyses possible with DMOD. These include tracing chains of causality in both backward and forward directions, backing the simulation up to points in time, determining how the value of a parameter evolved with time, identifying dependencies between parameters and events, and obtaining object-oriented views of a DMOD model. These analyses can be difficult to perform with conventional implementations of discrete-event simulation.

Of greater importance is the fact that DMOD programs can be thought of as statements of logic. Thus, the powerful abstractions, theorems, techniques, and heuristics of logic can be employed to first define, and then perform, even more complex types of analyses. Some of these are outlined in Section 6.0.

4.1 Tracing causality chains

For tracing chains of causality we make use of the fact that Prolog programs can be used not only to *compute* outputs, given inputs, but also to *verify* whether a given output corresponds to a given input. For tracing causality in the backward direction, let F be an event and H the history. We first compute what event caused F. As histories are sorted in decreasing order of time stamps, let a final segment of H be of the form [F|Hist_F]. Select an event E in Hist_F, and let a final segment of H be of the form [E|Hist_E]. Now, verify whether occurs(E,Hist_E,F,Hist_F,C) holds, and futhermore whether C is true in the context of Hist_F. If so, then E causes F. This step is executed repeatedly obtain a backward chain of causality starting at F.

For tracing causality in the forward direction, let E be an event and H the history. Let a final segment of H be of the form [E|Hist_E]. Evaluate the Prolog query occurs(E,Hist_E,F,Hist_F,C) to obtain F and C, where C contains the unbound variable Hist_F. Let a final segment of H be of the form [F|Hist]. Bind Hist_F to Hist, and evaluate C. If C is true, E causes F. This step is executed repeatedly to obtain a forward chain of causality starting at E.

4.2 Backing up simulation

The state of the simulation after event E occurs is fully characterized by the history up to E, and the event queue which prevailed immediately after E occurred. Simulation can be backed up to the point of time after E by restoring this history, and event queue. The event queue can be modified for exploring new possibilities. Procedure simulate can be easily modified to keep a record of the event queue prevailing after each event.

4.3 Tracing evolution of values of a parameter

The value of a parameter P can be computed after each event in the history to obtain a useful trace of how the value of P evolved with time.

4.4 Exploring dependencies

Dependencies between events and parameters, and between events and events can be computed quite easily. The occurs clauses are statements of the first type of dependencies. The value clauses are statements of the second type of dependencies.

4.5 Object-oriented views of model

An object-oriented view of a DMOD program can be obtained by listing, for each object, the set of parameters and their initial values, and the set of occurs, and value clauses relevant to that object. The relevant clauses are easily retrieved using the powerful symbolic manipulation facilities of Prolog.

5.0 RELATIONSHIP WITH PREVIOUS WORK

DMOD programs can roughly be thought of as statements of dependencies between events and events, and between events and parameters. These seem to represent the minimum amount of information which must be present, directly or indirectly, in any model of a given system built using the discrete-event simulation technique.

DMOD bears some resemblance to the event calculus of Kowalski [1986]. In both, events are central concepts, and the method of computing state from events is similar. However, the two have quite different underlying motivations. The latter is an attempt to formalize database updates, and solve the frame problem. It is not obvious how to do discrete-event simulation in it, in particular, to express causality rules of the form "if event E occurs at T then event F will occur at T1, T1>T, provided some other event does not occur between T and T1". It appears that reference to history must be maintained, and a mechanism for unscheduling events programmed, as proposed in DMOD.

Object-oriented programming is a popular approach to simulation e.g. in the papers in [Klahr & Waterman 1986]. However, the state-orientation of objects can again make it difficult to represent information about the past. Furthermore, a significant epistemological problem arises. In object-oriented programming, it is tacitly assumed that events occur as a result of conscious, intentional actions of objects, represented by message transmissions. However, there are many events which are caused unintentionally, which can be difficult to represent under the above assumption. Often these are represented by a god-like object but this can rapidly become very complex and cumbersome.

In DMOD, we remain neutral as to whether events are intentional, or unintentional. We only need to specify, from a high-level, objective point of view, how they occur. This seems to be conceptually much simpler.

Broda & Gregory [1984] show how to do discrete-event simulation in PARLOG, [Clark & Gregory 1986], a parallel logic programming language. Similarly, Li et al. [1988] show how to do discrete-event simulation in Communicating Sequential Prolog (CSP*), an extension of Prolog with the Time Warp [Jefferson 1985] communication mechanism. However, these formalisms deviate significantly from conventional logic so its tools have to be applied with significant caution. Furthermore, to fully exploit the power of these formalisms, systems have to be modeled as a set of deliberately communicating processes. Thus, the epistemological problem with the object-oriented approach may again arise.

Futo & Gergely [1982] describe T-Prolog, an extension of Prolog for discrete-event simulation. An interesting feature of it is that the model can be automatically modified by backtracking until the simulation exhibits some desirable behavior. However, T-Prolog also deviates significantly from conventional logic.

6.0 FUTURE DIRECTIONS

We are currently applying DMOD to modeling a real system, for the purpose of testing its limits. We are also studying how to perform more complex types of analyses, such as exploration, demand-driven simulation, model composition, aggregated explanation of simulation output, and computation of time instants at which certain conditions held. Finally, we are investigating the meaning of inheritance in the DMOD framework.

ACKNOWLEDGEMENTS

I am very grateful to Jeffrey Rothenberg, Iris Kameny, and Louis Miller for their valuable comments during the development of this paper.

REFERENCES

Abadi, M., Manna, Z. [1987]. Temporal logic programming. *Proceedings of IEEE symposium on logic programming*, San Francisco.

Broda, K., Gregory, S. [1984]. Discrete-event simulation in PARLOG. *Proceedings of second international conference on logic programming*, Uppsala University, Sweden.

Clark, K.L., Gregory, S. [1986]. PARLOG: Parallel programming in logic. *ACM transactions on programming languages and systems*, 8,1.

Communications of the ACM [1981]. Special issue on simulation and modeling, April.

Davis, M., Rosenschein, S., Shapiro, N. [1982]. Prospects and problems for a general modeling methodology. N-1801-RC, RAND Corporation, Santa Monica, CA.

Evans, G.W., Wallace, G.F., Sutherland, G.L. [1967]. *Simulation using digital computers*. Prentice-Hall, Englewoods Cliffs, N.J.

Futo, I., Szeredi, J. [1982]. T-Prolog: A very high level simulation system. Institute for coordination of computer techniques, Budapest, Hungary.

Jefferson, D. [1985]. Virtual Time. *ACM transactions on programming languages and systems*, July.

Kiviat, P.J. [1967]. Digital computer simulation: modeling concepts. RM-5378-PR, RAND Corporation, Santa Monica, CA.

Klahr, P., Waterman, D. (eds.) [1986]. *Expert Systems: Techniques, Tools, Applications*, Addison Wesley.

Kowalski, R. [1986]. Database updates in the event calculus. DoC 86/12, Department of computing, Imperial college, London.

Li, X., Unger, B., Cleary, J. [1988]. Communicating sequential Prolog. *Distributed Simulation*, (eds.) B. Unger, D. Jefferson. Society for computer simulation, San Diego, CA.

McCarthy, J., Hayes, P. [1969]. Some philosophical problems from the standpoint of artificial intelligence. In *Machine Intelligence*, (eds.) B. Meltzer, D. Michie, Edinburgh University Press, Edinburgh.

Zeigler, B. [1984]. *Multifacetted modelling and discrete-event simulation*. Academic Press, New York.

Advances in AI and Simulation
© 1989 By The Society for Computer
Simulation International
ISBN 0-911801-50-2

Scenario generation for knowledge-based simulation

Bruce Roberts
BBN Systems and Technologies Corporation
10 Moulton Street
Cambridge, MA 02138

ABSTRACT

We discuss techniques for increasing the effectiveness of knowledge–based simulations by facilitating the scenario generation process. Scenario generation includes the overall configuration of a simulation, the choice and disposition of its participants, and the initial specification of their many attributes and scripts. We assume an object–oriented simulation and draw examples from the domain of battlefield management, particularly command and control. Starting from an observation that the power and utility of large simulations is hindered by the exorbitant effort required to set up and run even a single scenario, we propose a set of realistic requirements and techniques to be incorporated into simulation environments, which could substantially reduce this effort. These techniques fall into four general categories: (1) increasing the expressive power of the user to talk about aggregates of objects and behaviors, (2) increasing the comprehensibility to the user of the scenario and the underlying simulation models, (3) allowing the user to build freely on existing work, and (4) allowing other systems to participate in the scenario generation process. The demands of scenario generation place requirements on the design of of the simulation environment itself that go beyond what is required to merely run a simulation.

INTRODUCTION

This paper discusses techniques for improving the utility and functionality of scenario generation for knowledge-based simulation systems. To focus the discussion, we will limit ourselves to the class of discrete-event object-oriented simulators exemplified by ROSS (Klahr and Faught 80; McArthur et al. 86) and KBS (Reddy et al. 86). Since we are specifically interested in simulations to support battlefield management, particularly command and control decisions, we will draw heavily on this domain for our examples. Previous object-oriented simulations built in this domain include TWIRL (Klahr et al. 84), BEM (Nugent and Wong 86), OPFOR (Downes-Martin and Saffi 87), and ALBM (ALBM 87).

To date, a major factor limiting the use of simulation technology has been the difficulty of creating the problem specifications—scenarios—which serve as input to the simulation. A scenario defines the complete starting state of a simulated world. It contains a vast amount of information since it must completely specify every individual object that participates in the simulation, their properties and relationships to other objects in the simulation. It also specifies the behavior of each type of entity: how objects of that type react to events. In addition, it specifies a script of actions (commands) for each individual object. The fact that each object can have its own properties, scripts, and reactions allows great flexibility and precision in modeling the real world, but at a cost in the magnitude and complexity of the specifications.

The creator of a scenario must manage a large quantity of interrelated information and have a high degree of familiarity with the domain itself and with the details of the world model underlying the simulation. This tends to restrict use of simulation systems to a limited audience of experts. In practice, it is rare for large simulations to be run for more than a single scenario because of the difficulty and expense of building them. Better scenario generators will make simulations more generally available and easier to use, and will make larger and more realistic models practical. Although

our proposals are targeted toward next-generation knowledge-based simulation systems, they are motivated by general requirements for composing and editing complex models, and should be applicable in part to existing and non-object oriented systems as well.

The scenario generator and the simulator combine to provide a simulation environment experienced by people with three different objectives: the simulation writer, an Implementer who deals in constructing illusions; the scenario writer, a problem solver with command of the domain; and ultimately a decision maker faced with choice and interpretation. Within this larger context, the tools available in the environment must contribute to all these objectives and support the basic cycle of specification, execution, and analysis that characterizes working with a simulation. Scenario generation has received scant attention, yet its needs affect the entire simulation environment.

CURRENT GOALS FOR SCENARIO GENERATION

In this section, we identify four functional goals for the scenario generation component of a simulation environment and suggest techniques for achieving them. First, increase the expressiveness of the user interaction in order to convey more instructions with fewer actions. Aggregating objects and behaviors, and using macro–operations to bundle complex or repetitious commands, are techniques for accomplishing this. Second, make the simulation system more comprehensible by using specialized interfaces for important types of data, building in self-description capability, and checking consistency. Third, recognize that scenarios evolve through many iterations by providing tools to retain, reuse, and distribute prior work. Fourth, allow scenario generator functionality to be embedded in other systems by making the programming interface uniform and extensible. We now elaborate each of these goals in turn.

Expressiveness

It should be easy to state the features one wants in a scenario, but the shear multitude of objects and their associated parameters make specification tedious. The primary goal of scenario generation should be to allow aggregate specification of objects and their behavior, with the system performing the appropriate translations from aggregate to individuals. This goal has two components: selection and modification.

Selecting objects makes use of different kinds of grouping operations. First, there are structural groupings arising from natural relationships in the domain; command, communication, and organic part/whole hierarchies are three important structural relationships in military domains. Second, there are situation dependent categories that become relevant to a particular scenario; e.g., "all the SAM sites at full readiness within 200 kilometers of Fulda Gap." Finally, a user may specify arbitrary collections extensionally, rather than intensionally; e.g., by pointing to icons on a map. In practice, these three kinds of grouping operations are intermixed to identify aggregates of objects in the scenario. Moreover, there may be multiple levels of aggregation. Aggregate objects must have an independent existence, so that the ability to reference the aggregate is not lost after the aggregate is first created or the simulation is run. For example, suppose we deploy a division at a certain position, but later decide to change our mind. So long as the system maintains the connection between the component units and the whole, it is always possible to tell the division to adopt new deployment; the system is able to access and reposition all of the division's components. Although our focus is on the scenario generation phase of simulation, it should be apparent that the ability to easily specify aggregates is useful to all phases of creating, monitoring, and analyzing a simulation. Aggregates provide a convenient handle tracing objects of interest as the simulation runs and give the user much greater flexibility for querying the model and reporting the outcome of the simulation.

Having once identified an aggregate, its attributes (e.g., speed fuel, location, strength) and its behaviors (e.g., move, sense, wait, defend) can then be modified. Aggregate specification requires intelligent help from the system in all but the most trivial cases. This knowledge is localized in translators, which convert operations performed on an aggregate into more primitive operations on its parts. Translators are the largest repository of knowledge in the scenario generator, and necessarily embody considerable domain expertise since they must deal with the subtleties in mapping between the corresponding meanings of the aggregate and its parts. For example, consider the relationship between the "location" of a division and that of its battalions, or "speed" of a tank platoon and its individual tanks, or "movement" of a squadron and the paths of its individual planes. An aggregate routing translator would convert a single MOVE command into a detailed sequence of individual movements. This feature allows one to define operators embodying common formations for large groups of units, such as a schema for a pincer attack, which would be laborious to specify on a unit-by-unit basis (Davidson and Russell 87; Downes-Martin and Saffi 87).

Distributing operations from an aggregate to its parts combines copying and allocating. Multiple translations are possible. For example, distributing a quantity of fuel to a tank platoon may be done *equally*, *proportionally* according to capacity, or *statistically* according to an empirically determined distribution. Positioning a tank platoon may invoke several independent translators that need to be reconciled; e.g., translators focused on terrain, doctrine, mission, or strength. Moving a platoon requires decomposing both the object and the action in order to be properly translated. The problem of defining translators has a reciprocal problem in the reporting the results or status of a simulation, where one needs to summarize across many individual properties to produce comprehensible reports.

A second major contributor to expressiveness in scenario generation is the support for macro-operations. Unlike aggregate operations, macro-operations are purely a syntactic device used to package a sequence of user commands into a single, new, easily invoked command. By using a fragment of a user's past interaction as a script from which to create a general procedure, the macro-operations extend the actions available to the user in ways both idiosyncratic and powerful. The new commands don't necessarily have to be invoked by typing or menu selection. Instead, by temporarily associating them with a gesture, the act of clicking on a visible object can apply the operation to it.

The subtleties of defining and using macros need to be addressed, since they greatly affect the utility of this mechanism. The seed for a macro can come from the main command history, or the commands associated with just one object. In either case, one must generalize the sequence by identifying and editing its internal references, which may refer to the target of the original operation, related objects, or constants. The subsequent applicability of a macro is enhanced by introducing conditionals. One is in effect "programming by example," and a full range of editing and debugging tools will be necessary.

Comprehensibility

A scenario should be easy to interpret and to change. This requires commands that are understandable and simple to use; displays that make information clear and accessible, and the results of each operation evident; and aids to understanding the structure of

the world model used by the simulation. We can categorize these needs as requirements on editing, self-description, and consistency.

The editing environment. Editing and display are complementary parts of the same task. Appropriate graphical displays can also provide the best means for manipulating the underlying data. Graphical presentations can be effective for summarizing data, increasing the density of information display, and simplifying the interpretation of complex relationships in data (Bocker et al. 86).

An editing environment is a collection of specialized editors, chosen to reflect the intrinsic properties of the data, and the varying needs of the user. The same data can be displayed (and edited) in multiple views (Kosy 86; Poltrock et al. 86), where each view supplies a different focus on the scenario, along with editing operations natural to the format of the displayed items. For example, to edit a mission, the routes would be displayed on a map as sequences of line segments, so that one could edit the routes by dragging the paths around with a mouse. On the other hand, to edit the mission schedule, a timeline would be displayed along which events could be positioned. This latter display emphasizes the temporal relations among events rather than the spatial ones.

Editors can incorporate knowledge of the simulation's world model and the state of the scenario to constrain the choices presented to the user. This makes valid options clear to the user, lessening the possibility for error and reducing screen and menu clutter. For example, a battlefield geometry editor that supports direct manipulation of areas, lines, and intersections should include ways of locking points to grid points, and enforcing constraints on boundaries between adjoining areas.

One can imagine a number of useful editors for common types of data. Directed graphs are appropriate for showing the many hierarchical relations that arise in scenarios: object type/subtype, group membership, communication nets, geographical areas, command flow, mission decomposition. Timelines and PERT charts show resource utilization and the timing of the events. Maps form the backdrop for many classes of geometric information: e.g., terrain, weather, cultural features, battlefield geometry, routes, targets. Line plots, histograms, and tables allow one to view and edit functional data that drives the simulation: e.g., attrition curves, strength profiles, probability distributions.

The prevalence of graphical displays is an area of significant overlap between the needs of scenario generation and those of the simulation environment as a whole.

Self-description. The simulation environment should contain descriptions of the models and their interactions, not just runnable code. Even the best browsing interface cannot make up for lack of model organization or poor design. Without good model descriptions, the scenario writer cannot know what is meaningful to specify, how to formulate his or her intentions, or the consequences of the specification. Properties of objects fall into groups, each contributing to a particular functional characteristic—mobility, for example. To act intelligently, the scenario writer needs to be able to discover these facts. A model description would contain this information, as well as the datatypes of the individual properties, suitable values, and defaults.

Collectively, the self-descriptive information about a simulation can be called a meta-model. A good meta-model helps to clarify the structure of the world model in the minds of its designers as well as its users. Consequently, a meta-model is best defined along with the simulation, not grafted on as part of a separate scenario generation component. An object-oriented programming style promotes, but does not ensure, the building of a meta-model. While some information can be inferred directly from the structure of the simulation (in the form of calling trees, and parameter usage), important information about the functional organization of the simulation must be supplied explicitly (in the form of message protocols and slot descriptors).

The meta-model attempts to describe the functioning of the model by recording those parameters of an individual that affect each of its behaviors; and those external factors that affect them in turn. This <u>causality lattice</u> makes the structure of the model clearer and would help the user appreciate both its capabilities and limitations.

As an example of how a meta-model would aid the scenario generation process, suppose that we want to model the effect of adding a new rangefinder to our tanks, one which will improve the accuracy of sighting by 20%. How do we represent this in the scenario? We tell the system to show us what parameters of tanks affect sighting. The system replies that no such parameter exists (explicitly) in the model. It then lists the functional categories of tank parameters and asks if any of those might supply a suitable alternative: e.g., movement, firing, command. We select firing parameters, and the list includes the item "firing accuracy," along with documentation explaining that this relates the likelihood of hitting the target to distance. We select this as the best place to approximate the effect of improved sighting ability, and invoke a graphical editor on the firing accuracy function so that our hit rate at long range is increased. We have used self-descriptive information to help us discover how to model a feature not provided directly by the simulation system.

Consistency. A simulation's self-knowledge can be applied to preserve consistency in scenario. Locally, type, range, and prototype information can be used to check the face validity of parameter values. Additional explicit constraints among attributes permit global checks across many interacting values and can serve as an implicit source of specification for missing values (Steele 80). These checks attempt to guarantee the internal consistency of the model, as well as its versimilitude; i.e., its faithfulness to reality.

Many constraints express themselves implicitly in translators, where they appear during the construction of a scenario as proposed values for parameters; e.g., "don't position tanks on too steep an incline," and "choose a route that remains invisible to enemy positions."

Consistency checking must be supported by large amounts of data: functional dependencies, datatype declarations, functional roles of parameters and behaviors (be they general variables, technological limits, or artifacts of the simulation), operation histories, etc. Fortunately, much of this data is also needed to support other features of the environment, so that the incremental cost of consistency checking is reduced.

Evolution

Creating a scenario is an iterative process that should take full advantage of prior work. Libraries of object prototypes and previously built examples provide ready-made sources of complex descriptions. For example, notional force structures, formations, weapons configurations, weather patterns, and many more details of a scenario could be recalled rather than generated afresh. The library may contain many kinds of entries. Besides examples of individuals, it is useful to be able to file away examples of composite structures, such as a layout of a division at the battalion level, or a template for an aerial formation. In knowledge-based simulation, where actors have goals and plans, it would be useful to be able to save instances of those as well. The library is useful both as a source of predefined cases that can be copied directly into a scenario, and as a source of examples which one might modify to fit a specific situation.

Any library's utility is only as good as its index. An object library can make full use of the type hierarchy relating stored items to provide access not just to individuals but to whole classes as well. Access by property value and property type provide other important means of retrieval. Once located, a library entry needs to be mapped onto the scenario under construction. Sometimes the whole entry is wanted, but often just a fragment of the entire entry is more useful, so the system must support filtering the properties in the library entry when applied to objects in the scenario. For example, one might copy only those parameters affecting ordinance from a saved

tank to an new one. Parameters in a scenario can be closely intertwined, with values of several parameters operating together to define behavior. This needs to be noted in the library entry, so that functionally related values are accessed as a group. Annotations on library entries, besides reminding browsers of assumptions not formally represented (author, purpose, etc.) also provide another basis for searching the library.

A significant aspect of scenario generation is the management of the scenarios themselves. Scenarios are objects in their own right, to which one can apply the same techniques as applied to other objects to organize, reference, and reuse them. As objects, scenarios possess their own properties and relations to other scenarios; for example, the outcome of a scenario might be its important distinguishing characteristic, or the set of all scenarios constituting a set of "what-if" explorations emanating from a common base scenario, or whether a scenario was generated by simulating an initial scenario up to a given state. The need to manipulate and filter fragments of a library entry is even more apparent for scenarios than for less complex objects. For example, one might want to extract only the Red offensive forces from a larger wargame, or its background terrain and weather conditions. Comparing scenarios is valuable for tracking modifications, verifying changes, reconciling different versions, and identifying the structural causes for the outcome of a simulation.

Embedding

The simulator itself may be part of a more comprehensive decision making environment from which specifications flow and to which results need to be reported. One should not assume that only *people* will constitute the user community for a simulation environment. For example, an external database of force positions might be used to provide direct input to a simulation, or the simulation make constitute the "what-if" component of an external planning system, to be run entirely under its control.

Parts of the scenario generation component itself may be delegated to separate modules that evolve over time to become more autonomous and independent. For example, consistency and validity checking are not localized functions, but require access to data throughout the system. Adding new rules and constraint checks should not disrupt the normal functioning of the system.

An open architecture, which provides a complete programmatic interface to the scenario generation component, is needed to promote modularity and to allow for extensions unforeseen by the original designers.*

FUTURE DIRECTIONS FOR SCENARIO GENERATION

Fully achieving the goals described in the previous section is an ambitious, but realistic task for knowledge–based simulation systems. In this section we present some areas of research that await further development before their full contribution can be felt. We will limit ourselves to those areas that impact the scenario generation process, since a full discussion of the future directions for knowledge–based simulation research would take us far beyond the scope of this paper. (Murray and Shepard 87), (Reddy et al. 86), and (Rothenberg 86) address this more general question in detail.

Designing Experiments

An experiment typically involves a number of coordinated scenarios. We have already discussed simple features for managing experiments; i.e., remembering and characterizing predefined scenarios, and the dependencies among them. Experimental design

---

* Systems frequently suffer from the assumption that there will always be a user controlling them interactively. In fact, there should be no functions accessible from the terminal which cannot be called directly, nor should the user have to resort to subterfuge to access useful functionality hidden in the internals. A good test of a simulation system is that it be possible to write programs that construct, alter, and run scenarios.

uses scenario generation as a component, and requires tools that would aid the planning, initialization, execution, and recording of multiple scenarios.

Sensitivity analysis is a simple class of experimental design. By automating the process of generating and running a sequence of scenarios that differ along a single prescribed dimension—e.g., a radar's effective range, or which of a set of divisions to deploy first—one greatly facilitates the use of a simulation to identify critical decisions and to evaluate the robustness of its results. Tools for sensitivity analysis would be used to explicitly describe changes from one run to another and to present the composite results.

Sensitivity analysis presumes that one knows what to vary and what to monitor; i.e., what features of the scenario might be most strongly implicated in the results. A more ambitious goal is a tool that aids in generating these hypotheses, and therefore goes one step further to help a user evaluate new or changed capabilities on the part of some object in the simulation by actually suggesting relevant scenarios. For example, one might look to the SACON intelligent assistant for the MARC structural-analysis package (Bennett and Engelmore 79) for a suggestion of how to achieve the goal of defining a scenario by its purpose rather than its content. SACON helps its users describe an item and environment in which to be tested, and then recommends how to set up MARC to accomplish it: what tests to run, how many cycles to request, and what kinds of failures to expect.

Integrating Planning with Scenario Specification

Mission planning is an important component of wargaming in which one elaborates high-level commands, taking into account the goals, current situation and presumed responses of other independent agents in the simulation. In practice, planning is a composite activity involving several specialized subsidiary planning agents; e.g., strategic, tactical, route, and fuel planners. The output of a these planners is a potential source of input to the scenario generator.

Simulation systems such as ALBM (ALBM 87), which uses simulation to evaluate partial or candidate plans, consider the planner a front-end to the system, so that planning occurs prior to, and independently of, scenario generation. A more integrated design would combine planning with scenario generation, regarding plan elaboration as a kind of *aggregate operator* that expanded high-level instructions into more detailed command sequences that drive the simulation. Continuing improvements in planners will lead to an increasingly declarative (goal–oriented) scenario specification languages.

More sophisticated simulations, in which intelligent agents generate plans (not just execute preassigned plans) as part of their normal behavior, require another kind of integration with the scenario generation process. In this case the planner itself becomes a part of the scenario and requires specialized tools to parameterize its resources and constraints.

Extending the World Model

So far in our discussions, we have treated the world model underlying the simulation as inviolate, while emphasizing the need to provide access and support for the scenario writer. He or she works within the constraints imposed by the model itself, and the tools we have outlined help to extrapolate and parameterize the model. An important line of research addresses this limitation by ask how the underlying model itself can be modified or extended. Pragmatically, any simulation environment will eventually be pushed beyond the scope of its original design, and a user will want to introduce new objects or behaviors not foreseen by the builders of the simulation. For example, someone will want to introduce helicopters into a simulation that contains only land forces. At this point the needs of the scenario writer become those of a simulation writer.

A plausible approach to model extensibility is to provide a well chosen set of primitive objects and behaviors from which a user can assemble new entities. These maximally composable primitives must be carefully crafted to ensure that they really partition the space of behaviors and functions naturally, so that a user can specify new functionality in an intuitive way. In our example, if the simulation of a tank was built out of such suitably general abstractions as position, mobility, fuel consumption, weaponry, and tactical formation, it is indeed possible to imagine using it as the basis for defining a helicopter. (Antonisse and Keller 88) discusses this approach in greater detail and points out the contribution of consistency provided by closed world model, even one closed only at the level of its primitives.

However good the primitives, one needs tools to aid access and understanding: libraries of datatypes, extended self–descriptive information (the meta–model), safeguards (consistency checks), structural and procedural editors. Providing intelligent access to the inner workings of a simulation is hindered by the presence of artifacts, those objects in the simulation that do not correspond to real objects in the domain. As (Rothenberg 86) notes, these artifacts are introduced for pragmatic reasons than than modeling ones; reasons of efficiency, simplicity, convenience, and necessity. In providing the user the ability to modify an object-oriented model, one relies on the understandability of the model to guide the user in altering it correctly. The problem with artifacts is that they may not correspond in any direct way to concepts the user understands, so the user's understanding of his domain provides no guidance in working with such items. Also, as simplifications, artifacts are more likely to require substantial modification when new capabilities are introduced. The net effect is that when the user tries to modify the model, it is the artifacts will cause him the most trouble and will absorb a disproportionate share of explanatory effort.

We wish to stress that artifacts are not necessarily bad. It is desirable that the system treat all distinct entities as objects, not just those which correspond to concrete elements in the (simulated) real world. There are many abstract objects, for instance, which will be easier to work with when treated uniformly as objects: strength profiles, functions, events, radio channels and transmissions (Klahr 86). This includes aggregate objects and artifacts. Conferring full-fledged object status improves the uniformity, comprehensibility, and extendibility of the system.

SUMMARY

Having discussed specific problems with current scenario generation practice, we then focused on ways that knowledge–based technology and sound user interface principles can be applied to them. Many of these techniques can be applied now in simplified form, although all would require some development work before realizing their full potential. We emphasized ways to reduce the effort required to create each scenario through the introduction of more powerful operators, especially operations that manipulate whole groups of objects and facilities for constructing sophisticated commands out of more basic ones. Closely related techniques would enable the user to build on previous work through the use of tools for maintaining libraries of prototypes, simple customization facilities, support for iterative refinement of scenarios, and experiment and scenario management. We described a number of ways to make the system more co-operative and understandable, including specialized editors and graphic displays, self-descriptive data, facilities to make the system self-documenting, and tools to help locate errors expeditiously. Finally, we stressed that the simulation system is a component in a larger effort to solve a set of problems, and therefore needs to be designed to interface with and make use of other tools and information that may be available.

ACKNOWLEDGMENTS

This work was funded by Rome Air Development Center, Griffiss AFB, under Contract No. F30602–87–D–0093.

The conclusions reported in this paper benefited greatly from lengthy conversations with my colleagues at BBN; especially Roland Zito–Wolf, Fred Seibel, William Salter, Stephen Deutsch, Andrew Veitch, Jeffrey Bergenthal, and Michael Crystal. Their collective experience provided a valuable crucible for developing and clarifying the ideas set forth here. Michael Hilton of RADC, an active proponent of knowledge–based simulation, must be credited with originally stimulating and focusing our attention on the requirements of scenario generation in a simulation environment.

BIBLIOGRAPHY

ALBM Team. 1987. "ALBM Detailed Design Plan." Technical Report TR-B.1.001, Defense Advanced Research Projects Agency (Aug.).

Antonisse, H. J. and K. S. Keller. 1988. "Strong Typing of Domain Terminology: Supporting Interactive and Automated Extensibility in Knowledge-Based Systems." Technical Report, MITRE Corporation (Jul.).

Bennett, J. S. and R. S. Engelmore. 1979. "Sacon: A Knowledge-Based Consultant for Structural Analysis." In *Proceedings of the Sixth International Joint Conference on Artificial Intelligence,* (Tokyo. Aug.), 47-49.

Bocker, H. G. Fischer, and H. Nieper. 1986. "The Enhancement of Understanding through Visual Representations." In *CHI-86 Human Factors in Computing Systems,* Marilyn Mantei and Peter Orbeton, eds., Boston, MA., 44-50.

Davidson, J. R. and R. L. Russell. 1987. "Soviet Forces Tactical Environment Model: An Object Oriented Simulation Tool." Technical Report 87W00165, The MITRE Corporation.

Downes-Martin, S. and M. Saffi. 1987. "SIMNET Semi-Automated OPFOR: A Functional Description Version 1.0." Technical Report 6555, Bolt Beranek and Newman Inc., Cambridge, MA (Sep.).

Klahr, P. 1986. "Expressibility in Ross: An object-oriented simulation system." In *AI Applied to Simulation,* Kerckhoffs, Vansteenkiste, Zeigler, eds., SCS Simulation Series 18:1, 136-139.

Klahr, P. and W. Faught. 1980. "Knowledge-Based Simulation." In *Proceedings of The First Annual National Conference on AI* (Stanford), 181-183.

Klahr, P., J. W. Ellis Jr., W. Giarla, S. Narain, E. M. Cesar Jr., S. R. Turner. 1984. "TWIRL: Tactical Warfare in the Ross Language." Technical Report R-3158-AF, The Rand Corporation (Oct.).

Kosy, D. W. 1986. "Menus, Logic, and English as Simulation Model Interfaces." In *Conference on Continuous System Simulation Languages*, Francois E. Cellier, Ph.D., ed. (Simulation Councils, Inc.), Jan., 57-63.

McArthur, D. J., P. Klahr and S. Narain. 1986. "Ross: An Object-oriented Language for Constructing Simulations." *Expert Systems Techniques, Tools and Applications.* Addison-Wesley Publishing Co., Chapter 3, 70-91.

Murray, K. I. and S. V. Sheppard. 1987. "Automatic Model Synthesis: Using Automatic Programming and Expert Systems Techniques Toward Simulation Modeling." In *Proceedings of the 1987 Winter Simulation Conference,* A. Thesen, H. Grant, and W. D. Kelton, eds. (Simulation Councils, Inc.), 534-542.

Nugent, R. O. and R. W. Wong. 1986. "The Battlefield Environment Model - An Army-level Object-oriented Simulation Model." In *Proceedings of the 1986 Summer Computer Simulation Conference,* R. Crosbie and P. Luker, eds. (Simulation Councils, Inc., Reno, NV, Jul.), 767-772.

Poltrock, S. E., D. D. Steiner and P. N. Tarlton. 1986. "Graphic Interfaces for Knolwedge-Based System Development." In *CHI-86 Human Factors in Computing Systems,* M. Mantei and P.Orbeton, eds. (Boston, MA, Apr.), 9-15.

Reddy, R.Y.V., M. S. Fox, N. Husain, and M. McRoberts. 1986. "The Knowledge-Based Simulation System." *IEEE Software* (Mar.), 26-37.

Rothenberg, J. 1986. "Object-Oriented Simulation: Where Do We Go From Here?" In *Proceedings of the Winter 1986 Simulation Conference,* J. Hendriksen and S. Roberts, eds., Simulation Councils, Inc., Washington, D.C., Dec., 464-469.

Steele Jr., G. L. 1980. "The Definition and Implementation of A Computer Programming Language Based on Constraints." Technical Report AI-TR-595, Artificial Intelligence Laboratory, MIT (Aug.)

Advances in AI and Simulation
© 1989 By The Society for Computer
Simulation International
ISBN 0-911801-50-2

An extension of an actor language towards discrete event simulation

Alain Senteni[*]*and Patrick Sallé*

Laboratoire LSI Université Paul Sabatier
118 Route de Narbonne 31062 Toulouse, France
E-mail: senteni@iro.umontreal.ca

Guy Lapalme

Département IRO, Université de Montréal
C.P. 6128, Succ A Montréal H3C 3J7, Québec Canada
E-mail: lapalme@iro.umontreal.ca

* also Faculté d'Education, Université de Sherbrooke,
Sherbrooke, Qc, CANADA

ABSTRACT

This paper proposes an extension of the actor language PLASMA towards discrete event simulation. First, we study discrete event simulation in the context of actors communicating by message passing, and we show that actors provide a tool for both process and event driven simulation. When a message is sent to an actor, it can be enclosed in an envelope. We propose the creation of a new type of envelope containing both message and virtual time at which this message should be sent. Envelopes of this kind alter the flow of messages, introducing simulation time as a new virtual dimension of the sequence of interpretation. Thus, the PLASMA interpretor considers the flow of simulated time and the usual sequence of messages at the same level, lightening considerably the writing of programs for simulation. This is completed by the creation of a new kind of form, enclosing a condition and a message, to allow for conditional sequencing - so called *waituntil* - among events or processes actors: the message in the form is sent only when the value of the condition becomes true, the condition being reevaluated at each simulation time step. These new dimensions of the actor paradigm provide an interesting toolbox for exploring the use of Artificial Intelligence languages in various styles of system simulation. By combining the actor language expressiveness with some dedicated features realizing either time or conditional sequencing of message transmission, we obtain a very interesting environment for the development of experimental simulation software.

INTRODUCTION

The contribution of AI languages to discrete event simulation has been already largely acknowledged by the simulation community. We propose in this paper an environment that belongs to the same vein, extending the promising actor paradigm to the domain of discrete event simulation. The initial actor interpreter that served as a basis for this work is called Plasma, a PLAnner-like System Modeled on Actors. Initially designed by Carl Hewitt at MIT (Hewitt, 77), the language was revisited at the LSI lab (Langages et Systèmes Informatiques) in Toulouse, France, by (Pomian 80), (Durieux 81)and (Salle 86 and 87), with a portable Plasma interpretor was developped on a LILA virtual machine (Carré et al. 84). Plasma is a lambda-language derived from Lisp and based on the concept of actors exchanging messages. To the application of a Lisp function to its arguments, Plasma substitutes that of the transmission of a message to an actor which will take care of it[1]. Previous experiments have shown that the actor methodology is quite powerful and flexible for the design of user-friendly interfaces, enabling an incremental and modular building of a system. We extend this approach to discrete event simulation, and we show that the dynamic nature of actors improves a great deal the isomorphism between the conceptual model and the code itself, making design, extension and debugging a lot easier. The actor methodology leads to the development of abstractions from a set of concrete experiments, making the building of a system comparable to the molding from a sketch, in much the same way as a sculptor works, this approach contrasting with a centralized one where everything has to be fixed at the beginning. Thus, a physical system can be modelled by defining and specializing autonomous processes, entities or events, able to exchange informations and cooperate. All styles of simulation modelling benefit from the highly expressive character of actors systems while it also releases the simulationist from the constraints of a predefined hierarchy.

[1] The appendix introduces the reader to the lexical elements of Plasma used in this paper.

Furthermore, we generalize Hewitt's idea of expressing control structures as patterns of passing messages to the introduction of simulated time as a sequencing dimension. We show how time sequencing can be easily done with time-referenced message transmissions, a new construct that includes to an usual transmission a release simulated date until which the transmission will be held. For this purpose, we will use a syntactic actor construct called an envelope. In actor languages, a message may be enclosed in an envelope, which, in addition to the message itself, may contain for instance another actor to which the reply should be sent. We define envelopes of a new type, containing both message and virtual time at which it should be sent. Those time-referenced messages alter the flow of message-transmission, making simulated time an integrated new dimension of sequencing, so that the extended actor interpreter considers at the same level the flow of simulated time and the usual sequence of messages, lightening a great deal the writing of simulation programs.

To be complete, a simulation language needs a general conditional sequencing statement. In the actor context, conditional sequencing among event or process actors is realised by the creation of a new kind of form, enclosing a condition and a message. The message in the form is sent only when the value of the condition becomes *true*, the condition being reevaluated at each simulation time step. As the condition may refer to the changing state of another actor in the model being simulated, this dimension provides a genuine conditional sequencing facility, equivalent to the traditional *waituntil* statement that can be found in some existing simulation languages. These extensions of the message-passing paradigm provide a complete toolbox for the exploration of various styles of discrete event simulation with actors. By combining the actor language expressiveness with some dedicated features realizing time or conditional sequencing of message transmission, we obtain a very interesting environment for developing experimental simulation software.

In the first section, we discuss the actor approach in general, referring to some previous experiences we had in domains other than simulation. In the second section, we show how actors provide a expressive environment for different styles of simulation, namely "Simula-like" processes or "Simscript-like" events. Third section studies the problem of time control and gives an example of the use of dated envelopes to improve the modeling of time, while fourth section finally describes a possible conditional sequencing feature and shows how it lightens the modeling of complex systems.

THE ACTOR APPROACH

The actor approach already proved to be quite interesting for the design of user-friendly graphical interfaces, where actors are physically represented by graphical objects with a specific *behavior* and *knowledge*. An actor interface for education was built ona Xerox 1109 at University of Montreal (Lapalme and Senteni 87) (Lemoyne, Senteni and Lapalme 88), showing how the actor methodology enables an incremental and modular building of a system.

The main feature of this method of system building is the absence of class hierarchies, allowing the work to be done using only instances which can be cloned and specialized to better suit the special needs of a new instance. The actor approach differs from a "class"ical one, such as in Smalltalk, because it does not imply the a priori definition a group of abstract concepts.

Sharing knowledge between actors is done by *delegation*, an interesting and economical mechanism that allows a sparsity of concepts when one designs and implements a system. Actors can refer to one another's knowledge or behavior, and therefore, can be specified only by their differences with other actors. An actor is not the end of a long conceptual chain in a hierarchy, and then, it becomes unnecessary to have a global idea of a system before starting its implementation. It is interesting to compare this approach with one using classes where abstractions have to be defined at first (class definitions: bottom-up reasoning) and then applied to the particular and concrete cases (instanciation: top-down reasoning): the path that actor systems follow is more "horizontal" and differential, an actor being sometimes used to define another one by analogy. As it is discussed in (Lieberman 86), paraphrasing Wittgenstein, it is often difficult to determine in advance the characteristics which will be necessary for the definition of a concept.

Actor languages appear as a very efficient tool to empirically develop complex systems. They allow the use of the object-oriented paradigm without forcing that of predefined formalisms. The actor concept enables one to define in a natural manner a simple formalism adapted to the application one has to deal with, going from the concrete to the abstract to finally come up with a general model which starts from a series of practical experiments, in contrast with the approach usually used in a system with class hierarchies. (Kreutzer 87) points out the advantages of using object-oriented languages to model physical systems, (Senteni, Sallé and Lapalme 88) show that actors constitute a step further towards a more flexible and evolutive environment. From these first experiences with the actor methodology, we can already mention that actors are an interesting dynamic approach to the concepts of object oriented methodology and a powerful tool for the definition of interactive environments.

SIMULATION WITH ACTORS

As simulation always refers to the physical world, we think that a concrete example will help exhibit the mechanisms of the main styles of simulation with actors, "Simula-like" process-actors and "Simscript-like" event-actors. Another important approach, the activity-scanning model is not studied in this paper. By scanning the whole model to decide what can happen next, we consider it closer to a production rules system where one cycles through a set of rules to change the state of the whole system. We see this approach as state-driven rather than clock or agenda driven, and therefore we consider it stands beyond the scope of this paper whose concern is rather the integration of a model of time to an actor interpretor.

For our purpose, we have chosen a simple classical "customers and teller" example, in which customers are waiting in a FIFO queue, arriving every *ta* (random uniform), to be served by a teller, taking *ts* (random uniform) simulated time units - "*similisecs*" - to serve one customer.

Process-Oriented Simulation with Actors

In a "Simula-like" style, a sequence of logically connected actions is refered to as a process actor, generated by a process generator, which can be understood as a dynamic equivalent of a subclass of the SIMULA process class (Dahl 66). We find in Plasma all the ingredients for a simple modelization of the idea of process. A *cell* - the only Plasma entity to which a value can be affected[2] - provides an actor with a private memory, able to represent the actor's state. In our example, the process *teller* will do nothing but change and recall its own state along the simulation computation; modelling its state will be the role of a cell, local to this actor.

A Coroutine Facility

Process-oriented modelling styles are based on conceptual concurrency. Quasi-concurrency, provided by the use of so-called "remanent variables" such as cells, is sufficient to define processes whose behavior is simple enough. However, for a more general endeavour, one must master coroutine techniques to interrupt the sequential flow. Plasma makes an extensive use of data encapsulation. For example, an actor evaluates as a *closure*, defining an environment local to the actor whose script may as well contain embedded blocks encapsulating local datas. These features make Plasma a very "closed" language: actors are independent entities communicating with others only by messages. In one such context, it is

---

[2] As Plasma uses static binding, atoms can't be affected.

hard to think of a global *detach/resum* mechanism, comparable to the one that exists in SIMULA and another method must be considered. In an actor language, an actor receives a message and in the meantime it receives a continuation for this message, specifying to whom the reply must be sent. This continuation corresponds to the stack management of calls and returns in Lispian languages. In the actor context, non-local exits such as ESCAPE, CATCH and THROW are realized through "*continuation catching*" . Coroutines are defined using this technique, proper to Plasma: the "*caught continuation*" suspends itself until it receives a message that wakes it up. One will create an actor whose behavior can be interrupted by "injecting" into the closure produced by the evaluation of the actor body, a *private resum*, knowing about the continuation that will be caught when the interruption will occur (Senteni and Sallé 88). Cells and coroutines constitute a complete toolkit for process interruption. Now, one can think of a wide range of process-actors, going from the simplest ones - an actor with simple behavior and no memory - to the most complex - an actor with a memory and a complex and interruptible behavior.

A Customer Process

```
(closure (cases
      (=>> Your_name
           Name)
      (=>> ?
          (SQS <= ["Activate (Gen_a_Customer <= "New)
               (Gen_a_Customer <= "NextArrival)])
          ((Teller <= "AvailableP)
           =>
           (cases (=>> true
                   (SQS <= ["Activate Teller (simtime)])
                   (Queue <= "Wait))
              (=>> false (Queue <= "Wait)) )))))
```

Figure 1: A customer process

A process generator for customers, *Gen_a_customer*, knows about the processes it instantiates, and gives them names: *process1, process2, process3,...* Its closure contains a random generator, *ta*, to issue the successive arriving times of customers with a uniform distribution. Each process may answer a specific request for its name - *Your_name* - or, when it receives any other request, may apply its behavior (Figure 1):

- Create one's successor. Schedule successor's execution at time: *<current simulated time> + <time interval to next arrival>*.

- Take one's turn in queue. Remove oneself from sequencing set.

- If teller is available, activate teller. Pass control to scheduling monitor.

- If teller is not available, pass control to scheduling monitor.
   One creates its successor whose execution will be scheduled at time:

   <current simulated time> + <time interval to next arrival>

just by sending the message:

   ["Activate (Gen_a_Customer <= "New) (Gen_a_Customer
   <= "NextArrival)])

to the scheduling monitor, the actor *SQS*. Firstly *New*, secondly *NextArrival* are then forwarded to the process generator, so that the monitor will receive an activation message including as its first part a process closure alike to the one in Figure 1, and as its second part, the activation time of this process. At that point, it will check if the teller is available. If it is, the current customer process will send to *SQS* the message:

   ["Activate Teller (simtime)])

to activate the teller[3]. *Queue* is a specialized actor that places the current process into a waiting line, in the meantime it desactivates this process, passing the control to the monitor. *Queue* actors' competence includes also statistics collection.

---

[3] *Simtime* is a standard actor that gives the current simulated time.

A Teller Process

The process *Teller* may recall its state, generate service durations with a random generator *ts*, and answer a few specific requests:

- "*Your_name* to identify,
- "*ServingFor* to produce a service duration,
- "*AvailableP* to produce teller's state (*true*/*false*),
- *Available* to change teller's state to *true*
- *Busy* will change it to *false*.

The behavior of process *Teller* (Figure 2) is quite simple:

- If *Queue* is empty, change one´s state to *true* (when its state is true, teller is available) and *Desactivate*.

- If *Queue* is not empty, change one´s state to *false*, then remove *Hold* for a random *ts* service time.   first customer in line.

Holding is done by sending to *SQS* the message:

["*Hold* (Teller <= "*ServingFor*)]

This behavior is cyclic and needs not to be a coroutine. After performing some simple actions, it escapes into simulated time. This makes sure that next time the teller is activated, the sequence of actions constituting its behavior will be resumed from the begining. For a more complex behavior that has to be interrupted between to actions, a coroutine actor would be recommended.

```
(Teller = (let (TellerState = '@true)
              (ts = (hasard <= 100))
          then
          (cases
          (=>> Your_name "Teller)
          (=>> ServingFor (ts <= []))
          (=>> AvailableP $TellerState )
          (=>> Available (TellerState <- true))
          (=>> Busy (TellerState <- false))
          (=>> ? ((Queue <= "QueueEmptyP)
                   =>
                  (cases (=>> true (Teller <= "Available)
                               (SQS <= "Desactivate))
                         (=>> ? (Teller <= "Busy)
                               (Queue <= "Next)
                               (SQS <= ["Hold
                                   (Teller <= "ServingFor)]) ))))

      )))
```

Figure 2: A teller process definition

Event-Oriented Simulation with Actors

Event-oriented simulation with actors can be performed using an *Event Scheduling Monitor (ESM)* very similar to the one that has been used for processes but expecting only *Activate* and *Desactivate* messages from the events. *Hold* messages are no longer relevant for an event can be perceived as a punctual process, with a null duration, and therefore, it never has to hold itself. Our example can be easily modelled in an event-oriented style with the four events *Hello* (Figure 3), *Start*, *Finish* and *Bye*, respectively figuring arrival and departure of a customer and beginning and end of the service[4].

```
(closure (cases
    (=>> Your_name Name)
    (=>> ? (ESM <= ["Activate (Gen_Hello <= "New)
              (Gen_Hello <= "TimeNextHello)])
       (Teller <= ["PleaseWait (Gen_a_Customer <= "New)])
       (ESM <= ["Activate (Gen_Start <= "New) (simtime)])
       (ESM <= "Desactivate) )))
```

Figure 3: An Hello event

In this approach, customer and teller are no longer concerned with time and are modelled as state-conscious passive entities whose state will be modified by the flow of events. The teller owns an *inQueue* and an *outQueue* and can produce their contents, and it also knows about its state.

A customer (Figure 4) knows about its name, and can record its entry/exit times, the latter being transmitted only at the end of the service.

```
(closure (cases
    (=>> Your_name Name)
    (=>> [Entry :t](EntryTime <- t))
    (=>> [Exit :t] (ExitTime <- t))
    (=>> EntryTime $EntryTime)
    (=>> ExitTime $ExitTime) ))
```

Figure 4: A passive customer entity

```
(=>> ?
    (Gen_a_Customer <= (at (Gen_a_Customer <="NextArrival) "New))
    (Queue <= ["Wait self])
    ((Teller <= "AvailableP)
     =>
     (cases (=>> true (Teller <= []))
            (=>> false []) )))
```

Figure 5: A time-referenced expression of customer behavior

TIME-REFERENCED MESSAGES

We introduce in this section a new paradigm for time sequencing which we call time-referenced message-passing, and which consists of associating, with a message, a simulated date until which its transmission will be held. The actor message-passing model uses envelopes, which, in many cases, will simply contain a message, but may as well contain other informations. A Plasma envelope is a form whose head is an envelope identifier. We are now going to show that time sequencing can be simplified in a significant way by the use of a new type of dedicated time-referenced envelopes, which we shall name "*at* envelopes" from the name of their identifier:

(at date message)

One such envelope allows for a transmission that makes a direct reference to a virtual time dimension (Jefferson 85).It evaluates as one of its kind, enclosing the evaluated values of the actors it encloses: if the value of *date* is *10* and that of *message* is "*Hello*, then the value of the *at* envelope above will be:

(at 10 Hello)

---

[4] A similar Simscript (Kiviat 68) example can be found at page 100 of (Kreutzer 86).

When it reads an *at* envelope, the extended Plasma interpretor inserts the corresponding transmission into a special stack, at a place that corresponds to the priority given by the time on the enveloppe. After achieving this, it returns the value *unbound* and carries on with the normal continuation of the current computation.

> *((at date2 "message2) => act)*
> *((at date1 "message1)=> act)*

In the program above, the two transmissions are evaluated in the order of the increasing dates and not that of the written sequence.

> *(act <= (at 12 "message))*

results in embedding an event notice such as:

> *["(act <= "message) 12]*

in a "sequencing stack", and carrying on with the usual continuation[5]. As soon as there is no continuation left, the interpretor starts evaluating the stack of held transmissions.

The sequencing set has now vanished from the customer's behavior (Figure 5) for it has been integrated to the interpretor, so we need no longer to make an explicit transmission to a monitor actor. We must also mention a change in the way one can adress the actor *Queue*. In this discipline, event notices are not available actors but rather hidden held transmissions.

> *(Queue <= ["Wait self])*

must then refer to the actor *self*, figuring the process that send the message. This transmission will not result in an escape, which will come up naturally from the continuations interplay.

CONDITIONAL TRANSMISSIONS

We need now a new paradigm for conditional sequencing to make our system complete. This will be done by generalizing the same operation that was used for time-sequencing to a new kind of forms, whose head is the standard atom *when*, in order to realize conditional sequencing:

> *(when true "message)*

is equivalent to *"message*, while:

> *(when false "message)*

is never forwarded since its condition is allways false. The interest of this type of transmissions lies in the possibility they offer to use by way of condition a predicate actor whose state can change along with its interaction with other actors of the model:

> *((when (predicate <= []) "message3) => act)*
> *((at date2 "message2) => act)*
> *((at date1 "message1)=> act)*

When *[]* is sent to *predicate*, it may not return *true*. In this case, the transmission will be held and the following *at* transmissions will be evaluated in the order of increasing times. However, each time one of these transmissions will be done, the held *when* transmission will be tried again in case *predicate* would have become *true*. Then, *message3* will be transmitted to the receiver *act*.

When forms constitute actually a general conditional sequencing statement which can be used to specify that an actor is waiting for a external condition to become true before it performs some action. This feature makes conditional sequencing within the reach of our interpretor, but we can as well use it for an ultimate simplification of the behavior of our favorite customer (Figure 6).

---

[5] The whole "quoted" transmission is stacked, so that its evaluation will we make it effective.

> *(=>> ?*
> *(Gen_a_Customer <= (at (Gen_a_Customer <="NextArrival) "New))*
> *(Queue <= ["Wait self])*
> *(Teller <= (when (Teller <= "AvailableP) [])))*

Figure 6: A minimal expression of customer behavior

There is a minimal expression of a customer behavior, whose code became almost isomorphic to the model description:

- create one´s successor, activate at time:
  <current simulated time> + <time interval to next arrival>
- put oneself in waiting line and desactivate
- when teller is available, activate teller.

CONCLUSION

Actor languages offer an interesting framework for the exploration of various styles of discrete event simulation and for the production of a good sampler of models in the main streams of the domain. However, the introduction of simulated time as an extra sequencing dimension brings to the fore a need for a specialized time control. (Hewitt 77) explains that one of the major benefits of the actor approach consists in replacing "hairy control structures" by patterns of passing messages. We showed that the introduction of a virtual time dimension appears as a drawback, for, in both models we are presenting in the context of standard actors, it puts the monitor at the same level as the actors representing the entities of the model, not bothering with the conceptual difference between them. This forces to a programming style in which time control is far too explicit, and where the transmissions of messages related only to the time sequencing are mixed with the ones related to process events or entities interactions. The lack of transparency of these control structures stands up against the expression fluency that makes the actor approach very attractive.

We showed that it is possible to offset this drawback by the creation of new patterns of actor transmissions, using time-referenced envelopes, that make simulated time a new dimension in the evaluation of a transmission. We presented on an example how the use of these new patterns of passing messages improves the isomorphism between the model description and the code itself. Then, we generalized this approach to the use of special forms for conditional transmissions, enlarging the scope of our interpretor to the modelling of systems in which the sequence of events depends not only on the simulated time, but also on the state of other components of the model. We showed how time-referenced and conditional transmissions could lead to a very sober and elegant style of simulation programming with actors.

REFERENCES

Carré F., Durieux J.L., Julien D., Sallé P. (1984) "LILA: Langage d'Implémentation pour Logique et Acteurs", Actes des Journées AFCET sur les langages Orientés Objets, Bulletin Bigre, p 68-85.

Dahl O.-J., Nygaard K. (1966) "SIMULA an ALGOL-Based Simulation Language", Communication of the ACM, Vol. 9, No. 9.

Durieux J.-L. (1981) "Sémantique des liaisons nom-valeur: application à l'implantation des lambda-langages", thèse d'état, Université Paul-Sabatier, Toulouse.

Hewitt C., (1977) "Viewing control structures as patterns of passing messages", Artificial Intelligence, Vol. 8.

Jefferson D.R. (1985) "Virtual Time", Communication of the ACM, Vol.7, No.3, p 404-425.

Kiviat P.J., Villanueva R., Markowitz H.M. (19868) "The Simscript II Programming Language", Prentice-Hall.

Kreutzer W. (1986) "System Simulation: Programming Styles and Languages", Addison Wesley Series in Computer Science.

Kreutzer W. (1987) "A Modeller's Workbench: Experiment in Object Oriented Simulation Programming", ECOOP'87 Proceedings, pp. 247-256, 1987.

Lapalme G., Sallé P. (1987) "Plasma: version 87", rapport interne, LSI, Université Paul-Sabatier, Toulouse.

Lapalme G., Senteni A. (1987) "Une application de la méthodologie acteur à la définition d'une interface conviviale", publication Université de Montréal, Dépt IRO.

Lemoyne G., Senteni, A., Lapalme, G. (1988) "Enseigner les relations mathématiques simples à l'aide d'acteurs directement manipulables", Intelligence Artificielle et Formation Proceedings, Lille, France.

Lieberman H. (1986) "Using Prototypical Objects to Implement Sared Behavior in Object Oriented Systems", OOPSLA'86 Proceedings. p214-223.

Pomian C. (1980) "Contribution à la définition et à l'implémentation du langage Plasma", thèse de 3ième cycle, Université Paul-Sabatier, Toulouse.

Sallé P. (1986) "Manuel d'Utilisation des interprètes Plasma, Alog et Actor", rapport Interne # 241, LSI, Université Paul-Sabatier, Toulouse.

Sallé P. (1987) "Langages d'Acteurs et Langages Objets: le langage Plasma", Interkibernetik '87, Tarragone.

Senteni A., Sallé P. (1988) "Coroutines et acteurs", document de travail, LSI, Université Paul-Sabatier, Toulouse.

Senteni A., Sallé P. and Lapalme, G. (1988) "The Impact of Different Ways of Sharing Behavior on Discrete-Event Modelling With Actors", submitted to ESM'89 Rome, Italy, June 7-9 1989.

Xerox Corporation (1986) "InterLisp-D Reference Manual"

APPENDIX

A Short Introduction to Plasma

For a complete description of the language, one should refer to (Sallé 86 and 87). However, the reader will find here all the elements needed for the comprehension of the few pieces of code presented in this article.

Plasma is a lambda-language, derived from Lisp, and based on the concept of actors communicating by message-passing. An ordinary function call to a function F with arguments A1, A2, ... An is replaced in Plasma by a transmission of message M to an actor ACT which will take care of it. This transmission is denoted by:

(ACT <= M) or (M => ACT)

To a Lisp function definition:

(defun F(X1...Xn)
                function body)

Plasma substitutes the definition of an actor receiver:

(ACT = (=>> filter
                actor body))

A receiver filters a message that it receives, and if the message matches the filter pattern, the body is evaluated in the environment produced by this pattern matching. If the matching fails, the message is forwarded to a standard default actor.

Primitive actors

The primitive actors are atomic values like integers and real e.g. (5 8 3.1416) and symbols e.g. (a23 anAtom). An actor can also be created by the operator quote, denoted by ", which returns the following actor without evaluation, as does the Lisp QUOTE function.

Sequences

Sequences of actors are denoted by brackets enclosing these actors: [...] e.g. [6 "red 4.5].

Standard actors

Standard actors are predefined ones, which could as well be given a metacircular definition in Plasma. The only difference with user-defined actors lies in the way some of them are called for. It may happen, as it is the case for simtime, that they are invoked as a Lisp function instead of by being sent a message. One will write (simtime) instead of the expected (simtime <= []).

Arithmetic actors

Arithmetic is done with predefined non-receiver actors named by the usual arithmetic operator. An addition is computed with (+ 2 3) and not (+ <= [2 3]).

Filters

A filter is an expression containing values to be found exactly in the message and variables to be bound to values of the message. A filter variable is indicated by a comma preceding the identifier (:). [Activate :process] matches a message containing two values "Activate and customer3, binding the filter variable process to the value of customer3. The transmission evaluation is fourfold: evaluation of the target, evaluation of the message, filtering of the message, evaluation of the body of the receiver. The filter itself is not evaluated. A sequence of 0 or more values can be matched by preceding the filter variable by an exclamation mark (!). So, [:x !:y] matches a sequence of 1 or more elements. x is then bound to the first element and y to the rest which can be empty.

Combined actors using cases

(cases
receiver_1
...
receiver_n)

creates a new actor whose competence extends to the treatment of any message that can be treated by any of the combined receivers. One such construct corresponds to the conditional one in other languages. The value returned by a cases actor is that returned by the first receiver which accepts the message.

Local actors

Local actors can be defined with a let construct:

(let def_1 ...def_n

then body)

where each def_i has the form:

(name = actor) or (name == actor)

In the latter case, the body of the actor uses the local definitions of the names being defined, as for the reclet constructs in Lisp.

(succ = (let (increment = 1)

then (=>> :x (+ x increment))))

evaluates as the closure: (closure (=>> :x (+ x increment))) defined in an environment in which increment is bound to 1.

Advances in AI and Simulation
© 1989 By The Society for Computer
Simulation International
ISBN 0-911801-50-2

Knowledge-based approach to modeling and simulation:
A tutorial

Adam C. Peck
Westinghouse Electric Corporation
Manufacturing Systems and Technology Center
9200 Berger Road
Columbia, MD 21046

The "knowledge-based" approach to modeling and simulation enhances the ability of the simulationist to represent a system of interest with just the right level of detail required to adequately model the real-world system. The "knowledge-based" approach includes a number of methodologies directed at representing knowledge: object-oriented programming, frame-based representation, and rule-based reasoning. Using artificial intelligence techniques such as those above for simulation results in an environment in which models can be developed rapidly. The resulting model structures are also easily understood and readily modified or extended.

This tutorial will review the basic concepts of object-oriented programming and frame-based representation. These concepts will then be discussed in relation to a simulation software package, SimKit.

Object-oriented programming includes the features of modularity, data abstraction, and data hiding. These features lay the foundation for a programming style that results in systems that tend to be portable and device independent. Maintainability, the property of easily fixing or changing the objects and relationships, and extensibility, the property of being easily altered to handle new requirements, are of major concern in examining the life cycle costs of a software system. Object-oriented programming provides a mechanism for enhancing maintainability and extensibility.

Frame-based representation has a long history in artificial intelligence. The major benefit of this representation is the ability to group into a class structure all the related features of an abstract class. The property of inheritance from superclasses to subclasses achieves a compactness not only in the programming software, but in the knowledge representation problem of adequately representing the system of interest, which may include quite complex entities and relationships.

SimKit is a product of IntelliCorp from Mountain View,CA. It runs on top of their Knowledge Engineering Environment (KEE) system. The process of how SimKit uses these concepts in building models and running simulations will be addressed in detail.

SimKit allows for the construction of a modular system of libraries and models. The libraries consist of object-classes and relationships that detail a generic system that is to be modeled, such as, a manufacturing plant. The model uses a library, or rather, a hierarchy of libraries, to configure the specific object-classes that make up a model.

The tutorial does not presume any background knowledge of artificial intelligence. The examples for model objects and modifications stress the modularity of components and the flexibility of the system. Although a familiarity with LISP would be useful, the concepts will be addressed at a high level, so a knowledge of LISP is not essential.

The goal of the tutorial is to show how a knowledge representation scheme allows for both rapid development and modification of models. It will be aimed at simulation practioners or managers who wish to broaden their understanding of some of the new tools available today in the simulation world.

Advances in AI and Simulation
© 1989 By The Society for Computer
Simulation International
ISBN 0-911801-50-2

Interfacing knowledge-based systems and simulators

Cynthia H. Kamhieh
Boeing Computer Services
Huntsville, Alabama

ABSTRACT

There are many potential simulator applications that may benefit from enhancement through the use of knowledge-based system (KBS) technology. Among these are reactive threat modeling, instructor task emulation for IOS automation, instructor emulation for embedded training (ET), and missing crew member emulation.

Inherent difficulties in interfacing KBS's to simulators arise dur to fundamental differences in temporal granularity and knowledge representation. In addition, real time processing issues for the coupled KBS/simulator systems must be resolved, along with problems relating to the ability of the KBS to do commonsense reasoning (e.g., time, space, etc.) about the simulated world.

This tutorial will cover the following topic areas in KBS/simulator interfacing:

(1) Temporal Granularity - Conversion of the time steps of a simulated world to "cognitive chunks" of time that represent meaningful events

(2) Temporal Reasoning - The natural nonmonotonicity of a simulated world, the frame problem, and reasoning about cause-effect relationships over time

(3) Knowledge Representation - The conversion between highly quantitative simulator data and numeric data structures, and the symbolic representations that are typically used for knowledge-based processing

(4) Real Time

(5) Verification and Validation of the knowledge-based system component in KBS/Simulator systems

(6) Specific KBS/Simulator Applications - Training, Simulator Control, and others of specific interest to attendees.

OUTLINE

I. Real Time

    A. Definition
       1. Time Characteristics
       2. Temporal Fidelity

    B. Knowledge-Based System Perspective on Real Time
       1. Event Orientation
       2. Subjectiveness of Time
       3. Temporal Process Modeling
       4. Variability in Temporal Modeling

II. Temporal Granularity/Reasoning

    A. Simulators
       1. Frame Level Granularity
       2. Stable Granularity
       3. Inter-frame Variability
       4. Frame Level Output

    B. Knowledge-Based Systems
       1. Event Level Granularity
       2. Variable Granularity
       3. Inter-event Variability
       4. Input Requirements / Event Level Output

III. Knowledge Representation

    A. Numeric vs. Symbolic Representation
       1. Knowledge-Based System Representational Characteristics

          a. Abstraction
          b. Logic-Based Knowledge Representation

       2. Simulator Representational Characteristics
       3. Qualitative Modeling of Objects/Processes in a Knowledge-Based System
       4. (Seemingly) Non-Deterministic Modeling of Objects/Processes in a Knowledge-Based System
       5. Quantitative Modeling of Objects/Processes in a Simulator

    B. The Interface
       1. Requirements of the Interface
       2. Characteristics of the Interface
       3. Representational Conversion/Mapping

          a. One-to-One
          b. Data Abstraction
          c. Data Fusion

IV. Verification and Validation

    A. Simulator Verification and Validation
       1. State-of-Practice
       2. Verification of System Specifications
       3. Validation of Algorithms, Physical Models, etc.

    B. Knowledge-Based System Verification and Validation
       1. State-of-Practice
       2. Verification of System Specifications
       3. Validation of Heuristics?
       4. Validation of Logical Systems

          a. Tractability
          b. Surface vs. Deep Validation

    C. Separate Validation of Coupled Systems vs.

Validation of the Coupled System as a
Whole

Advances in AI and Simulation
© 1989 By The Society for Computer
Simulation International
ISBN 0-911801-50-2

Introduction to neural networks

A. Martin Wildberger, Ph.D.   Kenneth A. Hickok
Chief Computer Scientist   Staff Analyst
General Physics Corporation
6700 Alexander Bell Drive
Columbia, MD 21044

ABSTRACT

This is an elementary tutorial introduction to the general field of neural networks and cognitive machines. It begins with a very brief discussion of natural and artificial neurons, the characteristics of neural networks in general and how they "learn". This is followed by a detailed description of the back-propagation paradigm. It includes a "walk-through" of the pseudocode for an implementation of a back-propagation network that learns to solve the "exclusive or" boolean operation.

NATURAL AND ARTIFICIAL NEURONS

The initial interest in constructing artificial neurons and artificial neural networks was their potential for use as a model of natural neural systems. It has been estimated that there are over 10^{10} neurons in the human nervous system. They come in many different sizes and shapes. The diagram, of a natural neuron, shown in figure 1, is generic and emphasizes just those characteristics that have been abstracted into the artificial neuron model most commonly used today.

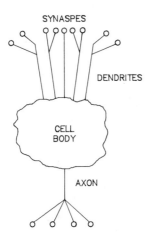

SYNASPES

DENDRITES

CELL BODY

AXON

Figure 1

Signals enter the neuron via its dendrites. The actual connection between the source of the signal and the dendrite is called a synapse. Any particular neuron may receive inputs from many other neurons via this dendrite structure and its synapses. The signals travel through the dendrites from the synapse into the cell body. The cell body combines the signals received and, if a threshold level is exceeded, the cell "fires", sending an electrical pulse down the axon. The axon terminates in a root-like structure which makes contact through multiple synapses with the dendrites of other neurons. There is considerable evidence that the rate of firing is influenced not just by the current inputs from other neurons, but also by the frequency with which the same inputs have triggered the same output in the past. This can be considered a form of learning, or, at least, of adaptation.

To construct an artificial neuron, we further abstract from this already over-simplified model and produce the diagram in figure 2. Different researchers call this structure by various names such as "unit", "processing element", or "neurode". We will use "neurode". In figure 2, the model of neurode "j" has inputs, s_i, from an external source or from other neurodes. Its own unique weights, W_{ij}, are applied to each of these inputs, summed, and converted by the neurode's "activation" function to produce a single output, s_j, which may be distributed to one or more other neurodes.

In this elementary model, the method of combining the inputs is assumed to be summation. A continuous activation function approximates a step function, and serves as a convenient representation of the threshold that appears to be present in the natural neuron. Specifying a particular set of weights gives the neurode a unique behavior. Modification of the weights allows the neurode to adapt or "learn".

The potential for learning is what makes computing with artificial neural networks significantly different than conventional programming. Rather than provide a fixed procedure to be followed in detail to solve a problem in a step-by-step manner, a relatively general purpose network is designed and then trained to improve its performance gradually.

Although it was originally devised as a model of the natural neuron, the neurode can also be treated as a particular kind of information processor, formally characterized by its activation function. From that point of view, all information that a neurode processes is local to it and private with respect to any other neurodes. Incoming signals and its own local memory (including its current weights) are the only determinates of its single output. These elementary processors only become

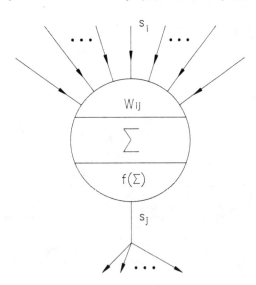

Figure 2

useful when combined in a network.

NEURAL NETWORKS

A neural network consists of more than one neurode (usually many) connected together through unidirectional information channels. Any possible combination of interconnections may be useful for a particular application, but the most common neural network architectures use a layered approach to simplify programming and aid human understanding of the system. For purposes of this tutorial, we will only consider layered architectures in which all neurodes in each layer send their outputs to all neurodes of the next layer and not to any other neurodes. Other architectures include connections that skip layers, that connect neurodes in the same layer, and that feed a neurode's output back to its own input, either directly or via other neurodes.

A neural network is characterized by its architecture or topology, the activation functions and weights of its neurodes, and the learning rule used to train it. A description of all of these constitutes the "paradigm" of the network.

The simplest layered neural network consists of just an input and an output layer, as shown in figure 3. Any additional layers inserted between the input and output layers are known as hidden layers. Figure 4 shows a network of three layers. There are two neurodes in the input layer, three in the hidden layer and only one neurode in the output layer.

Typically, the input layer serves only to accept data and distribute it to neurodes in subsequent layers. The input layer elements are not true neurodes and are not usually involved in any learning. They can be thought of as having only one input each and an identity activation function.

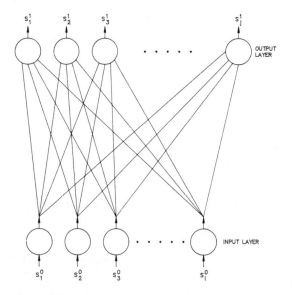

Figure 3

If we use the identity mapping as the activation function of the neurode in figure 2, it becomes an ADALINE (ADAptive LINear Element) originally designed by Widrow (Widrow 1962). [These are essentially the same as the "A cells" used in Rosenblatt's very early neural network, the PERCEPTRON (Rosenblatt 1962)]. If we use these linear neurodes in both layers of the two layer network of figure 3, the result is a unidirectional linear associator which, with minor modifications, could be either a MADALINE (multiple ADALINE) or a PERCEPTRON.

The basic purpose of the linear associator neural network is to learn to associate some number of input/output pairs of vectors, not necessarily of the same dimensionality. When presented with a "new" input vector that is close to one of the learned inputs, it should be able to output a vector that is close to the corresponding learned output. It is capable of being used as an associative memory device, as an encoding/decoding tool, or as an adaptive linear digital filter.

Although all the information in a neural network is local to the individual neurodes, any knowledge stored after training is represented globally across the whole network. Removal, damage, or other change to a single neurode affects the patterns, categories, or other knowledge of the entire network. In networks with large numbers of neurodes, many changes may take place before any significant effect is seen. On the

228

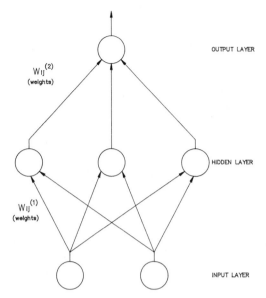

$W_{IJ}^{(2)}$
(weights)

OUTPUT LAYER

$W_{IJ}^{(1)}$
(weights)

HIDDEN LAYER

INPUT LAYER

Figure 4

one hand, this makes the network rather robust by providing a form of graceful degradation. On the other hand, it is often impossible to attribute specific aspects of behavior to an individual or single group of neurodes.

There are three basic approaches to training a neural network. In all three, a training set of examples is presented to the network and its output is observed. For "supervised learning" the correct output (target) must be known to the trainer. The network's output is compared with the target, and some or all neurode weights are adjusted based on the error. For "graded learning", only approximations to the correct outputs need be known. The network's output is periodically "graded" based on how close it matches the approximation. The "grade" is then used to adjust some or all weights. For "self-organization", only a representative sample of input data is needed. The outputs are observed until they have become stable and repeatable enough for practical use. Different network architectures and activation functions are needed for each of these approaches. This tutorial only treats supervised learning.

The modification of weights during the training phase does not take place via the network's unidirectional information passing channels. The weight changes are made by direct intervention in each neurode's local memory.

The mathematical formula that is used to adjust weights in either supervised or graded learning is known as a "learning rule". One commonly used learning rule modifies the weights of neurodes in such a way as to reduce the difference ("delta") between target value and the actual current output. It is variously called the delta rule, the Widrow-

Hoff learning rule, or the least mean square (LMS) rule. It's simplest form is

$$W_{ij}(t+1) = W_{ij}(t) + \Delta W_{ij}(t)$$

where t represents time and $\Delta W_{ij}(t)$ is the correction given by

$$\Delta W_{ij}(t) = \epsilon * (target_i - actual_i) * actual_i$$

where ϵ is a constant of proportionality known as the learning rate. This is an intuitively appealing approach to minimize the error as it is an approximation of a gradient descent procedure. This approach can, in fact, be proved to converge to the global minimum for the MADALINE network described previously. It is not possible to guarantee this result in the back propagation network shown in figure 4 and discussed in detail below. In practice, it is usually possible to gain the advantages of the more complex networks that can handle highly non-linear problems by judicious selection of learning rate and starting weights, and/or by the addition of a noise disturbance to avoid becoming trapped in local minima.

THE BACK PROPAGATION PARADIGM

Back propagation is a neural network paradigm that uses supervised learning to construct a transformation that maps input vectors into output vectors. Back propagation uses the Generalized Delta Rule (GDR) as its learning rule. The GDR is a generalization of the PERCEPTRON/MADALINE learning rule that allows for a non-linear, but differentiable, activation function and provides a method of updating the weights in a network so that known errors are minimized. Unlike the MADALINE network described above, the back propagation paradigm allows additional layers of neurodes between the input layer and the output layer to increase the computational ability of the network. back propagation networks have been demonstrated that solve problems that linear networks cannot solve (such as exclusive or).

The structure of back propagation is a multi-layered, fully connected, strictly feed-forward network. Back propagation networks have at least 3 layers of neurodes: an input layer, a hidden layer and an output layer. Some networks employ more than one hidden layer. Each neurode of layer n is connected to all the neurodes in layer (n+1). An example of a back propagation network is shown in figure 4.

Input neurodes act as described above to distribute the input signal to the first hidden layer. Hidden layer and output layer neurodes act as simple processors. To determine the level of activation for neurode i, first compute the weighted sum of the inputs, E_i. Thus

$$E_i = \Sigma W_{ij}s_j \qquad (1)$$

where the sum is taken over j, W_{ij} is the weight from the jth to the ith neurode and s_j is the output of the

j^{th} neurode. This can be done by calculating the scaler product of the input vector with the weight matrix, W.

The output of a neurode, s_i, is then determined by a non-linear function of E_i, so we have $s_i = f(E_i)$. This activation function, f, of the neuron, is usually the logistic function:

$$f(E_i) = 1/(1 + e^{-(E_i + T)}) \qquad (2)$$

where T is the threshold of a neurode and e is the exponential constant. The graph of this function is sigmoidal. It is roughly S-shaped, monotonically increasing and asymptotically approaches 0 and 1 for large positive or negative values of E_i.

The use of this activation function has several immediate effects. One is that the output of the network is limited to $(0,1)$ because E_i never reaches plus/minus infinity. (In the example that follows, to control the time needed for a network to learn a solution to the exclusive or operation, network outputs of 0.1 and 0.9 will be interpreted as 0 and 1.)

Another effect of using this activation function is that, in order to obtain output values that approach 0, E_i must be negative. Therefore, the weights of the network must be allowed to be both positive and negative.

Layer n is connected to layer (n+1) by weights that represent the strength of the connection between neurodes in different layers. The set of all the weights connecting the i neurodes in layer n to the j neurodes in layer (n+1) is an i x j matrix, $W^{(n)}$. $W_{ij}^{(n)}$ refers to the weight connecting the ith neurode in layer n to the jth neurode in layer (n+1).

THE GENERALIZED DELTA LEARNING RULE

The weights in the back propagation network are initialized to small random values (typically between -1 and 1.) As input/output pairs are presented to the network the weights are slowly adjusted according to the GDR.

The GDR has been derived by several different researchers (Werbos 1974, Parker 1982, Rumelhart et al. 1987.) While the derivation of the GDR is beyond the scope of this paper, a general understanding of the GDR equations will be useful prior to looking at our implementation. This specific implementation is based on a suggestion by Sejnowski and Lehky (1987).

The equation that defines the weights of a network at time (t+1) is

$$W_{ij}^{(n)}(t+1) = W_{ij}^{(n)}t + \epsilon \blacktriangle W_{ij}^{(n)} \qquad (3)$$

where ϵ is the learning rate and $\blacktriangle W_{ij}^{(n)}$ is a correction to the weight. In equation (3), the weight $W_{ij}^{(n)}$ at time (t+1) is equal to the weight at time t plus an amount that is proportional to the error due to that weight. To simplify equation (3)

we will set $\epsilon = 1$. As input/output pairs are presented to the network, $\blacktriangle W_{ij}^{(n)}$ is calculated as follows:

$$\blacktriangle W_{ij}^{(n)}(u+1) = \alpha \blacktriangle W_{ij}^{(n)}(u) + (1-\alpha) \delta_i^{(n+1)} s_j(n) \qquad (4)$$

where α is used as a smoothing parameter, $s_j^{(n)}$ represents the output of the jth neurode in layer n and $\delta_i^{(n+1)}$ is the error gradient of layer (n+1). This is done so that $\blacktriangle W_{ij}^{(n)}(u+1)$ is the running average of the error gradient.

Computing the error gradient for a layer, δ_i, for a layer is given by

$$\delta_i^{(n)} = (target_i - actual_i) f'(E_i). \qquad (5)$$

For the output layer we know the $target_i$ and we can observe the $actual_i$ output from the network. The derivative of the activation function, $f'(E_i)$, is $actual_i * (1 - actual_i)$, where "*" indicates multiplication. So for the output layer, N, we have

$$\delta_i^{(N)} = (target_i - actual_i) \\ * actual_i * (1-actual_i). \qquad (6)$$

This is easy to calculate because all the values are known. The problem comes when we look at the hidden layer(s). We don't have a known target for the hidden layer(s). To get around this $(target_i - actual_i)$ from equation 6 is replaced by the sum over j of the product of the error signals at layer (n+1) and the weights of the connections between the layers. Thus

$$\delta_i^{(n)} = \Sigma(\delta_j^{(n+1)} * W_{ij}^{(n)}) \\ * hidden_i * (1-hidden_i) \qquad (7)$$

This process is followed until the errors are propagated back through the entire network. After all errors are found through the above process the weights of the network can be updated according to equations 3 and 4 and the entire process repeated.

IMPLEMENTATION OF EXCLUSIVE OR

The pseudocode in figure 5 is an algorithm to implement exclusive or in a back propagation network with a single hidden layer and using the GDR as described above. Exclusive or is a boolean logic function that is true when only one of its inputs is true. If both inputs are true or both false the output from exclusive or is false. The pseudocode represents an abstraction from a working program written in C. A copy of the program is available from the authors on request.

The first two lines in figure 5 initialize the weight matrices, $W^{(1)}$ and $W^{(2)}$, to random values on the interval -1 to 1. Then the correction matrices, $\blacktriangle W^{(1)}$ and $\blacktriangle W^{(2)}$, are initialized to be the same size as $W^{(1)}$ and $W^{(2)}$ but with all elements of the matrices equal to zero.

Next, the process begins to loop until a condition is met that causes it to break out of the loop. The condition used to break the loop is that

```
W⁽¹⁾ = random[-1,1];
W⁽²⁾ = random[-1,1];
▲W⁽¹⁾ = zeros(W⁽¹⁾);
▲W⁽²⁾ = zeros(W⁽²⁾);
loop until broken
  old▲W⁽²⁾ = ▲W⁽²⁾;
  for k = (0 to 3, step 1)
    input = BIN(k);
    target = XOR(input);
    E⁽¹⁾ = input * W⁽¹⁾;
    hidden = f(E⁽¹⁾);
    E⁽²⁾ = hidden * W⁽²⁾;
    output = f(E⁽²⁾);
    if |target - output| > tolerance
      {
        δ⁽²⁾ = (target - output)
             * output * (1 - output);
        for j = (1 to 3, step 1)
        δⱼ⁽¹⁾ = δ⁽²⁾ * Wⱼ₁⁽²⁾
              * hiddenⱼ (1 - hiddenⱼ);
        for i = (1 to 2, step 1)
        for j = (1 to 3, step 1)
          {
            ▲Wᵢⱼ⁽¹⁾ = α * ▲Wᵢⱼ⁽¹⁾
                    + (1-α) * δⱼ⁽¹⁾
                    * inputᵢ;
            Wᵢⱼ⁽¹⁾ = Wᵢⱼ⁽¹⁾ + ▲Wᵢⱼ⁽¹⁾;
          }
        for i = (1 to 3, step 1)
          {
            ▲Wᵢ₁⁽²⁾ = α * ▲Wᵢ₁⁽²⁾
                    + (1-α) * δ⁽²⁾
                    * hiddenᵢ;
            Wᵢⱼ⁽²⁾ = Wᵢ₁⁽²⁾ + ▲Wᵢ₁⁽²⁾;
          }
      }
  if ▲W⁽²⁾ ≡ old▲W⁽²⁾ then break loop;
  end;
```

Figure 5

no change in the weights has taken place during the last iteration. To check this, the last (or old) $\Delta W^{(2)}$ is compared with the current $\Delta W^{(2)}$ at the bottom of the loop. A copy of the old $\Delta W^{(2)}$ is retained in each successive loop as "old$\Delta W^{(2)}$". If the old and current $\Delta W^{(2)}$ are identical, the loop is broken.

A "for" loop is used as a convenience to generate the four possible input patterns for the "exclusive or" operation. Inside the "for" loop, the loop index is first converted into its binary equivalent to get the actual input for the network. Then the target output is produced from a built-in exclusive or function.

Next, the forward pass through the network is calculated. First the vector of weighted sums, $E^{(1)}$, is obtained as the cross product of the input vector and the weight matrix connecting the input layer to the hidden layer, $W^{(1)}$. Then the output of the neurodes in the hidden layer is given by the sigmoidal activation function, $f(E^{(1)})$. $E^{(2)}$ is given by the product of the hidden layer state and the weight matrix $W^{(2)}$. The forward pass is completed with the calculation of the output of the network by putting $E^{(2)}$ through the activation function.

If the difference between the target and the actual network output is less than some tolerance, the network has responded correctly for this presentation and the weights do not need to be adjusted. However, if the difference is not within the tolerance the weights need to be adjusted.

To compute the updated weights we first obtain $\delta^{(1)}$, the error gradient of the output element. This is done by taking the product of the (target-actual) and the derivative of the activation function.

The three element vector that is the error gradient on the hidden layer, $\delta^{(1)}$, is computed next. A "for" loop is used with one pass for each neurode. When computing $\delta^{(1)}$, the target for the hidden layer is not known. To compensate for this $\delta^{(2)}$ is "back-propagated", moderated by the weight between a hidden layer neurode and the output neurode.

With all the δ terms known, the corrections to the weights and the updated weights can be calculated. Nested "for" loops are used to reference each element in $W^{(1)}$ and $\Delta W^{(1)}$. The correction, $\Delta W^{(1)}$, is proportional to the last correction and to the product of $\delta^{(1)}$ with the activation level of the unit that feeds it. The new weight, $W_{ij}^{(1)}$, is equal to the old weight plus the correction, $\Delta W^{(1)}$. This process is then repeated for the second layer of weights with the use of a single "for" loop as $W^{(2)}$ is a three by one matrix.

At the bottom of the loop the last weight change matrix and the current weight change matrix are compared. If they are identical the network has learned the mapping to within the desired tolerance level and the loop is broken. Otherwise control is passed back to the top of the loop and the process is repeated.

SUMMARY

This tutorial paper has described only a few basic concepts in neural networks. The particular paradigm of back propagation has been illustrated by a specialized program to solve the boolean exclusive or function. More general purpose tools are commercially available to develop neural networks using a variety of paradigms. Some provide for interactive specification of network topology, starting weights, activation functions, and/or learning rules (AI Expert 1988).

REFERENCES

AI Expert, vol. 3, no. 8 (August 1988.)

Parker, D. 1982. "Learning Logic." Invention report, S81-64, File 1, Office of Technology Licensing, Stanford University.

Rosenblatt, F. 1962. *Principles of Neurodynamics*, Spartan Books, Washington, DC.

Rumelhart, D., McClelland, J., and the PDP Research Group. 1986. *Parallel Distributed Processing: Explorations in the Microstructure of Cognition.* MIT Press, Cambridge, MA.

Sejnowski, T.J., and Lehky, S.R., "Neural Network Models of Visual Processing", Society of Neuroscience, (1987).

Werbos, P. 1974. "Beyond regression: New tools for prediction and analysis in the behavioral sciences." Ph.D. Thesis, Harvard University.

Widrow, B. 1962. "Generalization and Information Storage in Networks of ADALINE 'Neurons'," *Self-Organizing Systems*, ed. by M. C. Yovits, G. T. Jacobi, and G. D. Goldstein. Spartan Books, Washington D.C., pp 435-461.

ADDITIONAL BIBLIOGRAPHY

Anderson, J.A., and Rosenfield, E. (Eds.) 1988. *Neurocomputing: Foundations of Research*. MIT Press, Cambridge, MA.

Carpenter, G.A. and Grossberg, S. (Eds.) 1987. *Applied Optics: Special Issue on Neural Networks*. Volume 26, December 1.

Hopfield, J. J. 1982. "Neural Networks and Physical Systems with Collective Computational Abilities." *Proceedings of the National Academy of Sciences, USA*, v. 79 (April 1982) 2554-2558.

Kohonen, T. 1984. *Self-Organization and Associative Memory*. Springer-Verlag, Berlin.

Kohonen, T. 1980. *Content-Addressable Memories*. Springer-Verlag, Berlin.

Widrow, B. and S. D. Stearns 1985. *Adaptive Signal Processing*. Prentice Hall, Englewood Cliffs, NJ.

Advances in AI and Simulation
© 1989 By The Society for Computer
Simulation International
ISBN 0-911801-50-2

AI and simulation improve the system development and operations process

C. J. Golden
Ford Aerospace Corporation
1260 Crossman Avenue
Sunnyvale, CA 94089

ABSTRACT

An AI based modeling approach has been developed that allows a system to be simulated throughout all phases of its life and allows this simulation to be the basis of automated operations in the field. This approach provides the capability to assess changes made during one phase of the program on the system design as well as the ability to evaluate the impact on other phases of the program.

An example is provided that shows how this simulator can be developed and used as a vehicle for transfer of information from one phase of system development to another. Once the simulator has been developed, the person using it to perform trade studies or support operations can often describe actions performed in an algorithmic format. These algorithms can be programmed as "reasoning modules" that operate on the same simulator that the person used when performing the task manually. Therefore, this AI/simulation approach allows the developer/operator to gain insight into all phases of a system's lifetime, as well as provides a way to efficiently automate many of the development/ operations activities.

INTRODUCTION - THE SYSTEM DEVELOPMENT PROCESS

The development of a new or modified system begins with an analysis of mission requirements. Existing and planned systems are evaluated in terms of how well they meet new requirements and deficiencies are documented. Although the funding agency must complete this analysis before it can issue an RFP for a system or systems to correct these deficiencies, the contractors must also be able to perform this analysis so they can determine which system requirements are strong drivers to satisfying mission requirements and which are just "nice to have". The trade studies that determine which system design and operational approach is best in satisfying a set of system requirements cannot be effectively performed without a thorough knowledge of the mission requirements and operational environments involved.

Cost must be considered during the system design and operational approach trades made to determine the "best" system. Requirements are decomposed and functional block diagrams are developed. Usually functions are allocated to existing systems whenever possible to reduce costs. Also new systems are composed of existing hardware and software as much as possible to keep costs low. New development is identified and plans made to produce the new capability with the least amount of risk to system performance and support. Once the desired system is described functionally and components have been identified and sized for implementation, development proceeds, followed by test and implementation into the larger system. At this point logistic support and operational approaches derived during the mission analysis and system design phases are tested and implemented. Figure 1 shows the basic phases in the system development process. Once a new system is deployed, modifications must be made to it to accommodate new mission or operational requirements. These modifications follow the same processing the existing system as a baseline for comparison.

IMPROVEMENTS NEEDED IN INFORMATION TRANSFER

There are a wide variety of tools available to support the development process; however, they do not normally interface with each other so information from one phase of system development can be automatically transferred and used in other phases of development or operation. For example, system requirements are normally derived by modeling all facets of the mission and then applying a series of scenarios to the model to see what system performance is required to meet mission objectives. Quite often a number of independent mission specific models are used for the trade studies. Results are evaluated and an A spec is produced manually that documents system requirements. The design phase, which follows, allocates functions to hardware, software personnel and documentation, and determines system interface criteria. The B specs which result document the result of trades made to accommodate operational considerations, such as logistics support and maintenance. These trades are done using independent, models and are specific to the application. By the time the engineer using CAD/CASE tools receives the specifications, most information that went into all the trade studies required to produce the A and B specs is not readily available. Therefore the sensitivity of the final detailed system design to changes in scenario or other mission parameters cannot easily be evaluated. Similarly, when operators want to do something unplanned with the system, they should be able to easily evaluate the impact on the system and the mission. The information allowing such an evaluation was available during the requirements definition/preliminary design phases but is normally not available to the operator. Information available in one phase of the process should be available for all other phases of the process so existing tools can be used more effectively by the developer/operator.

AI - SIMULATION SOLUTION

An AI-simulation approach is being developed by Ford Aerospace that allows information applicable to one phase of the system lifetime to be accessed and used in other phases. This approach allows a developer/operator to evaluate consequences of changes on the total program, not only the small segment being addressed. The key to the approach is a flexible knowledge representation system that allows physical, conceptual and environmental entities or elements to

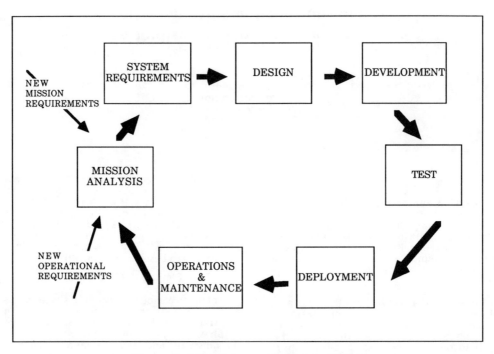

Figure 1. Basic Phases In System Development Process

be related in anyway the user chooses. Attributes and behavior are also defined by the user. The resultant knowledge base captures the same descriptive and process information that many rule-based systems contain. However it does not mix domain behavior with control processes. Figure 2 presents the way knowledge is stored in the simulator which can be used as a knowledge base for an expert system.

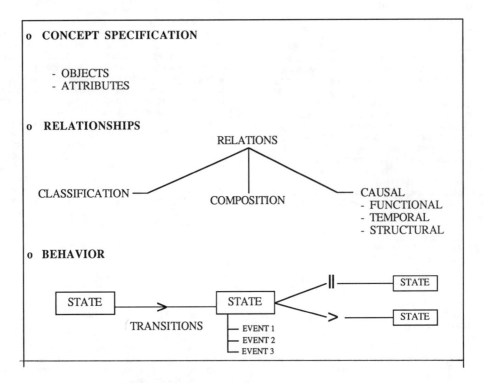

Figure 2. The Knowledge Representation System

After the domain has been described in the appropriate representation format, (i. e., modeled), simulations are run to validate that the performance is as expected or to see what characteristics of the elements involved still need to be changed before expected performance can be achieved. Sensitivity to changes in the model can be evaluated by noting the impact of changing attributes or behavior associated with any element on other domain elements. If the domain is a system that needs to be controlled once it is operational, then the knowledge base/simulator that is developed during the design process can be used to automate operations later. All that needs to be added is a "reasoning module" that approaches an analysis of the domain to accomplish a function much like a human would. The reasoning module could contain rules or an application specific algorithm, but generic reasoning processes, like causal diagnosis and resource planning are more useful.

During the development process, the "reasoning" performed by an engineer on the simulator/knowledge base to perform trade studies, define system interfaces, derive costs or other such functions can often be documented as algorithms. These algorithms can then be programmed to use the simulator/ knowledge base automatically and much of the routine effort associated with systems development can be automated. An example would be minimizing the cost of a system design. Cost models are available that provide estimates based on various fixed system parameters. The reasoning that an engineer applies during the trades to reduce costs while still meeting system requirements can often be automated once the engineer has worked with the domain model and the cost models manually for a while so he can describe his adjustment approach in logical terms.

KNOWLEDGE BASE TRANSFER EXAMPLE

An example of building an autonomous satellite system is provided to illustrate the concepts discussed above. From a total systems point of view, each satellite in the total constellation, the constellation with its data links, outside communication links, the ground links for health and status and mission control and the user of the mission data must be described in the knowledge base so trades on their performance characteristics can be performed to produce a "survivable" system. One of the many trades will determine how many functions will be performed on board the satellite in space. For example, it is relatively easy to put enough propellant on board for 6 months operations, if you know what will be performed over those 6 months. But what if an unexpected situation arises? How do you want the satellite to behave in this case? By varying the scenarios, the designers can determine what planned and unplanned situations the satellite should be able to handle autonomously and therefore how much propellant, as well as other resources, is needed.

Once the satellite's functional requirements have been established, the preliminary design can proceed. We have found that most companies reuse prior subsystem designs as much as possible. Therefore, the knowledge base built for a prior satellite subsystem can be "reused" and modified as required for the new satellite design. The designer can analyze the impact of adding and deleting functions to the basic system and how specific component failures impact the operations and maintenance functions. Therefore, levels of redundancy can be established and justified.

From these top level trades, a simulator, or model, of the satellite emerges. By accessing programs that derive component size and cost from existing or parametric data bases, total cost can be estimated. This process is summarized in the Prototyping Lab Section in Figure 3. The simulation/model knowledge base is so constructed that all the tools on the network can access the information and use it for further system development and documentation. If performance is not as expected at any point in the process, the actual results can be fed back into the simulator and total system impact evaluated. This capability is particularly important if new components must be substituted for those originally planned. The impact on operations and logistic support must be evaluated as well as on mission performance.

The simulation/model knowledge base is particularly important to the integration and test process since the system prototype it represents can be combined with existing systems (or models of them) and interface problems or operational problems identified before the detailed design phase starts.

The model (i. e., knowledge base) of the satellite can be tested just as the actual hardware is tested and therefore validated as a simulator. Figure 4 shows that the simulator of the satellite can be used during the design, development and test phases for trade studies and to simulate operations in a test bed. However, what is unique about this simulator is that reasoning modules can be added to it and the resultant AI system can be used first as a training and rehearsal aid before launch, second as an operator's aid in diagnosing and correcting satellite anomalies, third as an automated aid in situations where experts are not available and the system has been sufficiently validated, and finally as a basis for on-board autonomous operations in next-generation satellites.

SUMMARY

The key to information transfer between all phases of a system's development and operation is a properly constructed representation of the domain. The representation must allow interfaces to outside simulators to send and receive data as needed. It must be generic enough to be able to interface with the wide-variety of CAD/CASE tools available. It must be easy to change and document and have a graphics display that is easy to develop and use. Ford Aerospace has developed such a representation approach and is in the process of implementing it in various phases of the system development process.

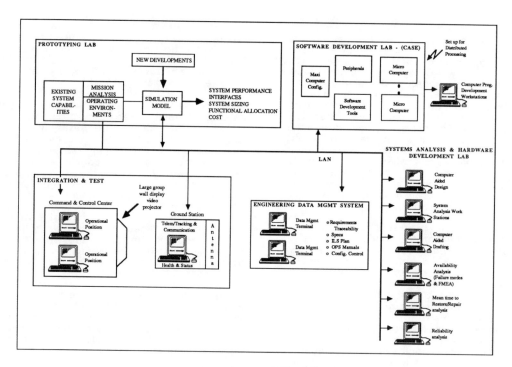

Figure 3. Integrated Tool Chest

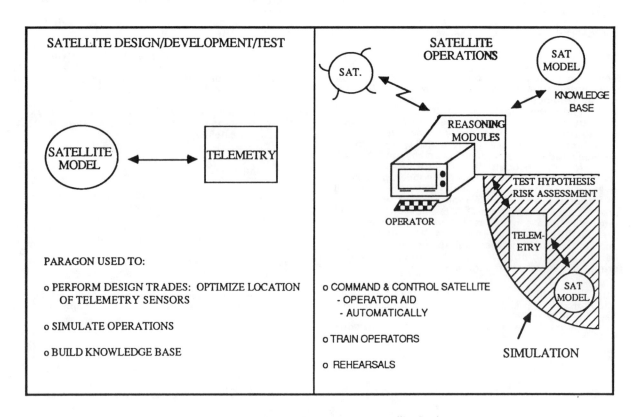

Figure 4. Operational Aid Evolves From Satellite Design

236

Advances in AI and Simulation
© 1989 By The Society for Computer
Simulation International
ISBN 0-911801-50-2

Configuration of automated electronic assembly systems using simulation

Detlef M. Weber
and
Colin L. Moodie
School of Industrial Engineering
Purdue University
West Lafayette,IN 47907

ABSTRACT

Many industrial companies are considering the implementation of automated manufacturing and assembly systems. The capital investment for these systems tends to be very high and an incorrect configuration of the system can prove to be very expensive. This has led management to require extensive planning processes before making a decision about an automation project.

At the end of this planning and design phase, the engineers of the design team have to prevail upon management the quality of their work and the advantages of the proposed system for the company. They have to justify their design under criteria such as cost, cost per product and return on investment. It is very difficult to predict the costs and the return on investment at that stage of planning and the engineers may be forced to make predictions and promises the implemented system cannot hold.

Simulation can provide the information for the economic justification of the automated manufacturing or assembly system. It can answer the managerial questions concerning cost and returns on investment.

INTRODUCTION

Many industrial companies are considering the implementation of automated manufacturing and assembly systems. The capital investment for these systems tends to be very high and an incorrect configuration of the system can prove to be very expensive. This has led management to require extensive planning processes before making a decision about an automation project.

Computer simulation has evolved into a very valuable tool for engineers in the process of designing the automated system. For example, simulation can be used to evaluate a system design, to compare different designs or to detect bottlenecks or problem aspects of a system. There are various other ways to apply simulation in the design of manufacturing or assembly systems.

The final step of every design phase for an automated manufacturing or assembly system is the presentation to the management of the company. The engineers of the design team must prevail upon the management the quality of their work and the advantages of the proposed system for the company.

This is a difficult situation for the engineers on the design team. Until this point, they have been involved with questions of technical feasibility, of manufacturing organization, material flow control, etc. Now they have to justify their design under criteria such as cost, cost per product and return on investment. In many cases, the management will not be satisfied with the results of their answers and will request more information and planning to achieve a better economic justification. The engineers may be forced to make predictions and promises that the implemented system cannot accommodate. This will diminish the standing of the engineers in the company and affect their careers.

We believe computer simulation can help in this stage of the planning and design of a manufacturing system. The simulation can provide the information for the economic justification of the automated manufacturing or assembly system. Simulation can answer the managerial questions concerning cost and return on investment.

In this paper, a computer simulation of an electronic device assembly facility is described. The objective of the simulation was to determine the optimal system configuration for the assembly task. The comparison of the alternative system configurations had to include engineering criteria in addition to the cost aspect.

A TYPICAL SITUATION

The management of a large company was considering automating the assembly of a product in their plant. Three other lines had been automated at an earlier time with varied degrees of success. The management had asked the engineer in charge to design a basic system configuration for this new automation project. The management wanted to know whether the different levels of success with the three lines was due to the varied system configurations of these three lines or due to other reasons like bad implementation, failure rate of the machinery, etc.

The engineer in charge had developed a basic system design for the new automated assembly line. The system configuration was similar to the configuration of the most modern automated assembly line. Still, the management and the corporate level remained hesitant. They requested more information and a thorough comparison of the three existing lines before deciding on the new automation project.

At this stage, the management and the engineer in charge decided to conduct a simulation study. The objective of the study was to compare the three existing automated assembly lines and other possible system configurations.

BACKGROUND

The company assembles electronic components in molded boxes as suppliers for other companies. The products are low cost items and there is considerable competition on the market. Each assembly line assembles a group of very similar products. The average batch size is 1,000 to 3,000 products.

About 60 to 80 assembly and testing operations are required for the assembly of one product and about 20 to 30 vibratory bowl feeders with picking devices feed the parts to the assembly devices. Some assembly devices place parts on the product, others fasten or solder the parts or perform miscellaneous operations (vacuum). At the end of the line a group of work stations adjust and test the assembled product.

A short investigation of the three existing automated assembly lines showed the configuration of the three lines differs in three aspects:
- the most modern line is a modularized, parallel line,

the other two are sequential lines,
- the most modern line has large buffers between the modules, the other two don't,
- the most modern line uses indexed rotary tables for the material transport in some modules, the other two use belt conveyors.

The two older automated assembly lines are identical in their general system configuration. Therefore, the comparison was limited to only two of the existing lines, the modularized, parallel and one sequential line.

The sequential line consists of 30 assembly work stations and 12 adjustment and testing work stations. The work stations are lined up along a belt conveyor. 24 vibratory bowl feeders provide parts to the assembly processes. The work stations operate upon the arrival of a tray with a half assembled product on it. The conveyor is controlled with a Programmable Logic Controller (PLC). Up to three trays with half assembled products can wait on the belt conveyor in front of a work station awaiting processing. Figure 1 shows the configuration of this line.

The parallel, modularized line consists of 47 assembly work stations and 11 adjustment and testing work stations. The center module consists of a belt conveyor, 30 work stations and 12 vibratory bowl feeders with a picking mechanism. Modules two and three assemble two sub-assemblies. The second module has 10 work stations and 5 vibratory bowl feeders. The sub-assembly is inserted to the center module at work station 14 of the center module. The third module has 8 work stations and 3 vibratory bowl feeders. The sub-assembly is inserted into the center module at work station 15. The fourth module, the testing module, receives the assembled products from work station 30 of the center module and tests them in 10 work stations. The material flow of the three sub-modules is performed by indexed rotary tables. One maintenance technician repairs and restarts down work stations. Three refill operators refeed empty vibratory bowl feeders and perform refeed operations for defective parts. Assembly devices and vibratory bowl feeders are equipped with sensors. The sensors check whether the assembly operation (assembly sensor) or the part picking operation (picking sensor) was correctly performed. If a picking error is detected, the part is abandoned and a new part loaded from the vibratory bowl feeder. If the assembly sensor detects an assembly error, it marks the tray bad. The assembly will be removed at the end of the line. The buffers between the modules can hold up to 100 subassemblies and between 0 and 3 products can wait in front of a work station for processing. Figure 2 shows the configuration of this line.

SIMULATION MODELS

We chose the modern, modularized assembly line as a reference model for our comparison. The number of work stations, the assembly times and the other data from this line were used to model the different system configurations. Five different simulation models were implemented.

Each model represents one system configuration. Model A represents the modern, modularized assembly line and serves as reference model for the comparison. Model A is shown in Figure 1.

Model B represents the system configuration for the older, sequential line. The work station data and other system specifications were taken from the reference model (modern, modularized line). This was necessary to make a comparison possible. Model B is shown in Figure 2.

Three additional models were designed and implemented. Model C tests the effect of decoupling buffers in a sequential line, model D tests the effect of refeed loops for rejected assemblies for the sequential line and model E tests the effects of refeed loops for the modularized line.

Model C represents a sequential line with three work-in-process buffers, similar to the sequential line (model B). The three buffers are inserted at stations 20, 35 and 45. The buffers have a decoupling effect. Model A has also three buffers but the modules operate in a parallel mode (The modules assemble sub-assemblies in parallel to the assembly of the main assembly). Module C operates in sequential mode. The first 20 assembly steps are performed on stations 1 to 20 in the first module. Then the assembly is fed as a whole to the next module and the next assembly steps are performed. This model was included to test the decoupling effect of buffers in general without the influence of the parallel operation. Model C is shown in Figure 3.

Model D again represents a sequential line similar to model B. Half-automatic refeed loops for defective assemblies have been added to the sequential line in this model. A common problem in automated assembly is the high number of assembly errors at assembly work stations (error rates from 1% to 10%). The assembly sensors in the existing lines detect these errors. Most rejects occur at a few work stations. Most of the half-finished assemblies are not destroyed and can be reentered at the work station of failure. In the existing systems, this is done manually at the end of a batch. The reinsertion work requires much time and labor. Currently, the overall reject rate for the modern, modularized line is 5 to 20%. Industrial experience with assembly lines showed that it is better to remove the defective assemblies after the erroneous operation and to reinsert it without an interruption operation.

This strategy is modeled in model D. The assembly sensor will remove the defective assembly right after the erroneous operation and place it on a waiting loop. From time to time a human operator will remove the defective parts, check the part and decide about its state. If the assembly can be reworked he will free it for reinsertion. An automatic insertion mechanism will put the assembly back into the line when there is space available in the input buffer of the work station. Figure 4 shows a schematic model of half-automatic refeed loop.

Model E models the same kind of refeed loops for the modularized line (model A).

SIMULATION EXPERIMENT

The SLAM II simulator by Pritsker & Associates was used for this simulation study. The software was operating on a IBM compatible PC/AT computer. A simple network model was implemented in SLAM II. Some Fortran subroutines were written and combined with the SLAM network to adapt the basic model to the specifics of the assembly task. The SLAM II network model is shown in Figure 5.

The main module of the SLAM II model represents one of the work stations. The entities, representing the assemblies are entered at a CREATE node whenever there is a space available on the belt conveyor. The first ATTRIBUTE of the entity specifies the next assembly process for this assembly. In the EVENT 1, a Fortran routine will read a file and identify the data for this assembly process (assembly time, transport time, and the number of the vibratory bowl feeder). The entity will occupy its place on the conveyor (acquire the RESOURCE transport) and will be transported to the work station. The transportation time is between 2 and 6 seconds. If the work station is operating on another assembly, it will wait on the conveyor. If the work station is available, the assembly will free the conveyor space and will be loaded into the work station (acquire the RESOURCE work station X with X being the number of the work station). The work station will process the assembly. with an operation time from 2 to 6 seconds. After the process, the assembly will occupy a place on the next section of the conveyor (if available) and free the work station. A Fortran function will determine randomly whether the assembly process has been erroneous or successful. This function basically models the assembly sensor. The entity will be passed back to EVENT 1 and will read the data for the next process from the data file. The whole process will be repeated on this entity until all operations have been performed. The entity will leave the system via a COLLECT node. The COLLECT node counts the number of finished assemblies and the average time in the system for these assemblies.

A second module of the SLAM II network models the vibratory bowl feeder. When the entity passes through EVENT 1, the data file will specify the connected vibratory bowl feeder. It will identify the feeder by its number or return a zero for no feeder. If a feeder is connected, the assembly will send a clone of itself to the vibratory bowl feeder module. The module will check whether the requested parts are available and will load them into the picking device. A Fortran function will randomly define picked parts to be erroneous (feeder sensor). When both the clone and the assembly arrive at the MATCH node (the original entity from the conveyor and the clone from the picking device), the assembly operation will be performed. At the end of this operation, the clone is eliminated in the ACCUMULATE node.

Three other modules model the refill operators, the work station break downs and the refeed loops (for models D and E).

The break down module randomly defines work stations to be down. This will trigger a request for the maintenance technician. If the RESOURCE maintenance technician is available, it will be scheduled, and after a random time the work station will be reset to operate. The RESOURCE maintenance technician is then freed.

The refill operators are modeled as RESOURCE with a capacity of three. Whenever a vibratory bowl feeder runs empty, a refill operation will be scheduled. A RESOURCE "refill operator", with a capacity of one is requested and acquired. After a random time, the supply for the part is reset to full load (400) and the RESOURCE refill operator is then freed. A similar process takes place if the refeed module requests an operator to check a the rejected assemblies in a refeed loop.

The refeed functions are modeled as a continuous loop. An EVENT node is checking the queues of rejected assemblies at the refeed functions in defined time intervals. If a queue at one work station has reached a length of more than 3 assemblies, the function will schedule a checking operation. A refill operator is requested from the RESOURCE of refill operators. The refill operator checks the assemblies and discards 10 to 20% of the parts because they cannot be reworked. The other assemblies are released to the reinsertion queue for being reinserted into the line.

All five models are tested for eight hours of simulated operation. Every hour a SUMMARY REPORT is created by the simulator showing the progress of operation and the measured data. Most of the data about RESOURCES, ACTIVITIES, FILES and variables are automatically collected by the simulator. The COLLECT node counts the entities that are finished and collects the information concerning them. Two additional Fortran routines collect the down times and the blocking due to part shortages. The two routines write the times to standard files.

An additional test was performed to evaluate the importance of the refill operators. In this test the initial part capacity of the vibratory bowl feeders was set very high. Therefore, no refill operation was required during the eight hours of simulated operation. The objective was to determine the effects of a parts shortage in the vibratory bowl feeder.

TEST RESULTS

The standard SUMMARY REPORTS of SLAM II produce a large volume of data. For the time-persistent variables, RESOURCES, FILES, ACTIVITIES and COLLECT nodes several data like minimum value, maximum value, current value, average value, standard deviation, number of observations etc. are returned.

In the model we used 58 time-persistent variables, 10 FILES, 9 ACTIVITIES and 62 RESOURCES. Each hourly SUMMARY REPORT had a length of 5 pages. The problem is to identify and extract the relevant information from this data volume and to match them to the model. In the study, 10 data types provided significant information for the comparison:

- THROUGHPUT. The COLLECT node provided the number of assemblies that had finished the assembly process successfully.
- LEAD TIME. The COLLECT node also provided the average time the assemblies had stayed in the system.
- ASSEMBLY REJECTS. For each work station the number of rejected assemblies were counted in a time-persistent variable.
- PART PICKING REJECT. For each vibratory bowl feeder, the number of rejected picking processes were counted in a time-persistent variable.
- NUMBER OF REFILL OPERATIONS. The number of refill operations were counted in an ACTIVITY (only the times that the bowl feeder ran empty).
- UTILIZATION OF WORK STATIONS. The RESOURCE statistics provided the work station utilization.
- UTILIZATION OF REFILL OPERATORS. The statistic for the RESOURCE refill operator measured the average utilization of the operators.
- UTILIZATION OF MAINTENANCE TECHNICIAN. The statistic for the RESOURCE maintenance technician measured his utilization.
- BUFFER QUEUES. The statistic for the FILES provided the average queue length, the maximal queue length and the average waiting time in the queue for the buffers between the modules.
- NUMBER OF REFEEDED ASSEMBLIES. For the models D and E, an ACTIVITY counted the number of assemblies reinserted into the assembly line.

Two more data were collected in separate files with Fortran functions. The first file collected the cumulative down time for each work station and the second file collected the cumulative empty time for each vibratory bowl feeder.

Some of these data need interpretation or computation to be meaningful. The utilization of the work stations can be used for identifying the bottlenecks and for measuring the overall performance of the system. For the evaluation of the overall performance the average utilization for all work station is more meaningful. The data part picking rejects, rejected assemblies, break down times and empty times are collected for each work station or bowl vibratory feeder. Again, the average value for each of these must be computed.

The resulting set of information would have been sufficient for most engineering applications. In our case an economic evaluation and comparison of the different system configurations was required, too.

The two data types, lead time and throughput, provided some indication for the economic performance of the different system configurations. Still, they do not provide sufficient information. Better throughput and lead time are not advantageous at all if achieved through higher cost. We found that the simulation had provided sufficient data to compute the material cost and the labor cost per product.

The computation of the labor cost per product is very simple. It is the sum of the cost for the maintenance technician and the refill operators for the time of operation divided by the throughput.

The computation of the material cost is more complex. The material cost consists of three components: the cost for rejected parts, for rejected assemblies and for finished assemblies. The cost of rejected parts is the sum of the number of rejects multiplied with the value of the parts. The reject data are collected for every vibratory bowl feeder, so an exact computation of the cost is possible even if the parts have different values. The cost of rejected assemblies is the sum of the costs of parts already assembled on these rejected assemblies. The reject data were collected for all work stations, again an exact computation is possible. Finally, the material value for finished products is the cumulative value of the parts in it. The sum of these three data is divided by the throughput and the material cost of a product is returned.

In a similar way, the investment costs per product and the miscellaneous cost per product could be computed. Miscellaneous cost contains components like energy cost, cost for operation materials like machine oil, administrative cost etc.

The most important simulation returns and computed data are summarized in Figure 6. In the next section, the results will be interpreted.

An additional test was performed for model B with an inexhaustible supply of parts in the vibratory bowl feeders. The objective of this experiment was to determine the influence of the part shortages on the throughput. The throughput increased approximately 50%.

EVALUATION

The most significant figure is throughput. For the modularized line model A, the throughput is significantly higher than for the sequential line (model B). The sequential, modularized line (model C) shows again a significant advantage over the sequential line (model B) but does not reach the performance of model A. This proves our theory. Both aspects, modularized configuration (buffers) and parallel operation of modules, contribute to the performance advantage. The reasons can be explained easily. The modules of the modularized system can continue to operate if one of the modules is blocked by a break down or a parts shortage (decoupling effect). The parallel operation of three of the modules (central, subassembly 1 and subassembly 2) reduces the lead time of the assembly operation and also the time for a changeover.

The reduction of changeover time is particularly important for assembly lines operating small size (100 - 1,000 parts) and medium size (1,000 - 10,000 parts) batches. A changeover requires the operators to wait until all parts of the batch have left the system: then, they perform the setup changes and restart the system. During this unloading and startup time the majority of work stations are idle for several minutes and capacity is unused. In model A, the parallel processing of three modules allows parallel unloading and restarting at three locations and, therefore, produces less idle times for the work stations. This effect can be observed in the simulations of models A and C. Model A with parallel operation gains a lead over model C with a sequential modularized operation in the first hour (10% better) and keeps, but does not expand, this advantage until the end of the eight hour period.

The refeed loops also demonstrated a significant impact on throughput. The two models with refeed loops (model D and E) showed again, significantly better results than their counterparts without refeed loops.

Another significant figure is the material cost per assembly. The relative number of rejects (ratio of rejected to good products per time interval) is about the same for all five models. However, this is a misleading figure. In the modular model, a reject of a product involves less material and less finished assembly steps than in the sequential system. For example, if work station 45 rejects an assembly 45 assembly steps and 24 components are lost for the sequential model but only 10 assembly steps and 5 components are lost in the modularized system. In the modularized parallel model, the work stations 36 to 45 assemble only a subassembly and not the entire product. As a result, the material costs for the modularized line are smaller than the material cost for the sequential or the sequential modularized line.

Not surprisingly, the labor cost per product is better for the modularized, parallel model compared to the two sequential models. The labor costs are the same for all models but the throughput for the modularized, parallel model is the highest.

The lead time for the modularized model is better than for the sequential models. The reason for this lies in the parallel operation of the modules and in the reduction of waiting times due to breakdowns and part shortages.

Machine utilization is also higher for the modular models. This indicates good performance because it matches with high throughput. If the throughput would be low and the utilization high, this would indicate that the utilization is a consequence of blocking.

CONCLUSION

The simulation study has provided the necessary information for engineering evaluation as well as for managerial decision making. Exact cost, throughput and lead time data showed that the performance of the modularized, parallel model is superior in its performance to the sequential and the modularized sequential model. The combination of high throughput and low cost proved that the performance of the parallel modularized system was achieved by better organization of the assembly process. The advantages of the modular approach are, in particular, significant in systems with frequent setup changes. Other data such as utilization data about work stations and transport system or queue data provide information that can be useful for optimization and improvement.

Also, it was shown that it might be of interest to consider refeed loops at work stations with a high reject rate. Normally it is not possible to consider this in the design of a new line because it is very difficult to identify reject locations without running the system. Therefore, a new assembly line should be designed in an adaptable way to allow the implementation of refeed loops when needed.

It could be the objective for several other simulation studies to determine the optimal number of modules, the optimal size of modules and the material flow system for each module. The criteria for these evaluations would be investment, throughput, setup and startup time, break down rate, operation cost, reject rates and, of course, the design of the product.

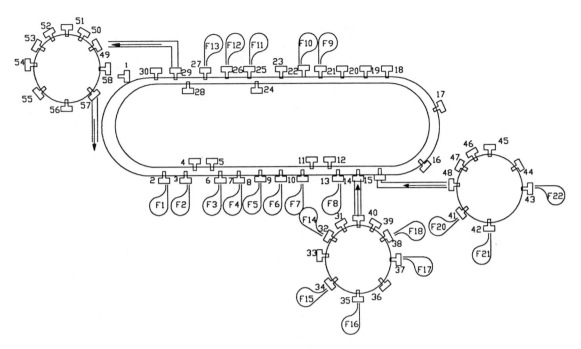

Figure 1. Modularized System Configuration

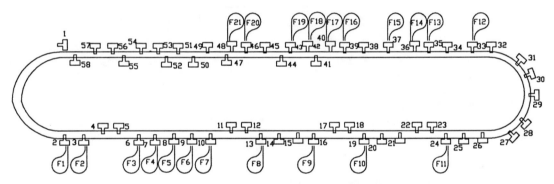

Figure 2. Sequential System Configuration

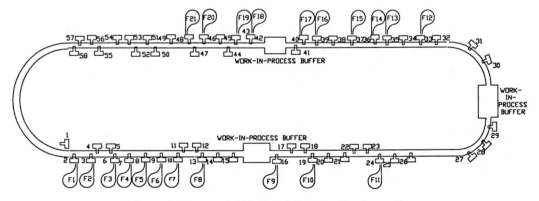

Figure 3. Sequential Buffered System Configuration

241

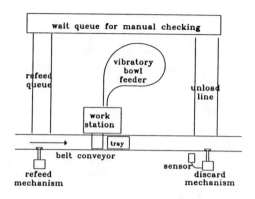

Figure 4. Refeed Loop

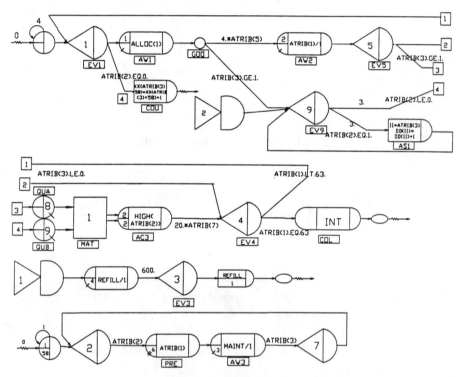

Figure 5. SLAM II Network

MODEL	THROUGH PUT	AVERAGE MACHINE UTILIZAT	AVERAGE LEAD TIME	NUMBER OF REJECTED ASSEMBLIES	NUMBER OF REJECTED PARTS	NUMBER OF REFEEDED ASSEMBLIES	MATERIAL COST PER PRODUCT	BLOCKING DUE TO MISS PARTS	AVERAGE DOWN TIME PER MACHINE	LABOR COST PER PRODUCT
A	1887	0.677	552	2582	972	0	47.37	5.4	6.38	38.16
B	1403	0.636	924	2823	799	0	50.64	5.9	6.11	51.32
C	1747	0.620	746	2559	981	0	48.81	5.5	6.32	41.21
D	1854	0.634	815	2169	852	842	47.88	6.0	5.84	38.83
E	1987	0.686	516	2451	920	920	47.34	6.4	5.83	36.60

Figure 6. Test Results

Advances in AI and Simulation
© 1989 By The Society for Computer
Simulation International
ISBN 0-911801-50-2

Simulation of Telephone Traffic for a
Real-Time Network Control Expert System

Michael St. Jacques and Delano Stevens

GTE
P. O. Box 290152
Temple Terrace, Florida 33687-0152

Abstract

A prototype simulation of traffic flow in the public telephone voice network is presented. The simulation generates telephone-switch performance statistics which are normally available in this type of network from live periodic switch reports. These performance statistics are being used in lieu of live data to exercise a real-time network management expert system. It was most important for the simulation to generate realistic data during periods with abnormally high traffic or under other unusual conditions. It was also known that the call activity for this type of model would normally be extremely high. To improve performance during calling overloads a simulation method called Event Grouping (EG) was devised in which call holding times were fixed allowable values corresponding to multiples of a constant integer time step. Evaluation of the EG method was accomplished by comparing generated results with a base-line model using a standard event-driven method. The simulation effort was begun in Prolog but abandoned because of problems with excessive memory use and inadequate performance. C was selected as an alternate and found to be extremely easy to use even for incorporation of expert heuristics into the model. A new method of approximating traffic rates for large trunk groups and a visual technique to curve fit calling pattern data were developed. The results of this study show that the EG method has little effect on model generated statistics and tends to improve performance under adverse network conditions.

Introduction

Despite recent introduction of central computer data collection and monitoring systems, managing the public telephone voice network today is a labor intensive process requiring high levels of expertise. In the belief that artificial intelligence techniques could improve this situation, a study was initiated by GTE in January, 1987 to investigate the feasibility of monitoring and controlling the public telephone voice network with real-time expert systems.

A small, rapid-prototype expert system with network management software and presentation displays (Kosieniak et al, 1988 and St. Jacques, 1988) was completed in June, 1987, and was met with enthusiastic support. A more extensive feasibility prototype was then begun which was designed to manage a portion of the metropolitan Tampa, FL network including 16 very active switches of various sizes, types and business-residential mix. It was not realistic to use the actual network during development because the switches could not be controlled to produce adverse conditions required to drive the expert system. Therefore, it was decided to create a computer model of network traffic. Recent reports on combining simulation and expert system technologies (Moser 1986 and O'Keefe and Roach 1987) added encouragement to the effort.

A major goal of the expert system was to sense the existence of potentially adverse, abnormal events, evaluate these events and correct them as soon as possible. Examples include radio contests or news events where a sudden flood of traffic saturates the network or isolates portions of it thereby impairing service to higher priority calls. Another example is a natural disaster which affects network equipment and pushes traffic levels dangerously high. These events and subsequent network performance in turn affect customer calling patterns. On a trunk which is experiencing severe cross-talk or static, holding times diminish significantly as calls are abandoned after a few seconds and retried. An increase in traffic is experienced as the result of a network difficulty. Therefore, it was decided to include expert heuristics in the simulation to accommodate these changes in customer calling patterns resulting from degraded network performance (i.e. an intelligent model).

It was known that call activity for this type of simulation would be extremely high during peak times and possibly worse during abnormal periods. Alone, the 16 switch Tampa sub-network would be responsible for normal peak traffic on the order of 300,000 calls per hour and much larger networks were ultimately to become simulation targets. Therefore, a number of performance improvement ideas were considered, but only one technique survived cursory evaluation. This method was named Event Grouping (EG) and is believed to be original and newly presented here. It involves restricting the possible call holding times to discrete integer values, all multiples of a constant simulation time-step and placing a limit on the maximum call holding time.

Two efforts were begun. One of these efforts, which is the focus of this paper, was aimed at determining the adequacy of network traffic statistics produced by the EG technique. This determination was accomplished with a small, easily evaluated symmetric network, by comparing EG results to statistics generated by a standard event-driven model (i.e. a theoretical model). The other effort (Mathis, 1989) handled the task of designing efficient code to implement the EG approach for the Tampa sub-network which would eventually drive the expert system. Although evaluation of the EG method for adequacy of results was the main thrust of the work some rough performance measures were made.

The remainder of this paper discusses the simplified network, normal calling patterns and the basis for the theoretical and EG methods. An unsuccessful Prolog implementation is presented followed by results and a summary. It is assumed that readers are familiar with Prolog and discrete-event simulation.

Simplified Network

A simplified, symmetric network devised to test simulation ideas is illustrated in Figure 1. This network consisted of 9 interconnected nodes labeled **A** through **I**, each representing a telephone switch (i.e. the device which connects customer telephones to the network). Eight switches were positioned on the perimeter with **E** in the center of the network

Network traffic consisted of telephone calls which originated at switches. Connections to other switches were made with trunks (circuits) which were logically gathered into trunk groups as they are in a real network. For example, the trunk group between

switches **A** and **B** contained 10 trunks and was called the **A-B** trunk group. A call required at least one trunk and a trunk handled a call in either direction, but not both simultaneously. Perimeter switches were directly connected to each neighbor switch and to the center switch **E**. To reach either neighbor switch, direct trunks were used but to reach non-neighboring switches calls were via-routed through **E**. Therefore, a call from **A** to **G** used a single trunk from both the **A-E** and **E-G** trunk groups.

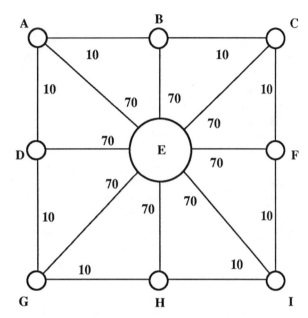

Figure 1. Simplified Network

Relative trunk group size was determined according to a postulated calling pattern which depended on the number of customers at each switch. In order to achieve the desired symmetry, it was established that each office, except **E**, would serve 10% of the total customers. Therefore, the 8 perimeter switches accounted for 80% of the total network's customers and 80% of the calls. The remaining 20% of the customers were connected to **E**.

At a given switch, the number of originating calls destined for another switch varied in accordance with the distribution of customers. For example, calls originating at **A** had a 10% probability of going to each perimeter switch and a 20% probability of going to **E**. Trunk groups from all perimeter offices to switch **E** also had to have enough trunks to handle calls which would via-route through **E**. The trunking configuration in Figure 1 accommodates this calling pattern.

Network Simulation

Telephone switches were simulated as non-queueing multi-server systems. Requests for service were telephone calls to other switches. The servers were trunks with the number of servers equal to the size of the trunk group. As a direct call was generated (e.g. from **A** to **B**), a single trunk was allocated for it and remained allocated (not usable by any other call) until the call ended. Calls via-routed through **E** were allocated two trunks. If the required trunks were unavailable at the required time, the call left the system unserviced. The service time of a call was its holding time (i.e. how long a customer would talk to another customer). The normal assumption of exponential service time was used (Mina, 1974). Call (event) generation was handled differently by each of the two simulations and will be discussed later.

Calling Pattern

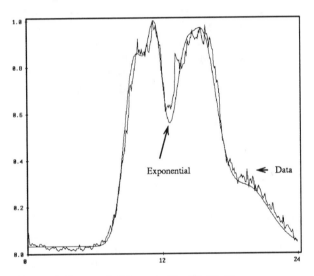

Figure 2. Dynamic Message Traffic Pattern.

In a real telephone network during a normal day, the message traffic pattern is dynamic. Figure 2 is a normalized representation showing actual calls originated throughout the day at a switch which services primarily business traffic. During the morning hours activity increases to a maximum which occurs at about 11:30 AM when people begin to leave for lunch. The lunchtime lull continues until about 1:30 PM when activity picks up again and builds to a second peak at about 2:30 PM. Then traffic diminishes during the rest of the afternoon. There is little activity during the evening hours on business phones. Residential trunks have a similar patterns.

Calling patterns were built into the models as a normalized, temporal load factor which was multiplied by a maximum traffic load. A set of exponential curves were developed and used to visually fit actual switch data with an equation thus allowing easy generation of a loading factor as a function of time. Figure 2 shows how well this curve fits the data.

Maximum Traffic Load

For maximum traffic :

$$E(n) = (m\rho) / E(ts) \qquad (1)$$

where $E(n)$ is the expected arrivals per unit time, ρ is the facility utilization, m is the number of servers and $E(ts)$ is the expected service time. For a non-queueing system ρ is calculated from the following:

$$P_b = [(m\rho)^m / m!] / \sum_{n=0}^{m} (m\rho)^n / n! \qquad (2)$$

where P_b is the blocking probability.

With trunking fixed (Figure 1), the number of calls generated at each switch to other switches ($E(n)$) was determined from a user input blocking probability and average holding time by solving (2) for ρ, then substituting ρ into (1). However, available tables for (2) were limited to fewer than the desired number of trunks (Network Career Advancement Institute, no date and Mina, 1974) Therefore, a tractable "trial and error" solution for ρ in (2) was created for large m which yielded acceptable results.

The Two Models

Both models consisted of a call generator, a routing algorithm and modules to keep track of trunk availability, compute statistics and increment time. Network management experts favor certain statistics over others (private communication and Bell Communications Research, 1987). Among the most important are trunk group percent occupancy (utilization) and the rates of attempts and connections. The models computed these statistics and reported them periodically. Options were available to model the entire simplified network or a single trunk group for which theoretical statistics were available. Also, the models could be run with a dynamic or constant traffic load. All code was written on a network of Sun Microsystems Workstations consisting of a Sun 3/260 which acted as a file server and two Sun 3/60 Workstations.

Theoretical Model

At the heart of this model was the "future-events chain," a term borrowed from the GPSS literature (Bobillier et al. 1976). The future-events chain was simply a list of yet to occur events which were ordered by the time at which they were scheduled to occur. The future-events chain was implemented as a linked list to allow easy merge/sorting of events as they were created. Only two types of events were required, call set-up and completion.

The simulation ran in the usual event-driven fashion. As an event was removed from the future-events chain and processed, time was incremented to the scheduled time of the next event on the chain. Therefore the time step was highly variable. During periods of relative inactivity, large time steps were common. During very busy periods, much smaller time steps were the rule. Time had to be implemented as a floating point variable to yield required accuracy.

If the encountered event was a call set-up, the route was determined and trunks allocated if possible. The call was then replaced on the future-events chain at its scheduled completion time to be removed when the simulation proceeded to that point. If no trunking was available the call was eliminated from further consideration with appropriate statistical updates. If the event was call-completion, the call was removed, trunks returned for use by other calls and appropriate statistics updated.

Five minutes (simulation time) was selected as a convenient time to interrupt the normal progression of the simulator to generate calls because statistics were available from real switches at this interval. The call generator determined how many calls to create according to the time of day and the type of switch (business or residence). Calls were created according to a Poisson distribution (Mina, 1974) and merge/sorted into the future events chain.

EG Model

The main difference between this model and the theoretical approach lies in the management of events. In the EG approach, the future-events chain was replaced with a future-events loop which accepted events only at defined integer time steps (hence the name Event Grouping). The future-events loop was a circular linked-list consisting of call-stacks each of which could hold many calls. At any given time during the simulation, one of these call stacks would be pointed to as the current stack.

Calls were generated every time-step, with the holding time rounded to the closest multiple of the constant time-step. Calls were constrained to begin and end at multiples of the time-step. In addition, an upper limit was set on the holding time so that no call would be created with a longer holding time than the maximum. The code was designed to accept any integer time step so that the effect of varying it could be observed. Common values were 6 seconds for the time step with a 10 minute maximum call holding time. The circular linked list required for this arrangement had 100 call stacks, one for each possible call holding time from 6 seconds to 600 seconds in increments of 6 seconds.

As calls were generated, trunk availability was checked. If required trunks were unavailable, the call was discarded but if the call could complete, it was placed on the future-events loop at the proper offset (i.e. a simplified merge/sort into the proper stack) according to the call holding time. For example, assume a simulation with 100 call-stacks and the current call-stack is 55. A call generated with a 6 second holding time is placed into the call-stack which will be current during the next sequential time-step (6 seconds from the present, i.e. stack 56). Likewise, a call with a 72 second holding time goes into stack 67 (55 + 72/6). Finally, a call with the maximum holding-time of 600 seconds is placed into stack 54 which was the current stack during the previous time step. The call placement algorithm was extremely simple and ran in constant time regardless of the number of stacks.

After all calls for a particular time step were placed in their appropriate position, time was incremented and the next call stack was addressed. Any calls in this next call stack were discarded (completed), appropriate statistics were updated and call generation was begun again.

Since call generation was accomplished at every time step and these were usually short, the fractional part of the number of calls to be generated was significant. Therefore, to properly account for all calls, the fractional part was considered to be a probability. An additional call was created if a random

246

number generator yielded a value less than the fractional part of the number of calls. For example, if 1.2 calls were required for a particular time step with a random number of 0.2 or less, another call was generated. Otherwise it was not. Resulting call patterns were approximately Poisson distributed.

Prolog Implementation

The simulation effort was begun in Prolog (Clocksin and Mellish, 1984) to take advantage of its declarative nature thus allowing rapid prototype development and easy incorporation of expert heuristics. Also it was desirable to test the capability of Prolog for this type of application. Call-stacks and required queues were implemented as difference-lists (Sterling and Shapiro, 1986) so that data was efficiently accessible from both ends of the data structure. Both recursive and "repeat-fail" versions were created and the code was "optimized" with direction and advice from the Prolog implementor (private communication). The optimization effort was aimed at eliminating multiple search paths during backtracking (i.e. determinant code).

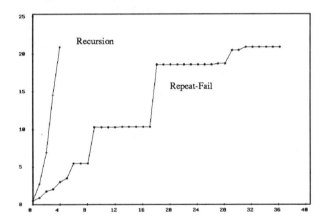

Figure 3. Prolog Memory Usage vs. Time.

Figure 3 shows memory allocation as a function of simulation time for both the repeat-fail and recursive versions of the EG model. These tests were run on a Sun Microsystems 3/260 Workstation with 16 megabytes of main memory and a 21 megabyte swap space under UNIX. No other processes were running. As the simulation progressed, the entire swap space was consumed within 4 minutes of simulation time for the recursive version and within 36 minutes for the repeat-fail version. A severe problem with the Prolog memory allocation functions was suspected (private communication).

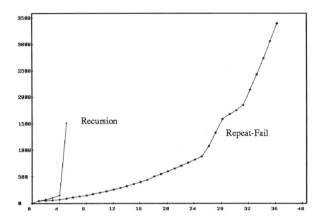

Figure 4. Prolog CPU Usage vs. Time.

Figure 4 shows the accumulation of CPU time for the same two tests. As the simulation progressed, the execution time remained relatively constant but the time devoted to garbage collections increased dramatically. Given these results, Prolog was abandoned and the models were written in C.

Results

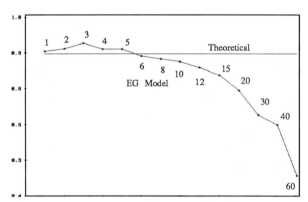

Figure 5. Predicted Utilization vs Time Step.

A number of tests were performed to determine the adequacy of statistics reported by the EG model. In all cases, results from the EG model were compared to those of the theoretical model. In addition, actual theoretical predictions were available for estimating the utilization of single trunk groups.

Figure 5 shows the computed average utilization of a single trunk group after a 20 hour steady-state test with the theoretical model (solid line). This value compares favorably with the theoretical prediction. Also shown are predictions of the EG model using various time-steps for the same conditions. The two models are within 1% for time-steps less than 12 seconds. As the time-step increases above 12 seconds, the correlation degrades. It was expected to observe degradation with increasing time step and encouraging to see such excellent agreement for lower values of time-step.

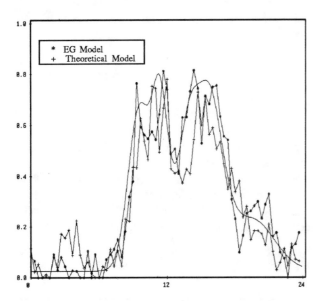

Figure 6. Model Performance, Dynamic Loading.

Another comparison was made between the theoretical and EG models for a case in which the entire network was simulated under dynamic load conditions. Figure 6 shows the utilization of a single trunk group during 24 hours of simulated time. A time-step of 6 seconds was selected for the EG model. Also shown for comparison is the temporal load curve. Although the theoretical model displays wider variability, the two are in close agreement. During the busy hours, the utilization is within 1% and the average over the entire day is within 0.2%.

The 6 second time-step for the EG model obviously resulted in a minimum call holding time of 6 seconds. Although excellent agreement was achieved for greater time-steps, 6 seconds was estimated as the time required for a caller to make a connection on a noisy circuit (excluding dialing and connection time) and to determine that a redial was required. In scenarios with frequent retries at minimum holding times it was desirable to use this value.

No benchmarking for CPU time was done with the models because the code was not optimized for per-

formance and it was decided that such results could be misleading. However it was noted that during periods of minimal activity, the theoretical model was about 4 times faster than the EG model, but during very busy periods or overload conditions the EG model was approximately 4 times faster.

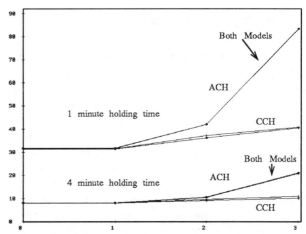

Figure 7. ACH and CCH During Upset.

As a final comparison, a series of runs were made to contrast the theoretical and EG models (6 second time-step) under adverse network conditions. Figure 7 illustrates model predictions of attempts/circuit-hour (ACH) and connections/circuit-hour (CCH) on a selected trunk group, through 3 report periods, during a buildup from normal call activity to 50% overload conditions. These parameters are frequently used by network managers as prime indicators. The lower set of curves are results for a trunk group with an average holding time of about 4 minutes while the upper set are based on an average holding time of about 1 minute. The two models show agreement within 0.2%.

Summary

Based on the previously described tests, it appears that the proposed EG approach adequately describes network statistics both under normal and adverse conditions. In addition, the EG approach demonstrates evidence of superior performance under conditions where an overload of traffic is being experienced. It is under these overload conditions for which it is desirable to obtain good performance for driving the expert system in real-time. Predictions with the EG model using various time-steps show excellent agreement with the theoretical model for time-steps less than 12 seconds. As the time-step increases above 12 seconds, the agreement degrades until the correlation becomes unacceptable. An implementation of the EG model for the 16 switch Tampa sub-network (Mathis, 1989) has been implemented using a 6 second time step and demonstrates excellent performance.

An approximation for the number of calls to be generated at each switch given a required blocking probability was presented and adequately approximates a solution for very large trunk groups. It is believed that this approximate solution will be useful for traffic engineering in real networks where very large trunk groups are common. Also, the visual curve fit technique based on exponentials will be useful for characterizing switch traffic patterns.

The Prolog implementation used for this study was inadequate for implementing models of this type because of memory allocation problems and performance. C served as an excellent alternative not only from a performance standpoint, but also for incorporation of expert heuristics into the models. As a result, it was decided to complete development of the expert system in C. This implementation went easily and yielded excellent performance.

Trademarks

Sun Workstations is a Registered Trademark of Sun Microsystems, Inc.
UNIX is a Registered Trademark of AT&T.

Acknowledgments

The authors express sincere appreciation to Messrs. P. Kosieniak, V. Mathis, B. Pilcher, L. Pollock and Dr. R. Walford for sharing their experience and expertise and helping to bring this work to a fruitful conclusion.

Bibliography

Bell Communications Research. 1987. *Network Management Handbook*. Bell Communications Research. Livingston, NJ. pp. 4-8 to 4-11.

Bobillier, P. A.; Kahan, B. C. and Probst, A. R. 1976. *Simulation with GPSS and GPSS V*. Prentice Hall, Englewood Cliffs, NJ. pp. 48-50.

Clocksin, W. and Mellish, C. 1984. *Programming in Prolog*, Springer-Verlag. New York, NY.

Kosieniak, P., Mathis, V., St. Jacques M. and Stevens D. 1988 "The NETWORK CONTROL ASSISTANT (NCA), a Real-time Prototype Expert System for Network Management." *Proceedings of the First International Conference on Industrial & Engineering Applications of Artificial Intelligence & Expert Systems IEA/AEI-88*. published by the Association for Computing Machinery (ACM). pp. 367-377.

Mathis, V. 1989. "GENSIM, An Interactive Discrete Event Simulator for Telephone Networks." *Proceedings, SCS Eastern Multiconference*. March 1989. Tampa, FL.

Mina, R. 1974. *Introduction to Teletraffic Engineering*. Telephony Publishing Corp. Chicago, IL. pp. 12-22.

Moser, J. G. 1986 "Integration of Artificial Intelligence and Simulation in a Comprehensive Decision-Support System." *Simulation*, Vol. 47, No. 6. Simulation Councils Inc. San Diego, CA. pp. 223-232.

Network Career Advancement Institute. No Date. *Network Planning and Design with New Technology*. Notes of course offered in 1987 by Network Career Advancement Institute, 202 Fashion Lane #113, Tustin, CA 92680. p. 2.3.35.

O'Keefe, R. M. and Roach, J. W. 1987. "Artificial Intelligence Approaches to Simulation." *Journal of the Operations Research Society*, Vol 38, No. 8. Operational Research Society Ltd. London, England. pp. 713-722

St. Jacques, M. 1988. "An Intelligent Telephone Switch Interface for a Real-time Network Control Expert System." *Artificial Intelligence in Engineering: Robotics and Processes*. Computational Mechanics Publications. Southhampton. pp. 371-385.

Sterling L. and Shapiro E. 1986 *The Art of Prolog: Advanced Programming Techniques*. MIT Press. Cambridge, MA. pp. 239-247.

Advances in AI and Simulation
© 1989 By The Society for Computer
Simulation International
ISBN 0-911801-50-2

Expert systems and simulation for training
test desk analyzers

Jeffery J. Howell
Microtel Learning Services
1795 Wilingdon Avenue
Burnaby, B.C., Canada V5C 5J2

ABSTRACT

The Test Desk Decision Support Tool (DST) and
Simulation was developed to assist in training the
British Columbia Telephone Company's craftsmen to
perform (in a Service Office position) as Test Desk
Analyzers. Test Desk Analyzers are responsible for
telephone circuit trouble analysis. The DST uses an
expert system shell coupled with a case-based
simulation to train technicians on the company's
telephone circuit trouble analysis procedures.

This paper discusses aspects of the development of
the Test Desk DST and Simulation, its use as a
training tool and other outcomes that result from this
application.

INTRODUCTION

The DST project was conceived in 1986 while
developing a case-based simulation for training
service office personnel how to use the 4TEL telephone
circuit testing system. Through a formal proposal
process, the project was deemed appropriate and
funding allocated the 2nd quarter of 1987.

The DST & Simulation was developed by Microtel
Learning Services (MLS) for the British Columbia
Telephone Company's Education Center. The main
project team was composed of two Microtel employees
(Jeff Howell and Drew Cuff), supplemented by two
part-time contract programmers and three part-time
telephone company subject matter experts.

Project personnel worked on a part-time basis from
November 1987 to February 1988 to develop a prototype
of the system. Alpha testing of the full system was
completed in June 1988 and Beta testing was completed
in August 1988. In September 1988, the DST was
implemented in classes at the Education Center.

BACKGROUND INFORMATION

Training people to perform their jobs in highly
technical and quickly changing environments is a not
an easy feat. Job training consists of transferring
to a job performer the skills, knowledge and attitudes
needed to perform that job. Specific knowledge is
needed about how and when to perform each task, how to
judge the outcomes of a performance and what new
actions to take based upon that judgment.

When we developed the Test Desk DST, we analyzed
the skills, knowledge, and attitudes processed by
journeymen Test Desk Analyzers.
The analysis process used was a combination of
Harless's "Front-end Analysis", Gagne'and Briggs' task
analysis and Meager & Pipe's performance analysis
techniques. The knowledge to be learned was arranged
following the Instructional Quality Inventory's
classification system for content: fact, rule, concept
(or category), principle, procedure (Wulfeck et al.).
The remainder of the development process followed the
International Telecommunication Union's (ITU) Training
Development Guidelines.

In our approach to training Test Desk Analyzers,
we knew that training of skills requires hands-on
repetition to achieve mastery learning. We also knew
that the "troubleshooting" process for circuit
analysis is primarily identification of concepts,
application of principles and execution of procedures.

In training troubleshooting processes, we
generally use a case study method. Case study is a
close examination of a particular problem to determine
what actions worked to solve the problem. The learner
then generalizes this information to other similar
problems. Another training technique that works well
is the Socratic method. This technique is modeled
after Socrates' method of using questions to lead his
pupils to discover the correct approach to a problem.

In our approach to creating the application for
training Test Desk Analyzers we used two assumptions.
First, simulations are excellent tools for training
technical personnel job related skills. Second, an
expert system should be an excellent resource for
training technical personnel knowledge about specific
job situations.

THE PROBLEM

The Test Desk Analyzer works in the telephone
company's Service Office. He/she is a fully qualified
technician with two or more years of technical school
and company provided training. They support the 611
Trouble Clerks in handling customer reported telephone
problems and perform routine analysis of telephone
network troubles. This position requires extensive
knowledge of the company's physical plant and
operating procedures. The analyzer works at newly
installed PC work stations that access multiple
company databases, newly created support applications
and a recently installed testing system. It is a
dynamic, high pressure environment that has impact on
the bottom line cost of operations.

The problem was two fold. The first was to train the new job holders. The second was to train the old job holders how to do their job with new tools. This problem can be viewed from two different perspectives. One from the telephone company's perspective and the other from the analyzer's.

The problem for the telephone company was both a time and money problem. The implementation of other new systems and equipment had created a large turnover of personnel. People with specialized skills currently doing circuit analysis were placed in key positions elsewhere in the company. Historically, it required over two years of classroom and on-the-job training to provide a Service Office with a fully qualified analyzer. New personnel were needed on the job far sooner than traditional methods had allowed.

Compounding the historical time requirement for training was the vast geographic distance British Columbia Telephone Company serves. The Province of British Columbia is two and a half times the size of the State of Texas in area. So travel costs for training are very high. Additionally, the data bases, testing tools and other applications used by the analyzers could not be partitioned nor access to production systems and telephone plant equipment arranged. Any hands-on training would require purchase and maintenance of new equipment and creation of specific data bases, all additional costs.

The problems from the analyzer's perspective were also of two types. As new systems and applications are brought on-line, old analyzers primarily require quick updating of their skills to use the new tools. Their old knowledge of troubleshooting was and is still valid in most cases. People new to the position required a background knowledge of company physical plant and operations, skills in how to use the databases and testing tools, and knowledge of circuit analysis procedures. Both old and new analyzers needed initial training to use their integrated work stations.

THE SOLUTION

Our solution to the problem was to develop an application that combined the qualities of a simulation with those of an expert system. A simulation would provide a controlled environment for reinforcing skills training on the data bases and testing system. An expert system would provide knowledge about analyzing circuit trouble reports in a dynamic environment.

This solution provided the advantages of extending limited instructor expertise, reduced equipment costs for training, protected in-service equipment and data bases, was transportable, and could be presented to a large number of trainees over a wide geographic area. We estimate that the application will save the company over $350,000 in equipment, data base programming, and operating costs over a three year period.

How The System Works

The expert system shell (used in the application) accesses a knowledge base containing information about analyzing faults in the company's telephone circuits. The co-resident case-based simulation replicates the company's business support applications, data bases and embedded testing systems. External programs track and record the users progress through the system. The application can be run on a personal computer or as part of a network.

The simulation and record keeping programs were written in the "C" language and occupy less than 64 K of RAM on a personal computer using an Intel 28286 processor with 640 K of RAM. The simulation displays are stored as ASCII file records for ease of update. Co-resident memory menus provide the user with control over the application.

The simulation uses a controlled case-based method of scenario presentation. Live data from the various systems the analyzer's use on the job were entered into ASCII data base records using screen capture techniques. These screen captures were locked together into cases that represent the status of the live systems when the scenario was created. The user can access any or all of the key information that was available to the analyzer when the case was first brought up and solved. External programs record the users analysis and routing of the trouble report and provide feedback on the correct actions that should be executed for each case. Cases are accessed randomly, so that the 100 cases will be seen in a different order each time the user resets the program.

The expert system uses Information Builder's Inc.'s Level5/PC shell and specifies a requirement of 512 K of RAM. The shell is a forward and backward chaining production rule system. The application contains over 600 facts and uses 120 rules in four chained knowledge bases that make use of shared variables and attributes. Data is entered into the knowledge base by the user via the keyboard and linked to the simulation through parameter passing from dBase III files.

User prompts and explanations of correct actions to be taken for each step in each case are presented by the expert system. Different routes through the knowledge base will be taken based upon user responses to questions and test results at each step. The simulation can be disassociated from the expert system. Then the expert system can be used as an exploratory "what if" tool by either the instructor or individual students.

Knowledge acquisition for the rule base was done as an adaptation of our training task analysis procedures. MLS follows the International Telecommunications Union (ITU) Training Development Guidelines when developing training systems. Our acquisition methodology was monitored by University of British Columbia research personnel operating under a Canadian National Research Council grant.

OUTCOMES OF THE SOLUTION

One major outcome of the training project is the building of a prototype version of the DST for field use. The field prototype utilizes the fault analysis knowledge base of the DST training system as an "intelligent job aid" to assist analyzers in making faster more accurate trouble routing. The next step is to build interfaces for the DST to the company's business support and testing systems. The interfaces will function somewhat like the training system's access to the case-based simulations and should show a marked increase in efficiency for the field prototype.

REFERENCES

IN A CONFERENCE PROCEEDINGS
Bult, T.; D. Peacocke; S. Rabie; V. Snarr; 1987. "An Interactive Expert System For Switch Maintenance." In Proceedings of the International Switching Symposium 1987. IEEE Communications Society, Piscataway, N.J., 0059-0065.

BOOK
Gagne', R.M. and L.J. Briggs. 1974. Principles of Instructional Design. Holt, Rinehart and Winston, New York.

A SPECIAL PUBLICATION:
Harless, J.H. 1982. Front-End Analysis Workshop, Harless Performance Guild, Inc., 218 Jackson Street, Newnan, Georgia.

A SPECIAL PUBLICATION:
International Telecommunication Union. 1979. Training Development Guidelines. Technical Cooperation Department/Training Division, Place des Nations - CH - 1211, Geneva, Switzerland.

BOOK
Mager, R.F.; P. Pipe. 1970. Analyzing Performance Problems. Pitman Learning, Inc., 6 Davis Drive, Belmont, California.

RESEARCH REPORT:
Wulfeck, W.H.; J.A. Ellis; R.E. Richards; N.D. Wood; M.D. Merrill. 1979. "Instructional Quality Inventory." Special Report, U. S. Navy Personnel Research and Development Center, San Diego, California.

Advances in AI and Simulation
© 1989 By The Society for Computer
Simulation International
ISBN 0-911801-50-2

GENSIM: An interactive discrete event simulator for telephone networks

Victor K. Mathis

GTE Data Services

P.O. Box 290152 DC B3-N

Tampa, Florida 33687

Contributors:

Perry M. Kosieniak   Delano C. Stevens   Michael G. St. Jacques

ABSTRACT

GENSIM, an interactive discrete event simulator for telephone networks, is a prototype simulation tool that has been developed to assist in the testing and demonstration of a real-time expert system aimed at network monitoring and control. It provides a high level simulation of telephone traffic for a network of switches and produces a series of switch reports (one per switch) every five real-time minutes. (The report data is a generic subset of the full data sets presented by actual GTE Stored Program Control (SPC) telephone switches.) The simulated report data is then forwarded to the expert system in lieu of actual real-world switch reports.

Under normal conditions the simulated network is loaded with calls statistically, taking into consideration the time of day, Poisson interarrival times, call rejection rates, interoffice trunk capacities, and standard queuing theory. Scenarios can be interjected and thus superimposed upon the otherwise "normal" telephone traffic. Thus unusual activity leading to focused calling, mass calling, partial and complete facility outages, and other potential network problems or concerns can be simulated on demand. A variety of switch controls, such as code blocks, call gaps, and reroutes can also be introduced to control the flow of traffic in the network. This paper discusses the implementation, features, and performance of the GENSIM simulator.

BACKGROUND

In January 1987 a study was initiated by GTE Data Services, Tampa, Florida, which investigated the feasibility of using expert systems technology to support a computerized network monitoring system in order to improve network management practices. Completed in December of 1987, this study produced a rapid prototype known as the Network Control Assistant (NCA), a real-time prototype expert system for network management. Written in Prolog and executed on an IBM PC/AT under PC-DOS, NCA successfully demonstrated the feasibility of using real-time expert systems to monitor and control the public telephone network.

In January 1988 work began on an engineering prototype successor to NCA. Known as GENESIS (GENeric Expert Systems with Intelligent Simulation), this prototype was developed on a network of Sun Workstations and written in C under UNIX. Intended to extend, enhance, and broaden the scope of the original NCA project, it includes among other things an expansion of the network under consideration from two central offices (a No. 2 EAX and a GTD-5 EAX) found in NCA to a sixteen office network consisting of No. 2 EAXs, GTD-5 EAXs, and a No. 3 EAX.

In the NCA project two live asynchronous data lines (one from a No. 2 EAX and one from a GTD-5

EAX) delivering real-world (nonsimulated) switch reports were used to drive the expert systems. NCA demonstrated the feasibility of capturing the switch report data from asynchronous teletype switch ports in real time, and of parsing and reasoning with the resultant data in an "intelligent" fashion. However, the NCA development team had little control over the adverse or exceptional conditions appearing in any given set of real world switch report data. This made the demonstration of a variety of potential scenarios difficult.

To solve this problem for GENESIS, a companion switch simulator was needed. An investigation of commercially available simulation tools failed to produce one that could adequately satisfy the major requirements of GENESIS, i.e. flexible real-time switch simulation of a 16-switch network under a volume of calls in the range of 20,000 to 30,000 per every 5 real time minutes. Thus a custom simulator (GENSIM) was conceived and developed to simulate the sixteen office network used in GENESIS, and to produce realistic simulated switch report data to drive GENESIS under a variety of scenarios. It is the GENSIM real-time multi-switch simulator which this paper addresses.

INTRODUCTION

GENSIM (GENesis SIMulator) is an interactive discrete event network simulator for telephone networks. It operates in real time and simulates a sixteen office (switch) telephone network which includes 157 trunk groups and 17,800 total network trunk circuits. This network, the GENESIS network, is based on sixteen predominant switches selected from a much larger network of switches located in the Tampa Bay area. GENSIM presently simulates this "subnetwork" as a closed network that requires all call activity to occur within this subnetwork, i.e. no TOLL calls, etc. (A future version of GENSIM is envisioned that will not have this constraint.)

Calls for the network are generated statistically and processed discretely, i.e. on a call-by-call basis. Support is built in for several potential scenarios as well as for the institution of controls at the given switches. Both scenarios and controls can be introduced interactively, while controls can also be received from GENESIS. Switch data for each office is "dumped" (to GENESIS) every five real-time minutes.

The GENSIM simulator was developed using Microsoft C on a 10 MHz IBM PS/2 Model 50 under DOS 3.3 with 640K RAM, a 20MB hard disk, and VGA color graphics. GENSIM uses Sun Microsystem's PC-NFS network file system to communicate with the Sun Workstation-based GENESIS system over an Ethernet local area network. It also uses Metagraphics' MetaWINDOW package for high-resolution graphics and windowing support. Under this configuration GENSIM is capable of transacting a maximum of approximately 35,000 phone calls network wide within a five minute scenario-free reporting period.

GENSIM ARCHITECTURE

GENSIM was designed with versatility, expandability, statistical integrity, and performance as primary considerations. The internal architecture consists of a number of independent processes (coroutines) which include a keyboard manager, a network call generator, and one process for each of the sixteen individual network switches. (In order to facilitate upward scalability and maximum portability to UNIX-based systems, the independent processes have been designed to simulate nonpreemptive multitasking within an unaltered DOS operating system environment.) A shared memory blackboard architecture is used for call queueing and interprocess communication via messages.

Visual interaction is accommodated through a set of high performance color graphics procedures. Multiple windows are utilized to display user inquiries, system output, switch statistics, call generation statistics, and even a graphical display of the network topology.

Switch Support

GENSIM presently demonstrates three types of GTE switches: the No. 2 EAX, the GTD-3 EAX, and the GTD-5 EAX. Nonetheless, their is sufficient versatility for including a variety of other manufactured telephone switches. The need for such "generic" flexibility is tied directly to the generic purpose envisioned for GENESIS, i.e. its need to monitor and control a wide variety of switches. Thus in reality the simulations need not be tied to any particular manufacturer's telephone switch.

Algorithms

Given the need to generate and fully process 20,000 to 30,000 calls within a 5 minute real time interval, special algorithmic techniques have been utilized in the actual implementation of GENSIM. The techniques used maximize simulator performance and flexibility while simultaneously minimizing the system memory requirements necessary for independently representing and tracking the 17000+ trunk circuits during call processing. This is accomplished with enough of the 640K memory left over to support the high performance high resolution color graphics and the PC-NFS device drivers required for Ethernet connectivity. In addition, GENSIM's call processing performance is both efficient enough and accurate enough to generate the sixteen realistic switch reports (about 30K total in condensed form), transport them to GENESIS, recycle the network, and begin a new call generation and reporting interval all within the allotted five real-time minutes.

Algorithmically GENSIM can support a network of virtually any size (number of offices), although both processing and memory constraints of a given hardware architecture dictate practical limits. The addition of an office essentially requires only the addition of another switch process, the inclusion of its trunking data into the global trunk group file, and modification of the call generator to account for the office based on its office profile.

Call Generation

Calls are generated point-to-point between two given offices within the network. This is essentially one step above generating actual phone numbers -- a step envisioned for a next version of GENSIM. In addition each call has associated with it a start time and potential hold and completion times. For each call processed within a simulation individual trunk circuits along a path from the call source to the call destination are seized, i.e. placed in use for that call and only that call for its duration. Additional calls must either utilize other circuits where possible or fail to be completed. This is consistent with the activity that occurs in real-world telephone networks.

CALL GENERATOR DESIGN

Given the requirements of the GENESIS project and the fact that its network was fashioned directly from switches and trunk groups in actual service in the Tampa Bay area, GENSIM's call generator has been designed to drive that network. To do this accurately and realistically, it was necessary to use the real-world trunking already established for the GENESIS network. This required a series of analyses to determine how to generate and distribute calls for a given network as opposed to configuring a network to meet the requirements of preexisting calling patterns and activity -- in a sense a form of "reverse engineering." These analyses steps were necessary in order for the simulator's output statistics to be consistent with those of the real world.

Call Distribution

Based on the known observation that telephone calls in a network tend to follow a Poisson distribution reflecting exponential interarrival times between calls, and also assuming that as a general rule telephone traffic engineers try to size office trunking typically for a 1% peak call rejection rate under normal peak activity, the distribution of calls required to meet these conditions was determined. This information provided the expected call source and sink capacities of the individual offices and the expected distribution of calls from any given office to each of the other offices. The resulting (static) call distribution patterns were tabularized for use by the call generator.

Call Start Times

During actual call generation each call requires associated start and hold times. Initially the start times of all calls were to have been drawn randomly from a continuous set of real values greater than or equal to a time t=0. Unfortunately the use of such an approach led to significant overhead in maintaining time-sorted queues of calls, especially considering the volume of calls needed to meet the demands of the GENESIS project. It was therefore considered that calls might be generated and processed in batches associated with small, sequentially order increments of time.

Test simulations conducted using each of the two approaches demonstrated that calls could be generated with Poisson interarrival times based on a discrete granularity of up to around 10 seconds (in 1 second increments) without significantly affecting the statistical accuracy of the simulation. In other words, the discrete call interval method produced results that approximated Poisson interarrival times well enough to be useful. (See associated paper entitled "Simulation of Telephone Traffic for a Real-Time Network Control Expert System" by M. St. Jacques and D. Stevens, also found in these proceedings.)

Based on the results of the discrete versus continuous call generation test simulations, the network call capacity requirements of the GENESIS network, and the need for maximum call generation and queueing performance, the discrete approach with 6 second time increments was selected for use in GENSIM. Therefore the GENSIM call generator produces all calls associated with a start time of t=0 seconds before those with a start time of t=6 seconds, and so on.

Call Hold Times

Exponential hold times are associated with the calls in order to maintain the correctness of the simulation model. These hold times vary around a predetermined average hold time that is maintained throughout the duration of a given GENSIM simulation. This average hold time takes into consideration the peak number of calls to be transacted in the network and the physical trunking of the network so that a simulated 1% peak call rejection rate is maintained for a fully loaded network.

Due to the added level of design complexity introduced by such factors, the present (initial) version of GENSIM maintains a uniform average hold time (typically 100 to 120 seconds) throughout the network and uses the same business/residence mix for each office. Ideally the average hold times of calls should vary from office to office and take into consideration the time of day, business versus residence mix, and other pertinent factors. A future version of GENSIM is envisioned which will take into consideration such factors on an office-by-office, i.e. switch-by-switch, basis to achieve a finer, more independent, and more flexible level of granularity in the simulation.

SCENARIOS

The present implementation of GENSIM supports four different scenarios that can be interjected into the network: Partial Facility Outage, Complete Facility Outage, Focused Calling, and Trunk Group Outage. For simplicity only one scenario can be active at a time. (A future version of GENSIM will allow for multiple simultaneous scenarios as well as additional ones.)

Briefly, a partial facility outage might result from a malfunction of a portion of a switch, causing an inability to process all of the calls for which it is responsible. On the other hand a complete facility outage implies that the entire switch at the office is down. No calls either incoming or outgoing can be processed by the switch.

Focused calling at an office might be caused by an event like a radio contest, where a much larger than normal surge of calls floods into a particular switch. The overloaded switch cannot process all of the calls due to a lack of hardware resources. In attempting to do so, however, it may "die" trying.

Trunk group outage refers to a situation where one or more trunks from one office to another are in some way damaged or cut. The result is a decrease in the call-carrying capacity of the trunk group such that many or even all of the calls destined for that affected trunk group may be "lost" before completing.

Each of these scenarios affects a switch's ability to function adequately in some way or another. Each one also impacts the overall network activity and may directly or indirectly affect one or more of the other switches in the network. The indicators of these scenarios appear in the switch report data generated during a given report interval. GENESIS uses this information to infer the problems, identify a given scenario, and recommend and possibly take actions to correct or at least alleviate the problems. It is GENSIM which simulates these scenarios to produce realistic report data analogous to that which would be seen in the real-world under the same conditions.

CONTROLS

GENSIM presently supports three different switch controls that can be used to alleviate problems in the network by managing and reducing call congestion: Code Blocks, Call Gaps, and Reroutes. (Other controls, such as Skip, Cancel-To, and Cancel-From, will be added in the future.) These are all controls associated with and used by one or more of the No. 2 EAX, GTD-3 EAX, and GTD-5 EAX SPC switches. GENSIM accepts the same control formats as the real switches and blocks, gaps, and reroutes traffic accordingly throughout the GENESIS network.

SUMMARY

GENSIM is an interactive discrete event simulator that simulates a sixteen office closed network using preexisting trunk capacities based on a real-world situation. Call generation, distribution, and processing under the assumptions of Poisson interarrival times, exponential hold times, and a 1% peak call rejection rate for peak normal traffic yields a statistical simulation of the network that produces realistic report data for each of the sixteen offices. GENSIM is able to simulate several different scenarios, respond to a number of switch controls, and still continue to produce realistic reports in real time. Calls are simulated and processed on a call-by-call basis and may total as many as 35,000 in a given five minute real-time interval under normal conditions (i.e. no scenarios) and normal reporting.

CONCLUSIONS

GENSIM has demonstrated the ability to perform high level discrete event simulations of telephone networks to yield realistic data that agrees reasonably well with that produced by lower level statistical simulations. In addition, for the small sacrifice in precision, GENSIM is able to accurately simulate a large real-world network in real-time! It has proven to be a valuable tool for assisting in the development of GENESIS. It also offers great potential as a stand-alone PC-based telephone network simulator. (Such a product does not seem to be commercially available at this point in time.)

TRADEMARKS

IBM is a registered trademark of the International Business Machines Corporation. IBM PC/AT, IBM PS/2, and PC-DOS are trademarks of the International Business Machines Corporation. Sun, Sun Microsystems, and PC-NFS are trademarks of Sun Microsystems, Inc. MetaWINDOW is a trademark of Metagraphics Software Corporation. UNIX is a trademark of AT&T Bell Laboratories. Microsoft is a registered trademark of Microsoft Corporation.

No. 2 EAX, GTD-3 EAX, and GTD-5 EAX are trademarks of GTE Corporation.

REFERENCES

Bell Communications Research, Inc. 1987. *Network Management Handbook*. Bell Communications Research, Inc.

Bobillier, P.A.; B.C. Kahan; and A.R. Probst. 1976. *Simulation with GPSS and GPSS V*. Prentice-Hall, Inc., Englewood Cliffs, N.J.

Kosieniak, P.M.; V.K. Mathis; D.C. Stevens; and M.G. St. Jacques. 1988. "The NETWORK CONTROL ASSISTANT (NCA), a Real-Time Prototype Expert System for Network Management." *First International Conference on Industrial and Engineering Applications of Artificial Intelligence and Expert Systems*.

AUTHOR INDEX

AUTHOR INDEX